European Dictatorships 1918–1945

Fourth edition

European Dictatorships 1918–1945 surveys the extraordinary circumstances leading to, and arising from, the transformation of over half of Europe's states to dictatorships between the First and the Second World Wars. From the notorious dictatorships of Mussolini, Hitler and Stalin to less well-known states and leaders, Stephen J. Lee scrutinizes the experiences of Russia, Germany, Italy, Spain, Portugal and central and eastern European states.

This fourth edition has been fully revised and updated throughout. New material for this edition includes:

- the most recent research on individual dictatorships
- a new chapter on the experiences of Europe's democracies at the hands of Germany, Italy and Russia
- an expanded chapter on Spain
- a new section on dictatorships beyond Europe, exploring the European and indigenous roots of dictatorships in Latin America, Asia and Africa.

Extensively illustrated with images, maps, tables and a comparative timeline, and supported by a companion website providing further resources for study (www.routledge.com/cw/lee), *European Dictatorships 1918–1945* is a clear, detailed and highly accessible analysis of the tumultuous events of early twentieth-century Europe.

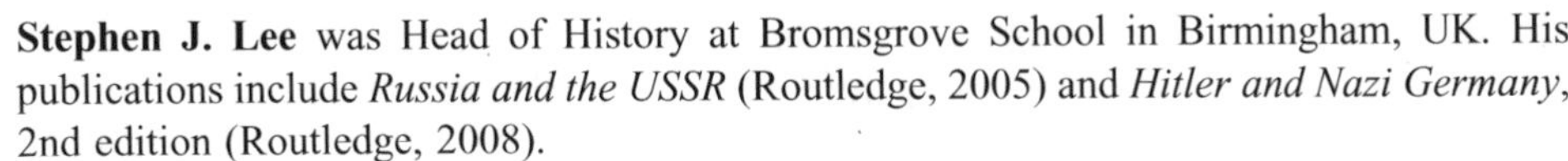

Stephen J. Lee was Head of History at Bromsgrove School in Birmingham, UK. His publications include *Russia and the USSR* (Routledge, 2005) and *Hitler and Nazi Germany*, 2nd edition (Routledge, 2008).

European Dictatorships 1918–1945

Fourth edition

Stephen J. Lee

LONDON AND NEW YORK

Fourth edition published 2016
by Routledge
2 Park Square, Milton Park, Abingdon, Oxon OX14 4RN

and by Routledge
711 Third Avenue, New York, NY 10017

Routledge is an imprint of the Taylor & Francis Group, an informa business

© 2016 Stephen J. Lee

The right of Stephen J. Lee to be identified as author of this work has been asserted by him in accordance with sections 77 and 78 of the Copyright, Designs and Patents Act 1988.

All rights reserved. No part of this book may be reprinted or reproduced or utilised in any form or by any electronic, mechanical, or other means, now known or hereafter invented, including photocopying and recording, or in any information storage or retrieval system, without permission in writing from the publishers.

Trademark notice: Product or corporate names may be trademarks or registered trademarks, and are used only for identification and explanation without intent to infringe.

First edition published 1987 by Methuen & Co. Ltd.

Second edition published 2000 by Routledge

Third edition published 2008 by Routledge

British Library Cataloguing-in-Publication Data
A catalogue record for this book is available from the British Library

Library of Congress Cataloging-in-Publication Data
Lee, Stephen J., 1945–
Title: European dictatorships, 1918–1945 / Stephen J. Lee.
Description: Fourth edition. | Milton Park, Abingdon, Oxon : Routledge, 2016.
Includes bibliographical references and index.
Identifiers: LCCN 2015050291| ISBN 9780415736138 (hardback : alkaline paper)
ISBN 9780415736145 (paperback : alkaline paper) | ISBN 9781315646176 (ebook)
LCSH: Europe—Politics and government—1918–1945. |
Dictators—Europe—History—20th century. |
Dictatorship—Europe—History—20th century.
Classification: LCC D727 .L37 2016 | DDC 320.444—dc23
LC record available at http://lccn.loc.gov/2015050291

ISBN: 978-0-415-73613-8 (hbk)
ISBN: 978-0-415-73614-5 (pbk)
ISBN: 978-1-315-64617-6 (ebk)

Typeset in Times New Roman and Gill Sans
by Florence Production Ltd, Stoodleigh, Devon, UK

Printed and bound in the United States of America
by Edwards Brothers Malloy on sustainably sourced paper.

Again, for Margaret and Charlotte

Contents

Illustrations

FIGURES

MAPS

TABLE

Dictatorships

Comparative timeline 1918–45

Dictatorships: comparative timeline 1918–45

	RUSSIA	ITALY	GERMANY
1917	Collapse of Tsarist regime (Feb/Mar) Provisional Government; Bolshevik Revolution (Oct/Nov); Cheka formed	Defeat by Austrians at Caporetto	Paschendaele; military dictatorship (OLH) under Hindenburg and Ludendorff
1918	Closure of Constituent Assembly; Treaty of Brest-Litovsk; Civil War; War Communism; Constitution of RSFSR	Armistice (Nov); establishment of *Fasci di Combattimento*	Surrender of Germany; end of Kaiserreich; proclamation of Republic; Spartacus uprising
1919	Civil War	(–1920) occupation of Fiume by D'Annunzio; political crisis; inflation; unemployment	Bavarian Soviet Republic; Treaty of Versailles; Constitution of Weimar Republic; formation of DAP
1920	Civil War; famine; war with Poland	Political crisis (Giolitti, Nitti)	Kapp Putsch; NSDAP – Twenty-Five Point Programme
1921	Famine; defeat by Poland; Treaty of Riga; Kronstadt Revolt; New Economic Policy	Formation of PNF; split between PSI and PCI; political crisis (Bonomi); violence organized by *ras* in rural areas	Reparations figure announced; formation of SA
1922	Cheka closed down; Lenin's stroke; Lenin's *Testament*; establishment of USSR	Political crisis (Bonomi, Facta); March on Rome (Oct); Mussolini appointed PM	Hyperinflation; Hitler's leadership of NSDAP
1923	Financial crisis; Codicil added to *Testament*	Acerbo electoral law; seizure of Corfu	French invasion of Ruhr; peak of hyperinflation; Rentenmark and Rentenbank; Hitler's Munich Putsch
1924	Death of Lenin; Triumvirate of Kamenev, Zinoviev, Stalin; codicil set aside; Constitution of USSR	Election: Fascists 404 seats; seizure of Fiume	Dawes Plan; two Reichstag elections; Hitler's imprisonment; *Mein Kampf*
1925	Trotsky dismissed as People's Commissar for War; Left Opposition of Trotsky, Kamenev, Zinoviev	Matteotti crisis and Aventine Secession; Battle for Grain; Locarno Pact; fundamental law; Vidoni Pact	Refounding of NSDAP; formation of SS; Locarno Pact; Hindenburg elected President
1926	Trotsky, Kamenev, Zinoviev removed from Politburo; Treaty of Berlin	OVRA; Rocco Law; Ministry of Corporations; youth organizations under ONB	German admission to League of Nations; Treaty of Berlin with USSR
1927	Approval of Socialism in One Country; Left Opposition expelled from Party; procurement crisis	Charter of Labour	
1928	Internal exile of Trotsky; Stalin's introduction of requisitioning	Electoral Law	Kellogg-Briand Pact; Reichstag election
1929	Defeat of Bukharin, Rykov, Tomsky; Trotsky exiled from USSR; First Five Year Plan; decision for collectivization	Lateran Treaty with Papacy; reflation of the lira	Himmler's leadership of SS; Young Plan; death of Stresemann; Wall Street crash
1930	Decree for collectivization and against kulaks; Stalin's article *Dizzy with Success*	National Council of Corporations	Reichstag election; collapse of Grand Coalition
1931	Renewal of Treaty of Berlin		Impact of collapse of Kredit Anstalt; Harzburg Front; formation of SD

LENIN 1917 – 24

STALIN 1924/9 – 53

MUSSOLINI 1922 – 43/5

	SPAIN & PORTUGAL	C & E EUROPE	BALKANS & TURKEY
1917			
1918		Surrender of Austria-Hungary; **Hungary:** Károlyi	Surrender of **Bulgaria** and **Turkey**
1919		**Austria:** Treaty of St Germain; **Hungary:** Béla Kun's regime	**Bulgaria:** Treaty of Neuilly
1920		**Hungary:** Treaty of Trianon; Regent Admiral Horthy (1920–43); **Poland:** Russian invasion	**Turkey:** Treaty of Sèvres; Little Entente (Romania, Yugoslavia, Czechoslovakia)
1921	**Spain:** defeat of Spanish troops by Riffians in Spanish Morocco	**Poland:** Piłsudski's defeat of Red Army; Treaty of Riga	**Yugoslavia:** Alexander I and Constitution
1922			**Turkey:** defeat of Greek forces; abolition of Ottoman Sultanate
1923	**Spain:** collapse of parliamentary system; coup by Miguel Primo de Rivera		**Turkey:** Treaty of Lausanne; Turkish Republic; **Bulgaria:** Stambuliski overthrown; **Romania:** Constitution
1924			**Albania:** Zogu's invasion and overthrow of Noli
1925			**Albania:** National Bank financed by Italy
1926	**Portugal:** coup of Gomes da Costa	**Poland:** Piłsudski's coup	**Turkey:** Civil code; **Greece:** General Pangalos
1927			**Albania:** military alliance with Italy; **Romania:** King Carol
1928	**Portugal:** Salazar placed in charge of finances		**Albania:** King Zog
1929			**Yugoslavia:** abolition of 1921 Constitution by Alexander
1930	**Spain:** fall of Primo de Rivera	**Hungary:** resignation of Bethlen	**Romania:** Iron Guard
1931	**Spain:** victory of Republicans in general election; abdication of Alfonso XIII; Second Republic; Constitution	**Austria:** collapse of Kredit Anstalt	**Turkey:** 1931 Manifesto; **Yugoslavia:** 1931 Constitution

PRIMO DE RIVERA 1923–30

BÉLA KUN 1919

HORTHY 1920–44

SMETONA

PIŁSUDSKI 1926–35

MUSTAFA KEMAL ATATÜRK 1923–38

ZOG 1928–39

	RUSSIA	ITALY	GERMANY
1932	Union of Writers; famine	Mussolini's *Political and Social Doctrine of Fascism*; Rocco criminal law	Two Reichstag elections; Hindenburg re-elected President
1933	Famine; opening of Belomor canal	IRI *(Istituto per la recostruzione industriale)*	Hitler Chancellor; Reichstag Fire; Enabling Act; ban on other parties; Gestapo; Concordat; withdrawal from League of Nations
1934	Second Five-Year Plan; assassination of Kirov	Syndicates replaced by national corporations	Death of Hindenburg; Night of the Long Knives; Hitler as Führer; Nazi–Polish Pact; Schacht's New Plan; Nuremberg Rallies
1935	Franco-Soviet Pact; Russo-Czechoslovak Pact; divorce made more difficult	Stresa Front; invasion of Abyssinia; Propaganda Ministry; workbooks *(libretto di lavoro)*	Nuremberg Laws
1936	Stalin's Constitution; abortion made illegal; show trial of Kamenev and Zinoviev	Involvement in Spanish Civil War; Rome–Berlin Axis	Remilitarization of the Rhineland; Anti-Comintern Pact; Four-Year Plan; Rome–Berlin Axis
1937	Purges; show trial of Piatakov and Sokolnikov	Membership of Anti-Comintern Pact; Ministry of Popular Culture	Papal encyclical *Mit brennender Sorge*
1938	Purges; show trial of Bukharin, Rykov, Yagoda	Manifesto on Race; Chamber of Fasces and Corporations; Fascist School Charter	Kristallnacht; Anschluss with Austria; annexation of Sudetenland
1939	Nazi–Soviet Non-Aggression Pact; occupation of E. Poland; Russo-Finnish War	Pact of Steel; invasion of Albania	Acquisition of Bohemia and Memel; Pact of Steel; Nazi–Soviet Pact; invasion of Poland
1940	Russo-Finnish War; assassination of Trotsky in Mexico	Involvement in Second World War	Conquest of Denmark, Norway, Netherlands, Belgium, France; Battle of Britain
1941	Invasion by Germany; resistance of Moscow and Leningrad	Defeat in Balkans and North Africa	Invasion of USSR
1942			Wannsee Conference; German defeat at El Alamein
1943	Soviet recapture of Stalingrad; Battle of Kursk; recapture of Kiev	Allied invasion of Italy; Italian surrender; dismissal of Mussolini; Salò Republic; German occupation of North	German defeat at Stalingrad and Kursk
1944	Recapture of Leningrad; Soviet advance into Poland and Balkans	Socialization law; deportation of Jews to German camps; civil war	'D' Day landings in Normandy; July Plot against Hitler
1945	Yalta and Potsdam Conferences	German withdrawal; collapse of Salò Republic; death of Mussolini	Allied invasion of Germany; Soviet occupation of Berlin; Hitler's suicide; surrender of Germany
1946–53	Fourth and Fifth FYP; Comecon, Zhdanov Decrees, Berlin Crisis, Leningrad Affair; death of Stalin		Germany zoned; divison between East and West Germany; Berlin blockade

STALIN 1924 / 9 – 53

MUSSOLINI 1922 – 43 / 45

HITLER 1933 –45

	SPAIN & PORTUGAL	C & E EUROPE	BALKANS & TURKEY
1932	**Portugal:** Salazar appointed PM; **Spain:** Statute on Catalonia; Law of Agrarian Reform	**Austria:** Dollfuss (1932-4); **Hungary:** Gömbös (1932-6)	
1933	**Portugal:** Constitution of *Estado Novo*; one-party system (UN); National Labour Statute; **Spain:** fall of Azaña's govt.		
1934	**Spain:** Asturias revolt	**Austria:** 1934 Constitution; civil war; Fatherland Front; assassination of Dollfuss; Schuschnigg (1934-8)	**Yugoslavia:** assassination of Alexander; Balkan Pact (Ro,Yu,Tu,Gr)
1935			**Turkey:** Treaty with USSR; **Bulgaria**: Manifesto of Boris; **Greece:** General Kondyles
1936	**Spain:** general election; invasions by Franco, Mola; help from Italy, Germany; Non-Intervention Committees	**Hungary:** Daranyi (1936-8) **Austria:** Austro-German Treaty	**Turkey:** membership of League of Nations; **Greece:** General Metaxas
1937	**Spain:** Franco's success in Malaga and Asturias; bombing of Guernica; Repub. success at Guadalajara, Teruel		**Bulgaria:** Constitution of Boris
1938	**Spain:** Catalonia cut off from Republican Castile; siege of Madrid; bombing of Barcelona	**Austria:** Seyss-Inquart; Anschluss; **Czechoslovakia:** lost Sudetenland; **Hungary:** First Vienna Award	**Turkey:** Atatürk succeeded by nönü; **Romania**: abolition of 1923 Constitution
1939	**Spain:** Final victory of Franco; end of Spanish Civil War	**Hungary:** Teleki (1939-41) **Austria:** Nazification	**Albania:** conquest by Italy and overthrow of Zog
1940	**Spain:** Meeting between Franco and Hitler at Hendaye; **Spain and Portugal:** neutrality in Second WW		**Yugoslavia:** Ustashi Croatia under Pavelić; **Romania:** Antonescu; **Greece:** invasion by Italy
1941		**Hungary:** troops for German invasion of Yugoslavia and USSR	**Albania:** resistance by NLC **Yugoslavia:** dismembered; **Greece:** invasion by Germany
1942			
1943			**Bulgaria:** death of Boris **Yugoslavia:** Tito's partisans
1944		**Hungary:** Horthy arrested by Germans; Szálasi's puppet regime	**Romania:** fall of Antonescu
1945		**Austria:** Democratic Republic	**Yugoslavia:** Federal People's Republic
1946–53	**Portugal:** membership of NATO 1949	Soviet-dominated regimes established in Poland, Hungary, Czechoslovakia	Soviet-dominated regimes established in Bulgaria, Romania. **Greece:** civil war 1946-9

SALAZAR 1932–68
FRANCE 1936–75
DOLLFUSS 1932-4
SCHUSCHNIGG 1934–8
SMETONA
PIŁSUDSKI 1926–35
ULMANIS, PÄTS
HORTHY 1920–44
SZÁLASI 1944-5
MUSTAFA KEMAL ATATÜRK 1923–38
ZOG 1929–39
METAXAS 1936–41
ANTONESCU 1940–4
PAVELIĆ 1941–3

Preface

Foreword to European Dictatorships 1918–1945 (Fourth Edition)

Stephen J. Lee – in tribute

Stephen Lee's many books derive their elegance from that restrained kind of passion which was quite his own. The aspect of his style which first commands the reader's attention is its quiet focus. Each sentence is measured, precise, saying neither more nor less than it needs to. Listen a little harder though, and you will sense an energy, even urgency in his prose. His books are all touched by the personal, too, in the dedications which sit at the front of each: 'For Margaret', 'For Max and Joan' and, later, 'For Charlotte'. History was his life force.

Stephen Lee (1945–2015) completed his first degree in African History in Zimbabwe (known then as Rhodesia), aged nineteen. On his return to the UK, he studied European History at St Peter's College, Oxford, and qualified as a secondary school teacher in 1968. From the beginning, his writing was intimately linked with his teaching. His wife, Margaret, like him a member of staff at Birkenhead High School for Girls in the 1970s, was struck by his meticulous and comprehensive teaching notes, and suggested that he work them up into publishable form. A contract with Methuen followed, and his first book, *Aspects of European History, 1494–1789*, was published in 1978. Then they came thick and fast, ranging in subject matter from Peter the Great, to Gladstone and Disraeli, to Hitler and Nazi Germany. His books have been translated into Estonian, Slovenian, Turkish and Japanese.

His career both as a teacher and as an author reached its zenith when he joined Bromsgrove School as Head of Department in 1991. He created a world there, decking every available bit of wall space with historical artefacts: coins and banknotes, newspaper cuttings, portraits of significant figures . . . Those who paid attention found great fun in his own resemblance to Lenin (an accident of genetics, not a look he cultivated). The building which, at that time, housed the History Department was originally a science lab, and he pinned up a notice near the entrance, with the motto 'We still experiment'. His lessons hummed with the same intense concentration as his books. Discipline was not something he usually needed to impose: it was the natural by-product of the interest and commitment which he expected his pupils to return. This expectation was justified, because one of his gifts was finding the right 'ways in' to a topic, presenting the material in a manner both rigorous and imaginative, and enabling students to explore. He touched many individual lives with his teaching, just as he helped to shape the field of secondary-level history through his writing.

So, reader, take this subject that he loved, and experiment.

Charlotte Lee, Cambridge and Worcestershire, August 2015

Prologue

The seventeen dictatorships, 1918–45

Europe between the two world wars consisted of a total of twenty-nine states. In 1920 all but three of these could be described as democracies in that they possessed a parliamentary system with elected governments, a range of political parties and at least some guarantees of individual rights. By the end of 1938, no fewer than sixteen of these had become dictatorships. Their leaders now had absolute power which was beyond the constraints of any constitution and which no longer depended upon elections. The dictators sought to perpetuate their authority by removing effective opposition, by restricting personal liberties and by applying heavy persuasion and force. Of the remaining twelve democracies, seven were torn apart between 1939 and 1940. Thus, by late 1940, only five democracies remained intact: the United Kingdom, Ireland, Sweden, Finland and Switzerland (see Map 1).

The first dictatorships were those of the far left, and involved the use of the term 'dictatorship of the proletariat' to indicate a phase in the development of the principles of communism (see p. 28). Lenin established the Bolshevik regime in Russia in October 1917 after the overthrow by force of the semi-liberal Provisional Government which, in turn, had disposed of the Tsarist Empire in March. Lenin's dictatorship was subsequently enlarged by Stalin, who came to power in 1924. Meanwhile, Hungary experienced a communist revolution in 1919 as Béla Kun tried to repeat the Bolshevik achievement. His regime, however, lasted only 133 days and eventually fell to counter-revolutionary forces. Although there were to be further attempts at installing a dictatorship of the proletariat in several other European countries during the 1920s and 1930s, none succeeded.

In fact, all but one of the other dictatorships came from the right of the political spectrum. Two of these, the most powerful, have been described as revolutionary. In 1922 Mussolini set the pattern for a number of other leaders by assuming control of Italy, and proceeded to impose the basic principles of Fascism. Eleven years later, in 1933, Hitler was appointed Chancellor in Germany and established a more ruthless regime – the Nazi Third Reich. Italy and Germany, initially rivals for control over central Europe, developed from the mid-1930s a working diplomatic partnership known as the Rome–Berlin Axis. With this they spread their influence widely in an effort to undermine the remaining democracies on the one hand and, on the other, to checkmate Soviet Russia.

The right also produced a series of more conservative dictatorships; these are often called authoritarian, in contrast to the totalitarian regimes of Italy and Germany and, indeed, of Stalin's Russia (see Chapter 9). Central and eastern Europe, completely reorganized after the First World War, succumbed to a series of strong men who promised an escape from the chaos of party conflict or the threat of communism. Hence, Horthy established control over Hungary in 1920 and Piłsudski over Poland in 1926. Austria moved to the right in 1932 under Dollfuss, whose regime was continued by Schuschnigg from 1934 until Austria's

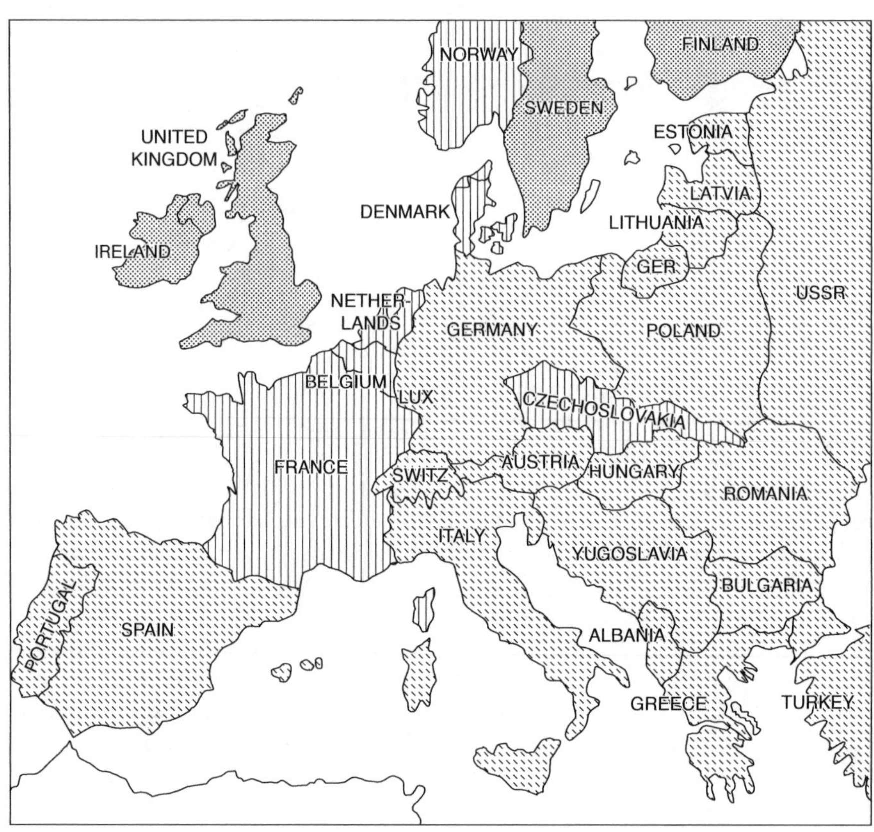

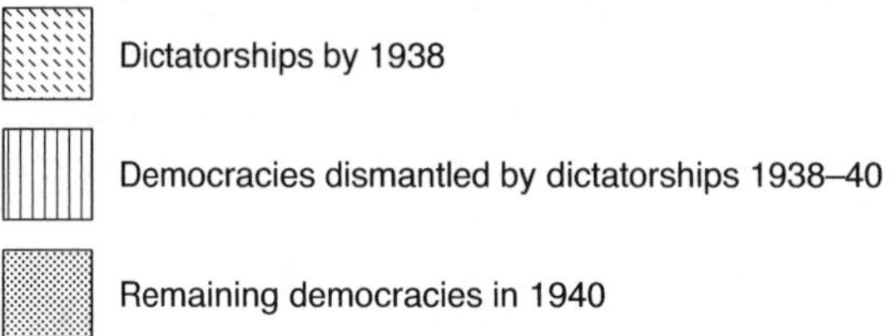

Map 1 The European dictatorships 1918–38/40

eventual absorption into Germany (1938). Even the tiny Baltic states adopted an authoritarian system: Lithuania fell to Smetona in 1926, Latvia to Ulmanis in 1934 and Estonia to Päts in the same year.

Dictatorships also emerged in all the states of south-eastern Europe, or the Balkans. Four of these were monarchies: Ahmet Zogu proclaimed himself King Zog of Albania in 1928; King Alexander assumed personal control of Yugoslavia in 1929; King Boris followed suit in Bulgaria in 1934; and, finally, King Carol dispensed with parliamentary government in Romania in 1938. The fifth Balkan state, Greece, experienced under Metaxas (1936–40) a more systematically organized form of authoritarianism which was influenced to some extent by Nazi methods.

The Iberian peninsula, meanwhile, had produced three strongmen. The first was General Miguel Primo de Rivera, Spanish dictator between 1923 and 1930. His regime, it is true, was succeeded by a democratic republic but this, in turn, was brought down by General Franco who led the Nationalists to victory over the Republicans in the Spanish Civil War. This conflict, which lasted from 1936 to 1939, also gave an opportunity to Hitler and Mussolini to pour military support into Franco's war effort and launch a combined offensive against the leftist supporters of the Republic; it did much, therefore, to increase the confidence and aggression of German and Italian diplomacy. Portugal's experience was less turbulent. From 1932 she was under the iron rule of Dr Antonio Salazar, who remained in power until 1968.

Between 1939 and 1941 no fewer than seven dictatorships (Poland, Lithuania, Albania, Yugoslavia, Greece, Latvia and Estonia) came under the direct rule of Germany or Italy. During the same period, seven democracies were dismantled – Czechoslovakia, Norway, Denmark, Holland, Belgium, Luxembourg and France – while, from 1941, the Third Reich made substantial inroads into Soviet Russia. Almost the entire continent, therefore, became part of the Nazi order, ruled either by governors appointed by Hitler or by puppet dictators. The latter were often leaders of fascist movements which had not succeeded in gaining power before 1939 but which now benefited from the military support of Germany. Examples included the Quisling regime in Norway, the Vichy administration in France, the Ustashi movement in Croatia, and Szálasi's Arrow Cross dictatorship in Hungary.

The fate of these regimes was tied to that of Nazi Germany; between 1944 and 1945 they all fell to the invading armies of the Soviet Union or Western Allies and to the internal resistance movements. After 1945, parliamentary democracy made a major comeback in western and central Europe, while Stalin's version of communism prevailed in eastern Europe. Right-wing dictatorship was therefore squeezed out of all but Spain and Portugal, and even here residual authoritarianism ended in 1975.

This leaves one dictatorship not so far considered – Mustafa Kemal Atatürk's regime in Turkey between 1923 and 1938. In many ways it stands out alone. His Turkey was the only one of the seventeen with its capital city – and most of its territory – outside Europe. It was unique in emerging from an absolutist regime without experiencing a transitional form of democracy. It was neither of the communist left nor of the fascist or conservative right. It did, however, have strong European influences, and its past and future show connections with Europe.

All the developments outlined in this Prologue will be given more detailed treatment throughout the rest of this book. Chapter 1 looks at the overall situation in Europe between the wars and the general preconditions for dictatorship. Chapter 2 provides a focus on the term 'dictatorship' itself and considers terms such as 'totalitarian' and 'authoritarian', 'left' and 'right', 'radical' and 'conservative', and pressures from 'above' and 'below'. It also deals with the ideological background and considers the meaning of Fascism, Nazism and Communism. Chapters 3, 4 and 5 examine the main developments in Russia, Italy and Germany – the 'big three' dictatorships. Chapter 6 provides, for the fourth edition, a considerably expanded treatment of Spain, the Spanish Civil War and Franco's regime, while Chapter 7 covers the different manifestations of dictatorship elsewhere – in Portugal, Austria, Hungary, Poland, Estonia, Latvia, Lithuania, Albania, Bulgaria, Yugoslavia, Romania, Greece and Turkey; it also provides a new introduction to dictatorships beyond Europe, especially in Latin America, Asia and Africa. Chapter 8, also new to this edition, looks at the fate of Europe's remaining democracies – at the seven that were dismantled by Germany or Russia, at the three remaining neutral and the two that stood defiant. Chapter 9 draws together, in a comparative survey, some of the main themes considered elsewhere, while the Epilogue concludes with a broad perspective of the period since 1945.

The overall aim is to examine ideas as well as details. Many of the issues dealt with are highly controversial, and will therefore be looked at from a variety of angles. During the past few decades there has been a vast outpouring of books on the inter-war period, initially on Nazi Germany and more recently on Soviet Russia. It is intended that the following chapters should reflect at least some of the more important theories: the second and third editions have updated these in line with recent research and therefore contain a number of arguments that differ substantially from those in the first edition. That is the way in which the study of history progresses.

This approach is based on the conviction, or hope, that most readers will find explanations as interesting and as important to them as factual detail. Where there are several explanations in direct conflict with each other there is plenty of scope for the reader to reflect and come to a personal decision.

Chapter 1

The setting for dictatorship

Europe experienced, between the wars, an unprecedented upheaval. Boundaries were altered in the most drastic way and numerous new states came into existence. Old-fashioned empires and the last remnants of autocracy had been swept away, to be replaced by constitutional democracies and the principle that each major ethnic group should be given the right to form its own nation. Naturally there was a heady optimism about the future and many shared the belief of H.G. Wells that the struggle between 1914 and 1918 had been the war to end wars. Yet the collapse of the old order was also a precondition for movements that were anti-democratic, and there was no guarantee that the new constitutions or boundaries would be indefinitely preserved.

The overall argument of this chapter is developed in six stages. First, Europe before the First World War was in a state of uncertainty, in many places in crisis. Trends were already in place that were released by the First World War and the peace settlement which followed it. The events of 1914–20 acted as a powerful catalyst, second, for internal change and, third, for the redrawing of boundaries. Fourth, these developments were in most cases associated with constitutional democracy and national self-determination. Such ideals were, however, soon threatened by serious underlying problems that, fifth, gave a boost to alternative systems in the form of left- or right-wing dictatorship. Finally, this process was accelerated by the worst economic crisis in recent history and by a complex international situation that saw the eventual association of dictatorship with militarism and war.

THE PERIOD BEFORE 1914

There has always been a tendency to see the period to 1914 as the climax of an order that was fundamentally stable when Europe had experienced the longest period of peace between major powers in its history. This was destroyed by the upheaval of the First World War, the radical effects of which created the environment for instability and dictatorship between 1918 and 1939. This picture is partly true, but it conceals major changes that were already taking place beneath the surface in pre-1914 Europe, and that were to provide at least some of the roots for inter-war developments. From this approach, the First World War cleared the way for changes that were already in progress. These affected economies, societies and political trends.

The pre-war period saw rapid technological development which amounted to a second wave of industrialization, along with an acceleration of communications and transport and an enhancement of scientific and medical knowledge. At the same time, there was also a massive population growth within Europe which more than offset the emigration from it. In most countries the most obvious social change was the growth of the working class, the result of industrialization. This class was becoming increasingly politically aware, as was the more traditional peasant class. Both exerted increasing influence, either through being enfranchised and participating in the early stages of mass politics or by the way in which the upper levels of society tried to shape policies to contain them. Either way, the politicization of the masses was proceeding before 1914.

So far, there has been little to dispel the positive image of the pre-war era. A great deal of attention, however, has been given by historians to a phenomenon associated with the so-called '*fin de siècle*'. According to Sternhell and others, there was a far-reaching 'intellectual crisis of the 1890s'.[1] This was beginning to shake the established thought of most of the nineteenth century which had been based on liberalism and materialism and which had pointed towards rational and progressive change. Examples of the new wave of anti-rationalism in philosophy and political thought are to be found in the works of Nietzsche in Germany, Bergson in France, Croce in Italy – all showing a reaction against positivism. The arts were also affected in a new wave of romanticism, epitomized by the operas of Wagner in Germany and by the departure from the accepted harmonic system in concertos and symphonies. There was a new interest in social psychology, especially in the emotional behaviour of the masses: the leading influence here was Le Bon in France. Throughout society, and especially in the universities, there was a growing emphasis placed on youth and renewal: this had enormous potential for the mass involvement of youth movements.

Politically, there were powerful critics of liberal parliamentarism, especially among Italian writers such as Mosca and Pareto. Even Marxism was affected by the transformation of ideas. Before the 1890s most Marxist organizations had aimed at a progressive change to a workers' state through the medium of social democratic parties. By the turn of the century, however, there was a growing force advocating violent revolution, which meant a pre-war split within many social democratic movements. The most obvious case was the crisis of the Russian Social Democrats in 1903 and the separation of the moderate Mensheviks from the more radical Bolsheviks under Lenin. Another major influence emerging on the far left was revolutionary syndicalism, developed by Sorel in France as an alternative to Marxism and using trade unionism as a revolutionary device to achieve political objectives. One of its early pre-war converts was Mussolini.

The far right also had its roots in this period. This adapted ideas relating to biology and evolution to generalized conceptions of humanity. The resultant social Darwinism transformed the more traditional patterns of racism and anti-Semitism. Especially influential were writers like Haeckel in Germany, Soury in France, and H.S. Chamberlain in Britain. Many far-right movements were already developing before the outbreak of the First World War. Action Française, set up in 1899, appealed to the masses in the form of 'integral nationalism'. Social Darwinism was highly influential elsewhere: for instance, in the Portuguese Integralismo Lusitano, and also in Spain and Greece. Germany experienced a series of movements and leagues which grew up during the 1890s, especially the Pan-German League and the Society for Germandom Abroad. There was also strong pressure for expansionism into eastern Europe and for the achievement of a continental Lebensraum as well as an overseas empire. Almost all of the far-right influences were *völkisch* and anti-Semitic: pre-1914 examples included the Anti-Semitic People's Party. Similar parties developed in Austria-Hungary, a diverse empire which comprised a dozen different ethnic groups. Particularly active were pan-German groups which favoured union between German-speaking Austria and Germany itself; Hitler came under the influence of these when he scratched out a living in pre-war Vienna.

Another, and even more complex, pre-1914 development was the convergence of the far left and the far right. This occurred especially in France, where the revolutionary syndicalism of Sorel synthesized with the radical nationalism of Maurras. The result was a dynamic conception of the state which would combine a corporatist society with expansionist militarism. This synthesis was to prove important in the development of Fascism in Italy as the syndicalism of Mussolini came eventually to fuse with the activism of D'Annunzio.

Traditional influences in Europe were also changing before the First World War. There was far more general instability than is often thought, especially in those regimes which were to become dictatorships during the 1920s and 1930s. As can be seen in Chapter 3, Tsarist Russia was in crisis in the sense that it was threatened by social and political upheaval. Austria-Hungary was also confronted by the possibility of internal collapse as the German and Magyar ruling groups were coming increasingly under pressure from the Slavs. Although more secure politically than Russia and more homogeneous than Austria-Hungary, Germany too had problems in the form of an increasingly assertive and numerous working class: this was considered intolerable by the ruling industrial and agricultural aristocracy. Italy's liberal regime had become increasingly unstable during the 1890s and attempted an unsuccessful experiment with a more authoritarian political structure. Even France and Britain were vulnerable – the former to pressures from the radical left and right, the latter to an unprecedented combination of constitutional and social crises between 1910 and 1914.

Since 1870, new states had come into existence in south-eastern Europe, while others struggled to be born. The whole process influenced the post-war settlement between 1919 and 1920. Already independent were Greece (1830) and, since 1878, Serbia, Romania and Bulgaria. Each of these considered itself incomplete and aimed for territorial fulfilment. There were also nationalist movements for independence among the Poles in Russia and among the different Slav groups in Austria-Hungary. Whether or not these aspirations were achieved depended on which side they found themselves on during the First World War. The Balkan states had also alternated between constitutionalism and political upheaval which produced periods of autocracy, a pattern which was similar to developments in Spain and Portugal.

All of these changes placed a strain on the structure of Europe, creating fissures and fault lines which would give way under the pressure of the First World War and its aftermath. There were, however, much darker forces at work. Although the glamorization of violence, the use of terror and the appeal of racial hatred are rightly associated with the later period, they all had their origins in pre-war Europe. Already war was considered by some a natural and desirable state. For example, Enrico Corradini and Giacomo Marinetti wrote in the *Italian Futurist Manifesto* in 1909: 'We want to glorify war – the only cure for the world', and they also extolled 'the beautiful ideas which kill'.[2] It is not difficult to see where Fascism and Mussolini derived some of their martial vigour. The targeting of minority groups was also in evidence. Anti-Semitism was rife in Tsarist Russia, with a series of violent pogroms occurring during the reigns of Alexander III (1881–94) and Nicholas II (1894–1917). It was also on the increase in Austria-Hungary, under the influence of prominent politicians and leaders such as Karl Lueger, Georg von Schönerer and the Archduke Franz Ferdinand. The young Hitler, then an Austrian subject, was certainly influenced by their ideas. There had even been evidence of genocide, although this had not yet been associated with anti-Semitism. The Ottoman Empire, the capital of which was in Europe, was the scene of the massacre of 200,000 Armenians between 1894 and 1896 and of a further 20,000 in 1909. Admittedly, the states of western and central Europe escaped the sort of scenes witnessed in eastern Europe and Anatolia. But all was by no means well in their overseas colonies. Overall, millions of indigenous peoples were killed through exploitation or massacres in areas like the Congo Free State, South West Africa and Tripoli. Europe was already becoming brutalized for the most brutal period in its history.

Far from experiencing underlying stability before 1914, Europe was therefore seething with unresolved problems and tensions. These were subsumed in 1914 by the greater emergency of war, only to re-emerge, considerably strengthened, in the peace which followed.

THE IMPACT OF THE FIRST WORLD WAR

The First World War was fought between the Entente powers and the Central powers. The former comprised Britain, France, Russia, Belgium, Serbia, Portugal and Montenegro, joined by Italy (1915), Romania (1916) and Greece (1917). The Central powers were Germany, Austria-Hungary, the Ottoman Empire and Bulgaria. Both sides expected at the outset a swift victory after a limited, nineteenth-century-style war. What in fact occurred was a massive onslaught, with a mobile front in eastern Europe and stalemate in the trenches of the western front. The total losses amounted to 13 million dead, of whom 2 million were Germans, 1.75 million Russians, 1.5 million Frenchmen, 1 million British and half a million Italians. Economies were drained, resources depleted, armies exhausted. Europe proved incapable of ending the conflict and it took the eventual involvement of the United States to tip the balance in favour of the Entente powers.

The impact of the struggle was considerable. During the 1920s the First World War epitomized all the evils to be avoided in the future. Twenty years later, however, it seemed to be eclipsed by the Second World War, particularly since the latter involved considerably greater loss of life and destruction. Then, as J.S. Hughes has argued, the further passage of time restored the original perspective. The First World War now appears fully as important as the Second – indeed, in certain respects, still more decisive in its effects.[3] It was, for example, a catalyst for revolution. It has long been accepted that military failure destabilizes a political system, destroys economic viability, mobilizes the masses, and undermines the normal capacity of the regime to deal with disturbances. The European state system was profoundly altered by the collapse of three empires, induced by defeat and privation.

The first of these was Tsarist Russia. By 1916 the German armies had penetrated deep into Russian territory on the Baltic, in Poland and the Ukraine. The Russian military response proved inadequate, and the supply of foodstuffs and raw materials was severely disrupted by communications difficulties. The government proved unable to cope, badly affected as it was by the periodic absences of the Tsar at the front. In February 1917 food riots erupted spontaneously in Petrograd, to which the official response was entirely inadequate; the regime's stability was destroyed by desertions from a destabilized army. The result was the abdication of the Tsar and the emergence of a Provisional Government which aimed eventually to operate a Western-style constitutional democracy. But this also made the mistake of seeking to snatch victory from defeat; further military disasters severely reduced its credibility and assisted the Bolsheviks in their revolution of October 1917. Within eight months, Russia had moved from autocracy, via a limited constitutional democracy, to communism: a remarkable transformation for a state which had historically been renowned for its resistance to political changes. Lenin made peace with the victorious Germans at Brest-Litovsk. The price he had to pay was to abandon Russian control over Finland, Estonia, Latvia, Lithuania and Poland – a very considerable loss of territory.

Of similar magnitude was the collapse of the Austro-Hungarian Empire. This had been Europe's most heterogeneous state, comprising thirteen separate ethnic groups, all of whom pulled in different directions. Two of these, the Germans of Austria and the Magyars of Hungary, had benefited most from the Ausgleich of 1867 which had created a Dual Monarchy, effectively under their control. The majority of the population, however, had been excluded from this agreement; Austria-Hungary contained a large proportion of Slavs, who could be subdivided into Czechs, Slovaks, Poles, Ukrainians, Serbs, Croats and Slovenes. These were already pressing for full political recognition, even autonomy, by 1914. The First World War wrecked the Austro-Hungarian economy and tore apart the political fabric of the empire as the various Slav leaders decided in 1918 to set up independent states rather than persist with a multiracial federation. By the time that the emperor surrendered to the Allies on 3 November 1918, his empire had dissolved into three smaller states – Austria, Hungary and Czechoslovakia – while the remaining areas were given up to Italy, Romania, Poland and the newly formed Southern Slav nation, eventually to be known as Yugoslavia.

The third empire to be destroyed as a direct result of the First World War was the Kaiser's Germany, or the Second Reich. The German war offensive, so successful against Russia, had been contained on the western front. The Western Allies, greatly assisted by American intervention, came close to breaking through the German lines in September 1918. Meanwhile, the German economy was being strangled by a British naval blockade. Under the threat of military defeat, the Second Reich was transformed into a constitutional republic, the Kaiser having no option but to abdicate on 9 November, two days before the German surrender.

By the end of 1918, eleven states covered the area once occupied by the three great empires (see Map 2). All but Russia were trying to adapt to Western-style parliamentary systems and this seemed to justify the belief of many that the war had become a struggle for democracy. Victory carried with it an element of idealism. The different peoples of Europe would be guaranteed separate statehood and given democratic constitutions. These, in turn, would ensure lasting peace by removing the irritants which had caused so many of Europe's most recent conflicts: harsh autocracy and unfulfilled nationalism. There is, therefore, a strong case for arguing that the First World War had a liberating effect. Further evidence for this can be seen in the profound social changes that occurred in all the states which took part. Particularly important was the increased influence of the middle class at the expense of the traditional aristocracy, the possibility of agrarian reforms and improved conditions for the peasantry, allowance for a greater political role for the working class and trade unionism and, finally, the emancipation and enfranchisement of women.

There is, however, another side to the picture. The First World War may well have created the conditions for the establishment of democratic regimes. But, at the same time it produced a series of obstacles which these new democracies proved unable to surmount. One of these was an underlying resentment of the terms of the peace settlements, which particularly affected Germany, Austria, Hungary and Russia; there was, from the outset, a powerful drive to revise them. Another obstacle was the prolonged economic instability which was aggravated by war debts and reparations payments. Even the destruction of the three empires had unintended side-effects. Some of the new dictatorships which emerged between the wars were built upon the mobilized masses and upon the ideologies which these autocracies had helped restrain – especially communism and fascism. It is arguable, therefore, that the war cleared the way for twentieth-century dictatorships by smashing nineteenth-century autocracies without providing a viable alternative.

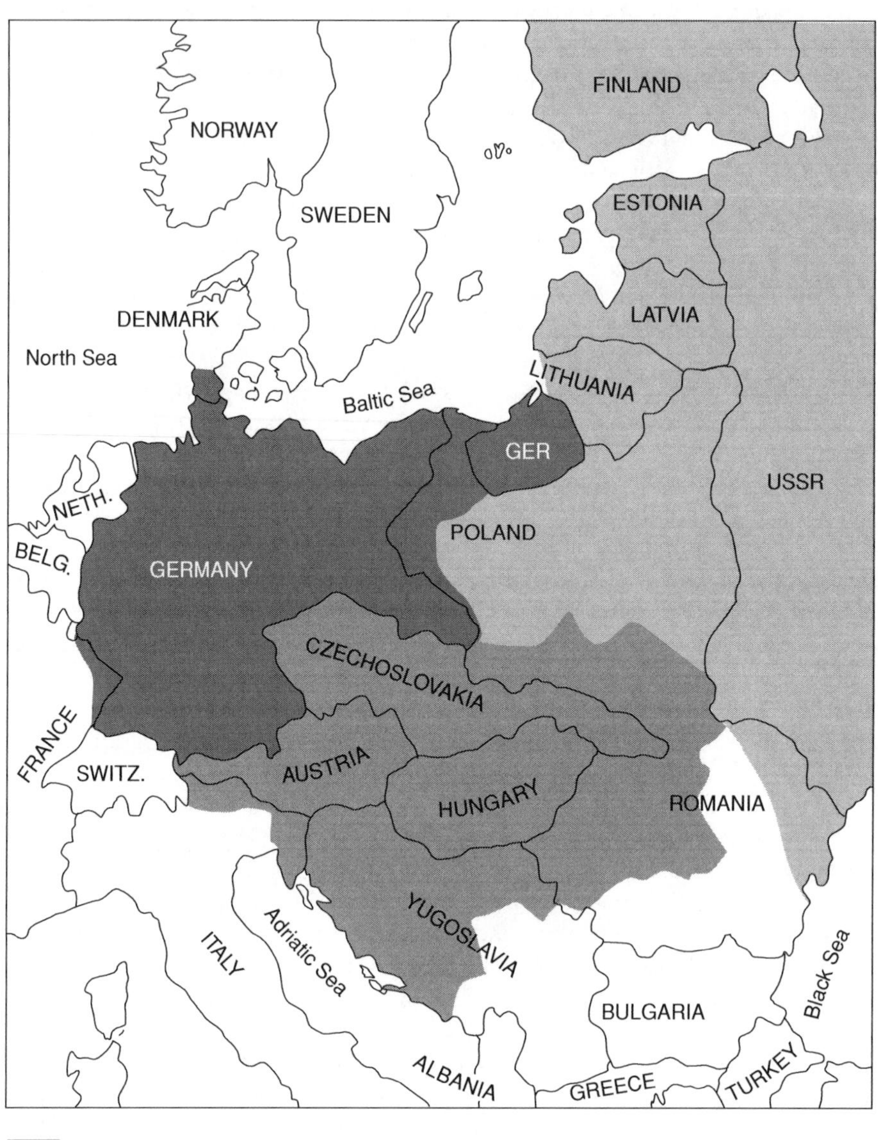

Map 2 The collapse of three empires and the emergence of the successor states

Was the First World War more important for inter-war changes than the developments which were already under way before 1914? The consensus is very much that it was. Bracher, for example, argues that 'In spite of their ideological prehistory, there can be no doubt that the new dictatorships of our century were principally a result of the 1914–18 war'.[4] Payne maintains that the war introduced 'a new brutalization of public life, a routinization of violence and authoritarianism, and a heightening of nationalist conflict and ambition, without which fascism could not have triumphed in key countries during the generation that followed'.[5] Kershaw goes even further. 'Without the First World War and its legacy', he argues, 'a Hitler would have been unimaginable as a leader of Germany.' He adds: 'Before 1914, Germany was a relatively non-violent society. After 1918 violence was one of its main features.'[6] A similar argument could be made for Lenin. It took the First World War to destroy both the Tsarist regime and the Provisional Government which followed it; it is possible that, without it, Russian autocracy might have evolved into a constitutionalist system instead.

But, in the cases of Germany and Russia, it is perhaps more appropriate to see the war as an accelerator (or even distorter) of pre-1914 developments rather than as an initiator of change in its own right. Recent research has shown Imperial Germany to have been a highly volatile society which may have been orderly on the surface but, nevertheless, seethed with conflicting pressures beneath. The traditional aristocracy, the landowning Junkers, along with the new industrialist aristocracy and upper middle class, were being increasingly threatened by the rapidly expanding urban working class (created by Germany's rapid industrialization after 1871). The outbreak of war was seen by the Imperial regime as a rallying of patriotic forces against social divisiveness – and therefore as a means of preserving the status quo. In actual fact, it released pre-1914 pressures: for example, the earlier division of socialism into evolutionary and revolutionary tendencies was confirmed during the war by the formation of the German Communist Party, a bitter enemy of the Social Democrats and of the constitutionalist system set up in Germany in 1919. The forces of the right were reshaped partly in response to this, the traditional conservatives eventually forming an understanding with the emergent far right against the left. By 1930 the majority of Germans did support anti-democratic parties but the underlying tensions were due to the period before 1914 as well as to the First World War.

Some historians have also pointed to the extreme vulnerability of Tsarist Russia even by 1914, arguing for the inevitability of its collapse with or without the war. Military defeat certainly accelerated the change of regime but the real crucible for the communist state which was eventually to emerge was the Russian Civil War. For one thing, it brought up to 5 million deaths, compared with the 2 million attributed to the First World War. For another, it destroyed any possibility of continuing the moderate political development initially made possible by the First World War; instead, the Civil War re-established a link between the methods of the old autocracy and the new dictatorship. The First World War may have cleared the way for Communism, but the Civil War gave it the authoritarian structure which many considered to be a throwback to the pre-war years. The ultimate embodiment of this was Stalin – the 'Red Tsar'.

THE PEACE SETTLEMENT AND ITS SIGNIFICANCE

Ten months before the end of the First World War, President Wilson announced in his Fourteen Points the expectations which he had for any future settlement:

> What we demand in this war . . . is that the world be made fit and safe to live in; and particularly that it be made safe for every peace-loving nation which, like our own, wishes to live its own life, determine its own institutions, be assured of justice and fair dealing by the other peoples of the world as against force and selfish aggression.[7]

What was needed, he continued, was a ban on secret diplomacy, guarantees of freedom of navigation on the high seas, the removal of economic barriers, the lowering of armaments levels, the evacuation of all occupied territory, the granting of self-determination to Europe's different peoples and the formation of a 'general association of nations'. This programme provided the set of ideals upon which the peace settlement was to be based.

Idealism, however, mingled with other motives. One was the satisfaction of wartime expansionist ambitions; the Secret Treaty of London (1915) had, for example, promised Italy extensive territorial gains at the expense of the Ottoman Empire and Austria-Hungary – a reward for joining the Entente powers rather than fulfilling an earlier commitment to Germany. Could such promises be squared with the principle of national self-determination? Another factor was public opinion. All the representatives gathering in Paris were under constant pressure from the media at home and from exhortations from politicians like Geddes to 'squeeze the German lemon until the pips squeak'. Finally, some delegates were obsessed with the need for providing security in the future, and regarded their priority as a settlement which would destroy Germany's military strength.

The actual negotiations were carried out in Paris by the Council of Ten. This consisted of two representatives from each of five powers: Britain and the dominions, France, the United States, Italy and Japan. But most of the work was done by President Wilson of the United States, British Prime Minister Lloyd George and French Premier Clemenceau. The usual picture of this trio is that Wilson was the idealist, having the advantage of American detachment from European problems. Clemenceau was concerned primarily with French security and revenge against Germany, while Lloyd George adopted a pragmatic approach, endeavouring to steer between Wilson and Clemenceau and to achieve by compromise a moderate and lasting solution. The Paris Settlement, therefore, reflected these three broad strategies, which can be seen at work in the individual treaties, named after the ring of towns around the outskirts of Paris or parts of the complex of Versailles.

Germany was dealt with by the Treaty of Versailles, signed on 28 June 1919. It affirmed, by Article 231, the prime responsibility of Germany and her allies for the outbreak of the First World War and, accordingly, made provision for territorial adjustments, demilitarization and economic compensation to the victorious Allies for the losses they had incurred. Germany was deprived of Alsace-Lorraine, Eupen and Malamedy, Northern Schleswig, Posen, West Prussia, parts of Southern Silesia, and all her overseas colonies. Limits were placed on her naval capacity, her army was restricted to 100,000 volunteers, and the Rhineland was demilitarized. A considerable quantity of rolling-stock and merchant shipping was also removed, while France was given exclusive rights to the coal-mines of the Saar region. Finally, provision was made for the payment of reparations by the German government, the total amount eventually being fixed in 1921 at 136,000 million gold marks. Altogether, Germany lost 13 per cent of her area, 12 per cent of her population, 16 per cent of her coal, 48 per cent of her iron, 15 per cent of her agricultural land and 10 per cent of her manufactures.

Opinion is divided as to whether this was a fair settlement. Historians of the 1920s, like W.H. Dawson, emphasized the harshness of a treaty which cut into German territory in a way which discriminated blatantly in favour of non-German populations. The result was that Germany's frontiers 'are literally bleeding. From them oozes out the life-blood, physical, spiritual and material of large populations.' More recent historiography has tended to redress the balance. Writers like J. Néré, M. Trachtenberg and W.A. McDougall put the case that France suffered far more heavily than Germany from the impact of war and that she therefore had a powerful claim to compensation and security. Indeed, considering that a German victory would have meant German control over much of Europe, the settlement drawn up by the Allies was remarkably moderate.

Time has therefore enabled a perspective to emerge. But perhaps the most important point is that contemporary statesmen strongly attacked the treaty, thereby giving ammunition to the German case that the treaty should be revised, even evaded. J.M. Keynes, the economist, was particularly critical; he argued that the settlement lacked wisdom, that the coal and iron provisions were 'inexpedient and disastrous' and that the indemnity being considered was far beyond Germany's means to pay.

He considered, indeed, that the treaty, 'by overstepping the limits of the possible, has in practice settled nothing'. This accorded very much with the German view that the treaty was a diktat, forced upon a defeated power, rather than a genuine negotiated settlement. By 1930 it was evident that a wide cross-section of the German political spectrum was extremely hostile to the Treaty of Versailles and that British politicians were increasingly aware of its shortcomings. The ultimate beneficiaries of both these trends were the parties of the right – the conservative National Party and the more radical Nazis. Hitler, especially, was to exploit the underlying resentment in Germany, while British politicians, affected by a belated attack of conscience, made excuses for his activities against the settlement. As will be shown in Chapter 5, the failure to uphold the Treaty of Versailles in the 1930s contributed greatly to the growing confidence and aggression of Nazi foreign policy.

Another part of the peace settlement concerned central and eastern Europe. Austria-Hungary was dealt with by the Treaties of St Germain (10 July 1919) and Trianon (4 June 1920), which were largely a recognition of a fait accompli, the collapse of the Habsburg monarchy. Czechoslovakia was formed out of the provinces of Bohemia, Moravia, Slovakia and Ruthenia; Transylvania and Bukovina were given to an enlarged Romania; Serbia received the Dalmatian coastline, Bosnia-Herzegovina, Croatia and Slovenia; while Trentino and South Tyrol were transferred to Italy. Bulgaria, meanwhile, was covered by the Treaty of Neuilly (27 November 1919) by which she lost the Aegean coastline, or Western Thrace, to Greece, parts of Macedonia to Yugoslavia, and Dobrudja to Romania. Elsewhere in eastern Europe, 1918 saw the emergence of Poland, Finland, Estonia, Latvia and Lithuania as independent states. Although the victorious Allies cancelled the Treaty of Brest-Litovsk between Germany and Russia, no attempt was made to return to Russia the territory which had been given up. Taken as a whole, all these settlements amounted to the greatest territorial transformation in European history.

The accompanying problems were also considerable. The new nations (or successor states) that replaced Austria-Hungary faced a series of crises, examined at length in Chapter 7. They all contained large disaffected ethnic minorities and struggled to achieve economic viability in cut-throat competition against each other. Austria and Hungary sought to revise the whole settlement, Austria by seeking union with Germany (prohibited by the Treaty of St Germain) and Hungary by trying to extend her frontiers at the expense of her neighbours. The overall result was that eastern Europe was fundamentally unstable and therefore vulnerable to political extremes. Italy, meanwhile, was thoroughly dissatisfied with her meagre gains at St Germain – certainly far fewer than had been guaranteed by the Secret Treaty of London (1915). Indeed, Mussolini found that resentment against the settlement had, by 1922, become a significant factor in boosting support for Fascism. Another resentful, and hence revisionist, power was Russia; Stalin had no intention of conceding permanently the territory lost at Brest-Litovsk or that lost to Poland by the Treaty of Riga (1920). He, too, had no underlying commitment to the post-war settlement and was not averse to helping upset it.

The final part of the peace settlement concerned the Ottoman Empire. This differed from the other changes drawn up by the victors in Paris in that it resulted in immediate chaos but longer-term stability, rather than the other way round. By the Treaty of Sèvres (20 August 1920), the Allies ended Turkey's rule over the Arab provinces in the Middle East. Of these, five were mandated: Iraq, Transjordan and Palestine to Britain, Syria and Lebanon to France; these were designated for self-rule in the longer term. The sixth area, the Hejaz, was joined to the rest of Arabia as an independent kingdom. Arrangements elsewhere were more controversial. Smyrna, an enclave in western Anatolia, was given to Greece for five years, after which its future would be subject to a plebiscite. Greece also received Eastern Thrace and the Aegean Islands, while Italy was allocated Rhodes and the Dodecanese. The Straits, comprising the Dardanelles and the Bosporus, were internationalized and the adjacent territory demilitarized. Although Sultan Mohammed VI was forced to sign the Treaty, there was fierce resistance from Turkish Nationalists under Mustafa Kemal. The Greeks were driven out, the Sultanate was overthrown and a new Turkish republic established. In September 1923 the Allies agreed, by the Treaty of Lausanne, to modify the territorial provisions of Sèvres. Eastern Thrace was restored to Turkey, providing a more substantial presence in Europe, and the Greeks were deprived of their entitlement to Smyrna. Stipulations in the Treaty of Sèvres for payment of an indemnity were also withdrawn. Alone among the areas dealt with by the peace settlement, Turkey's long-term future had been established by 1923 and the Second World War made no further adjustments to the changes already wrought by the First. Uniquely, also, an eastern European dictatorship was to avoid further conflict and, in the longer term, to evolve into a democracy.

THE CRISIS OF DEMOCRACY

The nineteenth century had seen the growth of parliamentary institutions in almost every European state. In many cases, however, there had been severe constraints on democracy, such as a limited franchise, strong executives, weak legislatures and, in central and eastern Europe, the persistence of royal autocracy. As we have seen, the First World War swept away these constraints, while President Wilson based his views of future stability on entrusting the different peoples of Europe not only with new states but with the power to run them. Cobban argues that 'The key to the understanding of Wilson's conception of self-determination is the fact that for him it was entirely a corollary of democratic theory.'[8] The basic assumption of many was that democracy could work and that it was the best guarantee of lasting peace.

What was meant by the democratic state? H. Kohn has listed some of the main characteristics of the democratic way of life. These include 'open minded critical enquiry' and 'mutual regard and compromise'; an opposition which functions as 'a legitimate partner in the democratic process'; a 'pluralistic view of values and associations'; a refusal to identify totally with 'one party or with one dogma'; recognition of the fundamental values of 'individual liberty'; and 'freedom of the enquiring mind'.[9] These features are common to all open democracies, whether republics or monarchies, and several devices were introduced after the First World War to try to give them effect.

These included the extension of the suffrage and the strengthening of the powers of parliaments. In much of central and eastern Europe a deliberate decision was made to use proportional representation, in the belief that this was the best means of conveying the popular will. The most influential type was the Belgian system, as adapted in 1918 by the Dutch. This related the number of votes cast to the size of party representation in parliament while, at the same time, allowing a national pool in which smaller groups could be included alongside the main parties. The general principle here was that the harmony and stability of the new democracies would be best served by a complete range of parties and interests. This device was therefore used in Germany, Poland, Austria, Czechoslovakia, Finland, Lithuania, Latvia and Estonia. Italy, Spain, Portugal and the Balkan states tried other variations on the democratic theme. The size of the electorate was also considerably enlarged by the extension of the franchise to women. Before 1914 women had had the vote only in Norway, Finland and Denmark. Britain followed in 1918 and 1928; Germany, Austria, Netherlands, Belgium, Poland, Estonia, Latvia and Russia between 1918 and 1919; Sweden in 1921; and Spain and Portugal after 1931.

Unfortunately, democracy everywhere soon came under serious strain. Economic crises included inflation in the early 1920s in Germany and a universal depression from 1929 onwards, aggravated by the raising of tariff barriers and the disruption of trade. Some states suffered racial instability as a result of conflicting ethnic groups. Others experienced social disruption caused by the growing hostility towards the regime of the different social classes – the business groups and capitalists, the professional middle class and small traders, peasants, farmers and workers. Economic, racial and social crises had a serious effect on political parties. Liberal parties were drained of supporters, especially in Germany; populist and Catholic parties managed to keep theirs, but consciously moved their policies to the right; conservatives became increasingly anti-democratic and authoritarian; and the parties of the left were torn between socialism and communism. In this state of flux what was needed everywhere was a secure political framework to restore stability and stiffen the resolve to preserve democracy.

This is precisely what was missing. The creators of the constitutions had been unduly optimistic in assuming that the expression of different viewpoints through party politics would automatically guarantee harmony. The unhappy experience of proportional representation demonstrated quite the reverse. K.J. Newman considers that proportional representation led to the disintegration of Italian democracy and seriously destabilized Germany. In multi-ethnic states like Poland and Yugoslavia it ensured that 'national, religious, ideological and regional groups' were irreconcilable.[10] It could certainly be argued that the majority voting system (or winner takes all) was more likely than proportional representation to maintain harmony. The reason was that it tended to produce a two-party system, in which each party was an alliance of interest groups prepared to compromise in order to present an acceptable image to the electorate; failure to do this would mean severe defeat, as seats in parliament were not designated in proportion to votes received. Proportional representation, by contrast, removed the necessity for groups to compromise within parties; the emphasis, rather, was on parties presenting as specific an image as possible and making a bid for a place in a subsequent coalition government. In other words, the majority voting system forced co-operation within parties before elections, while proportional representation relied on co-operation between parties *after* elections.

It is, of course, possible to criticize the majority voting system for being inadequately representative and for distorting electorates' decisions. It is also significant that most European democracies have, since 1945, reintroduced proportional representation. The important point, however, remains that the type of proportional representation adopted between the wars had no means of preventing splinter parties (a shortcoming now largely corrected) and coincided with an unusual number of crises. As a result, democracy became less a matter of how to deal with problems than of how to put together a government. A considerable amount of time and effort was spent trying to find a majority, necessitating exhaustive negotiation and horse-trading. In the process, the role of the prime minister or chancellor changed significantly; instead of acting as the head of a government putting across a package of proposals, he became a mediator between conflicting groups, desperately trying to retain power. This situation would be difficult enough in normal circumstances. At a time of national crisis it proved intolerable. The result was that, in some cases, the head of the government had many of his powers taken out of his hands by the head of state – the king in a monarchy, the president in a republic. The problem was that democracy had declining support during the 1920s and 1930s. Heinrich Müller, German Chancellor, said in 1930 that 'a democracy without democrats is an internal and external danger'. Here and elsewhere political parties failed to respond to the challenge. Liberal parties were generally weak and, in Germany, were divided into two. More secure were social democrats: where they could provide an alliance with the rural population, as in the Scandinavian countries, or with conservatives, as in Belgium, democracy survived. But in Austria and Germany they were to be superseded by a combination of the conservative and radical right – both profoundly anti-democratic. Spain and France tried a broad alliance of the left against the right, but this collapsed in military turmoil or political chaos. Meanwhile, support for European democracy from abroad gradually disintegrated. The United States, the original sponsor for Wilsonian democracy, withdrew into isolationism, while Baldwin's Britain regarded making a choice between the European right and left as equivalent to deciding between 'mumps and measles'. It is not surprising that democracy experienced growing disillusionment. Descriptions like 'the crisis of European democracy' were common currency in the 1920s and even earlier optimists like H.G. Wells now anticipated what would happen 'After Democracy'. There was widespread acceptance that the constitutions of 1919 and 1920 had been based too finely on juridical principles – at the expense of political realities. Hence they were not suited to deal with the exceptionally difficult practical economic and social problems which developed in the late 1920s and 1930s.

The trend away from democracy towards authoritarian rule was assisted by another defect which existed in some of the new constitutions. The constitution of the Weimar Republic in Germany was typical in that it provided a safeguard if things went wrong; Article 48 gave the president exceptional emergency powers when he needed them. Thus Germany became authoritarian during the Great Depression from 1931, providing a more amenable political atmosphere for the rise of Hitler. Over most of Europe it proved possible to graft dictatorship on to earlier democratic foundations. Only one regime, Bolshevik Russia, made a clean sweep of previous institutions. Others, including even Nazi Germany, retained much of the original constitutional framework until the very end. They did, however, amend the constitutions so as to make a mockery of the original principles and intentions. The main amendments were a ban on party politics and the strengthening of the executive at the expense of the legislature.

Finally, democracy was severely weakened by the absence of any really popular statesmen during the interwar years. The talent of men like Briand and Stresemann was unostentatious diplomacy which, although effective, rarely caught the public imagination. Churchill, who eventually did fill this gap, did not come into his own until 1940; indeed, R. Rhodes James has called his earlier career 'The Years of Failure'. Almost all the great personalities of the period were critics of democracy – Mussolini, Hitler, Piłsudski, Dollfuss, Primo de Rivera and many others. The masses were tempted by their charisma, sweeping promises and simple solutions. The nations' policies were increasingly taken out of the hands of larger political groups and the key decisions were personalized. This was to be one of the main characteristics of dictatorship and applies everywhere, including Stalin's Russia.

THE ROLE OF MODERNITY?

The decline of democracy and the rise of dictatorship in two of the states we shall cover has sometimes been associated with 'modernity' or 'modernization'. This has involved two major approaches, both of which have been applied to Italy and Germany. Some have stretched the point – and included Russia.

One approach emphasizes that these states all became dictatorships because this was their peculiar path to modernization. Germany, for example, missed out on the connection between industrialization and a strong middle-class liberal system as occurred in Britain, France or the United States. Instead, there was a tension between a growing capitalist economy on the one hand and pre-modern social influences on the other. The long-term result was an explosion producing the distortion known as Nazism. A similar case has been made for the rise of fascism in Italy. In the case of Russia, the relatively slow modernization under the Tsars resulted in a compensatory burst of social and economic change, especially under Stalin. These arguments are, however, too deterministic and are examined in Chapter 2.

A second approach is worth greater consideration at this point. Specific states did experience some disorientation as a result of modernization and were especially vulnerable to new communications technologies. This cannot be seen as a primary reason for the rise of dictatorship – but it does provide some explanation for the appeal which certain parties and regimes exerted.

Modernization was a key theme of the interwar period, having already accelerated in the decades before 1914 and through the First World War. Its impact was paradoxical. In some ways it brought recovery and consolidation. New production and management techniques, influenced respectively by Fordism and Taylorism in the United States, provided Weimar Germany with the basis for economic growth between 1924 and 1928. The development of new industries, especially motor cars, electricity and aircraft, helped compensate for the decline of the more traditional staple industries. Areas which particularly benefited were the Midlands and the South East in England, around the industrial areas of Paris, the north of Italy, especially Milan, and the Rhineland and Bavaria in Germany. Europe also experienced widespread cultural innovation in the work of Picasso, Schoenberg, Brecht and Gropius. At the same time, modernity also entailed more government involvement which in some areas sought greater uniformity; this aspect is described by Hoffmann as 'social interventionism and mass politics'.[11] Where there was social hardship, the cinema provided a means of relieving economic and social pressures, especially in Britain, where it became the main form of popular recreation.

Yet, despite these advantages, modernization could also be destabilizing. There was, for example, much resentment of Taylorism, as adapted to the European context by Bedaux in a process designed simply to speed up work. Extensive trade union opposition developed, resulting in an increase in strikes during the 1920s. In these circumstances many industrialists, especially in Italy and Germany, looked to more authoritarian systems which would be able to take action against unions – or perhaps abolish them altogether. Modernization could also create new divisions within society: this applied especially to Italy and Germany. The new sectors were not part of the traditional working class and were usually not unionized: this, in turn, meant that they developed an antipathy to the traditional parties of the left. In Germany and Italy they established close relations with new movements on the far right, of which advantage was also taken by I.G. Farben and the managers of Magneti Marelli.[12] One especially destabilizing facet of modernity was the impact of the First World War, which many saw as a modern crisis of civilization. The trauma was particularly profound in Italy and Germany, both of which experienced a yearning for something to compensate for the failure of the recent past. In Russia the effect had been multiplied by the Civil War, where parts of the country reverted to barbarism.

It is hardly surprising, therefore, that modernization should be seen as 'Janus-faced'. This description applies to three countries in particular, where modern technologies were used to achieve and implement state control while, at the same time, the systems from which modernization had arisen were roundly condemned. The ideologies of the far left and far right both brought alternative perceptions. They attacked modernity in one sense – for the dislocation and exploitation that it brought. They offered, as an antidote, alternative values, which, however, were combined with another vision of modernity.

The Soviet system, already installed by 1918, was based on the premise that modernization in a capitalist sense was destructive since it increased the exploitation of the masses by the few. The solution was therefore to modernize through collective measures in the interests of the proletariat. The Fascist parties and regimes had a more disingenuous view. Much of Europe's 'modernity', especially its cultural 'modernism', was despised as degenerate. The people of Italy and Germany were, they maintained, trapped between conflicting interest groups – capitalists and Communists, both of which were distorting modernization to their own purpose. Fascism therefore resorted to 'antimodern themes such as the folk and the purity of rural life, but did so for modern mobilizational purposes'.[13] Mussolini offered an ideology which would, in the words of Ben Ghiat, allow 'economic development without harm to social boundaries and national traditions'.[14] Fascists were, at the same time, committed to technological and scientific advance, although this was to be combined with the protection of traditional values.

In all cases the message was put across through one particular form of modernity – the technology of communications. In this the parties and regimes of the far left and far right excelled. They brought to bear all the persuasiveness of public speaking, magnified by loudspeakers and enhanced by a knowledge of crowd psychology. Mussolini and Hitler were particularly effective here, although Lenin and Trotsky had made an earlier breakthrough in the two years immediately after the Russian Revolution. The fascists and Nazis made full use of banners designed to modernize traditional images. This applied, for example, to the swastika, which was redesigned as a black geometric block placed at an angle on a white and red background; in it Hitler combined a revolutionary statement with what he (wrongly) regarded as an ancient Aryan symbol and the colours of the Kaiserreich. Extensive use was made of parades, uniforms and marching songs; in the latter phase of the Weimar Republic the Nazi Storm Troopers and the Communist Red Front claimed the streets as their own. Much has also been made of their modern approach to winning public support, as Hitler and Goebbels planned election campaigns and targeted different sectors of the electorate with specific promises. Once in power, they retained this support through mass rallies, concentrated use of the radio and simplified messages conveyed through posters and the cinema.

Once in power, the far left and right claimed modernization as their own and presented it in a form which, they claimed, harmonized with tradition (in Russia this tradition was revolutionary, in Italy and Germany pre-industrial). In Russia modernization was to be accomplished along Marxist lines. Although Lenin admired the efficiency of western production techniques, he deplored the economic structure which produced them. Hence the need for state controls, which were accelerated under Stalin. Modernity was also evident in the concept of 'gigantomania', in the development of new cities like Magnitogorsk, in the projection of the 'New Soviet Person', and in the Lamarckist 'scientific' stress on environment rather than heredity. In Fascist Italy modernization was to be presented in the form of advanced technology, produced by the New Fascist Man within the Fascist Century. At the same time, Mussolini devised in the Corporate State a blend of medieval guilds and modern controls, through which he claimed to remove the social tensions produced by capitalist modernization. In Germany Hitler created an Aryan mythology which he transplanted on to pre-industrial social values while creating a modern war machine and, in the ultimate twist, applying new technological principles to the destruction of a traditional racial 'enemy'.

Ultimately, the alternative approaches to modernization were to prove far more disruptive than those which they had replaced, as can be seen in Chapters 3, 4 and 5. Stalin's Five-Year Plans produced a severely distorted economy, Mussolini presided over a slowing Italian growth and Hitler created a system which eventually destroyed itself. Indeed, it could be argued that when modernization continued after the Second World War, it largely bypassed fascist and communist experiments with it.

But, of course, this was not apparent in the 1920s or the 1930s. The modern mobilizing techniques of incipient dictatorships carefully concealed their defective ideas about mobilizing modernity.

THE ECONOMIC CATALYST

J.M. Keynes observed in 1931: 'We are today in the middle of the greatest economic catastrophe – the greatest catastrophe due almost entirely to economic causes – of the modern world.'[15] He was referring to events generally known as the Great Depression. This was the nadir of the inter-war economy but, at the same time was part of a broader economic picture which needs to be examined. It is generally accepted that economic crises had profound political effects; although they were rarely the sole or specific cause of dictatorship, they certainly accelerated the process.

The first major crisis followed the First World War and the peace settlement. Before 1913, Europe had dominated world trade and industrial production. Concentration of four years of Total War, however, meant the loss of ground to the United States. Some European countries also experienced major upheavals as a result of revolution or the peace settlement. Russia, for example, went through a period of War Communism, followed by the New Economic Policy. The Bolsheviks also decided to repudiate all of Russia's pre-war debts, which particularly affected France. The emergence of eleven new states in eastern and central Europe destroyed the previous customs union in the area, impeded industrial development and promoted intense rivalry. In western Europe there was a considerable variation in post-war economic conditions. Italy underwent economic collapse which contributed to the rapid decline of effective parliamentary democracy and the rise of Mussolini. Britain and France both experienced post-war booms, but these were followed, after 1922, by a temporary general recession. Germany, meanwhile, was saddled by the Treaty of Versailles with reparations payments. The German government resented these deeply, and defaulted in 1923, at the same time printing paper money and effectively bringing about the collapse of the mark. In fact, the situation in the Weimar Republic epitomized everything which seemed most dangerous to Europe's economies: hyperinflation with threats to jobs and savings and a potential social upheaval.

In many cases, however, this first phase of economic malaise was dealt with effectively. The slump and inflation were both reversed and western Europe experienced a rapid increase in prosperity between 1924 and 1929. Several factors contributed to this. One was a more stable international situation; another was the resolution of the German reparations crisis by the Dawes Plan of 1924. But the most important reason was the beneficent influence of the United States – which contributed between 1925 and 1929 approximately $2,900 million in the form of investment in Europe. This helped settle the complex problem of post-war debts. American loans enabled Germany to make reparations payments to her former enemies in Europe, which, in turn, could make repayments on war loans to the United States. The more stable and rational system meant that industrial and agricultural output increased, while shipping and transport expanded rapidly. This was also a period of industrial rationalization or scientific management, which included the use of assembly-line techniques and the more economic employment of labour. In the international sphere, attempts were made to restore a fully functioning and stable exchange. Britain returned to the gold standard in 1925, followed by most other European countries by 1928. Meanwhile, in 1927, a conference met at Geneva to try to remove any remaining impediments to international trade. Overall, it seemed that Europe was experiencing unprecedented – and permanent – prosperity.

Our retrospective knowledge shows just how misplaced this confidence was. The recovery proved extremely fragile and a potential crisis lurked behind every apparent gain.

In the first place, much of eastern Europe was less affected by the upswing in prosperity. The Soviet Union was almost completely isolated, while the less industrialized economies of the successor states and the Balkans suffered severely from lower agricultural prices which benefited the consumer at the expense of the producer. Indeed, Poland, Albania and Lithuania were all lost to dictatorship during this period, the result of an interaction between economic stagnation and political crisis.

Second, western European industrial growth was not accompanied by a proportionate increase in the volume of trade. By 1925 Europe's industrial production was the same as that of 1913, but European share of world trade was down from 63 per cent to 52 per cent. It was clear, therefore, that Europe had not succeeded in fully replacing the markets lost during the First World War. The United States, in fact, hoped to prevent Europe from doing so. Experiencing a massive increase in industrial production and fearing competition from Europe, the United States imposed higher tariffs on imports. European countries, with the exception of Britain, followed suit. The result was a series of major obstacles to international trade which did much to reduce its overall volume.

A third problem was that the agricultural sector in western Europe and the United States went through a period of overproduction, largely because of more efficient farming methods. The result was a fall in agricultural prices of up to 30 per cent between the end of 1925 and autumn 1929. As in eastern Europe, the producer suffered and the erosion of his spending power eventually reduced the market for industrial goods. There were also political implications. In Germany, for example, small farmers had become destabilized and a prey to Nazism long before the onset of the Great Depression.

Fourth, industrial growth – the great economic achievement of the 1920s – was itself unsteady. It depended too heavily on American loans, mostly short term, and Germany borrowed at 2 per cent above normal interest rates. Any large-scale withdrawal of this investment would have devastating results. Even industrial rationalization or scientific management had its perils. By making it possible to reduce the size of the workforce, it added, even in prosperous times, to the unemployment figures. Before the onset of the Depression, Britain already had one million out of work and Germany had two million.

Finally, even the improvements made in international economic relations proved short-lived. The gold standard, for example, did not provide the anticipated stability, as its operation was distorted by the accumulation of most of the world's gold reserves in the United States. In general, Europe's recovery was so closely linked to the prosperity of the United States that the relationship could transmit disadvantages as well as benefits. To repeat the old metaphor, 'when America sneezes, the rest of the world catches cold'.

The more negative impact of the United States began to be felt from mid-1928. The quantity of American loans to Europe began to decrease, largely because of a boom in the domestic stock market. Investors were convinced that this would last indefinitely and that the prospects for returns on investment were far better at home than they were abroad. European economic growth was therefore already affected when, in October 1929, another savage blow was dealt by the Wall Street Crash. The sudden collapse of the US stock market was followed by further restrictions on American lending to Europe, thus depriving the latter of what had been a vital factor in its economic recovery. The real impact, however, was experienced in 1931 when the central European banking system was undermined. The crisis began with the collapse of the Austrian bank, Kredit Anstalt, and spread to Hungary, Czechoslovakia, Romania, Poland and Germany.

The economic impact was devastating. All the underlying deficiencies already referred to now came to the surface. By the end of 1932, for example, total world industrial production had declined by 30 per cent from 1929 levels and trade in manufactured goods by 42 per cent. During the same period, world food output fell by 11 per cent and the extraction of raw materials by 19 per cent. Of the individual countries, Germany was the most seriously affected: her 39 per cent decline in industrial production forced unemployment levels up to over 6 million. Other central European countries were also badly hit, including Austria and Czechoslovakia; the crisis was especially serious in Czechoslovakia's most highly industrialized region, the Sudetenland. Eastern Europe had suffered before the onset of the Depression from a drop in agricultural prices, but the Depression intensified the misery by destroying the trade in agricultural goods. The Soviet Union was, supposedly, insulated from the mainstream of the world economy because of her self-sufficiency and rigid economic planning. But even here the Depression had an impact. The Soviet Union depended for its own industrialization on imports of foreign machinery. These were paid for by exports of Soviet grain, the value of which declined steadily as a result of the fall in agricultural prices. Relatively, therefore, imports became more expensive.

The Great Depression presented a double aspect. In the words of Hughes, the crisis of capitalism also appeared as a crisis of liberalism and democracy. All the remaining parliamentary regimes came under severe strain. Some successfully preserved their political systems. The Scandinavian countries, especially Sweden and Denmark, made effective use of consensus politics to contain the emergency. Britain went through a political upheaval, but confined this to the parliamentary context by substituting a National Government for the usual bipartisan approach. France managed to hang on to democracy through the expedient of broad-based coalitions or Léon Blum's Popular Front of 1936. In most other European countries, however, democracy fell apart. Germany was the classic case. The broad-based coalition government of Müller collapsed in 1929, unable to agree a strategy to deal with the economic crisis. The subsequent shift to the right benefited the Nazis, and made possible the rise to power of Hitler by 1933. In eastern Europe, and in the Balkans and Portugal, there was an almost universal resort to emergency powers to replace already discredited parliamentary governments. The only real exception to this process was Spain, which actually progressed during the Depression from dictatorship to the democracy of the Second Republic. This could, however, be seen as a coincidence and, in any case, the Depression helped destabilize the republic and laid it open to the eventual counter-attack of the right in 1936.

How did the various governments come to terms with the problems caused by the Depression? Several policies were attempted. France refused to devalue its currency and, like Britain and Germany in 1931, relied on cutting government expenditure and carefully balancing the budget. Italy, Portugal and Austria tried variants of corporativism, and Nazi Germany introduced a drive for self-sufficiency, or autarky. The degree of success varied; by 1932 some countries were beginning to pull out of the Depression, and most were emerging by 1934. It seemed, therefore, that capitalism had survived the turmoil. The same, however, could not be said of democracy. For the capitalism which existed in most of Europe was no longer 'liberal capitalism' and no longer required the policies of 'liberal democratic' governments. Instead, a new type of 'economic nationalism' had emerged,[16] based on state control and the mobilization of labour and resources.

In one area economic recovery was delayed. The complex web of international trade was irreparably torn. The main reason for this was the collapse of any real international co-operation and the adoption of essentially national programmes of survival. There was only one compromise: the 1932 Lausanne Conference agreed to cut reparations by 90 per cent. However, the significance of this was overstated at the time, for Hitler proceeded after 1933 to ignore reparations totally. There were to be no other agreements. The World Economic Conference, convened in London in 1933, achieved nothing. All states were imposing high tariffs and drawing up bilateral or regional agreements which effectively destroyed free trade. Examples included the Oslo Group, comprising the Scandinavian countries, and the Ottawa Agreement of 1932 which covered the British Empire. France made similar arrangements with its colonies, while Germany drew up a series of trade pacts with the Balkan states which had profound political consequences (see Chapter 7).

The failure to provide a common approach to dealing with the world economic crisis also contributed to the rapid deterioration of international relations. The three major powers particularly responsible for this were Japan, Italy and Germany, all of which sought economic solutions in rearmament and aggression. The Italian invasion of Abyssinia, for example, was hastened by the withdrawal of American investments after 1929, which had the dual effect of removing all restraints on Italian foreign policy and encouraging Mussolini to reformulate his entire economic strategy. By far the greatest blow to the international system, however, was dealt by Germany. Hitler's Four-Year Plan was intended to prepare Germany for war by 1940, and the increase in military expenditure contributed greatly to the growing confidence and aggression of Hitler's foreign policy during the late 1930s. Dictatorship had finally forged its association with expansionism and militarism, whereas democracy, enervated by the Depression, clung desperately to the hope for peace.

Chapter 2

Types of dictatorship

The purpose of this chapter is to analyse the terms which will be used for the rest of this book. Some readers may, however, prefer to return to it after covering Chapters 3 to 7, and before looking at Chapter 9.

DICTATORSHIP AS A CONCEPT

Dictatorship is not a modern concept. Two thousand years ago, during the period of the Roman Republic, exceptional powers were sometimes given by the Senate to individual dictators such as Sulla and Julius Caesar. The intention was that the dictatorship would be temporary and that it would make it possible to take swift and effective action to deal with an emergency. There is some disagreement as to how the term should be applied today. Should it be used in its original form to describe the temporary exercise of emergency powers? Or can it now be applied in a much broader sense – as common usage suggests?

Buchheim argues that dictatorship should be seen as a temporary device. It is 'equally present in contemporary democratic republics' and involves the short-term suspension of the democratic process when quick and vigorous action is necessary.[1] Linz is more specific. Where the temporary suspension of the democratic process is in accordance with 'rules foreseen in the constitution of a regime', then the process should be called 'crisis government' or 'constitutional dictatorship'. But the term 'dictatorship' should be 'reserved' for 'interim crisis government that has not institutionalized itself and represents a break with institutionalized rules about accession to and exercise of power of the preceding regime, be it democratic, traditional or authoritarian'.[2]

Others take a less restricted view. According to Curtis, 'the meaning of the term has changed since Roman times. The essential ingredient of modern dictatorship is power; an emergency is not necessarily present.'[3] Brooker refers to the emergence, after the First World War, of 'a modernized form of dictatorship' which had 'a longer-term perspective than the previous forms'. But it had a characteristic feature – the possession of 'an official ideology and political party'; hence the 'most accurate categorical or conceptual description of the twentieth-century form of dictatorship' would be the 'ideological one-party state'. In this form, dictatorship was actually 'a more modern regime than democracy'.[4]

Even these four examples show an enormous range of possibilities. At one end of the spectrum we see 'dictatorship' as a temporary device to save an existing system. A little further along we encounter 'dictatorship' as a change not foreseen by that system. At the other end we move, via the permanent monopoly of power, to the monolithic ideological regime. One end of the spectrum might be seen as *exclusive*, in that it disallows anything but the original usage of the term; the other as *inclusive*, acknowledging that there are modern variants as well as earlier forms. Hence some historians writing on the twentieth century avoid referring to 'dictatorship' altogether; others, like Kershaw and Lewin, use it as an integral part of the title of one of their works – *Stalinism and Nazism: Dictatorships in Comparison*.[5]

This book has opted for the *inclusive* approach. Being tightly prescriptive about the use of words can lead to their elimination. There are, after all, similar debates over 'revolution' – but it is a term we still need. If the original understanding were exclusively employed we would be emphasizing revolution as a return to an earlier phase, as with the turn of a wheel. But in an *inclusive* sense we can refer to 'political, social, economic, scientific or cultural' revolution, or to revolution 'from above or below', as a 'sudden change of course' or as 'accelerated evolution'. The same should apply to 'dictatorship'. The important thing is to recognize that it can include alternative forms, which need to be defined by carefully chosen adjectives. In a sense, Linz did this with his use of the term 'constitutional dictatorship' while using an *exclusive* argument. Why, therefore, should we not refer, more *inclusively*, to 'military' or 'one-party' dictatorship, or to 'authoritarian' or 'totalitarian' dictatorship?

With this in mind, we might provide a provisional definition of 'dictatorship' based on three main characteristics. First, it is a regime whose power base is monopolized by a single group which cannot be removed. The type of group defines the type of dictatorship structure – 'personal', 'military', 'party' or, in Marxist terms, even 'class' ('dictatorship of the bourgeoisie' or 'dictatorship of the proletariat', for example). Second, 'dictatorship' involves the unchallengeable monopoly of controls by the power base over the population. This may range from 'temporary' or 'emergency' to 'permanent' or 'institutionalized'. Third, this may include the imposition of attitudes, ideas or an ideology. The type of attitudes or ideology will then indicate whether the dictatorship is 'authoritarian' or 'totalitarian', 'left' or 'right', 'Communist' or 'Fascist'.

The most significant feature about 'dictatorship' in an *inclusive* sense is, therefore, the defining characteristics which go with it. To these we now turn.

TOTALITARIAN OR AUTHORITARIAN REGIMES?

The terms most widely used by historians to describe different types of regime in the twentieth century are 'democratic' and 'non-democratic', 'authoritarian' and 'totalitarian', 'left' and 'right', 'communist' and 'fascist'. All of these can be used in different ways – or avoided altogether. This section will try to establish a framework which can apply a *type* to dictatorship, after considering various alternative approaches. As we have seen, not all historians like the word 'dictatorship' but our intention will be to qualify it by association with some of these other terms, rather than discard in favour of these terms.

The first distinction sometimes drawn is between 'democratic' and 'non-democratic'. Since all the regimes covered in this book were essentially 'non-democratic', this would not be particularly useful as a basic definition. It would contribute towards establishing which 'democratic' qualities each of them lacked but not towards defining the type of regime set up as an alternative.

A second possibility would be to distinguish between 'democratic' and 'authoritarian' systems. Generically, the latter is a system of government which is based on heavily centralized control and which dilutes or dispenses with a properly functioning parliamentary democracy. Used in its widest sense, 'authoritarian' would cover all forms of 'non-democratic' regime and hence all the examples dealt with in this book. Some historians confine themselves to this broad approach, while others, like Perlmutter, consider that 'authoritarianism' has sub-categories: thus 'When one speaks of "totalitarianism", one means an institutionalized authoritarian regime sustained by a combination of organization and ideology'.[6]

A third approach is to separate 'authoritarian' and 'totalitarian' rather than to see the latter as a branch of the former. Linz includes among 'authoritarian' regimes those which might be under military leadership or a non-totalitarian one-party system. The purpose of the authoritarian regime might be political demobilization and the pursuit of conservative or social policies which do not involve radicalization or mass mobilization.

This contrasts directly with the 'totalitarian' system[7]. According to Laqueur, the term was 'coined to cover common features of communist and fascist states', even though Mussolini had used it during the 1930s to describe the type of regime he was hoping to establish over the Italian people. Laqueur's statement was more relevant to the period immediately after the Second World War, when Western governments came to fear the Soviet Union – their former ally against Hitler – and to see much in common between communism and fascism. In the atmosphere of the Cold War, two systems were therefore conjoined under one classification. In an attempt to move away from loose generalization into more structured definition, historians since the 1950s have explained totalitarianism in a variety of ways. According to Friedrich and Brzezinski,[8] totalitarianism was a combination of 'an ideology, a single party typically led by one man, a terroristic police, a communications monopoly, a weapons monopoly, and a centrally directed economy'.[9] The ideology and the whole aim of the regime is 'total destruction and total reconstruction'.[10] Hence, the true totalitarian system moves step by step towards the achievement of its goals through the effective manipulation of the population. This makes full use of modern techniques of propaganda and indoctrination as well as of force. For Arendt the process is less orderly.[11] Radical ideology, she agrees, forms the basis of the totalitarian regime. There is, however, no coherent programme – only a restless movement 'to organise as many people as possible within its framework and to set and keep them in motion'.[12] The result is chaos rather than order, with new institutions overlapping traditional ones. The most important method used to bring the population into line is terror, since it cannot be assumed that other forms of socialization will be fully effective.

It should be pointed out that there are problems with the use of the term 'totalitarian'. The first concerns the regimes to which it should be applied. The original classification covered the USSR, Germany and Italy. Then the term was partially discredited by its Cold War extension to post-Stalinist Russia and its satellite states in eastern Europe. Gleeson, for example, describes totalitarianism as 'the great mobilizing and unifying concept of the Cold War'.[13] But should the term be applied to communist regimes *per se*? In the 1960s, at the height of the Cold War, Curtis argued: 'If communist countries are automatically viewed as totalitarian, with all the concept's pejorative connotations, they emerge not simply as the inevitable enemy but also as the embodiment of evil and of a heresy to be isolated.'[14]

This brings us to a second difficulty. Some historians have applied the term 'totalitarian' to certain 'democratic' regimes. In the early 1950s, for example, Talmon used the variant 'totalitarian democracy',[15] to describe the modern application of ideas and structures which first became apparent during the eighteenth century, especially the Jacobin phase of the French Revolution. This, however, has been applied only to the political *left* – and therefore excludes the ideologies and systems of the right like Fascism and Nazism. In effect, therefore, there have been two concurrent debates – one on whether the Soviet Union after Stalin was a totalitarian regime at all, the other on whether, if it *was* totalitarian, it was a democracy or a dictatorship.

The third complication is the more recent identification of 'strong' and 'weak' variants of totalitarianism. In the strong model, totalitarianism achieves total control over the population through conversion by methods such as socialization, indoctrination and force. The most important criterion for success is the degree to which the ideology and objectives of the regime are accomplished; the word 'strong' therefore reflects the structured or projective approach to change. By contrast, the weak model focuses on the way in which the regime exercises its power. The emphasis is on 'the practices of rule rather than its effects'. It stresses 'the actions of the regime, what the regime does as opposed to the degree of control it is able to wield'.[16] The word 'weak' is a reflection on the regime having to react to changes rather than being in control of them. Of the two, the weak model seems to offer more scope for effective analysis. For one thing, it is extremely difficult to define objectively how far a population within a totalitarian regime has been imbued with its ideology. It is far easier to assess the methods by which the regime has tried to achieve conformity. The strong model also implies that the regime is always in control, that power and decisions about the exercise of power are part of a 'top-down' process. The weak model, by contrast, allows for the existence of administrative confusion and for the influence of sectors of the population on the development of policy: this makes possible a 'bottom-up' analysis. In addition, the strong model would logically characterize an effective totalitarian regime as one which made decreasing use of terror. In the most extreme cases of totalitarian rule, the reverse happened, which also adheres more closely to the weak model.

With these difficulties, it is not surprising that the need for the term 'totalitarian' has been questioned altogether. Some historians now consider that it has been tainted by the ideological conflict of the Cold War; others have argued that recent research on Nazi Germany and Stalinist Russia has revealed so many deficiencies in the structure of their power that it can be doubted whether there ever has been a regime which can be properly described as 'totalitarian'. But the problem with this approach to terminology is that almost every word could be thrown out by purists, thus severely depleting the historian's vocabulary. As Tormey believes, it therefore 'seems as pointless to write off the concept of totalitarianism as it is to write off the concept of democracy'. In any case, there is always scope for the development of new definitions. One example of this is the recent focus on the 'sacralization of politics', which is covered in the chapters on Mussolini and Hitler.[17]

For the sake of clarity, this book will make a broad distinction between totalitarian and authoritarian. Both types of dictatorship dispensed with the normal processes of parliamentary government and were critical of democracy. Beyond that, however, their basic intentions differed.

Totalitarian regimes had a radical programme of change, and deliberately mobilized the masses to serve a 'revolutionary monopolist movement'. They were also permeated by an ideology or 'a quasi-religious philosophy with a claim to exclusivity'.[18] More specifically, totalitarian regimes possessed a distinctive ideology which formed a 'body of doctrine covering all vital parts of man's existence'.[19] Everything was in theory subordinated to it and attempts were to be made to restructure society according to its goals. Second, the political system was under the control of a single party, presided over by a leader who was invested with the cult of personality. This party aimed at mobilized mass support, particularly among the young, and generated paramilitary activity. Party politics were ended and the legislature brought under the control of the executive. Third, the individual was completely subordinated to the dictates of the state through a process of coercion and indoctrination. The former could involve 'a system of terror, whether physical or psychic, effected through party and secret police control'.[20] Indoctrination sought the destruction of cultural pluralism and the shaping of education, literature, art and music to the objectives of political ideology. Fourth, the totalitarian state sought to impose complete control over the economy by establishing the basic objectives and providing 'bureaucratic co-ordination of formerly independent corporate entities'.[21] In some respects the most 'totalitarian' of all the regimes may appear to have been Stalin's Russia, since it fulfilled all the categories mentioned. Marxism-Leninism was an all-embracing ideology which was used extensively as a social-engineering force. The Nazi regime, too, was totalitarian in that it was based on an ideology which was more extreme than any yet devised and which was imposed upon the population by extensive coercion and indoctrination. In Italy, however, radical theory was undermined by a remarkably persistent status quo. This places Fascist Italy on the borderline between totalitarianism and authoritarianism.

Authoritarian regimes, by contrast, used dictatorship in a conservative way, aiming to preserve traditional values and often the traditional social structure. This was to be accomplished neither by revolution nor by rousing the masses. Quite the contrary. As Bracher argues, authoritarian regimes arrived at the neutralization or 'immobilization of all other forces in the state'.[22] It is true that some had one or two common features with the totalitarian states. Greece, for example, sometimes imitated the Nazi security system and Metaxas was partly influenced by Hitler's ideology. Hungary under Gömbös and Poland after Piłsudski flirted with milder forms of fascism, while Austria under Dollfuss and Salazar's Portugal tried out local variants of corporativism. Several factors, however, prevent these and the other regimes from being regarded with Italy as even partly totalitarian. With the possible exception of Portugal, they lacked any consistent attempt to mobilize the masses behind the regime. In fact, quite the reverse: they aimed to neutralize and depoliticize. This was partly because their leaders relied upon traditional ideas, although in a regenerated form, and distrusted anything which was remotely radical or revolutionary. Finally, authoritarian leaders were content to let the individual remain within his traditional social context and there was rarely any attempt at mass indoctrination.

There remains one major issue. The terms 'authoritarian' and 'totalitarian' are generally used to classify a regime from a structural or static point of view. They do not, however, take account of *changes* within a regime – where it originates, how it develops and why it decays. There are two possible ways of dealing with this.

One is to allow an overlap between the terms at various points within a regime's history. An 'authoritarian' regime can, for example, tighten up into a 'totalitarian' one; indeed some, like Arendt, have argued that the 'authoritarian' regime of Lenin was eventually transformed into the 'totalitarianism' of Stalin. (Chapter 3, however, refutes this particular example.) Conversely, 'totalitarianism' can loosen or decay into more typically 'authoritarian' regimes; these have been called 'post-totalitarian authoritarian' and have been applied particularly to the communist systems in Europe after the Stalin era. Like the right-wing 'authoritarian' systems in Spain and Portugal, these eventually loosened up still further to enable the reintroduction of democratic influences. At this point it is no longer appropriate to call them 'dictatorships', although there is some controversy as to when, precisely, this occurred.

The other way of making terms such as 'authoritarian' and 'totalitarian' more dynamic is to develop a further description based on its ideological origins and purpose. Two main possibilities are fascist and communist. But others include looser terms such as nationalist or conservative.

THE IDEOLOGICAL BASIS OF DICTATORSHIP

Communism

The communist movements were based on a carefully formulated set of principles. The original ideas derived from Marx and Engels, who argued that all societies comprised two main parts – the base and the superstructure. The former was the prevailing economic structure (for example capitalism), the latter the political and social institutions of the ruling class. In order to change the institutions, or superstructure, it was essential to transform the base. This, in turn, involved the notion of class conflict, as the exploited classes sought to bring down their oppressors. Indeed, according to the *Communist Manifesto* (1848), 'The history of all human society, past and present, has been the history of class struggles.' This struggle operated by a dialectical process, by which the capitalist system inevitably developed its own opposite which would eventually destroy it. Hence, 'the bourgeoisie produces its own gravediggers'. Revolution, Marx considered, was a necessary function of this change for, in his words, 'force is the midwife of every old society pregnant with a new one'. After the revolution had been accomplished, a period known as the 'dictatorship of the proletariat' would begin, during which the bourgeois superstructure would be dismantled, private property would be abolished, production would be socialized and the proletariat would proclaim its triumph by eliminating all other classes. Gradually the 'dictatorship of the proletariat' would be transformed into the 'classless society' which would see an end to all need for force and coercion. According to Engels, 'The interference of the state power in social relations becomes superfluous in one sphere after another, and then dies away of itself.' The result is that state powers would be confined to purely administrative functions. In every other respect the state 'withers away'.

These theories were adapted to Russian conditions by Lenin, whose works of over twenty volumes covered all the different aspects of revolutionary activity, in the process bringing some major shifts to Marxist interpretation. Whereas Marx and Engels had looked to Germany as the most likely source of future change, Lenin added the significant twist that capitalism was most immediately vulnerable at the weakest link in its chain, rather than where it was most highly developed. In *Imperialism, the Highest Stage of Capitalism*, he maintained that the war revealed capitalism in decline everywhere, but the process of overthrowing old regimes would actually begin in Russia. Forcing the pace of the historical dialectic necessitated a tightly organized Central Committee, which consisted of dedicated professional revolutionaries. He regarded organization as essential, for 'Just as a blacksmith cannot seize the red hot iron, so the proletariat cannot directly seize power.' Marxism-Leninism, as the new synthesis came to be called, succeeded in overthrowing the western-style Provisional Government in Russia in October 1917. In the aftermath of the Revolution, Lenin established his own version of the 'dictatorship of the proletariat'. Considerable coercion was used to accomplish this, although he argued that the roles were now reversed: the 'majority' now suppressed the 'minority'.

Was this Leninist version a distortion of Marxism? The official Soviet view was that Lenin was adapting Marxism to new conditions, creating 'a mighty vehicle for the revolutionary transformation of the world'.[23] Against this, some western historians have put the case for a major distortion. Keep maintains that Lenin's regime pretended to be democratic, but 'Common to all Soviets was a form of organization that permitted them to be influenced – indeed, manipulated – by the radical activists.'[24] According to Pipes, 'his strategy owed precious little to Marxism and everything to an insatiable lust for power'.[25]

Rigby establishes a direct connection between the practice of Leninism and the power base of traditional Tsarism: 'the tendencies towards a mono-organisational order were indeed apparent in the old Russia.'[26]

Between 1918 and 1919 it looked as though it might, in the wake of the First World War, make spectacular gains elsewhere. The British Prime Minister, Lloyd George, said in 1919: 'The whole of Europe is filled with the spirit of revolution.' Yet, by 1929, the failure of the non-Russian communist parties to seize control had become apparent. Revolutions of the far left had collapsed in Bavaria, Hungary, Austria and the Po Valley in Italy. After 1920, communism, while remaining a spectre and constant threat, never succeeded in gaining power. Among the reasons, examined in Chapter 3, were the inconsistencies and defects of Stalin's foreign policy, which eventually weakened communism everywhere.

Further features were added to the ideology and practice of Communism by Stalin. He claimed that 'Socialism in One Country' was more in line with Marxism-Leninism as it had been developing up to 1924 than was Trotsky's variant – 'Permanent Revolution'. He used this to justify a strong domestic focus to socialist construction, as opposed to the internationalist approach of many other 'old Bolsheviks'. Second, in this construction, he placed particular emphasis on the 'dictatorship of the proletariat'. This, he said in 1930, 'represents the mightiest and most powerful authority of all forms of State that have ever existed.'[27] He thus abandoned the idea of the state 'withering away' and was able to intensify measures against any form of political opposition and, more importantly, against whole sectors of the population. Third, he explained the considerable increase in his own authority by reference to the original Marxist relationship between 'base' and 'superstructure'. He claimed to be updating an ideological adaptation already started by Lenin. Marx and Engels had argued that the economic 'base' gave rise to the political and social 'superstructure', the assumption being that economic transformation would come first. Stalin used the same metaphors but reversed their relationship. He argued that the superstructure needed to become 'the greatest active force' to 'assist its basis to take shape and acquire strength' and 'to help the new order to finish off and liquidate the old basis and the old classes'.[28] This directly justified the introduction of a centralized bureaucracy, and the reshaping of the economy through collectivization and industrial planning.

Was Stalinism the natural fulfilment of Marxism-Leninism – or a major distortion? The official Soviet line at the time was that Stalin had made major theoretical contributions in the process of ensuring that Moscow remained the centre of world communism. But after his death in 1953, few continued to believe that Stalin had advanced Marxist theory or that he was really the 'great educator' claimed as part of his personality cult. Instead, he was seen increasingly as the 'great opportunist', merely using ideological arguments to support policies he was making through other motives. Many saw Stalinism as a distortion of Leninism: these included sources as diverse as Soviet premier Khrushchev, the historian Tucker, and Lukács, the Hungarian revolutionary. Lukács said that 'Stalinism is not only an erroneous interpretation and a defective application of Marxism; it is, in fact, its negation. There are no longer any theorists. There are only tacticians.'[29] Another strand of interpretation has developed more recently: Stalinism *was* an ideological successor to Leninism, since it was Leninism which was responsible for the original distortion of Marxism. This has been emphasized by non-Soviet communist parties in western Europe, as well as by post-Soviet socialists. A possible viewpoint is that Lenin was a theorist of strategy, adapting Marxism to a new situation. Stalin was not a theorist, except in the limited ways already examined. But he used the Leninist approach to Marxism with his own special emphasis.

Fascism

The most extreme movement of the right is generally called Fascism. This was more diffuse than Marxism-Leninism and certainly much more difficult to explain. There are also controversies as to what type of support it attracted; where it was in the political spectrum; and where, when and why it appeared.

Two – complementary – definitions will do as a starting point. According to Blum, fascism was an 'ultranationalist, imperialist, and even racial ideology and political system'; it was 'entirely a European phenomenon closely tied to the personalities of Hitler and Mussolini'.[30] Paxton prefers to call it

> a form of political behaviour marked by obsessive preoccupation with political decline, humiliation, or victimhood and by compensatory cults of unity, energy and purity, in which a mass-based party of committed nationalist militants, working in uneasy but effective collaboration with traditional elite groups, abandons democratic liberties and pursues with redemptive violence and without ethical or legal restraints goals of internal cleansing and external expansion.[31]

Where did fascism originate? Here may be found widely divergent explanations. Marxist theories naturally put as much distance between fascism and communism as possible. They therefore reject the 'totalitarian' approach – either as a description of communism itself or as a method of finding common characteristics between communism and fascism. Instead, Marxists see fascism as a variant of capitalism. The earliest version of this was the interpretation advanced by the Communist International (Comintern) in 1933. As predicted by Lenin, capitalist societies were entering a period of crisis after the First World War. The reactionary capitalist elements manipulated the population through a mass movement capable of challenging the more genuinely revolutionary movement of the working class. In this sense it was the final and dying stage of bourgeois-capitalist domination, the fascist leaders being the 'agents' of capitalist controllers. A variant to this was the more nonconformist Marxist analysis provided by the Italian Communist, Gramsci, who pointed to the *political* crisis of capitalist states: fascism emerged as a radical populist alternative to the fading appeal of the ruling class – in an attempt to revive the capitalist drive.

These theories suffer from an over-structured interpretation of past trends, related entirely to the theory of class conflict and the ultimate struggle between the bourgeoisie and the proletariat, between the capitalist system and its inevitable successor. They were an attempt to read back into the works of Marx and Lenin the events of the twentieth century, without allowing for other influences and interpretations, based on more subtle nuances than class conflict and exploitation. A wide variety of these has been provided by non-Marxist explanations.

Some emphasize the climate of change between the late nineteenth and early twentieth centuries. Early non-Marxist arguments, advanced by the likes of Meinecke and Ritter, emphasized the moral crisis of European society, Fromm even referring to an 'escape from freedom and a refuge in submission'.[32] These, however, were somewhat sweeping, a reflection of disillusionment of the time but not convincing in the broader sweep of historical analysis. A similar, but more balanced theme has been taken by Blum, who sees fascism in the context of major changes in the climate of opinion of nineteenth- and early twentieth-century Europe.[33] He argues that 'The ideals of the Enlightenment and the French Revolution – rationalism, liberalism, democracy and egalitarianism – were increasingly challenged by new philosophical, scientific, pseudoscientific, and political precepts.'[34] Other interpretations focus on fascism as a reaction to other influences. Nolte, for example, argues that 'The origin of the Right lies always in the challenge of the Left.'[35] Elsewhere he defines fascism as 'an anti-revolutionary revolution of subversive conservatives'.[36] Hildebrand sees it rather as a reaction to development, the energy of fascism, coming from the resistance of residual 'elites to the egalitarian tendencies' of industrial society.[37] Others have cited agrarian societies in a crisis of modernization which threatened both landed elites and the peasantry. There is also a considerable emphasis on fascism as 'a reaction against the devastating impact of World War I' and the latter's 'unsettling aftermath on basically liberal nineteenth-century nations that failed to achieve social harmony'.[38] Among these, the recently united Italy and Germany were especially vulnerable.

Where in the political spectrum should fascism be placed? The majority view is that it belonged on the far right, in alliance with the conservative right which helped it into power. From this position it proceeded to expunge the centre and the left.

An interesting alternative, advanced by Sternhell, is that fascism was the result of a convergence between the far right and the far left, originating in turn-of-the-century France and spreading to Italy.[39] This does suggest the synthesis of nationalism and the syndicalist variant of socialism, without suggesting an ideological overlap with communism, which remained entirely distinct. It does not, however, apply to Nazi Germany. Another possibility is the extremism of the centre. Lipset maintains fascism depended on defections from the traditional liberal parties by middle classes feeling threatened by capitalism and communism.[40] This, however, provides a strong sociological explanation for the support of a movement going through an opportunist phase rather than an accurate placing of its theories.

Any attempt at a synthesis of fascism's characteristics is hazardous. Yet there were several obvious characteristics. It carried a belief in a radical change or revolution to end an existing condition of subjection or decadence and to achieve social transformation and rebirth. In the process, it rejected the two main alternatives of the early twentieth century and had a deep hatred of the British and French traditions of democracy (Hitler claimed, in *Mein Kampf*, that 'there is no principle which . . . is as false as that of parliamentarianism',[41] and of the revolutionary left, with its notions of class conflict and dictatorship of the proletariat). In terms of organization, fascist parties were presided over by an absolute leader who, in turn, was surrounded by all the trappings of a personality cult. At the lower levels were cadres and paramilitary outfits, intended to mobilize the masses and turn them against the establishment. In the context of the state, it combined single-party rule with the leadership principle (Führerprinzip or cult of the Duce) within the context of a totalitarian system which exerted control over all forms of communication and the economy. It also developed an alternative economic strategy to socialism and trade union power on the one hand and capitalism and big business on the other. It therefore offered a 'third way' which would seek to eliminate class conflict. Elsewhere it placed the emphasis firmly on conflict, applying the theory of the survival of the fittest to the social and political spheres and justifying both the crushing of the weak and ruthless military expansion. The result was a glorification of war which led to 'hypernationalist' policies. In Germany, this social Darwinism also underlay Hitler's racism and anti-Semitism.

Fascist movements drew support from a wide cross-section of the population, although with varying degrees of success from area to area. One receptive social group was the *lumpenproletariat*, the unemployed and displaced, although it should be said that most workers tended to support socialist or communist parties. Another was the rural population – both the peasantry and the estate owners. A third was the large number of former army officers and demobilized soldiers, veterans who were disillusioned by their treatment immediately after the First World War and, in some instances, shocked by the terms of the peace settlement. In the more industrialized countries, fascism drew its main support from the middle classes, who were profoundly affected and destabilized by the economic crises of the early 1920s and 1930s. Finally, capital and big business joined the bandwagon to try to find security against the threat of communism. Overall, fascism benefited greatly from the instability of the inter-war period and made the most of the 'flabbiness and the failures of the existing regimes'.[42]

At this stage it is necessary to sort out the various regimes of the right and establish which were fascist. The most obvious instance was Mussolini's Italy, where the term fascism originated, and which showed all the components already mentioned. Some authorities, like Sternhell, prefer to exclude Nazi Germany, but the general consensus is that a generic definition of fascism ought to include it. According to Kershaw, 'It might well be claimed that Nazism and Italian fascism were separate species within the same genus, without any implicit assumption that the two species ought to be well-nigh identical.'[43] Nolte refers to Nazism as 'radical fascism'[44] and Linz calls it a 'distinctive branch grafted on the fascist tree'.[45] Although Nazism did not consciously imitate Italian Fascism, there was considerable common ground in both organization and ideas. The most important differences were Hitler's emphasis on the racial community and anti-Semitism – neither of which was an integral part of Italian Fascism until 1938.

The other dictatorships of the right can be divided, before the Second World War, into two types: those which absorbed fascism and those which resisted it. The first did have significant fascist influences but these were mixed, in varying concentrations, with other factors. An example is Spain, where Franco balanced the fascist Falange Española (formed in 1933 by José Antonio Primo de Rivera) with the more traditional interests of the army, Church and monarchists; certainly the Falange never dominated the regime in the way that the Fascist Party prevailed in Italy. Another instance of a regime partially influenced by fascism can be seen in Austria, where Dollfuss introduced a conservative and clerical-inspired variant which has been dubbed both 'clerico-fascist' and 'Austrofascist'. A case has also been made for the existence of a quasi-fascist regime under Metaxas in Greece. Elsewhere, fascist movements were often regarded as disruptive and dangerous. In Hungary, Horthy had little sympathy with the Arrow Cross (formed by uniting several fascist groups in 1937), while King Carol of Romania tried to suppress the Iron Guard. The Polish leaders had no time for the Polish Falanga; there were also struggles between Päts and the Estonian Freedom Fighters, between Smetona and the Iron Wolf of Lithuania and between Latvia's Ulmanis and the Thunder Cross. Minority fascist movements also tried to cause upheaval in the democracies: for example, Action Française, the Dutch National Socialist Movement, the British Fascist Movement, Rex in Belgium and Lapua in Finland. There were also, in some countries, subnational or regionally based fascist parties; these included the Slovak People's Party and Ustashi in Croatia. Every one of these movements failed to gain power.

It appears, therefore, that fascism needed conditions of relative freedom in which to take over by itself. The ideal breeding grounds were the vulnerable democracies of Weimar Germany and liberal Italy. Elsewhere it failed to remove the inter-war authoritarian regimes which absorbed, diluted or rejected the totalitarian characteristics of fascism. Until, that is, an opportunity was provided during the upheaval of the Second World War. From 1941 onwards a series of fascist regimes came into existence as Nazi puppets – the Iron Guard in Romania, Arrow Cross in Hungary, the Slovak People's Party and the Ustashi in the Croatian part of dismembered Yugoslavia. All proved far more oppressive and vicious than the more traditional dictatorships which they replaced, but none survived the impending defeat of Nazi Germany. Although they all aspired to be totalitarian, they lacked the power base for independent existence. They represented little more than parasitic fascism.

Finally, on what timescale did fascism exist? Most authorities, including Griffin, focus on the inter-war period, with the main examples to be seen in Italy and Germany and smaller movements elsewhere. More controversially, Sternhell places the origins of fascism in pre-1914 France, from which it spread to Italy – but not to Germany; this, however, is essentially a minority view. Elements of fascism have also reappeared in Europe since the Second World War; these have been associated with the Movimento Sociale Italiano; the National Democratic Party (NPD), German Reich party (DRP) and Republican Party; Le Pen's National Front in France; and Zhirinovsky's Liberal Democratic party in Russia.

Other influences

In addition to fascism, Nazism and communism, there were other influences at play in inter-war Europe. These were not ideologies as such, but sometimes they assumed the force normally attributed to an ideology.

The closest to an ideology was nationalism. Indeed, it might be argued that nationalism is the only 'ism' which means exactly what it says: Sugar calls it one of the 'three dominant ideologies of the twentieth century', along with communism and fascism/Nazism.[46] On the other hand, it was too diffuse and widely variable to warrant such a connection. According to Minogue: although nationalism 'is a set of ideas', these 'add up less to a theory than to a rhetoric, a form of self-expression by which a certain kind of political excitement can be communicated from an elite to the masses'.[47] In any case, nationalism took a wide variety of forms, frequently with two or more reacting against each other within the same state. It was certainly present as a component in all systems of thought, whether in radical form in Italian fascism and German Nazism or in Stalin's Russification of communism. It was also integral, at the other end of the scale, to national self-determination, recognized by President Wilson and others as a legitimate liberal aspiration which was embodied in the formation of Czechoslovakia, Poland, Estonia, Latvia, Lithuania and Yugoslavia.

Between the two existed other forms of nationalism which shaped or influenced the authoritarian regimes of Europe during the 1920s and 1930s. One was integrationist nationalism, a powerful centrifugal force applied against internal ethnic minorities by authoritarian regimes: the main examples were measures against the Lithuanians, Belorussians and Ukrainians in Poland, and against the ethnic Hungarians in Romania. In addition, most authoritarian regimes discriminated in some form or other against Jews. Another variant was irredentist nationalism, or the pursuit of territorial claims. This was successfully applied by Piłsudski against Russia, but his authoritarian regime remained in Poland to protect the gains made in 1921. Hungary was less fortunate. A major influence on its foreign policy between the wars was resentment at the massive loss of territory imposed upon it by the Treaty of Trianon in 1919. Different again was the historic nationalism apparent in the longer-established nations of Portugal and Spain. Salazar's regime in Portugal fostered pride in imperial achievement – a form of sated nationalism – while Franco sought national regeneration inspired by Spain's more glorious past. There might also be combinations of these types of nationalism. One example was Hungary which experienced, under Szálasi, irredentism combined with a strong sense of the past in what he called Hungarism. Some nationalisms were also influenced by fascism, either by specific fascist movements operating within authoritarian regimes (like the Falange in Francoist Spain) or by authoritarian dictatorships in their later phase (Antonescu's Romania or Szálasi's Hungary).

Three other influences can be detected in Europe's authoritarian regimes, again in differing proportions. One was clericalism and the expression of a religion, normally Catholicism. This made its presence felt as a conservative force, mainly against communism, which the Church regarded as its greatest enemy. This was particularly prevalent in Spain during the Civil War, and in Austria under Dollfuss; it was also apparent in Poland and later in the disembodied states of Slovakia and Croatia. Regimes less affected by religious influences were Greece, Bulgaria, Romania and the Baltic states. Under Atatürk, Turkey's regime actively pursued the opposite – secularization and the removal of all political influence from Islamic bodies.

Another influence was conservatism. This acted either to maintain the status quo or to remove recent influences considered to have had a damaging impact. These 'influences' could include anything but were usually communism, socialism and movements on the far right. Hungary and Poland, for example, had a consistent record – until the late 1930s – of this type of reductionist conservatism. Alternatively, conservatism might be the bond which kept together an alliance of the centre to right against the countervailing forces of the moderate and far left. This was particularly the case in Spain, with Franco's National Front lined up against the Popular Front of the Republic.

The final factor, militarism, is more debatable. Although normally associated with the authoritarian right, military action has also been used against authoritarian systems as a force for change and reform, especially in pre-First World War Spain, Portugal and Turkey. But during the interwar period, military influences were normally adapted to conservative authoritarianism – most obviously in Piłsudski's Poland, Franco's Spain and Horthy's Hungary.

By and large, it is easier to define what ideologies the authoritarian regimes stood against than what they supported. This was because their fundamental purpose was not to mobilize or energize – but rather to prevent others from doing so. The one possible exception to this was Turkey, which used an authoritarian framework to achieve a radicalizing policy under western influences. This gave it the characteristics of a developmental dictatorship with a set of aims which was rather clearer than the others. But even Atatürk, who adopted certain principles, did not develop an ideology as such. Elsewhere the focus of authoritarian regimes was to impose severe restrictions on western democratic influences. In doing this they also prevented a fascist takeover. As we have already seen, the authoritarian establishment was usually strong enough to prevent the ascendancy of incipient totalitarian ideologies – at least until the latter began to expand from the base of their own regimes.

SUMMARY

The main argument of this chapter has been as follows. Although the term 'dictatorship' has attracted some controversy, it is more useful to see it in the more modern sense as a description of closed political systems which cannot be changed by the open democratic process. All regimes covered in this book were dictatorships at some point between 1918 and 1945.

'Dictatorship' should, however, be amplified by more specific reference to its type. The two most commonly used terms are 'authoritarian' and 'totalitarian'. 'Authoritarian' can be used as an overarching description of all closed systems. Or – as it is in this book – it can be distinguished from 'totalitarian'; as well as having a monolithic political base, the latter also involves a more explicit set of ideas and aims more directly to mobilize the mass of the people. Totalitarian systems include Stalinist Russia (Chapter 3), Fascist Italy

(Chapter 4) and Nazi Germany (Chapter 5). In the debate over Leninist Russia the preference here is for totalitarian rather than authoritarian, while the Soviet Union after Stalin could be described as evolving out of totalitarianism into a post-totalitarian authoritarian system. All the other regimes of the period (Chapter 7) were primarily authoritarian. This applies to Portugal, Spain under Primo de Rivera and Franco, Austria, Hungary, Poland, Estonia, Latvia, Lithuania, Albania, Yugoslavia, Greece, Romania, Bulgaria and Turkey (Chapter 7). For part of the wartime period some of these regimes came under the totalitarian control of Germany, Italy or the Soviet Union, or tried unsuccessfully to develop their own version of totalitarianism.

Related ideologies define the scope of totalitarian or authoritarian dictatorship. The two main ideologies of the inter-war period were communism and fascism. Both have been identified with totalitarianism within the state context (communism in the Soviet Union, fascism in Italy and Germany), although there has been some disagreement about the extent of their efficiency and about whether they overlap with authoritarian systems (the pre- and post-Stalinist regimes in Russia, for example). There has also been controversy as to whether fascism includes Nazism; the broad consensus is that it does, although as a different strand. In other cases fascism influenced regimes either briefly (Hungary under Szálasi) or as part of a broader coalition of the right (Spain under Franco or Austria under Dollfuss) which combined other influences not generally seen as ideological – clericalism, nationalism and militarism (Chapter 7). One non-Soviet regime was briefly communist after the First World War – Hungary under Béla Kun (Chapter 7). Other former dictatorships (Poland, Romania, Bulgaria, Hungary, Albania and Yugoslavia) became communist in the wake of the Second World War, while Estonia, Latvia and Lithuania were absorbed directly into the Soviet Union. For the moment, at least, fascism and the right gave way widely to communism and the left.

Chapter 3

Dictatorship in Russia

LENIN'S REGIME, 1917–24

Russia between 1917 and 1953 experienced two periods of dictatorship. The first was intended by Lenin to be a temporary dictatorship of the proletariat, a phase in the movement towards a communist system. The second was the more permanent and personalized dictatorship imposed by Stalin.

The revolution of October/November 1917

Soviet Russia was born in October/November 1917, when the Bolshevik Party, under Lenin, seized power in Petrograd and Moscow. In doing so it toppled the Provisional Government, mainly identified with the leadership of Alexander Kerensky. This, in turn, had replaced the regime of Tsar Nicholas II in March 1917.

Nicholas II's government had been severely weakened by a combination of military defeat at the hands of the Germans in the First World War, economic collapse and serious misgovernment. In March 1917 it was confronted by a largely spontaneous movement which began as a series of food riots and ended with the desertion of troops and security forces. When Nicholas II eventually abdicated on 15 March, two institutions claimed political authority. One was the Petrograd Soviet, a workers' council which was elected by soldiers and labourers. The other was the Provisional Government which had been set up by a committee of the Duma, a parliament which had been conceded reluctantly by the Tsar in 1905. The question now arising was: which of the two institutions – Soviet or Provisional Government – would provide the future power base?

There was nothing to indicate at this stage that the Bolsheviks would shortly be bidding for the control of Russia. They had played little part in the events of March and had no influence either in the Soviet or in the Provisional Government. The Soviet consisted mainly of Menshevik and Socialist Revolutionary deputies, while the Provisional Government, under Prince Lvov, was dominated by liberals and moderate conservatives – or Constitutional Democrats and Octobrists. Gradually, however, the Bolsheviks made their presence felt. Lenin returned from exile in Switzerland in April 1917 and set about making the Bolshevik Party the major organization of the working class. His intention was to take over the Soviet and use it to destroy the Provisional Government. For a while this seemed an impossible task. The Socialist Revolutionaries and Mensheviks within the Soviet were prepared to form a political partnership with the Provisional Government; this was cemented in the person of the Socialist Revolutionary Kerensky, who succeeded Lvov as head of the Provisional

Government on 20 July. Earlier in the same month Lenin had been seriously embarrassed by an abortive Bolshevik uprising; he had tried to prevent it on the grounds that it was premature. The Provisional Government ordered the raiding of the Bolshevik headquarters and issued warrants for the arrest of the Bolshevik leaders. Lenin escaped this only by going into hiding in Finland. It seemed, therefore, that the Provisional Government had triumphed and that the Bolsheviks had shot their bolt.

Through much of 1917, however, the Provisional Government faced serious difficulties which eventually worked in favour of the Bolsheviks. It maintained Russia's support for the Allies but, in the process, suffered further losses of territory to the Germans from July onwards. The economy, too, was in desperate trouble and the peasantry were openly seizing their landlords' estates in many of the rural areas. Kerensky, hoping to preside over an orderly land transfer, sent troops to deal with peasant violence, thus antagonizing a large part of the population. The Bolsheviks were able to take advantage of this policy and came out openly in support of the peasants. But the real crisis confronting the Provisional Government was the Kornilov Revolt. General Kornilov, Commander-in-Chief of the Russian army, tried in August/September to overthrow the Provisional Government and to substitute for it a military dictatorship that would, he hoped, drive back the German invader and deal with the internal threat of revolution. Kerensky could rely upon the Petrograd Soviet to mobilize support against Kornilov's troops, but he needed additional help if he were to save the Provisional Government. In desperation he turned to Bolshevik units known as Red Guards and agreed to arm them if they joined the defence of Petrograd. This decision saved the capital but placed the Provisional Government in grave peril. The liberals pulled out of the coalition with Kerensky, who was now left with a small fraction of his original support at a time when the Bolsheviks were growing in confidence.

By September the Bolsheviks had also become the most popular alternative to the Provisional Government. They had won majorities in the Petrograd and Moscow Soviets, and soon came to dominate most of the provincial soviets as well. From this, Lenin deduced that the time had come to seize the initiative and sweep Kerensky from power. The Petrograd Soviet was used as a front for Bolshevik revolutionary activity. Trotsky, its president, was also the overall co-ordinator of the impending coup, directing the activities of the newly formed Revolutionary Military Committee from his headquarters in the Smolny Institute. On the night of 6 November 1917, the Bolshevik Red Guards seized, with surprising ease and minimal bloodshed, the key installations of Petrograd. These included banks, telephone exchanges, railway stations and bridges. By 8 November the Winter Palace and the Admiralty Buildings, the administrative headquarters of the Provisional Government, had also been stormed. Kerensky had left the city to spend the rest of his life in exile.

Why were the Bolsheviks successful?

Lenin was assisted by three main factors. The first was the social and political situation between March and November, which gradually undermined the Provisional Government. The second was the growing popularity of the Bolsheviks during the course of 1917, which meant that they were able to harness a powerful undercurrent of revolutionary activism. And the third was the Bolsheviks' organization and strategy, which enabled them to take maximum advantage of the vulnerability of their opponents and the resentment of the urban and rural masses. Each of these has been the subject of controversy among historians, especially since 1991.

The weaknesses of the Provisional Government?

The Provisional Government has traditionally had a reputation for inefficiency and underachievement. This is not entirely just and attempts have been made to rehabilitate it. There was, nevertheless, an underlying problem which undermined its best efforts in the period between March and October 1917. This was the existence of a dual power base, referred to in the previous section. The Provisional Government consisted, at first, of Constitutional Democrats and Octobrists, and stood for the development of a Western type of parliamentary system. Established at the same time, the Petrograd Soviet comprised parties of the left, like the Mensheviks, Socialist Revolutionaries and ultimately the Bolsheviks. There were attempts to achieve collaboration between the two institutions. The Soviet, for example, passed an early resolution to co-operate with the Provisional Government laws in so far as they corresponded to the interests of the proletariat and the broad democratic masses of the people. Members of the Soviet were also drawn into the Provisional Government; Kerensky, a Socialist Revolutionary, was there from the start and several others joined the coalition governments of May and July.

These developments did not, however, guarantee political harmony. On the contrary, the Provisional Government and the Soviet pulled apart on conflicting policies over the continuation of the war and the distribution of land; to make matters worse, there was also dissension within the Provisional Government itself. The liberals pulled out of the government in August over the Kornilov Revolt so that Kerensky was left virtually isolated, presiding over a mere rump separated by an ever widening gulf from the Soviet. The latter was becoming increasingly radical and assertive, under the growing influence of the Bolsheviks, while Kerensky was becoming vulnerable to the accusation that his own claim to power was still untested by parliamentary election. In the words of one historian, it was a 'pre-legitimate regime'.

The Provisional Government was therefore inherently unstable and would have found survival difficult even in favourable circumstances. Its task, however, was rendered impossible by its military commitments. In the summer of 1917 it launched a great offensive against the Germans and Austrians in Galicia. This proved a disastrous failure, and from July onwards the Provisional Government faced the constant spectre of German advance. The Russian army was in imminent danger of collapse which, in itself, caused problems; mass desertions increased the level of instability, while, at the top, officers like Kornilov felt that they had little to lose by taking matters into their own hands. The Provisional Government's commitment to continuing the

1 Vladimir Ilyich Lenin, 1870–1924 (David King Collection)

war was one of the main reasons for its growing rift with the soviets and for the movement of the latter towards the Bolsheviks.

One further issue is worth brief examination. Why did the Socialist Revolutionaries and the Mensheviks in the Petrograd Soviet not take the initiative and set up an alternative to the Provisional Government? The answer is that they were considering this seriously and, but for the Bolshevik initiative in October, might well have done so. They were, however, hampered in taking decisive action by the different types of socialism which they represented; these could not easily have been reconciled. The Menshevik commitment was particularly strange. They were tied to a rigid version of Marxism which believed that the proletariat needed to help bring the bourgeoisie to power and then to wait, possibly for a long period, until capitalism had run its course before expecting the arrival of a socialist system. This justified co-operation with the liberals but hardly found favour with the Petrograd Soviet or with the first and second Congresses of Soviets which convened in June and October. (In his study of Menshevik strategy, Ascher asks the pertinent question: 'Had any class ever helped to make a revolution and then voluntarily stepped back to allow another to reap most of the benefits?'[1]) The Bolsheviks were therefore presented with a perfect opportunity to appeal to the radicals in the soviets through a series of promises in Lenin's *April Theses*. The result was a steady increase in Bolshevik influence which coincided with the deterioration of the Provisional Government. In the first Congress of Soviets (June 1917) the Bolsheviks had only 150 representatives to the Mensheviks' 248. By October the situation had been reversed; the Bolsheviks now had 300, the Mensheviks had 80 at the most.

An incident at the June meeting of the Congress of Soviets shows the contrasting attitudes to power of the Bolsheviks and other parties of the left. Tsereteli, one of the Menshevik leaders, argued that there was as yet no real alternative to the Provisional Government. He concluded: 'At the present moment there is no political party which would say, "Give the power into our hands, go away, we will take your place." There is no such party in Russia.' Lenin was heard to say from his seat, 'There is.'[2]

The influence of the masses?

It was once thought that the October Revolution was really a coup by a minority group against the real wishes of the population. In this respect, the key influence was the leadership and co-ordination of the Bolshevik Party, which planned and executed the transfer of power from the Provisional Government with military precision. In a sense, the acceptability of the new regime did not matter at first, since between 1918 and 1921 Lenin and Trotsky were able to transform the coup into a revolution.

This view has now been strongly challenged by a new wave of revisionist historians. This is largely because recent historical studies, of other European countries as well as Russia, have fundamentally reconsidered the way in which political power operates. It is now argued that there has been too much emphasis on the idea of power being a process which is exercised downwards, by leaders and organizations over peoples. Instead, there needs to be more recognition that leaders and organizations can be heavily influenced by pressures from below. The practical effect of the new perspective is that the Bolsheviks are now seen as being much more in line with the most immediate wishes of large parts of the population. Instead of forcing the pace of revolution by exploiting popular grievances, they were adapting their policies to enable them to move with a revolutionary current which already existed. The common people therefore had a vital influence on events. Acton's summary of this view is that, 'The driving force behind their intervention, their organizational activity and the shifts in their political allegiance was an essentially autonomous and rational pursuit of their own goals.'[3]

Which groups exerted the most influence on the Bolsheviks? One, which has in the past been greatly underestimated, was the peasantry. They provided a radical impetus, insisting on the return of the land to those who worked it and taking action to ensure that this happened. Peasant petitions also demanded justice through peasant courts, elected local authorities and more extensive education. Although there were frequent revolts, violence was not mindless but aimed at eliminating opposition to such designs. The Bolsheviks would have been unwise not to take note of such pressure. This explains the tactical adjustments to their policy made in the *April Theses* and subsequent pronouncements on land ownership, which were not exactly in line with Marxist collectivism. The urban workers also exerted pressure. The most active were the skilled workers, who tended to dominate the local soviets and factory committees. Like the peasants, they were radicalized by their own aspirations rather than by stimulus from the Bolsheviks. Elements within the army reacted in very much the same way. Their two main demands were for the democratization of the command and an early end to the war. This war weariness was less the result of external agitation, especially from the Bolsheviks, than from a deep welling up of discontent as a result of years of defeat and suffering. The resultant instability within the army was, of course, very widespread and would have led to further upheaval even if the Bolsheviks had not seized control in November 1917.

Rather than being manipulated themselves, therefore, these groups pressurized the Bolsheviks into taking action on their behalf. The Bolsheviks succeeded because they followed the trend rather than established it.

The organizational strengths of the Bolsheviks?

This more recent approach has implications for the whole question of the effectiveness of Bolshevik organization and leadership.

The argument which is now commonly used is that the Bolsheviks did not need to be effectively organized, since they rode to power on a wave of popular resentment. They were in a stronger position than their rivals, the Socialist Revolutionaries and the Mensheviks, who had sacrificed much of their credibility in 1917 by urging support for the policies of the Provisional Government. The Bolshevik Party was more democratic and decentralized than is often realized – precisely because this was the best way of adapting to the goals of the different sectors of society; centralized structures would have been a liability. The coup was carried out by Trotsky and the Military Revolutionary Committee in the name of the Soviet, which had a real influence over the decisions taken by the Bolsheviks against the Provisional Government. Whether or not the Soviet and the workers' committees approved of the seizure of power on 6–7 November, they were certainly not likely to try to prevent it, which meant that the Bolsheviks were given a clear path. It has therefore been argued that the Bolsheviks represented the general revolutionary trend in 1917 more effectively than any of the other parties precisely because they were not, at this stage, a centralized and conspiratorial organization.

Revisionist interpretations are based partly on new research and partly on a new emphasis. They should be considered but do not have to be accepted in full. There is one obstacle to the view that the popularity of the Bolsheviks made effective organization unnecessary. As soon as they had come to power the Bolsheviks arranged for an election of a new Constituent Assembly. Polling took place literally within weeks and the surprising result was that the

Bolsheviks lost heavily to the Socialist Revolutionaries. If the Bolsheviks were so successful in 1917 in reflecting public opinion, why did they not achieve a majority so soon after their successful seizure of power? Why, in particular, did they not experience a 'honeymoon period' with the electorate?

This may suggest a partial move back towards the more traditional view that the Bolsheviks *were* centrally focused. Certainly this was the attitude of Lenin himself, who had for many years emphasized the need for a tight party structure with a core of persons engaged in revolution as a profession. He gave the party a double objective in 1917. The first was to use organization on behalf of the masses to accomplish what the masses by themselves could not. The second was to take over the soviets, using them to legitimize the party's revolutionary activities. Lenin observed on 22 October: 'If we seize power today, we seize it not against the soviets but for them.'[4]

Effective organization would have been to no avail without a clear overall strategy. The basic principle of the Bolsheviks was to have a fixed long-term objective but a flexible short-term approach to it. The long-term aim was described in Lenin's *April Theses* as the 'transition from the first stage of the revolution, which gave power to the bourgeoisie . . . to the second stage, which should give the power into the hands of the proletariat and poorest strata of the peasantry'.[5] The short-term approach, however, would avoid any rigid or doctrinaire commitments. Above all, the right degree of force was essential at the right time; Lenin spoke of a judicious alternation between withdrawal and attack, depending on the strengths and weaknesses of the opponent. The Bolsheviks were, of course, fortunate in their leadership. Lenin, from the time of his return to Russia in April 1917, was the overall strategist of the revolution; he also dealt with internal divisions within the party and provided an authoritarian base which promoted a degree of discipline and unity which the other parties lacked. Above all, he was entirely responsible for the timing of the October Revolution. He had realized that the rising of July 1917 was premature and therefore urged restraint on that occasion. But by October he calculated that circumstances had changed sufficiently to warrant immediate action, and he urged: 'We must not wait! We may lose everything!'[6] From this point the initiative passed to Trotsky who used the Revolutionary Military Committee to take over the key installations in the capital.

However, while acknowledging that organization, conspiracy and timing were essential features of the Bolshevik Party, we should not lose sight of the balancing effect of revisionist ideas. A reasonable synthesis might go as follows. The Bolsheviks were not at this stage imposing their will on the people, nor were they shaping the revolution to their own design. Organization was therefore not essential for mobilizing support for revolution. Nevertheless, the situation in 1917 was highly volatile. Although the Bolsheviks had increased their popularity between March and October, it is possible to exaggerate the extent to which the peasantry had been won over. Quite possibly any transfer of allegiance was temporary, motivated by disillusionment with the indecisive policies of the Socialist Revolutionaries. The Bolsheviks would have been well aware of this and would have wanted to take maximum advantage of a situation which was only temporarily in their favour. This meant that they needed organization to take over the reins of power.

The survival of Bolshevik Russia: the Civil War, 1918–22

Seizing power was accomplished with surprising ease, but retaining it was to prove more difficult, as Lenin himself was all too aware. The most immediate threat was war – in two forms. The first was that the Great War, which had already been the catalyst in destroying

Tsarism and the Provisional Government, would bring down the Bolsheviks as well. The second was that the regime would be destroyed in a bloody civil war. Lenin might survive one form of conflict, but he could hardly survive both. He resolved, therefore, to end the struggle with which he had never agreed and in 1918 accepted the terms of the Treaty of Brest-Litovsk dictated by the Germans. He justified the enormous loss of territory by pointing to the greater good of saving the regime; hence 'a disgraceful peace is proper, because it is in the interest of the proletarian revolution and the regeneration of Russia'.[7] As a result, he was able to concentrate on dealing with the threats against the Bolsheviks.

Views have changed recently as to just what these were.[8] Traditionally, the Russian Civil War has been seen as a struggle between the Reds and the Whites. The Reds were aiming to save the Bolshevik Revolution and to extend it to all parts of the country, while the Whites sought to bring down the Bolshevik regime and to restore the previous system. The conflict was therefore about saving the October Revolution against attempts at counter-revolution. Revisionist historians now argue that there were actually two civil wars. One was the struggle between different strands of revolutionaries to control the revolution: this has been called the Red–Green civil war. The other – the Red–White civil war – was between one strand of revolution and attempts made to overthrow it.

Using the second approach, we can trace the conflict through three main stages. The first was the Red–Green war between the Bolsheviks and the Socialist Revolutionaries. The latter had set up rival governments to the east of the rather limited confines of Bolshevik rule. These were a real threat to Red control since they had a broad base of popular support. Several, however, were overthrown by military coups in the middle of 1918; the main instigators were such ex-Tsarist officers as Kolchak.

These became part of a broader White offensive against the Reds on all fronts between 1918 and 1920 – the second stage of the Civil War. The earliest attacks, which came from the south, were led by Kornilov, Deniken and Alexeyev. When these were contained in 1918, the southern initiative passed to Deniken alone and then, in 1920, to Wrangel. The eastern front saw extensive engagements with Kolchak's troops, culminating in the capture of Omsk by the Bolsheviks (1919). In the Baltic sector Yudenitch made a lunge for Petrograd but was driven back from the outer suburbs. Meanwhile, foreign expeditionary forces had landed, in support of the Whites, at Archangel and Murmansk in the north, as well as in the Crimea and the Caucasus. The Japanese penetrated far into eastern Siberia, via the port of Vladivostok. By 1920, however, the White armies had been repulsed by Trotsky's newly formed Red Army and the powers had all withdrawn their supporting troops.

This enabled the Bolsheviks to focus on the third and final stage: the revival of the Red–Green conflict between 1920 and 1922, as peasant armies, supported by the Socialist Revolutionaries, sought even at this late stage to remove Lenin's regime.

The Reasons for the Civil War?

The three phases of the Civil War had causes which were distinct and yet merged into each other.[9]

The first Red–Green phase (1917–18) was the direct result of rivalry between the Bolsheviks and the other revolutionary groups seeking to control the revolution. The Bolsheviks provoked the other parties by refusing to share power with them. Indeed, Lenin had seized power in October to prevent the formation of a broad-based government. He then rejected conciliatory proposals by the Socialist Revolutionaries, victors in the Constituent Assembly elections, to set up a coalition and instead dissolved the Assembly. The Socialist

Revolutionaries and other moderate socialists, such as the Mensheviks, resisted what they regarded as a drift to dictatorship; they tried to convince the workforce that it was now vital to overthrow Bolshevik rule and reconvene the Constituent Assembly. Nor was dissatisfaction with Bolshevism confined to Petrograd and Moscow. Early in 1918 the Yaroslavl soviets elected Menshevik majorities, while the Right SRs and Mensheviks scored similar successes in Riazan and Kursk. Within weeks there was widespread resistance to the Bolsheviks in the whole Volga region, including Samara and Yaroslavl, and the SRs established a directory at Ufa, which extended as far as the northern region around Archangel. Such widespread opposition was a real danger to the new Bolshevik regime which was, at this stage, by no means certain of survival.

Yet these same regions saw a swift transition from the Red–Green to the Red–White civil war. The links in the chain were a series of military coups conducted by ex-Tsarist officers. An attempt was made in September 1918 in Archangel, which failed; this was followed in November by another, in Omsk, which brought down the Socialist Revolutionary administration there. The new regime, under Admiral Kolchak, became the main focus of the westward offensive against the Bolsheviks. Other White thrusts from the Baltic and from the south emerged from the wreckage of moderate socialist governments. The overall effect was to transform the conflict from competing strands of revolution to a direct confrontation between revolution and counter-revolution. This was given an additional dimension by the intervention of the foreign powers on behalf of the Whites. Why did they do this? Britain, the United States, France, Italy and Japan aimed to return Russia to the war against Germany, an undertaking made by the Whites. In the process they hoped to restore a regime which would acknowledge the debts which Tsarist Russia had incurred from them during the process of industrialization and which would remove the threat of communism from the rest of Europe.

The Red–White civil war was largely over by late 1920. But the Bolsheviks were now confronted with a second Red–Green war. There was extensive upheaval in thirty-six provinces. By April 1921 there were 165 peasant armies in Russia, about 140 of which were connected with the SRs. The Bolsheviks simply referred to outbreaks of hooliganism and banditry, but clearly this was too dismissive. Other reasons are much more likely. For example, tension had now re-emerged between different revolutionary strands, which had been temporarily subsumed into the Red–White conflict. Many of the rebels again demanded an end to one-party dictatorship and a renewal of democratic elections. The slogans of the peasant armies were ‘Soviets without Communists’. Unrest was also the result of peasant fears of the food levy, grain requisitioning and early attempts at collective farming; another peasant slogan was ‘Down with State Monopoly on Grain Trade’. The Socialist Revolutionaries now tried to co-ordinate initially spontaneous uprisings into a second great effort to wrest control of the revolution from the Bolsheviks.

Despite these threats, the Bolsheviks had established control over the whole of Russia by 1922. The White armies had been forced to withdraw and many of the leaders of the Green enterprises were dead – either summarily shot by Red Army detachments or purged in a series of show trials. Bolshevik survival had therefore been transformed into victory.

Why did the Bolsheviks win the Civil War?

Again, the phases of the Civil War interacted with each other, to the advantage of the Bolshevik regime which, it should be remembered, was very much on the defensive. There is plenty of evidence that the Bolsheviks benefited from external or objective circumstances.

At the same time, they also made their own luck at crucial moments. It is rare for success to result without a combination of the two.

Lenin's initial policy to deal with the Green threat was crucial. He acted quickly to remove the German threat in March 1918 by signing the Treaty of Brest-Litovsk with Germany. This withdrew Russia from the First World War and enabled the Bolsheviks to focus on the internal situation. In August 1918 he also concluded a trade agreement, by which the Bolshevik government was to pay 6 billion marks and provide the Germans with one-quarter of the oil production of Baku on the Caspian Sea. In return the Red Army were able to take their focus off the west, especially the Ukraine, and switch their forces eastwards to deal with the rival revolutionary movements in the Volga area. This enabled them to recapture Kazan and Samara. Swain goes so far as to say that, by agreeing to the treaty, 'the Kaiser saved Lenin'.[10] Whether this guaranteed a permanent victory, however, is uncertain. The Socialist Revolutionaries were still securely ensconced in Ufa and the rival revolutionaries appeared evenly matched. Survival did not, at this stage, mean victory.

What made the crucial difference was the series of coups, conducted against the Greens by Kolchak and others in 1918. Again, Swain attributes enormous importance to this: the first phase of the conflict was ended 'not by Bolshevik victory in that war but by the armed action of White generals'.[11] Through their coups against the Socialist Revolutionaries, they 'changed the whole nature of the civil war'. They severely weakened the Green governments, which had been the greatest threat to the Bolsheviks. The Bolsheviks were actually better equipped to fight counter-revolutionaries than they were fellow revolutionaries. The new war forced many Greens to join with the Reds to deal with the common enemy. The catalyst for this was the Allied intervention on behalf of the Whites, which most Socialist Revolutionaries and Mensheviks found offensive. By December 1918 most areas saw negotiations between the Bolsheviks and other socialist parties; even the Socialist Revolutionaries sank their political differences with the Bolsheviks until victory could be accomplished against the Whites. This, of course, undermined their own chance of resisting the Bolsheviks in the longer term.

During the Red–White phase which followed, the Whites did a great deal to destroy their own bid for power. Their deficiencies were considerable. They were, according to Heretz, 'a large and disjointed agglomeration of forces operating on several fronts in diverse local circumstances'.[12] They had no real political base and even the areas through which they campaigned were not usually controlled by White governments: often they were under conflicting warlords or in the chaotic aftermath of disintegrating socialist governments. They also lacked a common strategy and failed to co-ordinate the separate campaigns of Yudenitch, Kolchak, Deniken and Wrangel; nor did the Whites and the supporting powers ever set up an overall war council. They entirely failed to appeal to the masses, particularly the peasantry. According to Kenez, the White generals 'did not systematically summarize their goals and beliefs. They never understood the importance of ideology and did not take ideas seriously. They had no body of doctrine and no overall leader.'[13] The rural populations tended to support the Bolsheviks as the lesser of two evils: they feared that the Whites would restore the powerful landlords and reimpose the former dues and obligations. In any case, the White armies lived off the land during their campaigns and therefore caused immense destruction through their foraging and looting.

Nor were the Whites greatly assisted by foreign intervention. According to Mawdsley, 'Contrary to what is often thought . . . the "fourteen power" anti-Bolshevik alliance that was featured in Soviet propaganda was a myth.'[14] Comparatively few Allied troops were sent to Russia and of these none participated in the battles. Keep lays particular stress on this point, attributing Bolshevik survival 'in part to sheer good luck'. Neither the Allies nor the Central powers were willing or able to take decisive action against them. The Bolsheviks 'were saved by the continuation of the war in the West, which held first priority in the thinking of all the protagonists'.[15] The Western powers were always lukewarm about supporting groups of nationalist conservatives who lacked even the pretence of a programme of reform. In addition, each Western government was internally divided as to whether to maintain the intervention after the end of 1918. Some ministers, especially in Britain, were receptive to anti-White public opinion which was being mobilized by trade union movements. Politicians such as Winston Churchill who wanted to continue an anti-Bolshevik crusade were very much in a minority. By 1920 Lloyd George's coalition government had decided to withdraw any remaining British forces – despite Churchill's pleas – while the French government had decided to switch to a more defensive anti-Bolshevik strategy by bolstering up Poland.

Meanwhile, the position of the Bolsheviks was greatly strengthened by several advantages which they possessed and the Whites did not. The Reds controlled all the internal lines of communication: they were therefore able to deal with emergencies as they occurred, switching their troops from one front to another. By contrast, the Whites had severe transport difficulties and found that the Trans-Siberian Railway was clogged through political and military disputes. The Bolsheviks were defending the industrial heartland which contained Russia's major cities, industrial centres and a rail network, which radiated outwards from Moscow. They also had the advantage of Trotsky's reorganization of the Red Army. He was able to increase the number of regular troops available to the Bolsheviks from 550,000 in September 1918 to 5.5 million by 1920; during the equivalent period, support for the Whites drained away so that the White troops were outnumbered by ten to one. Finally, the Bolsheviks had a clear and systematic ideology and used their control over all forms of communication to put across their propaganda. This undoubtedly had some effect on the civilian population.

Once they had dealt with the Whites the Bolsheviks were able to switch their attention back to the Greens. Although the military threat was more widespread than in 1918, the Green political and ideological infrastructure had in the meantime broken down. This meant that there could be no concerted anti-Bolshevik effort based on an alternative revolutionary strategy, as had existed in 1918. The peasant armies may have been temporarily stiffened by the guerrilla warfare of peasant leaders such as Antonov, but they were not up to resisting permanently the Bolshevik forces which had just gained experience from putting down the White armies. In any case, Lenin took political action to supplement the military campaigns of the Red Army. A crucial factor in bringing to an end the wave of peasant rebellions was the decision to end food requisitioning and to introduce the New Economic Policy in 1921. This meant that there was no longer a cause for which the peasantry needed to prolong its resistance.

Bolshevik victory was achieved at enormous cost. The Russian Civil War was, after the Taiping Rebellion in mid-nineteenth-century China, the most destructive in human history. The loss of life was far greater than that in the First World War. At least 900,000 were killed in the Red Army; the various peasant armies lost some 1 million; and no-one has ever managed to come up with a satisfactory estimate of White casualties. Civilian deaths were about 8.2 million, whether from disease, military atrocities or terror, the last of these accounting for anything up to 5 million. Destruction was massive and widespread, caused by deliberate sabotage or wanton looting. In some areas starvation was so prevalent that normal social structures completely broke down and cannibalism occurred. The economic impact was catastrophic, as agriculture was set back by several decades and the industrial developments which had occurred under Tsarism were extensively dislocated. The ways in which the Bolsheviks mobilized for victory also cast a shadow on the regime which they created.

The nationalities and the Civil War

So far we have dealt with the political, ideological and social elements of the Civil War. But there was a further dimension – the involvement of numerous different nationalities and ethnic groups within the former empire. Each of the three phases of the Civil War – Green, White and Green – was influenced, either directly or indirectly, by issues concerning these nationalities.

Who were they? The Russian Empire had consisted of well over sixty ethnic groups, ranging from the Slavs (Russians, Belorussians, Ukrainians, and Poles); Balts (Estonians, Latvians and Lithuanians); inhabitants of the Caucasus (including Georgians, Armenians and Azerbaijanis); and the peoples of Asiatic Russia, including those of Turkic origins (Kazakhs, Kyrgyz, Uzbeks, Tajiks and Turkmen) and those in Siberia (among whom were Komi, Udmurt, Mari, Mordva, Tartars, Chinese and Koreans). The Tsarist Empire had been build up by centuries of conquest and annexation, and consolidated by political centralization by the Russians, strongest of all the ethnic groups. Some, like the Finns, Poles and Ukrainians, had aimed over a century or more for independence or autonomy and their expectations had been strengthened by the collapse of the Tsarist government in February/March 1917. They and other nationalities therefore put pressure on the Provisional Government to guarantee self-determination. Such demands were less sympathetically received by parties of the centre and the right (such as the Constitutional Democrats and Octobrists) than by those of the left (the Bolsheviks, Mensheviks and Socialist Revolutionaries). The October Revolution, however, placed the Bolsheviks in a difficult position: they had become the new authoritarian status quo, which meant that many of the national minorities tended to align themselves with the Mensheviks and Socialist Revolutionaries. The process was accentuated by the threat of Russia's military defeat by the Germans. In March 1918 the Bolsheviks had to acknowledge, by the Peace of Brest-Litovsk, the cession of Finland, Poland, Ukraine and the Baltic States. They saw this as a pragmatic necessity to save the rest of Russia from counter-revolution and collapse. Other minority nationalities considered it an opportunity to secede from Bolshevik Russia with the support of parties like the Socialist Revolutionaries. Nationalist expectations therefore became caught up in the ideological and political rivalries between the Reds and Greens.

This overlay made the conflict more extensive and complex. As Jeremy Smith points out, 'the main engagements in the Russian Civil War of 1918–1920 were fought on the peripheries of the former Russian Empire, more often than not in the non-Russian lands'.[16] In the process, the Whites either promoted anti-Red feeling among the nationalities or, alternatively, had to deal with coalitions between the nationalities and the Greens before they could hope to come to grips with the Reds. This applied especially to the Deniken and Wrangel offensives in the Ukraine. For their part, the Bolsheviks saw national issues as a reservoir of ideological support for the Greens or of opportunist backing for the Whites. Since the greater overall popular support was for the Greens and since the initial White advances were through the peripheral regions of the former Empire, there was widespread chaos and even the prospect of the collapse of Bolshevik power.

In the longer term, however, this confusion actually worked in favour of the Reds and against the Whites, Greens and usually the nationalities themselves. The Whites, for example, were slowed down by ethnic issues, which offset any initial victories against the Greens. This gave the Reds a chance to organize against both. It also gave time for any anti-Red coalitions of nationalists with either Whites or Greens to fall apart, enabling the Reds to recover from any early reverses. Because of the peripheral nature of the Civil War the Reds had major strategic advantages as well. As we have already seen, they largely controlled the Russian hinterland, which greatly facilitated communications and troop movements. But there were also strong pockets of Red support among the Russian inhabitants of some of the urban centres in the regions dominated by the nationalities: an example of this was Kharkov, the Ukraine's second city. These provided the Reds with a series of stepping stones from the hinterland into the periphery, enabling them to drive back the White offensives and to mop up remaining resistance from the nationalities or the Green peasant armies.

But, although the complexity concerning the nationalities undoubtedly gave the Bolsheviks opportunities in wartime, the question was soon to arise as to how effectively they could be resolved with the return of peace. The nationalities issue therefore became part of the overall settlement of political, social and economic reforms made so urgent by the Civil War.

Creating the Bolshevik state, 1918–24

The creation of the Bolshevik state was the result both of the October Revolution and of the Civil War. How did the two relate to each other in the development of a new communist regime?

It has generally been argued that the Bolsheviks had come to power as the result of a limited coup in October 1917 and then proceeded to introduce the real revolution between 1918 and 1921 – as they had always intended. This revolution consisted of four key components. The first was the organization of Russia's people and resources to win the Civil War; this was the revolution mobilized. Second, the Bolsheviks took the decision to move away from a Western democratic system to a communist one based on the soviets; this was the essence of the political revolution. In the process they used coercion on a massive scale; the third constituent was therefore revolutionary terror. Fourth, the Bolsheviks aimed to introduce a revolutionary economy in the form of War Communism and to transform society through revolutionary egalitarianism. In all of these, the Bolsheviks had underlying ideological objectives and were therefore normally proactive. Not all of their changes succeeded. They were forced to backtrack on economic and social changes from 1921 and to concede that immediate changes were not going to be possible. However, any economic or social concessions were made possible only because the Bolsheviks retained a monopoly of political control throughout the whole period.

An altogether different view is possible – which is the one adopted in the next three sections. This moves away from the assumption that the Bolsheviks were solely designing a new system from above. Rather, they were also responding to pressures from below. This produces a perspective which is almost the mirror image of the first. The real revolution occurred not between 1918 and 1921, but in 1917: as we have already seen, the Bolsheviks had come to power in October by harnessing the full force of popular revolutionary feeling. Between 1918 and 1921, by contrast, they set about closing that revolution down, fearing the reviving popularity of the Socialist Revolutionaries and other moderate socialists. The Bolsheviks therefore resorted to changes which amounted in many respects to a *counter*-revolution. The mobilization of resources was initially intended to defeat the Green strand of popular revolution and to ensure that only the Red regime survived. The abandonment of Western parliamentary institutions, a direct response to the election victory of the Socialist Revolutionaries, was a means of permanently removing all other revolutionary parties. This was reinforced by the use of terror, which became the main device of counter-revolution. Economic policy was geared mainly to undermining other revolutionary influences. In the first Green and White phases this meant War Communism; in the second Green phase it meant the New Economic Policy. Social policies were more genuinely radical, but were partly a response to popular expectations for change and, in any case, were modified after 1921 in line with economic retreat.

The Bolsheviks justified many of their changes after 1918 by referring to ideological principles. Again, the two views differ in their approach to this. The traditional approach takes much of the ideological theory at face value. This assumes that Lenin and Trotsky were implementing from above policies and schemes which had already been planned. It is, however, more likely that they were constantly improvising in response to pressures beyond their immediate control and that ideology was usually a justification of policy introduced for essentially pragmatic reasons.

Political changes and terror

Shortly after the October Revolution one of the Menshevik leaders, Axelrod, said that 'the Bolshevik regime's days and weeks are numbered'.[17] He may have had good grounds for this, but events were to prove that the Bolsheviks were able to follow up their military survival in the Civil War with the consolidation of their internal political power.

The main development was the move away from a mixed democracy, with different types of representative institutions, towards a monolithic base. At first the Bolsheviks had been prepared to set up a new Western-style Constituent Assembly, which would coexist with the soviets, or workers' and soldiers' councils. But the elections held throughout Russia produced unexpected and inconvenient results. Out of a total of 41.81 million votes cast, the Bolsheviks won 9.84 million – more than the Mensheviks (1.37 million) or Constitutional Democrats (1.99 million), but considerably fewer than the Socialist Revolutionaries (17.05 million). The remaining votes were cast for other socialist or non-socialist parties or for ethnic or regional parties.[18] Despite performing strongly in Petrograd and Moscow, the Bolsheviks won only 23.54 per cent of the popular vote, compared with the SR share of 40.77 per cent and a combined 45.25 per cent for all non-Bolshevik socialist parties. Lenin decided on immediate pre-emptive action, closing the Assembly on 6 January 1918 after only one meeting. This was confirmed on 19 January by a resolution of the Central Executive Committee, which justified the decision on the grounds that the Constituent Assembly was 'expressive of the old correlation of political forces, when the conciliators and the Constitutional-Democrats were in power'. The Constituent Assembly was therefore 'bound to stand in the way of the October Revolution and Soviet power'.[19] This made it clear that the Bolsheviks considered the various soviets as a higher form of representation and that these should not now be challenged by a semi-western institution that contained a majority of politically-suspect deputies. In complete contrast, the Mensheviks and Socialist Revolutionaries saw the Constituent Assembly as the highest representative of popular opinion. The soviets had been pre-eminent only in times of emergency. Now that full elections had taken place, they should assume a subordinate role to the Assembly.

The dissolution of the Constituent Assembly has been seen as one of the key turning points in twentieth-century Russian history: it was, quite simply, the rejection of one constitutional system in favour of another. This has been widely acknowledged – but in two very different ways. One approach sees it as a means of keeping the Russian Revolution on track through the triumph of the democratic institutions that had emerged in October 1917. During most of the twentieth century the official Communist Party line was that 'the counter-revolutionary Constitutional-Democratic, Right Socialist-Revolutionary and Menshevik parties' had 'planned to overthrow Soviet rule through the Constituent Assembly'; hence soviet-based power 'was compelled to disband the Assembly'.[20] Some western observers have agreed with this. Rees, for example, argues that: 'Even before the October revolution the mass of workers understood clearly that the soviets were their organisations, responsive to their needs, and that the Assembly was a chimera of which they knew very little and from which they expected less.'[21] By and large, however, western historians see the end of the Constituent Assembly as a distortion of the whole process of democracy through the imposition of centralized Bolshevik power. According to Wade, the dissolution was in effect 'an announcement by the Bolsheviks that they would not give up governmental authority peacefully, by elections, but could be removed only by force'.[22] It also made civil war inevitable and 'laid the foundations of the political culture of the Soviet Union'.[23] This line is more convincing. The soviets did not provide for a fully democratic legislature; as Keep argues, Lenin 'conceived of the soviets as instruments of rule rather than sovereign bodies'.[24] Lenin's priority was to prevent any access to power other than by the Bolshevik Party. This meant that the soviets had to be part of a clearly defined political and constitutional structure that would maintain the status quo established in October 1917 – and prevent the emergence of any alternative.

Thus the key priority of all major political developments was that any innovation or modification should always be consistent with Bolshevik ideology. This applied, for example, to the 1918 Constitution, the first to be applied to the new state. Russia became a federation, the Russian Soviet Federated Socialist Republic (RSFSR), for which the All-Russian Congress of Soviets was the supreme legislature. Other powers were accorded to the Central Executive Committee (TsIK), which elected the government (Sovnarkom). A further step was taken with the formation of the USSR (Union of Soviet Socialist Republics) in 1922, a new constitution for which was officially introduced in January 1924. Both Constitutions were heavily influenced by the party. In 1902 Lenin had seen the Bolshevik Party as the vanguard of the proletariat and strictly limited its membership. In 1917 he followed a more pragmatic course to adapt the party to the wishes of the peasantry and soldiers as well as the industrial workers. But the pressures from below were perceived in 1918 as more negative and destructive, with the result that centralization was reinstituted, with the party Central Committee at the core. Within this were the broader Secretariat and the smaller organs of the Politburo and the Orgburo. Regional and local soviets or executives were dominated by parallel party committees, just as at the centre the Politburo controlled the Supreme Soviet, the Central Executive Committee and Sovnarkom. A Party resolution taken in March 1919 affirmed that 'the strictest the centralism and the most severe discipline are an absolute necessity'.[25] This effectively prevented other parties, especially the main rivals – Socialist Revolutionaries and Mensheviks – from gaining access. The Bolsheviks therefore departed from the western style of representative democracy whereby the party in power operated within the parameters of the constitution. Instead, Lenin ensured that the constitution was defined by the party; he therefore adhered to the statement he had made in 1906 on 'the intolerability of any criticism disrupting or impeding the unity of action decided on by the party'.[26]

The new system was enforced by rigorous action against all perceived opponents, of which there were many. These included Constitutional Democrats and other members of 'bourgeois' factions who became the enemy within an extended 'class war'; dissident nationalities who were subjected to mopping-up operations by the Red Army in the later stages of the Civil War; and anarchists, whose belief in unfettered liberty was considered a fundamental threat to the theory of the 'dictatorship of the proletariat'. Probably the greatest threat came from the non-Bolshevik revolutionaries, especially the Socialist Revolutionaries and Mensheviks. These were expelled from the soviets at all levels and public trials were held for twenty-two SR leaders in 1922. Meanwhile, a deliberate campaign of terror was conducted 'in the name and interest of the workers'[27] by the All-Russian Extraordinary Commission for the Suppression of Counter-Revolution, Speculation and Sabotage. Usually known as the Cheka, this was intended to 'prosecute and break up all acts of counter-revolution and sabotage all over Russia, no matter what their origin' and to 'bring before the Revolutionary Tribunal all counter-revolutionists and saboteurs'.[28] Under the leadership of Dzerzhinsky, it had powers of arrest and summary execution, killing over 140,000 people between December 1917 and February 1922, compared with 14,000 by the Okhrana during the reign of Nicholas II. Trotsky justified the bloodshed on the grounds that 'we shall not enter into the kingdom of socialism in white gloves on a polished floor'.[29] After the end of the emergency of the Civil War and War Communism, Lenin saw fit to end the more extreme activities of the Cheka, which was replaced in 1922 by the State Political Administration (GPU). This focused on strengthening 'revolutionary legality' but reducing the emphasis on 'revolutionary terror'. But the GPU and its successor in 1924, the Unified State Political Administration (OGPU), retained permanent coercive controls, whether these included systematic terror or not. The foundations and precedents were already in place for the later and more extensive Stalinist purges.

In spite of all these measures, the Bolshevik state was confronted by a surprisingly widespread internal opposition. This was to be expected between 1918 and 1920, the peak years of the Civil War, when the political future of the country was at stake; the Reds, after all, were confronted by the Greens, who had more widespread support. But the opposition actually reached its highest level in 1921, with 118 uprisings. The most significant was the Kronstadt Revolt, which followed open demands for 'soviets without Communists', elections by secret ballot and an end to the dictatorship of the Communist Party. Lenin referred to this as the 'the biggest . . . internal crisis' of the period.[30] The Bolsheviks took rigorous measures through the military conquests carried out against dissident peasants and nationalities by the Red Army in 1921 and 1922, while the Kronstadt Revolt was put down, with great bloodshed, by Trotsky and Tukhachevskii. But accompanying these measures were two compromises; these were certain concessions without, however, allowing any element of political opposition to re-emerge.

One concession was to the nationalities. Lenin's attitude to the nationalities issue had always been ambivalent and he was forced to try to resolve the fundamental contradiction that confronted him. On the one hand, Marxism as an ideology sought to transcend nationalism, on Marx's premise that 'the working man has no nation'. On the other hand, Lenin was forced to recognize the strength of nationalist feeling that had driven many in the peripheral areas to oppose the Reds in the Civil War. After their eventual defeat by the Red Army, they were included in a federal arrangement that was really an extended version of the RSFSR. The USSR was set up in 1922 to include not only Russia but also the Ukraine, Belorussia and Transcaucasia. The 1924 Constitution had a bicameral legislature, with a Soviet of the Nationalities as well as the Soviet of the Union, while the Republics also had their own institutions. In theory, each of the four Republics had the right to secede from the USSR, but this was rendered impossible in practice by the tight control of the Party within and over each of them. The principle of federalism was therefore another casualty to the practice of democratic centralism.

The other compromise was the New Economic Policy, an attempt to resolve Russia's turbulent economic developments between 1921 and 1924. To these we now turn.

Economic changes

Bolshevik ideology was based at least in part on the economic principles of Marxism. One of these was that any society consisted of a 'base' and a 'superstructure'. The base was the economic foundation upon which the society was built, while the superstructure comprised the political and social institutions that emerged from the base. Any change on the institutions therefore had to be accompanied by a transformation of the economy. Lenin's intention was to eliminate the division of society into classes and to increase the level of state control over all sectors. But the task was harder than he had envisaged, partly because of the extent of popular influence and opposition, and partly because of the rapidly changing circumstances between 1917 and 1924.

The result between these years was a wild oscillation of policies, leading to anything but a consistent application of a Marxist programme. Between November 1917 and mid-1918 economic changes were cautious. The Decree on Workers' Control, for example, provided for workers' management of the production, purchase and sale of products through 'elected organs' and local soviets of workers' control in the large cities.[31] At this stage, however, no attempts were made to nationalize any enterprises – other than banks, foreign trade and armaments works. Meanwhile, the Decree on Land confirmed the takeover by the peasantry of the nobles' estates; again, however, there was no provision for state control or large-scale collectivization of agriculture. Then, in June 1918, Lenin introduced the altogether more radical policy of War Communism. The Decree of Nationalization covered all large-scale enterprises, while the requisitioning of all grain surpluses greatly reduced the food stocks of the peasantry in order to supply the workers in the cities and the troops fighting the Whites. The results were chaos and extreme hardship. The monetary economy disintegrated, to be replaced by barter and black marketeering. Grain requisitioning led to a drastic decline in production as the peasantry lost incentives to produce more than for very basic needs. The inevitable shortage of food in the cities provoked strikes and riots – including the 1921 Kronstadt Revolt – which shook the very foundations of the Bolshevik regime. Faced with the worst crisis of his political life, Lenin now made a second major change. In 1921 he reversed War Communism by restoring a degree of capitalism and private enterprise through his more moderate New Economic Policy (NEP). The peasantry were now permitted to sell their surplus produce on payment of a tax, while 91 per cent of industrial enterprises were returned to private ownership or trusts. Results were not immediate since they were impeded by widespread famine between 1921 and 1922 and by a financial crisis in 1923. But, by the time of Lenin's death in 1924, recovery was well under way and, by 1926, the Russian economy had regained its 1913 production levels.

How have these changes been interpreted? As with other areas of the Bolshevik Revolution and Leninist state there has been a wide range of explanations, some Russian, others western.

One view is that the first stage reflected a policy that was moderate and fair but that it had to be interrupted to deal with the terrible situation caused by the Civil War. Lenin said later that 'War Communism was thrust upon us by war and ruin. It was not, nor could it be, a policy that corresponded to the economic tasks of the proletariat. It was a temporary measure'.[32] The NEP was introduced as quickly as possible as a measure of recovery, even though it involved the abandonment of some of the basic principles of War Communism. Official Soviet historiography later put a positive construction on this change: according to the *History of the Communist Party of the Soviet Union*, the shift of policy in 1921 demonstrated the Party's 'knowledge of the laws of social development', while 'the great Lenin showed his genius and scientific foresight'.[33] The disadvantage of this approach, however, is that it attributes the chaos and hardship of the period of War Communism to external factors, whereas they were just as likely to have been inflicted by the policy itself. Increased starvation, in turn, alienated the peasantry and provoked the second Green phase of the Civil War (see p. 42). These reservations have been strongly expressed by post-Soviet and anti-communist Russian historians. Volkogonov, for example, argued in 1994 that, far from reversing earlier moderate measures to deal with a crisis inflicted by civil war, Lenin actually used the war as justification for a radical approach that he had always preferred. In fact, War Communism was 'the basis and essence of Lenin's policy, and only its total collapse forced him to grab the lifebelt of the NEP'.[34] It has also been pointed out that the future regime of Stalin was to reverse the NEP in a return to coercive policies strongly reminiscent of War Communism.

Some Western historians had already followed a similar line to Volkogonov. In 1972, for example, Conquest maintained that Lenin imposed War Communism as a minority diktat from above. 'Bolshevik policies had proved economically disastrous' and their political implementation was 'detested by all classes'.[35] Thus the NEP was introduced only because the Bolsheviks were 'at the end of their tether'. Again, the implication is that War Communism, or something like it, had always been the preferred choice of the Bolsheviks. More recently, western revisionist historians have altered this approach by suggesting a different type of change. During the period of the October Revolution the Bolsheviks had been more receptive to influences from below and had tried to win over the peasantry. But, with the subsequent defection of much of the peasantry to the Socialist Revolutionaries and other Green factions, the Bolsheviks responded with tighter controls from above, of which War Communism was one of the key elements. For most Bolsheviks, including Lenin and Trotsky, the NEP was not a return to earlier moderation and 'bottom-up' influences; rather it was a tactical adjustment that was, in any case, strictly controlled by the Bolshevik monopoly of political power.

The position reached by 1924 was the apparent resolution of the previous inconsistencies in economic policies. This, however, raised the fundamental question as to how long the solution should last. Was the NEP merely an intermediate strategy which contained other long-term problems? Should the mixed economy be retained indefinitely, as Bukharin argued, or should socialism be accelerated – a course urged by Trotsky? As will be seen, this was to turn into a major dispute that overlapped the manoeuvring in the struggle for the political succession to Lenin.

Lenin: an assessment

Lenin was plagued by ill health during the last two years of his life. He suffered a stroke in May 1922 and, although he made a partial recovery, he never again played a full part in political life. His health deteriorated rapidly from March 1923 with the loss of speech and the onset of paralysis. On his death in January 1924 a post-mortem revealed that one of the two hemispheres of his brain had shrunk to the size of a walnut. The new leadership ignored one of his last wishes by having his body embalmed and placed on open display.

What are we to make of the period 1917–24? How should we interpret the dual process of revolution and consolidation? On the one hand, certain positive features are evident. Lenin led a party to electoral victory in the major soviets in Russia by October 1917, replacing the Mensheviks and Socialist Revolutionaries as the real spokesman of the urban workers. He used this new-found popularity to seize power and overturn a temporary regime which had clearly lost its way. He subsequently held the new state together against a series of counter-revolutionary attacks which were extensively backed by the major powers; eventually he expanded the frontiers almost to the previous limits of Tsarist Russia, thereby preventing the sort of disintegration which had already overtaken the Ottoman Empire and Austria-Hungary. Finally, he brought a dramatic change to the lives of the ordinary Russian people. The last social remnants of the Tsarist regime were swept away as the Bolsheviks confirmed the peasantry in possession of the nobles' estates; while measures were taken to end the exploitation of labour in industry by capitalists careless of such essentials as working conditions and health schemes.

There is, however, another picture. The cost of Russia's transformation was greater than she had ever experienced. Over 20 million lives were lost during a period of unprecedented conflict and destruction which affected the country – from the Polish frontier in the west to eastern Siberia, from Archangel in the north to the Caspian Sea in the south. It is possible to absolve Lenin from total responsibility for the ruin caused by the numerous military campaigns, but not from the unnecessary suffering and wastage caused by War Communism. And during the conflict with external enemies Lenin was strengthening the internal apparatus of coercion, establishing a one-party state and dispensing with more moderate forms of socialist democracy. In the process, he demolished one of history's promising what-might-have-beens.

This double-sided view is reflected in the controversies which have arisen over the two components of the period 1917–24: the Leninist revolution and the Leninist state.

At its most fundamental, the conflict of opinion concerns the very nature of the events which occurred in October 1917. The Bolshevik view was that the revolution was inevitable, part of a historical and dialectical process and representing, in Trotsky's words, the 'transfer of power from one class to another'.[36] A superior form of state was emerging; in this sense the revolution was, according to Lenin, a turning point in history, with the Bolsheviks directing and channelling the 'upsurge of the people'. The other contemporary explanation was advanced by Kerensky, a principal victim of Lenin's success. He saw the October coup as a freak occurrence and a 'perversion' of Russia's historical trends. He argued that a series of unfortunate events provided the opportunity for the Bolsheviks to 'break up the Provisional Government and stop the establishment of a democratic system in Russia'. Kornilov's attempt at dictatorship 'opened the door to the dictatorship of Lenin'; in fact, far from responding to any popular surge, Lenin succeeded 'only by way of conspiracy, only by way of treacherous armed struggle'.[37]

Lenin's interpretation was endorsed by official Soviet historiography. All other parties and types of democracy were mere throwbacks to a lower stage of historical development; hence, they could be thrown on the rubbish heap of history. Western historians, not confined to monolithic interpretation, vary in their approach. Some incline towards the conspiracy view of Kerensky. They see the Bolshevik Revolution as a distortion of socialism and Marxism used to construct a dictatorship which was by no means the logical outcome of previous trends. According to Gregor, the conspiracy was self-perpetuating, for 'the conspiratorial party of the revolution became a conspiratorial party of legitimacy'.[38] Others, such as Acton, see the Bolsheviks under Lenin as the only group successfully to tap into the real aspirations of the people. Christopher Hill adopts a Western Marxist position; to him, 'Lenin symbolizes the Russian Revolution as a movement of the poor and oppressed of the earth who have successfully risen against the great and powerful.'[39] This does not, however, harmonize with the revisionist view that Lenin may have been in tune with revolutionary fervour in 1917 but that he proceeded to close the revolution down after coming to power.

Another major controversy concerns the nature of Lenin's regime. One extreme has been put forcefully in Solzhenitsyn's *Gulag Archipelago*, published in 1974. One of the central themes of this book is that the October Revolution and the Bolshevik regime led inexorably to Stalinism, that they were one and the same process. In a review of the *Gulag Archipelago*, however, Mandel puts the reverse case, emphasizing the fundamental difference between the two regimes: the Bolshevik Revolution and the Stalinist counter-revolution.[40]

Some historians incline towards the case for continuity between Lenin and Stalin, although this is a criticism of Lenin rather than a rehabilitation of Stalin. A strong case is established by Leggett, who is convinced that terror was implicit in Leninism. Lenin's Cheka led ultimately to Stalin's NKVD (People's Commissariat of Internal Affairs – the forerunner of the KGB); consequently, 'it was Lenin who laid the police state foundations which made Stalin's monstrous feats technically possible'.[41] In the first volume of the latest biography of Stalin, Kotkin puts an even more forceful case. Although, he argues, Stalin was not affirmed as Lenin's legitimate successor, 'it bears reminding that the assertion that Stalin "usurped" power has an absurdist quality'. After all, Stalin's ascendancy owed much to 'Lenin's actions' and the 'Communist regime' had already come to power by a coup and 'questioned proletarians who dared to question the party's self-assigned monopoly.' Hence it is disingenuous to accuse Stalin 'of stealing what had already been stolen'.[42]

By contrast, E.H. Carr has argued that Lenin was sufficiently different to Stalin to have been likely 'to minimize and mitigate the element of coercion' had he lived to face Stalin's difficulties. Lenin was 'reared in a humane tradition, he enjoyed enormous prestige, great moral authority and powers of persuasion'. By contrast, 'Stalin had no moral authority whatever . . . He understood nothing but coercion, and from the first employed this openly and brutally.'[43] Mandel points out that whatever terror did exist under Lenin was a direct response to attempts at counter-revolution, to 'the White terror that came first' and the 'invasion of Soviet territory on seven different fronts'. Unlike Stalin, Lenin and Trotsky did not destroy the basis of justice. They did make mistakes in suppressing other parties and banning factions within the Communist Party itself, but these were direct responses to a desperate emergency and were conceived only as temporary measures.[44] Finally, Schapiro maintains that, despite being authoritarian in his methods, Lenin never destroyed the basic machinery of the various party organs. Stalin, on the other hand, ceased to use the party as a base of power, depending instead on a personal secretariat. He therefore exploited and abused Lenin's system – but, of course, the system had no inbuilt safeguards to prevent this from happening. Thus 'Stalinism was not a necessary consequence of Leninism, but it was nevertheless a possible result.'[45]

THE SUCCESSION, 1924–9

The struggle for power

During the last months of his effective rule, Lenin seemed increasingly concerned about the problem of his successor. In his *Testament* of December 1922 Lenin provided comments on the leading contenders. He mentioned, but passed over briefly, Kamenev, Zinoviev, Bukharin and Piatakov. He gave more attention to Trotsky, although he considered that he had become too heavily involved in administrative detail. When he came to consider Stalin he expressed real doubts: 'Comrade Stalin, having become General Secretary, has concentrated limitless power in his hands, and I am not certain that he will always be careful enough in his use of this power.' Shortly afterwards, in January 1923, Lenin added a codicil to the *Testament* urging the party to take action to remove Stalin from his post as General Secretary. He should, Lenin concluded, be replaced by 'some other person who is superior to Stalin only in one respect, namely, in being more tolerant, more loyal, more polite and more attentive to comrades'.[46] Before Lenin could do anything to prod the party into action, he was incapacitated by his second and third strokes.

When Lenin died in January 1924 the succession was still uncertain. At first Stalin's chances seemed remote, particularly in view of Lenin's *Testament* and its codicil, which were read out at a meeting of the party's Central Committee. But the other party members agreed that Stalin had improved his reputation during the course of 1923 and therefore voted to put aside the recommendations of the codicil. Meanwhile, Kamenev and Zinoviev had come to the conclusion that Trotsky was the main threat to the party's stability, partly because of his forceful personality and partly because of his close association with the army. Hence, they collaborated with Stalin and a power-sharing triumvirate emerged, with Stalin remaining in his post of General Secretary. But the triumvirate was to be only a temporary phase in the succession to Lenin. By 1929 Stalin was in total control, having overcome the challenges of all his possible rivals: Trotsky, Kamenev, Zinoviev and Bukharin. There appear to have been three main phases in this development.

The first was the emergence, between 1923 and 1925, of a major split between the triumvirate (Stalin, Kamenev and Zinoviev) and the isolated figure of Trotsky. This division was expressed in an ideological debate between 'Permanent Revolution' and 'Socialism in One Country'. Trotsky's strategy of Permanent Revolution emphasized rapid industrialization and the abolition of private farming at home. Abroad, Russia would promote the spread of revolution to the rest of Europe which would ensure the survival of Bolshevism. Socialism in One Country, advocated by Stalin, stressed the need to maintain the more moderate economic course of the NEP within Russia and to promote more positive relations with other countries to increase trade and attract foreign investment. Stalin was far less deeply committed to the economic principles of this right-wing strategy than Trotsky was to the left, his motive being the political one of isolating Trotsky. In this he succeeded. At the XIVth Party Congress in 1925 he received overwhelming support (although not from Kamenev and Zinoviev, both of whom opposed further concessions to the peasantry). Trotsky's political days were clearly numbered.

The second stage was the disposal of Kamenev and Zinoviev, which occurred between 1925 and 1927. Never one to share power for long, Stalin aligned himself with the most obvious rightist elements within the party, including Bukharin, Rykov and Tomsky. Between 1926 and 1927 Kamenev and Zinoviev made common cause with Trotsky, but it was too late. The Party Conference of 1927 gave its approval to Socialism in One Country and denounced Permanent Revolution. Trotsky was expelled from the Politburo, along with Kamenev and Zinoviev, and was exiled from Russia in 1929, while both Kamenev and Zinoviev were to perish in the purges of the 1930s.

The third stage was predictable: the elimination of Bukharin and the rest of the right, which was accomplished by 1929. The end of the 1920s also saw a hardening of Stalin's own economic ideas as he began to associate Socialism in One Country with the total transformation of industry at the expense of the peasantry – the programme of Trotsky, in effect, without the insistence on spreading revolution to the rest of Europe. This was strongly opposed by Bukharin, Rykov and Tomsky, who had always supported a moderate policy towards the peasantry. As Stalin gradually introduced measures against the wealthy peasantry, or kulaks, Bukharin, Rykov and Tomsky became more outspoken. Stalin accused them of plotting against the party's agreed strategy and forced them to resign from the Politburo and from their state offices.

By 1929 Stalin dominated the party and, through the party, the state more completely than Lenin had ever done. Ahead lay the sweeping economic changes and the purges. Bukharin compared him to Genghis Khan, adding 'Stalin will strangle us. He is an unprincipled intriguer who subordinates everything to his lust for power.'

Why Stalin?

Stalin was probably the least impressive of all the candidates for the succession. He was totally eclipsed by Trotsky in the October Revolution and never succeeded in winning the friendship and confidence of Lenin. He was even regarded as a plodder: Trotsky referred to him as 'the party's most eminent mediocrity'. This was to prove a serious underestimate. Stalin had skills that were less obvious – but more deadly. He was also able to benefit from a set of objective conditions that favoured mediocrity rather than brilliance. Beneath a bland exterior was a ruthless character. Sometimes posing as a moderate, he awaited the chance to eliminate other candidates for the leadership – Trotsky, then Zinoviev and Kamenev, and finally Bukharin. According to McCauley, Stalin was 'a very skilful politician who had a superb grasp of tactics, could predict behaviour extremely well and had an unerring eye for personal weaknesses'.[47] More recently, Kenez has described Stalin as a 'master of infighting' who would 'bide his time and come forward only when he possessed the political strength to defeat his opponents'.[48] This meant that he could take advantage of Bukharin's inability to convert a plausible interpretation of the NEP into a structured policy, of Kamenev's lack of a long-term vision, or of Zinoviev's weaknesses on organization. Indeed, Stalin was able eventually to dispense with all need for their support, since he had built up his own set of allies, especially Kalinin, Kuibyshev, Molotov and Voroshilov.

This was made possible by Stalin's organizational supremacy within the party. His vital appointment was to the post of General Secretary in 1922. Lenin had good reason to be concerned about Stalin's accumulation of power and influence. In controlling the party administration Stalin was responsible for appointments to various offices; hence he had the main voice in membership and promotion. Gradually he built up a steady base of support which made it possible for him to manoeuvre so effectively among his political rivals. The process operated as follows. The Communist Party was officially a democratic institution, in which the lowest level – the local parties – elected the Party Congress which, in turn, produced the membership of the Central Committee. The latter then elected the Politburo. But the composition of the local parties was determined by the Secretariat, which was under Stalin's control. It did not take long for Stalin's supporters to move into the upper levels of the party. There was an added incentive for these men: if Stalin's opponents could be removed from the highest offices then there would be a series of vacancies. It is hardly surprising, therefore, that Stalin's appointees should have been so willing to support him and that other prominent Bolsheviks were not accorded the respect which their experience perhaps deserved. Hence, as Kenez argues, Stalin 'skilfully removed from key positions the supporters of his opponents, replacing them with his own people'.[49]

Stalin's personal strengths were greatly assisted by the threat that Bolshevism was about to collapse into chaos. A crucial factor contributing to this was the failure of Trotsky's policy of spreading communism throughout Europe by revolution. His reputation was steadily undermined by the failure of the Spartacists to seize power in Germany in 1919 (see p. 172), and the overthrow of the Béla Kun regime in Hungary after only a few months (pp. 323–4). The benefit to Stalin was considerable. According to Colletti, 'The first rung of the ladder which was to carry Stalin to power was supplied by the Social-Democratic leaders who in January 1919 murdered Rosa Luxemburg and Karl Liebknecht . . . The remaining rungs were supplied by the reactionary wave which subsequently swept Europe'.[50] Stalin avoided being associated with international revolution, projecting instead a solid, traditionally Slavic appeal more in keeping with his own emphasis on Socialism in One Country – which was not dependent on the success of events outside Russia.

Stalin was able to take advantage of the internal wrangling over Bolshevik economic policy. The two strategies put forward during the 1920s were based on very different interpretations of the NEP. One was a planned retreat from the more radical policies of War Communism. This Bukharin and the rightists interpreted as meaning that the economy should now progress at the pace of 'the peasant's slowest nag'. The other, pressed by Trotsky and the leftists an increase in the pace of industrialization as the most effective means of implementing socialism. Russia was therefore caught up in a conflict which involved a new peasantry, the beneficiaries of the new capitalism allowed by the NEP, and the urban workers, who stood to gain more from accelerated socialism. Stalin was one of the few leading Bolsheviks able to manoeuvre between these extremes. In the early 1920s he tended towards the rightist conception of the NEP – until the procurement crisis of 1927 showed that the NEP was no longer working and therefore needed a rethink. Stalin's political struggle against Bukharin, Rykov was widely seen within the party as a balanced and considered reaction to an economic policy that had failed. Those who owed their positions to Stalin therefore seemed to have sound reasons for supporting him: he was credited with being able to read correctly the signs of the economic times. According to Silverman, 'Machine politics alone did not account for Stalin's "triumph"'; rather, 'the salient political fact' of 1928–9 was 'a growing climate of high party opinion'.[51] In all probability, it was a combination of the two.

Was Stalin's rise, therefore, the result of the calculation of a supremely rational, efficient and determined party leader able to use the efficient dictatorship already established by Lenin? Or was he the mediocrity that Trotsky described, with rather basic skills enhanced by circumstances? The verdict on this remains open. So, too, does the parallel dichotomy about what Stalin achieved once installed in power. E.H. Carr argued in the 1950s: 'More than almost any other great man in history, Stalin illustrates the thesis that circumstances make the man, not the man the circumstances.' This was quoted in 2014 by Kotkin, who added that Carr was 'utterly, eternally wrong'. Instead, Kotkin reaffirmed that 'Stalin made history, rearranging the entire socioeconomic landscape of one sixth of the earth'. The process required 'extraordinary maneuvering, browbeating, violence on his part'. He concluded that 'History, for better and for worse, is made by those who never give up'.[52] The following sections will take account of these views.

Why not Trotsky?

At first sight Trotsky might seem ideally placed to assume the mantle of Lenin. He had been the tactician of Lenin's strategy in October 1917; as President of the Petrograd Soviet

2 Joseph Stalin, 1879–1953, photo taken in 1927 (David King Collection)

he had organized the Revolutionary Military Committee which had seized power. During the chaotic months which followed he created the Red Army and, as Commissar for War, was instrumental in overcoming the threats from the Whites and foreign inverventionists. He has, indeed, been described as the 'dynamo of the militarised Bolshevik state'.[53] At the same time he made fundamental additions to Bolshevik doctrine, the most important of which was his emphasis on Permanent Revolution. He had considerable personal talents. He was unquestionably the greatest orator of the October Revolution, and was renowned for his intellect, statesmanship and administrative ability. Yet, for all these attributes, he found himself out of effective power by 1925, out of the party by 1927 and out of the country by 1929.

Part of the reason has already been provided – Stalin's rapid accumulation of power within the Bolshevik Party which enabled him to outmanoeuvre Trotsky. The rest of the explanation can be found in a number of serious disadvantages which helped turn some of Trotsky's apparent strengths into liabilities. The first was his incompatibility with other leading members of the party. He towered above them intellectually but in a way which brought him suspicion rather than respect. His whole attitude was profoundly influenced by contacts with western Europe. He therefore tended to play down Russian or Slavic achievements in culture and, in particular, in philosophy. After Lenin's death, however, the most influential of the Bolshevik leaders had little experience of the West and were therefore much more sympathetic to Stalin's pro-Slavic line. Hence, in January 1925 a resolution of the party's Central Committee condemned Trotskyism as 'a falsification of communism in the spirit of approximation to "European" patterns of pseudo-Marxism'.[54] As a 'westerner', Trotsky was also regarded as an intruder. He had avoided joining the Bolshevik Party until 1917 and had previously shown more sympathy for the Marxist principles of the Mensheviks. Lenin had found his assistance indispensable and had therefore given him rapid promotion, which was resented by others in the party.

It was therefore crucial for Trotsky to consolidate his own position within the party. This, however, is precisely what he neglected to do. The revolutionary leader and military organizer was unable to adapt to party politics; in Mikoyan's words, Trotsky 'is a man of State, not of the Party'.[55] This made him particularly unpopular with men who had tended to sink their own identities into the party organization. Kamenev, for example, complained that Trotsky entered the party as an individualist, 'who thought, and still thinks, that in the fundamental question of the revolution it is not the party, but he, comrade Trotsky, who is right'.[56] Throughout the period 1917–29 Trotsky persistently underestimated the suspicion in which he was held and took no effective measures to try to dispel it. His capacity for leadership and his ability to persuade were employed *outside* the party; as Carr observed, 'he had no talent for leadership among equals'.[57]

Soviet historians saw Trotsky as an incorrigible opportunist. This, however, is an exaggeration as, in many respects, he was just the opposite. He lacked all the essential components of patience, tact and timing and missed a unique opportunity to make a move against Stalin. He failed, in May 1924, to turn the knife in Stalin and even voted for the suspension of Lenin's codicil which would have removed Stalin from high office. The picture which emerges is of a politician completely out of his element, with no natural political instinct and no real understanding of how to exploit a particular situation.

After being expelled from Russia in 1929 Trotsky launched a series of verbal attacks on Stalin's regime. He criticized the growth of Stalin's personality cult; he was outspoken about Stalin's total failure to comprehend the threat of the Nazis in Germany in the early 1930s; and he wrote extensively on what he saw as Stalin's distortions of Marxism–Leninism. But, lacking a power base, he could be no more than a 'prophet in exile', to use the description of Deutscher.

STALIN'S RULE TO 1941

What kind of dictator was Stalin?

After establishing himself, Stalin ruthlessly extended his power and pushed ahead with his policies. The result was an extreme totalitarian dictatorship. Stalin went further than Lenin in imposing his own stamp on Russia. He exerted greater personal control over the Communist Party and, to ensure its permanence, he unleashed a flood of coercion and terror which was unprecedented and unparalleled. His use of the NKVD and the purges caused the deaths of many millions of Soviet people. This eliminated any serious threat to his position and enabled him to proceed to major economic changes in the form of forced collectivization and industrialization through three Five-Year Plans. He was also responsible for some major social and cultural changes under the collective description of Socialist Realism which, in turn, played a vital role in augmenting Stalin's own personality cult. Foreign policy, too, came under Stalin's direct control; he determined its overall rationale and dictated what course it should take. He was unquestionably one of the most ruthless and most pragmatic of all the statesmen contributing to the international scene between the wars.

This picture of Stalin is easily recognizable and is not really open to dispute. But huge changes have recently occurred in its corollary. It was once thought that Stalin's very ruthlessness ensured the efficiency of his system, and that the Soviet Union was a far better totalitarian model than, for example, Nazi Germany. Increasingly, however, the Stalinist regime is being seen as inefficient and even ramshackle. Far from managing to control the Soviet Union, he was often pushed by circumstances or by pressures from below. The overall argument for this can be summarized as follows. Although Stalin came to power partly through his own abilities, he was also greatly assisted by circumstance. Lenin's Bolshevik regime had run into the ground by 1921 and had had to resort to the New Economic Policy (NEP) and a general relaxation of the earlier radical socialism. By 1927, however, moderation was failing to deliver results, so that radicalism was revived with renewed energy. This coincided with Stalin's consolidation of power, so that he was able to take the initiative in launching a series of new programmes such as collectivization, the Five-Year Plans and political centralization. In this respect, Stalin was reactivating the earlier dynamism of the Bolsheviks and was stealing some of the policies for which he had condemned Trotsky to exile. He was determined to push ahead with this radicalism through economic and social change.

Far from being a model totalitarian dictatorship, however, the Stalinist political system was remarkably defective. The main problem was that there was less power at the centre than is commonly supposed. The core of both the administration and the party had enormous difficulty in exerting controls over local officials and institutions. Although Stalin took the initiative for most of the policies of the period 1929–41, he frequently lost control over their implementation as here the initiative passed to the localities. Usually what happened was that local officials and groups pressed on too enthusiastically in carrying out their orders, creating widespread chaos which then had to be dealt with by the centre applying the brakes. This, in turn, would result in local inertia so that again the centre had to recreate momentum. There were therefore violent swings of the pendulum: local interests sought to interpret central policies in the most favourable way, in response to which the centre had to take corrective action. As a general principle, therefore, Stalin's political power was used initially in a proactive way, but then became increasingly reactive. At times he came dangerously close to losing control altogether.

There were three examples of this. The first is the wave of purges that swept through the country during the 1930s and again after 1945. Stalin was certainly responsible for initiating these. But he found them hard to control and they assumed a momentum beyond what he had intended as local forces interpreted Stalin's orders in their own way, whether on collective farms or in factories. The incidence of terror therefore ebbed and flowed as Stalin sought to regain control. The second example is the economy. Stalin launched collectivization in 1928, only to find that it was implemented too rapidly as local party officials and detachments of the NKVD exceeded their quotas. When Stalin applied the brakes, the local interests became more defensive; this resulted in a second offensive, in which agricultural initiatives caught up with the purges. Third, Stalin's social changes were also subject to fluctuation. He did not simply reverse a more radical Bolshevik trend: this was already beginning to slow down under the influence of the NEP after 1921. Instead, Stalin actually attempted to revive the radical policies, especially in relation to the family and education, only to find that these added to the chaos of the early 1930s. He therefore swung back to supporting traditional social institutions and reviving conservative educational policies. This has been seen as a deliberate effort to underpin his personal authoritarian status. It could, however, be interpreted as a more instinctive reaction to escape the consequences of a programme that was not working.

None of this reduces the repressiveness of the Stalinist system. Stalin is still seen by most historians as perhaps the most ruthless dictator of the twentieth century, responsible for the deaths of many millions and prepared to make cynical use of terror on a massive scale. It remains extremely difficult to attempt to justify Stalin's actions or to rehabilitate Stalin as a character. But, as the following sections show, the extent of his control was often not in accordance with that of his brutality.

The political system: party, constitution and administration

The period 1929 to 1941 saw an apparently contradictory political development. On the one hand, Stalin gradually squeezed all signs of democracy out of the party, confirming his personal power and eliminating any possible rivals. On the other hand, changes in the Soviet constitution appeared to extend the range of democracy in the electoral system and some of the state institutions.

During the early 1930s the top levels of the party, especially the Central Committee, had taken vital decisions concerning economic planning and had greatly accelerated the collectivization of agriculture. At the same time, the party swelled its numbers and modified its organization to include more members from trade unions and factories. But the high point of the party was reached in 1934. The XVIIth Party Congress was full of euphoria and self-satisfaction at the scope of the party's achievements in industry. The next five years, however, saw drastic changes as Stalin reduced the top membership in systematic purges, as described in the next section; by 1939 none of the original Bolsheviks who had participated in the October Revolution was left. Stalin also restructured the party as a pyramid, with high grades being conferred as a reward for unquestioning loyalty.

Constitutional developments presented a strange contrast. The adoption in 1936 of a more progressive constitution coincided with Stalin's onslaught on the party. As part of the build-up, there was unprecedented preliminary discussion, with millions of people being consulted. A considerable change was introduced into the electoral system. Universal suffrage now applied to all over the age of eighteen, while voting was to be secret, direct and no longer weighted (as it had been in the 1918 and 1924 constitutions) in favour of the urban workers. The soviets, or legislative bodies, were also reformed. The new Supreme Soviet comprised two chambers, the Soviet of the Union, based on electoral districts, and the Soviet of the Nationalities, reflecting the regional and ethnic composition of the country as a whole. Article 30 of the constitution affirmed that collectively these were the supreme organ of state power. The Supreme Soviet elected a series of specialist committees and a thirty-three-man presidium for executive functions. The whole structure was undoubtedly an improvement and remained in existence until the largely insubstantial amendments made in Brezhnev's 1977 constitution.

How can one explain the disparity between developments in the party and the constitution? First, the 1936 constitution was made as progressive as possible in appearance in order to attract a favourable response from the West. The mid-1930s, after all, saw a growing concern within the Soviet Union about the spread of fascism and serious attempts by Stalin to foster popular fronts against it. Second, Stalin used the constitution as a means of diverting attention, internal and external, away from his purges. Hence, at a time when the party was being systematically drained of its top leadership, publicity was given to the constitution. This could well explain the remarkably restrained reaction of the West to events in the Soviet Union in the late 1930s. Third, the 1936 constitution was democratic in theory only. Many of the high-sounding principles were not implemented in practice and the supposed power of the Supreme Soviet remained under the direct supervision of Stalin himself. He therefore aimed to dominate the proceedings of the Soviet as directly as he controlled the party. In theory, there was nothing to stop him, at the centre, from pursuing any administrative policy he wanted.

But did this actually *work*? Revisionist historians have shown that we cannot take for granted a direct connection between totalitarianism and efficiency – whether in Fascist Italy, Nazi Germany or Stalinist Russia. The key point is that although dictatorship may well have been strengthened at the centre, this could not be fully effective unless it was properly implemented at local level, within both the state and the party. Centralized dictatorship had to operate outwards through effective channels or, to use a different metaphor, the influence of the apex had to seep down through all levels of the hierarchy.

There were widespread problems in the link between the central decision-making process and the localities: in the party, the administration, the factories, the collective farms and the army. Policies were issued by the leadership at the centre, but were not sufficiently specific. These were then variously interpreted by officials at different levels within the state and party, all of whom had their own aims and agendas. Local party secretaries defended the interests of their particular sector and interpreted orders from the centre as they saw fit. This, in turn, came in for criticism from the centre, which soon realized that policies were not being strictly adhered to. Stalin made frequent accusations that bureaucrats were impeding policy; in 1930, for example, he complained that local officials had become 'dizzy with success' in exceeding central quotas for collectivization. The centre therefore tried to restore discipline over the lower levels of management. Further waves of chaos followed in the localities as rank and file members now attacked their branch leaders or factory managers or collective farm chairmen. The latter retaliated by identifying trouble-makers and dealing with them summarily. The whole decision-making structure was therefore riddled with conflict and dissent. In the ensuing chaos the centre sought to restore a semblance of order, by adjusting, intensifying or ending particular campaigns.

Hence, the centre would eventually react to local influences. According to Arch Getty, 'Campaigns – including purges – could be stalled, sped up, aborted, or implemented in ways which suited local conditions and interests.'[58] Real power lay in local hands and with local party and government machinery. 'Even if one assumes Stalin's personality was the only or main factor in the initiation of policies, one must still explain the obvious disparities between central orders and local outcomes.'[59] The situation was further destabilized by the constant expansion of local officialdom. This made it increasingly difficult for the centre to control local officials without creating more officials, and thereby compounding the problem. Ironically, Stalinism, supposedly confined to the centre, in practice created the ideal conditions for 'little Stalins' in the localities. These were not a threat to the basis of Stalin's power, but they did threaten the effective enforcement of his policies.

Some historians consider that the 'revisionist' approach to Stalin's power has gone too far; the pendulum has therefore swung partially back towards the 'top-down' model. Rosenfeldt, for example, argues that Stalin managed to keep a high degree of control over the system via a Secret Department or Special Sector, which became, in effect, 'Stalin's personal secretariat'.[60] New investigations show that Stalin 'did in fact play an extremely important role in Soviet political life, that he constantly drove for an unprecedented degree of centralization, that all key initiatives or major decisions gradually came to lie with him.'[61] Pavlova argues that 'the strength of Stalin's power lay not in the organizational efficiency and discipline of the political machine, but in its potential to act and in particular in the far-reaching consequences of these actions'.[62] Quite so. It would be as pointless to remove Stalin from the equation as it would to remove Hitler. But the revisionist perspective has certain advantages which the traditional view by itself lacked. While not denying that Stalin was the overall initiator of policy, it removes the automatic connection between power and its successful implementation. Ruthlessness could well mean efficiency, but it could on occasions result also in chaos as local influences and cross-currents came to bear. This would explain the sudden changes, oscillations and swings as the top tried to correct the bottom's attempts to adapt to the direction imposed by the top. Seen in this light, Stalin had to give as much of his time to adjusting as to initiating, and to reacting as to planning.

The Terror

The most spectacular and notorious of all Stalin's policies was his deliberate creation of a state of total terror through a series of purges. The earliest of these affected the captains of industry and plant managers, of whom about 75 per cent were eliminated in the early 1930s.

From 1934 onwards the purges became more openly political, with the assassination of Kirov, Stalin's main potential rival. There then followed a series of spectacular show trials to deal with the party's most prominent figures, while below the surface Stalin's NKVD under Yagoda, Ezhov and Beria hunted down numberless unknowns. The first show trial (1936) disposed of Kamenev and Zinoviev; in the second, in 1937, Piatakov and Sokolnikov were accused of being the Anti-Soviet Trotskyist Centre. The third, in 1938, accounted for Bukharin, Rykov and even Yagoda – all on the charge of belonging to a bloc of right-wingers and Trotskyites. The army was also affected. In 1937 Marshal Tukhachevskii, hero of the Civil War years and now Commissar for Defence, was shot. All eleven deputy Commissars for Defence were executed, together with seventy-five out of the eighty members of the Supreme Military Council. The navy lost all eight of its admirals. Meanwhile, throughout the Soviet Union, something like 300,000 people were executed and 7 million put through the labour camps. By 1939 Stalin considered that the Terror had run its necessary course and decided to call a halt.

Causes

Although the enormity of Stalin's purges defies a completely logical explanation, a variety of motives has been suggested.

One is that Stalin had a disastrously flawed personality. Khrushchev, for example, later emphasized Stalin's brutality, vindictiveness, pathological distrust and sickly suspicion. More recently Tucker has maintained that, in addition to serving a political function, the show trials also rationalized Stalin's own paranoid tendency.[63] Grey, however, adopted a different approach, stressing that in launching the Terror, 'Stalin was acting not from cruelty or lust for power, but from the conviction that all real or potential opposition . . . must be uprooted or destroyed'. Although his methods were extreme and the results devastating, Stalin was part of a broader Russian autocratic tradition: 'Ivan the Terrible and Peter the Great, were the forerunners on whom Stalin directly patterned himself.'[64] Overy provided another explanation of Stalin's methods. 'Power with Stalin seems to have been power to preserve and enlarge the revolution and the state that represented it, not power simply for its own sake.'[65] In his recent biography Kotkin restores at least part of the importance of personal factors, while combining these with political objectives. 'The problems of revolution brought out the paranoia in Stalin, and Stalin brought out the paranoia inherent in the revolution.'[66]

A second reason for the purges is that Stalin was never one to resort to half measures. He aimed to wipe out the entire generation of Bolsheviks who had assisted Lenin between 1917 and 1924. This alone would guarantee Stalin as the sole heir to Lenin and would secure his position for a lifetime. Most of the threats to his power were latent and would possibly not reveal themselves for several years. They should, nevertheless, be dealt with as soon as possible. Since these latent threats were impossible to identify, a large number of people who would ultimately prove innocent of any form of opposition to Stalin would also have to go. It was only by having such a clean sweep that Stalin could make sure of eradicating those who would be a threat. In contrasting the liquidation programmes of Stalin and Hitler, Ulam points out that, by and large, the latter dealt with individuals and groups clearly identified as enemies of the Nazi regime.[67] However, 99 per cent of Stalin's victims were innocent of any opposition to the Soviet system and were loyal Soviet citizens.

A third explanation was economic: the rapidity of Stalin's proposed industrialization and the implementation of collective farming required a disciplined workforce and a compliant peasantry. In Stalin's eyes, this could only be achieved by coercion. In industry, measures had to be taken to force reluctant factory managers to implement the new policies, while peasant resistance to collectivization required ruthless measures from the dekulakization squads of the NKVD. As the pace of industrialization accelerated during the Second and Third Five-Year Plans the rapidly growing Gulag system of labour camps added further numbers to the workforce. Convict labour built the Belomor Canal, opened in 1933, and provided the mainstay of mining in Siberia, especially in the inhospitable Kolyma region. Terror was therefore inseparable from Stalin's vision of modernization: it removed obstacles from its introduction and it provided the impetus for its fulfilment.

Some historians have pointed to the importance of Stalin's reaction to external factors. There are two very different variants of this. On the one hand, Stalin was obsessed with the fear that the West would smash the Soviet regime before his industrialization programme was complete. It therefore made sense to adopt a pragmatic approach to foreign policy; Germany, the main threat, could be won over by a temporary policy of co-operation. Stalin found it no more difficult to collaborate with fascism than with any other European system, for he regarded it merely as a variant of Western capitalism. The old-style Bolsheviks, by contrast, were profoundly anti-fascist and saw Hitler as a far more deadly enemy than either France or Britain. According to Tucker and Conquest, Stalin therefore considered it essential to remove the anti-Hitler element to make possible the accommodation with Germany which eventually materialized in August 1939 in the Nazi–Soviet Non-Aggression Pact. Deutscher puts a different case. Stalin's main worry was that his regime would be destroyed from within – by internal revolt. There seemed little chance of this happening in 1936, unless, of course, some major external catastrophe occurred, which could lead to a revival of the scenario of the First World War; military crisis could well bring about a revolution. Stalin's solution was therefore to destroy any elements within Russia which could possibly take advantage of such a situation. The show trials dealt with these potential threats by magnifying the charge against them. They had to die as traitors, as perpetrators of crimes beyond the reach of reason. Only then could Stalin be sure that their execution would provoke no dangerous revulsion.[68]

All these explanations of the Terror have one thing in common. The decisions were taken by Stalin himself and were part of his determination to develop a new totalitarian system that covered all areas of Soviet life – the economy, society, politics and the military. He therefore carries the main responsibility for the vast loss of life and the extreme persecutions that these policies entailed. This much is still largely accepted. The assumption though was that Stalin was always fully in control and that he dictated the momentum and scope of the Terror. But it has now been questioned as to whether the Soviet administrative system was really that efficient – or able to impose its will so completely on the localities. Instead, some historians emphasize that there were 'bottom-up' reactions to 'top-down' orders, involving vast numbers of ordinary people and providing an additional momentum that went beyond Stalin's intentions.

The main example of this was to be found in the countryside. Decrees for collectivization were issued in a 'top-down' manner in 1929 by the All-Russian Central Executive Committee (or Council of People's Commissars), in line with Stalin's policy. These defined precisely who was to be classified as a wealthy peasant, or kulak, at the same time warning that dekulakization should not become an end in itself. But these instructions did not prevent a wave of terror developing as the dekulakization squads exceeded their instructions in a more chaotic 'bottom-up' response. This became so serious that Stalin had to stem the flow in 1930, accusing the squads of exceeding their instructions. When the campaign was resumed later that year, and extended between 1932 and 1934, the leadership attempted to exert more direct control over the local officials, again with limited success. This interaction between 'top-down' and 'bottom-up' forces has been strongly stressed by recent authorities. Viola distinguishes between the repressive policies which the state undoubtedly pursued and the methods used by cadres in the field to implement these. The latter were affected by a 'general political culture of the early 1930s', based on 'a mixture of traditional Russian fanaticism', and 'the unleashing of years of pent-up class rage and retribution'.[69] Some historians have gone even further. The repression and persecutions at local levels were manifestations of the breakdown of central control. Arch Getty, for example, argues: 'Stalin had initiated a movement with vague instructions and ambitious targets. As the process unfolded on the ground . . . it degenerated rapidly into chaotic and violent struggles based on local conditions.'[70]

Other sectors experienced similar dynamics. In industry there was widespread chaos as managers conflicted with the party and the workforce, all of which were pursing different interests. An additional complication was the Stakhanovite movement. Thurston argues that this created tension in factories as young Stakhanovites with personal and political ambitions upset the productivity balance which managers tried desperately to maintain. In turn, the latter became subject to accusations of wrecking and sabotage. 'Whatever its scope, as the terror unfolded the resentments and demands fostered by early Stakhanovism heightened tensions in industry.'[71] Much the same applies to the army. Reese claims that the party organizations within the armed forces experienced upheaval which was well beyond the control of the central administration.[72] Overall, Reese adds, the Terror may have 'begun at the center' but 'at the local level some people took advantage of it to settle personal scores.'[73]

Everywhere, therefore, local people had a real involvement in the Terror. Many were genuinely convinced that the economy was riddled with 'wreckers' and saboteurs who had to be brought to book. Here an important part was played by the show trials which helped whip up suspicion of and resentment against managers.[74] Peasants provided information and they testified at local *raion* trials (the local counterparts to the show trials). Paranoia spread through all levels of society, helping to maintain the momentum of terror at the lowest levels. Rittersporn maintains that the regime's emphasis on the 'subversive' activities of 'conspirators' interacted with traditional prejudices to produce an 'imagery of omnipresent subversion and conspiracy'.[75] According to Suny, 'The requirement to find enemies, to blame and punish, worked together with self-protection and self-promotion . . . to expand the Purges into a political holocaust'.[76]

To be fair, these arguments from the early 1990s – about the importance of popular influences – were provisional, pending further research in the light of access to the archives after the collapse of the Soviet Union. More recently, historians have tended to return – at least partially – to a more traditional approach, possibly because the archives themselves had been pruned of detailed evidence covering the Terror. Litvin and Keep neither confirm nor deny the strength of the revisionist case; instead, they see the 'popular input' as 'an *auxiliary* reason for the Terror's vast scope.[77] They argue that both approaches 'elucidate fundamental truths about Stalinism'. The traditional approach identified 'the monist urge of the Bolsheviks to gain mastery over social processes and human destinies', while the revisionists showed that 'intention "from above" was often foiled by unforeseen reaction "from below", which in turn demanded ever more draconian "solutions" from the leadership'.[78] This seems eminently reasonable. Very few historians, other than apologists for Stalin, would argue that he did *not* intend to inflict terror on an unprecedented scale or that he was *not* personally involved in countless decisions sending countless unfortunates to their deaths. But if we are to escape the simplistic conclusions of Khrushchev (see p. 63), we have to acknowledge that Stalin intended major changes in the economy, society and foreign policy, as well as the removal of all opposition and democracy within the party. These certainly involved unprecedented coercion at all levels. But coercion from the centre did not necessarily result in control over local areas, which meant that chaos often forced the adjustment of the degree of terror – sometimes to dilute it, but more often to exacerbate it in the name of discipline. The argument about chaos does not, therefore, reduce Stalin's responsibility.

Effects

The last section concluded that Stalin's terror was less carefully controlled and centralized than has often been thought. The corollary to this is that the effects are also less clear-cut and need partial reinterpretation.

It has been argued that the Terror was the chief method by which the party machinery of the Bolshevik state was transformed into the personalized totalitarian dictatorship of Stalin. As a result, Stalinism created a regime which was more consistently ruthless and pervasive even than that of Nazi Germany. There is some truth in this. Any capacity for debate about different strategies was certainly squeezed out of the centre of the party with the elimination of Kamenev, Zinoviev, Bukharin, Rykov and others. The chances of persuading Stalin to adopt a course different to what he had in mind, whether in economic or foreign policy, could never seriously arise after 1934. It could also be argued that the Terror was a necessary complement to the development of the Stalinist personality cult – the obverse side of the same coin. Paradoxically, the Terror also made it easier to introduce the 1936 Constitution, with more advanced democratic features than its predecessors; since these could easily be neutralized in practice they were never likely to provide any check to Stalin's overall power.

But terror has traditionally been seen as working in one way only – as tightening the political system and therefore enhancing the powers of dictatorship. Some historians have, however, suggested an alternative approach – that terror unintentionally unleashed confusion into the political system, thereby limiting the extent to which dictatorship could operate effectively. We have already seen how local groups in industry and the countryside interpreted central decisions. Normally such groups would have been cautious, but the Terror acted as a stimulus for greatly intensified activity. Hence, the result was more often the descent into chaos, with wild oscillations developing as first the local groups implemented the instructions of the centre in their own way before the centre attempted to restore an approved line. Paradoxically, terror was a democratizing force, although in a negative sense: it created a tyranny *of* the people quite as much as the traditional image of a tyranny *over* the people.

A similar controversy exists over the impact of terror on the economy. The top-down view is that, in giving an enormous boost to Stalin's authority, the Terror also provided a vital impetus for the development of a command economy based on centralized planning and imposed targets. Comparisons have been made between the rigidity of Stalin's methods on the one hand and, on the other, the greater flexibility of a mixed economic system that would have allowed for higher standards of living and far less suffering. Some have argued that only centralized planning, could have led to the rapid increases in heavy industry and armaments which eventually saved the Soviet Union from Germany. Others now maintain that the application of terror to the economy confused the lines of command, thereby undermining the whole Stalinist system. Two examples can be given of this. One was the approach to collectivization and dekulakization which, as we have seen, was conducted with excessive zeal by local party officials and the NKVD. The result was one of the greatest mass disobedience campaigns in the history of the twentieth century, aimed not at Stalin but at those who were interpreting his orders more freely than even he wanted. The second example is the impact of the Stakhanovites in industry. Their initiative, which was intended to promote an increase in productivity, helped slow it down. In the climate of terror, managers were understandably hostile to anyone who distorted their own implementation of industrial plans. This, in turn, made them targets for denunciation, with the result that the very people most likely to achieve local stability were removed. According to Acton, 'far from improving efficiency, the terror was manifestly damaging the economy'.[79]

This brings us to the impact of the Terror on the security of the Soviet Union. The purging of the armed forces cannot but have had a negative effect on Soviet defences. Experience was undoubtedly affected by the wholesale expulsion of officers. The real loss was of experience at the highest level, surely a crippling blow to any impending war effort. The result, it is generally argued, was a humiliating performance against Finland in the Northern War of 1939–40 and a disastrous collapse when the Germans invaded the Soviet Union in 1941. Yet, again, the impact of the Terror may have been exaggerated. Most of those purged in 1938 were not arrested but merely expelled from the party. Hence, the impact was more limited than once thought. It was originally estimated that the purges had accounted for between 25 per cent and 50 per cent of army officers. Estimates have put the figures at somewhere between 3.7 per cent and 7.7 per cent.[80] There are two main reasons for this disparity. One is a previous underestimate of the size of the officer class in the Red Army, the other the rapidity with which many were rehabilitated. Both of these points have the effect of diluting the impact of the Terror on the efficiency of the armed forces. In any case, many military expulsions from the army were not accompanied by loss of military rank. It has now been estimated that 30 per cent of army officers discharged between 1937 and 1939 were reinstated.[81] This was part of the policy of the central authorities to reduce the scale of denunciations. At the XVIIIth Party Congress in March 1939, for example, it was said:

> Political organs and party organizations often expel party members far too light-heartedly. The party commissions of the Political Administration of the Red Army find it necessary to reinstate about 50 per cent of the expelled men because the expulsions were unjustified.[82]

It seems, therefore, that measures were being taken to correct the severity of the purges well before the German invasion.

Finally – and most important of all – how can we measure the impact of the Terror in terms of the suffering it caused to the people? The number of victims is colossal – but controversial. Accurate estimates have always been open to dispute and the release of official material from the Soviet archives after the onset of *glasnost* only served to accentuate this. The total number of deaths according to Nove and Wheatcroft was between 4 million and 11 million – significantly lower than Conquest's estimate of 20 million. Soviet figures, released in 1989 point to the execution of 681,692 people between 1937 and 1938 and a total of 786,098 between 1930 and 1953.[83] Estimates of prison populations also vary. Rosefielde puts them at 10 million and Conquest at 8 million in 1938 (increasing to 12 million by 1952); Nove and Wheatcroft put the peak figure at 5.5 million in 1953, closer to Soviet estimates of up to 4 million in labour camps. There is also a major difficulty in distinguishing between those who died as a direct result of a purge and those whose deaths were caused by famine or diseases associated with Stalin's agricultural policies. Inevitably, comparisons have been made between the Terror inflicted in the Soviet Union and that carried out by the Nazis. The Soviet purges had no equivalent to the directly targeted racial extermination implemented with technological efficiency by the Nazi regime. Yet the majority of Soviet citizens were dragged into the direct path of the Terror, whereas most Germans (or at least those who were not racially excluded from the *Volksgemeinschaft*) were not. Strangely, the main instigator of the Soviet terror was not as widely hated and feared as was once thought. This was because the population was largely affected at the local level by officials acting partly on their own initiative to interpret Stalin's orders. The man who was most directly responsible for the death of millions of innocent victims was widely seen as the main hope for bringing the Terror to an end.

The economy under Stalin

Economic change was Stalin's immediate priority once his authority had been confirmed. He intended to transform the Soviet Union into a superpower by equipping it with a huge industrial base. The process began in 1929 and continued, with the interruption of war, until his death in 1953. Lenin's New Economic Policy had allowed limited private enterprise in the agricultural and industrial sectors. The peasantry were permitted to grow grain for the market, under licence, while most of the smaller industrial enterprises were denationalized. By the time of Lenin's death, the NEP had attracted widespread support and its continuation was urged by the 'rightists' within the party, including Bukharin, Rykov and Tomsky. Some, however, considered that a more appropriate strategy would be rapid industrialization and the introduction of collective farming. Trotsky, in particular, favoured this approach as part of his strategy of Permanent Revolution.

At first, Stalin favoured the continuation of the NEP, which he associated with Socialism in One Country. By 1928, however, he had reversed the NEP and associated Socialism in One Country with collectivized agriculture and rapid industrialization. How can we explain this apparent turnabout in economic policy? The following analysis shows that, in both cases, Stalin was at the same time reacting to events beyond his immediate control while trying to push the economy in a new direction. The result was bound to be a large measure of confusion.

Collectivization

Between 1926 and 1927 Russia experienced a major crisis in food procurement, as only 17 per cent of all grain harvested by the peasantry reached the urban workers. Stalin's response to this was to bring back requisitioning – previously used between 1918 and 1921. This proved too be the first step in a longer-term policy that ended the NEP and the introduction of collectivization. How, precisely, the procurement crisis led to this is now open to debate. One view is that Stalin used the crisis as an excuse to impose, from above, his own preconceptions on the economy. The other is that he was pushed by circumstances, and pressures from below, into emergency and makeshift measures.

By the first argument, Stalin was the prime mover of economic change. He saw two possibilities for the future of the Soviet economy, 'There is the capitalist way, which is to enlarge the agricultural units by introducing capitalism in agriculture'; the alternative was 'the socialist way, which is to set up collective and state farms'. The latter was preferable, since it would provide the means for using agriculture as a way of subsidizing industry and developing socialism. The problem was how to persuade an innately conservative part of society to accept the role of being in the forefront of this socialist advancement. It was becoming increasingly unlikely that they could be won over voluntarily since the NEP seemed to be evolving away from communist principles: the movement was very much towards the search for fair prices by the peasant producer. Stalin was convinced that all this needed to change – quickly. He therefore launched a revolution from above to break with the economic trend of the NEP and to herd the peasantry into collectives. He was also determined to tighten his political control over the party: according to Brovkin, his move was therefore 'a pre-emptive strike on the central party–state apparatus'.[84] In essence, Stalin used the procurement crisis as an excuse to destroy an economic system which was working economically in order to gain full political control. It was a deliberate and calculated policy which went against the natural course that Russia was taking. It marked the beginning of the Stalinist revolution.

There is, however, a very different perspective. Stalin was not in control of the changes in agriculture from 1927. He did not impose collectivization as a policy decision: instead, he stumbled into it with neither planning nor forethought. The reason was that the NEP was not working and the attitudes of both peasants and workers forced him into a fundamental change of policy. The procurement crisis occurred because industry was failing to provide the goods for the peasants to buy: hence they held on to their grain. Since it could not satisfy basic consumer needs, the NEP had failed. Stalin therefore had no choice. According to Lewin, 'The market mechanism of NEP, which had worked wonders at the start simply by following its natural course, had in the end led the regime into an impasse.' Hence, when faced with the procurement crisis, Stalin reacted instinctively by operating 'the lever whose use he best understood; he resorted to force'. Nevertheless, 'When he manipulated this particular lever in January 1928, Stalin did not know where the process set in motion by his "emergency measures" would ultimately lead him.'[85] It may even be that Russia was moving away from the NEP anyway – and that Stalin simply went with the momentum. Arch Getty maintains that, although Stalin was officially responsible for collectivization, he was strongly influenced by 'the social, economic and political environment that he did not create'.[86]

These explanations seem to be mutually exclusive. But are they? Both emphasize Stalin's willingness to use force: this could be seen as the common and most important factor in the change of economic direction. The consolidation of personal power was his most important consideration, which meant that political criteria dominated the economic. It is unlikely that he would have had a long-term economic blueprint for implementing socialism. At the same time, he could certainly have developed a socialist strategy as a solution to his immediate political difficulties. In 1927 he faced the prospect of political humiliation caused by the procurement crisis. The alternatives were to make further concessions by continuing the NEP or to take a tougher line by ending it. The latter was more attractive since it would also enable him to cut down his remaining opponents, like Bukharin, who favoured the continuation of the NEP. He therefore took an economic decision for political reasons. It was not systematically planned – but, at the same time, he did not simply drift into it. He reacted to circumstances to enhance his power. Once the power was secure he could convert reactive measures into something resembling projective plans.

These were based on the principle of collectivization. The rationale which Stalin now produced was that the existing organization of agriculture was a major obstacle to the country's overall economic development. Existing grain supplies were inadequate to feed the industrial workers in the cities. The basic reason for this was the pattern of land ownership, which was based on fragmentation into small individual holdings. This led to a capitalist mentality which promoted individual rather than collective values; the procurement crisis could therefore be explained as the result of selfish hoarding. As the reasons were simplified, the solutions could be made clearer. Temporary requisitioning in 1928 led inexorably towards collectivization, officially announced in 1929. Private land was now to be brought within collective farms (*kolkhozy*) or state farms (*sovkhozy*). The end of private property would, in turn, remove the remaining cause of class divisions: this meant that the main target were the kulaks, the landowning peasants who had prospered under the NEP. Finally, and above all, agricultural changes could be used to assist the country's industrial transformation.

Industrialization

As in agriculture, the reasons for Stalin's industrial policies are now open to debate. Did he dictate the process from above or was he pushed by pressures from below? The former model may attribute too much to the decision of one man. As important as the initiatives from above, it is now argued, were pressures from below. Stalin was under considerable social pressure exerted by the industrial working class whose interests were out of line with the more conservative peasantry. The working class wanted readily available food and job security, both of which depended on a compliant peasantry. The latter, however, needed higher commodity prices to enable them to buy more consumer goods. The problem was that consumer goods would not guarantee job security for the workers or state investment in industry. Hence, there was a tension between agriculture and industry, which was bound to affect the decisions taken from above in the name of the various groups. By this analysis, Stalin reacted to the needs of the working class in the cities, just as he had to the dangers posed by the peasantry over the procurement crisis.

This, however, should not obscure the importance of Stalin's own influence on industrialization. By 1927 he had moved towards taking command of an economy which, through the NEP, had been left for a while to take its own course. As we have already seen, this was due partly to Stalin's own accumulation of power, and partly to problems within the economy which required his attention. Stalin therefore developed a series of priorities related to the future security of his own regime. This meant an emphasis on heavy industry and, in particular, on armaments. These decisions were taken by Stalin himself for reasons which were partly political and partly a reaction to the conflicting pressures of sub-groups. Once his position was secure, however, he was able to present a more coherent overall strategy with a clearer underlying logic. Two of his priorities stand out.

The first was Soviet Russia's very survival. Stalin took over Trotsky's emphasis on the threats of capitalist encirclement by the West. He then welded this anti-capitalism to a basic commitment to Russia's self-sufficiency, or Socialism in One Country. In February 1931 he summarized his position as follows:

> We are fifty to a hundred years behind the advanced countries. We must make good this distance in ten years. Either we do it or we shall be crushed. That is what our obligations to the workers and peasants of the USSR dictate to us.[87]

From the start, therefore, Stalin was moving the Soviet economy on to a war footing. This placed the emphasis on heavy industry at the expense of light or consumer industry, since iron, steel and heavy machinery could more easily be converted to armaments production. It could also be adapted to a change in Soviet military strategy which occurred during the 1930s: Stalin came under the influence of military theorists who believed that the Soviet Union should move on the offensive and prepare for a pre-emptive strike at a time of its own choosing. This meant the building and stockpiling of massive amounts of armaments. Through the industrial Five-Year Plans Stalin therefore gradually moved the motive from defence against the West to the preparation of an offensive against it.

The other motive was ideological: industrialization was the only fully reliable means of developing a socialist economy. Any genuine intention to ditch the NEP was bound to mean a reorientation from agriculture to industry, since the NEP had been geared to the former. Stalin had come to accept that Socialism in One Country had to enlarge the urban proletariat and that the socialist way of doing this was through state control of industry. Any such development would involve curbing the consumer sector, which tended to strengthen capitalism. If capitalism was to be eradicated from the Soviet Union, action had to be taken against the class most likely to try to preserve it. Hence, Stalin was able to justify using the peasantry to subsidize industrial development and to reduce the emphasis on consumerism. The reorganization of agriculture would therefore make possible accelerated industrialization, thereby bringing the Soviet Union's social structure more into line with the classless society. Stalin was enough of a Marxist to be able to justify pragmatic decisions with retrospective ideology.

The impact of Stalin's agricultural policies

If one of the purposes of collectivization was to end private property, a key criterion for success was surely the number of units collectivized. The process was implemented with remarkable speed. The proportion of collective holdings increased from 23.6 per cent in 1930 to 52.7 per cent in 1931, 61.5 per cent in 1932, 66.4 per cent in 1933, 71.4 per cent in 1934, 83.2 per cent in 1935, 89.6 per cent in 1936 and, finally, 98 per cent by 1941. Unfortunately, all this occurred too quickly. The process spiralled out of Stalin's control as the centre of administration lost the initiative to the local party officials, local industrial managers and local officials of the secret police, the NKVD. Stalin became so concerned about their frantic activities that he accused them of being 'dizzy with success' and called a halt in 1931. As the local officials fell into line with the new instructions, inertia set in and Stalin had to start the whole process up again. Throughout the period the pendulum swung violently backwards and forwards as the centre launched policies which became distorted in their operation locally. The results were administrative chaos and a decline in productivity. The figures for grain harvests declined between 1928 and 1929 from 73.3 million tons to 71.7 million. After a temporary recovery to 83.5 million tons in 1930, the decline continued to 69.5 million in 1931 and 69.6 million in 1932. There were even more dramatic losses in livestock over the same period: the number of pigs declined from 70 million to 34 million, sheep and goats from 146 to 42 million and pigs from 26 million to 9 million.

The impact on the peasantry was disastrous. It has been argued that this was partly self-induced: the result of deliberate defiance sparked by fear and the threat of massive collective resistance. Alternatively, agricultural production was sacrificed to hunt for kulaks as class enemies. As a result, local conditions became so volatile that it became physically impossible in some areas to fulfil even the normal agricultural processes of sowing, harvesting and breeding. Either way, the result was misery – although the extent of this did vary. Nationally, food consumption dropped between 1928 and 1932: bread from 250 kilos per head to 215 and potatoes from 141 to 125. But these figures do not show that the countryside was far worse off than the cities. Between 1932 and 1933 areas like the Ukraine experienced a major famine. Some authorities have calculated that between 5 and 7 million people in the Soviet Union – mostly in the Ukraine – died from starvation as a direct result of the policies of collectivization. There was also an unprecedented upheaval in Russian society. Peasants were turned against each other, as the kulak minority fell victim to the less affluent, who, in turn, were affected by mass hysteria and panic. This had a knock-on effect on the urban areas as factories, workshops and munitions were overwhelmed by the influx of millions of desperate peasants seeking employment and survival.

Are there any arguments at all in defence of Stalin's agricultural policies? It was once held that collectivization did, at least, help to subsidize Soviet industrial growth, thereby avoiding any dependence on western loans. But even this has now been challenged on the grounds that it would have been administratively impossible to transfer resources effectively from one sector to the other. Instead, agricultural changes *impeded* industrial growth: the transfer of population was too rapid for industry to absorb, which meant huge administrative problems and worsening social conditions. Recent arguments have stressed that there was no net flow of resources from agriculture to industry; if anything, agriculture benefited from industrial input, especially in the form of machine tractor stations. Unusually for any historical assessment, conclusions now seem uniformly negative. It could certainly be argued that the most vulnerable area of the Soviet economy between the Stalin and Gorbachev eras was agriculture.

The impact of Stalin's industrial policies

In 1928 Stalin introduced the First Five-Year Plan which was intended to transform the industrial base of the Soviet Union. The organization of this was the responsibility of the State Planning Bureau, or Gosplan. The emphasis was placed on heavy industry rather than on consumer goods, and especially on coal, steel, oil, electricity and armaments. The Second and Third Five-Year Plans followed in 1933 and 1937, the last of these being interrupted by the German invasion of the Soviet Union in 1941.

But did they work? Stalin has certainly been credited with the development of heavy industry. He did not, as is sometimes suggested, lay the actual foundations for this. The Tsars had developed a considerable industrial capacity, based on five main centres: Moscow (textiles), Petrograd (heavy industry), the Donetz region (coalfields), Baku (oil) and the Ukraine (iron and steel). Lenin added plans for widespread electrification and for the development of the Urals. Stalin did, however, enhance the scale of heavy industry: he was responsible for the emphasis on 'gigantomania' – the construction of new industrial cities such as Magnitogorsk and the expansion of heavy plant and steel production. The increase was considerable: the First Five-Year Plan (1928–32) raised steel production from 3 to 6 million tons, coal from 35 to 64 million and oil from 12 to 21 million; the Second Five-Year Plan (1933–7) increased the figures to 18 million tons for steel, 128 million for coal and 26 million for oil. The last complete figures for the Third Five-Year Plan before it was interrupted by the 1941 German invasion were 18 million, 150 million and 26 million, respectively.

There was also a positive impact on employment: far higher levels were achieved than had been anticipated at the outset of the First Five-Year Plan. Instead of the 3.9 million expected in state industry by 1922–3, the number reached 6.4 million. The pace then slowed to 7.9 million by 1937 and 8.3 million by 1940. The bulk of these were peasants leaving the countryside. Urban populations also increased dramatically by something like 200,000 per month, or by a total of 30 million between 1926 and 1930. Unemployment ceased to be a serious factor since the magnet of industrialization brought in ever increasing numbers from the countryside and enabled more ambitious targets to be established for projects in heavy industry. In the process, Stalin generated the capital and labour necessary for such developments from within the Soviet Union itself. This was the purpose of subordinating agriculture to industrialization. Stalin therefore effectively sealed Russia off from the West and enabled the country to progress amid its hostility. Ultimately, Stalin's industrialization assisted the Soviet Union's survival in the Second World War. According to Hutchings, 'One can hardly doubt that if there had been a slower build-up of industry, the attack would have been successful and world history would have evolved quite differently.'[88] In a more direct sense, heavy industrialization had made it possible for the Soviet Union to rearm. In 1933 defence comprised 4 per cent of the industrial budget; by 1937 it had risen to 17 per cent and by 1940 to 33 per cent. Heavy industrialization therefore translated into ultimate survival.

All these points are part of the traditional argument which credits Stalin with the development of Soviet industrial infrastructure through ruthlessly centralized control. Although this is still widely supported, a number of reservations have now been added.

Although Stalin did try to set an overall agenda, based on accelerating heavy industry, the effectiveness of the planning mechanism has been called into question. Recent research has shown that setting targets did not in itself constitute planning. It was one thing for the central administration, including Gosplan, to draw up target figures for the different components of industry, but quite another to develop the mechanism whereby these might be achieved systematically. Hence, the ruthlessness of the Stalinist dictatorship did not necessarily produce efficiency in the promotion of heavy industry. There was, for example, little overall consistency in the pace of the Five-Year Plans. This was due largely to the disruption caused by local influences. Local managers had to protect themselves by exaggerating their needs for investment and by hoarding materials to ensure that they had sufficient supplies. This meant shortages elsewhere and a consequent lack of overall balance. There was a lack of harmony between the different sectors of the economy. Soviet industrial development was, in fact, well behind that of the United States. The latter benefited from auxiliary developments which enhanced industrialization, including transport, services and managerial and accounting expertise.[89] Many of these were provided by private enterprise. This was missing in the Soviet Union, which meant that the initiative had to be taken by the state.

The effects of this were generally negative. According to Shearer, having a 'command-administrative economy' was not the same as having 'a planned one'.[90] Instead, there was administrative chaos, which had serious consequences when the Hitler invaded the Soviet Union in June 1941. This was because all the mechanisms of the Five-Year Plans had been geared towards the country fighting an offensive war, whereas what the situation in 1941 needed was a defensive response. Centralized administrative control actually had to be loosened to achieve the levels and types of mobilization for an effective fight-back. This theory is in direct contrast to the argument that Russia defeated Germany because of planning. On the contrary, Russia achieved this *despite* planning.

There is much less disagreement about the serious side-effects of industrialization. Russia was unique in European history in experiencing an industrial revolution that produced no corresponding improvements in the quality of life of her inhabitants. As will be seen in the next section there was, instead, massive social upheaval. There was serious overcrowding in the cities and the huge dormitories and other shared accommodation resulted in squalor and social disruption. There was an inherent contradiction in the whole process. The agricultural and industrial transformation, that was intended to modernize Russia, actually tore apart its social fabric. This made it more difficult to stabilize working patterns but easier to exploit the population and the fear to which it was constantly exposed.

The final evaluation of the effect of Stalin's industrialization returns to the cause. Starving the consumer sector to develop heavy industry can be seen in two ways: either it was a deliberate strategy to create an industrial superpower with a compliant population or it was the result of inefficient planning worsened by local chaos. If it was the first, then any imbalance was part of a design and the overall result was efficient industrialization bought at a high price. If, however, it was the second, then the process of industrialization was almost as badly flawed as that of agricultural change. This, in turn, raises the possibility that the price was not only too high, but unnecessary.

Society under Stalin

Overall patterns of change

There were major changes in all areas of Soviet society during the 1920s and 1930s. But the *way* in which they occurred provides a perspective on Stalin's overall rule. The earlier historical view focused on a shift from the experimentation carried out by the Bolsheviks under Lenin to a more disciplined approach under Stalin, who revived traditional authority but with a totalitarian emphasis. This undoubtedly occurred – but in a more disorganized and haphazard way than was originally suggested.

Earlier arguments stressed the fundamental differences between Lenin and Stalin, accounting for changes in social policy in two ways. First, the Bolshevik period of experimentation brought with it the threat of social breakdown, with the extreme side-effects threatening the pace of economic change. And second, Stalin had instinctive preferences for more traditional forms of authority to deal with the backlash, since these enabled him to adopt a 'top-down' approach in the ruthless imposition of his power. This transition has, however, been oversimplified, suggesting a bloc change between two different systems. More recent interpretations have suggested a more complex – but convincing – explanation of the process, emphasizing its untidy variations between experimentation, reaction and adjustment. The Bolsheviks had already begun to relax their own radical measures from 1921 onwards – the time of the NEP. Stalin, by contrast, attempted at first to revive the flagging radical policies in the late 1920s and early 1930s to add momentum to his main priorities – economic transformation and rearmament. The problem was that he lost some of the initiative to local forces, whether in the form of over-enthusiastic officials or a resistant workforce. As we have already seen, both exerted pressures 'from below' which distorted the intentions from above. It was therefore necessary to impose more discipline which, in turn, brought about the need for further adjustments.

This overall pattern was further complicated by the varying paces of change for the different areas of society considered in this section. It was more straightforward in the cases of social equality, women and the family, but more variable for religion, education and culture.

The basic Marxist tenets of equality were not directly challenged by either the Bolsheviks or their successors. These included classlessness and equality between individuals, gender and nationalities. Changes, however, took place in how these were applied. The Bolsheviks preferred a more literal and absolute interpretation of equality: in their attempt to eliminate all social distinctions, they removed the insignia of rank within the Red Army, narrowed differentials in wages, and took a strict line on gender equality, promoting women within the central political system in a way that was unheard of in the dictatorships of the far right. They also intended to weaken the family in order to liberate women and ensure the greater influence of the state over the individual. In promoting cultural equality they even dispensed with authoritarian figures like conductors in orchestras.

At first Stalin went along with these changes and even tried to accelerate them during the 1920s. But when his economic policies encountered the impediments of strict egalitarianism, he rapidly came to the conclusion that the more traditional forms of hierarchy had to be restored. He therefore reintroduced all traditional distinctions of army rank, along with insignia and epaulettes (which were now given an exaggerated size, as were the army and navy caps). He also developed a new hierarchy within the party and industry to ensure that his instructions were fully implemented. In economic policy he realized that the earlier methods of enforcing equality had interfered with economic growth. In order to create a disciplined workforce, he ended the practice of 'wage equalization', arguing that it had nothing to do with socialism. He considered it essential to draw up new scales 'which would take into account the difference between skilled and unskilled labour'.[91] Hence, the old Marxist principle of 'from each according to his ability, to each according to his needs' was modified under Stalin to 'from each according to his ability, to each according to his work'.

But this policy had mixed results. On the one hand, by increasing incentives it did accelerate the momentum of industrial change. On the other, such incentives were, in practice, highly selective. The only real beneficiaries were the Stakhanovites, or shock workers who acted as an example to the rest of the workforce by exceeding their quotas. As we have already seen, these were a mixed blessing anyway, since they frequently threw into chaos any attempts by local factory managers to work out how to implement their targets. Managers and local officials were, in turn under suspicion for either exceeding their instructions, or dragging their heels. This meant that, although the egalitarian principle was eventually redefined by Stalin, adjustments had to be made throughout the 1930s which could not help but affect the different sectors of society.

Women and the family

In contrast to fascist Italy, authoritarian Spain and Nazi Germany, women and the family were not automatically connected during the early Bolshevik regime. Official policy between 1917 and 1926 had been to destroy institutions that represented the traditional order, especially the family. In her treatise *The New Morality and the Working Class* (1918) Alexandra Kollontai had stated that 'the old type of family has seen its day'.[92] Emphasis was placed instead on gender equality. Divorce was made extremely easy by the Decrees of December 1917, while bigamy and abortion were no longer criminalized; indeed, the latter was allowed by the Decree of November 1920.[93] Stalin's view swung from one extreme to the other. At first, during the 1920s and early 1930s, he continued social radicalism as the best means of promoting his target of rapid economic change. He was also of the view that genuine equality had to operate between individuals within an all-embracing state rather than through an officially sanctioned hierarchy. Later, however, he moved away from the early radicalism of the Bolsheviks, reinstating the close connection between women and the family within a more traditional social structure.

Like most Bolsheviks, Stalin had initially followed the Marxist attitude that the family was a means of bourgeois control and capitalist exploitation and that the measures against it were the only means of building socialism. This was in contrast to Nazi, fascist and conservative conceptions, all of which saw the family as an essential means of transmitting values and allegiances, whether political, economic or ideological. Most of Stalin's early measures were therefore against the family and marriage. In the interests of industrial advancement, labour laws frequently separated husbands and wives for work in different areas, ignoring any individual appeals made against this. Abortions were justified on the grounds that they enhanced the freedom of women and, at the same time, prolonged their active service to the state.

Stalin's conversion to a different course was the consequence of the devastating social backlash of these policies. Women experienced a host of problems. They had less legal protection against unwelcome sexual pressures, fewer guarantees of support from husbands or partners, while inadequate care facilities for their children meant that they faced the 'double burden' of domestic roles and the expectation of increased contributions to the workforce. More important for Stalin was the impact of earlier policies on population growth, with all the implications for labour shortages. In many of the urban areas, there were more abortions than live births: Leningrad in 1934 had 42 abortions per 1,000 population compared with 15.9 births,[94] while the figures for Moscow in the same year were 154,000 abortions to 57,000 births. The main reason for this was that the migrant labour to the cities made a desperate attempt to limit the size of their families because of cramped and squalid living conditions. The weakening of the family released widespread social problems. Loss of control and discipline among children meant an increase in juvenile delinquency, hooliganism, gang warfare and riotous behaviour, all of which placed pressure on the state and on judicial processes. Overall, as Timasheff argues: 'The disintegration of the family did not disturb the Communists, since this is precisely what they wanted to achieve, but they were disturbed by quite a few collateral effects of the disorganization.'[95]

This certainly applied to Stalin. He probably spared little thought for the anguish caused by the sexual exploitation of women, the trauma of broken families, or the break-up of personal relationships. But there is no question that he was so concerned about the impact on economic growth and social stability that he felt impelled to introduce major changes from 1936 onwards. His priorities were to enlarge and stabilize the workforce and restore a form of social control through which state discipline would operate. He therefore reversed his policy on the family and reverted to a more traditional emphasis on its importance. His views were reflected in a *Pravda* editorial (28 May 1936) on official discussion about the abolition of legal abortion. This indicates how far attitudes had been reversed since the Bolshevik era. 'When we speak of strengthening the Soviet family, we are speaking precisely of the struggle against the survivals of a bourgeois attitude toward marriage, women and children. So-called "free love" and all disorderly sex life are bourgeois through and through.'[96] The regime now attached more importance to the marriage process in registry offices and to the issue of official marriage certificates; wedding rings were actually introduced in state shops from 1936. Divorce was made more difficult from 1936 through greater restrictions, tighter conditions and higher fees. In the same year abortion was abolished in all cases except where there was a risk of the transmission of hereditary diseases or a threat to the health of the mother. Within the revived family there was now a greater emphasis on the relationship between mother and child, which earlier policies had both questioned and weakened. Stalin even introduced a new cult of motherhood, with posters depicting mothers with babies in their arms, and new state honours were accorded to women with a large number of births. Nowhere is the contradiction of Stalinism greater than in its reluctant but determined acceptance of family.

How beneficial to women were Stalin's changes? In theory women experienced many new advantages. By Article 122 of the 1936 Constitution, they were 'accorded equal rights with men in all spheres of economic, state, social and political life'. These gave women 'equally with men the right to work, payment for work, rest, social insurance and education' and also 'state protection of the interests of mother and child, pregnancy, leave with pay', and provision of 'a wide network of maternity homes, nurseries and kindergartens'.[97] In practice the impact was mixed. It is true that women experienced greater security as a result of tightening the obligations of men within the marriage settlement. There was also a larger proportion of women in higher education and the professions than in Germany and Italy. On the other hand, they were still not strongly represented politically. Although they accounted for 15 per cent of the membership of the lower levels of the party, there were none at the higher levels, in contrast with the situation in the Lenin era. Above all, there is little evidence that the 'double burden' had been eased. More generous maternity provision would normally reduce the number of women in the workforce; the latter, however, actually increased in Leningrad from 44.3 per cent of the total in 1935 to 49.6 per cent in 1937.[98] The revived importance of marriage placed more emphasis on women's role as homemakers and child-bearers – without, however, reducing the consequent problems in continuing to be a major part of the labour market. Stalin's revision of the egalitarian laws also had an adverse impact on women, who were particularly affected by the increasing differentials in pay. There were also inadequate attempts to control the misogynistic tendencies that had always existed in the workforce.

Extensive research has now been done on women's attitudes throughout the Stalin era. One of the more surprising revelations is the strength of these attitudes, especially in the opposition shown to the enforcement of collectivization in the rural areas which ran parallel to the first Five-Year Plan. There were numerous 'women's riots' (*Bab'i bunty*) which, according to Viola, 'proved the most effective form of opposition to the Soviet state'.[99] Certainly there was no equivalent action by women in Fascist Italy or Nazi Germany. Less spectacular, but no less deeply felt was the continuing resentment against the 'double burden', especially in towns. This remained until the end of the Soviet Union – and beyond. Even as late as the 1970s and 1980s women continued to experience its impact: the average time per week taken in shopping and queuing for limited food supplies was nineteen hours. Divorce remained high and many women in the Slavic regions of the Soviet Union had as many as nineteen abortions in their lifetime. Improvements had certainly occurred after 1936 and again after 1956. But these were relative only to the harshness of life in the 1920s and early 1930s.

Religion

Stalin's policies towards religion followed a more complex pattern of change and counter-change. They involved a more frequent swing of the pendulum than in other areas, probably through his periodic attempts to compensate for earlier policies that had not worked properly. What had started as adjustments became major changes, which were then considered to have got out of control. Stalin's ambivalence towards religion did not help here. He had permanently lost any attraction to it as a result of his early experiences at an Orthodox seminary; instead he had become an ardent Marxist and claimed to be second only to Lenin in adapting Marxist theory to Russian conditions. He preferred, therefore, to undermine religion whenever possible – and certainly when he felt that the need arose. But he was enough of an opportunist to see the advantages of religious support when he adjusted to more traditional policies in other fields. At first he followed his preferences. He attacked religion as a threat to the advancement of communism and he accelerated the campaign for atheism which had started under Lenin.

From 1928, for example, church steeples were pulled down by volunteers in the League of the Godless. Decrees the following year prohibited religious worship for all but registered congregations and placed a blanket ban on attempts at conversion to religious belief; particularly affected by these restrictions were evangelical groups like the Baptists. The Orthodox Church suffered a reduction in the number of clergy, many of whom were arrested and deported to labour camps. This period lasted until 1934, when official policy relaxed its pressure on religion as part of a more general easing that also affected the economy and society. The new approach was formalized by Article 124 of the 1936 Constitution, which guaranteed 'freedom of conscience' and 'freedom of religious worship'. This was, however, balanced by an undertaking that the right to 'anti-religious propaganda shall be recognised for all citizens'.[100] The effectiveness of such activity declined and, by 1938, membership of the League of the Godless had fallen threefold from the 1932 figure.[101] By contrast, church attendance increased, especially during key festivals such as Easter and Christmas, while the 1937 census (eventually cancelled by the government) suggested that over 50 per cent of the population admitted to having religious beliefs.

By 1937–8 the pendulum swung back against religion, which became caught up in the era of the purges. The main reason for this was a perception that most denominations had over-asserted themselves during the preceding period of respite. Priests were accused of extending their freedom to practise religion into promoting anti-atheist activity and involving themselves in social and political issues. All religious denominations were affected by the purges: a disproportionate number of victims were clergy and religious believers. The mass closure of churches resembled that of earlier times: for example, Leningrad had only five in 1938, compared with thirty-three in 1937.[102] Then, from 1939, the most extreme measures were removed, allowing the pendulum to swing back towards the centre. The outbreak of war in 1941 made a further difference as, according to Davies, the regime was 'forced to recognise the strength of popular belief' and 'turned to the Church in its hour of need'.[103] During the struggle with Germany, the Orthodox Patriarchate, abolished during the radical period, was re-established to provide a focus for Russian patriotism. Ward argues that the newly formulated policy led unofficially to a 'Church-State concordat'.[104] Stalin preferred the Orthodox Church to the Catholics and Protestants, largely because he was more confident that the Orthodox hierarchy would be able to restrain its laity from activities that might threaten the wartime agreement. On the other hand, where Stalin felt that there would be little benefit to the regime, concessions were much less likely. There was no let-up for the Jews who, in the circumstances, were hardly likely to support the German invaders, nor for the Muslims, the majority of whom were outside the German invasion path.

The impact of Stalin's policies towards religion proved less damaging in the longer term than at the time. Stalin's successors, especially Khrushchev and Brezhnev, were no more successful in undermining the Christian churches, which experienced a major resurgence after the collapse of the Soviet Union in 1991. The experience of Jews was more uncertain. For the remainder of Stalin's regime there was a significant increase in official and popular anti-Semitism. This was especially distressing since it came on top of the policy of systematic extermination carried out by the Einsatzgruppen during the German invasion. The war had a mixed legacy. On the one hand, Russia now contained (after the United

States) the largest concentration of Jews in the world. On the other, the post-Stalinist era saw increased pressure for emigration from the Soviet Union, especially to Israel. Islam was also under strong suspicion, partly for its cohesive ideology and partly for the social bond it provided in Asiatic republics like Kazakhstan and Uzbekistan. Stalin reduced the 26,000 mosques in the Soviet Union in 1921 to 1,312 by 1942 and ensured that Islamic courts were abolished. But Islam was not permanently weakened. Its abiding social influence among the population, in the form of large families and hostility to birth control or abortion, along with the less extensive war damage in central Asia, meant that the population increased more rapidly in the Muslim regions than in the Slavic areas. This had enormous implications for the future: Islam outlived not only Stalinism but the Soviet Union itself.

Education and culture

Education underwent a similar transformation to the social changes outlined above. Under Lenin during the 1920s educational theory had favoured relaxed discipline and group activity in schools based heavily on Marxist ideas. At first Stalin intensified the Leninist approach. In history, for example, the books of Pokrovskii emphasized the negative heritage of the Tsarist and capitalist past. This seemed to harmonize with Stalin's plans to modernize industry and accelerate socialism. By 1934, however, Stalin had completely changed his approach. He reintroduced formal learning, examinations and grades, and the full authority of the teacher. Another example of revived conservatism was the restoration of school uniforms, including compulsory pigtails for girls. History now placed a positive slant on the Tsarist past and created heroic figures out of Ivan the Terrible and Peter the Great. Stalin also reversed the tendency of the 1920s to base access to higher education on social criteria. Thus, instead of favouring applicants from the proletariat, Stalin insisted that the demands of technology would be best served by selecting candidates with the highest academic qualifications. As in other areas, his educational changes were an attempt to wrest the initiative back from the radical dynamic which had spiralled out of control by the end of the 1920s.

Much has now been written about the impact of Stalin's initial radicalism and subsequent conservatism in education. Both phases had advantages and disadvantages. During the 'radical' period, from 1927 to 1931, there were huge increases in institutions and enrolments. The priority of Narkompros (People's Commissariat for Enlightenment) was to create education for the masses. Numerically this seemed to work. Schools increased from 118,558 in 1927–8 to 166,275 by 1933, and pupils from 7.9 to 9.7 million. During the same period 1,466 specialist institutes came into existence in higher education, student numbers increasing from 168,500 to 458,300. Soon, however, the benefits of an expanding base gave way to the problems of declining quality: in 1931, Narkompros was criticized by the party for falling short on educational standards, in particular for general knowledge. The end of the radical phase brought a revival of standards, partly through the restoration of formal content such as the theoretical element of the sciences, and partly through the reintroduction of entrance requirements based on academic success. This meant a change in the social intake of students. Access to higher education once again favoured the more articulate sectors of society and the automatic preference previously given to the proletariat was ended. It seems, therefore, that overall numbers benefited from the radical phase, while improved standards resulted from the return to traditional policies.

The official line intruded also into culture. At first, Stalin was even more radical than the Bolsheviks. Art and literature were used to publicize the Five-Year Plans and collectivization. 'Artistic brigades' were set up, under RAPP or the Russian Association of Proletarian Writers. As in other fields, however, complications soon emerged. Works of real merit declined, while local application of artistic criteria allowed mediocrity to flourish in an atmosphere of repressive confusion. Clearly something had to be done to instil order and raise standards. In 1932, therefore, RAPP was replaced by the Union of Writers, which redefined cultural criteria in accordance with 'Socialist Realism'. This laid down direct guidelines so that writers would mobilize the masses and aim consciously to be engineers of the human soul. All literary works must also provide 'a truthful, historically concrete depiction of reality in its revolutionary development'.[105] In 1958, the writer Sholokhov provided a more straightforward description of Socialist Realism as 'that which is written for the Soviet government in simple, comprehensible, artistic language'.[106] Stalin was also susceptible to Russian tradition, showing a liking for Russian stories and folk tunes. His own view of Socialist Realism, therefore, was that it was 'National in form, Socialist in content',[107] in effect a synthesis of socialist change and highlights from the past.

Again, the results were mixed. On the one hand, he reduced all art forms to state subservience, which had obvious implications for quality. Painting was used directly for political propaganda, which meant that most works were stilted or conveyed blatant untruths about collectivization. The most common themes were contented peasants, industrious workers with Stakhanovite aspirations, and the paternalist qualities of Stalin himself. Architecture was even more directly controlled by the state, since plans and designs could rarely be achieved without state funding. Priority was given to prestige projects, which formed an integral part of the regime's obsession with gigantomania. On the other hand, the Soviet Union experienced something akin to a renaissance in music and film. Composers were able to work more successfully under Stalin's constraints than under Hitler's. The output of Prokofiev, Khachaturian, Kabalevsky and, above all, Shostakovich was impressive by any standard, and the Soviet Union had a greater musical output than any other dictatorship of the twentieth century. Film, too, was used more subtly in Russia than in Germany, and Sergei Eisenstein directed *October*, *Battleship Potemkin* and *Ivan the Terrible*, all abiding masterpieces.

Overall, Stalin moved from an early acceleration of Bolshevik radicalism to a revival of past traditions. This has usually been put down to a deliberate policy on his part. It might, however, be more appropriate to see it as a response to initial failure. As the regime appeared increasingly ramshackle he had to abandon radicalism and attempt to restore authoritarianism through more reliable traditions. The later policies were generally more beneficial – or less harmful – than his earlier ones. The fracturing of society by collectivization and enforced industrialization was predominantly negative, while the revival of traditional values provided greater stability for social and cultural developments. Without exception, however, the changes were introduced to bolster an insecure dictatorship. As a result, the main casualty of all Stalin's policies, whether radical or traditional, was the individual.

Support, opposition and resistance

We have seen from the previous sections in this chapter that the impact of Stalin's policies on the Soviet population was massive. As a direct result of his policies people throughout the Soviet Union experienced disruption and relocation, famine and starvation, class war against the kulaks, repression of religious groups, and incarceration within the gulag system. Earlier historical views emphasized that the people were crushed into total subjection, or at least into conformity, by a monstrous totalitarian system. This is, of course, hard to discount, especially when the all-pervasive presence of the NKVD and the high-profile and exemplary purges and show trials are taken into account. But, as in the case of Nazi Germany, recent historians have drawn attention to the various shadings of public opinion, from open support, through outward conformity and passive acceptance, to cautious opposition and direct resistance. The type of response therefore depended on the actual relationship between the individual or group and the regime.

Open and voluntary support for the regime came from those who benefited from it or from those who were convinced by its ideology or propaganda. Many of the younger members of society were effectively indoctrinated within Komsomol and questioned or rejected many of the more traditional values. A new elite of workers grew out of the Stalinist economic system and, like the Stakhanovites, were held up and rewarded by it, benefiting particularly from the end of wage equalization. The command economy created a vastly expanded bureaucracy, with many managerial positions dependent on Stalin's economic policies. Even more obviously, the security services, especially the NKVD, depended on unquestioning loyalty to the regime. As the Party extended its roots into all the Republics of the USSR, those who became involved in it developed as yet another elite, with reason to prefer this new Sovietization to the old national identity. Overarching all of these commitments to particular roles was the total loyalty accorded to Stalin – part of the 'personality cult' condemned in 1956 by Khrushchev. To an extent this was a substitute for the more abstruse ideological details with which much of the population found it so difficult to identify. Partly because of the cult, Stalin escaped much of the opprobrium heaped on his officials, remaining in the public view detached from the policies he set in motion.

Open support needs to be distinguished from outward conformity and passive acceptance. The latter tended to come from those who had not become part of a new elite, but from those who nevertheless depended upon the state for their basic livelihood. Fitzpatrick has argued that: 'The state was the monopoly distributor of goods and services, which meant that allocation – the power to decide who got what – was one of its most important functions.'[108] This meant that the state held individuals under its control more than any other association, whether the family or local community. The state could therefore go some way to enforcing compliance. Or to put it the other way round, the very survival of individuals and groups often depended on co-operation with the state. Hence, according to Fitzpatrick: '*Homo Sovieticus* was a ring-puller, a time-server, a freeloader, a mouther of slogans, and much more. But above all, he was a survivor.'[109] Never was this more applicable than during the late 1930s, when survival could mean collaboration with the NKVD and playing an integral part in the 'endemic' terror.

At times there would be grumbling, hostility and disobedience. Most of this was cautious and restrained, but NKVD soundings showed that the unpopularity of the regime existed in most towns, although it was more embedded in the villages.[110] This was caused by a variety of factors. The most widespread was resentment of the low standard of living which had not been improved by the low priority given in Stalin's policies to consumer goods; this was exacerbated by envy of those who were clearly better off because of their elite status or political placements. The result was the most common of all manifestations of civil disobedience: the spread of the black market was in defiance of all the state regulations which aimed to kill off any elements of capitalism, especially at local level.

With the end of the Cold War and the collapse of the Soviet Union, the opening of official archives has produced considerable evidence of more fundamental opposition, even resistance. According to Viola,

> The wider story of resistance reveals an entire world within the Stalinist dictatorship, a semi-autonomous world of many layers, cultures, and languages of existence, experience, and survival that coexisted with, evolved within, interacted with, and at times bypassed the larger and seemingly omnipresent reality of Stalinism.[111]

A variety of examples of resistance has been identified. During the First Five-Year Plan there were widespread strikes by industrial workers; in 1932 there were also uprisings against food shortages and cuts in rations in the Lower Volga region, the Ivanovo Industrial region, Ukraine, Belorussia, and even the Urals and western Siberia. Particularly apparent was peasant resistance to enforced collectivization amidst the general chaos of enforcement by local officials, especially in provinces like Riazan. Women were often at the forefront of such incidents. McDonald explains that

> Men were much more likely to be arrested for protest than women and tended to stay on the sidelines unless the women were threatened. Only then could peasant men step in on the grounds that they were defending their womenfolk.[112]

As well as gender, sexuality became a focus for small-group resistance: in open defiance of criminal laws, there was an increase in organizations of and partnerships between homosexual men. Finally, the closest any groups came to outright rebellion against the Soviet state were representatives of the various nationalities who questioned the whole basis of their inclusion into the USSR. To these we now turn.

The nationalities under Stalin

Stalin had considerable knowledge of the non-Russian nationalities – more, in fact, than Lenin. Born in Georgia, he had extensive experience of transcaucasian politics and problems. In 1913 he wrote *Marxism and the National Question*; his appointment by Lenin as Commissar for Nationalities (1917) was the first of his major posts, to which he subsequently added liaison official between the Orgburo and the Politburo (1919) and Secretary General of the Communist Party (1922). Increasingly he abandoned his Georgian roots and Russified himself, in much the same way that Hitler, the Austrian, became Germanized and Napoleon, the Corsican, regarded himself as French. The significance of this background was threefold. He understood the aspirations of the non-Russian nationalities and knew the concessions they wanted; he was prepared to grant some of these. At the same time, he had developed sufficient control over the Party to neutralize these concessions in practice. And, because of his own conversion, he was willing to expand Russian influence beyond any limits achieved by the Tsars.

There were certainly some positive indicators for the nationalities during the 1930s. The 1936 Constitution was intended as a showcase for the Soviet Union and was widely praised in the West. For one thing, the concept of federalism was considerably widened. The eleven republics, reconstituted from the four of 1924, were the RSFSR, Ukraine, Belorussia, Armenia, Azerbaijan, Georgia, Uzbekistan, Tajikistan, Kazakhstan, Turkmenia and Kirghizia. This seemed broadly in line with the extension of political rights to all sectors of the population through a new and equal suffrage from the age of twenty. There was also an apparent attempt to balance social and ethnic representation in the form of a bicameral Supreme Soviet, the Soviet of the Union being elected through equal constituencies, the Soviet of the Nationalities representing the nationally-based republics. This was not dissimilar to the structure of the United States Congress, with its House of Representatives based on constituencies and the Senate representing the States themselves. Article 13 of the 1936 Constitution affirmed that 'the Union of Soviet Socialist Republics is a federal state, formed on the basis of the voluntary union' of 'Soviet Socialist Republics', which were 'equal in rights'. There was even a statutory provision for ending this union; by Article 17, 'the right freely to secede from the USSR is reserved to each constituent republic'.[113] Could it be that the Stalinist regime had provided a new and more equitable balance between the demands and needs of the social and ethnic sectors of the Soviet Union?

In theory, perhaps. But there developed an ever-increasing gap between theory and practice. Stalin continued – and intensified – the trend established by Lenin: subjecting the Republics to the Communist Party and thereby strengthening the ties imposed by democratic centralism. Under Stalin the process was taken a step further with the imposition of personal control of the party – so that even the concept of 'democratic' centralism became questionable. At the same time, Russians controlled the membership of the CPSU and virtually monopolized the key organs. Aspiring apparatchiks of non-Russian origins, such as Khrushchev from the Ukraine, had to accept the logic of the channels of power radiating outwards from Moscow. They therefore hastened to Russify themselves as an essential step towards controlling the Party and – through careful appointments – the nationalities. Stalin also aimed deliberately at cultural assimilation. Although he allowed cultural diversity in theory, this was in practice subjected to creeping Russification. Since the Five-Year Plans involved centralization, the language used throughout was Russian; this applied also to the army and the central organs of the Party. Russification was also apparent in 'Socialist Realism' (see p. 80). Even the Soviet Union's historic focus was essentially Russian as Stalin revived the reputations of Alexander Nevsky, Ivan the Terrible and Peter the Great.

But attempts to control the nationalities went beyond this – into the realm of terror. These were applied to all sectors – including the kulaks among the peasantry, the industrial managers and workforce, the membership of the CPSU, and the armed forces. Peasants in the Ukraine, for example, were perceived as a double threat – for their resistance to collectivization after 1929 and for their potential separatism. The Kazakhs were seen in very much the same way. Indeed, under Stalin, mass repression was often conducted *primarily* through ethnic channels. This applied particularly to the quotas of victims for each republic and each area. The appropriate branches of the NKVD intensified the pressure on the unfortunate inhabitants in an attempt to exceed the quota. In this way the channels frequently flooded and systematic targeting turned into mass slaughter. In other cases, economic and social policies became doubly repressive in certain areas. Hence the Ukraine was targeted for the most intensive action against kulaks and other 'saboteurs' during the collectivization campaign between 1929 and 1931, with the mass requisitioning of grain resulting in famine and the death of at least 10 million Ukrainian peasants through starvation.

A particular characteristic of the Stalin era was the deportation of entire ethnic groups and their relocation in other parts of the Soviet Union. Mawdsley provides three reasons for this. One was the development of a system initially related to the deportation of kulaks and peasants who resisted the implementation of collectivization; the network of labour camps and the system of 'special settlers' could readily be adapted to ethnic groups. Another reason was the pressure of external events, especially in the Far East. When Japan invaded northern China in 1937, the Soviet authorities authorized the resettlement of the Korean minorities to the central Asian Soviet Republics of Kazakhstan and Uzbekistan. Third, the Soviet annexation between 1939 and 1940 of eastern Poland, the Baltic States, Bessarabia and parts of Finland provided new subject peoples who were subsequently thinned out by deportations to Siberia and central Asia. Among those resettled were 390,000 Poles and 180,000 Romanians, Ukrainians, Latvians, Estonians and Lithuanians.[114] This provided the setting for the more extensive and extreme persecution of the national minorities, which occurred after the German invasion of the Soviet Union in 1941.

SOVIET FOREIGN POLICY, 1918–41

The foreign policy of Lenin and Stalin was highly complex, and involved numerous zigzags. At its best, it was skilful, confident and effective; at its worst, it was blundering, uncertain and ruinous. Throughout the period there was an internal conflict between ideological motives on the one hand and, on the other, a pragmatism which bordered on cynicism.

1918–24

The new Bolshevik leaders displayed an intense ideological hostility to the Western powers, believing in the inevitability of their eventual collapse and also in the necessity of this as a precondition for the survival of communism. Trotsky argued that this collapse must be accelerated by Russia: 'Either the Russian Revolution will create a revolutionary movement in Europe, or the European powers will destroy the Russian Revolution.'[115] At the same time, Lenin had to take into account the immediate situation in which he found himself and make policy adjustments as he considered necessary. This meant that he was forced to make agreements with Western powers in a style of diplomacy which was essentially pragmatic. Although he also encouraged foreign revolutionary activity, as ideology seemed to demand, this became a lesser priority.

There were two reasons for this apparent turnabout. The first was the influence of external developments. From the time of the October Revolution until the death of Lenin the Bolsheviks had to adapt to the pressure exerted on Russia by Western powers. This was far more important than that exerted by the Bolsheviks on the West. The second factor was even more important. Throughout the period the Bolsheviks remained vulnerable to internal pressure from the Russian population. This did much to condition their response to the West. Faced with these two interrelated influences, Lenin had to adapt rather than devise: his foreign policy had to be more reactive than projective.

This became apparent almost as soon as the Bolsheviks had seized power. Ideology suggested using the First World War to spread revolution among the working classes of the capitalist powers. Common sense, however, dictated withdrawal from the war as quickly as possible. Russia's continued involvement had already brought down the Tsarist regime and the Provisional Governmnent; why should the Bolsheviks now succeed where these others had failed? The revolutionary impetus would almost certainly continue. Just as the Provisional Government had fallen to the Bolsheviks, so the Bolsheviks were, in turn, vulnerable to the Socialist Revolutionaries who were establishing separatist governments to the east of the areas under Lenin's control. To make matters worse, it was becoming apparent that the bulk of the population was swinging its support behind the Socialist Revolutionaries early in 1918. The Red revolution was therefore in danger of being overtaken by a Green revolution. Marxists – Lenin and Trotsky included – were only too aware of the importance of war as a catalyst for such a change. After all, 'war is the locomotive of history' and, to use a different metaphor, acts as the 'midwife for every old society pregnant with a new one'. While being optimistic that history was on their side, the Bolsheviks were more pessimistic about the indiscriminate impact of war.

As soon as he had come to power, therefore, Lenin issued a decree which called upon 'all warring peoples and their governments to begin negotiations immediately for a just and democratic peace, a peace without annexation and indemnities'. Unfortunately, Russia's negotiations with Germany at Brest-Litovsk at the end of 1917 hit a major snag. The Germans insisted that Russia surrender, as the price for peace, Finland, Lithuania, Poland and the Ukraine. The Russian delegation withdrew from the talks in February 1918 but was forced to return. This was partly because the Germans had renewed their military offensive and partly because the Socialist Revolutionaries were applying increasing pressure in the Urals and the Volga region. In March 1918, therefore, the Bolsheviks conceded, in the Treaty of Brest-Litovsk, to all the German demands. This enabled the Bolsheviks to deal more immediately with their internal opponents, the Greens, and with the growing threat of the Whites and their Western support.

It might be thought that the Civil War gave the Bolsheviks ample reason for permanent hostility to the West. After all, the latter had provided supplies to the Whites through Murmansk, Archangel, the Black Sea, the Caucasus and Vladivostok. Although this intervention failed, there was to be further anti-Bolshevik action, in the form of aid to Poland. In 1920, a Polish invasion conquered much of the Ukraine. The Red Army launched a counter-attack, coming within striking distance of Warsaw, but a second Polish offensive was made possible by extensive reforms carried out by Marshal Piłsudski and French help provided through General Weygand. By the Treaty of Riga (1921) Russia suffered its second territorial amputation in three years. Yet the period after 1921 saw attempts by Lenin's regime to come to terms with the West. There were two main reasons for this.

The first was pressure from within. Although the Whites had been defeated in the Civil War and the Socialist Revolutionaries reduced to a splintered opposition, the Bolsheviks were faced from 1920 with a wave of resentment from the peasantry. There were widespread revolts and peasant wars, largely in reaction to the unpopular policy of War Communism. The introduction of the New Economic Policy in 1921 was a tactical retreat which also required a different attitude to the Western powers. The priority was now the end of Soviet isolation and the acceptance of coexistence with capitalism. This would enable Soviet Russia to concentrate on industrial growth in an attempt to create a balanced economy. It might even be necessary to attract Western investment. According to Kamenev in 1921, 'We can, of course, restore our economy by the heroic effort of the working masses. But we cannot develop it fast enough to prevent the capitalist countries from overtaking us, unless we call in foreign capital.'[116] There was, however, more to it than that. By 1921 the Bolsheviks had come to the conclusion that they could not hope to control the population of Russia *and* engage in an offensive against capitalism.

The second reason for the search for coexistence was the failure of the Bolshevik hope that a revolutionary flame would spread across Europe, consuming Russia's enemies. The year 1919 had brought high expectations but eventual disappointment. The left-wing socialist regimes of Bavaria and Hungary were overthrown, while the communist uprising in Berlin was put down, in January 1919, with considerable bloodshed. Clearly world revolution was further off than had originally been hoped. There was a powerful irony here. Trotsky and Lenin had believed that Bolshevik organization would be sufficient to activate revolutions against the regimes in the leading capitalist states. In other words, a 'top-down' communist initiative would promote a 'bottom-up' campaign against capitalism. In fact, the reverse occurred. The 'bottom-up' threat came from within Russia, forcing the Bolshevik leadership to take a 'top-down' decision to live with capitalism rather than to try to destroy it.

Between 1921 and 1924 the Bolsheviks therefore reversed the connection between diplomacy and revolution. Marxist theory had previously emphasized revolution as the main strand of foreign policy, with diplomacy a method of adjustment. In the light of experience between 1918 and 1921, however, Lenin focused on diplomacy in practice, although he continued to use revolution as a subordinate theme.

Diplomacy produced some real gains for the Soviet government: in 1921 and 1924, for example, trade agreements were drawn up with Britain. But the real target for Soviet activity was Germany, isolated and resentful after the harsh terms of the Versailles Settlement. As Lenin had stated in his 1920 speech, 'Germany is one of the strongest advanced capitalist countries, it cannot put up with the Versailles Treaty . . . Here is a situation we must utilize.'[117] He did. The Soviet Foreign Minister, Chicherin, conducted secret negotiations with Rathenau, his German counterpart. These reached their climax in Genoa in 1922. Ostensibly, Russia and Germany were themselves objects of discussion among the other powers, but the tables were turned when the Russo-German Treaty of Rapallo was announced. Germany became the first state to extend full diplomatic recognition to Bolshevik Russia; both countries agreed to expand trade, and Germany would provide credits and investment for Russian industry. Rapallo is usually seen as a diplomatic victory and a vindication of Lenin's approach. It succeeded in splitting the Western powers and destroyed any immediate chance of a united Western response to communism.

Meanwhile, Lenin continued to use revolutionary activity and propaganda as a subsidiary device in his foreign policy. In March 1919 he established Comintern (Communist International) to co-ordinate communist movements and to bring them under the overall direction of Moscow. In 1920 Comintern based its whole structure on that of the Soviet Communist Party and declared itself to be 'a single Communist Party having branches in different countries'.[118] Its purpose was to promote radical activity and to weaken anti-Soviet policies pursued by Western governments. At the same time Lenin established relations with 'countries of the East' (a term which has now been replaced by 'less developed countries') to encourage them to throw off Western influence. It did not matter that most of these countries were themselves anti-communist. The important thing was they were also anti-imperialist; wars of liberation in the colonies could be just as damaging for the Western powers as internal revolution.

The overall impression was that ideology was subordinated to practicality. At the same time, Lenin clearly did not relish what he was doing. He could not, of course, admit that he was being forced in this direction by pressures from within Russia since this would not fit well with Bolshevik claims to be leading the revolution rather than merely reacting to it. Hence, he described his diplomacy with the West as a temporary expedient, a mere diversion until the preferred policy of worldwide revolution could be resumed. The main advantage, as he saw it, was that diplomacy would enable Russia to work on the differences between the various capitalist states. In a speech to Moscow party activists in December 1920, he argued:

> So long as we have not won the whole world, so long as we remain economically and militarily weaker than what is left of the capitalist world, we must stick to the rule: be able to exploit the contradictions and oppositions between the imperialists.[119]

He saw three particularly important areas of discord: in the Pacific between the United States and Japan; the differences between the United States and Europe; and, above all, the gap between the wartime Allies and defeated Germany. One – or more – of these was bound to provide communism with opportunities in the future.

1924–39

Stalin's foreign policy was so complex that it is the subject of considerable controversy. This section will, therefore, provide a brief outline of the main developments and then attempt to interpret their meaning.

At first the Soviet government succeeded in extending its respectability. It gained diplomatic recognition, in 1924, from Britain, France, Italy and Japan. In 1926 a second agreement was drawn up between Russia and Germany; the Berlin Treaty was, in effect, a neutrality pact which also renewed the various agreements made at Rapallo. There were, however, complications in Soviet relations with the West. In 1927, for example, the British government broke off diplomatic relations after ordering the Soviet embassy in London to be raided. By the end of the 1920s Stalin was deliberately playing down friendship with the West. He argued that the Soviet Union no longer needed any form of Western economic assistance and that, in any case, capitalism would be destroyed by an economic crisis. He decided to keep open the contact with Germany by renewing, in 1931, the Treaty of Berlin, but he made no attempt to assist the Weimar Republic to prevent the rise of Nazism between 1931 and 1933 and even restrained the German Communist Party (KPD) under Thälmann from collaborating with the German Social Democrats (SPD). Indeed, Stalin saw the latter as merely another manifestation of that same crisis of capitalism which had increased Hitler's support; hence, social democracy was the 'moderate wing of Fascism'.[120] Stalin's insistence that the SPD were unworthy of power because they were social fascists certainly played a part in destroying any meaningful opposition to the Nazis, who came to power in January 1933.

Between 1933 and 1934 Stalin attempted to maintain close relations between Russia and Germany. In 1935, however, he appeared to change course and to draw up agreements to contain Germany. Two examples are the Soviet–French and Soviet–Czechoslovak Treaties of Mutual Assistance. Meanwhile, Stalin had also secured Russia's entry into the League of Nations and from 1935 he sponsored the growth of popular fronts throughout Europe in which communists, socialists and liberals were encouraged to resist fascism. By 1938, however, Stalin was clearly envisaging further alterations in Soviet foreign policy, while 1939 saw separate negotiations between Russia and, on the one hand, Britain and France and, on the other, Nazi Germany. In August 1939 Stalin eventually settled for Germany and the foreign ministers of the two powers, Molotov and von Ribbentrop, formally signed the Nazi–Soviet Non-Aggression Pact.

This somewhat tortuous route to Soviet security has often puzzled Western observers. It is, however, possible to examine Stalin's motives on two levels. First, what was the underlying aim of his relations with other powers throughout the period as a whole? Second, and arising from this, why did he pursue particular policies at various stages between 1924 and 1939?

The underlying motive seems to have been to provide security from abroad for the construction of communism at home. This would eventually enable the Soviet Union to turn its power outwards. In Stalin's own words, 'Our banner remains, as before, the banner of peace. But if war breaks out, we shall not be able to sit with folded hands – we shall have to make a move, but the move will come last.' Stalin assumed 'hostility from all imperialist powers and, therefore, the need to keep them divided'.[121] Short-term security therefore merged with prospects for long-term offensives. From this basic assumption, three priorities followed logically.

The first was the transformation of Russia into an industrial superpower: this would give the military base necessary for survival. In justifying his policy of Socialism in One Country and the introduction of the planning system, Stalin constantly harped on the theme of Soviet insecurity. In February 1931, for example, he said, 'We have lagged fifty to a hundred years behind the leading countries. We must cover this distance in ten years. Either we do that or they crush us.'[122] The second priority was to safeguard the Soviet Union, while this reconstruction was under way, by not precipitating attacks from the West. Stalin therefore opted for Socialism in One Country rather than Permanent Revolution, which might well upset the external situation to Russia's internal disadvantage. The third, and more distant, option was eventual military involvement to defeat the capitalist West: this would both ensure Soviet security and enable the recovery of territory lost by the treaties of Brest-Litovsk (1918) and Riga (1921).

In his approach to foreign policy, therefore, Stalin gave priority to rapid internal growth regulated by a planning mechanism, short- or medium-term external security, and long-term military intervention. This was not a blueprint but a series of fairly general objectives which linked the economy to industrial and military mobilization. It was, however, much more difficult to decide what specific line of foreign policy was most likely to achieve them. This is where historians have disagreed with each other. Broadly, they have followed two lines of argument.

The first is based on the so-called 'Rapallo' approach. Stalin tried to continue the special relationship established with Germany by the Treaty of Rapallo in 1922. This made sense for a number of reasons. Rapallo and its successor, the Treaty of Berlin (1926), secured for the Soviet Union investment and military co-operation from Germany. It put pressure on Poland, which had, after all, won the Russo-Polish War of 1920–1. It might even have neutralized the Anglo-French combination. This was an important consideration since Britain and France were always likely to be hostile to Russia. Sooner or later, Russia's special relationship with Germany would pay off, especially if the latter could be enticed into a conflict with the other capitalist powers. In this event, Soviet involvement could be used, in Stalin's words, to 'throw the decisive weight onto the scales, the weight that could be preponderant'.[123] The second view is quite different. Stalin adopted a multilateral approach based on improved relations with Britain and France, rather than a bilateral relationship with Germany. This 'collective security' strategy would have two main advantages. It would allow the Soviet Union a more pivotal role in European diplomacy while, at the same time, building relations with the two countries most likely to constrain Germany, always the main potential threat to Russia.

Are these two interpretations entirely antagonistic? By one analysis, the Nazi–Soviet Non-Aggression Pact of August 1939 was a logical and direct consequence of a long-term strategy. Stalin's main hope, it is argued, was that Germany and the West would tear each other apart and that Russia would be well placed to pick up the pieces. One of the main reasons for Stalin's willingness to see the Nazis in power in Germany was that they would be much more likely than a democratic regime to attack the West. Another reason was that the alternative – a collaboration between the SPD and KPD – would be highly embarrassing to Stalin. The SPD were pro-Western and were therefore likely to reduce the chance of a split between capitalist powers. Hitler's rise, it would seem, suited Stalin perfectly. Of course, Hitler's policies from 1934 onwards were more forceful than Stalin had anticipated and it was therefore necessary to take steps to contain Germany and to remind Hitler that Germany had no option but to consider an eventual deal with Russia. But the collaboration between the Soviet Union and the Western powers was never more than a temporary expedient, designed to last until Stalin was able to return to his preferred policy. The opportunity came in August 1939 and the Nazi–Soviet Pact represented, in Tucker's words, 'the fruition of

Stalin's whole complex conception of the means of Soviet survival in a hostile world and emergence into a commanding international position'.[124] A new war was now inevitable, a war which Stalin could help start. Then, from a position of neutrality, he could watch the combatants exhaust themselves. He could then involve Russia, claim territory and sponsor revolutionary movements to create a ring of socialist states.[125]

All this has a certain logic. But it is stronger in its analysis of the general purpose of Soviet rearmament than it is in explaining the details of Soviet diplomacy. For one thing, it attributes to Stalin the sort of long-term diplomatic objectives which amount almost to a blueprint. The very considerable changes in Stalin's foreign policy are seen as mere tactical deviations in pursuit of a long-term strategy. But might they not actually have been a change of long-term strategy as a result of short-term indecision, uncertainty and awareness of previous errors? Within two years of Hitler's rise to power, Stalin realized that Nazism was far more resilient than he had expected. The only answer was a total change of strategy, to end the connection established with Germany in the 1920s and to seek accommodation with the West and Czechoslovakia. Stalin also ordered communists everywhere to collaborate with socialists, in direct contrast to his previous policy towards the German communists and socialists. The eventual switch back to Germany can be explained by the events of 1938. The Anschluss and the crisis over Czechoslovakia showed the West in the worst possible light. Stalin was forced to the conclusion that the Western powers were unreliable allies. It appeared that they would now allow Germany to rearm and expand without hindrance. In 1939 Stalin had two options open to him. He could maintain the Soviet friendship with France and extend it to Britain – but with more definite and specific military commitments. Or he could seek agreement with Germany and draw up a territorial settlement which would eliminate any possible cause of conflict. During the first half of 1939 Stalin seemed willing to incline towards either alternative but was eventually infuriated by the unwillingness of Neville Chamberlain, the British Prime Minister, to meet his terms. In August 1939, therefore, he informed the Politburo of his decision to do a deal with Hitler. In this perspective, the Nazi–Soviet Non-Aggression Pact can be seen as one of two last-minute alternatives, rather than as the logical outcome of all Stalin's previous policies.

This line reveals a very different Stalin. Had he been as consistent as Tucker maintains, he would have had to transcend not only Chamberlain and Daladier – admittedly not too difficult – but even Hitler, whose forward planning has now been called into question by a whole battery of historians. Stalin was no better as a diplomat than his contemporaries. Perhaps he was worse. Indeed, his whole commitment to foreign policy has been open to dispute. According to Haslam, he 'took only a sporadic interest' in this area; 'on the whole, Stalin abstained from direct intervention and contented himself with merely reviewing and approving . . . Even the process of review was occasionally delegated to others.'[126] We could go further down the road opened by Haslam. The zigzag in policy shows the impact of subordinates, upon whom Stalin relied to extract him from previous errors. For example, Soviet agreements with France in 1935, together with the promotion of broad anti-fascist fronts all over Europe, owed much to Foreign Minister Litvinov, who sought to improve Soviet relations with the West through involvement in the League of Nations. But Stalin had become convinced by 1938 that collective security had been destroyed by Anglo-French appeasement towards Germany. He now blamed Litvinov for having involved the Soviet Union too closely with France and replaced him with Molotov, who was more in favour of moving towards Germany. Hence Stalin was influenced by advisers – until things went wrong and he needed someone to blame. By this approach, Stalin was no more in control of Soviet foreign policy than he was of many aspects of his domestic policy.

The Nazi–Soviet Pact and the period 1939–41

The terms of the pact may be summarized as follows. Germany and Russia undertook 'to desist from any act of violence, any aggressive action, and any attack on each other, either individually or jointly with other Powers'. Should either become involved in any conflict, the other would remain strictly neutral. Neither would 'participate in any grouping of Powers whatsoever that is directly or indirectly aimed at the other party'.[127] Accompanying the Non-Aggression Pact was a secret additional protocol which provided for the demarcation of spheres of influence in eastern Europe, including Poland. The two countries proceeded almost immediately to implement this. Stalin invaded Poland on 17 September 1939, two weeks after the start of the German Blitzkrieg from the west. The Red Army encountered comparatively little resistance, for the Polish airforce had been obliterated by the Luftwaffe and the Polish army had already been defeated by the German Panzer divisions. A further agreement followed between the two powers, partitioning Poland for the fourth time in that unhappy country's history. The Soviet Union regained the Belorussian and Ukrainian areas lost to Poland in the war of 1920–1. From this point Russia and Germany shared a common frontier and maintained an uncomfortable coexistence – until Hitler broke this by launching an invasion in June 1941.

The Non-Aggression Pact and its accompanying protocol put into perspective every other initiative taken since Stalin's assumption of full control in 1929. Not surprisingly, two very different interpretations can be advanced about whether it was a success. These depend on whether the pact was the outcome of a long-term plan or whether it was put together at the last minute to compensate for all the frustrations and difficulties which had occurred during the 1930s.

The first case is that Stalin had always intended to come to terms with Germany. This had been a long and difficult process, involving several changes of direction on the way. But the Non-Aggression Pact achieved much of what he had wanted. Hitler would now feel more confident to attack Poland, thereby provoking France and Britain. Stalin would be able, through the secret protocol, to recover Soviet territory lost to Poland in 1921, secure in the knowledge that Britain and France still regarded the limit of the Polish state as the Curzon Line. Russia would also be able to restore the economic connections with Germany that had originated at Rapallo. Seen in this light, therefore, the Pact was the culmination of everything that Stalin had planned. There is, however, an alternative approach. Rather than the long-sought outcome of a long-term strategy, the Pact was merely one of the unforeseen events in a long sequence of dislocating changes in Soviet foreign policy; far from being in control of the situation, Stalin seized the Pact with Germany as a lifeline once he had become aware of the failure of previous attempts to co-operate with France and Britain. The protocol has also been misinterpreted. It contained no specific partition of Poland – but rather a more general agreement on spheres of influence in eastern Europe. In fact, Stalin invaded eastern Poland partly to limit the extent of the German advance; Roberts goes so far as to say that 'The partition of Poland in September 1939 was the direct result not of the Nazi-Soviet pact but of the unforeseen rapidity of the Polish military collapse'.[128] Again, Stalin was reacting rather than planning.

How necessary was the Nazi–Soviet pact for Russia? Soviet historians argued that 'subsequent events revealed that this step was the only correct one under the circumstances. By taking it, the USSR was able to continue peaceful construction for nearly two years and to strengthen its defences'.[129] It has also been suggested that between 1939 and 1941 Stalin was able to create a buffer zone in eastern Europe, without which the impact of the 1941 invasion would have been even worse than it proved to be. There are, however, alternative arguments based on the proposition that the pact was *not* necessary for Russia. Laqueur maintains that, without it, Hitler would not necessarily have invaded in 1939. He was, after all, too preoccupied with Poland, Britain and France to draw off divisions for yet another campaign. More telling is the observation that even if Hitler *had* moved immediately, the Soviet Union could well have been better off. By 1941 German military production had grown proportionately more rapidly than the Soviet Union's, enabling Hitler to launch in Operation Barbarossa the sort of offensive that would have been impossible in 1939.[130] Besides, Russia lost any strategic advantage in 1940 with the fall of France and the inability of Britain to launch a direct attack on the continent. This more than cancelled out any benefits gained by Stalin from territorial acquisitions after the Nazi–Soviet pact. The notion of an advantageous respite between 1939 and 1941 is therefore simplistic.

Even if it were not, there is plenty of evidence that Stalin misused those two years. At the end of 1939, for example, he involved the Soviet Union in a war with Finland – to push back the Finnish frontier from the outer suburbs of Leningrad and to secure facilities for a naval base near the mouth of the Gulf of Finland. The Winter War proved more difficult than Stalin had anticipated and the Red Army experienced a number of humiliating reverses while struggling towards its objectives. It also showed up Russia's military deficiencies and bankrupted her diplomatic reputation to the extent that she was expelled from the League of Nations. In all probability these failings convinced Hitler that he could afford to attack the Soviet Union sooner rather than later. Stalin's other activities aggravated Hitler further between 1940 and 1941: dissatisfied with Soviet gains from the 1939 pact, he put pressure on Hitler to make further concessions, especially in the Balkans. There were also diplomatic complications. In September 1940, Germany, Japan and Italy concluded a Three-Power Pact, which Stalin was invited to join. But when Molotov, the Soviet Foreign Minister, visited Berlin in November 1940, he refused to adhere to this pact until the remaining Soviet demands in eastern Europe had all been met. According to Grey, this meeting probably confirmed Hitler's decision to invade Russia in 1941.[131] Yet, even when it became obvious that Soviet relations with Germany were deteriorating rapidly, Stalin showed little awareness of any threat of invasion. He assumed – wrongly – that this would not happen without an ultimatum and that he would have time to make any necessary Soviet concessions. Worse still, he ignored all warnings that Hitler was about to launch an attack. Further details, and the reasons for his errors, are dealt with in the next section.

THE GREAT PATRIOTIC WAR, 1941–5

The invasion of 1941 and Soviet defeat, 1941–2

Operation Barbarossa was launched by Hitler on the Soviet Union on 22 June 1941. Other states soon followed in declaring war on Russia, especially Romania, Italy, Slovakia, Finland and Hungary. The invasion force totalled over 3 million men in 162 divisions, the greatest in the whole of human history to that date. The objective was no less than the total destruction of the USSR.

At first, German troops were remarkably successful. Their advance was divided into three prongs – against Leningrad in the north, Moscow in the centre and Kiev in the south. By the end of 1941 the whole of the Baltic coastline had been conquered, Leningrad was under siege and the Germans were within 25 miles of Moscow. Although the attempt on the capital had failed, most of the Ukraine was occupied, including Kiev, Kharkov and

Odessa, and the Crimea was under German control. When the offensive was resumed in the spring and summer of 1942 the main advances came in the south with the crossing of the Don and the capture of the oilfields of the Caucasus. By August 1942 the Germans had reached the Volga and Stalingrad. During the early phases of the invasion the Soviet armies folded like cardboard. German tanks, for example, advanced an unprecedented 250 kilometres within the first three days and, within the first three months, the Wehrmacht killed more than 1 million Russians and took 1 million prisoners. Hitler told his generals at the outset: 'We have only to kick in the door and the whole rotten structure will come crashing down.'[132] The results seemed to justify this confidence. The Germans had captured an area that extended 600 kilometres from west to east and 1,500 from north to south, while 56.7 per cent of all Soviet losses in the war were incurred in the initial shattering campaign of 1941–2. The Soviet workforce initially fell from 66 million to 35 million and the construction of industry accomplished within the Five-Year Plans was threatened with total destruction.

How can we explain this sensational collapse? The Soviet vindication was the numerical superiority of German armaments in 1941. This simply will not do. Soviet forces outnumbered the Germans and, at the time of the invasion, the Soviet Union possessed 24,000 tanks (compared with the Germans' 3,400). Western historians have tended to focus on the element of surprise and Stalin's defective strategy before and at the time of the invasion. This is nearer the mark but now needs to be considered within the context of recent research into the specific ways in which Russia prepared for war. The combination of newer and long-established views suggests two closely related reasons. First, during the 1930s, Soviet military infrastructure had been prepared for the type of war that Stalin had considered most likely in the future. Second, however, Stalin blundered into a war of the type – and in circumstances – that he had *not* envisaged.

The first of these has been given prominence in studies based on recent research. During the 1930s a key purpose of Stalin's Five-Year Plans was to prepare Russia for Total War by means of rapid industrialization. But his was not to be the traditional pattern of defensive warfare to repel invaders. Instead, Stalin had been converted to a new strategy by military theoreticians like Varfolomeev and Triandafilov. They argued that since defensive measures had not worked for Russia between 1914 and 1918, the Soviet Union should in future prepare to deliver a swift and crushing blow through 'the conduct of operations of annihilation'.[133] To do this the Soviet Union would need to deploy all its forces as soon as war broke out to deliver a sudden and decisive blow. Hence the priority of the Five-Year Plans was rearmament in preparation for an offensive war and, throughout the 1930s, tanks, artillery pieces, aircraft and small weapons were produced and stockpiled on a large scale.

It has, indeed, been argued that Stalin was preparing a pre-emptive strike on Germany, which Hitler foiled by launching his invasion first. This theory was originally advanced at the end of the 1980s by V. Rezun, a Soviet defector and former intelligence official. Writing under the pseudonym Suvorov, he presented, in 1990, an account of Stalin's intentions to attack Germany in June 1941.[134] The controversy about the claim has been intense. Radzinsky[135] inclines towards Suvorov's proposition on the grounds that Chief-of-Staff Zhukov drew up a document warning of an impending blow from Germany and recommending that Stalin 'anticipate the enemy and attack the German army at the moment when it is the process of deploying and before it has time to organize its front and the coordination of its various arms'.[136] Attack should be concentrated south-west, to separate Germany from its southern allies. This seemed to be in accord with Stalin's general views on war. In May 1941 a directive from Stalin stated that his regime should implement Lenin's intention to defeat capitalism 'just as soon as we are strong enough' and that 'any war waged by the Soviet Union is a just one'.[137] Among those who are more doubtful that Stalin was planning an invasion are Mawdsley,[138] Volkogonov[139] and McDermott.[140] Navigating carefully between contrary points of view, Uldricks argues that Stalin's speech hinting at aggression was deliberately leaked as a warning to Hitler not to invade. Furthermore, Stalin turned down Marshal Zhukov's proposals for a Soviet strike. The evidence is therefore circumstantial, and a direct assumption that Stalin was planning an imminent attack on Germany ignores the inconsistencies of Soviet foreign policy as a 'frequently shifting balance of elements involving both appeasement and resistance'.[141] Instead, it makes more sense to see a Soviet offensive as one of Stalin's longer-term options. As Litvin and Keep argue, 'Had Hitler *not* invaded, Stalin might have launched a strike later, but this is to enter the realm of hypothesis'.[142]

The real issue not so much that Stalin had planned a war in 1941, but rather that he had allowed his thinking about the type of war he would wage in the future to blind him to the threat in the present. The German invasion in June 1941 did not come without warning and there is plenty of long-established evidence that Stalin wilfully ignored the threat posed by Germany at the time, entirely misjudging the situation and committing colossal blunders. The most basic of these was to misinterpret Hitler's intentions. Stalin considered that, for all his pronouncements, Hitler was fundamentally a pragmatist and, as such, would not commit the major blunder of fighting a war on two fronts. After all, Hitler was still involved in the west: Britain was still undefeated and the United States was becoming increasingly hostile to Germany. Logically, therefore, Hitler would want to avoid conflict with Russia – at least for the time being. Stalin could therefore expect plenty of warning of any deterioration in relations between Germany and Russia, which could be repaired, if needed, by well-timed concessions. The most pressing danger, as Stalin saw it, was not to give Russia sufficient time in preparing for successful Total War by *provoking* Hitler into immediate action.

This attitude was behind the mistakes that Stalin committed early in 1941, which delivered up Russia to Hitler's attack. Stalin was totally unreceptive to warnings from British intelligence in April of German troop concentrations near the Soviet border. Stalin's reasoning was that Churchill was trying to provoke a conflict between Germany and Russia which would open up a war on two fronts – to the benefit of Britain. At the time, this was not an unreasonable assumption. But he also ignored intelligence reports from his own agents. On 20 March, for example, General Golikov, the head of military intelligence, forwarded to Stalin information he had received about the build-up of German troops in the border areas. Similarly, in May, Admiral Kuznetzov quoted the German naval attaché in Berlin that war was imminent, but Stalin dismissed the evidence as having been planted. Vital information was also received from the pro-Soviet German agent in Japan, as well as from the Soviet embassy in Berlin. Both gave the precise date of the intended attack – 22 June 1941. Stalin rejected these warnings on the grounds that they did not conform to his interpretation of Hitler's character and intentions. He has been strongly criticized for this – from the 1950s to the present. In his destalinization campaign in 1956, Khrushchev accused Stalin of deliberately ignoring the warnings of a German invasion threat and regarding the beginning of the attack 'as only a provocative action on the part of several undisciplined sections of the German Army'. Khrushchev concluded that 'everything was ignored; warnings of certain army commanders, declarations of deserters from the enemy army, and even the open hostility of the enemy'.[143] According to Mezhiritsky, 'Stalin was illiterate in military matters' and was 'mesmerized by the dogma that Germany wouldn't undertake a war on two fronts'. Since he had 'indicated a deadline for the Red Army to be ready for war –

apparently in May 1942' – Stalin 'clung to this deadline'.[144] Even those more inclined to defend Stalin on many issues specifically exclude his conduct in the first half of 1941. Grey refers to 'a series of desperate attempts to appease Hitler' and 'painful efforts to avoid even the semblance of provocation'.[145] There is therefore general agreement that 'The causes of this disastrous behaviour lay in Moscow with Stalin'.[146]

Not surprisingly Stalin was personally devastated by this turn of events, although it is not entirely clear what happened next. The usual view is that he experienced a breakdown and for the first ten days after the invasion confined himself to his *dacha*, in isolation from his officials, only to recover his resolution by the beginning of July. Just how much he contributed personally to the administrative changes, in preparation for the fight-back, remains unclear. It is certainly true that the first radio announcement of the invasion was made by Molotov on 22 June and that Stalin's broadcast did not follow until 3 July. It is significant that part of this was a justification of his previous policy. Referring to the 1939 Non-Aggression Pact, he pointed out that 'We secured our country peace for a year and a half and the opportunity of preparing our forces to repulse fascist Germany should she risk an attack on our country despite the pact'.[147] The credibility of this is reduced by two factors. First, as we have seen, Stalin was preparing for a future offensive war by the Soviet Union. And second, his actions at the last minute actually undermined the capacity of the Red Army to resist Hitler's attack. As the German armies moved up to and over the frontier Stalin had interpreted this as a minor breach of discipline and ordered Soviet units to fall back to avoid provoking a larger onslaught. He had even issued orders against the mobilization of reserves. It seems, therefore, that Stalin did not use the Non-Aggression Pact to defend the Soviet Union; if anything, his own policies nullified any advantages it might once have had.

The threat was not only the rapidity of German advance during the first weeks: the momentum was maintained for several months which could not be stopped. Long-term preparations for an offensive war now prevented a realistic short-term response in the form of an orderly retreat. The result was a rout on all fronts. Yet even at this stage the leadership failed to adjust its strategic thinking. Even while the Germans were nearing Moscow, Kiev and Leningrad, official propaganda denied that there had been any reverses and that such references amounted to 'defeatism' – to be dealt with severely. This delayed the possibility of tactical retreat until it was too late. There were also longer-term blunders that contributed to the military paralysis of 1941: these went back to some of Stalin's extreme policies during the 1930s. One was the decapitation of the Red Army's leadership during the purges which meant that many of the senior officers facing the Wehrmacht in 1941 had relatively little direct experience. Another problem, again attributable to the period of Terror, was a massive increase in political interference in military matters. Because of the chaos that the Terror had produced, this involvement was often controlled by political and military 'illiterates'. Beneath Stalin's own blunders there were therefore many lesser incompetents, suddenly exposed by the emergency of the German invasion.[148] Another damaging legacy from the 1930s was an enormous residue of resentment and dissatisfaction with Stalin's regime. Here, social and economic hardship caused by forced collectivization overlapped nationalist resentments as millions of Belorussians, Ukrainians, Georgians and peoples in the Baltic states initially welcomed the Germans as liberators. According to Fischer, up to 2 million inhabitants of the Soviet Union fought for the German armies.[149]

In summary, the war that the Soviet Union fought between 1941 and 1942 was not the one that Stalin had anticipated. He had been mobilizing the Soviet Union for conflict in the unspecified future. This would take the form of Total War and would be followed by swift victory. Instead, what Russia actually experienced was swift defeat, followed by Total War. The German invasion therefore came as a profound shock to the whole military strategy of the Soviet Union, as the diplomacy of Stalin destroyed any initiative that Russia might have had. How could the Soviet state possibly hope to survive?

Revival and victory: 1943–5

The furthest extent of the German advance was reached towards the end of 1942. From this stage onwards the occupying forces were slowly but steadily driven back by the unremitting counter-offensive of the Red Army, made possible by a remarkable national revival.

The first major Soviet achievement was the successful defence of Moscow by Marshal Zhukov. This was made possible by the withdrawal of Soviet troops from the Far East to strengthen the capital. (It seems that this time Stalin decided to believe the news of the Soviet agent in Tokyo, Richard Sorge, that Japan was about to launch an attack on the United States, not on Russia.) The Battle for Moscow tested the German army to its utmost and, although the German advance continued in 1942, it was directed against the south, not against the capital. Stalin decided to focus the Soviet counter-attack on the city of Stalingrad, which was eventually captured by Zhukov early in 1943. This was undoubtedly the turning-point of the war and was followed in July 1943 by a Soviet victory in the tank battle at Kursk. From this time onwards the Soviet advance proved irresistible. Kiev was liberated by November 1943 and Leningrad early in 1944. During the first half of 1944 the Germans were finally forced out of Russian territory while, in the second half, the Red Army advanced into the Nazi-occupied states of eastern Europe. Most of Poland was captured, although virtually no assistance was provided by Stalin to the Warsaw revolt against the Germans, which was eventually put down with great brutality. Romania was forced to surrender in August and Bulgaria in September, while in October the Yugoslav resistance forces under Tito were assisted by the Russians to liberate Belgrade from German occupation. A final effort from the north-east resulted, in January 1945, in the fall of Warsaw and the conquest of the rest of Poland. From February 1945 Zhukov concentrated on the advance on Berlin. The capital was besieged and heavily bombarded, eventually falling in April after savage street-to-street fighting.

Considering the initial collapse between 1941 and 1942, the Soviet Union therefore made the most remarkable military recovery between 1943 and 1945. Plenty of reasons have been given for this transformation. One is the recovery of Stalin from the crisis of confidence he experienced in the first weeks of the attack and the effectiveness of his subsequent leadership. A second was the importance of the first three Five-Year Plans, which meant that the Soviet Union was able to outproduce Germany in war *matériel*. Third, new military strategies were adopted, which proved far more effective than the woeful performance in 1941. Fourth, the Soviet Union was able to liberate itself, with relatively little assistance from its western Allies. This owed much to the fifth factor, the surge of patriotism that facilitated Soviet recovery. Finally, Stalin owed much to the mistakes made by Hitler, who lost the war as much as Stalin won it. These are all traditional explanations. Although most are broadly correct, they need some refining in the light of recent research; it is also essential to place more emphasis on them in combination with each other. Doing this provides a few surprising twists to long-held assumptions.

Stalin's personal recovery restored him to full leadership, enabling him to make the structural changes necessary to mobilize the Soviet Union's remaining strengths. Grey emphasizes his ability to learn from earlier mistakes both in his military strategy and in his choice of subordinates. 'With his disciplined mind and tenacious memory, he developed considerable military expertise and technical knowledge.'[150] He also made effective administrative adjustments, dismantling part of the previous system and setting up two new institutions, Stavka as the general headquarters and GOKO as the State Defence Committee. The latter was given powers to conduct all aspects of the war and comprised Molotov, Voroshilov, Malenkov and Beria. Under the overall authority of Stalin as People's Commissar for Defence, GOKO replaced the more complex party channels of communication, ending the earlier state of administrative confusion and making possible a more rational approach to economic and military planning. But some historians have questioned the extent to which Stalin himself should receive the credit for all this. Volkogonov, for example,[151] maintains that Stalin had 'no professional military knowledge' and that the Soviet people eventually prevailed not because of Stalin but in spite of him. According to Lewin, the recovered Stalin still continued to dominate the administration to such an extent that other members were afraid to show initiative. These, however, are minority views. The general consensus is that Stalin *did* change the way in which he ran the Soviet Union and that he was personally responsible for at least some of the improvements that resulted.

Military recovery was based on the Soviet Union's eventual ability to outproduce Germany and sustain the massive losses inflicted on the Red Army. The usual argument is that the first three Five-Year Plans had geared the Soviet economy to Total War and could produce more armaments than the more limited Blitzkrieg-based German economy. There had also been a long-term shift of resources into Siberia which meant that 20 per cent of the country's industrial capacity was outside Europe by 1941. This was enhanced by the transfer of factories eastwards to enable the continued production of weapons beyond the range of the German attack. While this interpretation is sound enough, the conclusion usually drawn from it is not. It has often been assumed that Soviet recovery was due to the full implementation of Stalin's command economy: more armaments were produced after 1942 because the planning system was stepped up a gear. This intensification of previous controls has now been challenged: historians like Sapir have shown that the reverse occurred. The mobilized economy developed by the first three Five-Year Plans had been basically inefficient, weakened by the tensions between central and local decision making. The crisis of war stimulated a more efficient approach: interference by the centre with the local bodies was reduced and more local initiative was allowed in the meeting of central armaments targets. From 1943 local production was based on local decisions about the supply of raw materials and the most effective methods of using labour resources. Market forces therefore became more significant than central administrative constraints. This led to the paradox, pointed out by Sapir, that the earlier 'mobilisation economy had to be at least partially demobilised to achieve war mobilisation'.[152] But it worked. The whole process was possible because the types of weapons and components were kept deliberately unsophisticated, which meant that they were quick to build, easy to maintain and inexpensive to replace.

These changes in the command economy delivered overwhelming numbers of tanks, aircraft, artillery pieces and small weapons to wherever on the front they were required. These enabled Soviet forces to overwhelm the German Wehrmacht. Among the most important of these were the Katyusha rocket-launchers, the SUS (self-propelled artillery), heavy mortars, and the T-34 tank, which was admitted by one of the German commanders, General Guderian, to be superior to anything in the panzer divisions. German vehicles were not equipped for winter conditions and did not even have antifreeze (something that the Soviet vehicles did not need as they ran on diesel). The initial German superiority in the air was soon reversed as the Soviet airforce was provided with fourteen new types of aircraft, including the Il-2, nicknamed the 'Golden Plane' by Soviet pilots and the 'Black Death' by the Germans.

Soviet military recovery was, therefore, due to more appropriate styles of leadership and more efficient use of economic resources. These were accompanied by a new strategy which departed from the unqualified emphasis on 'offensive' warfare developed during the 1930s. Instead, it was now considered more appropriate to combine the more traditional defensive approach with a devastating counter-attack whenever this became possible. Zhukov's advice to Stalin in April 1943 showed this line of thought:

> I consider it inadvisable for our forces to go over to the offensive in the very first days of the campaign . . . It would be better to make the enemy first exhaust himself against our defences, and knock out his tanks and then, bringing up fresh reserves, to go over to a general offensive which would finally finish off his main force.[153]

The result was a close co-ordination between partisan warfare and the massive thrusts of the Soviet forces at Kursk in 1943, followed by the invasion of Poland and the Balkans in 1944. This meant the end of Blitzkrieg for the Germans and the beginning of the type of Soviet offensive which had been anticipated in the 1930s. Clearly, the army had to be given more initiative to implement these military changes. This was another example of the partial reversal of an inter-war policy – in this instance the politicization of the army was abandoned. After the catastrophe of 1941 and 1942 Stalin allowed a much greater degree of military initiative. He promoted to supreme command able officers like Zhukov, Tolbukhin, Konev, Malinovsky, Vatutin and Rossakovsky. He also allowed crucial military decisions to be taken at the front. Hitler, by contrast, allowed the destruction of the German army at Stalingrad by refusing to let von Paulus conduct an orderly withdrawal.

Stalin and Soviet historians always maintained that the Soviet Union liberated itself and that any economic and military assistance given from outside provided only a small contribution to Soviet victory. Recently, however, western historians have come to see external help as vital. US and British aid provided large quantities of back-up equipment and transport facilities, including trucks, jeeps and rolling stock. This filled gaps in Soviet infrastructure, enabling Soviet factories to concentrate on producing armaments. As a result, Soviet armies could move more quickly than they could otherwise have done from the defensive to the offensive. Harrison also maintains that, although halting the German advance 'was conducted largely on the basis of Soviet domestic supply', the subsequent pursuit of the Wehrmacht and the ability 'to project Soviet military power into the heart of Europe' were based 'significantly on western resources'.[154] The western Allies also contributed substantially to the Soviet Union's military fight back against the German invasion. Although Stalin accused them of using up Soviet lives by their refusal to invade France until 1944, they had already been involved in a second front in North Africa from 1942 and had invaded Italy in 1943. In the process, they drew off divisions vitally needed by the Wehrmacht on the Russian front. British and American bombing raids over Germany also restricted the amount of war *matériel* that could be produced by the Reich in 1944 and 1945 by which time, of course, the German presence in the east had to be scaled down to resist the rapid advances in the west. The interaction between events on different fronts is now strongly emphasized as being of benefit to both the Red Army and the Western Allies.[155]

The patriotic response was also crucial to Soviet success, although the connection between the 'people's war' and Stalin's leadership has recently been reassessed. On the one hand, there were contradictory policies from above to control the popular response and to maximize patriotism. These involved both the harshest repression and unusually moderate concessions. Repression included the elimination of those who were suspected of having already collaborated with the Germans in 1941 and 1942, or those who might do so in the future. This went beyond the arrest and execution of individuals to the transportation of whole peoples from their homelands to remote parts of central Asia and Siberia: victims included Balkars, Chechens, Karachais, Meshkhetians, Crimean Tartars and many Ukrainians, Balts and Cossacks. The intention was to remove any core for future mass rebellions and any distraction to the intensification of a patriotic response which was ideologically Soviet and historically Russian. Stalin's more moderate policies were designed to strengthen commitment and patriotic support to 'Mother Russia'. Hence he granted concessions to the Russian Orthodox Church in exchange for the latter's efforts to mobilize patriotic sentiment. The regime also relaxed some of the harsher measures previously used to enforce collectivization and tolerated at least some elements of a market economy. Soviet citizens were targeted by propaganda which stressed the connections with the Russian past. The 'Great Patriotic War' against Hitler was therefore a parallel to the 'Great Fatherland War' against Napoleon, while Russian figures from the past were resurrected in Eisenstein's films *Ivan the Terrible* and *Alexander Nevsky*. A typical view of Stalin's wartime measures is that they were therefore a 'combination of permissiveness with drastic punitive measures' or the introduction of 'permissive elements into a basically draconian practice'.[156] At the same time, Russia experienced a huge upsurge of patriotism from below, which far transcended Stalin's measures. The self-sacrifice of the citizens of Leningrad in the face of the German siege, or of the Red Army at Stalingrad and Kursk, or the resistance of the partisans behind enemy lines, was unprecedented in its scale, even in Russian history.

It has, finally, been argued that Hitler contributed as much as Stalin to the outcome of the war between Germany and Russia. Certainly, Soviet recovery from defeat was paralleled by the German collapse from victory. This happened in three ways. First, the impetus of the German attack was sustainable only in the short term, whereas Soviet strength lay in longer-term endurance which wore out the enemy. This was due, at least in part, to a contrast between Hitler and Stalin, from which the latter benefited. Hitler's military strategy initially proved spectacularly successful but failed to deliver final victory within the timescale he had envisaged; from 1942 onwards he refused to modify his policy of maintaining German positions at all costs or allowing for orderly withdrawal and regrouping. For all his faults, Stalin was able to take advantage of this; he showed some willingness to learn from previous mistakes, whereas Hitler obstinately refused to accept the importance of German numerical inferiority in crucial areas such as Moscow in 1941 and Stalingrad in 1942–3. Although both had able commanders, Hitler was less willing to take advice after 1941 from Guderian or von Paulus than Stalin was from Zhukov. Second, the misrule of captured territories, especially the Ukraine and Belorussia, undermined any goodwill the Germans originally encountered from their peoples. Nazi brutality, based on extreme racial arrogance, put into perspective the earlier ruthlessness of Stalin's economic policies. Even elements of the Nazi regime saw the dangers of this. In October 1942, Bräutigam, the head of the Main Political Department in the Reich Ministry of the Eastern Territories, strongly criticized the Reich's policy. In a memorandum he described the wishes of the Soviet population as 'incredibly modest', adding that an administration 'not intent simply on plunder and exploitation' would have 'kindled the greatest enthusiasm' and 'put at our disposal a mass consisting of millions'.[157] In not promoting regional autonomy (as he had already done in some occupied areas in western Europe), Hitler missed the opportunity of enlisting a wave of anti-Soviet ethnic support. Instead, German occupation was a vital catalyst for a Soviet patriotic revival. Third, growing German problems allowed the recovery of Soviet production. The German economy had not been geared to such a major undertaking as the destruction of the Soviet Union: it had been mobilized only for short-term partial war, whereas the Soviet economy had in the 1930s been prepared for long-term Total War. Hitler had relied on a series of rapid victories followed by the absorption of the infrastructures of his conquests; in Russia, however, Blitzkrieg had reached its limit and the conversion to Total War (see p. 241) never succeeded in achieving overall victory. The Soviet economy had the reverse experience: it was made more effective by the relaxation of some of the earlier constraints.

Relations with the West, 1941–5

When Germany attacked Russia in June 1941 Stalin's whole attitude to Hitler underwent a profound change. He hastened to seek the co-operation of those Western countries which he had previously suspected. Hence, in 1941, the Anglo-Soviet Mutual Assistance Pact was drawn up, followed in 1942 by the twenty-year Anglo-Soviet Treaty of Alliance. Stalin also concluded a Lend-Lease agreement with the United States worth $11 billion. When the United States entered the war against Germany, the Grand Alliance was formed (although no document was actually signed), aimed at bringing down the Nazi regime. However, collaboration was never complete. Throughout the war there existed an undercurrent of distrust which grew stronger as the need for unity receded. This distrust went back as far as the foundation of the Bolshevik state and was largely ideological: Trotsky, for instance, had once referred to Lenin and Wilson as the 'apocalyptic antipodes of our time'. But there were also specific irritants throughout the period 1941–5 which were particularly apparent at the major wartime conferences – at Tehran (November to December 1943), Yalta (February 1945) and Potsdam (July to August 1945).

The first of these irritants was military. Stalin wanted an active alliance and no repetition of the 'sitskrieg' which had been the West's response to Hitler's Blitzkrieg against Poland in August 1939. He considered it vitally important for the Western Allies to open up a second front in France to draw off between forty and sixty German divisions from the Russian sector. He made his first request for this to Churchill in July 1941. In August 1942 Churchill visited Moscow to disclose his plans for Operation Torch – to be opened up, however, in North Africa. Stalin's reaction was bitter disillusionment: 'All is clear', he told his associates. 'They want us to bleed white in order to dictate to us their terms later on.'[158] The Anglo-American landings in North Africa did help matters but Stalin did not regard them as a justifiable substitute for an attack on France. This finally came in June 1944, although by this stage Stalin was accusing the Anglo-American forces of advancing into Germany as quickly as possible in order to minimize Soviet conquests in central and eastern Europe.

The second main breach concerned the frontiers and regimes of eastern Europe. The most significant of these was Poland. Britain and the United States were prepared, at Yalta and Potsdam, to concede the Curzon Line as Poland's frontier, thus allowing the USSR to retain all the Polish territory conquered in 1939. But at the same time they were profoundly unhappy about the possibility of permanent Soviet control over Polish institutions; hence their insistence on the Yalta Declaration on Liberated Europe, by which the powers undertook to assist the liberated states to create democratic institutions of their own choice. This, of course, produced an inevitable difference of interpretation between the Western powers, who hoped for the installation of liberal democracies, and the Soviet Union, which had always intended to promote revolutionary communist regimes. Above all, Stalin was determined to develop a buffer zone between Russia and the West, or a glacis of friendly socialist states. Clearly this would be a major post-war issue.

The outcome of the war, and of the disagreements with the Western Allies, was clearly in Russia's favour. Stalin had, by the middle of 1945, every reason to feel satisfied with the Soviet position in Europe. Nazi Germany had been smashed and partially dismembered by the principle of zoning agreed at Yalta and Potsdam. All the gains made by Russia as a result of the Nazi–Soviet Pact of 1939 were retained, namely eastern Poland, the Baltic states and part of Romania. Indeed, Soviet expansion went beyond the 1939 limits, also encompassing parts of East Prussia and Czechoslovakia. In the Far East, Russia had gained, in return for minimal participation in the war against Japan, Sakhalin and the Kurile Islands, which had been ceded by Tsarist Russia in 1905 and 1875, respectively. The sphere of Soviet control extended far beyond these enlarged frontiers. Moscow now dominated a huge socialist arc comprising Poland, Czechoslovakia, Hungary, Romania and Bulgaria, together with the Soviet zone of Germany. At last the USSR seemed to have both security and the means to spread communism into the heart of Europe. Many of Stalin's expectations had therefore been realized. The capitalist states had come into conflict with each other and the end result had been the strengthening of the Soviet Union and the opportunity to spread Soviet influence.

The cost

It was not until 1956 that the full extent of Soviet losses in the Second World War were revealed. It is now known that they are the heaviest suffered by any country in history as the result of an invasion by another power.

The most devastating impact was on the population, both military and civilian: 5.7 million Russian soldiers surrendered to the Germans, of whom 3.3 million subsequently died in captivity. The German High Command bore direct responsibility for the appalling conditions faced by Russian prisoners-of-war; an order stated that the Bolshevik soldier lost all claims to treatment as an honourable opponent in accordance with the Geneva Convention. The occupying forces also treated Russian civilians with extreme brutality. The Slavs were seen as a subhuman race and the Reichsleiter of the east, Rosenberg, aimed at no less than the national disintegration of the USSR. Overall, the Soviet Union lost between 26 and 27 million people, compared with 375,000 Britons, 405,000 Americans and 600,000 French people. The total looks even worse when placed on top of previous losses. Estimates vary widely, but some point to 13.5 million in the First World War, Civil War, epidemics and starvation; and up to 20 million during the 1930s in the famine and purges. To this can be added a shortfall of births between 1914 and 1945 of well over 90 million, equivalent to the combined actual post-war population of Germany and France.[159]

Destruction of property was also on a massive scale. Details were released as early as 1947. According to Molotov, the Germans destroyed 1,710 towns and 70,000 villages, 31,850 industrial enterprises and 98,000 collective farms. The sufferings of two Soviet cities are particularly well known. Leningrad experienced a siege which lasted for 900 days and the eventual casualty figure for this one city was greater than that of all the Western Allies combined. The suffering was the direct result of starvation, dystrophy and scurvy, as well as German bombing and bombardment. Stalingrad, meanwhile, was totally devastated. Russian and German troops fought over each street, and then in the ruins and rubble. An official Soviet description reads as follows:

> In the trenches carved out in the steep banks of the Volga, in gullies and the shells of ruined houses, in the cellars of bombed buildings the Soviet soldiers fought to the last to defend the city. The German forces launched 700 attacks and every step forward cost them tremendous losses . . . Between 500 and 1,200 splinters of bombs, shells and grenades per square metre were found on the slopes of Mamai Hill, one of the main centres of the fighting, after the Battle of Stalingrad had at last come to an end.[160]

Hutchings has placed Soviet sufferings in perspective by comparing the losses inflicted in the two World Wars. Population losses in the Second World War were 50 per cent larger, but the population of 1941 was much greater than that of 1913. Russia during the Second World War experienced greater economic destruction than in the First, but substantially less disruption, largely because the industrial base of 1941 was much greater than that of 1913. There was a significant contrast in the pattern of destruction; in the First World War industry suffered more severely than agriculture, while the reverse was true in the Second. Indeed, after 1945, agriculture remained a serious problem long after factories and houses had been rebuilt. A key question was how Stalin would adapt his policies to deal with this specific problem.

As it turned out in the longer term, the extent of destruction was to be an issue for the very survival of the Soviet Union. Just as the Civil War had helped shape Bolshevism into a repressive communist bureaucracy, so the experience of the Second World War proved to be a major factor in its inability to change. Stalin won the war – but could he survive the peace?

The treatment of the nationalities, 1941–5

The Soviet Union's federal structure, established in 1922 and extended in 1936, was maintained through the war. The territories taken between 1939 and 1945 were added and the same principles of national self-determination were applied. The official line on the role of all the peoples of the Soviet Union in the war can be seen in an extract from *A Short History of the Communist Party of the Soviet Union*:

> The Soviet people won their historic victory in the Great Patriotic War because of the socialist social and state system that had been established in the USSR, because the workers and peasants, all the peoples of the Soviet Union, were bound together in real friendship, because the Communist Party had fostered and encouraged this friendship.[161]

Significantly, this edition was published in 1970 and, because of the destalinization campaign of the late 1950s, refers to the leadership of the 'Communist Party' rather than to 'Stalin'. It also conceals a major trauma affecting the ethnic groups within the Soviet Union during wartime.

For most Russians the tight constraints of the 1930s were relaxed between 1941 and 1945 in a desperate effort to focus on winning the war. For the nationalities, however, the repression became increasingly severe. Stalin was obsessed with the fear of potential betrayal by non-Russian groups within the USSR and went to extreme lengths to neutralize this possibility. Whole communities were uprooted from their homelands and transplanted to other – more remote and barren – areas, a process organized by Beria and the NKVD and carried out by the Red Army. The first affected were Koreans, Poles, Ukrainians, and the peoples of the Baltic, some of whom had already been removed before 1941. Then, after the German invasion in 1941, Stalin ordered the deportation of 400,000 ethnic Germans to Siberia and central Asia. A similar fate befell 69,000 Turkic Karachaians and 93,000 Kalmyks in 1943 and 500,000 Chechens and Ingush, 340,000 Balkars and 180,000 Crimean Tartars during the course of 1944. Their autonomous republics and districts within the RSFSR were all dissolved and removed from the records. The later deportations were unnecessary in strategic terms since the Germans had long since been forced out of the regions concerned. According to Mawdsley, 'They can only be seen as a grand ethnic punishment or an extreme version of the prophylactic counter-insurgency.'[162] It could also be argued that Stalin was using the opportunity to revert to a policy of Russification – but in a much more extreme form than it had ever been applied before.

Further deportations came even after the victory over Nazi Germany as the Soviet frontier was consolidated against the possibility of any future invasion from the west. Particularly indiscriminate was the treatment of Ukrainians, Estonians, Latvians and Lithuanians, all of whom were accused of collaborating with the German invaders. It is true that there were Wehrmacht and SS units formed from among these nationalities, although subsequent measures were applied with little attempt to target those actually involved. As for the Jewish minorities, those who escaped the Einsatzgruppen of the SS or deportation to the Nazi death camps, faced a ban on the practice of their religion, the closure of their institutions, and a prohibition on their publications. During the so-called Doctor's Plot, fifteen Jewish leaders were tried and executed in August 1952, a virtual re-enactment of the show trials of the late 1930s.

1945–53: MATURE DICTATORSHIP?

The regime and the man behind it, 1945–53

Stalin was unique among the dictators covered in this book in that he emerged as a victor in 1945. Others had committed suicide, or been executed or sent into exile, or had survived only by keeping their countries out of the conflict. In theory, Stalin's position should have been unassailable.

The broad outline of the regime often referred to as 'High Stalinism' is as follows. Stalin gave absolute priority to consolidating his personal control over the Soviet Union through the implementation of a series of changes from 1945 onwards. In many cases these reversed the wartime policies introduced after the German invasion of June 1941. Among the state institutions, the Council of People's Commissars, or Sovnarkom, became the USSR Council of Ministers and acquired a new inner Presidium. The state bureaucracy was increased in size, the eighteen People's Commissariats becoming forty-eight Ministries by 1947. At the same time, Stalin ended GOKO, the State Defence Committee, which had played such a vital administrative role during the war. There were also changes at the centre of the party, as the Politburo was replaced by another Presidium in 1952. This had a much larger membership, which Stalin rarely consulted, preferring the advice of a smaller, informal and ever-changing core. Although Stalin maintained the party (in 1952 renamed the CPSU) as a cement to keep the Soviet Union together while maintaining the fiction of 'voluntary' federalism, it was a shadow of its former self: for example, no party congresses were held between 1939 and 1952. The army, too, became less influential, with the demotion of Zhukov and other key generals, and the subordination of military officials to political commissars.

New organizational controls were accompanied by another round of purges – directed at the army and the party, which Stalin targeted in the Leningrad Affair. This resulted in the trial and execution of party leaders and war heroes, such as Voznesensky, who had done what they could to organize resistance to the German siege. Stalin also sought to strengthen his grip on society at large through the 1946 Zhdanov degrees. These tightened working practices and reimposed on the arts the full force of Socialist Realism, which had been relaxed during the war. Control over society and the arts in what is usually known as the Zhdanovschina was at first directed at ideology, before expanding into other areas of culture and society. Underlying the whole system was the intensification of terror. The NKVD, under the direction of Beria, continued to take its toll through renewed persecution. Action against the nationalities which had collaborated with the Germans during the Great Patriotic War was extended to a new campaign against 'kulaks' and anyone questioning the reintroduction of collective farming. Soldiers in the Red Army who had been held as prisoners of war by the Germans were suspected as collaborators; many therefore found themselves transferred to Gulag camps, the number of which grew rapidly after 1945. Finally, the Soviet Union experienced a wave of virulent anti-Semitism, unquestionably exacerbated by Stalin's own views and punitive actions.

There is now a wide variety of interpretations about this period of Stalin's dictatorship. Most historians agree that Stalin's health and some of his mental facilities were on the decline, that he was obsessed with self-glorification and that he reached a new peak of ruthlessness. So where is the focus of the controversy?

The original approach to 'late Stalinism' acknowledged that Stalin was infatuated with power. But some biographers placed the emphasis on what Stalin tried to *do* with it. Deutscher, for example, focused more on the paradox between Stalin's pursuit of two policies, 'nationalist' and 'revolutionary',[163] less on arbitrary nature of Stalin's personality. He also tried to anticipate Stalin's longer-term contributions to Soviet power. Both approaches are understandable in view of the date of Deutscher's publication: 1949 – well before the extreme revelations brought by Khrushchev's destalinization campaign of 1956. Ian Grey also emphasized the *purpose* of Stalin's measures rather than the personality that produced them. As we have already seen, he placed Stalin's megalomania firmly within Russia's autocratic tradition, stressing the use of his ever-increasing authority to impose long-term solutions to the destruction his country had experienced in wartime.[164] Other historians made more of the sheer brutality of the later regime, of Stalin's grip based on fear and new purges. But the corollary was still that, up to the time of his death in 1953, Stalin's ascendancy was total, based on new centralizing measures to consolidate his authority and the removal of all perceived threats to the regime. These enabled him to launch a campaign of reconstruction in industry and to reimpose collectivization in agriculture. He achieved his original objective of making the Soviet Union a superpower and extended Russian control, for the first time, over most of eastern Europe. Victory in the war was therefore the means by which the totalitarian measures of the 1930s reached their logical completion in the late 1940s. Stalinism was fulfilled in a period of 'mature dictatorship' and Stalin himself came closer than either Hitler or Mussolini to achieving totalitarian goals. It is true that his organizational changes created internal tensions. But, if there was a degree of chaos, it was planned – as a guarantee of Stalin's own power. There is therefore a possible parallel with Bracher's explanation of 'organized chaos' in Nazi Germany.

Or is there more of a case for linking late Stalinism with the Broszat thesis on Hitler's regime: that chaos was more spontaneous and erratic?

During the 1990s, no doubt as side-effect of the sensational collapse of the Soviet Union in 1991, a new approach emerged to explain Stalin's post-war dictatorship. This emphasized its arbitrary nature and, at times, its breathtaking incompetence. The period 1945–53 was *not* one of dictatorship fulfilled. All the problems that had confronted Stalin before 1941 now returned in full measure so that, far from being settled into 'mature dictatorship', he was as insecure as ever. If Stalin remained arbitrary and despotic, this was not because he was now so settled that he could do whatever he wanted. His increasingly irrational behaviour was his response to threats to his system and a very real fear that it might break up. Age and the war had taken their toll, and it was clear that Stalin was now deteriorating physically and mentally, adding hugely to the chaos. Kenez, for example, emphasized that Stalin had built up a 'surrogate ideology of hero worship'; that, 'isolated from Soviet reality', he had 'formed an imaginary picture of the world around him'; and that 'he became the primary victim' of his own propaganda.[165] Ward's assessment of Stalin was equally striking. 'This was no self-confident tyrant in charge of a smoothly functioning totalitarian regime but a sickly old man; unpredictable, dangerous, lied to by terrified subordinates, presiding over a ramshackly bureaucracy.'[166] If anything, victory had increased Stalin's difficulties. His personal ascendancy, far from reaching a new peak after 1945, was more seriously challenged than at any time since 1929. The paradox, pointed out by Ward, is that 'whilst the Russo-German conflict strengthened the regime and legitimized the Generalissimo as a symbol of the will to victory, Stalin's personal power was threatened'.[167] The success of the Red Army raised the spectre Stalin had always feared – that the regime would be militarized and Stalin himself would be the target of an internal coup. This explains why he demoted Zhukov and wound up GOKO. He therefore repoliticized the regime, but even here was obsessed with the possibility that future challenges to his authority might emerge from the centre of the party. This is why he avoided summoning the key party organs and launched new rounds of purges. His policies after 1945 were initiated for defensive reasons, from a position of weakness rather than from one of strength: Stalin's priority was to recover rather than to sublimate his power.

But has this approach gone too far in the opposite direction? There has certainly been a partial swing of the historiographical pendulum towards the original emphasis on Stalin as both ruthless and effective. Two main examples can be cited. First, 'late Stalinism' was not necessarily in headlong decline. Some historians have pointed up Stalin's remaining strengths. According to McDermott, he 'obstinately and tenaciously clung to the reins of power, even as his mental and physical capacities began to desert him by the early 1950s'. He was still in complete control of decision making and of the secret police. He also remained 'vindictive, suspicious and murderously dangerous'. Hence 'The Stalin who emerges is more complex, but certainly no less a tyrant.'[168] Second, there has been some emphasis on a purposeful long-term strategy to implement a consistent ideology. After their research into the Soviet archives, Gorlizki and Khleyniuk[169] attribute to Stalin motives for his policies that were based on a greater degree of political logic than had previously been allowed – a closer approximation to the earlier interpretation of a powerful Stalin. But, as McDermott stresses, they added another dimension. Stalin was motivated not just by the intensification of his power base, but also by the pursuit of a 'separate, respected and powerful socialist system'.[170] Harassing his subordinates, manipulating the various committees and constantly changing their membership did not, therefore, 'contradict his wider political objectives'.

As we have seen elsewhere in this book, the major dictators have been recently been given more credit for developing longer-term ideas and visions, however distorted these may still seem. But, at some future time, the pendulum may well turn again.

Stalin's post-war economic policies

Stalin's main priority after 1945 was the reconstruction of Soviet industries and agriculture after the appalling destruction caused by the war with Germany. He decided in 1945 to return to his economic strategies of the 1930s, including central planning and collectivization. The Fourth and Fifth Five-Year Plans (1946–50 and 1950–5) again placed the emphasis on collective farming and the development of heavy industry at the expense of consumer goods. Such measures are usually explained as an intensification of the command economy as the most effective means of reconstruction. This, however, fails to take into account that many of Stalin's measures after 1945 were retrogressive. The inefficiencies of the 1930s were all revived in the formal planning system. Despite its failings in the 1930s, collectivization was not only revived but intensified: the *kolkhozy* increased in size and their number was reduced from 252,000 to 76,000. The recentralization of industrial planning was also a step backward, especially after the success of the partial demobilization of the economy during the war. In effect, Stalin missed the opportunity to continue the more progressive wartime policies and thereby abandon the more blatant failures of formal planning.

There were some positive achievements, however. As during the 1930s, Stalin pushed the Soviet Union further in the direction of the status of a superpower. Considerable investment was also channelled into the nuclear industry, again for military reasons. By 1949 the Soviet Union possessed the atomic bomb and, by 1951, the hydrogen bomb. By 1950 it was also announced that all the targets of the Fourth Five-Year Plan had been exceeded and that the overall industrial base was now substantially larger than it had been in 1940. But the deficiencies were as obvious as they had been during the 1930s. The emphasis on heavy industry meant the continuing neglect of the Soviet consumer. The conditions of the workforce were also very harsh. The forty-eight-hour week was regarded as a minimum; workers were unable to choose their jobs or to move to other areas; industrial discipline remained especially severe; and wages were based on piece work. But the Achilles' heel of the Soviet economy was undoubtedly agriculture. The 1946 harvest, for example, produced only 40 per cent of the crop of 1913. The problem was aggravated by low investment, as agriculture received only 7.3 per cent of the total available in the Fourth Five-Year Plan. There was also widespread discontent with the *kolkhozy*, with their artificially low prices for agricultural produce and a lack of incentives.

Although recovery did occur between 1945 and 1953, it was much slower than that accomplished by West Germany or Japan. In a real sense the infrastructural damage inflicted by the Second World War was permanent because it was dealt with by the inappropriate measures from the 1930s rather than new measures anticipating the 1950s. The emphasis was very much on restoration rather than renewal. As we have seen, however, this was in line with Stalin's political perspectives.

Stalin's post-war foreign policy

The last years of Stalin's rule saw the extension of Soviet control over the countries of eastern Europe and the intensification of the Cold War with the western powers. The two processes were of course interconnected, as one constantly reacted with the other.

From 1945 onwards Stalin was determined to spread Soviet influence wherever possible, especially to those areas liberated by the Red Army from Nazi rule. He enforced and institutionalized Soviet hegemony by four main methods. The first was through territorial acquisition: Estonia, Latvia and Lithuania were directly integrated into the Soviet Union, along with the area taken by Poland in 1921, the easternmost part of Czechoslovakia and parts of northern Romania. Second, this redefining of Soviet frontiers provided direct military access to East Germany, Poland, Czechoslovakia, Hungary and Romania. The security of this zone was guaranteed by a steady increase in the number of Soviet troops, which reached 5.5 million by the early 1950s. Third, Stalin ensured Soviet political domination by the communist takeover of eastern European governments that had started in 1945 as coalitions and broad fronts. Two examples of this process were the replacement Tildy and Beneš, the original coalition leaders of Hungary and Czechoslovakia, by hard-line Stalinist regimes under Rákosi and Gottwald respectively. Fourth, Stalin institutionalized Soviet ideological and economic control over eastern Europe through multilateral organizations like the Communist Information Bureau (Cominform) and the Council for Mutual Economic Assistance (CMEA or Comecon). The latter was designed to co-ordinate the economies of eastern Europe and to direct Czech, Polish and Hungarian trade towards the Soviet Union, thereby creating an almost self-sufficient commercial block. The one major multilateral body that came *after* Stalin was the Warsaw Pact or Warsaw Treaty Organization, a military alliance set up in 1956.

The result was a steady increase in tension between the Soviet Union and the West. The ideological confrontation was now more intense than at any time since the creation of the Bolshevik state. In a major speech on 9 February 1946 Stalin announced that he would abide by the basic principles of Marxism–Leninism, and proceeded to attack the capitalist powers as instigators of the Second World War. In the following month Churchill openly criticized Stalin's policy in eastern Europe. His speech, delivered in Fulton, Missouri, contained the famous sentence: 'From Stettin in the Baltic to Trieste in the Adriatic an iron curtain has descended across the continent.' The Cold War was subsequently hardened by two open declarations of policy. One was the Truman Doctrine (1947) which promised military or economic aid to Greece and Turkey and 'support for peoples who are resisting attempted subjugation by armed minorities or by outside pressures'.[171] The promise of economic aid was subsequently implemented by the Marshall Plan. Stalin's response was the so-called Zhdanov Line. In a speech in 1947 Zhdanov warned of the new threat of the capitalist West: 'The cardinal purpose of the imperialist camp is to strengthen imperialism, to hatch a new imperialist war, to combat socialism and democracy, and to support reactionary and anti-democratic pro-Fascist regimes and movements everywhere.'[172] The only answer, he concluded, was to tighten Soviet control – in the ways already outlined.

Tension between the Soviet Union and the West was also apparent in areas beyond eastern Europe. One of the earliest confrontations was the Iranian crisis (1945–6), in which the continued Soviet occupation of the northern part of Iran was challenged by the United States and Britain. The threat of armed conflict was eventually averted when, in 1946, Soviet troops were withdrawn in return for oil concessions. Back in Europe, the Cold War entered a particularly dangerous phase in 1948 with the Berlin Crisis. Stalin attempted to squeeze out the Western presence from Berlin by closing off the supply routes which connected West Berlin to the Western zones of occupied Germany. This policy, however, backfired. The British and Americans airlifted sufficient quantities of food and fuel to supply West Berlin, and Stalin was unable to prevent this for fear of American nuclear retaliation. The Berlin blockade had another undesirable side-effect for Stalin. It convinced the West of the need for a more systematic defence pact against Soviet aggression in Europe: hence the formation of the North Atlantic Treaty Organization (NATO). Soviet involvement in the Far East met with mixed success, especially over the Korean War (1950–3). When Soviet-backed North Korea invaded the South, the latter was assisted by United Nations forces, comprising mainly Americans. Stalin was forced to watch while the newly established communist regime in China came to the rescue of North Korea. From now on the Soviet Union had a major rival in the communist world.

Traditional interpretations of the motives of Stalin's foreign policy focus mainly on his response to external pressures on the Soviet Union. Because he now completely dominated the political system *within* the Soviet Union he was able to determine this response, whether he was dealing with the western powers or the eastern European satellite states. The key events of the Cold War were therefore activated – even calculated – from above. But this perspective now needs to be balanced with another. It is true that Stalin *did* take the key decisions that led to the events already outlined. Yet, as we have also seen, the political system within which he operated was somewhat flawed. As a result there were internal pressures within the Soviet Union that helped shape the responses of 'the Boss' to the new satellite states and the West.

This was partly due to the paradoxical impact of the Great Patriotic War (1941–5) and its aftermath. On the one hand, the Soviet Union had been strengthened by a strong patriotic response and the success of the army in preventing the disintegration of its various components. On the other hand, once the war had been won, military victory seemed to threaten Stalin's personal power by creating alternative models for political leadership and reducing the need for patriotism to the point of regional self-denial. Stalin therefore acted to strengthen his dictatorship – but by reintroducing the political coercion and command economy of the 1930s to replace the more relaxed measures that operated during the war. Just as he had once used the threat of the West to justify the harshness of collectivization and the terror of the purges, Stalin came to depend on a new conflict with the post-war western powers to maintain his power internally. Hence domestic crises were frequently explained, in the language of the Cold War, as the results of external ideological threats. He also used this to justify the tightening of his control over eastern Europe which, he stressed, would protect both the Soviet Union and the new communist regimes that had come into existence by 1948. He also used the subjection of Poles and Hungarians to guarantee his control over Ukrainians and Belorussians.

Different cases can be made as to whether or not Stalin succeeded in his policies towards eastern Europe and the western powers.

In eastern Europe the Soviet Union seemed, by the end of Stalin's rule, to have achieved unprecedented security. Trotsky's earlier attempts to achieve Soviet influence in the area through revolution had all ended in failure. Stalin, by contrast, had succeeded in inflicting upon it military conquest, political influence and ideological control. The result was in total contrast to the hostility of all the states in eastern Europe shown to the Soviet Union before 1941, when Bulgaria, Hungary and Romania had even aligned themselves with Nazi Germany. What Churchill referred to in 1947 as the Iron Curtain contained an area that could now also be called a glacis, or open killing ground sloping up to a fortress, which offered new strategic defence to the Soviet Union against the western powers or any future German threat. Yet there is another side to all this, which became more apparent in the longer term. The imposition of totalitarian regimes may have subdued the region for the rest of Stalin's lifetime, but this also created future resentment and unrest, with which his successors had to deal – as in Hungary (1956), Czechoslovakia (1968), Romania during the 1970s and Poland from 1981. Meanwhile Stalin had entirely failed to dominate Tito's Yugoslavia, and Hoxha's regime in Albania was able in the late 1950s to align itself with China. By the end of the 1980s, the whole panoply of Soviet controls had fallen apart; the ultimate irony is that all the states that had once been within Stalin's glacis eventually moved towards multilateral western organizations like NATO and the European Union – to shed forever the memory of the Warsaw Pact and Comecon.

How effectively did Stalin fare with the western powers? Again, there are examples of success and failure. After 1945 the Soviet Union emerged as one of the world's two superpowers and a military supremacy over a large part of the continent that had never existed before. With the development of the atomic and hydrogen bombs in 1949 and 1951, Stalin also seemed to have closed the gap in technology where the west originally led. Again, however, Stalin's policies recoiled on the Soviet Union in the longer term. The west responded in a more concerted way – through the Truman Doctrine and NATO – than it had ever done in the inter-war period. Stalin did not have everything his own way – even within the immediate area of his control. He was, after all, obliged to back down over his Berlin blockade (1948–9). Indeed, there is a line of thought that the Soviet Union's power was still vulnerable, despite the obvious advances it had made. According to Kennedy-Pipe, 'The Cold War was not a competition of equals: rather, it was an unequal struggle between one strong regime, the United States, and one fragile regime, the Soviet Union'.[173] It has also been argued that in trying to compete with the United States, Stalin and his successors placed intolerable strains on the Soviet economy; even the reforms of Andropov and Gorbachev in the 1980s failed to prevent this leading to the collapse of the Soviet Union in 1991.

The death of a dictator

All this brings us back full-circle to Stalin's vulnerability. By 1953 Stalin had become more insecure than ever; in Ward's phrase, he was 'raging, like Lear, against failure and mortality'.[174] This made him more dangerous than ever, especially to his subordinates, who feared a revival of the great fear of 1938. In fact, Stalin was about to launch a new purge, but this was prevented by his death in March 1953. He was staying at his country *dacha* in Kuntsevo, where he suffered a stroke. When he did not make an appearance on 1 March, none of his staff dared find out the reason. As Stalin's absence lengthened into days, the officer on duty contacted Stalin's senior associates – Beria, Malenkov, Khrushchev and Bulganin. They came quickly to the residence to find Stalin lying on his bedroom floor. Stalin's body was embalmed and placed next to Lenin's in the mausoleum. There it remained until 1961 when, on the orders of Khrushchev, it was cremated and buried in the Kremlin Wall.

Stalin's death had obvious implications for his system. Would this die with him? This was the case with almost every other dictator covered in this book. Or would his – alone – outlive the founder?

REFLECTIONS ON STALIN'S DICTATORSHIP

This chapter has considered the merits and defects of Stalin's individual policies before 1941, during the Great Patriotic War, and after 1945. This final section will provide some overall views of Stalin's rule, concentrating on three questions.

What was the basis of Stalin's power?

We have seen that Stalin rose to power through his control over the party and sought to maintain it by means of social discipline and purges. Throughout his rule, however, there were four factors which gave Stalinism its distinctive character: ideology, historical tradition, personality cult and, of course, terror.

Stalin was not originally renowned as a philosopher, but he aimed to establish himself as an authority on Marxism and to adapt Marxism to the needs of an industrializing society. He wrote four major works: *Marxism and the National Question* (1913), *Foundations of Leninism* (1924), *Marxism and Linguistics* (1950) and *Economic Problems of Socialism in the USSR* (1952). He always prefaced any major policy statements with ideological references, even in his speeches to the people during the Second World War. He succeeded in turning Marxist principles upside down in order to justify his enormous personal powers. As a result, Stalin has been disowned by most Marxists, who denounce his use of their ideology to construct a totalitarian state.

Stalin did not, however, base his power entirely on ideology. Most of the early Bolsheviks, especially Lenin, Trotsky, Bukharin, Kamenev and Zinoviev, had been Westernized Russians who had turned against their Slavic inheritance – political, social and cultural. Stalin, by contrast, was profoundly Slavic and quite deliberately revived an interest in an earlier phase of Russian history. He was particularly fascinated by Ivan the Terrible (1533–84), with whom he seemed in many ways to identify. Ivan had been confronted by opposition from the landed nobility, or boyars, under their spokesman Prince Andrei Kurbsky; this paralleled Stalin's problems with dissidents within the party, led by Trotsky. Ivan tackled the problem by initiating a series of purges carried out by the *oprichniki* (horsemen who carried, as the emblem of their special authority, brooms and dogs' heads attached to their saddles). This may well have been one influence behind Stalin's purges and the activities of the NKVD. Stalin insisted on the official rehabilitation of this most unpopular of tsars and ordered Eisenstein to produce an epic biographical film. He also restored pride in other periods of the Russian past and, during the Second World War, patriotism was deliberately linked to ideology. In the words of Tucker, 'Stalin merged Marx with Ivan the Terrible.'[175] He also developed an almost tsarist attitude to power, but with his version of Marxism taking the place of Divine Right.

This brings us to the personal basis of Stalin's power. During the period 1929–53 Stalin constructed the most elaborate personality cult in history. An extract from an official history read:

> Stalin is the brilliant leader and teacher of the Party, the great strategist of the Socialist revolution, military commander and guide of the Soviet state. With the name of Stalin in their hearts, the collective farmers toiled devotedly in the fields to supply the Red Army

3 Joseph Stalin, late in life, c.1952 (David King Collection)

> and the cities with food, and industry with raw materials. Stalin's name is cherished by the boys and girls of the Socialist land.

On Stalin's seventieth birthday so many letters of congratulations and greetings were sent to *Pravda* that it took three years to publish them. The Soviet Union was filled with Stalin statues and busts, and numerous cities and towns were named after him.

In part this cult of personality was developed to cover Stalin's personal deficiencies and lack of charisma. Mediocrity and facelessness had assisted his rise to power, as his contemporaries had not seen Stalin as a danger until it was too late. But mediocrity bred insecurity, and insecurity was certainly a factor in Stalin's campaign to eliminate the entire 1917 crop of Bolsheviks and to project himself as the only true successor to Lenin – the best Leninist.[176] Ulam provides another explanation for the cult:

> Stalin was a butcher, who had sent tens and hundreds of thousands of men, women and children to be tortured and shot on the strength of a diseased imagination. The cult acted as a safeguard or a barrier keeping him from stepping over into actual insanity.[177]

He needed, it could be argued, to be reassured by overwhelming acclamation that he was pursuing the right policies after all. In effect, therefore, Stalin practised the ultimate in self-delusion, and indoctrinated himself.

How effective was Stalin's power?

Stalin's search for power was therefore total and the methods he used were more extreme than those of his contemporaries – Hitler and Mussolini included. For decades historians

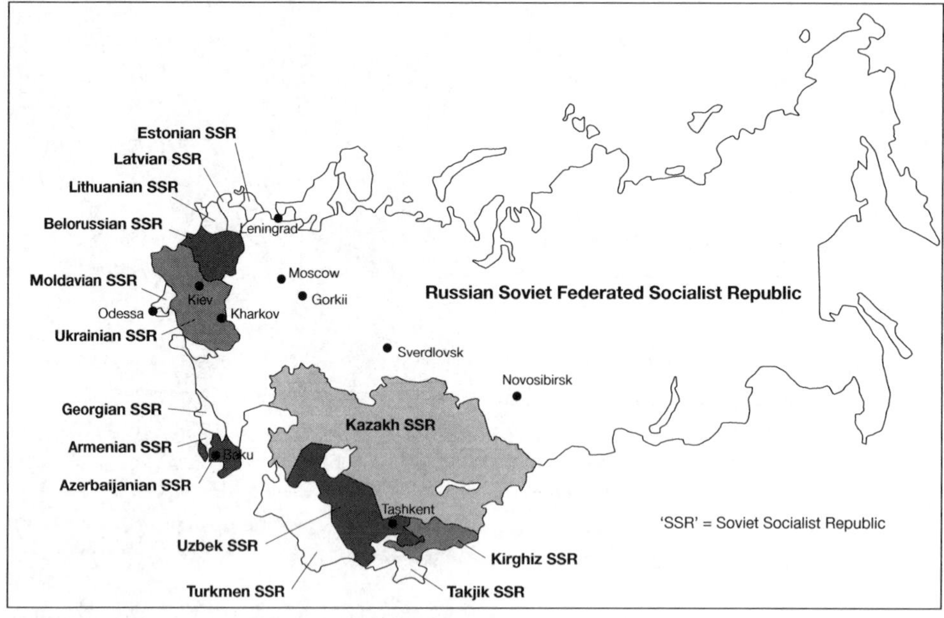

Map 3 The Soviet Union in the later phase of Stalin's rule

and students in the West have seen an automatic connection between method and result. Stalin, it has been assumed, was both ruthless in his pursuit of power and efficient in his use of it, with the first point leading directly to the second. Ruthlessness and efficiency combined to create a form of totalitarianism which was more complete than that of Nazi Germany. Stalin was fully in control of internal developments. He created an industrial infrastructure through an effective planning system; he cut down possible opposition by directly instigating purges; he changed the people's cultural and social perceptions; and he pursued a foreign policy which, with occasional changes in tactics, had an overall strategy.

Because of these developments, and despite the suffering inflicted, the Soviet Union was able to inflict defeat on Nazi Germany. This followed a disastrous initial response, in which Stalin completely misinterpreted Hitler's intentions. But Stalin's subsequent recovery interacted with the long-term economic and military preparation, and with the centralization already instilled, to overcome the much more limited military and economic base of Nazi Germany. Victory also strengthened Stalin's position after 1945. He restored the power and the planning system which he had employed during the 1930s and ensured compliance through a new set of purges. He also spread Soviet influence across eastern Europe and set the pace in the development of the Cold War. In all respects, this was the period of 'mature dictatorship'.

Almost all parts of this chapter on Russia have put forward a different approach, one which has gained ground rapidly since 1991. By this interpretation, Stalin's regime was ruthless but not, as a direct consequence, efficient. Totalitarianism was fundamentally flawed: this was especially apparent during the 1930s and in domestic policy. As we have seen, Stalin sought to centralize a political and economic system which kept falling to local initiatives. As a result, central correctives had to be applied, which meant that Stalin's policies were as much reactive as they were planned. Similarly, his foreign policy had to be put on to corrected courses, partly because of earlier errors of judgement and partly because of circumstances beyond his control. The war with Germany initially paralysed the whole system. The economic planning of the 1930s had been geared to mobilizing Russia for an offensive campaign, whereas Stalin's inappropriate diplomacy necessitated a defensive response which could not immediately be delivered. Major changes were, however, introduced to transform the situation. Soviet production was made more efficient, paradoxically, by partially demobilizing the economic structure to enhance military mobilization. The Soviet Union defeated Germany because it was able to transcend the limits of Stalinism from the 1930s.

After 1945, however, Stalin's position was vulnerable to the very forces which had been responsible for military victory. He therefore had to reinstitute the sort of control which had existed during the 1930s but which had been relaxed during the war. But this was an expression of insecurity rather than 'mature dictatorship'. There was also an element of desperation about Soviet expansion in Europe. In part, it was a response to circumstances, in part a means of justifying internal policies, a rerun of the interaction between foreign and domestic policy during the early 1930s. As had always been the case, ruthlessness did not necessarily engender efficiency; as often as not, it was itself a reaction to inefficiency. As a system, Stalinist totalitarianism tended to use up more than it created.

Was Stalin necessary?

The most recent verdict on Stalin is therefore largely unfavourable. This was not, however, always the case.

Among Western writers, the most ardent defender of Stalin was Ian Grey, who deliberately set out to redress what he considered a long-standing bias against Stalin. Many historians, he argued, have been influenced by Trotsky's vilification of Stalin. In reality, Stalin may have had defects, but he also possessed a 'great and highly disciplined intelligence' together with 'single-mindedness' and 'implacable will'. He was totally dedicated to 'the two causes of Russia and Marxism–Leninism', in the service of which 'no sacrifice was too great'. His ruthless measures were therefore applied for a higher objective. Throughout the purges Stalin 'showed an extraordinary self-control and did not lose sight of his purpose'. In the last analysis, Stalin could claim that 'Soviet Russia had become stronger as a result of his grandiose campaigns of industrialization, collectivization and social transformation.'[178]

Before 1991 most Western historians followed a more ambivalent approach. Their argument was that Stalin constructed the most brutal dictatorship and used appalling methods, but his achievement was considerable. His industrialization drive, in particular, made possible eventual victory against fascism and the subsequent development of the Soviet Union into one of the two superpowers. McCauley argued:

> One may dismiss Stalin as a tyrant, as an evil man whom the USSR could have done without. On the other hand, it is possible to argue that he rendered the Soviet people a service which may eventually be seen as his greatest achievement. It is quite probable that had the USSR not gone through the forced industrialisation of the 1930s she would have succumbed to the German onslaught of 1941.[179]

E.H. Carr believed that Stalin was necessary, in that he was 'an agent of history', produced by the circumstances following the Bolshevik Revolution. If Stalin had not set in motion the process of industrialization, someone else would have done. In this respect, Stalin was 'the great executor of revolutionary policy'. He was, however, a man of opposites. He combined immense achievements with utter brutality: he was, in Carr's words 'an emancipator and a tyrant'.

The main dissenting voice against this line was Ulam, who chose to lay much more stress on Stalin's deficiencies, believing that Russia would have been much better off without him. He refuted the argument that Stalin's industrialization programme dragged Russia into the twentieth century; on the contrary, much faster progress would have been made by an alternative regime – possibly even by Tsarist Russia. It is also inappropriate to argue that Stalin paved the way for victory in the Second World War; if anything, he impeded it by his earlier liquidation of vast numbers of people who would have been useful to the war effort.

This approach anticipated the most recent analysis which has emerged since the collapse of the Soviet Union at the end of 1991. Previous views that Stalin was necessary were based on the assumption that he developed and controlled a system which worked; disagreement focused on the cost of this system. Revisionist historians have, however, shown that the system did not necessarily work and that Stalin was not always in control. Perhaps the most telling argument is that the Soviet Union was able to defeat Nazi Germany only by dismantling the planning system which had been developed during the 1930s – the very system which has always been considered to have been Stalin's main contribution to the victory over Nazism. If this argument is true, then the whole essence of Stalin's achievement is undermined. It is possible to pursue the argument further. Stalin's Five-Year Plans were based on the premise of a future offensive by the Soviet Union. This conditioned Stalin's diplomacy and delivered up to Hitler the opportunity for a surprise attack in 1941. Stalin's system would have collapsed but for the dismantling of that system and the reversion to a more traditional form of warfare.

Such an argument would make Stalin redundant in the history of Soviet survival, let alone that of Soviet development. Yet the answer is not that simple. The question which must also be considered is whether the Soviet Union could have produced sufficient war *matériel* as a result of the dismantling of the Five-Year Plans if the Five-Year Plans had never existed in the first place. In other words, it is possible to criticize Stalin's methods while acknowledging that he had a vital role to play in preparing the Soviet Union for war. The result may have been the wrong war but at least the infrastructure was there. It may have been the wrong infrastructure for the particular war, but the infrastructure could be modified to bring about a different type of war. In other words, Stalin's system was unpicked by him in the face of emergency to produce a new and less dogmatic method, which helped produce victory. This appears not only to vindicate Stalin, but to make him crucial for the very survival of the Soviet Union.

Until, that is, we consider the impact of Stalinism on the future. We now have the advantage of a longer perspective. Previously the ultimate criterion for success or failure was victory or defeat in the Second World War: this was bound eventually to vindicate Stalin. But we are now aware of the ultimate paradox of Soviet history: that the regime which survived Hitler died of old age in 1991. This, too, was Stalin's legacy.

It used to be thought that Stalin's victory in the war had created a hardened system which was fully in control of a totalitarian dictatorship within and which pursued the Cold War outside. Stalin was predominant: small wonder that he should have been criticized by his successor, Khrushchev, who felt that he was in the shadow of Stalin's monolith. The destalinization campaign which was launched in 1956 was therefore an attempt to escape from the shadow and restore the light of Lenin's legitimate succession. The problem was that Stalinism kept reappearing as the forceful strand of Soviet development. When Khrushchev was overthrown in 1964, for the failures of agricultural reforms and for his action in the Cuban Missile Crisis, Stalinism made a partial return in the policies of Brezhnev; from 1964 and 1981, the Soviet Union re-established its military and nuclear credibility. Between 1985 and 1991 Gorbachev sought to end the Cold War and reorganize the Soviet economy, only to face attempted overthrow by neo-Stalinists under Yaneyev. The post-Soviet regime of Yeltsin also experienced opposition from groups nostalgic for the Stalinist past – and the association which it still enjoyed with power and efficiency.

There is now an altogether different perspective. Stalin reached his peak during the war *despite* his system. When he attempted to restore his system after the war, he fell into a decline which led to a crumbling of his regime. Stalin was not a posthumous threat to Khrushchev because of his strength, but because of his weakness. And that weakness was the way in which Stalin had personally distorted the communist system, which had somehow survived in spite of him. Khrushchev therefore removed Stalin from history not to destroy an entrenched system but to clear away its wreckage. Perhaps Khrushchev was the first to realize that the Soviet Union had survived *despite* Stalinism, not *because of* it. As events turned out, the negative legacy of Stalinism proved stronger than the positive. Khrushchev fell in 1964 at least partly because of his experiments to rehabilitate agriculture. Brezhnev and Kosygin failed on the same ground, while Gorbachev failed in his efforts to Westernize the economy through perestroika largely because of the inflexibility of the Stalinist system. The ultimate failure of Stalin, therefore, was to create a system which could not survive in peace as well as it had done in war.

Chapter 4

Dictatorship in Italy

Italy was the first of the major European states to seek salvation in the policies of the radical right, and Mussolini was the first of a succession of fascist dictators. Yet there has always been a puzzling element about Mussolini's rule. Although his influence was profound, he is often derided as a buffoon. In 1919, for example, the socialist Giacinto Serrati described him as 'a rabbit; a phenomenal rabbit; he roars. Observers who do not know him mistake him for a lion.'[1] In 1961, A.J.P. Taylor called him 'a vain, blundering boaster without either ideas or aims'.[2] 'Fascism', he added, 'was a façade. There was nothing behind it but show and empty rhetoric.'[3] There have also been references to Mussolini as a 'sawdust Caesar'.

With views like this it has often been difficult to take Mussolini and Italian Fascism seriously. Yet this is precisely what we have to do if we are to avoid trivializing a topic which has as much historical significance as Stalin's Russia or Hitler's Germany. The key to understanding the Italian dictatorship is not to assume that it was simple but, rather, to accept that it was complex. By avoiding the simplistic, recent analyses have provided plenty of lines which can be pursued. This chapter aims to look at some of them.

THE RISE OF MUSSOLINI TO 1922: AN OUTLINE

From the beginning of his stormy career in journalism and politics until he became Prime Minister in 1922, Mussolini underwent a series of major shifts in the direction of his beliefs and tactics.

His original radicalism was of the left, not of the right. He leaned towards revolutionary socialism, thought in terms of class struggle and uncompromisingly condemned nationalism and imperialism, particularly Italy's conquest of Tripoli in 1912. He was a member of the PSI (Italian Socialist Party) and in 1912 was appointed editor of the newspaper *Avanti* by the party's militants. Through *Avanti* he aimed to promote popular revolutionary fervour, while at the same time attempting to enter Italian politics legally; he failed, however, to win a parliamentary seat in the 1913 elections. Throughout 1914 he devoted his energies to putting the case against Italian involvement in the First World War.

Then occurred the first of Mussolini's changes. By 1915 he was pressing openly for Italy to join the fighting; clearly his ideological views were built on shifting sands. He was promptly deprived of his editorship of *Avanti* and was expelled from the PSI. He succeeded, however, in acquiring his own paper, *Il Popolo d'Italia*, in which he wedded war with revolutionary fervour, using slogans like 'Who has steel has bread' and 'Revolution is an idea which has found bayonets'. His own personal contribution to the Italian war effort was a spell of loyal but undistinguished military service, ended in 1917 by wounds received after a grenade exploded in his trench.

In March 1919 Mussolini presided over a meeting in Milan which gave birth to the Fascio di Combattimento. The Fasci soon spread to some seventy other cities and towns, where they established themselves as local political movements with local programmes. At the national level, the Fascio di Combattimento identified as its enemies a surprisingly large number of groups: organized labour (especially the trade unions and the PSI), capitalism and big business, the monarchy and even the Church. Not surprisingly, the Fascists failed to win a single parliamentary seat in the 1919 elections, and the Socialists mocked Mussolini by burying an effigy of Fascism in Milan.

These developments induced Mussolini to undergo, in 1921, a second change. This time he was prepared to abandon his revolutionary inclination and prepare fascism for a parliamentary struggle. Hence, he set up a political party (the PNF or Partito Nazionale Fascista) and appealed to as wide a cross-section of society as he could by targeting the enemies to socialism and the threat of red revolution. This strategy was more successful, and in 1921 the Fascist Party won thirty-five parliamentary seats.

But broadening the appeal and abandoning open revolution did not mean less violence. On the contrary, black-shirted Fascist squads launched numerous attacks on the left. They were given their opportunity by a wave of strikes organized in the cities by the trade unions and the PSI, as well as by action taken in rural areas by peasant leagues against landowners. Throughout 1920 and 1921 militant workers and peasants were intimidated into submission, through beatings and being forced to consume castor oil and live toads. All over Italy Fascist activities were directed by local leaders (or *ras*). One of the most successful of these was Balbo, who captured Ferrara and much of Romagna from the Socialists in May 1922. The Socialists responded in August with an appeal for a general strike as a protest against Fascist violence, but this played further into Mussolini's hands. It took the Fascists only one day to smash the threat and thus to emerge as the main safeguard against industrial disruption.

Meanwhile, the post-war Italian governments had become increasingly unstable and unpopular. A succession of prime ministers sought to contain what they saw as a threat from the left and, in the process, came to depend on the parliamentary support of the Fascist Party. Even so, Mussolini had nowhere near sufficient electoral backing to establish an alternative government; the best he could reasonably have expected was an invitation to play a minor role in Prime Minister Facta's cabinet. Yet 1922 saw a spectacular political development: the replacement of Facta by Mussolini.

This occurred as the result of a threat of force from Mussolini and a reaction of near panic from the government. On his way to the Fascist Party Congress in Naples in October 1922, Mussolini stopped off in Rome to demand at least five cabinet ministries. In Naples he made preparations for a Fascist march on Rome to seize power if his conditions were not met. Facta urged King Victor Emmanuel III to declare martial law so that the threat could be countered by force. The King refused and, mindful of the Fascist contingents gathering outside Rome, invited Mussolini to join a coalition government. Sensing the possibility of total capitulation, Mussolini declined. On 29 October Mussolini, then in Milan, received a request from the King to form his own government. This was followed shortly afterwards by the much heralded March on Rome as Mussolini, now Prime Minister, paraded his henchmen through the streets and announced the beginning of a new era.

THE RISE OF MUSSOLINI TO 1922: AN EXPLANATION

Four reasons can be given for Mussolini's success by the end of 1922. First, Italy itself had undergone a prolonged crisis before 1914, and again more acutely from 1919, in which conventional political and economic solutions no longer worked. Second, during the same period, a new ideology had grown out of this crisis, providing Mussolini with an alternative route to power. Third, this new movement attracted the support of a cross-section of a society thoroughly disillusioned with the existing establishment. And fourth, Mussolini's leadership and strategy gave to this movement a versatility and vitality which contrasted all too obviously with a tired and dull government.

Underlying instability, 1861–1922

Italy had been united as a liberal parliamentary regime but, in the era between Cavour and Mussolini, lacked political stability. There was a rapid succession of ministries: twenty-two between 1860 and 1900 (an average of 1.8 years each), nine between 1900 and 1914 (1.6 years each) and seven between 1914 and 1922 (1.1 years each). At first, parties were not clearly defined and government depended on a consensus reached between the different political groups, a process known as *trasformismo*. Unfortunately, this could be maintained only by the distribution of favours and offices, a corrupt system which kept political power in the hands of the very few.

There were several attempts to achieve political stability before 1914. During a period of political crisis in the 1890s a conservative politician, Crispi, tried to convert the state into a more authoritarian regime, based on that of Bismarck's Germany. Although this failed at the time, the potential was not lost on future politicians. For the moment, however, a more liberal line was followed in the decade before 1914 as Giolitti (Prime Minister 1903–5, 1906–9 and 1911–14) tried to reform the whole process by seeking the co-operation of the Catholic Church and the Socialists, and by introducing near-universal manhood suffrage in 1912. Giolitti's critics, however, argued that his efforts were already in trouble by 1914 and that Italian politics had not been able to adjust to mass participation. These experiences were to be enormously important in the early 1920s. Pollard maintains that 'Fascism was to be the agent of reaction on behalf of the grouping of forces which had been at work in the End of the Century Crisis'.[4] In this respect, the roots of Mussolini's solution to the crisis of Italian constitutionalism can be seen in the 1890s. Giolitti, in the meantime, failed to build up a system to prevent this development: 'It is no exaggeration to say that Giolitti's failure to launch Italy on the path of a representative, mass democracy in the pre-war years helped open the way for Mussolini and Fascism in the post-war period.'[5]

Two contrasting traditions had therefore appeared within the Italian political system. One was the liberal experience of power, which was moderate but also corrupt and uncertain. The other was the authoritarian backlash which seemed to offer something more substantial and secure – if, that is, it could ever be achieved. Clearly a major upheaval was needed to turn prospect into reality.

This was provided by the First World War; in the words of De Grand, it 'marked a rupture in the course of Italian political development'.[6] In effect, it pushed Italy from instability into crisis. The traditional governing groups were split in their attitude to the war. Giolitti remained consistently opposed, while the wartime prime ministers, Salandra, Boselli and Orlando, could neither co-operate with him nor do without him. The result was a paralysis of parliamentary government, which was worsened by Italy's military defeat at the hands of the Austrians at Caporetto in 1917. The regime was reprieved only by the Italian victory in 1918 at Vittorio Veneto against an Austria which was falling to pieces internally. Governments were also under pressure from the threat of economic collapse and social disruption. The total cost of the war was 148,000 million lire, over twice the total expenditure of all Italian governments between 1861 and 1913.[7] The economic base was weakened by huge budget deficits and by unbalanced trade and industrial production. It has been estimated that, by 1919, exports covered only 36 per cent of Italy's imports. Furthermore, the growth of industrial production between 1915 and 1918 had been geared so directly to the war effort that it could not be maintained by the requirements of the post-war home market. Unemployment soared, with demobilization mainly responsible for the total of two million unemployed by the end of 1919. Inflation had also become a fact of life, with the cost of living in 1919 about four times that of 1913.

With this gloomy economic background, it appeared that Italy had emerged from the war with all the potential for violent confrontation. On the one hand, the urban and rural working classes were desperate to prevent any further decline in their standard of living. On the other, the industrialists and landowners feared that demands for increased wages and employment protection would raise costs and threaten productivity and profits. The situation was further complicated by the impoverishment of a large part of the lower middle class which became radical and assertive, distrusting labour and capital alike. The crucial issue from 1919 was whether the post-war governments could salvage the liberal approach and pull these conflicting forces back together for the collective national good.

Giolitti, Prime Minister between June 1920 and July 1921, made some attempt but found that all hope of consensus politics had now been dashed. The Socialist Party (PSI) and the majority of the unions were militant in their demands, the lower middle classes were no longer dependable as moderate voters, and the whole political scene was further complicated by the emergence of the Italian Popular Party (PPI), a large Catholic grouping. The only real hope for stability was a coalition which included Italy's two largest parties, the Socialists and the PPI. However, the gap between them was unbridgeable. Giolitti and his successors, Bonomi (1921–2) and Facta (1922), therefore, operated in a political vacuum. Increasingly, they came to depend on the Fascists – but in a way which was underhand, unparliamentary and ultimately suicidal. Unable to resolve the growing crisis between labour and capital, and ever conscious of the threat of revolution, the governments tacitly allowed the Fascists to take direct and often brutal action against unions and peasant leagues. This was the last resort of a government which seemed to have lost the will to govern.

Even so, the crisis of liberal government does not fully explain the ease with which the handover was made to Mussolini and authoritarianism in 1922. After all, Mussolini was appointed Prime Minister with a parliamentary base of only 35 seats out of 535. The reason seems to be that 1922 was a low point in government stability, with both the Prime Minister and the King contemplating disaster. Facta was in a caretaker role and was clearly hoping that Giolitti would be able to resume power. His immediate concern was to try to prevent Mussolini from pre-empting this changeover, which is why he was prepared to confront him with the threat of martial law. The King, however, had different concerns. In the event of a confrontation between the Fascists and the army, the latter might desert or there could be a civil war. In either event, he could well be forced to abdicate. To him, therefore, Mussolini seemed a safer alternative to Giolitti.

There is one final point. The fact that Mussolini had only 7 per cent of the seats in parliament did not matter too much. Such a proportion was not unprecedented, as a number of previous governments had been built on similarly insubstantial foundations. The assumption was that a coalition would be quickly added around the core – perhaps the usual combination of Liberals and Popolari. Only this time, the core would prove stronger because it was more authoritarian. Perhaps this is what the King had in mind: giving more energy to a failing liberal system while restraining the authoritarian alternative.

Or perhaps there was no such calculation and Mussolini and the Fascist movement were simply the beneficiaries of collective government indecision. Either way, the influence of both Mussolini and Fascism must have increased phenomenally over a short period for such decisions to have been made.

The emergence of a Fascist movement

Fascism did not, as is sometimes suggested, spontaneously ignite in post-war Italy. It had a longer history than that and the ingredients which made it so combustible had been a long time in the mixing. Nor was Fascism simply a superficial set of slogans designed to give an appearance of an ideology to the personal pretensions of Mussolini. Instead, Fascism and Mussolini were separate identities, although they came together in a symbiotic relationship. Fascism was a magnet for widely divergent views and ideas, taking followers from all other parts of the political spectrum. Normally the far left and the far right are seen as the two poles on the political spectrum, separated from each other by all the other political positions. Fascism was uniquely the result of what happened when the far left and far right came together, in the process bypassing the more moderate sectors. This shortcut enabled it to attract a far wider range of support than any of Italy's more traditional political parties.

Mussolini himself started on the far left. His early beliefs were influenced by a combination of Marxism and syndicalism, the latter inspired by the French revolutionary theorist Sorel. At he same time, he was able to become a full member of the more conventional Socialist Party (PSI), thus merging three separate strands of the left. Among the more genuine syndicalists was Rossoni, with whom Mussolini joined, along with radical Italian Republicans, in promoting the pro-war cause in 1914, in the process leaving the PSI. Already he and others from the far left were moving towards co-operation with the right.

Meanwhile an alternative and more radical right had also been emerging in Italy. Gabriele D'Annunzio reflected the widespread disappointment in the way Italy had been united: the process seemed incomplete, lacking in poetry and action. Hence the far right had strongly theatrical inclinations. It was also all too aware that Italian aspirations were not being taken seriously in Europe. Other activists included Marinetti (who, as a Futurist, emphasized the importance of power and the application of modern technology to war), Corradini, a strong critic of 'ignoble socialism', Federzoni and Rocco. In 1910 they established the Italian National Organization, which called for an authoritarian regime and a power cult connected with ancient Rome. This was of future importance in establishing contacts with the conservative power base, especially business and the Church.

So far there may not appear much in common between the two extremes. But by 1914 they had come to share a strong antipathy to the liberal regime in Italy and to the main alternative – socialism. From that stage onwards the dissident left and right began to collaborate. The catalyst was the involvement of Italy in the First World War. Nationalist and Syndicalist squads actively campaigned in favour of Italy joining the war, calling themselves Revolutionary Action Groups (Fasci di Azione Rivoluzionaria). Mussolini, now converted to the idea of Italian intervention, resigned from *Avanti* and founded *Il Popolo d'Italia*. He therefore allied with the far right, although he retained his attachment to some of the key ideas of the left. D'Annunzio was also strongly in favour of Italian participation in the war. He focused on the prospects of empire and imperialism, while at the same time meeting the syndicalism of the left as a means of achieving a more radical economic organization.

If the war brought co-operation between left and right, the peace which followed helped turn this into convergence. Italy emerged disillusioned and heavily indebted to the Allies. Political instability worsened and in the ensuing chaos the two strands now intertwined to produce the characteristic components of Fascism. Mussolini concentrated on organization, instituting the Fascio di Combattimento for activists of the far left. When this failed to develop properly he turned to a second wave of organization at a local level in the form of the *ras*, before finally opting for the level of a political party. By this time, Mussolini had adapted his syndicalist origins to the realities of the Italian political situation. Meanwhile, D'Annunzio was adding the theatrical elements to Fascism. His involvement in the Fiume escapade immediately after the war produced the uniforms, slogans and rituals which were soon to become an integral part of Fascism. Those who returned from Fiume also became prominent in the *ras* squads. The realignment which was Fascism was completed by the fusion of the Nationalist Association with the Fascist Party in 1923. This meant a major shift of fascism to the right and the strengthening of the links with the Italian establishment.

Two historical debates have arisen from these developments. The first concerns the *roots* of Italian Fascism. Sternhell argues that the left–right convergence occurred first in France, with the convergence of Sorelian syndicalism and the ultra-nationalism of Maurras. This convergence was transmitted to Italy along the same two channels, in effect making France the seedbed of Fascism. In both France and Italy, Fascism originated from the rejection of the tradition of the Enlightenment.[8] Critics of this approach question the extent to which France could have provided such a continuous influence, as well as the neatness of the syndicalist–nationalist synthesis. The process was messier and involved a great deal of pulling and tugging between different Italian-based factions (see Roberts). A similar case could be made against Gregor's view that Fascism was already a coherent and fully-formed ideology by the time that Mussolini had taken power, with all its strands in place. Instead, according to Roberts, Mussolini had to 'balance personnel and innovations in order to foster a façade of consensus'.[9]

Yet for all the positioning and repositioning of the various pieces, one thing remains clear. What became Fascism had an extraordinary magnetism for groups as widely divergent as revolutionary syndicalists, futurists, revolutionary republicans and ultra-nationalists. It was able to absorb them and, in the process, create its own left–right polarity. The process did not make for long-term stability but it was of vital importance to gain support for Mussolini's rise to power, with which we are concerned at the moment. The next question which needs to be answered is: why did Fascism increase in popularity during the crucial years of Italy's political instability?

Support for Fascism

The emblem eventually adopted for the Fascist Party was the fasces, a bundle of rods with a protruding axe-head, carried by magistrates in ancient Rome. These rods came to symbolize the various groups supporting Fascism, individually weak but deriving a collective strength from being bound together. Certainly Fascism appealed to a wide cross-section of society at a time when the prevailing atmosphere was one of political instability and economic insecurity. To many people, Fascism offered an alternative to a narrowly based and discredited government on the one hand and, on the other, the upheaval of a socialist revolution.

The original support for Fascism came from war veterans – young, aggressive and, according to Gregor, 'irretrievably lost to organized socialism and ill-disposed toward the commonplaces of the traditional parties'.[10] Most of them were fiercely patriotic; they denounced the mutilated peace of the Paris Settlement and their ardour was fired by the occupation of Fiume in 1919–20 by D'Annunzio. The Italian army was generally sympathetic towards the Fascists, although two attitudes tended to prevail: the lower levels participated enthusiastically in Fascist rallies and diverted a considerable amount of military equipment and arms, while the officer corps tried to keep discipline within the army without actually attacking Fascism. On the civilian scene, the *carabinieri* which, as the constabulary, was the main force of law and order, openly sympathized with Fascism and stood aside when attacks were directed at trade unionists.

The backbone of Fascism has long been considered to have been the lower middle class, especially small shopkeepers, artisans and clerical workers.[11] This normally moderate sector of society had been destabilized by the process of industrialization and by the economic difficulties caused by the war. They were the casualties of changes occurring all over central Europe, and the sociologist Seymour Lipset has called them the 'displaced masses'. They were caught between the rival forces of labour and capital and spurned the solutions of the socialist left, for these would involve a further depression of their status and their being levelled down into the working class. Hence, in De Grand's words, they saw the Fascist movement as 'the long sought instrument of bourgeois resurgence',[12] since it promised an end to industrial disruption and revolutionary socialism on the one hand while, on the other, it seemed ready to curb the power of big business. De Felice goes even further: for him, 'Fascism as a movement was the idealisation, the desire of an emerging middle class.'[13]

In terms of its sheer influence, however, the agrarian sector has until recently been underestimated. At first most of the support came from the landlords and estate owners. Their contacts with Fascism emerged from fear of the left. In the 1920 elections the PSI won control over many of the cities, including Milan and Bologna, along with twenty-five provincial councils and 2,200 district councils. In these circumstances the traditional ruling elites lost their predominance. At the same time they were also facing pressures from the labour markets and the peasant leagues. This meant that the traditional groups were greatly assisted by the Fascist attacks on peasant strikers. During the first half of 1921 Fascist squads destroyed 119 labour chambers, 107 co-operatives and 83 peasant league offices.

Yet there is evidence that even more substantial numbers of the peasantry were won over. These were mainly the smaller-scale peasant proprietors who were alienated by the undertaking of the PSI to collectivize the land. Some 500,000 people had managed to acquire ownership of land since 1918 and, even if the amount was meagre, they were determined not to lose it to socialism. There was therefore an active preference for the later Fascist policy of small land grants given to individual cultivators rather than the socialist alternatives.[14] Thus Fascism appealed to the cravings of two separate sectors of the landed interest. The fact that these two sectors opposed each other was one example of the inherent contradiction within Fascist support. Mussolini was even surprised by the extent of peasant support, as he had originally seen Fascism as an urban phenomenon.[15] The rural situation is highly complex and is an area where further research is particularly needed.

Industry produced the most dramatic class rupture in post-war Italy and it is scarcely surprising that the great industrialists should have backed Fascism. Because Mussolini's followers battered the unions into submission, the industrialists were willing to provide large donations; two examples were Alberto Pirelli, the tyre magnate, and Giovanni Agnelli of Fiat. Then, during the course of 1921, a number of workers joined the Fascist movement. The main reason for this was the growing crisis of socialism. The PSI split in 1921 and a separate Communist Party was established under the influence of Gramsci. The organization of the socialist movement became even more decentralized and provincial, which meant that the attacks of the Fascists rarely met co-ordinated resistance. Those workers who defected from what they saw as a sinking ship were also attracted by the emergence of alternatives to the unions – the Fascist syndicates.

Finally, there were sectors who assisted Fascism indirectly: although they could not bring themselves to support Fascism openly they were at least prepared to tolerate it in a way which would have been out of the question with, for example, socialism. One of these groups was the political establishment, whose attitude has already been examined. Another was the aristocratic class, who were appeased by Mussolini's willingness to end his attacks on the monarchy: he said in Udine in September 1922, 'Now I really believe that the regime can be profoundly altered without touching the monarchy . . . Therefore, we shall not make the monarchy part of our campaign.'[16] The Queen Mother, Margherita, and the King's cousin, the Duke of Aosta, rapidly became admirers of Fascism. A third sector was the Catholic Church. This was won over by the moderation in Mussolini's stance by June 1921, when he was asserting in parliament: 'Fascism neither practises nor preaches anti-clericalism.'[17] The Church also took its cue from Pope Pius XI who, from the time of his election in 1922, remained on good terms with Mussolini. The Church undoubtedly considered a communist revolution to be the main threat. Mussolini, by contrast, had abandoned atheism and had come to accept that 'the Latin and Imperial traditions of Rome are today represented by Catholicism'.[18]

The role of Mussolini himself

A distinction has already been drawn between Italian Fascism and Mussolini. The former possessed considerable independent momentum, as was shown by the widespread local support gained in 1920 and 1921. But Fascism was also diffuse and incoherent, likely to dissipate unless given a national structure and identity. This is what Mussolini provided.

His first contribution to Fascism was its organization. It is true that he had an enormous struggle to achieve any sort of centralization in 1921 and that local activism would continue, undisciplined, for several years to come. He did, however, give Fascism its vital foothold in parliament, and the PFI gained respectability and political credibility which transcended purely local interests. He was also able to establish links between local activist groups, so that Fascism could claim to be a national movement as well as a national party. In the process, he provided a much needed synthesis between different parts. Augusto De Marsanich observed in 1922 that the party was often 'revealed as a mosaic' and that in such circumstances 'only the intellect and will of Mussolini can still control and direct us.'[19]

Second, Mussolini showed the importance of opportunism and action rather than a fixed ideology. Admittedly, he sometimes hesitated: Balbo, for example, is supposed to have prodded him into action over the March on Rome by telling him: 'We are going, either with you or without you. Make up your mind.'[20] He was also strongly inclined to intuitive behaviour and he lacked a policy or a programme. He did, however, succeed in projecting himself as a flexible pragmatist and he managed to cover up any erratic or inconsistent views. He once explained: 'Only maniacs never change. New facts can call for new positions.'[21] He claimed that his was a doctrine of action, and he saw his strength as having neither an overall system nor, after 1919, an ideological straitjacket. This pragmatism enabled him to make full use of the chaotic conditions in post-war Italy. He could use the largely spontaneous Fascist campaigns of pressure and violence in order to satisfy the popular craving for positive action; at the same time, he could pretend that Fascism was moderate in parliament, so winning the grudging approval of the government.

This brings us to Mussolini's personal leadership. His career has been presented as one of bluster and bluff – in huge proportions. But then the early 1920s were a period in which outrageous bluff had a better than usual chance of success. Mussolini applied all his journalistic skills and tricks to attract popular attention and support. He also learned, from D'Annunzio during the Fiume escapade, how to create a sense of power among his followers, even incorporating into the Fascist movement the war-cry of the Arditi: 'Ayah, ayah, alala!'. His personal attributes, according to Hibbert, included 'a physical stance not yet devitalised by illness, a style of oratory, staccato, tautophonic and responsive, not yet ridiculed by caricature and a personal charm not yet atrophied by adulation'.[22] With this presence, he was able to act his way into power.

For this is what happened. He played upon the post-war crisis, making it appear that Fascism really did have the strength to smash socialism and remould society, and that it could disrupt the functioning of parliamentary politics. No chances were taken by the politicians, and Mussolini was given more respect than his strength perhaps deserved; this would explain the capitulation of Facta and Victor Emmanuel when they were put under threat in October 1922. The counterpart to Mussolini, the destroyer, was the constructive statesman who, alone, could reconcile, rally and unite; under his leadership 'Fascism would draw its sword to cut the many Gordian Knots which enmesh and strangle Italian life.'[23] This personification of power had inherent dangers as, eventually, the bluff turned inwards and, as Mack Smith argues, Mussolini fell victim to his own delusions.[24]

MUSSOLINI'S DICTATORSHIP, 1922–43

Between 1922 and 1943 Mussolini established, at least in theory, all the institutions and devices associated with the totalitarian state. The foundation was the Fascist ideology, upon which was set a one-party system and all the paraphernalia of the personality cult. Popular support was guaranteed by indoctrination and, where necessary, coercion, while the economy was brought under a corporative system and geared to the needs of war. This section will examine the attempts to develop a dictatorship, the extent to which these actually changed Italy, and whether they worked in practice. Below the surface there are indications that the totalitarian state was extremely precarious. Fascist ideology was a makeshift alliance of different interests, the political institutions retained a surprisingly large number of non-Fascist influences, and the processes of indoctrination, coercion and corporativism were never completed. Above all, foreign policy eventually destabilized the whole system.

The stages in Mussolini's dictatorship

Although the individual components of Mussolini's dictatorship are complex, there is a discernible chronological trend to which they all at least partly relate.

The period between October 1922 and January 1925 saw Mussolini coming to terms with his appointment as Prime Minister and his attempts to make that power more substantial and permanent without, however, making radical changes based on ideology. Then, between 1925 and 1929, he aimed more consciously to step up the process of creating a Fascist regime, in the process using the term 'totalitarian' for the first time at the annual congress of the PNF in June 1925. A degree of stability seemed to have been achieved by 1930, in both domestic and foreign policies.

This was, however, subsequently threatened by the economic pressures of the Great Depression. During the early 1930s, therefore, Mussolini moved more definitely towards a

4 Benito Mussolini, photo taken in 1923 (© Hulton Archive/Getty)

concept of the 'corporate state' and tried to integrate the various forms of totalitarian control. The problem was that the regime needed a more obvious appearance of success. Mussolini sought this in a more active foreign policy, which involved his dictatorship in a series of wars. This meant another round of radical changes in the late 1930s; these were the result partly of domestic pressures and partly of influences from Nazi Germany. The result was, in Morgan's words, that 'Between 1936 and 1940 the regime consciously stepped up and intensified its attempts to "fascistise" Italian society.'[25] This broke the earlier balance and consensus within Italy and meant the intensification of repression on the one hand and of opposition on the other.

Meanwhile, Italy's economic infrastructure, seriously weakened between 1936 and 1939 by constant exposure to war, was tested to the point of collapse by Mussolini's disastrous decision to enter the Second World War. Although Mussolini attempted between 1943 and 1945 to recreate something of the original dynamism of Fascism, by this time he had become no more than a Nazi puppet within a small part of northern Italy.

The ideology of Fascism

In 1932 Mussolini penned the basic ideas of the movement, clearly and emphatically, in his *Political and Social Doctrine of Fascism*. Fascism, he said, was anti-communist, anti-socialist and strongly opposed to an economic conception of history. He denied that class war can be the preponderant force in the transformation of society. Fascism was also anti-democratic, denouncing the whole complex system of democratic ideology. It was certainly authoritarian: 'The foundation of Fascism is the conception of the State. Fascism conceives of the State as an absolute.' Finally, it promoted territorial expansion as an 'essential manifestation of vitality'.[26]

On the negative side, this definition was a hotchpotch of the ideas of conflicting sub-movements and sub-ideologies, of which De Grand has identified no fewer than five.[27] The first was national syndicalism which, in its emphasis on creating syndicates of workers and managers, was initially republican, anticlerical and vaguely socialistic. The second was rural fascism, which was anti-urban, anti-modern and anti-industrial. The third was technocratic fascism; because it accepted industrialization, and all the implications of modernization, it differed markedly from rural fascism. The fourth was conservative fascism; with its industrial, agrarian, monarchist and Catholic connections, it was basically traditional, pragmatic and non-ideological. The fifth was nationalist fascism, perhaps the most coherent version with an emphasis on an aggressive foreign policy and an authoritarian political system. In addition to this five-way division between the strategies of these groups, there were other gaps. National syndicalism and technocratic fascism were both radical. They regarded themselves as the logical outcome of western Europe's revolutionary heritage, although they restored the emphasis on order and social harmony rather than individualism and liberal democracy. By contrast, conservative and nationalist fascism rejected Europe's revolutionary tradition altogether; their purpose was not to rationalize the French Revolution but to do away with it. This wide range of attitudes may originally have helped Fascism to gain popular support but, once the Fascist regime had been established, it proved a source of weakness. The Fascist state lacked the sort of monolithic base which Stalin's version of Marxism–Leninism gave to the Soviet Union.

Fascism was therefore an eclectic ideology, or one in which diverse components were loosely stuck together. This was perceived even at the time. De Marsanich observed in 1922 that 'our party is revealed as a mosaic' and that there was 'a multiplicity of interpretations made by Fascists themselves so that each individual believes in his own type of Fascism'.[28] This was partly because of the different strands which contributed to the emergence of the ideology. We have already seen the broad convergence of the radical right and radical left. Within this framework came the more specific views of a number of individuals bringing with them the wreckage of their previous attachments. Hence, radicals of the left included Arpinati, an anarchist, and Bianchi and Rossoni, both revolutionary anarchists. To the right flocked radicals influenced by D'Annunzio, followed by Catholics, conservatives and monarchists. Mussolini was always conscious that Fascism had never been able to develop the sort of synthesis normally attributed to Marxism–Leninism. He gave reasons for this in 1932, as an introduction to the attempts to define Fascism: 'The years which preceded the March on Rome were ones in which the overriding need for action did not allow us the possibility of profound philosophical enquiries or complete doctrinal elaborations.'[29]

From these puzzling observations we may draw several conclusions. First, because Fascism was so eclectic, support was the most important issue. This meant that the leadership was always influenced by views and developments from below. As a result, the real issue was mobilization of support rather than purity or correctness of belief. But this had further consequences. Mobilization at the expense of ideology meant depoliticization. The contraction of ideology left a gap. This had to be filled by leadership as a pragmatic attraction rather than as an ideological principle. As will be seen, this meant that a tension was to develop between the ideology and the leader who purported to represent it.

Political power and institutions

Mussolini had come to power in extraordinary circumstances. From the end of 1922 he was therefore in charge of an emergency government. In fact, he presided over two coalitions. One was the multi-party cabinet, in which he was now Prime Minister; the other comprised the different strands of the Fascist movement, of which he was the Duce, or Leader. From this not very promising beginning, Mussolini gradually converted a semi-liberal regime to a one-party dictatorship.

The process was complex and often confused. Between 1922 and 1925 Mussolini settled for modifying the constitution to enhance his position in government. Then, following the Matteotti Crisis, Mussolini set up from 1925 onwards a different type of regime, in which two priorities emerged. One was to squeeze any remnants of democracy out of Italy's constitutional system through the advancement of Fascism. But the other was to adapt Fascism to Italy's traditions by wringing much of the radicalism out of the Fascist Party.

The regime therefore developed a dual momentum. In one sense, it has been seen as revolutionary, with an acceleration into the institutions of dictatorship. At the same time, the wilder nature of Fascism was being tamed: its momentum was being slowed to make it more acceptable to Italian traditions. The result of this was political confusion as the processes of change and continuity frequently tripped each other up, so that Mussolini himself became the only figure able to reconcile the contradiction. This explains his enormously enhanced position and the extent of his personality cult.

Initial coexistence with the liberal regime

In 1922 Mussolini headed a cabinet in which there were four Fascists and ten non-Fascists. Since his party had only 7 per cent of the seats in the lower chamber of parliament, Mussolini had, at first, to be cautious and conciliatory. He lulled the other deputies into a sense of security by promising that he would defend, not destroy, the constitution. The former governing parties seemed to have given up completely. Nitti, an ex-Prime Minister, was convinced that 'The Fascist experiment must be carried out without interference: there should be no opposition from our side.'[30] The King, meanwhile, was prepared to grant Mussolini emergency powers for one year. As a result, Mussolini gradually built up his credibility. This was shown when, in 1923, the Fascist Party (PNF) absorbed the Italian Nationalist Association (ANI) and one of the latter's leaders, Federzoni, joined Mussolini's government.

The problem for Mussolini with this early constitutional arrangement was, of course, that he could always be removed. The only thing that could prevent him from suffering the same fate as Orlando or Giolitti was to establish a secure Fascist majority in the chamber. This would then provide opportunities for the establishment of a permanent dictatorship in the future. Mussolini managed to persuade the chamber that his intention was constructive, not revolutionary. In a mood of revulsion against Italy's habit of producing brief and unstable ministries, the chamber passed the Acerbo electoral law in 1923. This stated that the party, or bloc, with a 25 per cent poll would automatically have a two-thirds majority in the parliament and would therefore form the government. The Italian electorate confirmed Mussolini's power in the election of April 1924 by giving the Fascists 4.5 million votes (64 per cent of those who voted) and control over 404 seats. The combined vote for the opposition was about 2.5 million. From this time onwards Mussolini could claim a genuine electoral mandate and therefore pursue more radical policies with fewer inhibitions.

In view of the previous electoral performance of the Fascists, this was a colossal victory. The main reason for this success has been put down to Fascism's 'Big List'. This involved the defection of candidates

5 Benito Mussolini, 1883–1945
(© Popperfoto/Getty)

from other parties – thirteen from the Popolari and eighty from the liberals and conservatives. The support of major candidates like Orlando was especially important. Such defectors were crucial in bringing electoral support which Mussolini would not otherwise have had. In addition, Fascist intimidation had a considerable impact on the election process, putting off much of the potential opposition vote. A divided left was another crucial factor: in 1924 there were three parties, the original PSI, the reformist PSU under Matteotti and the PCI under Gramsci. The working class was still an undecided constituency, but it was not mobilized against Fascism. According to Pollard, 'United, the working-class parties might have robbed Mussolini of his victory.'[31]

The election result was a sensation. Mussolini was jubilant and could afford to disregard the claims of the PSU leader, Matteotti, that the election was invalid because of the extent of Fascist violence and intimidation. He could not, however, ignore what happened next.

The turning-point: the Matteotti Crisis

In June 1924 Matteotti was seized outside his house, bundled into a Lancia and stabbed to death. His body was discovered two months later in a shallow grave on the outskirts of Rome. It soon became evident that the crime had been committed by over-zealous Fascists. The impact of this was enormous: Payne considers it 'the most serious crisis Mussolini would experience before World War II'.[32] The media turned against Mussolini, and many of the recent converts to Fascism now hastened to desert. The murder was seen as a direct blow at the Italian constitution by the Fascist Party, especially since the car was traced back to Mussolini's private office. More significantly, the support built up in the 1924 election now threatened to unravel: Mussolini's two-thirds majority had represented the decision of only one-third of the electorate – and many of their votes had been delivered to the PNF via the defections of the normal recipients of their votes. The Matteotti affair threatened a major revival of the opposition, as Mussolini was criticized by Giolitti, Orlando, Salandra, and others who, for the previous three years, had been either supportive or mute.

Mussolini's recovery, however, was rapid and his subsequent actions illustrate his opportunism. The Socialist deputies withdrew from parliament, as a protest, in what came to be known as the Aventine Secession. Their intention was to show that parliamentary democracy was dead and to force the King to dismiss a discredited government. In fact, this proved to be the wrong strategy. The Aventine Secession undercut the position of Giolitti, who remained within parliament, and allowed Mussolini the opportunity to seize the initiative and defend the integrity of the chamber against pressures from outside. It also gave the King a reason to wait on events rather than to make an immediate decision.

If the crisis was the worst Mussolini faced in peacetime, his recovery from it was certainly the most pronounced. He reshaped his government by removing compromised Fascists such as Finzi and De Bono; he attacked the Socialist deputies for reneging on their parliamentary responsibilities; and he held out an olive branch to the parties which were on the brink of deserting their alliance with Fascism. Probably the most influential speech of his career was made to parliament on 3 January 1925: 'Very well,' he said, 'I now declare before this assembly and before the entire Italian people that I assume, I alone, moral and historical responsibility for all that has happened.' He brought everything, however, within the broad scope of the Fascist movement, losing the specific incident within the general: 'If Fascism has been nothing more than castor oil and the truncheon, instead of being a proud passion of the best part of Italian youth, then I am to blame.'[33] By confessing to everything – and therefore to nothing – Mussolini regained the initiative. He emerged as a statesman prepared to take on burdens rather than as a politician confronted by a crime. The opposition, meanwhile, appeared to have given up. Mussolini proceeded to hammer home his advantage by refusing to allow the Aventine Secessionists to return to their places within the chamber.

The significance of the Matteotti Crisis was enormous: indeed, it is often seen as a turning-point in the development of the Fascist regime. Once Mussolini had recovered his confidence and control, he clearly had to do something more permanent to stabilize the political situation. In a series of measures usually described as a 'second wave', he resorted to a programme which has been seen as both revolutionary and conservative, which broke with the past while retaining some of its traditions.

Political 'revolution'?

From January 1925 onwards, Mussolini accelerated towards the establishment of a dictatorship. This involved the destruction of the Italian liberal state which had been in continuous existence since 1861. It is not surprising that this process is sometimes considered to be a 'Fascist revolution'.

The first component of the 'revolution' was the destruction of parliamentary sovereignty. This meant the swift dismantling of the opposition. The Secessionists were prevented by force from resuming their seats in parliament, while in 1926 other anti-Fascists were told that their electoral mandate was no longer valid. Many of the leaders went into exile, including the Liberal Nitti and the PCI member Togliatti. Gramsci was jailed and died in 1936. The one-party state was formalized in May 1928 by the introduction of a new electoral law; this ensured that all parliamentary candidates would be selected by the Fascist Grand Council from lists submitted by confederations of employers and employees. The final list had to be voted for as a whole by the electorate. In effect, parliamentary elections had been replaced by a plebiscitary dictatorship. The process was completed when, in 1938, the Chamber of Deputies was abolished and replaced by the Chamber of Fasces and Corporations.

A second purpose of the political 'revolution' was to strengthen the executive powers and to free them from any dependence on the legislature. Instead, the executive had considerable freedom of action. This meant the massive consolidation of Mussolini's personal powers. A fundamental law, passed in 1925, altered the constitution to make him responsible to the King rather than the legislature. Then, in January 1926, he was empowered to govern by decree, a process which was to be used over 100,000 times by 1943. During the late 1920s he also accumulated offices on an unprecedented scale. In 1929, for example, he was personally responsible for eight key ministries: foreign affairs, the interior, war, navy, aviation, colonies, corporations and public works. This authority was accompanied by the deliberate inflation of Mussolini's own image in the creation of the cult of the Duce (this is examined further on pp. 129–30).

A third component of radical political change was the reorganization of the Fascist Party to enable it to meet the responsibilities of dictatorship. Originally it had been localized in its composition, and there was a faction which demanded a permanently decentralized organization and a limited membership. Eventually, however, the centralist viewpoint prevailed. The radicals of the party, led by Farinacci, wanted a carefully organized machine to ensure that the policies of Fascism could be uniformly implemented. The first step was the establishment in 1922 of the Fascist Grand Council, under the control of Mussolini himself. Then, during the Matteotti Crisis, the original party bosses at local level were purged and a new structure came into being, based on the principles of centralized direction and widespread party membership. In 1928 the Fascist Party Grand Council was made 'the supreme organ that coordinates all activities of the regime'.[34] Meanwhile, in 1926 a Special Tribunal for the Defence of the State was set up to deal with suspected anti-Fascists – another blow against the liberal tradition of political and ideological diversity.

The late 1920s saw a fourth example of radical Fascism. Mussolini had always been strongly influenced by revolutionary syndicalism and, once his power was secure against any opposition, he proceeded to implement it. In September 1926 he laid the foundation of the corporate state in the form of twelve national syndicates, under a Ministry of Corporations that was also established. The process was completed in 1934 when the syndicates were replaced by national corporations. The corporate state was merged into the political system by the replacement of a directly elected parliament by a corporative chamber; this, in turn, was reorganized as the Chamber of Fasces and Corporations.

There were, finally, developments in ideology. Attempts were made in the early 1930s to stabilize and define the Fascist revolution by giving its ideas a more dynamic appearance. An article, written in 1932, for the *Enciclopedia Italiana* hailed the 'Fascist century', and anticipated the wave of imperial expansion. We are left, therefore, with a picture of an ideological dictatorship operated, with immense executive authority, through a one-party system. All this seems to have been constructed on the ruins of the liberal state: it must, therefore, have been a 'revolution'.

. . . or political 'continuity'?

A closer look, however, reveals some surprising inconsistencies in this picture. There is evidence that Fascism conceded at least as much to tradition as it managed to change it. Mussolini left a considerable part of the previous political structure intact. After all, he had said in August 1921: 'For me fascism is not an end in itself. It is the means to re-establish national equilibrium.'[35] This stopped the Fascist 'revolution' from attacking some of the traditional bases of Italy – the monarchy, the Church and the army. In order to prevent these from being openly threatened, Mussolini took as many measures to constrain the Fascist Party as he did to advance it. Indeed, the constitution of the party (1929) explicitly provided for the subordination of the party to the state. Although Fascist ministers were prominent in government departments, in each case they were under the ultimate authority of Mussolini himself.

At the local level the submission of party officials to the traditional authorities, the prefects, was even more pronounced. Mussolini's circular to prefects of 5 January 1927 read:

> I solemnly affirm that the prefect is the highest authority of the state in the province. He is the direct representative of the central executive power. All citizens, and in particular those having the great privilege and supreme honour of supporting fascism, owe respect and obedience to the highest political representative of the fascist regime and must work under him to make his task easier.[36]

Mussolini even referred to the need to deal with any violent actions by the *squadristi*: 'The prefects must prevent this happening by using all means at their disposal, I repeat by using all means at their disposal.'[37] Other major local officials, such as the mayors, tended to be agrarian notables rather than Fascist activists – and the latter were again expected to follow orders.

The party was therefore controlled at all levels. According to Payne, 'One of the most striking features of the regime was that the political dictatorship also became a dictatorship over the party rather than of the party.'[38] To make this possible, radicalism was removed from the party. Some 60,000 of the more violent members were removed from its ranks, and new members were only admitted from the youth movements: this ensured their loyalty and obedience. The party increased in size from 300,000 in 1921 to over five million by 1943, in which middle-class membership predominated. The core of the party was also constrained. In theory the Fascist Grand Council was the supreme co-ordinating body; in practice it operated under the direct control of Mussolini himself, whose priority was to ensure that it did not replace the traditional state institutions

Several historians have deduced from these developments that there was an overall party depoliticization. 'Beginning in the late 1920s,' Tannenbaum argues, 'the party became the servant of the State rather than its ruler.'[39] This, according to Payne, means that 'There was no "Fascist revolution", save at the top.' Indeed, 'State administration changed comparatively little.'[40] If there was 'not a revolution', then what happened must have been 'an authoritarian compromise'.[41]

A political vacuum filled by the 'cult of the Duce' . . .

Revolution or continuity? The two approaches can be seen as entirely different interpretations of how Mussolini consolidated his power, each complete in itself. Or they may have been two different strategies used by Mussolini as circumstances allowed or dictated. The latter is more likely, since common sense suggests that there were elements of both political revolution and political continuity between 1922 and 1939.

Assuming that revolution and continuity could develop together, logic would next suggest an uneasy and contradictory relationship between the two. Yet, on the surface, Mussolini appeared to have achieved a one-party state, based on an overriding ideology, without eradicating Italy's traditional institutions. In an illusion of order and harmony, Mussolini had managed to avoid a direct confrontation between party and state by injecting revolutionary dynamism into traditional institutions. The trouble with this interpretation is that it underestimates the turbulent impact of one upon the other. On the surface, there may well have been order and collaboration between Fascism and traditional Italy, but beneath the surface there was seething unrest as numerous members of the Fascist Party and the *squadristi* came into direct confrontation with the equivalent layers of state officialdom. Especially important was the conflict between local Fascist leaders on the one hand and the prefects and mayors on the other. Numerous complaints reached Mussolini about the way in which state authorities and the Church were flouting Fascist ideology. Mussolini must have been aware that the harmony between the party and the traditional institutions was only superficial. Indeed, after 1930, he became increasingly disillusioned with the most important of these, the monarchy. Why, therefore, was he prepared to tolerate such an unsatisfactory situation?

One view is that the conflict was deliberately created. Mussolini was able to construct an overall relationship between the party and the state which ensured the survival of both. At the same time, he aimed to create conflict and discord below the surface in order to promote his own position and to make himself indispensable. Lyttelton, for example, maintains that Mussolini 'deliberately fostered untidiness and illogicality in the structure of government'.[42] This was because he intended to rule by balancing the different elements which made up the state and the party. His basic fear was that one or more of these elements might eventually challenge his authority, and the greatest immediate threat seemed to come from the Fascist Party itself. Hence, he took the drastic but logical step of depoliticizing the regime. The result was a strange paradox: the strength of Fascism depended on the weakness of Fascist organizations. Or, to put it another way, a movement which was famed for its activism was encouraged by its leader to show inactivity. Mussolini was deliberately creating a vacuum in the political and administrative structure where one would normally expect to find a ruling class or elite. The explanation of this was that Mussolini was opposed to the emergence of any group which was likely to compete with him for power and public support. The gap was filled by the cult of the Duce,[43] or Mussolinianism, and Fascism was restrained so that this could predominate. The cult of the Duce was not an essential part of the Fascist programme, but rather an elaborate superstructure imposed on top of it. As far as Mussolini was concerned, however, it was the whole point of his rule; after all, he had once said, 'If Fascism does not follow me, no one can make me follow Fascism.'[44]

There is much to be said for this approach. It gives more meaning to the cult of the Duce than does the view of Taylor that Mussolini was a 'vain, blustering boaster'. It also separates Mussolinianism from Fascism and shows that the former did not arise from the latter but, in fact, lived in tension with it. On the other hand, it assumes that Mussolini's dictatorship was dictated from above – that the cult of the Duce forced itself into the political vacuum contrived by Mussolini himself.

It is difficult to imagine a personality cult being sustained entirely on a created need. It is more likely to be the deliberate intensification of a need which was already there. An additional dimension was therefore necessary. Mussolinianism was as much the response to pressures from below as it was to calculations from above. The cult of the Duce met a deep psychological need and therefore responded to public demand rather than creating it. In their situation the population found hero worship an essential antidote to fear since it provided hope and as near as they were likely to get to certainty. Ideology needed to be personified so that the irrational could be rationalized and projections turned into realities. The personality cult could succeed only if the projection of the personality was accepted by the people. In a very real sense, therefore, Mussolini was a reflection of popular aspirations. Mussolinianism was an extension of his skills of oratory: he adjusted to the crowd in order to sway it.

Mussolini's position was therefore doubly strong, but simultaneously doubly precarious. During the 1920s and 1930s he could exist through a combination of radicalism and conservatism, smoothing over conflict on the surface while allowing it to seethe underneath. He could do this because he was sustained by popular adulation, which he strengthened through speeches, role modelling and sloganizing. Of the three major dictators he was at one moment the most acclaimed and at another the most reviled (his eventual fate, at the hands of the system and the people, is dealt with on p. 166).

. . . or the 'sacralization of Italian politics'?

It is, however, possible to reverse the argument. The style and ritual were not so much the result of Mussolini's attempts to impose his own presence within a political vacuum. Rather, they were the penetration of a new dynamism into the state itself. This type of approach has been advanced by modern historian Emilio Gentile[45] who puts a case for Fascist Italy being part of a general trend for the 'sacralization of politics', in which modern political movements take on 'aspects of religion' in 'their ideology'. They do this through 'the ways in which they socialize and integrate', in the 'formulation of a body of beliefs', the 'fideistic cult of their leaders' and 'the adoption of ritual and symbolism'.[46] This institutes 'a lay religion' aimed at creating subjects 'dedicated body and soul to the nation'.[47]

There are certain advantages to this interpretation. First, it takes Mussolini and Italian Fascism seriously again by pushing back previous approaches that underestimate their importance – either by openly ridiculing Mussolini's posturing or by focusing on the papering-over effect of Fascist ceremony. In re-examining arguments about substance and style, Gentile reintegrates Fascism and Mussolinianism rather than seeing the two in tension with Mussolini deliberately creating a void to fill it himself. This also re-establishes the case for Fascist Italy being a totalitarian state after the constant questioning by some historians. At the same time, Gentile avoids overstating the strengthening effect 'sacralization' or underestimating its negative side-effects. 'In the enterprise of spreading its doctrine and arousing the masses to faith in its dogmas, obedience to its commandments, and the assimilation of its ethics and its life-style, Fascism spent a considerable capital of energy diverting those energies from other fields that might perhaps have been more important for the interests both of the regime and of the people.'[48]

There are, however, problems with the 'sacralization' theory. Does it go too far in the opposite direction to those of structural chaos and Mussolinianism? In correcting the approach to Mussolini's regime as an absurdity – and by reviving the connections between the ideology, the system and the leader – perhaps it has done too much to depersonalize the whole system. Are the personal appeal, eccentricities and inconsistencies of Mussolini himself now understated? Does 'sacralization' create a function out of the personal nature of the adulation of the Duce and understate the tensions this sometimes brought to the whole Fascist Party and movement? After all, such conflicts were the *real* distractions from the coherence of Fascism. There are also deficiencies with the very term 'sacralization'. Admittedly there were instances of direct parallels between political and religious liturgy: an example of this was the Fascist credo. Yet making this too conscious a policy – as a parallel liturgy covering all areas, rather than an occasional piece of unfortunate plagiarism – would surely have undermined the undoubted sympathy that the Catholic Church had for Mussolini and Fascism. After all, the papacy had been explicit in its condemnation of secularism and atheism. Its preference for fascism over communism rested on its certainty that the former would defend the Catholic tradition against attempts to undermine it.

Indoctrination and culture

While altering the base of political power, Mussolini also sought to establish a new national identity for the Italian people. This followed broadly the same pattern as the political developments within Italy. In the first three years the changes were relatively slow, followed by a more adventurous approach between 1925 and 1929, but as yet without any radical ideological input: this was increased as a result of the Great Depression between 1930 and 1934. The most significant developments in indoctrination occurred after 1935, with the invasion of Ethiopia and the growing influence of Nazi Germany. Mussolini's aim was to create New Fascist man, who would live in the 'century of Fascism'. For this, it was essential to have the full participation of all Italians.[49] Mussolini's method to guarantee this would be 'totalitarian'; this was a term he first used in a speech to the Fascist Party Congress in June 1925 – in which he referred to the 'totalitarian will' of Fascism.[50] The whole process of what Falasca-Zamponi has called an 'aesthetic-totalitarian project'[51] involved the exaltation of violence, which was 'sanctified' as 'the premise for Italy's renewal'.[52]

But it had to be controlled and focused on Fascism, the new state and the Duce. All allegiance was to be directed to Mussolini himself. His short stature and partial baldness were disguised by a ramrod-straight stance and a shaven head, both of which were intended to give him a 'Roman' appearance. His demagoguery remained impressive, based on the unsubtle belief that 'the crowd loves strong men'. Falasca-Zamponi provides the following description: 'He talked with tight teeth; words were assembled in groups and distanced by pauses; each unit of words was pronounced with a measured rhythmical style.' This was accentuated by his head leaning 'halfway back, his eyes almost out of their sockets, his chin and mouth forward'. In fact, 'The speech became one of the main elements through which the spectacle of Mussolini's power unfolded.'[53] Mussolini summed up his intentions on the balcony thus: 'mine are not speeches in the traditional sense of the word. They are elocutions, a touch between my soul and yours, my heart and your hearts'.[54] He was also portrayed as an expert rider, aviator, fencer, racing driver and violinist. The public were also assailed by slogans such as 'The Duce is always right!' and 'Believe! Obey! Fight!'.

It might be thought that education would play a crucial role in the new order, but changes were slow at first and subject to subsequent modification. In 1923 the Education Minister, Gentile, introduced a structure specifically intended to create a new elite: technical education was separated from the classical courses which became the passport to university education, and a rigid examination system was applied. This, however, came under universal criticism from parents and was so difficult to operate that Fedele, Gentile's successor, had to modify it from 1925 onwards. After 1929 there was more of an effort to Fascistize schools under the Ministry of National Education, which replaced the earlier Ministry of Public Instruction. The process was accelerated by Bottai in 1936. Textbooks became a state monopoly; the number of approved history texts, for instance, was reduced from 317 to 1, while a junior Italian reader informed solemn eight-year-olds that 'the eyes of the Duce are on every one of you'. From 1938 racism was openly practised and taught in the classroom, while 1939 saw the introduction of the Fascist School Charter. By and large, however, education was not one of the more successful examples of indoctrination. There were too many loopholes and evasions and, in the universities, underground resistance to and contempt for so-called Fascist values.

Hence, the regime came to place more emphasis on the organization of youth groups outside the school sector. Again, the pace gradually intensified. Initially the whole process was very haphazard. From 1926, however, the youth organizations were grouped into the Opera Nazionale Balilla (ONB). During the 1930s the stages of these became more clearly defined. At the age of four, boys became Sons of the She-Wolf; at eight they joined the Balilla, before moving to the Avanguardisti at fourteen and finally the Fascist Levy at eighteen. The creed of the Balilla blatantly superimposed a doctored version of Italian history on a twisted religious format:

> I believe in Rome the Eternal, the mother of my country, and in Italy, her eldest daughter, who was born in her virginal bosom by the grace of God; who suffered through the barbarian invasions, was crucified and buried, who descended to the grave, and was raised from the dead in the nineteenth century, who ascended into heaven in her glory in 1918 and 1922 and who is seated on the right hand of her mother Rome; who for this reason shall come to judge the living and the dead. I believe in the genius of Mussolini, in our Holy Father Fascism, in the communion of the martyrs, in the conversion of Italians and in the resurrection of the Empire.[55]

This was principally part of the more radical wave which occurred after 1936. The organization was further tightened as all sections of youth were brought under the collective Gioventu del Littorio (GIL) in 1937, membership of which was made compulsory in 1939.

How effective were these organizations? It is true that a large proportion of Italy's youth responded enthusiastically to Fascism. They were, for example, given opportunities for outdoor recreation which had previously been lacking. On the other hand, membership of these paramilitary organizations was by no means universal, as some 40 per cent of the age group between eight and eighteen managed to avoid joining them. The proportion was much higher among girls, many of whom were not given a sufficiently fulfilling role to compensate for the subservience which Fascism expected of them in society. Recent research has also shown that the youth groups were more influential in the urban than in the rural areas, in the north and centre rather than in the south, and in the middle classes rather than in the peasantry or working classes.

Fascism also tried to organize the population at large, through the OND or Dopolavoro. Although set up in 1925, this really came into its own during the Great Depression as a means of ensuring the total commitment of the workforce. It co-ordinated the various different work schemes and clubs, and promoted library, radio, sports and recreation facilities. The next stage was the emergence of the OND as a full ministry in 1935, with the intention of providing for a more fully co-ordinated use of the mass media for the purpose of indoctrination. This is another example of the increased radicalization from the mid-1930s, but did not develop into anything like the more sophisticated systems of the KdF and SdA in Germany.

That Mussolini considered the control of the press to be a major priority was hardly surprising, in view of his own experience as a newspaper editor. Early measures included the suppression of many papers by the exceptional decrees of 1926 and, in 1928, the compulsory registration of all journalists with the Fascist Journalist Association. The press office under Rossi controlled news and censorship. The process was extended in the early 1930s when the press office came under the control of Polverelli. He increased the control over individual journalists and was responsible for the development of the cult of the Duce in the press. He managed to exert effective control over what was published; in difficult cases the government called upon the local prefects to enforce its decisions. Further changes were made when Ciano established the Ministry for Press and Propaganda – another example of radicalization for the purpose of presenting the Ethiopian campaign in the most positive way. By and large, Mussolini's regime of journalism was more successful than most other elements of the totalitarian state. There was, however, a price: constant distortion of the facts about Italy's record in her three wars led eventually to the entire government being misinformed. Mussolini, in particular, lost all contact with reality, even though – or because – he spent several hours each day reading the newspapers.

Cultural output was, on the whole, more diverse in Italy than in either Germany or the Soviet Union. There was less attempt to create a grand style and there was more receptiveness to outside influences. According to Pollard, 'There was no such thing as a "Fascist culture", even less a cultural revolution in Italy. What Fascist Italy lacked was a clear cultural programme and strategy.'[56] This began to change, however, from 1935 onwards when Mussolini expressed increasing concern about the preoccupation of Italians with art for art's sake. Instead, he insisted, it was now necessary to develop a more utilitarian approach which would help reinforce Italy's expansionist and martial roles.[57] Attempts were later made to institutionalize the control of culture through two bodies set up in the 1930s. The first was the Propaganda Ministry (1935), with the Ministry of Popular Culture following in 1937.

The latter tried to regulate music, literature, art and the cinema. But it was never as efficient as the measures used by Goebbels to Nazify German art and literature or the Socialist Realism of Stalin.

One of the more popular forms of culture was the cinema which, according to Mussolini, was 'the strongest weapon'. This provides a more detailed example of the incomplete nature of Fascist control. On the one hand, there was an increase in institutions and regulations. A film institute was set up in 1925, followed, in 1934, by the Office for Cinematography. The government insisted on quotas (100 films were to be made in 1937) and tried to dictate the themes of major epics. On the other hand, such controls were far from total. Most films were produced by private enterprise and were not geared to the state's propaganda requirements. Indeed, Fascism's lack of cultural awareness alienated the younger generation of film directors, like De Santis and Visconti, who aimed at realism rather than distortion. Thus, ultimately, Mussolini's 'strongest weapon . . . was turned against Fascism itself'.[58]

The overall impression, therefore, must be that the Fascist state failed to exert the type of control over ideas which is normally associated with totalitarianism. The traditional liberal culture proved impossible to eradicate, even through the more radical impulses of the 1930s. The negative result was that Mussolini was able to attract less total popular commitment than either Hitler or Stalin through culture. The positive side was that there was less to expunge after the end of the Fascist regime. Bosworth, for one, has shown that there is more continuity in Italian culture, before and after 1945, than is commonly realized.[59]

Coercion

Indoctrination is invariably linked to coercion. The use of force had been implicit in the Fascist movement from the beginning and a system of repression was gradually constructed. The Law on the Defence of the State was established in 1926. This provided for terms of imprisonment for anyone attempting to reconstitute an opposition party, or attempting to propagate 'doctrines, opinions or methods' of such organizations.[60] These offences would be tried by a Special Tribunal for the Defence of the State. The following year saw the formation of a secret police, or OVRA (Opera Voluntaria per la Repressione Antifascista). Those who experienced the full pressure of these organs were mainly ex-politicians and dissidents who refused to take the oath of loyalty to the regime, although, from the late 1930s, the apparatus was also used to enforce a policy of anti-Semitism.

How effective was this system? On the one hand, it was clearly part of the paraphernalia to exert control over the population and to eliminate alternative ideas. Historians accept that the intention was to facilitate subjection. According to Morgan, 'the police's preventive and repressive powers were now so extensive and pervasive as to create a real climate of fear and repression'.[61] The Fascist regime operated on the joint principles of conversion and coercion. Support for the system was therefore engendered in a repressive atmosphere which was intended to remove any element of choice. Ultimately the effectiveness of the conversion depended partly on the strength of the propaganda and indoctrination but partly on the fear of the consequences of evasion. During the 1930s about 20,000 actions were taken by the police every week, many of these being initiated on the basis of information received from people known to the accused. This meant that repression was assisted by the people themselves within a general and widespread fear of recrimination.

The scope of repression was therefore considerable. But the degree of terror it employed was not. OVRA was not equivalent to the SS in Germany or the NKVD in the Soviet Union. Nor was there any fundamental change in criminal justice to correspond with the creation of the People's Court in Germany: within Italy the legal system continued to operate much as it had always done, despite the so-called Fascistization of the regime. The death penalty was used only nine times between 1927 and 1940 while, of the 4,805 cases actually brought to court, 3,904 ended in acquittal. During the entire Fascist period 5,000 people were given prison sentences for political reasons and 10,000 sent into political exile.[62]

There is, not surprisingly, a broad consensus about the Fascist police state which has been unaffected by any other interpretations concerning Mussolini. During the 1990s, Payne argued that 'In Italy the Mussolini regime was brutal and repressive, but not murderous and bloodthirsty';[63] according to Whittam, the 'threat posed by this mysterious organisation [OVRA] . . . was more important than its actual activities',[64] while Pollard maintained that 'Though life was no joke for dissidents in Fascist Italy, it was eminently preferable to their fate in the other two totalitarian states.'[65] Such views only reinforce the earlier conclusion of Cassels that 'The Fascist regime used terror, but was not in any real sense based on terror.'

Anti-semitism and racism

Nowhere is there a greater contrast in the earlier and later policies of Mussolini than in the treatment of Italy's Jewish population.

During the 1920s anti-Semitism was hardly an issue. There were, it is true, some anti-Semitic influences from France – and especially from Maurras. A few Fascists, such as Preziosi and Farinacci, tried to propagate them, but they did not translate easily into practice. Italy had always been less affected than other parts of Europe by anti-Semitism, largely because Jews had never amounted to more than one in a thousand of the total population. Individual Jews had joined the Fascist Party in the early 1920s: ironically the proportion of their membership was well above the overall national average. Mussolini had seen no problem with this. His approach to Fascism had been on the left-wing, syndicalist strand, which meant that he had no instinct for the anti-Semitism of the right. Indeed, he had originally denounced Nazi racism as 'unscientific and absurd',[66] going so far as to ensure full legal status for Italian Jews in 1932 and, from 1933, to give sanctuary to 9,000 Jewish exiles from Germany.

Then came a dramatic reversal of attitudes and policy. In July 1938 a Manifesto on Race was drawn up by Mussolini and ten professors as a scientific exposition of Fascist racial doctrine. It proclaimed that 'the population of Italy is of Aryan origins and its civilization is Aryan', that 'there now exists a pure Italian race and that Jews do not belong to the Italian race'.[67] It was followed by decrees banning intermarriage between Jews and non-Jews and removing Jews from prominent positions in finance, education and politics. Property restrictions were also imposed and any Jews who had entered Italy since 1919 were to be repatriated.

These changes took Italy by surprise and were immediately associated with growing influences from Nazi Germany. Some historians still agree with this. De Felice maintains that Mussolini 'introduced state antisemitism in Italy . . . because of his basic conviction that, to render the Italian–German alliance iron-hard, it was necessary to eliminate every strident contrast between the two regimes'.[68] It would be pointless to deny this external channel of influence. By 1938 Mussolini needed Hitler's support in Europe and the Rome–Berlin Axis was moving steadily towards a military alliance. It therefore made sense to bring Fascist ideology more into line with Nazi racism. Even if, as Pollard maintains, there is no evidence that Hitler put pressure on Mussolini to make this change, it is possible that Mussolini felt 'out of step with almost every other Fascist movement'.[69] It was no coincidence that Hungary and Romania also introduced anti-Semitic legislation in 1938.

But there is a tendency to go too far in this direction and to assume that anti-Semitism was entirely an external transplant into Italy. There was, on the contrary, a powerful influence within Italy for the change of policy – the conquest of Ethiopia between 1935 and 1937. This made race a more important public issue and resulted in direct access to anti-Semitism. Admittedly, 'one can argue equally logically that Italy had already ruled an empire (Eritrea, Somalia and Libya) for fifty years before the invasion of Ethiopia without developing any discernible anti-Semitic tendencies'.[70] On the other hand, the circumstances of the conquest of Ethiopia carried extreme connotations of racial 'inferiority'. The whole process was unusually brutal, involving the use of mustard gas, and there were also fears of miscegenation between the considerable number of Italian troops and the indigenous population. Racism therefore became ingrained in the later phase of Fascist ideology. Mussolini needed to prepare the Italian people for a role of future domination over 'inferior' peoples, in very much the same way that Aryan domination was being projected for eastern Europe.

Italian anti-Semitism was an extension of this vision. The connection was, of course, suggested by developments within Germany. This does not, however, remove the indigenous origins. Given the changing situation in foreign and imperial policy during the second half of the 1930s, Mussolini had his own reasons for revising his views about the Jews. This was partly because a small number of Jews were beginning to draw attention to themselves – thereby creating unintended pressure from below. Two issues proved especially important. The first was the opposition of Italian Zionists to Mussolini's proposals to take over the Palestinian mandate from Britain. The second, and more important, was the courageous criticism by Jewish intellectuals of the Italian campaign in Ethiopia. Mussolini promptly resorted to the traditional European response of using an identifiable target as a scapegoat. The stance on Palestine and Ethiopia must indicate a Jewish 'conspiracy', which was behind the decision of the League of Nations to impose sanctions against Italy. It was the 'conspiracy' theory rather than direct pressure from Germany which brought Fascist Italy into the mainstream of anti-Semitism – another traditional European response.

The policy was, however, intensified by competition with Germany. Mussolini felt under increasing pressure to compete with Hitler for seniority within the partnership between Italy and Germany. This involved creating an Italian counterpart to the German master race, and Mussolini's special ingredient was racial purity. Hence, 'While the racial composition of the other European nations has altered considerably even in recent periods, the grand lines of racial composition have remained essentially the same in Italy during the last thousand years.'[71] The only blot on this record were the Jews, who comprised non-European racial elements and had never been assimilated in Italy.

Mussolini's anti-Semitism was never the focal point of Fascist ideology; nor did it become the heart of consuming obsession. Policies against the Jews were therefore perceived as being out of place in Italy. Such actions were neither popular nor accepted: they were widely resented. In asking 'Why, unfortunately, did Italy have to go and imitate Germany?'[72] Pope Pius XI was voicing both the Catholic conscience and the secular misgivings of those who saw the creeping influence of Nazism in Italy. In the event, the racial decrees were never applied effectively, another illustration of the incomplete nature of the totalitarian state. During the Second World War there were no large-scale shipments of Italian Jews to Nazi camps until the Germans occupied northern Italy in 1943; elsewhere anti-Semitic legislation gradually lapsed, especially after the fall of Mussolini.

Mussolini's attitude to racism and anti-Semitism can, in the final analysis, be seen as a barometer of the pressures on Fascism. During his rise to power, anti-Semitism was one of the right-wing strands of Fascist ideology which he could entirely ignore. Nor, during the 1920s, was there any reason to target the Jews: they were entirely outside his attempts to carry through a Fascist revolution while keeping traditional institutions intact. As the regime entered economic difficulties during the Great Depression there was still no search for a Jewish scapegoat, the reverse of the situation in Germany. It was the conquest of Ethiopia, itself a radical response to growing internal pressures, which produced a powerful current of racism. The anti-Semitic channel developed with the aforementioned Jewish criticism of Mussolini's objectives. The diplomatic link with Hitler suggested what measures should be applied in Italy – but these were part of an overall intensification of Fascism in Italy in the period leading up to the Second World War. As Whittam argues, 'Mussolini sought to reinvigorate the regime by his racial programme and his foreign policy.'[73]

This, however, carried the risk of upsetting the earlier consensus and creating more resentment. Radicalism would lead to further war and Mussolini was gambling on military victory as a universal panacea. As it turned out, the regime fell into the vortex of defeat but, according to Morgan, it was the contemporary perceptions of anti-Semitism in Italy that 'shaped the Italian people's response to the Fascist regime in the late 1930s'.[74] This, in turn, has been seen as the 'triumph of old humanitarian values over new Fascist principles'.[75]

Relations between church and state

There was no natural affinity between the Church and Fascism. After all, Mussolini had once been a strident atheist and very few of the Fascist leaders were practising Catholics. Both sides, however, had much to gain from ending the deep rift between Church and state which went far back to the era of Italian unification. Mussolini claimed the credit for this reconciliation, arguing that the 'serenity of relations' was 'a tribute to the Fascist regime'.[76] In fact, the healing was started by Orlando, Prime Minister between 1917 and 1919. It could, however, be argued that the process was greatly accelerated by the Fascist government.

The highlights were the three agreements of 1929. The Lateran Treaty settled the question of the Pope's temporal power by restoring the Vatican City to his sovereignty. The Concordat defined more carefully the role of the Church in the Fascist state. Catholicism was to be the sole religion of the state, religious instruction would return to schools, and Church marriages would be given full validity. In a third agreement the papacy was compensated for financial losses, incurred in the nineteenth century, by the payment of 750 million lire in cash and 1,000 million in state bonds.

Why was this arrangement reached – and what was hoped to develop from it? Each side had its own, somewhat contrasting, view. The Pope hoped that Fascism would provide a better medium than the former liberal state for the revival of Catholic influence over the secular power. Mussolini hoped that the support of the Church would provide more security and stability for Fascism. Although he was acknowledging that Fascism was not now going to replace traditional Catholic virtues, the agreement meant that Mussolini could concentrate on those areas in which Fascism could be more actively extended – the economy, education and foreign policy.

Two views have recently been advanced as to the wisdom of the Lateran Treaty. The first, very much in line with the traditional perspective, is Morgan's argument that 'the Conciliation was probably the most important contribution to the consolidation of the Fascist government in power on a wider basis of support and consent'.[77] The alternative approach is that Mussolini was to some extent duped. Bosworth, for example, comments that the 'uneasy relationship between Fascism and Catholicism' was 'a meeting between a long-sighted Church and a short-sighted regime'.[78] There are elements of truth in both. On the one hand, Mussolini was able to use the agreement to considerable political advantage. On the other, he also found himself in conflict with an institution which had no intention of yielding the essential pressure points of its power.

Mussolini's gains are readily apparent. He had, after all, succeeded in gaining the support of a power which had been hostile to successive governments for a period of fifty years. Pius XI claimed that the Lateran Accords 'brought God to Italy and Italy to God'.[79] The Vatican was therefore willing to urge the electorate to vote for the Fascist list in 1929 and 1934. There was also strong support for Mussolini's policies on population increase, the family and divorce. Above all, there was a considerable overlap of interest between the government and the papacy in foreign policy.[80] Cardinal Shuster, for example, compared the invasion of Ethiopia with the Crusades, while Pius XI openly justified Mussolini's participation in the Spanish Civil War on the grounds that he was helping contain the main enemy of Christianity: 'The first, the greatest and now the general peril is certainly Communism in all its forms and degrees.'[81] This attitude met with the overwhelming approval of the upper levels in the Church's hierarchy.

On the other hand, Mussolini never succeeded in subordinating the Church to the full control of the state; it could even be said that the Church emerged strengthened from the relationship and came eventually to threaten the Fascist state. Three issues proved especially contentious. In the first place, Mussolini's insistence on controlling the minds of the young was bound to lead to conflict. In 1931 the Pope protested in his encyclical *Non abbiamo bisogno* against Fascist attempts to close down youth clubs and to monopolize education. The Church won a number of concessions in the form of the 1931 Accords which allowed involvement in specifically religious activities for youth groups. Second, the Pope reacted with hostility to that part of Mussolini's racial legislation in 1938 which forbade intermarriage between Italians and Jews: this was on the grounds that Jews could no longer be converted to Catholicism. In the process, the Church found itself in harmony with Italian public opinion which opposed racism for more general reasons. Finally, there were underlying tensions throughout the period between the Pope's vision of an Italy reconverted to Catholicism and Mussolini's vision of a sacralized Rome – an eternal secular Italy based on the principles of ancient Rome. Again, the survival of the Church in the 1930s meant that the papacy could restore its claim to represent the conscience of Italians – once the regime was threatened with the spectre of defeat.

The extent to which Catholicism helped to undermine the Fascist regime in its critical period is examined on page 146. Key roles were played by Catholic Action, an organization of laymen which had been established by the Pope in 1922, by the FUCI (Federazione Universitari Cattolici Italiani), a university-based movement of Catholic students and intellectuals, and the Movimento Laurienti. It has to be said that, if Mussolini's deal with the Church consolidated Fascism in the 1930s, it also enabled Catholicism to gather its own strength against Fascism in the early 1940s.

Economic policies

The overall trend in economic policy was from initial free enterprise to state intervention and control. The process was complex. In summary, the regime's approach to the economy was, until 1925, a continuation of earlier liberal policies. An attempt was then made to increase state control without going the whole way to establishing a socialist base. Mussolini's solution was a compromise: a partnership between the state and private economic enterprise in the form of 'corporativism'. The corporate state was gradually set up between 1926 and 1934 and was widely publicized. It was not, however, particularly effective. Instead of using it as a means of harmonizing economic policy, Mussolini increased government control outside the scope of corporativism. The result was a confusion of institutions and often a conflict of aims.

The main development between 1926 and 1934 was the emergence of the corporate state. The idea of corporativism was not new; it was based partly on medieval guilds and corporations and partly on the revolutionary syndicalism of Georges Sorel, an early influence on Mussolini. The basic intention was to replace the old sectional interests (such as trade unions and employers' organizations) which so often produced conflicts between labour and capital. Instead, the Rocco Law of 1926 recognized seven branches of economic activity: industry, agriculture, internal transport, merchant marine, banking, commerce and intellectual work. These were formed into syndicates, under the control of the Ministry of Corporations, also established in 1926. The system was further refined by the creation in 1930 of the National Council of Corporations and the organization of economic activity into twenty-two more specialized corporations by 1934. By 1938 this process was brought into the political system with the creation of the Chamber of Fasces and Corporations in place of the old Chamber of Deputies.

In theory, corporativism was the Fascist alternative to socialism on the left and undiluted capitalism on the right. The so-called 'third way' would increase state control over the economy without destroying private enterprise and it could be adapted to the new Fascist institutions. In particular, it was a means by which Italy could be helped to tackle the pressures of the Great Depression. In practice, however, the whole system proved inefficient and cumbersome. It failed to provide any sort of consensus between employers and workers and was almost entirely excluded from any real decision-making on the economy. Historians have always been critical of its practical applications. Cassels remarks that 'the corporative state was a true child of Mussolini: the great poseur brought forth an organism which was a travesty of what it purported to be'.[82] According to Pollard, 'In reality, in the corporations and other new government agencies Fascism had created a vast, largely useless apparatus.'[83] The corporate state has been seen largely as a means of sharing power between Fascism and the economic interests of the landowners and industrialists. It was more about creating a subservient labour force than about providing a structure capable of undertaking genuine economic change. Hence, in the words of Tannenbaum, 'Fascist Italy had complete control over the labour force and very little control over the nation's economic structure.'[84]

Increasingly, the whole structure of corporativism was ignored and policies pursued outside its scope. In terms of finance, industry and agriculture, the government pursued separate lines. In each case these originated in the 1920s and were intensified during the 1930s. They managed, however, to remain largely beyond the gravitational pull of corporativism.

Between 1922 and 1925 Finance Minister De Stefani followed a traditional course of balanced budgets, avoided price fixing and subsidies, and withdrew government involvement in industry. From the mid-1920s, however, the views of Mussolini became more influential. These were based as much on the dictates of national prestige as on sound economic thought. He was obsessed, in particular, with the value of the Italian currency, declaring: 'I shall defend the Italian lira to my last breath.' In 1929 the lira was reflated to the level of 90 to the pound sterling, a decision which seriously undermined Italy's competitiveness as an exporter and which probably brought on recession even before the impact of the Great Depression. During the 1930s the government imposed increasingly tight financial controls which, from 1936, became an integral part of the policy of autarky (self-sufficiency) necessitated by war. This was the most radical phase of Mussolini's economic policy, corresponding with the acceleration of changes in other areas. The impetus for such decisions was certainly not a corporate one: it came from Mussolini's priorities in foreign policy and from pressures from heavy industry.

Fascism always favoured heavy industry at the expense of light (or consumer) industry, because of the former's close association with armaments. At first the emphasis was on encouraging private enterprise and leaving untouched private concerns like Fiat, Montecatini Chemicals and Pirelli Rubber. With the onset of the Great Depression, however, the government became more heavily involved by introducing schemes for job-sharing and for rescuing those industries in difficulty. In 1933 it set up the IRI (Istituto per la Recostruzione Industriale) to channel state investment into those industries which were considered most vital. The policy of autarky brought more rigid controls and centralization. By 1939, according to De Grand, the IRI controlled 77 per cent of pig-iron production, 45 per cent of steel production, 80 per cent of naval construction and 90 per cent of shipping.[85] Morgan points to the separation between these developments and the corporate state. The organization of the IRI was parallel to corporativism, rather than integrated into it, and therefore 'resembled a "consortial" rather than a "corporate" state'.[86]

In some respects, industry recovered reasonably well from the impact of the Great Depression. Between 1936 and 1940 it overtook agriculture for the first time in Italian history as the largest single contributor to the GNP (34 per cent as opposed to 29 per cent).[87] Imports had dropped considerably by 1939 when compared with the levels of 1928: raw materials by 12 per cent, semi-finished articles by 40 per cent and finished articles by 48 per cent. Meanwhile, industrial production as a whole had risen by 9 per cent. These figures were offset, however, by the persistence of serious weaknesses in the Italian industrial sector. Mussolini's policies failed to remove the huge disparity between north and south, while Italy remained affected by low productivity, high costs and a decline in domestic consumption. Overall, Italy's recovery from the effects of depression was slower than that of any other European power. What made the situation intolerable, however, was the exposure of an inadequate industrial infrastructure to the constant pressures of military conflict – in the form of the invasion of Ethiopia (1935–6), involvement in the Spanish Civil War (1936–9) and the invasion and occupation of Albania (1939). It is hardly surprising that Italy was defeated so rapidly during the Second World War: the country had already been brought to the point of exhaustion by policies which undermined any reconstruction which had been managed. It has to be said that neither the policies nor the reconstruction had much to do with the corporate state.

The most important development in agriculture was the drive for self-sufficiency in grain which was intended to improve Italy's balance of trade with the rest of Europe and with North America. Characteristically, Mussolini introduced the 1925 campaign as the Battle for Grain and, amid massive publicity, was photographed reaping, or driving tractors. The battle succeeded in increasing grain production by 50 per cent between 1922 and 1930 and by 100 per cent between 1922 and 1939. This was, however, largely at the expense of other crops like fruit and olives which would have been more suited to the additional land given over to grain.

Mussolini also sought to create extra arable land, through reclamation schemes, and extra people, through a higher birth rate. The former was accomplished by schemes like the draining of the Pontine Marshes. The latter was attempted by the Battle for Births, the aim of which was to double Italy's population within a generation. The reasoning behind such a dramatic demographic change was that a static population reflects a decay of national vitality and that a larger population would be essential for the empire which Mussolini was in the process of creating. The incentives for larger families included the payment of benefits for children, the imposition of extra taxation on single people and giving priority in employment to fathers. The whole scheme, however, failed in its objective: between 1921 and 1925 there had been 29.9 births per 1,000 people, whereas between 1936 and 1940 this had declined to 23.1 per 1,000, due partly to the mobilization of men to fight in Mussolini's foreign wars.

It is difficult to avoid a negative overall assessment of Fascist economic policy. The 'third way' of corporativism was attractive in theory but irrelevant in practice. The economy was taken forward instead by a process of mobilization, based on increasingly direct government intervention. The result was a confusion of two strategies which had implications also for social policies.

The social consequences of Mussolini's regime

The impact on social classes

Before 1922 Mussolini claimed that Fascism represented the interests of all classes. By 1939, however, it was evident that any real benefits had accrued only to a small minority – the great industrialists, the estate owners and those members of the middle class serving in the Fascist bureaucracy. For the majority of Italians, by contrast, the quality of life deteriorated.

The industrialists were able to depend on a permanent alliance with the government. The 1925 Vidoni Pact and the Charter of Labour (1927) greatly increased their powers while destroying the capacity of the trade unions to resist. The corporate state, too, was loaded in favour of employers, who continued to be represented by their traditional spokesmen, while the workforce had to depend on government lackeys. Thus all forms of industry, from mass production to small-scale sweatshops, were free from official regulations. Of course, parts of industry were adversely affected by the Great Depression, but they were given top priority by the government after 1933, either through investment from the IRI or through official approval of the spread of cartels. The latter effectively reduced competition between the industrial giants, making life easier at the top but also preventing any substantial modernization.

The landed gentry also maintained their status despite the Depression. They were helped by government policies which were intended to maintain a large rural labour pool. In 1930, for example, the movement of rural workers to cities was allowed only by permission of local prefects, while in 1935 special workbooks (*libretto di lavoro*) were introduced. Also, despite Mussolini's original belief that Italy was a country of small landholders, the large estates were maintained undiminished. By 1930 the large landowners, who accounted for 0.5 per cent of the population, owned nearly 42 per cent of the land; the small landholders, 87 per cent of the rural population, owned a mere 13 per cent.

The lower middle class experienced mixed fortunes. Those in private enterprise were adversely affected by the economic circumstances of the 1930s, but those who entered state service did reasonably well for themselves. The complexity of the administration and the growth of the corporate state produced large numbers of civil service jobs. On the whole, wages were reasonably high and the fringe benefits considerable.

The rest of Italian society suffered severely, mainly for the same reasons that the upper classes benefited. The urban workers were tied down by the regulations introduced by the industrialists with government approval, and were also intimidated by the fact of high unemployment (about two million by 1932). The peasantry and agricultural workers were so badly affected that many defied government edicts and moved to the cities (particularly Rome, Milan and Turin) to swell the slum population. They were driven to this by a reduction in agricultural wages of up to 40 per cent during the 1930s. The working masses as a whole experienced a comparable decline in living standards; it has been estimated that the index of real wages fell between 1925 and 1938 by 11 per cent. Food became more expensive because, although retail prices moved downwards, they did not correspond to the reduction in wages. Moreover, Mussolini's obsession with the Battle for Grain meant the neglect of other foodstuffs and the wasteful use of marginal land. Hence, a whole range of essentials and luxury items like meat, fruit, vegetables, butter, sugar, wine and coffee became too expensive for many urban and rural workers. Mussolini recognized this development; he also justified it and, in the process, turned his back on his original guarantee of material well-being for all. 'We must', he said in 1936, 'rid our minds of the idea that what we have called the days of prosperity may return.'[88]

The impact on women

Fascism had always stressed that gender inequality was natural, whereas class differences were artificial.[89] The intention was that men should fill the occupations and the armed services, while the role of women was to manage the home and produce the population that Italy needed.

The usual view is that, as a result, their status was deliberately and systematically repressed. Women were not given political rights: the undertaking in the 1919 Fascist Programme for women's suffrage was applied only in 1925 – to local elections only – but these were abolished a year later. Although the *fasci feminili* gave women direct access to the fascist movement, its role was essentially non-political and involved only attending rallies and organizing charitable enterprises. It was always under the control of the PNF, which consistently opposed advancing the powers of women in politics or employment. Women were also constrained from seeking social emancipation. Both the press and the PNF condemned the behaviour of women in France or Britain, contrasting the '*donna crisi*' with the Italian paragon – the '*donna madre*'. By the Battle for Births (1927) the latter were placed firmly in the roles of childbearing, family management and the homemaking sciences. This was underpinned by the Rocco Criminal Law of 1932 which banned contraception, sterilization and abortion, as well as enhancing the husband's authority over his wife in both financial and legal terms. Other measures included marriage loans, the waiving of school taxes for 'large families' (redefined in 1934 as comprising eight or more children) and 'premiums' paid for multiple births. During the 1930s a spate of edicts also restricted the participation of women in most branches of employment. By 1938 women were permitted to take up to no more than 10 per cent of the total jobs available. In some areas it was even more restrictive. From the 1920s women were prohibited from teaching philosophy, modern languages and, above all, history, while in the early 1930s women were barred from competitive entry to state employment.

The impact of Fascism on women was therefore fundamentally negative. Nevertheless, two further factors need to be considered.

One is that the Fascist treatment of women was not particularly radical in a society that was already patriarchal and anti-feminist. Almost all of Mussolini's laws on women had the full backing of the Catholic Church. According to Bosworth, 'Fascist State and Catholic Church were generally in patriarchal concord about the proper place of women in society'.[90] Caldwell agrees: the Fascist insistence on the primacy of motherhood for women 'has to be read in conjunction with these Catholic traditions, which precede the period of Fascism but reinforce the tendency to regard women primarily as biological reproducers and nurturers'.[91] If anything, De Grand maintains, the Fascist regime 'found itself increasingly dependent on the moral power of the Church to achieve its demographic aims'.[92] What Mussolini did was not, therefore, revolutionary, but rather an intensification of existing trends.

The second point is that the impact of Fascism was uneven at the best of times. This was because the policies relating to women were constantly contradicted by other needs. For example, the population policy demanded an emphasis on the maternal role, while the crisis in the standard of living, which affected many Italians, made it more sensible to have smaller families. Far from increasing under Mussolini, Italy's rate of population growth was actually lower during the Fascist era than it had been before 1914. By the late 1930s the birth rate was at 23 per 1,000 inhabitants, compared with over 30 before 1914.[93] This was often the result of a direct challenge to official policy. According to de Grazia, 'Fascism spoke of the family as the pillar of the state, but family survival strategies in the face of terrible economic want accentuated the antistatist tendencies of Italian civil society'.[94] Despite the inducements, the number of marriages per annum hardly changed: between 1921 and 1928 there were 8.17 per 1,000 people, rising to 8.9 by 1937 but dropping back to 7.3 by 1938.[95] Nor did employment policies relating to women work out as intended. The percentage of women in the agricultural workforce was 44.7 in 1921 and 39 in 1936; the equivalent proportion of women in industry was 34.4 per cent in 1921 and 33.1 per cent in 1936.[96] Indeed, attempts to remove women from employment had to be reversed towards the end of the 1930s as the mobilization of men for war brought increased pressures on industry.

The overall outcome was clearly mixed. On the one hand, social constraints on women were successfully maintained, but only because these had the force of tradition and, above all, the Catholic Church behind them. On the other hand, where the Fascist state tried to enforce changes they encountered the problem of trying to resolve competing priorities. The most important of these was a series of wars which, from 1935 onwards, imposed problems that could not be offset. The increase in population did not happen; even if it had, it would have had no impact on Fascist Italy's capacity to mobilize effectively until well into the 1940s. This would have been much too late. The only way out was to allow women back into the workforce on a major scale, thereby breaking one of the key social tenets of Italian Fascism.

Benefits to Italy?

Did Fascism confer any real social benefits upon Italy? Some have, indeed, been identified. According to Gregor,[97] Fascist social welfare legislation compared favourably with the more advanced European nations and in some respects was more progressive. To take some examples, old-age pensions and unemployment benefits were both increased and medical care improved to the point that there was an appreciable decline in infant mortality and tuberculosis. Pollard maintains that the emphasis on increasing the birth rate led to 'the first attempt in Italian history to provide a universal and comprehensive antenatal care system and was thus one of the first steps in the establishment of an Italian National Health Service'.[98] Welfare expenditure also rose impressively – from 7 per cent of the budget in 1930 to 20 per cent in 1940, while the state spent 400 million lire on school-building between 1922 and 1942, compared with a mere 60 million spent between 1862 and 1922. Finally, the party provided welfare agencies known as EOAs (*ente opere assistenziali*) which co-ordinated relief funds for the unemployed, especially during the winter months. This has been seen as a 'capillary' structure which enhanced the general flow of relief to where it was most needed.[99]

On the other hand, state benefits, valuable though they were, could not in themselves make up for the heavy loss in earning power. In any case, many Italians dropped through any safety nets spread by the state. About 400,000 people lived in hovels made of mud and sticks, while others lived ten to a room. Poverty remained deeply rooted throughout the rural south where other forms of control also remained intact. Duggan's work has shown that Fascism made comparatively little impact on the Mafia. Although the regime claimed to have eradicated this criminal organization, all that happened was the development of a dual system. 'What was distinctive about Sicily in the 1930s was not that the mafia had been destroyed, but that the authorities could not use the word to describe the chaos.'[100] Hence, Fascism was unable to release this highly traditionalist brake on its few attempts at modernization.

Was it entirely the fault of the Fascist regime that so many Italians faced impoverishment? After all, the Italian economy had always been vulnerable and during the 1930s other industrial nations also suffered severely as a result of the Great Depression. While allowing for this, it is still possible to attribute many of Italy's problems directly to Fascist policy. The policies of the 1920s, especially the revaluation of the lira, pushed Italy into recession before the Depression, and possible recovery in the 1930s was slowed down by preparation for war. It could be argued that even the population policy contributed directly to the falling standard of living. When the United States cut its annual quota of Italian immigrants to 4,000 in 1924, Mussolini did everything possible to promote migration from the United States to Italy. This reduced the remittances sent to Italy by workers in the United States by something like 90 per cent: from five billion lire per annum to 500 million. Given this ambivalent relationship between what Fascism inherited and what it did, we need to turn now to the attitudes of the people who were affected.

Attitudes to Mussolini's regime

Recent research on Germany and Russia has shown that the populations of these two countries were more involved in the actions of the regimes than was originally thought. Conversely, there was also more opposition. Much less research has been done on this in Italy, but it would be surprising if the same overall trend had not applied there as well. De Felice anticipated the first part of the argument when he maintained in 1974 that Mussolini had extensive support within Italy, especially during the 1930s. What is more difficult to accept, however, is that the support remained constant. Indeed, it now seems that Mussolini's regime was more subject to fluctuations than those of Hitler or Stalin and that there were more obvious peaks and troughs.

The first of the peaks was the 1924 election, which showed popular confidence that Mussolini could provide a political stability which had eluded the liberal governments. The second was the 1929 election in which some 90 per cent of Italian voters supported the regime. Even allowing for the absence of any real electoral alternative, this was not entirely a distortion of public political opinion. By 1929 many Italians had concluded that Fascism was offering a real chance of economic recovery as well as becoming more moderate by coming to terms with the Catholic Church; Mussolini appeared to be achieving a balance between totalitarian rule and respect for traditional institutions. The third peak in Mussolini's popularity came with the Italian conquest of Ethiopia between 1935 and 1936 which provided military victory, enhanced Italian nationalist aspirations and offered the prospects of increased international status.

Between these high points in the regime there were, however, alarming dips in public confidence. The first of these occurred in 1924 over the Matteotti Crisis: the turn of events so shocked the parliament and the press that the public response appeared to endanger the very base of Mussolini's government. The second trough, between 1932 and 1935, was caused by growing economic problems; these probably had a direct impact on Mussolini's decision to invade Ethiopia (see p. 136). The euphoria after military success was followed by a third downturn as a result of the increasing commitments to Hitler and the introduction of unpopular anti-Semitic policies. Mussolini never succeeded in regaining his former credibility and the disastrous involvement in the Second World War from 1940 onwards resulted in demands for his dismissal in 1943.

Beneath this zigzag response to Mussolini's leadership and policies there was a more consistent underlying attitude. As we saw in the previous section, estate owners had every reason to support Fascism whatever the aberrations of the moment, as did the leading industrialists and the clerical sections of the middle class. Other groups, such as the industrial and agricultural working classes, were more ambivalent, some joining the adulation in the peak periods, others remaining loyal to outlawed political groups such as the Socialists or Communists. The latter were to experience a sudden resurgence from 1943. Much of the population also managed to evade full participation in the activities sponsored by the regime even though it professed loyalty. This applied, for example, to 40 per cent of young people managing to keep out of 'compulsory' Fascist youth movements, as well as to lay Catholics who chipped away at the secularizing influence of Fascism in the schools. Mussolini's regime, therefore, was never as deeply rooted as those of Hitler and Stalin.

The attitudes of two groups are worth a more detailed examination: women and Catholics. These accounted for a substantial majority of the population.

The previous section considered how women were affected by Fascist social policies. How they reacted is more problematic. The reason for this is that Fascism was continuing and accentuating a traditional undercurrent within Italian society while, at the same time, also encountering cross-currents. The attitudes to women differed in the north and the south, the former coming more into line with liberalizing movements in Britain, France and the United States, the latter remaining more traditionalist. Hence, the changes brought by Fascism were more obvious in Milan and Turin than in Naples and Palermo. Women would also have had a wide variety of attitudes, which can be stereotyped only to a certain degree. Many in the middle classes would have strongly resented the impediments placed upon their professional development; others, however, would have been won over by the renewed emphasis on the family. The majority would have been unconvinced by the new twist given by Fascism to the traditional message of anti-feminism but would have resigned themselves to the inevitable, especially during the period of the Depression. For most, the key factor was the impact of Fascist policies on the family, which meant a growing concern about the expenditure on armaments at the expense of consumerism. Above all, the hectic foreign policy pursued by Mussolini from 1935 onwards proved thoroughly disruptive to family life. This more than offset any appeal that Fascism might originally have had as a guarantor of family cohesion, whereas in Germany Nazism proved less disruptive, at least until 1939.

Catholic attitudes to Mussolini were also ambivalent. At first the Church hierarchy was won over by the Lateran agreements of 1929 and largely approved of what Mussolini did until the late 1930s. The Catholic laity, however, showed a lack of enthusiasm for the compromise between Church and state. The main ground of conflict was education. Catholic organizations, especially the youth wing of Catholic Action, continued to compete with the Balilla. This meant initially a division between the upper levels of the hierarchy and the rest of the Church. The leadership eventually came more into line with the laity in 1938 as a result of the introduction of the racial laws and the closer diplomatic relationship between Mussolini and Hitler.

But throughout the period it was Catholic Action, an organization for laymen, which took on the government. The main area of contention was the type of education intended for Italy's youth. An agreement was reached in 1931 whereby Catholic Action would confine its recreational and educational activities to a purely religious content and would not try to undermine Fascist ideology. By 1939, however, Catholic Action had developed a number of institutions for youth which drew membership away from the Fascist paramilitary organizations and which directly competed with official social and cultural groups. It seemed that while approving Mussolini's fight against alien beliefs abroad, within Italy the Church competed aggressively with Fascism for the soul of the people.

There were also political implications. Two other organizations sprang up in the 1930s – the FUCI, for university students and staff, and the Movimento Laureati which aimed, quite deliberately, to foster a new order. Together with Catholic Action, these proved to be a potential opposition. Indeed, according to a police report in Milan in 1935, Movimento Laureati could form 'in a few hours, the strongest and most important political party in Italy'.[101] As the Fascist regime entered a period of crisis after 1939, Catholic leaders began to take a direct initiative. Aldo Moro, for example, revitalized the FUCI, and what was almost an alternative government formed around De Gasperi in 1943. Bitterly disillusioned by military defeat, Italians eventually shook off Fascism and returned in part to the traditional left, in part to Catholic politics – this time in the form of the Christian Democratic Party.

Overall, the attitude of the Italian mass of the population was still tacitly loyal to the regime in 1939, despite the hardships faced. From 1941, however, discontent grew rapidly as opposition turned into resistance and disobedience into insurrection and civil war. This was the result of Italy's catastrophic involvement in the Second World War – the culmination of an adventurist foreign policy, to which we now turn.

MUSSOLINI'S FOREIGN POLICY, 1922–40

Did Mussolini have a foreign policy?

In his first speech as Prime Minister to the Chamber of Deputies (1922), Mussolini proclaimed that 'Foreign policy is the area which especially preoccupies us.' His intention, he said on another occasion, was simple: 'I want to make Italy great, respected and feared.' He undertook to end Italy's traditional backstage role in European diplomacy; instead of picking up the scraps left by other powers in their rivalries with each other, Italy would seize the diplomatic initiative. As a result, she would be able to secure a revision of the post-First World War settlement – that 'mutilated victory' – and extensive territory in the Mediterranean and Africa.

Historians have not, however, been inclined to take Mussolini particularly seriously. At a very early stage in post-war historiography, he was attacked for being inconsistent and a dupe to Hitler. Salvemini wrote in 1953 that he was 'an irresponsible improviser, half madman, half criminal, gifted only – but to the highest degree – in the arts of "propaganda" and mystification'.[102] This view was more or less duplicated by A.J.P. Taylor in 1961:

> Everything about Fascism was a fraud. The social peril from which it saved Italy was a fraud; the revolution by which it seized power was a fraud; the ability and policy of Mussolini were fraudulent. Fascist rule was corrupt, incompetent, empty; Mussolini himself was a vain, blundering boaster without either ideas or aims.[103]

From the late 1960s historians responded to the opening of the Italian archives by providing more complex interpretations but, even so, there has been nothing like the sort of debate which has been caused by the foreign policies of Hitler and Stalin.

This section will, therefore, attempt an overall perspective on Mussolini's foreign policy which uses some of the themes applied to Germany and Russia. Mussolini is as entitled as any other leader to be considered a serious player on the European scene. Like Hitler, he combined traditional objectives with a new radical vision of the future. Like both Hitler and Stalin, he was an opportunist who took advantage of situations as they arose while, on occasions, seeking to force the pace through more projective action. Like them, he scored successes and made mistakes, although, in his case, the latter were predominant. In addition, there was in Italy, as in Germany and Russia, a close interconnection between foreign policy and domestic issues.

In outline, Fascist foreign policy was an amalgam of three main components. The first was a continuation of Italy's traditional objectives, which had been apparent before the First World War. The liberal state, established in 1861 and completed in 1870, had sought to increase its influence in Europe in a variety of ways. Diplomatically, it had allied with Germany and Austria-Hungary in 1882 and had also sought to expand Italy's influence within the Mediterranean and in the Balkans. An empire had been formed in Eritrea and Tripoli, and an attempt had been made to conquer Ethiopia, which failed on the plains of Adowa in 1896. By 1914 Italy was still unfulfilled as a major power and its involvement in the First World War was due to a calculated gamble, in the Treaty of London, that it was more likely to achieve its objectives on the side of Britain and France. Several of the objectives constantly referred to by Mussolini were therefore pre-Fascist. Italy already had expansionist aspirations in its immediate vicinity – conscious that it alone had not benefited here from the collapse of the Ottoman Empire in Europe. Italy was already a state with imperialist ambitions which were given more urgency by the 'martyrs' of Adowa. And Italy was already conscious of its importance in European diplomacy, with any decision to change sides being likely to affect the overall balance of power. Hence, there was nothing new about Mussolini's focus on the Balkans and the Mediterranean, his talk of conquest in Ethiopia, and his policies of 'equidistance' and side-changing in Europe.

The second element was a strong sense of disillusionment which followed the Paris Peace Settlement of 1919. Italy's gains by the Treaty of St Germain had been confined to South Tyrol and Trentino. This meant that Italy's share of territory from the collapsed Austria-Hungary was less than that received by Poland, Romania or Yugoslavia. There was no compensation in Istria, despite strong Italian representation for this at the Paris Conference, and nothing at all was forthcoming from the Turkish islands in the Aegean. Italy was, therefore, already a revisionist state. Nationalist and liberal parties attacked the settlement in parliament and post-war governments were half embarrassed, half pleased by the antics of D'Annunzio in Fiume. On coming to power in 1922 Mussolini therefore inherited an immediate agenda as well as longer-term aspirations.

What, then did Mussolini provide? This was the third component. His vision for the future was based on the past – both recent and distant. The recent past had produced a united Italy, a country and a people seeking an identity based upon a modern nation state. This priority can be called 'etatism', with the focus on the state itself. The distant past provided traditions of power based on the Roman Empire. Mussolini sought to revive this heritage by giving Italy another base – the 'imperium', or empire, which would eventually transcend etatism. This overall aim has, however, attracted considerable controversy – both in its conception and in its attempted fulfilment.

Some historians, mainly Italian, deny that Mussolini had long-term grandiose schemes for imperial expansion;[104] others, like Knox,[105] Kallis,[106] Rodogno[107] and Mallet,[108] consider that such aims were fundamental to Mussolini's foreign policy. There are also differences of opinion as to whether Mussolini had a natural affinity with Nazi Germany. One view, advanced by A.J.P. Taylor, De Felice and others, is that he stumbled into an eventual alliance with Hitler by antagonizing Britain and France after 1935: a more positive version is that Mussolini deliberately pursued 'equidistance' (a careful manoeuvring between the powers to Italy's advantage) until events forced him to opt for Germany. According to Mallett, however, these views are now outdated. A combination with Germany was always Mussolini's preferred choice, since Britain and France were always the main impediments to Mussolini's main geopolitical objective – Italian control over the Mediterranean, north and east Africa,[109] while Kallis and Rodogno point to numerous parallels in German and Italian expansionism.

Overall, it seems that any significant turning point in Mussolini's foreign policy came after 1935, with the invasion of Ethiopia. *Before* that there were two possibilities: either Mussolini followed a largely opportunistic course, or he was unable to embark on longer-term objectives because events had not yet moved in his favour. *After* 1935 there could also be two main explanations for his actions. On the one hand, he was forced towards Germany by the elimination of possible co-operation with Britain and France. On the other, changing circumstances in Europe made it easier for Mussolini to achieve the diplomatic and military partnership he had always preferred. These approaches will be integrated into the following sections.

The development of Mussolini's foreign policy

Between 1922 and 1940 Mussolini's foreign policy underwent major changes. The first phase (1922–9) saw his aspirations being constrained in Europe while Italian colonial rule became increasingly brutal in north Africa. During the second phase (1930–5) Mussolini moved towards agreement with Britain and France, for reasons to be analysed. The turning point came in 1935 with the Italian invasion of Abyssinia and the third phase (1935–40) was dominated by a growing commitment to Germany and hostility towards Britain and France. Attempts to make sense of these contradictory developments have produced a variety of explanations which, in recent years, have grown increasingly complex.

Phase I: 1922–9

During the 1920s Mussolini's foreign policy appeared erratic, alternating between aggression and conciliation. Mussolini was tempted by the prospect of revising the Treaty of St Germain in Italy's favour and of expanding Italy in line with the broader imperial vision he was already showing by 1922. He was, however, constrained by the growth of collective security abroad and by the need to play himself into power at home. The result was a period in which nothing much happened for Italy in Europe apart from pinpointed aggression against Corfu and Fiume, and an attempt at anti-French diplomacy. As yet there were no opportunities to challenge British naval power in the Mediterranean or British and French predominance in north and east Africa: without an ally there was simply no prospect of Italy attempting either of these. As Mussolini realized from 1927, the only feasible possibility here was Germany, a fellow revisionist state with resentment against the Peace Settlement of 1919. But Germany was tightly constrained militarily, and the political ideology and base of the Weimar Republic had very little in common with those of Fascist Italy. Even by 1929 there seemed little chance that Italy would be joined in Europe by a second fascist regime under Hitler and Nazism. All that Mussolini could do in the 1920s was to apply pressure to Europe's diplomatic fabric to see where there might be a chance of swift glory cheaply bought while, at the same time, consolidating Italy's imperial control in Africa. In Europe Mussolini was forced to accept outcomes that were well short of his aims and to play the diplomat himself. The energy of Fascism was more apparent in Africa where there were fewer constraints on the regime's aggression and brutality.

The first instance of aggression was the Corfu Incident. On 21 August 1923 General Tellini and four other Italians were assassinated by terrorists while working for a boundary commission which was marking the border between Greece and Albania. Mussolini seized the opportunity to browbeat Greece, demanding compensation of 50 million lire and an official apology. When these did not materialize, he ordered the occupation of the Greek island of Corfu, clearly his original intention. Greece, however, appealed to the League of Nations which, in turn, referred the whole matter to arbitration by the Conference of Ambassadors. The outcome was a compromise which Mussolini accepted, with extreme reluctance, under strong British diplomatic pressure. Italian marines were pulled out of Corfu on 27 September and the Greek government paid the 50 million lire, but did not apologize. Within two weeks of the settlement of the Corfu Crisis, Mussolini tried again, this time more successfully. He installed an Italian commandant in Fiume, a city whose status was in dispute as it was claimed by both Italy and Yugoslavia. In this instance, Yugoslavia had no alternative but to agree to the Italian occupation as her main ally, France, was militarily involved in the Ruhr. Mussolini's victory was formalized in 1924 by the Pact of Rome.

By 1925, however, Mussolini was showing a more reasonable face – this time to the European powers. Gustav Stresemann, Aristide Briand and Austen Chamberlain, foreign ministers of Germany, France and Britain, were committed to international co-operation and the construction of a system of collective security. Mussolini was at first reluctant to involve Italy in any specific scheme, as it would limit his chances of a future diplomatic coup. Increasingly, however, he came under pressure from two directions. Externally, he was persuaded by French and British diplomats and was courted by Chamberlain, who particularly wanted Mussolini's participation. Internally, the more traditional and non-Fascist career diplomats of the Italian Foreign Ministry brought all their persuasiveness to bear.[110] The result was Mussolini's signature on the Locarno Pact. Partly as a result of this concession, British opinion of Mussolini became more favourable. Over Corfu he had shown a petulant outburst which seemed to go against the pragmatic trend of Italian diplomacy; Locarno seemed to indicate that he had at last moved to a more moderate and sensible course – in the tradition of Cavour.[111]

Or had he? Elsewhere in Europe Mussolini was doing what he could to destabilize the international scene. It could be argued that he was trying to make up for his lack of influence in western Europe by pressing particularly hard for advantages in the Balkans. He was resolutely hostile to French efforts to influence eastern Europe through a series of alliances. More fundamentally, Mussolini had conceived a deep dislike for France. This was partly ideological, as France harboured most of Italy's anti-Fascist exiles. It was also partly strategic, as France seemed to block the way to Italy's expansion in the Mediterranean and Africa. Hence, he tried to destroy the French system in eastern Europe and, in the process, to penetrate the Balkans. His main target was the French-sponsored Little Entente of Yugoslavia, Romania and Czechoslovakia. At first it appeared that he might break this by peaceful means. In 1924 he drew up a commercial agreement with Czechoslovakia and a treaty of friendship with Yugoslavia. But then he overreached himself in a sudden lunge for territory and glory. He became involved in the Albanian Civil War, supporting the rebel Noli against Yugoslavia's protégé, Zogu. Although Italy came to establish a virtual protectorate over Albania, Mussolini lost the chance to detach Yugoslavia from the French system. Indeed, the Little Entente tightened and Mussolini felt obliged to attempt to sponsor a counter-bloc consisting of Albania, Hungary and Bulgaria.

How successful had Mussolini been by 1929? On the one hand, his policies had been confined to the achievement of the possible: Mussolini's objectives were based at this stage on a limited etatist base and seemed to lack the broader sweep of the imperium. He was clearly frustrated by the restrictions imposed upon him by Italy's limited infrastructure but had not yet developed the confidence (or recklessness) to try to break through these. The positive side was that he was highly rated by British leaders. Churchill called him 'Roman genius in person' and Austen Chamberlain said, 'I trust his word when given and think we might easily go far before finding an Italian with whom it would be as easy for the British Government to work.'[112] On the other hand, there was still much unfinished business. Italy remained outflanked by French influence in the Balkans and there were times when the Locarno Pact seemed a major disadvantage; in helping guarantee the Rhine, Mussolini had freed French and German attention, which could now wander to central Europe, and Austria.

During this period Mussolini looked beyond Italy's shores and frontiers for the achievement of his more grandiose designs for Italy. Although there was – as yet – no chance of achieving a new Roman imperium in Europe and the Mediterranean, he *could* consolidate Italy's position in north and east Africa, thereby promoting Italian expansion from the periphery towards the centre rather than by the more conventional Roman way. He aimed at this stage to consolidate Italian control over Eritrea and Somaliland in east Africa and over Libya in north Africa. Mussolini had aspirations for linking these together by future conquests in Ethiopia, the Sudan and possibly Egypt. An enlarged Italian empire would confirm Italy's claim to be a major European power and provide an outlet for the future expansion of Italy's population. This scenario for a new Roman empire might seem far-fetched in the 1920s – until we remember that Hitler was at the same time developing ideas for Germany's Lebensraum in eastern Europe. The difference was that Mussolini was already Prime Minister of Italy, whereas Hitler had just served a prison sentence on a charge of treason.

Mussolini's main focus in the 1920s was north Africa. Libya had been held by Italy as a colony since 1912, but virtually nothing had been done to administer or develop it and Italian control had loosened. Mussolini visited it in 1926 and made it the target of special plans for the future. These included new urban centres, land reclamation and the attraction of tourism. Between 1928 and 1933 Libya was 'pacified' by Badoglio and Graziani – which involved removing a population of some 100,000 from parts of the interior. This was conducted with deliberate ferocity and brutality and the concentration camps set up on the coast brought many deaths from starvation and disease. In dealing with a local rebellion from 1931, led by Omar el-Mukhtar, the Italians bombed civilians with poison gas.[113] Altogether, it has been estimated that one-tenth of Libya's population perished under Fascism.[114] This was shrouded in secrecy, even after the end of the fascist regime in Italy. It is significant as the exception to Mussolini's otherwise restrained external policies during the 1920s and early 1930s, showing that restraint was imposed upon him rather than chosen by him. It was also an indicator for the future, showing the potential of Fascism for racism overseas and providing the experience and testing ground for later expansion in Ethiopia.

Phase 2: 1930–5

The European situation changed between 1929 and 1934 as a result of the Great Depression. Multilateral co-operation through international institutions began to give way to bilateral agreements and rivalries. This situation clearly benefited Mussolini, since it gave him more room within which to manoeuvre.

It has usually been argued that Mussolini aimed to make a more definite mark on European diplomacy through the pursuit of a more consistent and reasoned policy. In this way he would emerge, as he had always intended, as Europe's senior statesman and arbiter. It has been argued that, at this stage, Mussolini was capable of a shrewd and realistic assessment of the European scene. His new device was to promote rival blocs, with Italy acting as mediator and maintaining a calculated equidistance between the powers involved. On one side would be France and Britain. On the other would be Germany, increasingly revisionist and determined to undermine the Versailles Settlement. Mussolini would commit Italy to neither; instead, he would create tensions or, alternatively, promote détente in such a way that Italy would always be the beneficiary. He may even have thought that Britain and France would become so dependent on Italian co-operation in containing Germany that they would have to grant major concessions in the Mediterranean and Africa. Should they ever take Italy for granted, Mussolini could always exert diplomatic pressure on them by producing the German card, or backing German revisionist claims. Either way, etatism would eventually expand into the imperium.

Before long, the argument continues, Mussolini found this card unplayable, for Germany came to pose an even greater threat to Italian interests than had France. The source of the trouble was Austria. It was well known that the German right had long favoured the absorption of this rump of the former Austro-Hungarian Empire, a danger which increased with Hitler's appointment as Chancellor in January 1933. Mussolini was desperately anxious to avoid this Anschluss, since he regarded Austria as an Italian client state and as a military buffer zone. A crisis occurred in 1934 when the Austrian Nazi Party was involved in the assassination of the Austrian Chancellor, Dollfuss. Fearing that Hitler would use the chaos within Austria as an excuse to annex it, Mussolini sent Italian troops to the frontier. Meanwhile, he was forced to swallow his previous prejudices and seek closer ties with France – who also dreaded the prospect of an enlarged Germany. He therefore dropped his designs on the Balkans, and in January 1935 formed an accord with France. This was followed, in April, by the Stresa Front in which Mussolini joined Britain and France in condemning German rearmament, announced by Hitler in the previous month. Although forced by events in Austria to abandon his preferred strategy of equidistance, Mussolini seemed, nevertheless, to have recovered a degree of diplomatic security. He also took part in discussions with French foreign minister Laval in January 1935 which would allow Mussolini a free hand in Ethiopia in return for continuing Italian diplomatic support over Germany. The end of equidistance therefore gave way to the pursuit of the imperium.

More recent interpretations have called into question both the intended permanence of 'equidistance' and the extent of Mussolini's alienation from Germany. Instead, the Duce was biding his time until he could extract more favourable terms from the Führer which would enable him to pursue Italian expansion at the expense of British and French interests. The pressure on Hitler imposed by the Stresa front was to Mussolini a manoeuvre rather than a change of course and could easily be reversed in the future. As we have seen elsewhere, this approach takes Mussolini more seriously by acknowledging that he had long-term objectives. Nevertheless it may well underestimate the instinctive dislike and distrust that Mussolini had for Hitler in the period 1933–6. He had already criticized Nazi racial policies; he had also considered Nazism a sufficient threat to justify sending Italian troops to the Austrian frontier after the assassination of Dollfuss in 1934. In any case, how much did Mussolini actually need German military support in 1935? Irrespective of his longer-term aims at their expense, it might have made more sense to boost Italy's imperialism with the tacit agreement of Britain and France. Germany was as yet unproven as a revived military power: the remilitarization of the Rhineland and the beginning of the Four-Year Plan began only in 1936. In 1935, therefore, Mussolini opted openly for Italian action in east Africa, ending the period of Italian containment but keeping his options open for the future. He was confident that this would be a success.

Phase 3: 1935–40

From 1935 Italy became involved in a period of hectic activity, behaving in every way like an expansionist power with further imperial ambitions in both Africa and Europe. Mussolini began by launching an invasion on Ethiopia in 1935, moved on to providing military assistance to Franco and the Nationalists in Spain, and then seized Albania in 1939. In the process, Italy gravitated towards Germany in three stages – the Rome–Berlin Axis (1936), the Anti-Comintern Pact (1937) and the Pact of Steel (1939). This course led Italy into an ultimately disastrous war in 1940.

The Ethiopian War was sparked by the Wal Wal Incident. In December 1934 a party of Italians was fired upon at an oasis on the Ethiopian side of the border with Italian Somaliland. An immediate apology was demanded from Ethiopia, since Italy claimed the right to use Wal Wal. The matter was, however, referred to the League of Nations, while Italy prepared, over the next ten months, for a full-scale invasion of Ethiopia. All seemed well for Mussolini, particularly since Britain and France were unwilling to condemn his attitude. When the League eventually refused to apportion blame for the Wal Wal Incident, Mussolini decided to go ahead with the invasion; this commenced, from Eritrea, in October 1935, under the leadership of Graziani and De Bono. Italian troops won a major victory at Adowa, erasing the humiliating memory of defeat there in 1896. In November, however, a sinister development occurred with Badoglio's use of poison gas against Ethiopian troops and civilians. This time the League responded more decisively by applying, from October, economic sanctions against Italy. Unfortunately, these were largely ineffectual since they excluded vital materials like oil, coal, iron and steel. It also appeared that Britain and France were willing to connive at Mussolini's conquests. The Hoare–Laval Pact of December 1935 would have given Italy northern and southern Ethiopia, leaving an independent state in the centre. This scheme was leaked to the press and eventually howled down by public opinion. Nevertheless, nothing was done to prevent the Italian advance on Addis Ababa, which fell in May 1936.

The Ethiopian War was a turning point in Italian policy, for which various reasons have been given. More traditional views have emphasized Mussolini's inconsistency. A.J.P. Taylor confessed to being mystified by Mussolini's decision for action in Africa in 1935 at a time when Germany was still threatening Austria. This threat did, however, dictate a speedy conquest to enable Italy to prevent further German threats in central Europe. Some historians have attributed Mussolini's decision to a determination to allow no further delay in completing the task of conquest that had failed so disastrously at the first attempt in 1896. The international situation had to be favourable, which involved some fine calculations on Mussolini's part: 1935 provided a more favourable chance than Mussolini had had before – provided that he could produce a quick result. Others, such as Cassels, Mack Smith and De Felice consider that internal dynamics explain the apparent inconsistency of Mussolini's actions. Rearmament was essential to reactivate the economy after a period of decline brought on by the Depression. Fascism had stalled ideologically and needed renewed impetus, while social cohesion and support would be strengthened by military success.

There are, however, dissenting voices. 'Taken as a whole, none of these explanations have stood the test of time.'[115] Mallett's summary of the arguments against these includes three main points. First, the impact of the Depression was largely over by 1934 and social cohesion was not threatened, since there was no real challenge to the political supremacy of Fascism, 'Italy being a one-party dictatorial state with a mostly efficient internal security apparatus'.[116] Second, there had been a long-standing commitment to imperial expansion and to domination of the Mediterranean, which meant that Italy would have to come eventually into conflict with Britain and France. 'Works that have examined more closely Mussolini's thinking over the period from January 1935 onwards have confirmed that, for him, an Italian annexation of Ethiopia marked not a limited phase of overseas expansion, but, on the contrary, only the beginning of a more ambitious imperial policy.' Third, this would entail future expansion into the Sudan and possibly Egypt and therefore conflict with Britain. According to recent research into the Italian archives, Mussolini ordered Italian forces to prepare for attacks on the Royal Navy if necessary. He was greatly assisted by the low-key approach taken by the Baldwin government in Britain which, at this stage, was anxious to avoid any possibility of direct conflict with Italy.[117]

Far apart though these views appear to be, they are not entirely mutually exclusive. There is certainly a strong case for saying that expansion in the Mediterranean and into Ethiopia were part of a long-term geopolitical ambition – even if this risked the possibility of conflict with Britain and France and necessitated a future alliance with Germany. The Ethiopian venture was, therefore, more than a desperate attempt to seek a distraction from problems within Italy or an opportunist exploitation of favourable international circumstances. Yet to place all – or even most – of the emphasis on the pursuit of a project for its own sake is not entirely convincing either. Mussolini may well have been holding back on the pursuit of long-term aims before 1935. But what made 1935 the decisive turning point in his foreign policy? Mussolini was still at odds with Germany over Austria, while Hitler had yet to provide any convincing evidence that Germany would provide the military support and military strength that Italy would need to challenge Britain and France. There was still an area of considerable uncertainty and Mussolini was taking as much of a chance as ever, as

Taylor pointed out. Yet the Taylorian explanation that Mussolini was a blunderer is also unconvincing. Mussolini must have had sound reasons for concluding that 1935 was the right time to launch the invasion of Ethiopia. This is where the argument for the favourable international situation still applies – just as it does to the opportunities provided to the achievement of Hitler's objectives between 1936 and 1939. And committing Italy to such a vast undertaking must also have been integral to Italy's domestic needs, interpreted by Mussolini as the emergence from economic crisis into a new era of accelerated Fascism based on popular enthusiasm mobilized by intensified propaganda. The motivation was therefore long-term but the means of achieving it was more immediate.

The Ethiopian War had momentous results. By one argument, it narrowed the range of Mussolini's future diplomatic options. Britain and France were alienated by the method of conquest and were never to trust Mussolini again. Germany was considerably strengthened, as Hitler used Mussolini's involvement in Africa, together with the diversion this caused to Britain and France, to remilitarize the Rhineland in 1936. Mussolini had seriously miscalculated; Hitler had reacted far more rapidly than he had expected and, to make matters worse, Austria was more vulnerable than ever before. From 1936 Germany exerted a profound influence on Italy, based on growing diplomatic confidence and military strength. Within Italy this influence took the form of a racial programme, while externally Mussolini was hoping to synchronize his own ideology with Hitler's Nazism to produce a century of Fascism.

This line has, however, been questioned as being too dismissive and a more positive interpretation of Mussolini's approach has been suggested. By 1936 Mussolini was more concerned with challenging Britain and France than with preventing Germany's expansion into Austria. Indeed, Italian concessions over Austria could be used as a means of persuading Hitler to back Mussolini against Britain, thereby ending any need for Mussolini to try to regain Britain's goodwill. Hence, according to Bell, 'From being a member of an anti-German coalition, Italy began to cultivate German friendship'.[118] The implication is that Mussolini made a definite decision to move Italy towards Germany, rather than being forced away from Britain and France. In addition, Mallett points out that recently released archival material 'leaves little room for doubt that in the aftermath of the Ethiopian Crisis of 1935–6 Mussolini actively courted Hitler's Germany, and aligned Italian policy closely to that of the Reich'.[119]

Although such interpretations do acknowledge that Mussolini was more in control of Italy's foreign policy after 1935 than was once thought, they do not indicate that he followed the most appropriate course. From 1936 a policy of consolidation would have made most sense, giving Italy the chance to replace losses caused by the Ethiopian War. Yet even before this conflict had ended Mussolini had made another commitment – this time to assisting Franco's National Front against the Spanish Republic. Involvement in the Spanish Civil War was motivated partly by an obsessive hatred of left-wing popular-front governments. The future, he wanted to proclaim, lay with Fascism, nationalism and right-wing militarism. It might well be possible to establish Italian influence over a series of fascist or semi-fascist states in the Mediterranean; influence over Spain, for example, could well lead to control over Salazar's Portugal. In strategic terms, this would weaken Britain's naval position in the western Mediterranean and make Gibraltar extremely vulnerable. It would mean that the Soviet Union would lose Spain as a potential ally and that France would be outflanked by three hostile states – Spain, Italy and Germany. There was also a military motive for involvement, as Italy could test the efficiency of her armed forces in a different theatre of war. Italian contributions to the Nationalist cause were considerable. By 1937 50,000 Italian troops were active in Spain and the total death toll had reached 6,000.

Mussolini also provided 763 aircraft and 1,672 tons of bombs, 950 tanks and 7,663 motor vehicles, 1,930 cannon and 240,747 small arms, and the use of 91 warships – all at a total cost of 14 billion lire.[120] Admittedly, other governments became involved; Hitler also supplied Franco, and Stalin assisted the Republic. There is no doubt, however, that Italy's sacrifices were by far the largest.

To what effect? Italy's involvement has usually been seen as a major blunder. Certainly Mussolini was unable to make up the loss of equipment before the outbreak of the Second World War. This was to prove very serious. Both Britain and France, convinced that Italy was now irrevocably hostile, began from 1937 to rearm at a pace which Italy, with her smaller industrial base, could not match. While all the other major powers were stronger in 1939 than they had been in 1936, Italy was undeniably weaker. The full extent of her vulnerability was not yet known, but clues were provided by the humiliation of the Italians by Spanish Republican forces at Guadalajara. Nor was there any real gratitude from Franco, who would agree only to guarantee Spanish neutrality in any conflict between Italy and another power. More than ever, Mussolini had to depend on Germany. He tried to ignore the uncomfortable truth that war, and the policy of autarky which accompanied it, had disrupted Italian trade and allowed Germany to penetrate Italy's markets in the Balkans. He therefore had to swallow his personal dislike of Hitler and give Italy up to what F.W.D. Deakin has termed the 'Brutal Friendship'. Again, this has been questioned by the more recent argument that Mussolini was actively preparing the way for a stronger relationship with Germany in preparation for taking on British and French influence; the emphasis is now very much on the 'aggressive and pro-Nazi characteristics of the Duce's policies'.[121]

This connection between Italy and Germany was formalized by the Rome–Berlin Axis, a term first used by Mussolini in a speech delivered in Milan on 1 November 1936. This followed a visit by the Italian Foreign Minister, Ciano, to Berlin and Berchtesgaden to secure an agreement on joint intervention in Spain. Both Germany and Italy were well satisfied. Germany had succeeded in pulling Italy into her corner. As von Hassell, German ambassador in Rome, had observed, the Spanish Civil War was reinforcing the lesson of the Ethiopian War and Italy was realizing 'the advisability of confronting the western powers shoulder-to-shoulder with Germany'.[122] The Axis was further tightened by the signing of the Anti-Comintern Pact with Germany and Japan in November 1937 and the Pact of Steel (May 1939) which committed Germany and Italy to mutual support in any offensive or defensive war. Italy, for her part, was momentarily enjoying the sensation of power. In 1937 Ciano exulted: 'The situation of 1935 has been transformed. Italy has broken out of her isolation: she is in the centre of the most formidable political and military combination which has ever existed.'[123]

Unfortunately for Mussolini, Germany's seniority in the Rome–Berlin Axis soon became obvious. Hitler forced the pace, and some of his actions showed open contempt for Mussolini. In March 1938, for example, he gave Rome only a few hours' notice before sending German troops into Austria. This has been seen as the beginning of the end of Fascist Italy as 'the shadow of the predatory and overwhelming force of pan-Germanism' fell over her.[124] It is true that Mussolini managed to regain some of his stature as a mediator at the Munich Conference in September 1938, but this was because it suited Hitler to cast Mussolini temporarily in this role, before returning to his customary offhand manner. On two occasions in 1939 Mussolini was given virtually no advance notice of German intentions: the occupation of Bohemia in March and the conclusion of the Nazi–Soviet Pact in August. Yet, amazingly, Mussolini's government failed to monitor the wording of the Pact of Steel which bound Italy militarily to Germany; instead, Ciano virtually gave a blank cheque to his German counterpart, von Ribbentrop. Mussolini was also deceived over Hitler's timetable. He had assumed in May 1939 that Germany was not intending to fight a war before 1943 at the earliest. When Germany invaded Poland in September 1939, Mussolini was severely embarrassed by Italy's total inadequacy to meet the commitments of the Pact of Steel. Ciano had to submit to Berlin a list of strategic *matériel* urgently needed by Italy. When Germany offered only a small quantity, Mussolini had no option but to seek from Hitler a temporary release from his military obligations. Part of the problem was that Italy's resources had been overextended by Mussolini's attack on Albania in April; he could not afford now to rush into a conflict with France and Britain which Hitler had so inconveniently provoked. Even so, for a man with such a huge ego, this peace was a humiliation, to be reversed at the earliest opportunity.

Conclusions 1922–40

Overall, Mussolini's foreign policy had definable long-term aims. These involved converting etatism into the imperium – in the Mediterranean, Africa and Europe. They would involve challenging Britain and France as the containing powers and also as the anti-revisionist guarantors of the Versailles settlement. But such aims could only be latent between 1922 and 1935; during this period small gains could be made through opportunism, which related to short-term methodology rather than to overall ambition. The fulfilment of this ambition began in 1935, the turning point at which Mussolini committed Italy to Germany as an essential part of his challenge to Britain and France in the Mediterranean and Africa. The problem was that the extension of Italy's base by Mussolini beyond the traditional overseas imperial one could not be achieved with Italy's resources. This was to be Mussolini's real failure.

The interconnection between foreign policy and domestic issues

It has become increasingly common in historical writing to point out the close links between foreign and domestic policies. Much has been made of the attempts made by rulers like Napoleon III and Wilhelm II to mobilize popular support and maintain domestic harmony through the deliberate use of aggressive diplomacy, territorial expansion and war. Most observers see the same tendency in Mussolini's policy and would agree with Morgan's assessment that the 'customary separation of foreign and domestic matters' can be 'artificial and distorting'. Instead, 'Internal and external policies were explicitly linked and interacted in a synchronised way.'[125]

There is, however, some difference over the extent of his calculation, especially over the decision to invade Ethiopia. Perhaps the grandest conception has been put forward by De Felice, who sees Fascism as a 'revolutionary phenomenon' which aimed at the 'mobilization of the masses and the creation of a new kind of man'.[126] This had not been accomplished during the 1920s by domestic policies and clearly a new impetus was needed. This would be external expansion; hence 'the Ethiopian question was not only one of waging war, but also principally of creating the new Fascism after the conquest of the empire'.[127] In terms of generating a new spirit and mobilizing support behind the Duce, the Ethiopian War was Mussolini's political masterpiece and his greatest success.

Another Italian writer, Carocci, emphasizes the search for an instant remedy rather than the achievement of a grand design. By 1935, he argues, the situation at home was potentially dangerous:

> People all over the country felt indifferent to the regime, detached from it. In order to overcome these feelings, in order to galvanise the masses and try to break the vicious circle of economic crisis, more drastic and more attractive measures were needed.[128]

De Grand partly disagrees with this – but in terms of the timing rather than the principle. He maintains that the decision was not born of desperation; there were 'no compelling economic imperatives in Italy for expansion in 1934 and 1935. The worst crisis of the depression had been overcome.'[129] Nevertheless, he adds, the decision for the invasion was made at the peak of the economic crisis in 1932. Mack Smith argues that the purpose of Mussolini's foreign policy was to bolster his prestige, which by the mid-1930s had been affected by economic strain. The device used was propaganda on a massive scale; indeed, 'any history of Mussolini's foreign policy has to be . . . a history of propaganda'.[130] The whole process created an addiction; the addiction led to self-delusion. Increasingly Mussolini was misled by his own pronouncements, pursued erratic policies and ignored basic facts. Such an argument was also adopted by contemporaries of Mussolini. Salvemini, an exile from Fascist Italy, identified Mussolini as 'a buffoon, a sawdust Caesar', living hand-to-mouth in a desperate effort to make his foreign exploits rally support for his domestic measures and to stabilize the base of his regime.

Some historians remain unconvinced by this type of argument. Knox, for one, sees in Mussolini's expansionism a genuine vision – equivalent to Hitler's quest for Lebensraum.[131] Foreign policy did not proceed from 'internal social or political pressures'. Indeed, what happened in the 1930s was the opposite of 'social imperialism'. To extend this line of reasoning, it might be said that Fascism was an ebullient ideology which had to turn outwards in order to seek sublimation in struggle, militarism and conquest. This approach would reduce the emphasis on domestic problems in the mid-1930s. It could be argued that Mussolini's personality cult had already won the battle for popular acceptance and support; it now had to be justified by action. After all, Italians had been led to believe, it was better to live 'one day as a lion than a thousand years as a lamb'.

WAR AND COLLAPSE, 1940–5

Italy in the Second World War

Italy's neutrality, announced by Mussolini on 3 September 1939, came to an end with his declaration of war on Britain and France on 10 June 1940. Why did he change his mind?

During the intervening months the situation in Europe had been transformed. Hitler's Blitzkrieg had crushed Poland within four weeks and his offensive in the west had brought the collapse of Norway, Holland and Belgium. Mussolini, therefore, felt that he had little to fear. Italy would not be committing herself to a prolonged struggle, as France was on the point of defeat and it was only a matter of time before Britain fell. Hence, there was a chance for Mussolini to erase the humiliating memory of non-belligerence by joining Hitler as an equal partner in a great Axis offensive. He envisaged a short conflict, lasting perhaps only a few weeks, and followed by a conference at which Italy would receive the spoils due to a victorious power.

These expectations were not fulfilled. Italian troops made slow progress in the Alpine War against a severely weakened France, managing to win only a few square miles of territory. The main disappointment was that Hitler was unwilling to hand France's North African colonies to Italy, preferring to leave them and the French Mediterranean fleet under

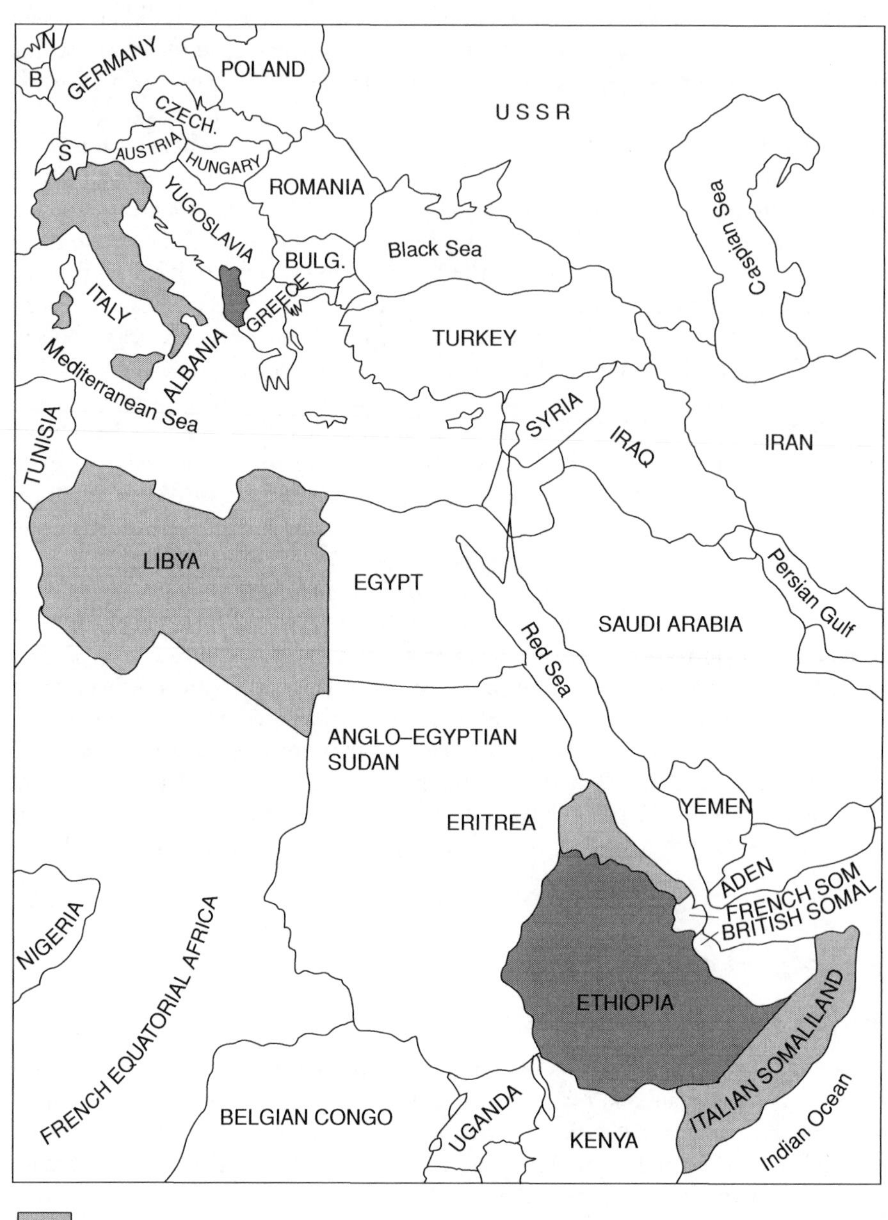

Map 4 The Italian overseas empire by 1939

the puppet Vichy regime to ensure the latter's permanent collaboration with Germany. Nor could Mussolini expect easy compensation in the form of British territory in Africa: the Royal Navy was still active in the Mediterranean and the long-awaited German invasion of Britain had not materialized. Once again there was the danger that Italy would play a totally subordinate role to Germany – unless, of course, Mussolini could regain the initiative.

He attempted to do so in the 'parallel war'. The intention was to develop an Italian sphere of influence in the Balkans and North Africa, leaving Germany to dominate northern Europe. Hence, in September 1940, he launched an Italian invasion of British Egypt from Libya and, in October, attacked Greece. But his hopes of a new Roman Empire covering most of the eastern Mediterranean were swiftly shattered. The Greeks repulsed the Italian attack and Hitler had to mount an extensive rescue operation in the Balkans in 1941; when, eventually, Greece and Yugoslavia did fall, it was to the Germans not the Italians. The British, meanwhile, counter-attacked from Egypt, achieving major successes under Wavell early in 1941. Again, the Germans had to take over and Mussolini was partly relieved, partly humiliated by the successful campaigns of Rommel. No rescue was possible, however, in the Horn of Africa where, during the course of 1941, Italy lost to British Empire troops her prized colonies of Somaliland, Eritrea and Ethiopia.

Floundering badly in the sort of prolonged war which he had not anticipated, Mussolini became increasingly desperate and irrational. He proved entirely willing to go along with Hitler in widening the scope of the war. In 1941, for example, he pressed on Hitler a total of 61,000 Italian troops to assist the German invasion of the Soviet Union. In the same year he declared war on the United States in the naïve belief that America was a degenerate power which could never adapt a consumer-based economy to military needs. He placed increasing emphasis on ideology, envisaging an ultimate Fascist triumph over the forces and theories of Bolshevism and liberal democracy. Yet, despite his attempts to retain at least some influence over the Axis alliance, the reality was that Italy's dependence on Germany was now total.

The trouble was that Germany was now beginning to lose ground. From late 1942 German forces in North Africa and on the eastern front were heavily assailed by Montgomery, Eisenhower and Zhukov. Hitler's priority was the Russian campaign, which involved drawing off German troops and supplies from North Africa. This sealed Italy's fate. The Western Allies won back North Africa early in 1943 and, at the Casablanca Conference, agreed that the first attacks on Axis-controlled Europe should be directed against Italy as its 'soft underbelly'. Consequently, British and American troops landed in Sicily in July 1943. Even before they crossed over to mainland Italy, Mussolini had been removed from power. On 8 September the new Italian government officially surrendered to the Allies. The Germans, however, occupied northern Italy, delaying final victory for the next eighteen months.

Reasons for the Italian defeat

One of the main factors in the Italian defeat was the series of disastrous decisions taken by Mussolini himself, often against the advice of his ministers. The first of these was to commence hostilities in June 1940 with the full knowledge that the Italian Commission on War Production had warned that Italy could not sustain a single year of warfare until 1949. The second was to initiate a 'parallel war' when it seemed unlikely that Germany would co-operate with Italian designs on French colonies; Mussolini's invasion of Greece in October 1940 was a botched attempt to gain territory in the other direction to compensate for this disappointment. The third error was to commit Italy so lightly and with so little thought of the consequences against the world's two industrial and military giants, the United States and the Soviet Union. The former played a vital part in rolling back the Axis occupation of North Africa, while the latter drained off the Axis troops needed to prevent this. Of the three mistakes, the first was the most catastrophic, as it made Italy entirely dependent on German military success. Hitler destroyed Mussolini's chances of swift victory by broadening his own objectives to fit into his own visionary scheme, and the invasion of Russia doomed Fascist Italy long before it brought about the collapse of the Third Reich.

Italy's armed forces were inadequate to the demands placed upon them by Mussolini. Earlier losses incurred in the Ethiopian War (1935–6) and the Spanish Civil War (1936–9) had not been made up and there was, by 1940, a hollow ring to Mussolini's boast that Italy could mobilize 8 million men within hours. In fact, the Italian army in 1940 comprised a total of 3 million men, who were inadequately supplied with 1.3 million rifles (of 1891 design); the most reliable weapons proved to be those captured from the Austrians at the end of the First World War. The army had only 42,000 vehicles, including obsolete tanks and armoured cars which could be pierced by rifle fire. Ignorant of these deficiencies, Mussolini gambled everything on a lightning war – or *guerra lampo* – the equivalent to Hitler's Blitzkrieg. In practice this strategy was inoperable, partly because Italy had no equivalent to Germany's panzer divisions and partly because Italian generals were intensely suspicious of such methods; they regarded the tank as having little practical application to the demands of warfare either in Europe or in North Africa. The army was also poorly organized and the mobilization of August 1939 was so inept that it is doubtful whether Italy could have entered the war at that stage even if Mussolini had decided to do so. There was virtually no co-operation with either the German government or the German High Command, in complete contrast to the joint planning undertaken by the Western Allies in their conquest of North Africa and France.

Of the other two services, the navy was the better equipped and had actually been admired by Hitler in the mid-1930s. Yet here, too, there were serious deficiencies. Italian warships were designed essentially for speed, which meant that their heavy fuel consumption limited their effective range to 6,500 miles. No aircraft carriers were built, as Mussolini believed that Italy was herself a 'natural aircraft carrier'. Although eight battleships were under construction in 1939, the incredible fact remains that not one of them hit an enemy ship with its shells. Italy did possess the world's largest fleet of submarines but they were notoriously slow to submerge and losses amounted to 10 per cent within the first weeks of war. Italy's airforce was also defective. Mussolini had once boasted that he could make the skies black with Italian aircraft, but in reality Italian production was far below that of the other Axis powers, Germany and Japan. The quality was also suspect, and the RAF had comparatively little difficulty in knocking out the Fiat CR 42, the Fiat G 50 and the Macchi MC 200. Matters were made even worse by the refusal of the airforce leadership to co-ordinate its plans with the army and navy. Unlike the Luftwaffe and the RAF, the Italian airforce always demanded, and received, special autonomy. This was part of a long-term rivalry between the three services, which made combined operations virtually impossible. Hence, according to Whittam, 'Military weakness had been built into the regime from the very start.'[132]

Underlying Italy's military weakness was a severely limited economic and industrial base. Mussolini's policy of self-sufficiency had failed to solve the problem of the shortage of strategic *matériel* and, as we have seen, Germany was slow to respond to Ciano's appeals for help in August 1939. Italy went against the overall trend for industrial nations by experiencing between 1940 and 1943 a decrease in production of 35 per cent in industry and 25 per cent in agriculture. The figure which most effectively conveys Italy's limitations as an industrial power is that for steel production: 2.4 million tons in 1939, compared with Britain's 13.4 million and Germany's 22.5 million. This meant that Italy had serious problems in converting her limited industrial infrastructure to sustained warfare. Kennedy estimates that Italy's 'war potential' in 1937 was only 2.5 per cent of the combined total of all the great powers, compared with Germany's 14.4 per cent, Britain's 10.2 per cent and the Soviet Union's 14.0 per cent.[133] Between 1940 and 1941 Italy's expenditure on armaments rose from $0.75 billion to $1.0 billion: the comparable figures for Britain over the same period were $3.5 billion and $6 billion.[134]

The problem was, of course, partly historic, as Italy had industrialized at a later stage than her competitors. But the responsibility rests also with the policies of Fascism, as Italy was less prepared for war in 1940 even than she had been in 1915. Germany was able to increase its levels of production from 1941 onwards by converting to 'Total War'; Italy, however, was already in economic overdrive by 1940. It is often thought that Germany had to help Mussolini by shoring up Italy from then onwards. This certainly applied militarily, but there is more doubt concerning economic contributions. Indeed, the overall balance may even have worked against Italy; according to Morgan, 'Germany began to extract more from Italy than she gave.'[135] For example, Germany made use of 350,000 Italian workers, many of whom were skilled specialists. This was partly responsible for the growing internal resentment which brought about the collapse of Mussolini's regime in 1943.

Italy as 'conqueror'

This might be seen as an unusual heading, for two reasons. One is that Italy's martial role in the Second World War was, as we have seen, brought to a comparatively swift end. The other is that some historians, especially A.J.P. Taylor, have created a stereotype of the absurdity of Mussolini's regime. Yet there is another side to this rather negative picture. Italian Fascism did have extensive ambitions for conquest and domination and, for a while, developed an actual taste for both. And, with his special relationship with Hitler, Mussolini was, for a while, able to implement some of his ambitions. At its peak, the Italian empire comprised both African colonies and European subject states. The former consisted of Eritrea and Somaliland (annexed from 1886 onwards), Libya (taken from the Ottoman Empire in 1912 and 'pacified' between 1923 and 1934), Ethiopia (invaded and conquered between 1935 and 1936), and part of Egypt. Italy's European possessions were Albania (taken in 1939), Slovenia, Croatia and Montenegro, parts of Greece (1941–3) and south-eastern France (1940–3).

The impetus behind Italy's empire was threefold. First, it was an intensified version of traditional colonialism. Ever since the late nineteenth century Italy had competed with Britain, France, Portugal and Germany for colonial possessions. In this respect, Mussolini inherited the concept of empire as a 'right' of a great power and as a means of achieving equality of international status with Britain and France in particular. Second, the extension of territorial control into Europe as well seemed to have been guaranteed by the 1915 secret Treaty of London – by which Italy had been promised South Tyrol, Trentino, parts of Dalmatia and Turkey, and the Dodecanese Islands – as an inducement to enter the Great War on the side of the Allies. Third, Mussolini took Italy's aspirations beyond both of these. Under his rule Italy had much in common with Nazi Germany. In the words of Kallis, the leaders of both regimes 'repeated the themes of constant struggle, elitism and living space with a consistency . . . which could not be dismissed a priori as mere propaganda or bluff'.[136] Nevertheless, certain features of expansionism were more specific to Italy than to Germany: Mussolini placed heavy emphasis on the Roman past, which he equated with Fascist Italy and, in particular, with Italy's further 'Roman' expansion in the Mediterranean and Africa.[137] New attention has also been brought to the purpose and style of Italian occupation by Rodogno, who argues that, in contrast to the earlier colonial empires, 'Fascism intended to impose on . . . the European peoples what the British and French had imposed on Africa and Asia'.[138]

In the end, Italy's African colonies had all conquered by the Allies before the invasion of Italy in 1943. The possessions in Europe were formally ceded by the terms of the armistice signed with the Allies but this was inoperative since they were taken over by German occupation, from which the Germans had to be dislodged by a combination of resistance movements and Allied intervention. In effect, however, Italy ceased to be an empire of any description in September 1943. Her brief experience of practising conquest and occupation raises an issue which has been an uncomfortable one for post-war Italy – war crimes. Italy has long been seen as a victim of Fascist buffoonery and of more sinister Nazi influence – and therefore, in part at least, as a victim. But the increasing seriousness given to Mussolini as a genuine dictator carries with it some culpability for the actions of a repressive totalitarian regime, however flawed this was in practice. Rodogno maintains that 'Although the Italians were not the "race of conquerors" that Mussolini wanted, they were nevertheless capable of brutality and violence'.[139] Admittedly the war crimes of Fascist Italy were fewer in total terms than those inflicted by German or Japanese occupations or by puppet dictatorships like the Ustasha in Croatia, or through the internal measures of Stalin in the Soviet Union and Franco in Spain. But there *were* massacres, heavy casualties in concentration camps, and calculated retaliation against civilians, whether in overseas colonies or in European territories; in Libya and Ethiopia, of course, there was also the extensive use of mustard gas. There has long been some reluctance to consider these outside the more general excesses of European colonial rule or the regrettable side-effects of twentieth-century warfare. But in the final analysis, can any country be both 'conqueror' and 'victim'?

The fall of Mussolini

Military disaster provoked a wave of disillusionment with Mussolini's regime. Taken in by his own propaganda, the Duce was totally unaware of the dangers; as Mack Smith observes, 'he had got used to living in cloud-cuckoo land'.[140] There was increasingly widespread opposition to German ideological and military influence; in March and April 1943 there were extensive strikes and protests, which the police were powerless to prevent.[141] There was also resentment at the rapid fall in living conditions: Italians had to put up with some of the worst hardships suffered by civilians anywhere in Europe. There was, finally, pressure for peace from those traditional groups which had once collaborated with Fascism – the industrialists and military leaders like Badoglio and Caviglia. Even the Church tried to disentangle itself from the regime, and now swung its support behind the King rather than Mussolini. The Fascist Party proved incapable of rallying the population to face adversity and was itself demoralized by the internal convulsions brought about by Mussolini himself.

Indeed, Mussolini set in motion the chain reaction of events which led to his collapse. In February 1943 he sacked Grandi, Bottai and others from high office within the Fascist Party. This provoked a set of conspiracies in which De Grand has identified two main elements. The first involved the traditionalist pre-Fascist politicians and military leaders, the second the moderate Fascists who hoped to dump Mussolini and replace him with Caviglia. With the Allied landings in Sicily, the conspirators decided on drastic measures. At a session of the Fascist Grand Council in July 1943 Mussolini was attacked by Grandi, Bottai and Ciano for his conduct of the war. They called for the full restoration of the legal organs of the state and the dismissal of Mussolini himself. This motion was eventually carried by nineteen votes to seven and Grandi explained the decision to the bewildered Duce: 'You believe you have the devotion of the people . . . You lost it the day you tied Italy to Germany.'[142] The following day Mussolini was dismissed by King Victor Emmanuel and imprisoned at the Gran Sasso. Marshal Badoglio was appointed as the new Prime Minister.

Why was Mussolini so powerless to prevent this startling turn of events? The answer lies in the delicate balance between the different powers and institutions within Italy, which Mussolini had been so careful to maintain. Under the strain of war this balance was destroyed and Mussolini was left without any political protection. During the 1930s he had missed the opportunity of giving the Fascist Party greater unity and had deliberately encouraged the growth of cliques in order to pursue a policy of divide and rule. This recoiled on him in 1943; he could rely on only a single group led by Farinacci, while the majority of the Fascist leaders turned against him, charging him with having deliberately distorted the Fascist movement. This meant, in Pollard's description, that 'The overthrow of Fascism when it came was essentially a "palace revolution".'[143]

Mussolini's vulnerability was intensified by the existence of an alternative form of leadership in Italy. Unlike Hitler, Mussolini had never assumed all the powers of head of state. The monarchy, which had been left intact, became a rallying point for the Italian army in 1943, while the coup against Mussolini was backed by Victor Emmanuel himself. In addition, Mussolini never placed his personal stamp on the Italian army. The oath of allegiance, for example, was still to the state and not to the Duce in person. Nor had he managed to create an entirely loyal military elite like Hitler's Waffen SS. He had also been less careful than Hitler in anticipating trouble from his generals, and had not taken the trouble to shuffle their positions to prevent plotting or the build-up of opposition. Even his intelligence service was defective, for he was taken completely by surprise by the July coup. Despite his known contempt for Mussolini, Hitler was astounded by the suddenness of the Duce's fall and asked: 'What is this sort of Fascism which melts like snow before the sun?'

THE ITALIAN SOCIAL REPUBLIC (RSI), 1943–5

Mussolini was rescued from the Abruzzo mountain stronghold of Gran Sasso on 12 September 1943 by a German glider-borne expedition. He was taken to Germany, where plans were made for the formation of a new Fascist state in that part of Italy which had not yet been occupied by the Allies. The intention was that Rome would remain the capital, but this was the next target of the Allies and its fall was thought to be imminent. The headquarters were therefore placed at the safer location of Salò on Lake Garda, although different ministries of the new government were spread across northern Italy. The area covered included the cities of Turin, Genoa, Milan, Verona, Padua, Venice and Bologna. The leadership was provided by three main types of Fascist. There were pro-Nazis like Pavolini, Ricci, Farinacci and Preziosi; opportunists like Graziani, who had no military future under the royal government in Rome; and those, like Pini, who remained devoted to Mussolini himself.

A 'return to the beginning'?

It has been said that the new Repubblica Sociale Italiana (RSI), alternatively known as the Salò Republic, represents a return to the beginning of the Fascist movement.

The plot of 25 July showed Mussolini how treacherous the monarchy and the old establishment could be. In a speech on 18 September, the day on which the Republic was proclaimed, Mussolini stated: 'It is not the regime that has betrayed the monarchy', but rather 'the monarchy that has betrayed the regime'. Shorn of his alliance with this, and other, traditional institutions, Mussolini was free to revive his early ideological preferences. Once again, he became anti-monarchist ('When a monarchy fails in its duties, it loses every reason for being') and displayed the kind of radicalism that once again attacked capitalism. Instead of allying with industrialists, he now intended to 'annihilate the parasitic plutocracies . . . and make labour the object of our economy and the indestructible foundation of the state'.[144] This meant that 'The state we want to establish will be national and social in the highest sense of the word; that is, it will be Fascist, this returning to our origins'. This was implemented by a new programme devised at Verona in November 1943, followed by the socialization law of February 1944. Key industries were to be nationalized, workers were to participate in factory and business management, land reform was to be initiated and there were to be wage and price controls. Overall Mussolini hoped to rebuild the original connection between radical nationalists, syndicalist workers and activist *squadristi*. It was intended as a complete reversal of the earlier trend of abandoning radicalism in a compromise with traditionalism.

From the start, however, the RSI proved a pale imitation, even a mockery, of the early Fascist movement. For one thing, it had few military powers. Since 600,000 Italians were now in internment camps in Germany, the Italian forces had been substantially reduced. Indeed, it is unlikely that there were more than 45,000 plus 80,000 conscripts and up to 50,000 elsewhere.[145] This meant that Mussolini had lost all control over Italy's destiny and was now heavily dependent on Germany. All decisions made by the Republic had to go through German Ambassador Rahn, or SS General Wolff, while eight north-eastern provinces in South Tyrol, Venetia and the Adriatic were removed from the Republic and placed under direct German administration. Pollard points out the similarity between the Salò Republic and other puppet regimes such as Vichy France, Tiso's Slovakia and Pavelic's Croatia.[146] In addition, the Republic held few of the former attractions for the various sectors of the population. Workers and peasants, who had once deserted the left for Fascism, now abandoned Fascism to return to the socialist and communist left. They took part in strikes and demonstrations and joined the Italian resistance movement. Industrialists saw no advantages to Mussolini's new radicalism and did everything in their power to prevent the implementation of the 1944 Decree Law. By 1945, therefore, only a few dozen enterprises had been nationalized. Finally, the mainstay of Fascism, the lower middle class, became resentful at the decline of living standards caused by prolonging the war against the Allies. They, too, switched their allegiance and once more craved parliamentary politics. It seemed that Italy had been jolted back into its pre-Fascist course. The RSI had become totally inappropriate.

The collapse of the Italian Social Republic, although delayed by eighteen months, was inevitable. It was rent with dissension as extremists like Farinacci and Pavolini hunted down the traitors of 25 July, to the alarm of the moderates. The Republic seemed to focus on revenge rather than unity; at Verona, for example, Ciano and several others were found guilty of treason and executed in January 1944. Mussolini himself became bitterly disillusioned and cursed the Italian people for what he called their soft character and dislike of vigorous action. He came to the conclusion that Italy was not, after all, the historical heir to ancient Rome, but a nation of serfs. As for his government, it was almost entirely in foreign hands. northern Italy had been divided into two sectors – one under German administration, the other under German influence. In the latter, which included the republic, the German army introduced a set of institutions that ran parallel to those of Mussolini and also controlled the entire network of communications between Mussolini's ministries. Mussolini's survival therefore depended entirely on German military fortunes.

Struggles in the north

Meanwhile, the RSI was confronted by growing internal opposition from many sectors of the population. This included a revival of political movements, especially the Communists (PCI), Socialists (PSI), Liberals (PLI), Christian Democrats (DC) and Actionists (Pd'A). These came together after the announcement of Mussolini's dismissal, forming the Committee of National Liberation (CNL). Part of the intention was to offset the appearance of being totally dependent on the Allies by playing a part in Italian liberation from both Nazism and Fascism. The Germans were, however, still very much in control in the north, while the newly constituted Fascist regime at first seemed to have sufficient strength, in the RSI police contingents and the National Republican Army under Graziani, to contain the opposition. The question therefore was: who would overcome this remaining obstacle – and how?

The view of the Allies was that the Italian resistance was not particularly effective and might be an encumbrance in their military campaigns against the Germans. Certainly the Allies undertook the main task of driving the latter back: first in the Battle of Monte Cassino; then, four months later by the occupation of Rome; then by breaking through the Gothic Line, north of Florence; and finally by advancing across the plains of northern Italy into the foothills of the Alps, where the Germans surrendered in April 1945. The resistance did, however, play an increasingly important role. Their numbers swelled from an initial 9,000 to 90,000 by the spring of 1944 and 250,000 by April 1945.[147] The Communists established the Garibaldi brigades from the middle of 1944, especially in Piedmont. Their purpose was to attack the German armed forces, the Fascist regime, and the industries and communications assisting the Axis war effort. There were also Patriotic Action groups (GA) which were largely independently operating cells, carrying out attacks on German and Fascist personnel and installations; these were denounced by Mussolini's governments as 'terrorists'. In all areas women played a vital role, with 35,000 in direct combat, and 70,000 in Women's Defence Groups, communications, organization and supplies.

How has this struggle been interpreted? Immediately after the end of the war and in the emergence of a new democratic Italy, the emphasis was on a united resistance that had included all Italians who were not actually Fascist. Resistance organizations liberated Italian towns and villages, in many cases before the actual arrival of the Allies. This approach was agreed by all political groups, including Social Democrats and Communists and was the basis of the work of historians such as Battaglia, who links the leadership of the Communists and the Italian proletariat with the driving force of popular patriotism.[148] Most historians see the communists as part of a broader spectrum. Procacci, for instance, maintains that the resistance 'was above all a very wide political movement. It had been the achievement not only of the workers who had sabotaged and the men of the military formations who had fought, but also of the peasants who had fed them and the priests who had hidden them'.[149]

Some, however, place more emphasis on the complex cross-currents of a 'civil war'. Pavone, for example, provides a detailed analysis of the personal as well as political views of combatants on both sides.[150] It has even been argued – for example by De Felice – that the majority of Italians did not contribute directly to either the Resistance or to the RSI, but were trapped *between* the two sides. The vicious nature of the struggle is emphasized by Mack Smith, who describes the 'growing fever of terroristic reprisal and counter reprisal'.[151] Finally, there have been suggestions of a 'class war' within the 'civil war', between those wanted to strengthen the position of the Communist Party in the future and those who feared the prospects of Communist political dominance. It has been pointed out that the resistance gave the Communists a disproportionate influence in Italian local government and made the PCI the largest Communist party outside eastern Europe.

Four 'struggles' have therefore been identified. The main war was the continuing military conflict between the Allies, on one side, and the Germans and Italian forces of the RSI on the other. This was accompanied by a popular Italian uprising, against both the RSI and the German occupation in the north, supported by a wide variety of social groups and political parties. The other two struggles are more contentious. One is a minority and vicious civil war between two bitter ideological opponents, from which the majority of the population tried to disengage. The other is a class war with the rivals, especially the Communists, seeking to build up their strength in anticipation of a new post-war Italy. The scope for further research into this whole area is therefore considerable.

The end

In April 1945 German resistance finally collapsed as the Allies broke through the Commacchio Line and the Argento Gap. After the surrender of General Wolff to the Allies, Mussolini fled from Milan with his mistress, Clara Petacci. They were picked up by partisans on the Lake Como road and, on 28 April, were shot against the gates of a villa. The final indignity was the public exhibition of their mutilated corpses, along with those of Farinacci and other leading Fascists, in the Piazzale Loreto in Milan. By a cruel irony, Mussolini had once said (referring to the martial spirit of Fascism) that 'Everybody dies the death that corresponds to his character.'[152]

REFLECTIONS ON MUSSOLINI'S DICTATORSHIP

The ideology

The relationship between Mussolini and Fascism has been seen – broadly – in three different ways. One emphasis is on Fascism as empty rhetoric or as a mere extension of Mussolini's vacuous ideas. A.J.P. Taylor dismisses Fascism as a 'fraud'. 'Everything about Fascism was a fraud. The social peril from which it saved Italy was a fraud; the revolution by which it seized power was a fraud.'[153] Others have focused on Mussolini's opportunism and the basic absence of ideology. The striking thing about Fascism, argues Halperin, 'was its identity with a single individual'. Fascism was 'fundamentally nothing but Mussolinianism'. Its identity with Mussolini gave it 'tremendous rhetorical dash' but also 'accounted for its extraordinary intellectual poverty'.[154] Fermi finds Mussolini's political ideas 'shallow or objectionable, or both',[155] while his 'doctrine of government' could be summed up 'in the words of one of those slogans of fascism which were soon to appear everywhere, in the press, on the sides of houses, along main roads and railways'.[156]

An alternative – and less dismissive – approach is that Fascism was a real force, created by Mussolini and adapted as he went along. There is, however, a particular focus on the political history of Fascism, especially as it impacted on Mussolini personally. This is common in some (but not all) biographies of Mussolini. Mack Smith, for example, maintains that 'Italian fascism was more than just Mussolini.' However, 'the quirks of character in this one man were a crucial factor in both its successes and failures.'[157] Sometimes there is a tendency not to distinguish between Fascism and the Fascist Party;[158] ideology, as such, is given little coverage beyond the actual application of ideas in action within the Party and the Fasci di Combattimento. A more distinctive role is attributed to Mussolini by Gregor. Fascism had more collective origins, formed by the ideas of men like Gentile, Michels, Papini, Malaparte, Prezzolini and Croce. Mussolini had merged these to organize 'a belief system' that was 'intellectually coherent' even before the Fascist movement was formed. Hence, 'There are few historians today who can insist that neither Fascism nor Mussolini had an ideology.'[159]

The third possibility is that Fascism was a serious entity – with or without Mussolini. There was a strong ideological undercurrent, to which Mussolini contributed, but not infrequently, a conflict developed between them as one of them shifted position. Roberts argues that 'Fascism was a messy mixture, and its centre of gravity changed as the regime evolved'.[160] Nevertheless, its ideology should not be trivialized. Its texts provide 'serious debate' over corporativism, 'serious rethinking of the Hegelian ethical state for a mass age', and 'serious discussion of the scope of Giuseppe Mazzini in the light and outcome of Marxism'.[161] The very complexity of the contributions to Fascism and the 'contradictions among the founding impulses' helped produce 'the impasse' that affected 'the regime's later phase' and the 'increased centrality of the Cult of the Duce'.[162]

The first approach is overstated and either precedes or ignores the considerable amount of work done on Fascist ideology since the late 1960s. Its main deficiency is that it confuses the issue with Mussolinianism, which can be given a separate, if overlapping identity. The second approach takes Fascism more seriously but perhaps attributes too much importance to Mussolini, either as its founder or as the co-ordinator of its different components. The third captures the diverse nature of Fascism and the internal contradictions which this subsequently engendered, although it tends to associate the centrality of Mussolini with distortion and conflict. Mussolini had the capacity both to reconcile the strands of Fascism, especially during the 1920s, and, during the 1930s, to try to radicalize Fascism with a new infusion of his own ideas: this is where the distortions occurred which some Fascists – and not a few historians – attributed to the growing influence of Nazism. This restores the initiative – but not the control – to Mussolini.

The Duce

There has always been a negative image of Mussolini, emphasizing the grotesque, incompetent and hollow features of his leadership and his regime. Mussolini was, for example, 'a vain, blundering boaster without either ideas or aims'.[163] The image of the buffoon, however, trivializes Italy's Fascist experience and encourages unhelpful stereotypes about both the dictator and his country. Instead, it is worth recalling his two contemporary images. During the 1920s he was widely praised as a 'statesman' in Europe and as a 'reconciler' at home. In the 1930s, his own propaganda asserted his claim to be a warrior and to have introduced a more dynamic phase of Fascism. The question which arises is whether this was the same man, or whether he underwent a fundamental change.

It could be argued that the Mussolini of the 1920s was under constraints which the same Mussolini had blown away by the 1930s: in other words, there was an underlying continuity in his aims. As De Grand argues, 'Despite this instability in Fascist policy, Mussolini's personal beliefs remained constant.'[164] What changed was the degree of his intervention to implement those beliefs.

Quite simply, during the 1920s he had no choice. His domestic policy involved having to build a consensus to stabilize his control over the state. He was, after all, still constrained by the King as head of state, by a largely conservative civil service and by the universalism of the Catholic Church. His best prospects lay in swift pieces of legislation which received official sanction. His foreign policy was restricted by Italy's military and economic base. Again he was obliged to confine himself to small offensives and to play the diplomatic role in international relations. The one exception was in the colonies, where – for anyone who cared to notice – Mussolini's more extreme ideas were unleashed from the start. But generally the restrained Mussolini was actually quite successful and at this stage attracted admiration rather than ridicule. What changed? Not Mussolini: during the 1930s he began to pursue his earlier objectives – as the constraints were lifted. This was not because things became easier, but because they became more difficult and chaotic. At home Italy was hit by depression, abroad it was threatened by a more assertive Germany. Mussolini's fear was that the impetus of Fascism was slowing down. He therefore revived it by accelerating corporativism, then autarky, while abroad he went all out for imperialism and expansion.

It is often asked whether Mussolini was a pragmatist or ideologue. He was, of course, both. During the 1920s his approach to power was pragmatic and authoritarian, while he set up the ideological consensus. There were ideological initiatives – such as the launching of corporativism; but there were also reconciliations, especially with Catholicism. Then, during the 1930s, occurred what De Felice has called the 'totalitarian turn' and a greater emphasis on ideology. The impetus behind this is controversial. De Grand argues that Fascism had reached 'an ideological dead-end'.[165] The implication is that Mussolini had to try something new. De Felice, by contrast, attributes the turn the momentum established by success in Ethiopia. Between the two comes Bosworth's argument that he might 'somehow at last spark a genuine revolution' and 'paradoxically sustain the ageing and tiring Mussolini through further years of office'.[166] Whichever of these applies, the late 1930s brought an injection of radicalism to Fascism and to the regime itself.

The problem was that the 'totalitarian' turn damaged Italy's infrastructure and threatened the consensus which had been established during the 1920s with the social, industrial and religious establishment. By contrast with where the 'turn' was now taking Italy, the framework of the regime in the 1920s had, been 'conservative-authoritarian'.[167] It was a major error in terms of Fascism's political stability – but the last chance to achieve Mussolini's real objectives for Fascism.

The regime

Nazi Germany and Stalinist Russia have always been considered radical and extreme: the term 'moderate' appears very rarely and tends to be used only by apologists. Fascist Italy is different. Two faces are genuinely perceived – the moderate as well as the extreme. Italian Fascism is seen as milder than Nazism or Stalinism in the sense of being less organized and systematically ruthless. According to Halperin, 'Neither as potent nor as efficient as Nazism, fascism was less brutal and more widely imitated than its German counterpart.'[168] Ridley goes further:

> But in a number of ways it was milder than Nazi Germany and Stalinist Russia or the royal despotisms of the sixteenth and seventeenth centuries. It resembled more closely Tsarist Russia in the nineteenth century, Metternich's Austria, or the France of Napoleon I and Napoleon III.[169]

The strong implication here is that Fascist Italy belonged to the authoritarian category of dictatorships, not the totalitarian.

There is something to be said for this view, and examples can be found at various points in this chapter. The OVRA was far less intrusive than the Gestapo or NKVD and there was never any equivalent of the SS. Italy was considerably less repressive internally than Francoist Spain and other more conservative regimes. Nor was there any equivalent of the redemptive and eliminationist influences in the anti-Semitism shown in Nazi ideology. The Fascist regime was based on a broad consensus and was officially sanctioned by the Catholic Church. The penetrative power of Fascism was also weakened by pronounced inefficiency – sometimes to grotesque and comical levels. Finally, the Fascist ideology itself was at least partially influenced by the ideas of Giovanni Gentile who, according to Gregor, was its conscience – 'a conscience singularly missing from National Socialism, and Marxist–Leninist totalitarianisms'.[170]

It has also been argued that there was an overlap between Fascist Italy and the more traditionally liberal regimes. This has been shown in two ways. First, the economic policies of De Stefani in the 1920s owed as much to liberal economic principles as to Fascism. Second, and more controversially, it has been said that modern liberal states have pursued policies which have themselves verged on the ruthless, thereby coming close to overlapping with fascism. According to Kedward, 'What looks like a revisionist, less severe approach to Mussolini's Italy is in many ways paving the way for a more severe critique of authoritarian liberal regimes.'[171] This could even point to 'ways in which fascism of the Italian variety and an exceptional liberalism converge'.[172] The contrast between Italy and some of the democratic states has been overdrawn, given the harshness of some of the latter's economic policies and the measures taken against trade unions and dissent.

This is not, however, the whole story. There is another, very different perspective, which takes into account all developments under Fascist rule, not just those which created a moderate consensus. The essential point is that the Fascist regime within Italy changed as it developed. As it established itself during the 1920s it was bound to have liberal influences. But these were not permanent. But, according to Bosworth, it was a distorted derivation. 'Fascism was as surely the bastard, post-First World War child of liberalism as communism was of social democracy.'[173] Moderate influences can themselves be radicalized, as happened during the 1930s. We have already seen that the Fascist regime became more assertively ideological during its second decade. This was when it began to move towards Nazism as well as towards Nazi Germany. Although some of the Nazi race science was unacceptable, Italian scientists were developing their own variant and formed part of a new racial initiative which came from Rome. Racism was part of a larger re-education programme to accelerate the development of the 'fascist man'. Mussolini's legislation in 1937 included a ban on Africans to citizenship – they could only ever be subjects: this compared with Germany's Nuremberg Laws in 1935. To Mussolini, anti-Semitism was not simply a by-product of the Nazi influence but a hardening of the whole context of Fascism. Because it upset the earlier consensus it was, of course, difficult to impose. This was a reflection on the regime's organizational deficiencies rather than on any moderation on its part. Mussolini went on to authorize the intensification of racial theory and made it one of the key influences in the Salò Republic from 1943.

Fascism has sometimes been said to have followed a form of 'spiritual racism' to distinguish it from Nazism. This is discounted by Fascist attitudes and polices in Africa from the very beginning of the regime. The thread linking Libya and Ethiopia finally emerged in Italy itself from the mid-1930s. Fascism not only had the potential for brutality on a substantial scale, but also *was* brutal. Marshal Badoglio wrote to Graziani in 1930: 'But now the course has been set and we must carry it out to the end, even if the entire population of Cyrenaica must perish.'[174] In Libya the regime set up concentration camps and experimentation with poison gas. According to De Grand: 'The empire became a gigantic testing ground for a Fascism that sought to free itself from any constraints.'[175] This, indeed, is where totalitarianism would be more completely imposed than in Italy itself. Ethiopia, too, was the scene for Fascist brutality unaffected by any degree of moderation. Mussolini himself authorized unconstrained warfare, pressing for the use of gas and for the 'gradual liquidation' of the rebellious population.[176] It is true that the scale of the killing was much smaller than that in Bolshevik Russia and Nazi-controlled eastern Europe. Nevertheless, it showed the same ferocity and gratuitousness; what it lacked was the same degree of efficiency and infrastructure. The colonial experience does, indeed, show 'what Fascism was really about'.[177]

Chapter 5

Dictatorship in Germany

Adolf Hitler was appointed Chancellor on 30 January 1933. His rise to power and the decline of the Weimar Republic are sufficiently complex to justify a preliminary section relating the main developments up to that date before proceeding to look at explanations.

THE WEIMAR REPUBLIC AND THE RISE OF HITLER, 1918–33

The formation and development of the Weimar Republic, 1918–29

The Weimar Republic was born of military defeat and revolution at the end of the First World War. Under the threat of military collapse the Kaiser's Second Reich was transformed into the Weimar Republic during what has come to be known as the 'German Revolution'.[1]

This occurred in two phases. The first was a revolution from above as, early in October 1918, the military establishment handed over power to a civilian cabinet. The High Command, under Ludendorff and Hindenburg, sensed the inevitability of defeat and tried to ease the way towards an armistice with the Allies by advising Kaiser Wilhelm II to appoint Prince Max of Baden as Chancellor. A powerful underlying motive was the army's desire to avoid any direct blame for Germany's surrender, when it came. The Allied response, however, was unfavourable; President Wilson argued that the German power structure was still intact and that he could deal only with a genuine democracy. Prince Max now prevailed upon the Kaiser to dismiss Ludendorff from his command and it seemed that, despite the Allies' reservations, the Second Reich had the most genuinely representative government since its formation in 1871.

The second phase was a revolution from below which brought down the Second Reich altogether. In late October and early November the sailors of the German fleet mutinied in Kiel and Wilhelmshaven, while military discipline was also subverted in Hamburg and Cologne. Similarly dramatic events occurred in the south, as Kurt Eisner declared Bavaria an independent republic. Prince Max, fearing the complete disintegration of Germany, resigned on 9 November, to be replaced as Chancellor by the leader of the Social Democrats, Friedrich Ebert. On the same day the Kaiser and the lesser German rulers abdicated, and a republic was proclaimed by another Social Democrat, Philipp Scheidemann, from the balcony of the Reichstag building in Berlin. Scheidemann's concluding words were: 'The old and rotten – the monarchy – has broken down. Long live the new! Long live the German Republic.'[2] Two days later, on 11 November, Germany signed an armistice with the Allies.

But the German Revolution was not yet complete. The country now experienced a brief period of civil war as rival groups of the left competed for power. The main contenders were the Social Democrats (SPD) and two more radical groups, the Independent Socialists (USPD) and the Spartacists. At first a Provisional Government was established, comprising both the SPD and the USPD. The former, however, were afraid that Germany might follow the example of Russia the year before, and that the Provisional Government would be destroyed by a coup from the radical left, perhaps from the Spartacists. To prevent this, Chancellor Ebert made a controversial deal with the army commander, General Groener, to put down any Bolshevik-style revolution which might occur. The test was not long in coming. In December the Independent Socialists withdrew from the government, while the Spartacists (who now called themselves Communists) demanded the 'sovietization' of Germany and the continuation of the revolution. The SPD put down subsequent Spartacist demonstrations in January 1919, and in the violence and bloodshed the two Communist leaders, Karl Liebknecht and Rosa Luxemburg, were killed. A second Spartacist uprising was suppressed, with much greater bloodshed, in March, while, in April, troops were sent to overthrow the Republic of Soviets which had just been proclaimed in Bavaria. Moderate socialism now appeared safe from the far left, but the latter neither forgot nor forgave the experience of 1919.

During this crisis a move was made towards establishing permanent institutions. Elections were held in January 1919 and a Constituent Assembly convened in Weimar, away from the street violence of Berlin. Three of the moderate parties formed a coalition government: the Centre Party (Z), the Democratic Party (DDP) and the Social Democrats (SPD). In opposition to the coalition were the parties of the right – the Nationalists (DNVP) and the People's Party (DVP) – as well as the Independent Socialists (USPD) of the far left. The Communists (KPD) did not contest this election. Ebert now became the first President of the Republic, with Scheidemann his Chancellor until June 1919.

Meanwhile, a constitution was being drafted by a special committee under the jurist Hugo Preuss. Eventually promulgated in August 1919, this embodied many advanced principles of democracy and borrowed freely from the experience of England, France and the United States. The main terms were as follows. The head of state was to be the President, elected every seven years by universal suffrage. He was given, by Article 48 of the constitution, emergency powers: 'In the event that the public order and security are seriously disturbed or endangered, the Reich President may take the measures necessary for their restoration.'[3] The head of the government was to be the Chancellor, appointed by the President and needing the support of the majority of the legislature, or Reichstag. The Reichstag, elected by universal suffrage by means of proportional representation, would be able to deal with legislation, defence, foreign policy, trade, finance and security. The last section of the constitution carefully itemized the various 'rights and duties of the Germans'.[4]

By the end of 1919, therefore, the republic had overcome pressures from the far left and had acquired a legal framework. The question now arising was: could it survive? The next fourteen years saw, in succession, a period of instability and severe problems (1919–23), a remarkable recovery and a period of consolidation (1923–9) and, finally, the crisis which eventually destroyed the republic (1929–33).

The most serious obstacle to the new government in 1919 was the signing of the Treaty of Versailles with the victorious Allies. The German delegation was horrified by the harshness of the terms but the Allies were determined not to make major modifications. In June, Scheidemann resigned as Chancellor in protest but his successor, Bauer, eventually agreed to accept the treaty. Versailles was to prove a millstone around the neck of the republic, and had much to do with the second problem of this early period: inflation. The devaluation of the mark started during the war but was aggravated by demobilization and by the stiff reparations imposed, under a provision in the Treaty of Versailles, in 1921. Speculation, massive overprinting of paper money and the French occupation of the Ruhr in 1923 all completed the collapse of the mark in November 1923 to 16,000 million to the pound. Savings were wiped out overnight and, for a few weeks, barter unofficially replaced the use of coinage. During the same years, political challenges compounded the difficulties of the republic. One example was the Kapp Putsch (1920), an unsuccessful but frightening attempt by the far right to seize power in Berlin; another putsch was tried by Hitler in Munich (1923) in circumstances described in the next section.

Nevertheless, the period 1923–9 saw a remarkable recovery and greater stability. This is generally known as the 'Stresemann era' because of the profound influence exerted by this leader of the DVP, first as Chancellor in 1923 and then as Foreign Minister until 1929. Vital economic developments included the stabilization of the currency in the form of the Rentenmark and an agreement on reparations with the Allies in 1924 known as the Dawes Plan. Massive investment followed, mostly from the United States, which enabled German industry to recover almost to 1913 levels, despite the loss of resources and land in 1919. At the same time, Stresemann stabilized Germany's relations with the rest of Europe. He followed the 1922 treaty with Russia with another in 1926, participated in a collective defence pact with four other countries at Locarno in 1925, and took Germany into the League of Nations in 1926. Underlying these achievements was a period of relative political stability as coalition governments functioned more or less effectively, lubricated by the political diplomacy of Stresemann himself.

These halcyon years did not last. Stresemann died in 1929, a year in which Germany was suddenly confronted by economic catastrophe. Meanwhile, lurking in the background, and preparing to take advantage of any such change of fortune, were Hitler and the Nazis.

The early years of the Nazi movement, 1918–29

Many Germans were bitterly opposed to the revolution of 1918, blaming Jews, socialists, liberals and Catholics for the fall of the Second Reich and military defeat. Particularly resentful were the *völkisch* groups which sprang up all over the country and issued racialist and anti-liberal propaganda.

One of these was the German Workers' Party (DAP), formed by Anton Drexler in Munich in January 1919. It was joined, in September 1919, by an Austrian with unfulfilled artistic pretensions who had fought in a Bavarian regiment in the German army throughout the First World War. Hitler blamed the republic for Germany's surrender and openly expressed his 'hatred for the originators of this dastardly crime'.[5] He rose rapidly to the position of the party's theorist and chief propaganda officer, and his talent as a public speaker was apparent even at this early stage. In February 1920 he headed a committee which devised the party's twenty-five-point programme, consisting of a variety of nationalist, socialist, corporativist and racialist principles. Meanwhile, the name was extended to 'National Socialist German Workers' Party' (NSDAP), commonly abbreviated to 'Nazi'. Branches were organized beyond Munich and support came from disbanded soldiers and from some elements of the army, or Reichswehr. The mouthpiece of the NSDAP was the *People's Observer* (*Völkischer Beobachter*), acquired in 1920. The next stage was Hitler's rise to the leadership of the party. By mid-1921 he was in dispute with the committee under Drexler over the question of organization and strategy. Eventually he outmanoeuvred Drexler and was elected Party Chairman in July. He immediately decided to demonstrate that the NSDAP was radically different from all traditional 'bourgeois' parties and to centralize everything, especially propaganda, on Munich. The movement was given teeth by the formation, in July 1921, of the Sturmabteilung (SA), a violent paramilitary organization intended, in the words of the newly named *Völkischer Beobachter*, 'to develop in the hearts of our young supporters a tremendous desire for action'.[6] The SA proceeded to intimidate opponents, disrupt other parties' meetings and engage in bloody clashes in the streets. Hitler developed a sense of irresistible power and overwhelming confidence, and was prepared to prove the *Beobachter*'s maxim that 'history does not make men, but men history'.

Mussolini, it seemed, had demonstrated this in his March on Rome in 1922. Could Hitler do the same in 1923? The republic was experiencing a many-sided crisis at least as serious as that confronted by the Italian monarchy. Hitler hoped to march on Berlin with the support of the right-wing Commissioner of Bavaria, Gustav von Kahr, and the Bavarian armed forces; the majority of the Reichswehr would then be won over. In November 1923, 600 SA men, under Hitler's command, took over a meeting being addressed by Kahr in the Bürgerbräu Keller, one of Munich's largest beer halls. Kahr, even at gunpoint, refused to support the putsch and an SA street demonstration the following morning was dispersed by the Bavarian police. Hitler's attempt at power therefore ended in ignominious failure and he was put on trial for treason. He was, however, treated leniently by sympathetic judges, and was sentenced to five years' imprisonment in Landsberg Castle. He served just over one year, in comfortable conditions which enabled him to write the first volume of *Mein Kampf* (*My Struggle*). On his emergence from captivity in December 1924 he found the NSDAP in total disarray; in his absence it had disintegrated into warring factions. Hitler was not displeased with this, as it guaranteed his own indispensability and meant that he was well placed to resume control.

During his internment Hitler had time to develop a more systematic version of his ideas and aims. Up to this point they had developed untidily over three main stages. During his early life in Vienna (1907–13) he had been profoundly influenced by anti-Semitic literature and the political utterances of Karl Lueger. He had also developed a deep hatred of the multi-ethnic empire of Austria-Hungary, identifying instead with the newer German nation. His experiences of the war and its immediate aftermath (1914–19) left him with a burning resentment, a drive for vengeance and a deep hatred of the far left. The period 1920–4 saw the fusion of anti-Semitism and anti-Communism and the development of a vision of expansion by Germany against the 'inferior races' of eastern Europe; this would follow the preliminary revolution and internal reordering within Germany. According to Kershaw, 'By the mid 1920s, then, Hitler had developed a rounded philosophy which offered him a complete view of the world, its ills and how to overcome them. Its substance never changed down to his death.'[7] This substance is considered briefly in Chapter 2.

When he refounded the NSDAP in February 1925, Hitler emphasized the need for a change of strategy. Until November 1923 he had assumed that the Weimar Republic could be overthrown directly. But the failure of the Putsch showed that democratic government was more resilient in Germany than in Italy. Hitler would therefore have to settle for a constitutional or 'legal' path to power. This did not mean a fundamental conversion to the principles of constitutional democracy; on the contrary, parliamentary politics would be the means, not the end. Revolution was still the ultimate aim, but would now be the result of achieving power rather than the means by which power would be achieved. For the time being it would be necessary, in Hitler's words, 'to hold our noses and enter the Reichstag alongside Marxist and Catholic deputies'. At the same time, he saw a continuing need for the SA and paramilitary influences. In fact, Hitler now led the Nazis at two levels. On the surface they were a parliamentary party, aiming at gaining electoral support at the expense of their rivals. Below the surface they remained a mass movement, committed to gaining mass support. Their chance would come in the future, after the victory of the 'legal' approach.

To accomplish this change of strategy it was necessary to extend the Party's appeal. The Nazi Party had to move away from its narrow working-class base. It could not hope to compete effectively for the working-class vote with a moderate SPD and a revolutionary KPD. Instead, Hitler decided to reformulate parts of the 1920 Party programme so as to appeal to different parts of the population. This meant that he had to move away from socialism; in 1927 he told his economic adviser, Keppler, that the economic goals of the original programme were now 'unusable'. By attacking socialism and the left, Hitler began to exercise more of an appeal to the middle classes and the right. This meant that Hitler increased the emphasis on nationalism, on the 'stab in the back' and 'November Criminals' myths of 1918 and the Versailles diktat of 1919.

Despite this new approach, the period 1925–9 proved exceptionally difficult for the Nazi Party and the movement. In the first place, Hitler was confronted by opposition from north German leaders, especially Gregor Strasser, who considered that the party's ideology should place heavier stress on socialism and the nationalization of key industries. Hitler eventually gained unquestioned ascendancy over the northern units of the party at the Bamberg Conference (February 1926) in which he out-argued Strasser and, by the force of his rhetoric, won over one of his arch critics, Josef Goebbels. (The latter had, only a short time before, demanded the expulsion of the 'petty bourgeois Adolf Hitler'!) The overall result of this victory was that Hitler tightened his control and established the monolithic structure he had always sought. In the subsequent reorganization, cadres of dedicated activists were set up in the basic party units, the *Gau*, under the control of the officials, or *Gauleiters*, who were appointed by Hitler himself.

The second and more intractable problem of this period was the stability of the republic and the poor electoral performance of the NSDAP. In the Reichstag election of December 1924, for example, the NSDAP acquired only fourteen seats, making it the least significant of the national parties in terms of electoral support; its performance in 1928 was even poorer, resulting in only twelve seats. Yet the party was nothing if not resilient. It showed a remarkable capacity to survive these hard times and switched its campaign from the cities to the rural areas, which agricultural depression had made more volatile. The *Völkischer Beobachter* observed in May 1928: 'The election results from the rural areas in particular have proved that with a smaller expenditure of energy, money and time, better results can be achieved there than in the big cities.'[8] The party therefore developed an electoral base which expanded rapidly as Germany came under the grip of economic recession.

The years of crisis, 1929–33

The origins of the Great Depression are dealt with in Chapter 1. Of all the industrial states, Germany was undoubtedly the most vulnerable to a sudden downturn in economic conditions. Her industry was heavily dependent on foreign investment to the tune of 5 billion marks per annum by 1928. Her banking system was geared to the use of short-term loans for long-term enterprises and, as a result, was potentially very vulnerable. As the Depression deepened, foreign loans were withdrawn and the banking system eventually collapsed in 1931. Meanwhile, industrial output had to be cut back through lack of investment and the contraction of overseas markets. The boom years of the late 1920s came to an abrupt end with a dramatic rise in the number of bankruptcies. The inevitable result was a rapid increase in unemployment, from two million in 1929 to 3.5 million in 1930, 4.4 million in 1931 and over six million in 1932.

The Depression dealt a devastating blow to democracy in Germany. Chancellor Müller's coalition fell apart on 27 March 1930 over the question of cutting dole payments. Since the power of the Chancellor depended on the support of the Reichstag and the economic crisis had made collaboration between political parties more difficult, the initiative now passed to the President. The republic's second President, elected in 1925, was Field Marshal Hindenburg. Very much a product of the old establishment of the Second Reich, he had an authoritarian approach to politics. During the stable years he had had no option but to play an inactive role in the manoeuvring for power between the various parties. From 1930, however, he was able to fill the vacuum left by the sudden death of consensus politics. Under the influence of one of his main advisers, General Schleicher, Hindenburg appointed the Centre Party leader, Brüning, as Chancellor. When Brüning tried to introduce a deflationary budget it was rejected by the Reichstag. Hindenburg sought to enforce it by presidential decree, under Article 48 of the constitution. The Reichstag objected to this course, with the result that Hindenburg agreed to Brüning's request for an election in September 1930. The results proved disappointing to Brüning and he was forced to carry on without the support of the Reichstag. He resorted increasingly to the use of presidential decrees so that, by the time of his fall in May 1932, parliamentary democracy had virtually disappeared.

Meanwhile, the NSDAP was rapidly expanding the base of its support. It was geared to take full advantage of the republic's crisis, as Hitler arranged mass rallies, travelling speakers and a flood of material from the propaganda department. The Reichstag election of 1930 was a triumph for the NSDAP, which secured 6.5 million votes and increased its representation from 12 to 107 seats, thus becoming the second largest party in the Reichstag. Hitler capitalized on this success by cultivating connections with the traditional right, including the Nationalists (DNVP), the army, industrialists like Thyssen, and agriculturalists; this alliance was formalized in the Harzburg Front of October 1931, directed against the republic's policies and record. In January 1932 Hitler made a direct appeal to German industrialists in his Düsseldorf speech, denouncing parliamentary democracy and highlighting the 'Bolshevik threat'. He was carefully establishing his credentials as an anti-revolutionary.

Hitler's self-confidence was now at its peak and he challenged Hindenburg for the presidency. The 1932 election ran to two ballots. On the first, Hindenburg obtained 18.7 million votes (49.6 per cent of the total), Hitler 11.3 million (30.1 per cent) and Thälmann, the Communist leader, 5 million (13 per cent). On the second ballot Hindenburg secured an overall majority with 19.4 million (53 per cent) to Hitler's 13.4 million (26.8 per cent) and Thälmann's 3.8 million (10.2 per cent). This result was a disappointment to Hitler, who had expended a massive effort to no avail. The only other possibility was now to try for the second most important office – the chancellorship.

In this he was to prove more successful, and ultimately he came to power by the back-door methods of diplomacy and intrigue rather than over the threshold of electoral support. The process was highly complex, involving President Hindenburg, General Schleicher and an aristocrat, Franz von Papen.

The first stage was the collapse of Brüning's government in May 1932, largely because it had lost the support of those who mattered, namely the President and his retinue. Schleicher had been alienated by Brüning's decision to ban Hitler's SA, and Hindenburg by a proposal to take over bankrupt Junker estates for use by landless peasants. Hindenburg therefore pushed Brüning into resignation and Papen was installed as the new Chancellor, the first in the history of the republic not to have the basis of party support. Hitler agreed not to oppose the new government in exchange for the removal of the ban on the SA and new Reichstag elections. The latter, held in July 1932, showed another sensational swing to the NSDAP, which now became easily the largest party, with 230 seats and 37.3 per cent of the popular vote. When Hitler was invited by Papen to join his cabinet he demanded, instead, the chancellorship. This was refused, however, by President Hindenburg. Papen then tried to weaken the position of the NSDAP by calling yet another Reichstag election in November 1932. This time the NSDAP lost electoral support, declining to 196 seats in the Reichstag and 33.1 per cent of the vote. Clearly Hitler's popularity had peaked and it would have come as no great surprise if the Nazi phenomenon had faded to its semi-obscurity of the late 1920s. This was due partly to a slight upswing in the economy and partly to the disillusionment of part of the electorate as Nazi violence and intimidation intensified on the streets. Already in 1930 the Prussian state government tried to curb this by banning outdoor meetings and parades, along with SA uniforms. The extent of the criminality of the SA was to be evident in 1932: within one month of an emergency decree, issued by Papen to legalize the SA, 99 people had been killed and 1,125 wounded in street attacks.[9] Then on 10 August nine uniformed SA men broke into a miner's home in Potempa in Upper Silesia, beating and torturing him to death. In the subsequent court case the assailants were sentenced to death and Hitler did his reputation little good by delivering an impassioned appeal in their support. No one could claim that the Nazi movement had not already shown its violent credentials before 1933.

But then events swung back in Hitler's favour. Papen proved incapable of holding power for very long and the chancellorship went to Schleicher, who had managed to convince Hindenburg that he could broaden the base of his support by detaching members of the NSDAP from their support for Hitler. In this he failed dismally; the only Nazi who seemed interested in his offer was Strasser, who was promptly thrown out of the party. Meanwhile, Papen felt sufficiently slighted by Schleicher to intrigue against him with Hitler. In January 1933 Papen persuaded Hindenburg to appoint Hitler as Chancellor in a coalition government which would contain only three Nazis and which would be carefully monitored by Papen as Hitler's deputy. Schleicher had tried to keep his own government afloat by asking for further emergency powers. These Hindenburg was not prepared to grant, since he now had an alternative. On 30 January 1933 he confirmed Hitler's appointment, believing that sufficient precautions had been taken to tame the radicalism of the NSDAP. In fact, Hitler proceeded to destroy the Weimar Republic within weeks of his coming to power. Only one more election was to be held before Germany was subsumed into the Third Reich.

EXPLANATIONS OF THE RISE OF HITLER

The rise of Hitler involved distinct processes which, although connected, did not lead inevitably from one to the other. One was the collapse of democracy within the Weimar Republic and the development after 1930 of an authoritarian regime which was hostile to the whole basis of the republic. Another was the emergence of an entirely new form of right-wing movement which, under Hitler, eventually replaced this authoritarian system with a totalitarian regime. The latter could not have occurred without the former: Hitler's rise was accomplished through the collapse of the republic. But this collapse was not necessarily tied to a historical trend leading inevitably to Nazism; it could have been followed by an alternative system.

An explanation as to why Hitler became Chancellor can be advanced in three stages. First, the Weimar Republic became increasingly destabilized with the disintegration of effective democracy. Second, Nazism emerged as a dynamic movement which was capable of gaining support from a substantial part of an electorate which had become disillusioned with the republic. And third, the conservative right provided a channel which enabled this new dynamic to penetrate and force open the flawed structure. The whole picture is complex, and it is necessary to avoid any one-sided or oversimplified view.

The vulnerability of Weimar democracy

The bedrock of any democracy is its constitution. As we have seen, the constitution of the Weimar Republic had certain advanced democratic features, including the enfranchisement of all men and women at twenty, and a form of proportional representation which guaranteed one seat in the Reichstag for every 60,000 votes cast. It also made it necessary for the Chancellor and his cabinet to have the support of a majority in the Reichstag, thus ensuring that the executive would at all times be responsible to the legislature. Yet several problems soon emerged to negate these positive features, making the constitution extremely difficult to operate.

One was the tendency of proportional representation to encourage the proliferation of parties. When this was associated with the need for majority government, it became evident that everything would depend on the assembling of coalitions. At first this seemed theoretically simple. The three parties most responsible for the formation of the republic – the SPD, the Centre and the DDP – earned in the 1919 elections 76 per cent of the vote, which translated into 78 per cent of the seats. But in the election of 1920 their support dropped to only 48 per cent of the vote, which meant that government became dependent on other parties as well. The eventual solution was the support of Stresemann, who brought in part of the DVP. Unfortunately, this was offset between 1923 and 1928 by the withdrawal of the SPD into opposition. It even became necessary to bring into two cabinets several right-wing politicians from the DNVP. This, of course, meant that the base of the government was broadening all the time, which made more difficult any concerted decision-making. Serious enough in the favourable economic climate between 1924 and 1928, this became an intolerable handicap when Germany was struck by the Great Depression. The result was the collapse of the normal process of democracy as, under Brüning and his successors, the government no longer sought the regular mandate of the Reichstag. This led, between 1930 and 1933, to the authoritarian phase of the Weimar Republic, which, in turn, provided the opportunity for Hitler in 1932 and 1933.

Some historians and recent German politicians have identified an undercurrent of anti-democratic feeling which severely damaged the fabric of the republic. According to Snyder, the new regime was seen as a 'stopgap' and 'from the days of its origin the Weimar Republic was unwanted and unloved'. Theodor Heuss, the first President of West Germany, maintained that 'Germany never conquered democracy for herself.'[10] It could certainly be argued that democracy was handed down from above in 1918, without any serious attempt to change the existing civil service or the judicial and military elites. Below the surface of a democratic constitution, therefore, was a profoundly conservative base, with no commitment – emotional or intellectual – to a republic. Certain sections of the community could have become permanently reconciled to the new system – for example, the proletariat and the middle classes. These, however, were severely affected by the impact of the 1923 and 1929 economic crises. Much of the population was highly vulnerable to right-wing ideas and organizations. A strong tradition of anti-Western and anti-democratic thought was maintained by writers and activists like Moeller, van den Bruck and Junger, who induced widespread nostalgia for the Second Reich and anticipation of a Third. The response of much of the population was to criticize the Weimar politicians for their facelessness and to turn to more authoritarian figures like Hindenburg and, ultimately, Hitler. Throughout the period 1918–33, therefore, the onus was always upon democracy to show that it was a better system than the authoritarian models of the past. Many people remained highly sceptical.

Unfortunately, the image of democracy was not strengthened by the performance of the political parties. According to Fraenkel, these failed to fulfil 'the functions which devolve upon them in a constitutional pluralistic Parliamentary democracy'.[11] The traditional right – the DNVP – maintained a consistent hostility to the republic. They attacked it at every opportunity and eventually welcomed its demise. Indeed, in collaborating openly with Hitler's NSDAP, they provided the channel for his appointment.

The more moderate Centre Party did manage to keep a respectable level of support, attracting over 50 per cent of the Catholic vote. It had, however, little appeal to Protestants, despite professing to be primarily a 'Christian' party. But the most damaging impact of the Centre Party was its swing to the right. This occurred in two stages. In 1928 Monsignor Kaas took over from Wilhelm Marx as party leader, emphasizing the party's clerical attachments and undermining its ability to reconcile the moderate parties on secular issues. Then, after 1930, the Centre displayed an unfortunate willingness to adapt to presidential dictatorship. Once Müller had withdrawn the SPD from government, Brüning was content to rely upon President Hindenburg to issue emergency decrees under Article 48 of the constitution. Thus, after playing a key role in upholding democracy, the Centre delivered the first blows against it.

The liberal part of the political spectrum was also badly flawed. Germany had developed the unique phenomenon of two varieties of liberalism. To the left of centre, the DDP represented the political and social freedoms which made their way into the constitution, while the DVP, on the right, merged liberal economic theory with nationalism and authority. The two parties rarely collaborated, except during the period of Stresemann's ascendancy, and neither was able to maintain the support of the middle classes, which should have been their natural constituency. In part, this was because they were never able to appeal to the 'diverse social and economic interests' which constituted the 'material base' of the middle classes.[12] The result was to be a devastating change in voting behaviour as, after 1928, the DDP and DVP lost almost all their electoral support to the Nazis. This defection was the greatest single factor in converting the latter from a fringe to a mass party. In a very real sense, therefore, fascism emerged from the ruins of liberalism.

It might be thought that the best chance of upholding the republic came from the left wing. After all, the parties of the left had fairly consistent support, ranging from 45.5 per cent of the vote in 1919 to 36.9 per cent in November 1932. Unfortunately, the left was also fragmented into two segments (three for the brief period 1919–23). The bitter rivalry between the SPD and the KPD was the legacy of the German Revolution of 1918–19. The KPD never forgot the bloodshed of January 1919 and regarded the SPD, who had put down their attempted coup, as class enemies. There was also a profound ideological gap. Thälmann, the KPD leader, was influenced by Stalin's belief that social democracy was not essentially different to fascism and that they were both manifestations of capitalism. He argued, indeed, that the greatest threat to German communism lay in the SPD, 'in the social democracy which gains the trust of the masses through fraud and treachery'.[13] He believed that the Depression would act as a great catalyst for changes in the voting pattern and that the KPD would pull in the working-class vote in much the same way as the NSDAP was benefiting from the support of the middle classes. (The KPD did make certain inroads; for example, in July 1932 it reduced the SPD's share of the vote to 21.6 per cent and boosted its own to 14.3 per cent. But it never became a mass party to rival the NSDAP.) Thälmann also hoped that, if Hitler were to achieve power, he would soon be overthrown by a proletarian revolution organized by the KPD; in this sense, a fascist regime would be a 'temporary intermediate development'. As far as Thälmann was concerned, therefore, there was no reason to co-operate with the other parties in preventing the accession of Hitler.

If the SPD so distrusted the KPD, could it not have made more of its links with other groups? Herein lies the SPD's greatest failing. Although by far the most important influence behind the formation of the republic, it never quite managed to sustain a role in government proportionate to its size in the Reichstag. In the words of Hiden, 'They failed to make of their early association with the bourgeois parties, or so-called "democratic middle" of DDP, Centre and DVP, a lasting and constructive partnership.'[14] They refused, for example, to be involved in the government of the republic during the crucial period between 1923 and 1928. The SPD remained during the period of the Weimar Republic essentially a party of the working class and made very few inroads into the middle classes. This was in contrast to the British Labour Party which sought greater middle-class support as it became the main alternative to the Conservatives. Part of the problem for the SPD at this stage was that it was limited by attachments to its trade union movement and was concerned that any attempt at a more concerted appeal to the middle classes would lose it votes to the Communists.

Chapter 1 referred to the importance of a catalyst in the breakdown of parliamentary systems. This was particularly important in the case of Germany, where economic crisis destabilized the whole social structure, with serious side-effects for the political system. Two stages were involved in the process – inflation and depression. General Morgan of the Disarmament Commission said of the former: 'Inflation has destroyed the equipoise of society. It has ruined the middle classes and impoverished the workers . . . Inflation has undermined the political basis of the Republic and concentrated all real power in the hands of a few, namely the great industrialists.' In fact, a period of recovery followed this perhaps premature diagnosis. But the real significance of inflation was that any future economic crisis would be bound to have a doubly serious impact. Hence, from 1929 the Depression radicalized sections of the population which inflation had already rendered unstable, turning them either to the extreme right or to the far left. It also destroyed any possibility of political consensus and, as we have seen, returned Germany to the practice of authoritarian government.

6 Adolf Hitler, 1889–1945, at Berchtesgaden (© Popperfoto/Getty)

The strength and appeal of the Nazis

The rise of Hitler was also due to a number of active factors. To be examined in this section are the role of propaganda and organization, Hitler's strategy and identification of key issues, and the importance of his own personality and influence. Also of vital importance is the support given to the NSDAP by different sections of the population.

The success of the Nazi movement is inevitably associated with the highly skilled use of propaganda and the development of an efficient organization. In these respects it was far ahead of all the other German parties, including the KPD. The importance which Hitler attached to propaganda and organization can be seen clearly in several extracts from *Mein Kampf*: 'The function of propaganda', he argued, 'is to attract supporters, the function of organization is to win members.' He continued:

> Propaganda works on the general public from the standpoint of an idea and makes them ripe for the victory of this idea, while the organization achieves victory by the persistent, organic, and militant union of those supporters who seem willing and able to carry on the fight for victory.

Or, to put it another way:

> The first task of propaganda is to win people for subsequent organization; the first task of organization is to win men for the continuation of propaganda. The second task of propaganda is the disruption of the existing state of affairs and the permeation of this state of affairs with the new doctrine, while the second task of organization must be the struggle for power, thus to achieve the final success of the doctrine.[15]

The manifestations of propaganda were numerous. Albert Speer later asserted that 'Hitler was one of the first to be able to avail himself of the means of modern technology'. Admittedly, he was unable to make effective use of radio until after coming to power and establishing a monopoly over this medium, but he did use numerous other means, including loudspeakers, provocative posters and bands. Above all, he depended on the power of the spoken word, which he always considered more important than written material. He had a profound insight into the collective emotions of crowds and believed that his message to them had to be kept simple, striking and memorable: 'The receptivity of the great masses is very limited, their intelligence is small, but their power of forgetting is enormous.' Hence, propaganda 'must be limited to a very few points',[16] which must be constantly repeated to establish them as incontrovertible facts. It was also vital to make the individual feel important only in the context of the crowd and to establish stereotyped enemies and targets by means, if necessary, of 'the big lie'. Organization, of course, was essential for the maintenance of mass commitment: hence the vast number of marches and rallies, the uniforms and paramilitary drill, and the street fights with Communists and Social Democrats. The whole process was intended to prepare the movement to seize power when the opportunity arose.

The identification of this opportunity depended on Hitler's strategy and timing. His first bid for power was defective, based, as it was, on the mistaken belief that he could imitate Mussolini's successful March on Rome. But the failure of the Munich Putsch in 1923 was followed by a more skilful adaptation to a dual role of legality in party politics which drew attention away from the radicalism of his mass movement. This course lulled the suspicions of the republican government, which considered the KPD as a more serious threat and, as a result, underestimated the revolutionary potential of the Nazis. It also enabled Hitler to appear as a more moderate politician to those sectors of society who had previously been put off by the gutter politics of the early years of the movement. Along with this overall change in strategy, Hitler aimed constantly to reformulate the party programme so as to appeal to different parts of the population as they became alienated from the republic. In 1927 he told his economic adviser, Keppler, that the economic goals of the original programme were now 'unusable'. He considered that some of the details of the 1920 document were too doctrinaire and he was more prepared than some of the more orthodox Nazi leaders to be flexible and pragmatic in the presentation of a party image. He went so far as to establish a section within the organization to identify the reasons for different types of public discontent and to develop specific remedies which would appeal to different social groups. As Stachura has put it, the 'NSDAP revealed itself to be perhaps the most tactically flexible and opportunistic political movement in the Republic.'[17]

In developing a broad appeal for the Nazi movement, Hitler relied on the projection of general issues for the consumption of the population as a whole, and specific issues for the different classes. An example of the former was his attack on the republic's foreign policy. Taking advantage of the unpopularity of the Versailles Settlement, Hitler was able to implant upon the national consciousness terms like 'November Criminals' and the 'stab in the back'. Bullock adds:

> His was a closed mind, impervious to argument or doubt. It was thanks to this assurance that he possessed the key to history, and with it could unlock the future as well, that he was able to exploit tactical opportunities, without any risk of losing sight of his objectives.[18]

He also slammed the policy of détente pursued by Stresemann: 'our people must be delivered from the hopeless confusion of international convictions and educated consciously and systematically to fanatical Nationalism'. Another mainline policy, guaranteed to be taken seriously across most of the political spectrum, was anti-communism; this is seen by Hamilton as one of the most important of all Hitler's appeals.[19] Finally, he made effective use of the deep undercurrent of anti-Semitism in Germany, making the Jews scapegoats for all of Germany's evils, whether in the form of callous capitalism or revolutionary communism. Above all, he made a permanent and intentionally damaging connection between the regime and the detested minority, developing the concept of the 'Jew Republic'.

What was the importance of the personal role of Hitler in the rise of the Nazi movement? Emphasis is usually placed on his charismatic leadership and an almost demoniac willpower. Trevor-Roper, for example, maintains that 'His own firm belief in his messianic mission was perhaps the most important element in the extraordinary power of his personality.'[20] He also possessed, according to Bullock, a 'sense of opportunity and timing'. This was the right combination of characteristics to take advantage of the troubles of the Weimar Republic since Hitler was at his best when destroying a system by exploiting its crises. He later experienced much greater difficulty when he had to defend his own system which, in turn, came under threat in the second phase of the Second World War. At this stage, Hitler's personality was to become a major liability to the Nazi movement and to Germany's military survival.

The final issue which needs to be examined is the basis of support for National Socialism. Much research has been carried out on the defection to the NSDAP during the late 1920s and early 1930s. It was once thought that Nazism appealed mainly to the middle classes, with substantial additions from the working class and from the upper levels of society who were, nevertheless, more reluctant to shift from their original political allegiances. Now, however, the tendency is to assume more general and widespread support for Hitler.

It is still possible to say that the middle classes made up the largest single proportion of Nazi support, and that their defection from their traditional parties was vitally important in converting Nazism into a mass movement. During the 1920s they had voted in large numbers for the DDP and the DVP, although some also supported the DNVP and, if they were Catholic, the Centre. Some historians, like Childers, have argued that the basis for the middle-class movement towards the NSDAP had been established during the late 1920s, even before the onset of Depression from 1929.[21] Others maintain that the flow occurred only after 1929, making it a direct result of the Great Depression. The middle classes found unbearable the impact of a second economic crisis which destroyed the apparent recovery from the first. The psychological blow was so profound that they made an uncharacteristic move away from the moderate centre to the radical right. These two interpretations can be harmonized. The older section of the middle class, comprising artisans, small retailers and peasant farmers, formed the core of the support for Hitler and were showing support for him before the Depression: theirs was a disillusionment with the structure and policies of the republic itself. To these was subsequently added the weight of much of the new middle class – the non-manual employees, civil servants and teachers – who aligned themselves with Nazism as a direct result of the Depression. It is possible that they were moving in this direction anyway. But the simple fact is that the NSDAP secured only twelve seats in the Reichstag election of 1928; it therefore took the Depression to convert a trickle of middle-class support into a flood.

There is a further controversy over the connection between Nazism and the working class. It was once strongly argued that the working class remained largely loyal to the parties of the left which, in any case, had a distinctively proletarian appeal. The KPD was especially class-based and its support increased during the Reichstag elections of 1930 and 1932. Although the SPD lost seats, it came nowhere near the collapse suffered by the parties of the centre, clearly indicating that it retained the bulk of its support. By this analysis, the proletariat was less drawn to Nazism because, in the words of Stachura, 'The Party was unable to establish a significant working-class constituency because it did not develop a coherent interpretation of "German Socialism".' This was partly because Hitler's 'innate contempt and distrust of the proletariat remained paramount'.[22] Other historians, such as Mühlberger, are not convinced by the 'middle-class thesis' of Nazism.[23] Recent research has tended to support the view that working-class input was substantial. Studies of Nazi membership records show something like 40 per cent of the membership coming from the working class, while 60 per cent of the SA were of the same origins. Parallel research on electoral trends has, through computer analysis of statistical data, produced very similar voting results. According to Fischer, 'a good 40 per cent of the NSDAP's voters were working class, remarkably similar to the proportion of workers in the party itself'.[24] Again, there is a possible synthesis between two interpretations. On the one hand, the working class never came to provide the largest body of support for Nazism: in that respect, the original views seem correct. On the other hand, it is possible to overestimate the continued loyalty of the working class to the parties of the left. After 1928 substantial shifts did occur: the growth of the Communists was more than offset by the decline of the SPD. The latter shrank by between a quarter and a third: these lost votes almost certainly went straight to the Nazis. Thus, although the NSDAP was not primarily a working-class party and the majority of workers remained with the parties of the left, the inflow of working-class support for Nazism was still a vital factor in the conversion of Nazism into a mass movement.

The attitudes of the upper classes to Nazism were largely pragmatic. Landowners, businessmen and industrialists saw in Hitler the prospect of safety from the threats of communism and socialism on the left. Arguably, they saw beyond this and looked to Nazism to deliver over to them a disciplined and constrained workforce. They looked to Hitler to undo the pro-trade union and welfare policies of most of the governments of the Weimar Republic. Even those who distrusted the violence and vulgarities of the Nazi movement were still likely to be supporting it indirectly. It was unlikely that the affluent sectors of German society after 1929 voted in significant numbers for any party to the left of the DNVP, and the DNVP itself was in close collaboration with the NSDAP after Hugenberg assumed the leadership. Hence, the Nazis benefited considerably from the respectability, publicity and funding brought by a relatively narrow but highly influential sector of society.

To some extent, the appeal of Nazism transcended class barriers altogether. The three more general categories usually considered most important are religious denomination, gender and age. There is no doubt that the Protestants were more likely than Catholics to vote Nazi. They had no existing party base, whereas the Centre Party held the Catholic vote even at the height of the economic and political crisis. Many were also profoundly suspicious of the Weimar Republic, which, as we have seen, they identified mainly with Catholic and working-class values. On the whole, they had far more affection for the memory of the Kaiser's rule and were not, therefore, averse to another change of regime. As far as gender is concerned, the Nazis managed to make up for an early imbalance in their support. Before 1930 the majority of women were more right wing in their voting behaviour than men; yet the majority of Nazi votes came from men rather than women. By 1933 there was a more even split as many women became convinced that Hitler was the best prospect for bolstering the institution of the family in troubled times; this probably counteracted the earlier and well-founded suspicion that Nazism was profoundly anti-feminist. Finally, the Nazi movement had a powerful generational impact. It appealed directly to youth, partly through its dynamism and attack on traditional ideas and institutions, partly through the oversimplified solutions to the problem of unemployment. Young men, more than any other section of the community, were prepared to submerge their identity and to respond to Hitler's appeal to the crowd instinct.

It is difficult to escape the conclusion that during the later period of the Weimar Republic the NSDAP was the most heterogeneous party in Germany. It included people from the complete range of social backgrounds, even though the precise proportion of these may be open to debate and controversy. Hitler alone managed to create a radical movement with which he could transform into fanaticism the desperation of a profoundly disturbed people.

The channel to power provided by the conservative right

After 1928, therefore, Hitler succeeded in collecting for the NSDAP much of the electorate which had become disillusioned with the republic's manifest deficiencies. This was essential for Hitler's rise to prominence but it does not fully explain his rise to *power*. A further step was needed – a means of forcing a way in through the republic's fissures. This was greatly assisted by the drift to authoritarian rule within the republic after 1929, in which democracy was systematically undermined by the conservative right. This, in turn, led to an opportunist alliance between the conservative right and the Nazis as the former tried to use the latter to sweep away democracy and strengthen the conservative–authoritarian base.

Ironically, the initial drift to authoritarianism was made possible by the constitution itself which, in Article 48, allowed the President to assume emergency powers should he consider these necessary. The first President, Ebert, had used Article 48 constructively to maintain the stability of the new democracy. But his successor, Hindenburg, was a very different proposition. His election in 1925 has been seen as a major disaster for the republic: he was an authoritarian and military figure, with a considerable suspicion of the whole parliamentary process. Eyck comments that 'No matter how Hindenburg might comport himself in the immediate future his election as president of Germany was a triumph of nationalism and militarism and a heavy defeat for the Republic and parliamentary government.'[25] Hindenburg brushed aside the problem of finding a parliamentary majority by exercising presidential decree powers allowed by Article 48. According to Boldt, the use of decree laws increased from five in 1930 to forty-four in 1931 and sixty in 1932, while sittings of the Reichstag declined from ninety-four in 1930 to forty-one in 1931 and a mere thirteen in 1932.[26] This trend effectively ended the role of party politics. The situation deteriorated further after the fall of Brüning in 1932 as Papen and Schleicher were both determined to avoid any return to parliamentary sovereignty.

But why were the conservative right willing to allow Hitler and the radical right to benefit from this? The explanation seems to be that the conservative right (which included the DNVP, some of the army command, President Hindenburg and Chancellors Papen and Schleicher) intended to use Nazism for their own purpose. They believed that the republic had outlived its usefulness and that any return to the party politics of the 1920s was impossible. Instead, conservative constitutional theorists argued in *Unsere Partei* that the party system would eventually fracture and be replaced by a broad front. For this reason, the DNVP therefore aimed to create a broad 'movement' of the right which would also include the NSDAP. The latter could be used for its radical impetus. It had the capacity to destroy the republic, but once that was achieved it would be brought into line with the more conservative objectives of the DNVP. The collaboration between the Nazis and the DNVP was crucial; Hiden goes so far as to say that it 'played handmaiden to Adolf Hitler and his movement at the close of the 1920s'.[27] This strategy, which eventually proved to be fatally flawed, provided Hitler with access to power. His appointment as Chancellor was due to a fortuitous circumstance – the personal rivalry between the last two Chancellors, Papen and Schleicher. The latter faced a political crisis when, in January 1933, the Reichstag challenged his use of Article 48. The constitution provided a loophole in that the President could dissolve the Reichstag and call an election. But, having already done this twice in 1932, Hindenburg preferred to find an alternative Chancellor. This explains his receptiveness to Papen's recommendation that Hitler should be appointed, with himself given a watching brief as Vice-Chancellor.

Hence, Hitler came to power largely through a conspiracy. Yet this does not mean that the Nazis did little themselves to achieve it. The conservative right would not have been so willing to collaborate with a weak fringe group. It was evident to them that the NSDAP had managed more effectively than any other party to mobilize popular discontent against the republic. Hitler appeared to them an elemental force whom they intended to use in their own way. But there is a final irony. Hitler came to power as the support for the Nazis was starting to ebb: after all the vote for the Nazis fell back slightly in the second election of 1932 and it seemed a reasonable assumption that Hitler's popularity with the electorate had peaked. This, the conservative politicians calculated, would make Hitler easier to manipulate. Nazism appeared sufficiently strong to be directed against parliamentary democracy but not strong enough to challenge the authoritarian conservatives. It was a flaring flame which would destroy the republic and then die back into the traditional authoritarianism which would be all that was left.

The politicians who gave Hitler power in this way made the most ghastly political blunder in the whole of Germany's history.

THE THIRD REICH, 1933–45

Dictatorship established, 1933–4

When he was appointed Chancellor on 30 January 1933, Hitler's power was by no means absolute. He had only three Nazis in his cabinet and he was constrained by Papen who, in his position as Vice-Chancellor, had to be involved in any contacts between the Chancellor and President. Another problem was that Hitler had no emergency powers beyond those which Hindenburg was prepared, under Article 48 of the constitution, to grant him. It seemed, therefore, that Papen was fully justified in believing that Hitler could be tamed. Within two months, Papen argued, 'we will have pushed Hitler so far into a corner that he'll squeak'.[28] Yet, within six months, all constraints had been eliminated. Hitler was able to kick away the ladder by which he had ascended to power and establish a dictatorship based in effect on a permanent state of emergency.

Hitler's first priority was to strengthen the position of the NSDAP in the Reichstag so that he could use the latter to force through measures to change the constitution. He intended, in other words, to use the democratic process to destroy democracy. He therefore demanded immediate elections, and the Reichstag was dissolved on 1 February, two days after his appointment as Chancellor. In the election campaign which followed, Hitler had two major advantages over the other parties. First, he had more direct access to the media, especially radio; this he used more effectively than any previous politician, thereby enhancing the electoral appeal of the NSDAP. Second, he was able to use emergency powers to weaken the position of some of his opponents. For example, the decree of 4 February made it possible to control the meetings of other parties. It also enabled Goering to draft a special police order in Prussia to the effect that the 'activities of subversive organizations are . . . to be combated with the most drastic measures'. Indeed, 'failure to act is more serious than errors committed in acting'.[29] Even more extreme measures were allowed by the decree of 28 February which suspended many personal liberties 'until further notice'. The pretext for this was a much publicized attempt to burn down the Reichstag building on 27 February. It used to be thought that this was a deliberate ploy by the Nazis to cast the blame on the Communists and SPD. It is now generally believed that the fire was the work of a single individual, van der Lubbe, and not part of an organized plot. Whatever the truth, however, the event was exploited by Hitler to the utmost. He was empowered to suspend various articles of the constitution and to take over the power of the state governments if necessary.

The election results were announced on 5 March. They showed considerable gains for the NSDAP when compared with the results of the elections of November 1932. The Nazi vote increased from 11.7 million to 17.2 million and its percentage of the total from 33.1 to 43.9. Hitler's partners, the DNVP, gained 200,000 votes and an extra seat. The Centre Party made marginal increases and the SPD remained about the same. Real losses were experienced by the DVP and other middle-class parties, and also by the Communists.

Three reasons can be given for Hitler's gains. The first is that his tactic in calling an immediate election completely unsettled his opponents. Most of the non-Nazis in his first cabinet had meekly submitted to this demand for a dissolution and, according to Broszat, 'were guilty of the first fateful blow against the concept of containing Hitler'. Second, there appears to have been a degree of resignation in the Reichstag itself as the deputies failed to use the Committee for the Protection of Parliamentary Rights effectively; this might have challenged Hitler's demand for an election as being too hasty. And third, the Nazi monopoly of the state media and extensive use of emergency decrees cut away much of the opposition's capacity to present an effective case against Hitler.

But the process of establishing a dictatorship was not yet complete, for the NSDAP still lacked an overall majority in the Reichstag. What happened next was a new offensive as the constitution was stormed from below, at the level of local government, and from above, within the Reichstag itself.

Recent historical studies have drawn attention to the importance of Nazi pressure in the individual states, or *Länder*, in many cases amounting to a 'terrorist, revolutionary movement'.[30] In March 1933 SA and SS squads went into action, taking over town halls, police headquarters and newspapers. The resulting chaos was usually so serious that the central government had to intervene via the Minister of the Interior, Wilhelm Frick. Nazis were appointed to the local office of Police Commissioner and, on 7 April, a new law allowed for the installation of special Reich governors in all states. In effect, therefore, Nazi rule was imposed at the local level throughout Germany even before dictatorship had been completed at the centre. Nevertheless, Hitler was conscious of the need to restrain some of the wilder Nazi activists in case they should impede the revolution from above – which was now well under way.

The Reichstag reconvened on 21 March 1933. Hitler now intended to secure the passage of an Enabling Act which would radically reduce the Reichstag's powers. Such a major constitutional change, however, needed a two-thirds-majority vote, which the NSDAP and their allies, the DNVP, did not between them possess. Hitler's solution was ingenious. First, he used the emergency decree of 28 February to expel from the Reichstag all Communist deputies. He then negotiated with the Centre Party an agreement whereby the latter would vote for the Enabling Act in return for special guarantees for the Churches. Hitler was very reassuring on this point. He saw in Christianity 'the most important factors for the maintenance of our society' and would therefore 'permit and guarantee to the Christian denominations the enjoyment of their due influence in schools and education'.[31] On 23 March 1933 the Enabling Act secured its required majority, with only the SPD voting against it. Its terms virtually destroyed parliamentary powers by allowing the Chancellor to issue laws without consulting the Reichstag.

The changes now gathered momentum as the new power was used to eliminate other political parties. Between March and July all parties apart from the NSDAP were forced to wind themselves up. The whole process culminated in the law of 14 July 1933 'Against the Establishment of Parties' which declared it a criminal offence to organize any political grouping outside the NSDAP. Another election was held in November 1933, in which a single party list was put to the electorate for its approval. The result was that the NSDAP took all the seats in the Reichstag. Germany was officially a one-party state.

Why did the opposition give up? The most obvious reason is that it had no choice. The parties of the left were smashed by the government's emergency powers. The Communists, for example, were prevented from taking their seats in the Reichstag, and the SPD were banned outright in June. The Centre Party gave up any pretence at political opposition in return for a guarantee of religious freedom; it liquidated itself voluntarily. Even the DNVP was unable to keep itself afloat as its leaders found it increasingly obvious that they no longer had any hold on the political monster they had helped create. President Hindenburg, no admirer of the party system, made no attempt to interfere with Hitler's assault on the opposition, for fear of provoking a more violent and radical constitutional upheaval.

By the middle of 1933 Hitler was still not completely secure. His position could be upset either by the radical wing of his party or by the army. The most likely threat was that undisciplined action by the former could provoke a counter-blow from the latter.

The destructive capacity of the Nazi radicals had been evident in March 1933 when the rank and file had brought about at local level changes which were far more sweeping than Hitler had intended. The SA were especially violent and the party leadership regretted its earlier failure to tame them. By the middle of 1933 there were also demands for a new Nazi revolution. Ernst Röhm, for example, wanted to extend the scope of the SA so that the German army would be absorbed into it. Röhm expressed the disillusionment of the radical Nazis with Hitler's apparent caution: 'A tremendous victory has been won,' he argued, 'but not absolute victory.' He added: 'The SA and SS will not tolerate the German revolution going to sleep.'[32] Hitler was unimpressed by such views. He was particularly anxious to keep the support of those very interests under attack by Röhm. He was also opposed to radicalism for its own sake: 'Revolution is not a permanent condition . . . The stream of revolution once released must be guided into the secure bed of evolution.'[33] Further provocative activities were therefore to stop. Accordingly, Frick's circular of 6 October 1933 instructed the activists that 'These infringements and excesses must now cease once and for all.'[34]

What made Hitler particularly wary of antagonizing the army was that he hoped shortly to become President. Hindenburg was approaching death and the army, if threatened by the Nazis, might prevail upon him to nominate a successor. Alternatively, the army might attempt a coup against Hitler, with or without Hindenburg's approval. Hitler would be able to counter this coup with the help of the SA, but this would make him a virtual prisoner of the radicals. He could, however, adopt another course: he could crush the SA with the support of the army and, over a period, establish the same influence over the military commanders as he had over the politicians. There would be more chance of total penetration and control if Nazification was slow and cautious. The army had good reason to co-operate with Hitler: it hated the programme of the SA and was particularly averse to Röhm's aim to see 'the grey rock' of the Reichswehr submerged in the 'brown flood' of the SA. The dislike was mutual: the SA despised the aristocratic connections of the army officers, while the army regarded the SA leadership as uncouth upstarts. The Reichswehr commanders saw Hitler as the moderate who would seek to preserve at least some of the traditional values. They were therefore prepared to do a deal with Hitler; they would stand back while Hitler took whatever measures he considered necessary against his own delinquents. They would even intervene to save Hitler from the SA if necessary.

As events turned out, their help was not required. By the beginning of July 1934, the SA leadership had been cut down by Hitler's elite corps, the SS. The 'Night of the Long Knives' claimed the lives of Röhm, Strasser and many other Nazis who were considered disruptive. A grateful army was now prepared to concede to Hitler the office of head of state. When Hindenburg died five weeks later, Hitler succeeded him as Reich President, adding the title of Führer for good measure. The army took an oath of personal allegiance: 'I swear before God to give my unconditional obedience to Adolf Hitler, Führer of the Reich and of the German People, Supreme Commander.'[35]

Was there a 'legal revolution'?

The political changes accomplished between 1933 and 1934 have often been referred to as a 'legal revolution'. Two interpretations can be applied to this: one with the emphasis on *legal*, the other stressing the concept of *revolution*. Hitler's appointment as Chancellor in January 1933 had been due partly to the broadening electoral appeal of the Nazis from 1931, in line with his strategy of legality after 1923, and partly to intensified Nazi activism and violence in the streets. This contradiction – the seizure of power (*Machtergreifung*) accomplished 'legally'– now continued until the destruction of the Republic was complete.

Was it 'legal'?

The Nazis took care to build a logical progression towards dictatorship, each stage dependent on the last, thereby providing a facade of legality. For example the Enabling Act, or 'Law for Terminating the Suffering of the People and Nation' of 24 March 1933, contained within its preamble the words: 'The Reichstag has passed the following law, which has been approved by the Reichsrat. The requirements of legal constitutional change having been met, it is being proclaimed herewith.'[36] This part was a direct reference to the Constitution of the Weimar Republic, Article 76 of which had stated that: 'acts . . . amending the Constitution can take effect only if two-thirds of the legal number of members are present and at least two-thirds of those present consent'.[37] To secure the necessary two-thirds majority the government used the emergency powers under Article 48 of the Weimar Constitution to exclude the Communists from the Reichstag. Once passed, the Enabling Act became the 'legal' means by which the Chancellor could use his new executive powers to alter other parts of the political process. After all, under Article 1 of the Enabling Act, 'the government also is authorized to pass laws' the latter being 'issued by the Chancellor and published in the official gazette'.[38]

Under this economical and highly convenient arrangement, further legislation followed. The Law of 31 March for the 'Coordination of the *Länder* of the Reich' reorganized the whole structure of local state governments; the Law of 7 April for 'the restoration of the professional Civil Service' purged the administration of non-Aryans and political opponents; the 'Law against the New Formation of Parties' (14 July) confirmed that: 'The sole political party existing in Germany is the National Socialist German Workers' Party.'[39] Just over a year later, the 'Law Concerning the Head of the German State' (1 August 1934) used the same formula laid down in the Enabling Act to combine the office of President with that of Chancellor.[40] In each case, therefore, the 'legality' of Hitler's abolition of previous constitutional safeguards was justified by amendments to the constitution itself through the process of 'legal constitutional change'.

This circuitous piece of logic is open to extensive criticism. After all, Hitler's main intention was to use some of the powers allowed by the Weimar constitution to destroy other areas which these were intended to protect. This meant that the way in which the *letter* of the law was observed was entirely contrary to the *spirit* of that law. Hitler's objective was nothing less than the end of the Weimar democratic system. He achieved this in three ways, all under the procedures allowed by the Enabling Act. First, he converted precautionary powers, allowed to the President in an emergency, into a convenient method by which the Chancellor could bypass the legislature on a regular basis. Article 48 had been included in the Weimar Constitution to preserve democracy against potential enemies, whereas the Enabling Act was based on the premise that democracy was itself the enemy. Second, the entire federal system, integral to the Weimar Constitution, was undermined by the withdrawal of the autonomous power of the *Länder*. Third, the destruction of the multi-party system – a basic ingredient of the Weimar Constitution – changed the whole purpose of voting. Instead of voting for a government that would prepare legislation through the Reichstag, the electorate now expressed its occasional approval, in a plebiscite, for major measures introduced by the government by the process of edict. And fourth, the previous separation between the head of state and the head of government, a necessary component of any democratic system, was destroyed by the absorption of the presidency and the chancellorship into the Führer.

The whole notion of 'legality' was therefore a mockery. A democratic constitution was not amended by due process of law: it was destroyed by anti-democrats who targeted its emergency provisions against the constitution itself. Modern historians confirm this view. Bracher, for example, refers to 'the purely formalistic conception of a "legal" seizure of power'.[41] The purpose of the 'legality tactic' was to surround 'this new type of totalitarian power seizure with its seductive aura', making all legal, political, or even intellectual resistance difficult', indeed 'well-nigh impossible'.[42] Even if Hitler's appointment in January 1933 was legal, the subsequent extension of his powers was not. According to Leitz, 'Hitler, clearly, did not seize power. However, the rapid progress of events which began with Hitler's appointment and ended on 2 August 1934 with the union of the offices of president and chancellor in the person of the "Führer and Reich Chancellor Adolf Hitler" did amount to a seizure of complete power'.[43]

Finally, there is considerable doubt as to whether the Nazis even observed the *letter* of the Constitution. Hitler's 'legal' changes were accompanied by pressure and violence – of the very type that the constitution had originally been conceived to prevent. After all, Article 48 had been intended for presidential use to put down mass activism, not to unleash it against selected constitutional targets. Hildebrand refers to 'Nazi terrorist tactics' and maintains that 'it was often difficult to distinguish terroristic from legal measures'.[44] The key reason for the two-thirds majority behind the Enabling Act was the exclusion and imprisonment of the Communist deputies elected to the Reichstag two weeks earlier; there were also attempts, by SA intimidation and threats of violence, to prevent the Social Democrats from casting their votes against the Enabling Act. Similarly, the state governments were forced by mass pressure to accept the reduction of their constitutional powers. Pressure therefore made impossible any challenge to the use of 'legality' – in a way that was clearly illegal.

Was it a 'revolution'?

In view of what has already been said, perhaps it is more appropriate to describe the accumulation of political power by Hitler as 'revolutionary'. But here the thrust of the argument can be put into reverse. The very notion of 'step-by-step' change – and its dependence on previous constitutional provisions – is not normally seen as a 'revolutionary' process.

Hitler's institutional changes were strictly limited in terms of the destruction of previous systems. After all, the Weimar Constitution was never formally abolished and the Reichstag and Reichsrat remained intact as the legislature. The existing ministries in the central government were retained; the posts (for example, the Foreign Minister, Interior Minister, Finance Minister and Ministers for Economics, Justice, Defence, Food, Posts, Labour and Transport) were remarkably similar to those within the Weimar Republic. Much the same applied to the civil service and even the federal structure. The Nazification of the institutions of the Weimar Republic occurred in such a way as to minimize the chances of a sudden break with the past, probably to prevent the possible accumulation of opposition. All this bears little resemblance to the revolution within Russia. Lenin had taken the decision to remove any remaining connection with Western-style legislatures and to substitute a new legislative system based on the soviets. The government, too, was new, based on the Central Executive Committee and its inner core, the Politburo. The post-Tsarist system introduced by the Provisional Government was swept away, to be replaced by Lenin's 1918 Constitution, as amended by Stalin in 1924 and 1936. Even the earlier attempt at change in Germany (1918–19) seems to warrant the description of 'revolution' more directly that the process of Nazification between 1933 and 1934). After all, the Communist-inspired *Räterepublik* of 1919 followed the Bolshevik approach in a populist replacement of western institutions with councils and soviets. It is true that the Nazis had their own populist undercurrent, which featured particularly in the 1933 'town-hall revolutions'; but this was brought to heel by Hitler in the Night of the Long Knives once it had become apparent that Röhm was exceeding the powers allowed to him by the Führer.

Yet are the arguments *against* the Nazi regime being 'revolutionary' any more convincing than those *for* its 'legality'? Or, to put the case the other way round, disputing its legality helps, for two reasons, to confirm that it *was* revolutionary. First, we have already seen that the basic *purpose* of regime was nothing less than the destruction of constitutional democracy. In whatever way this was to be achieved, it was still a seizure of power – conforming to Hitler's notion of *Machtergreifung*. Although the institutions of the Weimar Constitution still existed (even with some of their previous functions) they had none of their previous *powers*. Indeed, these powers were now exercised by new institutions that had been imposed alongside the existing ones: the extent of this is examined more fully in the next section. Why should the substitution of power to duplicated institutions be considered any less revolutionary than the establishment of entirely new ones? The 'substance' of power was what counted, not the 'shadow'. Second, the whole process involved a revolutionary undercurrent that had always been apparent in the Nazi movement. It is true that Röhm's attempted changes in 1934 were crushed. But these could be seen as a *tactical* challenge to the direction Hitler was taken. This is, after all, a common feature of revolutions, whether in the form of Robespierre against Danton or Stalin against Trotsky. What counts in the end is the monopoly of coercive power held by the main revolutionary faction. In the case of the Nazi 'revolution' this control was just as clear as in the Soviet equivalent. The disciplining of the SA was accomplished by the SS, the innermost core of the SA that had emerged by 1934 to become a separate entity. The ultimate purpose to which this new institution was put must even be considered to have exceeded the customary parameters of 'revolution'. Not only had the SS come to control the operation of many state powers by 1941; it was also the means whereby Nazi racial policies were to be achieved. The Holocaust went beyond revolution. But it arose from it.

Party, government and leadership

By the end of 1934 Hitler had, to all intents and purposes, destroyed the Weimar Republic. The constitution of 1919 was never formally abrogated but all opposition parties had been eliminated, individual rights withdrawn, the Reichstag's control over the government ended, and all the major offices of state concentrated into the hands of one man. Democracy had been superseded by dictatorship and institutionalized terror. The traditional view is that this was efficient and tightly organized, with Hitler in total control. This view has, however, undergone modification. It is now argued that the German dictatorship was far less orderly than used to be supposed; indeed, there were elements of chaos. Basically, there existed in the Third Reich two competing trends. One was the revolutionary activism of the Nazi movement, the other the persistence of traditional institutions and structures. The result was duplication, overlapping and conflict, evidence of which can be seen at the levels both of central and local governments.

Despite the so-called 'Nazi revolution', central government experienced a surprising degree of continuity. All the former ministries were retained, and their powers were even increased by the Enabling Act. The civil service continued to function; in the words of Noakes and Pridham, it was a 'bureaucracy of high competence and long traditions'.[45] There was certainly no attempt to destroy existing institutions and to replace them with new NSDAP organs. Hitler was never overenthusiastic about the idea of undiluted party rule, but preferred to develop parallel institutions, which generally competed with each other. There were several examples of this process. One was the appointment of Special Deputies who were outside the government ministries but fulfilled similar functions to ministers. Hence, Todt, as General Inspector for German Roads, overlapped and came into conflict with the Minister of Transport, while the Youth Leader of the Reich had powers which impinged on those of the Minister of Education.[46]

The confusion was compounded by the development of a third layer of personnel, who were outside the scope both of the normal ministers and of the parallel party functionaries. These included the office of the Deputy Führer, the Four-Year Plan Office (along, confusingly, with its six ministries), and the SS/Gestapo/SD complex under the authority of Himmler. All this resulted in widespread inefficiency. The main problems were the duplication of functions between agencies and growing conflict between officials. On numerous occasions appeals were made to the Führer himself to arbitrate in disputes between them. His response was to distance himself from routine disputes and to rely upon Hess as a mediator. Faced with this sort of problem, it is hardly surprising that there was a threat of creeping inertia among subordinates as officials at all levels shied away from taking responsibility through fear of making a mistake – not of policy but of jurisdiction.

Untidiness and overlapping were also apparent in local government, where two main types of authority jostled for power. The first type comprised the traditional authorities, under the Minister-President of each state. This office was retained even when the Reich was reconstructed in January 1934 and the federal system weakened. The Minister-President was regarded as a useful post in the Nazi regime and was subordinated to the central government's Ministry of the Interior. Meanwhile, a second type of official had emerged – one which was based more directly on the party. Hitler decided to appoint ten Reich Governors from among the most prominent of the Party *Gauleiters*; their purpose was to enforce the Führer's edicts and orders. What happened was open competition and conflict between the Ministers-President and the Governors, each complaining regularly to central government about the activities of the other.

What was the reason for this curious state of affairs? Two broad explanations have been advanced by historians. One is that Hitler did all this on purpose. The 'intentionalists' argue that Hitler deliberately set his institutions and officials against each other in order to maintain his own position as the only one who could manoeuvre between them. Bracher, for example, maintains that Hitler remained detached from the struggles between officials: 'the antagonisms of power were only resolved in the key position of the omnipotent Führer'; indeed 'the dictator held a key position precisely because of the confusion of conflicting power groups'.[47] Similarly, Hildebrand believes that 'The confusion of functions among a multitude of mutually hostile authorities made it necessary and possible for the Führer to take decisions in every case of dispute, and can be regarded as a foundation of his power.'[48]

An alternative position is taken by historians usually categorized as 'structuralists' or 'functionalists'. They stress that any chaos was entirely unintended and that it resulted from confusion and neglect. Far from deliberately distancing himself from competing officials in order to maintain his position, Hitler was simply showing incompetence and administrative weakness. According to Broszat, 'The authoritative Führer's will was expressed only irregularly, unsystematically and incoherently.'[49] Mommsen maintains that 'Instead of functioning as a balancing element in the government, Hitler disrupted the conduct of affairs by continually acting on sudden impulses, each one different, and partly by delaying decisions on current matters.'[50]

The debate has been given a new dimension by Kershaw's use of the concept of 'working towards the Führer', a term quoted from Hitler's state secretaries in the mid-1930s. Kershaw maintains that Hitler provided the essential goals, such as territorial expansion eastwards and the removal of Jews and other race 'enemies'; Hitler was also the 'unifier', 'activator' and 'enabler' in the Third Reich. In these ways he provided the impetus between radical policies. Yet the actual implementation of policy was 'largely brought about by others, without Hitler's clear direction'.[51] Hence Hitler was not trying to create chaos in order to create his own position. That was the result of others acting on the 'will of the Führer' as they interpreted it.

Which of these is the more likely scenario? As is often the case in historical interpretation, a judicious combination of the two schools is possible. There is no doubt that Hitler did whatever he could to fragment potential opposition: indeed, he had already welcomed the partial collapse of the party while he was in Landsberg prison. It is not, therefore, beyond the realms of possibility that he welcomed discordance within the state in order to regulate his subordinates and prevent the emergence of 'overmighty' barons. The 'intentionalists' therefore have a point. On the other hand, it is difficult to imagine this being planned. The deliberate projection of chaos carries enormous risks which may seem justifiable in retrospect but which can hardly have been chanced at the time. In any case, if the original 'legal revolution' had been 'planned' on the basis of the simplest and most direct route to dictatorship, what would have been the logic in complicating the process by deliberately creating overlapping bureaucratic layers? The balance of credibility therefore switches here to the 'structuralists'. But only when considering the origins of the chaos; once we focus on its continuation, Bracher's perspective makes more sense. Conceding that the chaos was unintended, what possible motive could Hitler have had for tolerating it unless it was in his interests to do so? Would it be too much to assume that, having adjusted his approach to taking power by 1933 and to consolidating it by 1934, Hitler would have been unable to correct any aberrations thrown up in the process? It is more likely that it suited Hitler to live with the chaos which had emerged despite his efforts because this was an effective way of cancelling out trouble-makers within the party. Broszat therefore convincingly explains the origins of the Nazi administrative chaos, with Bracher providing the vital reason for its continuation.

Coercion and terror

Changes in the political system were accompanied and reinforced by the transformation of the institutions of justice and of law and order. The basic principles of the law were radically altered while, at the same time, there developed an enormously powerful apparatus of coercion and terror. In effect, the Third Reich was under a perpetual state of emergency.

The legal system was altered in both theory and practice. Hitler disliked the 'liberal' and 'formalistic' elements of legal theory. Instead, he insisted that the basis of law should be the 'healthy popular feeling' and 'welfare of the national community'.[52] In practice, the 'legal revolution' brought government control over the whole judiciary. Judges were appointed on the basis of their loyalty and part of their training had to include 'a serious study of National Socialism and its ideological foundations'.[53] For a while the process of Nazification was incomplete, as Minister of Justice Gürtner was not himself a Nazi. On his death in 1941, however, he was succeeded by Thierack, and the whole judicial system slid under the control of the SS.

The latter was not the original force of Nazi coercion. This unofficial power belonged to the Sturmabteilung (SA). Formed in 1921, this had been responsible for much of the Nazi violence during the period of the Weimar Republic and the opening year of the Third Reich. After the purge of 1934, however, the SA's role was severely restricted. Although it continued to provide street activists and bully-boys (as, for example, in their central role in Kristallnacht in 1938), as well as some of the massed ranks for official ceremonies and rallies, most of its powers and influence passed to the SS. The leaders of the SA, Lutze (1934–43) and Schepmann (1943–5), had nothing like the authority wielded by Röhm before his execution in 1934. Instead, Germany came under the thrall of a different set of institutions collectively known as the SS/Gestapo/SD complex which was responsible for all areas of policing and security – and for much else besides.

The SS

The SS/Gestapo/SD complex grew from three separate strands to form a network that covered all areas of policing and security. The SS (Schutzstaffeln) originated in 1925 as the elite within the SA and came under the leadership of Himmler in 1929. The SD (Sicherheitsdienst) was set up in 1931 as the NSDAP's internal police force. The Gestapo (Geheime Staatspolizei) was established in Prussia by Goering in April 1933 and was initially accountable to the Ministry of the Interior. Gradually the three strands came together. In 1934 Himmler became the effective head of the Gestapo, to which he added the position of Reichsführer SS. The process was officially recognized in Hitler's decree of 17 June 1936 'to unify the control of police duties in the Reich'. From this stage onwards the SS expanded even further. It penetrated the army by means of the SS Special Service Troops (SS-Verfügungstruppe – SS VT); from this was created the Waffen SS, the divisions at the forefront of every military campaign. Finally, the SS took over from the SA the organization of the concentration camps, manning them with the Death's Head Formations (SS-Totenkopfverbände), while the genocide programme from 1941 came under the control of the Reich Security Main Office (Reichssicherheitshauptamt or RSHA).

The functions of the SS/Gestapo/SD complex became ever more extensive. As well as security and policing, the SS underpinned the racial emphasis of the *Volksgemeinschaft* more completely than did any of the state institutions. The SS also played a vital role in seizing and administering German conquests in eastern Europe; above all, it was responsible for implementing much of the Nazi extermination programmes, first through the Einsatzgruppen, then through working to death in concentration camps or gas chambers in the extermination camps. The main victims were 'anti-social elements' such as 'Jews, Gypsies, Russians and Ukrainians, Poles with sentences of more than three years, Czechs and Germans with sentences of more than eight years'.[54] Another key area of SS involvement was the economy, where it ran a large number of industrial enterprises through the Main Administrative Office for Business and Commerce. Finally, Himmler even brought the SS into matters of religion. In 1937 he maintained that it was part of 'the mission of the SS to give the German people over the next fifty years the non-Christian ideological foundations for a way of life appropriate to their character'. At first his views had comparatively little influence, largely because Hitler at the outset maintained a pragmatic connection with the

Christian churches, especially through the 1933 Concordat, and frowned at anything that might disrupt this. The real influence of the SS came during the late 1930s and the period of war, when Hitler and other Nazi leaders accepted Himmler's assertions that Christianity was pacifist, unpatriotic and pro-Jewish. By then the SS had extensively incorporated paganism into its ritual and had led Nazism into a strongly anti-Christian stance that was not shared by the majority of Germans.

These developments altered the whole balance of the Nazi state. At first the regime had been a compromise between party influences on the one hand and, on the other, the traditional forces in the administration, army and business. In 1933 and 1934, the period of the so-called 'legal revolution', the SS played a subordinate role. Increasingly, however, it became independent of both the party and the state, although two recent historians have disagreed about the extent of the actual influence of the SS or as to whether the Nazi state was converted into an 'SS state'.

Browder sees the SS as a constantly expanding entity that exerted huge influence on the whole development of Nazism: it went beyond anything originally envisaged by Hitler, who had initially considered the priority to be measures to maintain domestic control during his pursuit of an active foreign policy. Although Hitler 'did not have to be persuaded to adopt a police-state system like the one Himmler offered', he did have to abandon his customary principle of divide and rule in concentrating 'enormous powers in Himmler's hands'. As for the later policies of imperialism and genocide, 'These required the SS state'.[55] Browder maintains that the SS helped shape Hitler's policy here. 'Hitler had not yet formulated clear lines of action that required the existence of the SS-police system.' Therefore, 'It was only after the emergence of that machinery that the potential for radical solutions to "racial problems" came into view as a correlated result.'[56]

Kitchen, on the other hand, emphasizes the limits of SS power and the strength of opposition to it. Although the SS did indeed have 'a vast commercial and industrial empire', this had to be 'constantly defended against the claims of the military'. In the process, 'many a round was lost, and the SS were never able to achieve its aim of turning Nazi Germany into an SS state'.[57] There was, for example, some resistance from Wehrmacht officers to SS attempts at infiltration and control, even though there was a surprising degree of co-operation over action involving atrocities. A later – and more serious – breach opened up between the SS and the NSDAP. From 1943 onwards Bormann controlled the party more effectively than had any of his predecessors, acting increasingly as 'Hitler's Cerberus'.[58] Despite the enormous powers he had accumulated, Himmler found himself increasingly restricted in his direct contacts with the Führer. Goebbels, too, counted for more in the political elite once he had been appointed Plenipotentiary for Total War from July 1944. Bitter rivalries also developed between the SS, the government ministries and the new layers of administration in eastern Europe. For example, Himmler clashed with Foreign Minister Ribbentrop over policy towards Romania in 1941: Himmler and the SS supported the Iron Guard in their bid for power, while Ribbentrop persuaded Hitler to back Antonescu. At the same time Himmler was criticized by Governor Hans Frank over the SS deportations of Poles and Jews into the Central Government, which disrupted Frank's plans for the creation of a German colony with a successful economy.

There were also multiple internal flaws *within* the SS: these included administrative conflicts between the multiple branches and the various units within these branches. There were questions as to the precise role of the SD and the relationship of the Gestapo with Sipo and Kripo, while the WVHA's interests in twenty concentration camps and 165 work camps, as an integral part of the SS commercial enterprises, came into direct conflict with the RSHA over the extermination of potential labourers.[59] Above all, there were bitter, and frequently public, antagonisms between individuals. The most significant of these was Himmler's differences with Heydrich until the latter's assassination in 1942. Heydrich was a ruthless pragmatist, while Himmler was governed more by the principles of 'racial purity', based on the 'values of blood and selection'.[60] According to Höhne, 'the SS world was a bizarre and nonsensical affair, devoid of all logic'. As such, 'it was anything but an organization constructed and directed on some diabolically efficient system: it was the product of accident and automatism. The real history of the SS is a story of idealists and criminals, of place-seekers and romantics: it is the history of the most fantastic association of men imaginable'.[61] This may be seen as going too far. After all, might not the last point apply to the story of Nazism generally? But, given that the 'fantastic' did occur, the SS should be seen as playing a vital structural role in its realization. This makes more sense than seeing the SS merely as a 'fantastic' part of the Nazi system.

An overall conclusion might be this. The SS under Himmler was the most completely totalitarian part of the Nazi regime and, while it was expanding, provided the strongest impetus behind the most radical measures of Nazism. During the first half of the war it might even be seen as a state within a state. But it had too many internal structural defects and personal conflicts to overcome the pressures mounting against it from the NSDAP and the Wehrmacht. It eventually imploded under the threat of imminent defeat by the Allies – especially by the Red Army in Berlin in 1945. The SS was, therefore, better at expansion than it was at consolidation.

The Gestapo

The Gestapo (*Geheimestaatspolizei*), along with Kripo (*Kriminalpolizei*), was a section of Sipo (*Sicherheitspolizei*), although it is far better known than these other two institutions within the SS orbit. Its main leader, under Himmler, was Heydrich, followed, after the latter's death in 1942, by Müller and Best. Along with the Soviet KGB, the Gestapo became the twentieth century's epitome of the effective and all-embracing totalitarian police force affecting the entire population. But how true is this picture?

Earlier historians tended to regard the Gestapo as a success story. Crankshaw, for example, considered it a 'highly professional corps'.[62] According to Schultz, 'scarcely a politically significant initiative against the National Socialist regime went undetected'.[63] Delarue maintains, 'Never before, in no other land and at no other time, had an organisation attained such a comprehensive penetration of society, possessed such power'.[64] More recent views, by contrast, have stressed that the reputation of the Gestapo is a myth that derives from its own propaganda. Gellately, for example believes that 'The Gestapo's reputation for brutality no doubt assisted the police in the accomplishment of its tasks, but brutality alone . . . does not provide a satisfactory explanation for its effective functioning'.[65] Mallman and Paul argue that the Gestapo was insufficiently equipped to carry out its directives and that it had to rely on information volunteered by members of the public. Recent local studies show that 'the Gestapo at local level was hardly an imposing detective organization, but rather an under-staffed, under-bureaucratized agency, limping along behind the permanent inflation of its tasks'.[66] This applied to Gestapo headquarters in Stettin, Koslin, Hanover, Bremen, Dortmund, Düsseldorf, Würzburg and other areas. The outbreak of war aggravated the problem with a further decline in the number of staff. Inexperienced officials replaced those who had been conscripted into the Wehrmacht. The total membership of the Gestapo was little more than 32,000, of which only half were fully concerned with the task of political policing.[67] In the circumstances it could function only through the enormous number of denunciations which came from a generally compliant population. Some authorities have even asserted that the effectiveness of the Gestapo was superseded by the East German police force, the Stasi, itself directly influenced by the Soviet NKVD and KGB. This is a clear indication that the totalitarian policing methods of Stalin's Russia have been considered more effective than those of Hitler's Germany.

The latest interpretations have returned to a more central position, where the Gestapo now reassumes its capacity for inflicting terror on the population without being totally dependent on the latter's complicity. Burleigh, for example, questions the focus on 'desk-bound policemen, almost buried under the avalanche of denunciations from ordinary citizens'. Instead, 'The Gestapo's primary task was to destroy political and clerical opposition. It was clearly highly effective' in smashing Communist resistance which sank 'without trace between 1939 and 1941'.[68] According to Evans, the emphasis on a 'self-policing' society underestimates the 'terror and intimidation in the functioning of the Third Reich'.[69] Johnson believes that the stress on denunciations tends to 'underestimate and obscure' the capability of the Gestapo and to 'overestimate the culpability of ordinary German citizens'.[70]

Between them, these changes in approach provide a good example of the way in which historical interpretation typically works. In this case, the pendulum starts with a swing towards the 'top-down' effectiveness of a totalitarian institution. This is later replaced by a sweep towards a greater emphasis on a 'bottom-up' collusion from the population, followed in turn by a partial return to the 'top-down' explanation, although with some acknowledgement of popular co-operation. There are other examples of similar historiographical patterns elsewhere in this chapter and in other parts of this book.

Indoctrination and propaganda

According to Goebbels, reconciliation with – or neutrality towards – the new regime was insufficient. 'Rather', he said at a press conference on 15 March 1933, 'we want to work on people until they have capitulated to us, until they grasp ideologically that what is happening in Germany today not only must be accepted but also can be accepted'.[71] Eighteen months later, at a Nazi Party Congress in Nuremberg, he emphasized the importance of propaganda in accomplishing this. 'Among the arts with which one rules a people, it ranks in first place.' Indeed, 'there exists no sector of public life which can escape its influence'.[72]

An administrative infrastructure was clearly needed to co-ordinate the transmission of ideology. This was developed by two changes. The first increased the power of the Ministry of Education over the states, or *Länder*, to remove the possible threat of local particularism to the achievement of educational conformity. The second established a new Ministry for People's Enlightenment and Propaganda in 1933. Under the overall control of Goebbels, this eventually comprised a series of chambers for press, radio, theatre, music, creative arts and film. In theory the regime now had the power to apply negative censorship in whatever form it considered necessary and, more constructively, to shape the development of culture at all levels.

How effectively did these institutions carry out the regime's intentions? Any assessment needs to make a distinction between 'propaganda' and 'indoctrination'. It is true that the two were connected in that indoctrination of the population involved regular exposure to official propaganda. There were, however, separate features. Indoctrination was a process carried out largely in education, the youth movements, the workplace and the armed forces. Propaganda made more direct use of channels such as radio, cinema and the press. Indoctrination was a continuous, long-term process, whereas propaganda provided the highlights.

Indoctrination, education and youth movements

The methods used to indoctrinate Germany's youth were nothing if not thorough. The main intention was to indoctrinate, to implant fixed ideas and doctrines, rather than to open minds. Hence, Hitler once said, 'When an opponent declares "I will not come over to your side", I calmly say, "Your child belongs to us already."' The subjects primarily affected were history, which emphasized Nordic, Nazi and military themes; science, based strongly on Nazi race theories; and literature, which was virulently anti-Semitic. The school curriculum also received the additions of race study and eugenics, used as vehicles for Nazi ideology. In some areas 'elite' schools were established, the most important of which were the Napolas (to educate future government and military personnel), the Adolf Hitler Schools and the Castles of Order. Teachers were recruited and kept for their ideological conformity, their main obligation being 'to defend without reservation the National Socialist state'.[73] To guarantee this degree of loyalty, membership of the Nationalsozialistische Lehrerbund (NSLB), or Nazi Teachers' Association, was compulsory. The impact of these measures was considerable, creating among the young an emotional commitment to the regime which was often absent in the adult population. The universities were also the target of a regime which both despised and feared the academic world. Again the emphasis was on ideological conformity. The Minister of Culture told the universities in 1933: 'From now on, it will not be your job to determine whether something is true, but whether it is in the spirit of the National Socialist revolution.'[74] To enforce this new approach to higher learning, the government deprived university senates of their authority and assumed control of the appointment of rectors.

In many ways, however, the educational process was flawed. Changes were held up by constant argument between administrative and party organs. For example, the Ministry of Education continued to use the guidelines of the Weimar Republic largely because it could not agree with the party headquarters the shape of their replacement. The conflict between Ley and Rust on the one hand and Bormann and Hess on the other meant that the new regulations for elementary education were delayed until 1939, while secondary schools were served little better. This had two unfortunate side-effects for the Nazis. One was the dilution of the content of the curriculum by more traditional influences than was originally intended. The other was the persistence of confusion within the schools themselves as to the precise means of delivering the curriculum. Gestapo reports were full of references to unsatisfactory teachers; but many of these were probably confused rather than deliberately uncooperative. There was also a serious decline in educational standards. A typical complaint expressed by the army was that 'Many of the candidates applying for commissions display a simply inconceivable lack of elementary knowledge.'[75] Vocational and technical schools frequently claimed that basic ignorance seriously impeded normal coverage of the curriculum. There were also problems in higher education: Nazi policies led inevitably to a decline in the standard of scientific research, especially with the abolition of the 'Jewish Physics' of Albert Einstein. Ultimately Germany paid a heavy penalty for this straitjacket on academic freedom, losing against the Western Allies the race to develop the atomic bomb.

Indoctrination was also attempted by means of mobilization through the youth movements. All young people were to be trained for a future role. In the case of boys this was military service, while for girls the emphasis was on preparation for marriage and motherhood. To ensure the martial and marital message did get through, boys and girls were co-opted into the Hitler Youth. This was subdivided into several components. Boys joined the Deutsches Jungvolk (DJ) at the age of ten, proceeding at fourteen into the Hitlerjugend (HJ). Similarly, girls entered the Jungmädelbund (JM) at ten and the Bund Deutscher Madel (BDM) at fourteen. The whole organization was placed under the control of Baldur von Shirach as the Reichsjugendführer. Total membership of the Hitler Youth grew from 2.3 million in 1933 to 7 million in 1939, increasing during the same period from 30.4 per cent to 77.2 per cent of the 10–18 age group.

How important was the Hitler Youth in the Nazi system? In some respects the varied activities had widespread appeal, initially appearing as a challenge to more conservative forms of authority and giving youth a sense of collective power. Earlier historians tended to emphasize the seductive nature of the various sections: Jarman, for example, wrote in the 1950s that 'it was a real punishment to remain, for any reason, outside'. Children 'wanted to march and sing and salute' and 'to enjoy the wonderful, exciting life' that was organized for them or 'to go to the Nazi camps'.[76] There was also a tendency to dwell on the success of the whole process of indoctrination. There may well be some truth in both of these points, especially during the earlier stages of the movement. It had widespread appeal, giving youth excitement and a sense of collective power; within it there was also extensive adulation for the Führer himself. But more recently historians have stressed the failings of the Hitler Youth. The whole organization suffered from administrative imbalance: this time the conflict was between the Ministry of Education and the Reich Youth Leadership over underlying objectives and priorities. This meant that the Hitler Youth and the education system frequently diverged. It also lost part of its attraction to many young people as it came to be seen as part of the new establishment. This is particularly strongly put by Peukert.[77] According to the latter, 'The more the Hitler Youth arrogated state powers to itself, and the more completely young people were assimilated into the organisation, the more clearly visible became an emergent pattern of youth nonconformity.' As a result, significant numbers sought 'their own unregimented styles in spontaneous groups and gangs'.[78] This accelerated rapidly with the emergence of the Edelweiss Pirates and Navajos (see p. 211) and the further proliferation of dissident subcultures under the impact of war.

Yet it should not be deduced from this that the Hitler Youth lost its direct impact. It was rather that its overall emphasis *changed* over time. Although there had been some decline in its general appeal and its capacity to generate enthusiasm, there was, by contrast, a strengthening of its more specific contributions to the Nazi system. The work of Rempel and Harvey[79] provide two examples of this. Rempel shows the growing importance of the boys' section of the Hitler Youth as a source of recruitment to the SS, providing constant replenishment during the war years. The female equivalent, emphasized by Harvey, was the recruitment of many former members of the BDM for service in the *Volkstumskampf*; this involved an important non-military contribution to the Germanization of conquered territories in the East. There is also evidence that the Hitler Youth system lost none of the intensity of its powers to indoctrinate, even if declining proportions of its membership were affected. After all, among the most fanatical of Hitler's last-ditch resistance fighters against the invading Allies in 1945 were recruits from the Hitler Youth who filled some of the gaps left in the collapsing Wehrmacht.

Propaganda and culture

The main target of indoctrination was youth, while propaganda and culture affected the entire population. The institution mainly responsible was the Ministry of People's Enlightenment and Propaganda which fulfilled two functions. In the words of Goebbels, the minister in charge, 'popular enlightenment is essentially something passive; propaganda, on the other hand, is something active'. Propaganda had to dominate. 'It is not enough to reconcile people more or less to our regime, to move them towards a position of neutrality towards us.' Instead, it was essential to 'work on people until they are addicted to us'.[80] As with the indoctrination of youth, the impact of propaganda and the new culture met with a mixed degree of success.

The Nazis gave priority to the radio since this increased the impression of personal contact between the people and their leader, thereby enhancing the effectiveness of the Führer cult. Goebbels was convinced that the Reich had to make full use of technology to enable state propaganda to reach the masses. Increased access to radio sets was, of course, an essential prerequisite for the success of this approach. This was achieved, with ownership of sets increased from 25 per cent of households in 1932 to 70 per cent by 1939, the largest proportion anywhere in the world. These were all brought into a web of the Reich Broadcasting Corporation, over which the government established control in 1933. Radio was also used to generate a feeling of collective loyalty by communal listening to Hitler's speeches, which were relayed by loudspeakers specially set up factories, stores, offices and blocks of flats. For the vast majority of the population the radio provided the most abiding impression of the Führer that they were ever likely to have. As such this component of propaganda must go down as a considerable success.

Film proved a more difficult medium and the regime used it less effectively than it did radio. The most accomplished film was not necessarily the most influential. Riefenstahl's *Triumph of the Will* was commissioned by Hitler himself as a record of the Nuremberg rallies of 1934. Technically a brilliant achievement, it created a multi-layered image of Nazism which brought in all elements of society and directly fostered the Führer cult. On the other hand, it was too long for most audiences, who sometimes reacted negatively to the repetition of the same types of scene. During the war years the anti-Semitic component of films became more extreme; here, however, Hitler's vision of what was likely to engage the public was less effective than that of Goebbels. *The Eternal Jew*, commissioned by Hitler and directed by Hippler, was so crude that audiences were repelled by the images created. The anti-Semitic message was conveyed more skilfully through a feature film, *Jud Süss*. By this stage, Goebbels had learned how to introduce propaganda as a subliminal message within the context of a story with which the viewers could identify. This applied also to his attempts to engender a spirit of resistance to the Allies with his film on Frederick the Great. But such developments came too late to have anything but a peripheral effect on the morale of a population facing imminent defeat.

At first it proved more difficult to subordinate the press to propaganda. One reason was that it had had longer to develop under private ownership, whereas the more recent technology of the radio could be brought more easily under state control. Another was that the number of newspapers had greatly increased during the period of the Weimar Republic to a total of over 4,700: these covered a diversity of views, attitudes and allegiances. Gradually, however, the government extended its powers. State-owned newspapers increased from 2.5 per cent of the total in 1933 to 82 per cent by the end of the Nazi era. The German News Agency (DNB) was set up to control the activities and output of journalists, who were made responsible to the state rather than to their editors. There were also regulations for the presentation of news features, with detailed guidelines on the line to take. It was, for example, forbidden to show photographs showing government ministers drinking alcohol in case these should give the mistaken impression that they were taking their responsibilities lightly. The result was a less stimulating read for those among the public who avoided the official Nazi propaganda of the *Völkischer Beobachter* or the virulent extremes of Streicher's *Der Stürmer*. The decline in German readership was therefore hardly surprising.

The Nazis attempted to introduce a new cultural policy, or *Kulturpolitik*; according to Welch, they were 'the first party systematically to organize the entire cultural life of a nation'.[81] But this, too, produced problems. The Ministry of People's Enlightenment and Propaganda found much in the arts that was suspect or even objectionable but never quite succeeded in promoting an alternative. Traditional literature, art and music were severely pruned, with the intention of allowing the growth of a new and distinctive Nazi culture. The results were generally negative. Literature experienced a complete void; music experienced some new activity; and art developed rapidly – but with work of low quality.

Literature was heavily affected by preventive censorship. This involved book-burning sessions, mobilized by the SA, and the removal of over 2,500 German authors from the approved lists. To some extent, destruction was cathartic – the relief of pent-up anti-intellectualism. It could never seriously have been the preliminary to an alternative Nazi literature. It discouraged any diversity of viewpoints and individual experience, seeking instead to stereotype collectivism. Within this atmosphere any chance of creating much of an 'official' literature disappeared, even supposing that the population would have been allowed any time to read it.

The visual arts were more successfully used by the Nazis in inculcating basic 'blood and soil' values. Painters like Kampf and Ziegler were able to provide pictorial stereotypes of physical appearance, of women as mothers and home-minders, and of men in a variety of martial roles. Such images reinforced the roles already developed through the institutions of indoctrination, such as the BDM and the HJ. On the negative side, the result was a form of art which was bland and lacking in talent: the vacuum produced by preventive censorship was filled with mediocrity. Of all the art forms, it was architecture which held the deepest interest for Hitler; it would, after all, be the visible measure of the expected millennium of Nazi rule. Hitler made the revealing comment in 1937 that 'the greater the demands the state makes upon its people, the more imposing it must appear to them'. He therefore became obsessively involved in designs for the rebuilding of Berlin and Nuremberg – plans eventually scrapped because of their unsurpassed ugliness.

The Nazi regime ended the period of musical experimentation which had been a major cultural feature of the Weimar Republic. The works of Schoenberg and Berg were considered un-German, while those of Mendelssohn were banned as 'Jewish'. Yet the majority of German or Austrian composers were unaffected and retained their place as part of Germany's cultural heritage. The Nazis did, however, use certain composers as the spearhead of their cultural penetration: foremost among these was Wagner, whose *Ring* cycle was seen by Hitler as the musical embodiment of *völkisch* values. Contemporary composers like Richard Strauss and Carl Orff had ambivalent attitudes. They managed to coexist with the regime and produce work which outlived the Reich. In this sense the quality of the Reich's musical output was superior to the work of painters like Kampf and Ziegler, but the result was less distinctively Nazi. Overall, Nazi culture was ephemeral and, unlike Socialist Realism in Russia, had no lasting impact.

Indoctrination, propaganda and the test of war

The ultimate test of the success of Nazi propaganda was whether the people of Germany could be brought to accept the experience of war. Throughout the Nazi era there were really two levels of propaganda: one put across Hitler's basic ideology, the other made pragmatic adjustments to fit the needs of the moment. Up to 1939, pragmatism frequently diluted ideology, giving rise to considerable theoretical inconsistency in Hitler's ideas. During this period Hitler was presented as a man of peace and yet all the processes of indoctrination and propaganda emphasized struggle and its martial refinement.

The period 1939–45 tended to bring together more completely the man and his ideas. This occurred in two stages. The first was the acclimatization of the people to the idea of war, achieved through the emphasis on Blitzkrieg, or 'lightning war'. Logically this fitted in with the notion of easy conquest achieved by the 'master race', and while it lasted it was a considerable success: Hitler probably reached the peak of his popularity in 1940, at the time of the fall of France. During the second stage, however, propaganda had to acclimatize the people to the experience of war. At first Goebbels scored a propaganda success in his 'total war' speech in 1941, but in the longer term there was a clear decline in popular enthusiasm. From 1943 the main characteristic shown by German civilians was fortitude in the face of adversity and destruction, not a fanatical desire to achieve a world vision. By this stage, Nazi propaganda and indoctrination had not so much failed as become irrelevant.

Women in the Third Reich

Women played a crucial role in electing and supporting the Nazis: according to Boak: 'the NSDAP received more votes from women than from men in some areas before 1932 and throughout the Reich in 1932'.[82] Hitler was also massively popular with women, although the adulation for him was not extended to most of his subordinates. For many years after the fall of the Reich the assumption was that women submitted totally to the regime receiving, in return, inducements for marriage and childbearing as compensation for being deprived of equality of opportunity and higher-level careers. They tended to be seen as generalized masses with a common pattern of behaviour and an overall inertness, deprived of any scope for individual achievement other than in the home environment. But recent historiography, to which major contributions have been made by women, has moved away from this approach by integrating women more fully into the mainstream of German life. As such, they would have had the full range of views about Hitler and Nazism – and would have played a more active role in the Reich. This is not to deny the existence of gender-based exploitation but, rather, to question the extent of its enervating impact.

That Nazism was an 'overtly misogynistic movement'[83] can certainly be seen in the views of the Nazi leadership that women had a limited and clearly defined role. In a rally at Nuremberg in 1934 Hitler said that 'man's world is the State', while 'the world of the woman is a smaller world. For her the world is her husband, her family, her children and her house'.[84] According to Goebbels: 'The mission of woman is to be beautiful and to bring children into the world . . . the female prettifies herself for her mate and hatches the eggs for him.'[85] The emphasis on reproductive and domestic functions produced an overall policy to remove women from the top levels of the civil service, law, medicine and politics. At all stages there was a heavy stress on women's racial 'responsibilities'. The opportunity to qualify was also affected, the number of female university students falling by nearly three-quarters between 1933 and 1939. Instead, girls were given a narrow education and were indoctrinated to their role in the BDM. The rules for selecting a marriage partner, issued by the Nazi Racial Policy Bureau, included instructions like: 'Being a German, only choose a spouse of similar or related blood' and 'your duty is to produce at least four offspring in order to ensure the future of the national stock'.[86] Once married, women were induced to stay at home by new marriage credits and child bonuses.

Yet these measures were never particularly successful. The general decline of unemployment created a new demand for labour. The result was the steady recruitment of women into both agriculture and industry, the total reaching 5.2 million by 1938. In any case, it has been established by Stephenson that the exclusion of non-Aryans and political opponents 'from influential or promoted positions in thoroughgoing purges in 1933' meant that 'German male labour and professional expertise were not alone sufficient for the regime's ambitions'. Hence women were encouraged to enter the employment market, 'even areas that had previously been designated "men's" jobs'.[87] For some women, therefore, the Nazi regime brought further opportunities than had been available under the Weimar Republic. This applied especially to women who had few formal qualifications but wished to be involved in political activism. Nor were overt Nazi policies fully enforced in the professions, from which women were far from fully excluded. Women remained in teaching, medicine, the law and the civil service, although most were in lower positions or women's sections. Opportunities increased during the war with the shortage of men in the professions, although many of the highly qualified never regained their former status. Even the bulwark of Nazi racial policy – the family – was not fully protected. Divorce rates increased more rapidly than marriage rates in Nazi Germany, while the number of births fell far short of expectations: the overall pattern had been a gradual decline in the Weimar Republic followed by a gradual increase in the Third Reich – but only to earlier Republic levels.

It is now recognized that the Nazi system 'rested on a female hierarchy as well as a male chain of command'.[88] The largest organization within this was the *NS-Frauenschaft* (NSF or Nazi Women's Group) which also co-ordinated the *Deutsches Frauenwerk* (DFW or German Women's Enterprise) and the Women's Labour Service. By 1935 about eleven million out of the country's thirty-five million females belonged to the *NS-Frauenschaft* and were willing to support the ideas and beliefs of Nazism. Women were responsible for implementing the increasing number of laws affecting social planning by providing the details and names of those who were Jews or racially or socially 'unfit'; many of the latter were eventually subjected to sterilization or 'euthanasia'. Women also organized the redistribution of Jewish property that had been confiscated. Above all, women leaders exercised a profound influence on the German family, regarding it, in the words of Koonz, as 'an invasion route that could give them access to every German's most personal values and decisions'.[89] A detailed analysis has also been provided of women's involvement in *Volkstumskampf*, the Germanization of the East.[90] Initially this meant the borderlands, then from 1939 the occupied areas of Poland and other eastern areas. According to Harvey, volunteers created 'model communities and a model domestic culture as the bedrock of the future German nation'.[91] Young women, who had been fully 'socialized' and inducted into Nazi ideology through the BDM and the Women's Labour Service, provided help and advice – not always appreciated by the local population – on the welfare of mothers and families. Sometimes they went beyond this in carrying out the more penetrative policies of occupation such as the redistribution of property confiscated from Poles to new or existing German settlers.[92]

More attention is now also paid to individual leaders within this system. The most significant was Gertrud Scholtz-Klink, the leader of the *NS-Frauenschaft*/DFW and the Women's Labour Service. Although never acknowledged as in any way equal to her male counterparts, she nevertheless had administrative ability and exerted considerable influence over a total of seven million women. Auguste Reber-Gruber, meanwhile, supervised 100,000 women teachers in Germany. To her, the purpose of education was to mould 'German girls as the carriers of the National Socialist point of view'.[93] She was more distrusted than Scholtz-Klink by male administrators because she was more combative and less diplomatic or submissive. Sophie Rogge-Berne was more openly feminist than either of these, arguing in 1937 that it was misguided to remove women from the professions since 'Women doctors could give aid and comfort to fatigued mothers. Women teachers would be most suited to instruct adolescent girls. Women jurists would be most qualified for dealing with cases involving children'.[94]

The 'female hierarchy' was supposed to harmonize with the rest of the administrative structure. In fact, it contributed to contradictions and tensions within that structure. A fundamental conflict developed between the submissive role of womanhood in the racial state on the one hand and their part in their more active involvement in the economy and Lebensraum on the other. It was extremely difficult to combine the two. Hitler's ideas about the subservience of women, although integral to his larger racial vision, actually impeded the achievement of the expansion he wanted. Conflict arose with his subordinates as Hitler rejected pleas from Speer, Sauckel and others for the conscription of women to the wartime workforce or for the increase in women's wages. This partially explains the huge increase in conscripted and slave labour from conquered territories – which was still not sufficient given the ever-increasing threat to Germany from the western Allies and the Soviet Union. Goebbels forced the issue with his official announcement of Total War in 1943, which meant that women were finally drafted into wartime work. Another example of the tension within the policy towards women was Himmler's obsession with Aryan breeding, which produced fissures within already established policy. Giving full credibility to unmarried mothers and instituting the policy of Lebensborn increased the gap between parts of the Nazi leadership, official morality and the Catholic Church.[95] Even the involvement of women in the *Volkstumskampf* created tensions within the increasingly complex administrative machinery for the conquered territories. Their work frequently crossed the conventional line of the female role, which resentful male administrators saw them as transgressing. As in almost every other area of Reich administration there was therefore a degree of confusion and conflict.

If women were more active in the Nazi regime than was once thought, what implications does this have for their responsibility for the actions taken in the name of that regime? It has always been acknowledged that a number of women contributed to some of the worst crimes of the Nazi era, especially the 3,000 female warders in concentration camps (such as Irma Griese at Auschwitz and Ilse Koch at Buchenwald); at the same time, the vast majority of women have been considered submissive to a regime that in many ways victimized them. More recently, as we have seen, the emphasis has moved to a more widely spread complicity in the enforcement of Nazi ideas. As Koonz argues, 'Over time, Nazi women, no less than men, destroyed the ethical vision, debased humane traditions, and rendered decent people helpless.' Yet, she continues 'other women, as victims and resisters, risked their lives to ensure Nazi defeat and preserve their own ideals'.[96] The extent of their opposition ranged, as with men, from mild dissent to active campaigning (as with Sophie Scholl in White Rose) and secret work for SOPADE. Yet the emphasis on women's complicity or opposition has been accompanied by acknowledgement of their victimhood, but in a more gender-specific sense – the rape of hundreds of thousands of women and girls by invading armies in 1945, especially in the east.[97]

Relations with the churches

Germany has, since the Reformation, been divided between the Protestant north and the mainly Catholic south. Both denominations had been highly suspicious of what they saw as the blatant secularism of the Weimar Republic and were prepared to do a deal with the Nazi regime. Hitler's initial attitude was reassuring. He said in the Reichstag on 23 March 1933 that Christianity was 'the unshakeable foundation of the moral and ethical life of our people'.[98] There was, however, some doubt as to whether this was the real policy of the Nazis or merely a precaution to maintain a measure of support while the regime consolidated. The passage of time soon pointed to the latter.

The Protestant Churches were prepared to welcome the arrival of the Nazi regime, regarding the Weimar Republic as un-German and ungodly. According to Steinbach, many of the Protestant clergy 'welcomed the Nazis' seizure of power because they mistook it for the reestablishment of "order" and traditional state authority'.[99] Hitler took only six months to exploit this. In July 1933 the twenty-eight provincial Protestant Churches (Landeskirchen) were centralized into a single Reich Church, which soon came under Reich Bishop Müller. Then, in 1935, the Reich Church was placed under the control of Hans Kerrl, Minister of Church Affairs. There was also increasing evidence of the infiltration of Nazi values, with the establishment of the DC (German Christians). This sect managed to combine Christian beliefs with racism, anti-Semitism and Führer-worship, laying itself open to the accusation that it was the 'SA of Jesus Christ'. In opposition to the DC there emerged the Confessional Church, under the leadership of Pastor Niemoller. It retained its political detachment from the Nazi regime and, perhaps because of this, was banned in 1937, Niemoller himself being interned in a concentration camp.

The Catholic Church was also willing to collaborate with Hitler in 1933. The Centre Party, still a political arm of Catholicism, had supported Hitler's Enabling Act (March 1933) in return for certain religious guarantees from the government. This compromise was followed, in the same year, by the Concordat, drawn up by Cardinal Pacelli for the Church and by von Papen for the political authorities. This promised continuing freedom of worship, the protection of denominational schools and the right to publish and distribute pastoral letters. In exchange, the Church agreed to withdraw totally from active politics; the Centre Party, for instance, dissolved itself voluntarily. The Nazis, however, soon subverted the agreement. Various organizations, like the Cross and Eagle League and the Working Group of Catholic Germans, sought to disseminate Nazi values, while the government deliberately discredited the clergy by holding public 'immorality' trials involving nuns and monks. By 1937 the situation had deteriorated so badly that Pope Pius XI abandoned his earlier neutrality and issued an encyclical called *Mit brennender Sorge* ('With Deep Anxiety') which was strongly critical of government measures. This was followed by growing disillusionment within the Catholic Church and real doubts about ultimate Nazi intentions towards religion.

By the late 1930s these intentions had come out into the open. As the Churches reacted with hostility to government attempts to Nazify them, many party officials inclined increasingly to non-Christian forms of religion. One example was the German Faith Movement, which introduced pagan ceremonies (widely used by SS officials) and virulently attacked the most sacred tenets of Christianity. According to *Sigrune*, the journal of the German Faith Movement, 'Jesus was a cowardly Jewish lout who had certain adventures during his years of indiscretion.'[100] Two prominent Nazis were particularly anti-Christian; Julius Streicher, notorious anti-Semite and pornographer, claimed that the Crucifixion was an instance of Jewish ritual murder. Martin Bormann declared in 1941 that 'The concepts of National Socialism and Christianity are irreconcilable . . . Our National Socialist ideology is far loftier than the concepts of Christianity, which in their essential points have been taken over from Jewry.'[101] Hitler's own views were more ambivalent. On the one hand, the ideas of Rosenberg, Himmler and Bormann did not impress him and, according to Burleigh, 'both neo-paganism and efforts to Nazify Christianity itself were second-order considerations, at least for Hitler himself'.[102] On the other hand, there was a definite 'sacralization of politics' within the Hitler cult. Burleigh emphasizes his grandiose conceptions. 'He saw himself as the last chance for mankind before the onset of cosmic desolation, should the race war he envisaged have the wrong outcome.'[103] Hitler also became increasingly impatient with the Judaic roots of Christianity, with its claims to universality and with its emphasis on such virtues as compassion and forgiveness; these simply did not fit into the needs of Nazism. Nor did the focus on individual salvation.

> To the Christian doctrine of the infinite significance of the human soul . . . I oppose . . . the saving doctrine of the nothingness and insignificance of the individual human being, and of his continued existence in the visible immortality of the nation.[104]

Did Nazi persecution inflict any lasting damage? Kershaw provides several examples of the resilience of Christianity in Germany. During the 1930s there was no significant decline in Church membership, while an increase occurred during the war years. Meanwhile, the clergy managed to maintain a considerable influence over the laity. In the long term, the impact of the Churches on politics was strengthened, as was shown in the Catholic base of post-war Germany's CDU (Christian Democratic Union). Everything, therefore, 'points to the conclusion that Nazi policy failed categorically to break down religious allegiances'.[105]

Support and opposition

A considerable amount of research has now been done into the reactions of the German people to the Nazi regime. This partly challenges the traditional view that the population was terrorized into compliance, that support was enforced and that opposition was rare. Recent interpretation has followed two trends. One has been to question the ability of the totalitarian state to impose such total domination. The other shows that the population was far more active in expressing its views than was once thought. The implications of this are, on the one hand, that the regime must have experienced a considerable degree of willing support to enable it to function properly, while, on the other, there were substantial numbers of people who showed varying forms of defiance. Modern studies have put the focus on the people as much as on the institutions, and have come up with some intriguing results.

Support

Support has a variety of meanings and shades. It can be active, showing direct commitment through personal conviction. Or it can be tacit – the absence of opposition through either indifference or fear. Both types existed in Nazi Germany.

Active support existed for several reasons, the most important being the personal popularity of Hitler himself. This was picked up by a number of external visitors, including the former British prime minister, Lloyd George, who wrote in the *Daily Express* in 1936: 'The old trust him, the young idolise him. It is not the admiration accorded to a popular leader. It is the worship of a national hero who has saved his country from utter despondency and degradation.' He went as far as to say: 'He is the George Washington of Germany – the man who won for his country independence from all her oppressors.' Lloyd George acknowledged that this description 'may appear extravagant'. Yet, 'all the same it is the bare truth'.[106] Hitler benefited from the widespread disillusionment with the institutions, leadership and politics of the Weimar period, offering to each sector of the population a vision for the future that replaced the divisions of a fractured class structure with the unifying force of the Volksgemeinschaft. Yet, while offering something new, he confirmed his legitimacy by projecting his regime in line with those of the past. Like the First Reich, the Third would last for a thousand years, fulfilling the interrupted destiny of the Kaiserreich, which Hitler acknowledged as the 'Second'. By doing this, he could claim to have rescued Germany from the distortions it had suffered under the Weimar Republic, a travesty that had come into existence after the defeat in the First World War. In this way he managed to feed into the former ruling class's myth of the 'stab in the back' and the weakening of Germany's military strength by Social Democrats, Communists and, above all, Jews. He therefore thrived on the situation he found because he seemed to offer hope – and national salvation.

Indeed, Hitler maintained that 'we are not a movement. We are a religion'.[107] He therefore demanded absolute and unconditional faith in his leadership, while the regime and its opportunities for power and publicity provided the basis for the same 'sacralization of politics' that was seen in Mussolini's Italy (see p. 130). Hitler showed a combination of dedication to his people while, at the same time, being kept apart from them – except when he appeared before them to dedicate to them his achievements on their behalf. Unlike Mussolini, Hitler based his life on self-denial, declining to portray himself as the epitome of the masculine virtues. Whether or not he lacked Mussolini's machismo, the people interpreted his role as being above normal human needs. The whole Hitler myth was amply reinforced by Goebbels, who employed all his talents for propaganda and display on the Führer's behalf. Goebbels admired Hitler's 'creativity' as that of a 'genuine artist, no matter in what field he may be working'.[108] In many ways Goebbels was the better speaker, with a more commanding and vibrant voice. But he lacked Hitler's presence and used his own abilities to develop the aura of the man he worshipped. The extent of Hitler's perceived 'divinity' was made apparent in German cinemas in the mid-1930s when the opening scene of Riefenstahl's documentary, *Triumph of the Will*, showed Hitler descending, godlike, from the clouds on his visit by aircraft to the Nuremberg rally.

The reality, of course, could not have been more different. Hitler the man projected an array of negative images. He had a harsh voice and, in the words of Waite, an 'unimpressive, even ludicrous figure', who looked like an 'apprentice waiter in a second-class Viennese cafe'.[109] His personality was also prone to childish tempers, humourlessness, inflexibility, and an obsession with his health that led to his total dependence on the quack ministrations of his personal doctor, Morel.

Yet he had a second appeal: strangely, he was seen during the 1930s as a moderate, able and willing to provide reassurance. In the early stages of his power he took care that his political changes were technically constitutional. He also emphasized that he was upholding traditional virtues and, until the outbreak of war, he professed to have religious beliefs. The public had confidence in his ability to control his more unsavoury subordinates. None of these ever approached the popularity achieved by Hitler. Goebbels was despised for his extreme views and mocked for his diminutive stature and a deformed foot; Himmler was seen as the epitome of ordinariness, Heydrich of ruthlessness, Goering of ostentation, Ley of boorishness and Bormann of remoteness. Some, like Streicher, were actively loathed, although Hitler himself secretly enjoyed the grotesque lies published about Jews in *Der Stürmer*. Yet all were part of a system that many Germans felt that Hitler could control, whether by the process of government he had instituted or by occasional culls like the Night of the Long Knives in 1934. Hitler was also careful to allow others to take the lead in anti-Semitic denunciations; examples include Röhm and the SA in the anti-Jewish boycotts in 1933, Goebbels's organization of Kristallnacht in 1938, and the moves by Himmler and Heydrich towards extermination programmes. From this it should not be interpreted (as it has been by a small minority of historians) that Hitler was not involved in the decisions for the Holocaust, but rather that much of the population mistakenly saw him as a force against extremism. In fact, the whole process was disguised by the concept of 'working towards the Führer'.

Until 1941, at least, Hitler's popularity was based on a third criterion, the measure of success. Public support reached regular peaks with the withdrawal from League of Nations Disarmament Conference (1933) and subsequent rearmament, the Remilitarization of the Rhineland (1936), the Anschluss, and the incorporation of the Sudetenland (1938) – all of which contrasted with the seemingly pacific policies of Stresemann and the cautious obstructiveness of Brüning. The public's misgivings about the outbreak of war were dispelled by the rapid conquests of Poland in 1939 and of Denmark, Norway, the Low Countries and France in 1940. Even those with a vested interest in undermining Hitler's position admitted the strength of his appeal. The Social Democratic Party in Exile (SOPADE) drew up a number of reports. One of these stated that 'Many people are convinced that Germany's foreign-policy demands are justified and cannot be passed over. The last few days have been marked by big fresh advances in the Führer's personal reputation'.[110]

Many Germans were not deceived by the Führer cult or by the projection of Hitler's image as a moderate. Yet there was no means of expressing disapproval without crossing the boundary into illegal dissent or even treason. Constitutional changes in 1933 had destroyed any possibility of voting for any other parties. In any case, the 'step-by-step' approach of the 'legal revolution' had made opposition appear not only illegal but also illogical: why should the system now be challenged when earlier stages within the same process had not been? Opposition needs above all to be justified; for this there needs to be at least a foundation of popular support. This was largely lacking: either for the positive reasons already given or for fear of punitive action from the Gestapo and other security organs. These did their job well in threatening the minority with dire consequences – and by enlisting the active support of the majority as informers. Unlike Stalinist Russia, Nazi Germany did not develop a system of terror that threatened the population at large. Rather, terror was directed at the minority – either for racial reasons or against active dissent. For most Germans, therefore, it made sense either to give the Führer their active support or tacitly to accept his rule for fear of the consequences of doing otherwise.

Looking at the levels of support from different sectors of the population has, in the past, produced a number of arguments that have been assessed in various ways: some have been maintained, others modified and a few fundamentally challenged. The attitudes of women have already been considered (see p. 184). We now turn to the various social classes and the armed forces.

It was once widely accepted that the upper and middle classes were enthusiastic supporters of the regime since they had brought Hitler to power in the first place. There is still much to confirm this. The business sector, for example, had supported Hitler from the outset, mainly out of fear of communism. During the Third Reich the great industrialists threw in their lot with Hitler because his policies delivered to them a disciplined workforce deprived of any means of collective bargaining. Although Marxist historians may have exaggerated the influence of 'monopoly capital' on Nazism (and, indeed, on fascism generally), there remains little doubt that the industrial barons and the Nazi regime co-operated closely with each other. The Four-Year Plan and mobilization for the war effort produced an even closer identity, while major industrial enterprises like Krupp and I.G. Farben were eventually implicated in the worst excesses of Nazi occupation.

The attitudes of the middle classes are, it has now been pointed out, more difficult to disentangle. Some had voted for Hitler well before 1933 and became key elements in the support for his regime. Other sections, however, found themselves in a more ambiguous position. The small landowners, or German peasantry, had always been seen by Hitler as the basis of any 'blood and soil' policy in the future construction of the Volksgemeinschaft. They had welcomed this elevation of their status by voting heavily for the Nazis in 1928, 1930 and 1933. In practice, however, their position became more marginalized after 1933. They benefited least from economic recovery and were adversely affected by the Reich Entailed Law. But any doubts they might have felt was never turned into direct opposition to the regime: the small farmers may have cooled in their perception of Nazi economic policy but they continued to support the leadership. Small businesses also had a mixed experience. Those which were efficient thrived and continued to worship the Führer. Those that were already struggling by the mid-1930s went under; they were, in effect, 'proletarianized' and had to settle for the limited benefits offered by the institutions aimed at the working class. As for the 'white-collar' sector, or the 'new middle class', this was attracted less to the 'blood and soil' ethos of Nazism than to the rapid growth of the bureaucratic state, which offered it opportunities for employment and advancement as officials. This also guaranteed support for the system into which they were drawn.

It was once argued that the working class were less favourable to Hitler before 1933 and that they remained more resistant to Nazi influence – at least until the parties they had traditionally supported, the SPD and the KPD, had been crushed by his regime. It is true that they had some cause for grievance: they benefited less from the economic recovery of Germany after 1933, their wages were held down while their working hours increased and their contributions to a rising GDP remained unacknowledged. Yet the vast majority settled down into tacit support for the regime, increasingly drawn into the activities and diversions offered by the KDF and SDA. It has now been pointed out that much of the working class considered itself better off under the Nazis. According to Mason, 'the Nazi economic "miracle"' convinced many workers that 'things were getting better, especially as, for most of them, the point of reference was not the best years of the Weimar Republic but the more recent depths of the Depression'.[111] In any case, individual opposition would have been rendered futile by the extensive use of modern production methods, including the whole assembly-line process. The whole process was accentuated by war, which meant that 'Firm integration into traditional socio-cultural milieux was shaken'.[112] This made possible a growing loyalty to the leadership from the very people who had once been suspicious of it: contemporary SOPADE reports pointed out that 'There is no mistaking the enormous personal gains in credibility and prestige that Hitler has made, mainly perhaps among workers'.[113] Indeed, during the campaigns in eastern Europe, many of the most enthusiastic soldiers were recruits from the working class.

This brings us to the attitude of the army to Hitler's regime. It has always been held that most of the army was systematically Nazified, partly through its oath of personal allegiance to Hitler and the adoption of the swastika insignia on uniforms. It was also acknowledged that the army was grateful to Hitler for his action against Röhm and the SA in the Night of the Long Knives. The Wehrmacht, as the army was renamed in 1938, was therefore fundamentally loyal to the Nazi regime. For many years, however, the prevailing view was that it was the SS, not the Wehrmacht, which committed the atrocities in the occupied territories in eastern Europe. More recent research has since shown that the army played an integral part in the shooting of civilians in Poland, Belorussia and the Ukraine, whether in direct co-operation with the Einsatzgruppen or through the use of its own police battalions. There was also a surprising degree of complicity among soldiers, even reservists. Bartov, for example, argues that even members of the working class, once supporters of the left, could be transformed into 'brutalized and fanaticized soldiers'.[114]

Overall, greater emphasis is now placed on the voluntary support shown for the regime by most of the population and on the extent of complicity at all levels. Three historians present a particularly disturbing picture. Mallman and Paul argue that the Gestapo relied on information volunteered by large numbers of people against each other – much of it unsolicited.[115] Goldhagen goes further by insisting that the slaughter of Jews in eastern Europe was carried out by willing recruits to the German army as well as by the more experienced SS.[116] It is, of course, possible to go too far in this direction and to underestimate the capacity of the SS and Gestapo to terrorize the population. It is also important not to underestimate the courage of those who opposed.

Opposition and resistance

Accompanying the growing emphasis on support for the Nazi regime has been the increased attention given by historians to opposition and resistance. This has been due to detailed research into Gestapo archives and the development of the argument that Nazi Germany was less effective as a totalitarian regime than was once thought.

Opposition existed in four main forms. Three of these expressed reservations about certain aspects of the regime but fell far short of demanding an overall change to it. The first consisted of minor dissent – nothing more serious than everyday grumbling and complaining; the second took the form of social 'deviance', mainly by youth groups that rebelled against authority; and the third comprised more carefully targeted opposition to specific policies, with the purpose of getting these changed. The fourth category was a more fundamental rejection of what the regime stood for. In part this was provoked by the removal of any distinction between legal opposition and illegal or treasonable activity; this meant that some groups challenged the regime as a whole rather than reacting to or aiming to change certain manifestations of its behaviour. Bearing this in mind, we can identify a political or ideological resistance and a military resistance which plotted to overthrow the regime and make peace with Germany's external enemies. There was, of course, some overlap between these four categories. Everyday grumbling might grow into social deviance among some groups or more targeted opposition in others. Under the impact of war, the distinction between the categories was further compacted as political resistance overlapped with military plotting as part of a broader resistance that came even to include elements of social deviance.

Minor dissent and grumbling were far more common than other forms of opposition. According to Kershaw, 'The extent of disillusionment and discontent in almost all sections of the population, rooted in socio-economic experience of daily life, is remarkable'.[117] Most grumbling was sparked by problems of everyday life rather than beliefs or political tenets. These were the result of subordinating the consumer market to the Four-Year Plan's emphasis on rearmament and heavy industry, with the consequent increase in working hours, controls over wage levels and compulsory membership of the KdF. But, widespread as the grumbling was, it was subject to two main constraints. One was the amount of information gathered by the Gestapo from voluntary denunciations on all matters, some very trivial. Another was the personal popularity of Hitler, for reasons already discussed. The targets of most resentment were either faceless Nazi bureaucracy or individual henchmen, the butt of numerous popular jokes. In any case, there was no clear vision as to what could replace the Nazi regime which, for all its inconveniences, most Germans still preferred to the Weimar Republic. According to one SOPADE report, 'This is especially so among the Mittelstand and the peasantry. These social strata are least of all ready to fight seriously against the regime because they knew least of all what they should fight for.'[118]

Social deviance was apparent mainly amongst a minority of boys and girls between the ages of fourteen and eighteen who had become disillusioned with the Hitler Youth. The main drive was rebellion against authority, especially Nazi authority. There were also cultural influences from Britain and the United States, which gradually inculcated an acceptance of western values. This was especially apparent during the war, which increased the alienation of rebel youth through tightened controls by further expectations of labour and military service and more extreme discipline within the Hitler Youth.

Youth dissidents were of two broad types – gangs, which were predominantly working class, and the Swing movement, which was drawn from the more affluent middle class. The largest of the gangs was the Edelweiss Pirates (*Edelweisspiraten*) which sprang up from 1938, mainly in the Rhineland. Subdivisions included the Kittelbach Pirates from Düsseldorf, the Roving Dudes of Essen and the Navajos from Cologne. Most were escapees from the Hitler Youth, which they now targeted as their prime enemies. Shouting their slogan ('Eternal war on the Hitler Youth') they ambushed and beat up members of that organization. During the war they also defied official restrictions on movement by going on long hikes, during which they showed a more relaxed sexuality than the authorities liked. They also gathered up Allied propaganda leaflets dropped from the air and distributed them through letterboxes, provided sanctuary for deserters from the Wehrmacht and assisted the escape of British and American pilots who had been shot down over the Ruhr. Their most drastic action was the assassination of the head of the Gestapo in Cologne in the autumn of 1944.[119] The Swing movement was more widely spread across the cities of Germany, from Hamburg to Berlin and from Stettin to Dresden. They were strongly influenced by American jazz, which was particularly provocative to a regime that regarded jazz as 'negro' music and therefore as 'degenerate'. Among the more affluent members of Swing youth were the 'English casuals' who dressed in the height of English fashion and spoke English where possible. Needless to say, this did not go down well in wartime Germany.

The Nazi regime was frustrated and embarrassed by both types of youth movement. According to an official SA report in 1941, 'The HJ are taking their lives into their hands when they go out on the streets',[120] while in 1942 the Reich Youth Leadership maintained that the development of dissident groups was increasing during the war 'to such a degree that one must speak of a serious risk of the political, moral and criminal subversion of youth'.[121] The authorities tried a variety of measures to contain the situation.[122] Sometimes they ignored some of their less extreme activities as childish pranks. More commonly the Gestapo, with the help of the Hitler Youth, rounded up offenders, shaved and branded their heads, and sent them to youth concentration camps or reform schools. Occasionally the Gestapo went the whole way – staging public hangings of members of the Edelweiss Pirates, as in Cologne in November 1944. But part of the difficulty confronting the authorities was tracking down the leadership. The gangs were not political movements or conspiratorial organizations with clearly defined structures; they were normally seen as less of a threat than resistance groups and therefore given less attention by already hard-pressed officials.

A third form of opposition was expressed over specific issues by individuals, groups or institutions. The main example of this was the reaction of the churches, which criticized the regime on three occasions before 1942. In 1933 Pastor Niemöller objected to the Nazi reorganization of the Protestant churches, while in 1937, there were Catholic protests about their schools being required to display portraits of Hitler in the place of crucifixes. Clergy from both denominations later attacked the euthanasia programme; the Bishop of Limburg wrote in August 1941 that 'All God-fearing people feel that this extermination of the helpless is an almighty crime'.[123]

These developments were to show that opposition from the Catholics was more likely to succeed than from the Protestants. The latter were more fundamentally divided and had nothing of the international status held by the Catholic Church. In addition, the Protestants were trying to resist a fundamental bureaucratic change, whereas the Catholics took on the government over an initial matter of detail, resulting in compromise whereby Hitler's portrait and a crucifix could both be displayed. The outcome of the protests against euthanasia was somewhat different: although religious objections did bring about changes, these were mainly based on increased secrecy to remove the policy altogether from public attention. In some cases, Catholic protests failed outright: these were usually on more general matters of principle. For example, the regime made no concessions over the 1937 Papal Encyclical *Mit brennender Sorge*: 'With burning anxiety and mounting unease we have observed for some time the way of suffering of the Church'.[124] Cardinal Galen's 1941 protest against police powers used in Nazi Germany also fell on deaf ears: 'Justice is the state's foundation. We lament, we regard with great concern, the evidence of how this foundation is being shaken today', especially since 'The regular courts have no say over the jurisdiction by decree of the Secret Police'.[125] The same applied to the Protestant Bishop Würm's complaint to the Chancellery in December 1943: 'I must state that we Christians feel that this policy of destroying the Jews to be a grave wrong.'[126]

All denominations had reservations which prevented the mobilization of a more general Christian opposition to the regime. They feared the threats to Germany from the east, especially, in Galen's words, 'the assaults of godless Bolshevism'.[127] On the other hand, the regime never succeeded in its attempts during wartime to undermine Christianity. The latter began to contribute to areas of resistance but remained most effective as a residue of the public conscience. A prime example of this was Dietrich Bonhoeffer who, according to Hamerow, 'remained convinced that the struggle against the Third Reich's religious policies could not be separated from the struggle against its political, military or racial policies'.[128]

The last category can be described as political opposition and conspiratorial military resistance. These often merged and challenged the whole basis of the regime rather than seeking redress on a specific issue. The two largest parties in opposition to the Nazis were the Social Democrats (SPD) and the Communists (KPD). The 1933 ban on all parties other than the NSDAP meant that any political opposition in the future would automatically constitute treasonable resistance. The KPD had more organizational cells within Germany and were more openly revolutionary. Broszat emphasizes the considerable differences between the two. The Communists tended to be younger and 'socially disenfranchised', whereas the Social Democrats were generally well established skilled workers who 'who enjoyed the respect of their non-Socialist neighbours'.[129] Tactically, 'the Communists tended to support a more radical political creed and the Social Democrats a more pragmatic one'.[130] They also looked to different areas for external support. The Social Democrats abroad, known as SOPADE, were based initially in Prague, then in Paris under the leadership of Ernst Schumacher, whereas the KPD had direct connections with Moscow. The Social Democrats concentrated on acquiring accurate information about the state of public opinion about the regime, in the form of SOPADE reports, although these were usually discouraging and did not lead directly to attempts to dislodge the regime. The Communists were more ambitious in this respect but were impeded by the tortuous foreign policy of Stalin: during the late 1930s they were constrained by Stalin's increasingly pro-German feelers, culminating in the Nazi–Soviet Pact in August 1939. It was not until 1941, when Hitler invaded the Soviet Union, that the Communists began to make a comeback, largely under the tutelage of Stalin, who switched his entire emphasis to direct support for the KPD. At the same time, the Soviet Union had a profound mistrust of the Social Democrats as 'lackeys of capitalism'. Smaller groups, meanwhile, also pursued a political agenda. Student organizations like White Rose (*Weisse Rose*), led by Hans and Sophie Scholl, distributed leaflets at Munich University criticizing Hitler's leadership, especially after the failures at Stalingrad in 1943. Some of those involved were executed for treason, even though no violence was involved.

Some elements of opposition in the army had existed before the outbreak of war in 1939. General Beck had secretly tried to get Hitler removed from power in 1938 and at the same time urged the British government to stand firm in resisting Hitler's claims over the Sudetenland. He was joined during the war by a number of other officers who became convinced that Hitler had to be overthrown. Usually conservative, often Prussian and sometimes members of the former aristocracy, they included von Tresckow, Schlabrendorff and von Quirnheim. The most spectacular act of defiance was Stauffenberg's plot to blow up Hitler at the Wolf's Lair in July 1944. This and other conspiracies widened to include political elements as well; many of the civilians involved were conservatives who had opposed the Weimar Republic and wanted to avoid any possibility of a return to this. Nevertheless, like the military resistance, they were convinced that Hitler had to be removed and the Allies persuaded to agree to an armistice. Among the most influential were von Koltke, von Wartenburg, former Mayor of Leipzig Goerdeler, and the former German ambassador to Rome, von Hassell.

Political and military resistance faced enormous problems. The greatest was the loyalty to Hitler embedded in the German people and reinforced by institutional oaths of allegiance in the army and government departments that severely restricted recruitment to resistance groups. It is significant that military plots were aimed specifically at Hitler. This was partly because, despite the latter's monstrous aberrations after 1941, his distorted racial policies and colossal military mistakes, there still existed an almost unadulterated trust in his ability to deliver eventual German victory. Or perhaps this amounted to an absolute certainty that it would be impossible to persuade others that his personal judgement was wrong. He therefore had to be removed from the scene if there was to be any chance of achieving peace and of saving Germany from total destruction. Beyond that, however, there were different plans for the future between the various political components of the resistance. For example, younger conservatives like Count von Moltke and Count von Wartenburg, who dominated the Kreisau Circle, aimed at establishing a new Germany based on direct elections at lower, or *Kreis*, levels, followed by indirect elections for the Länder and Reichstag. Germany might then be integrated into a federal Europe. Others, like Goerdeler and von Hassell, preferred a more authoritarian system with the power to govern by decree, reversible only by a two-thirds majority in the Reichstag. In any case, the Allies proved highly unwilling to negotiate. All the Allied leaders had come to regard Hitler as greater liability to Germany than to their own advance in 1944 and 1945. Hence they continued to insist on unconditional surrender, a demand which cut ground from under German resistance. It is a measure of the latter's courage that the less likely a negotiated peace seemed, the more important it became to show that had been at least some active defiance.

One type of reaction to Nazi rule is especially difficult to categorize: from the victims of Nazi persecution, or the outcasts from the *Volksgemeinschaft* (see pp. 223–4). In many cases, any form of opposition or resistance was impossible, given the helplessness of the victims. Those who had any capacity to react would generally try to avoid drawing attention to themselves. But some did try to follow one or more of the strategies already covered. Everyday dissent and grumbling would hardly have been a sensible option but membership of dissident youth groups might well offer some protection. Attempts were also made by bodies like the National Representative Organization of Jews in Germany (*Reichsvertretung der Juden in Deutschland*) to try to defend the status and interests of Jews as recognized during the Weimar Republic. When these proved ineffectual, attention switched to flight abroad which, contrary to earlier beliefs, was a course that most German Jews wanted to take.[131]

Joining resistance movements was more difficult for Jews in Germany than in German-occupied Europe, for two main reasons. Areas like Poland, Latvia, Lithuania and Belarus had larger concentrations of Jews. Although these were often subjected to the hatred of other indigenous groups, they were also able to contribute to partisan movements against German occupation. This, of course, was impossible in Germany, which lacked any popular uprising, even if there was a growing acceptance of the need for military-based resistance. Nevertheless, individual German Jews did contribute to political resistance movements like the Communists and Social Democrats or fought for the International Brigades in the Spanish Civil War.

The overall deduction to be drawn from these different strands is a complex one. In theory, the Nazi state was totalitarian in that it eradicated institutions allowing the formal expression of dissent and opposition and then proceeded to use the SS and Gestapo to pick off individual manifestations of anti-Nazi behaviour. By and large, this combined process was successful: there was, after all, never any real threat to the regime except for the occasional act of violence. And yet the fact that opposition did develop in such a variety of forms indicates that totalitarianism was only partly successful. The regime frequently had to make concessions on specific issues; it faced a general increase in deviant behaviour and, during the war, it provoked the coalescence of normally incompatible groups. It is possible to go further. Peukert argues that the *Volksgemeinschaft* had not been achieved by 1939 and that the internal harmony of the system needed increasingly to be maintained by diverting public opinion against minority groups whether inside or outside Germany. 'Terror accordingly bit ever deeper' from the 'margins of society into its heart'.[132]

The Nazi economy

Hitler's main ideas

According to Bracher, 'At no time did National Socialism develop a consistent economic or social theory'.[133] It is true that Hitler was in no sense an economist. Unlike Marxism, the ideology of Nazism had no underlying economic component: there was no equivalent to the notion of political change occurring through the dialectical conflict between classes exerting their economic interest. Nazism was fundamentally racist and *völkisch* in its conception and economic factors were always subordinate to this. It would therefore be inappropriate to seek in it any autonomous economic strategy. Yet Hitler's policies towards the economy were influenced by four main priorities. First, he aimed to create an autarkic system that would enable Germany to establish and sustain a broader hegemony within Europe. He intended, second, to target the lands to the east. Third, since this would inevitably involve expansion and conflict, the economic infrastructure would have to sustain a large increase in military expenditure. But, fourth, this would have to be done without severely depressing living standards and thereby risking the loss of support from the German people.

How did these components fit together? The 1920s saw the emergence of Hitler's ambitions for Lebensraum which underlay all his ideas about the ultimate purpose of economic change. Instead of following a predominantly internal socialist policy, as championed by Gregor Strasser, he committed himself to expansionist nationalism, based on the twin pillars of Lebensraum and autarky. These were emphasized in the second volume of *Mein Kampf*, published in 1925, and in his *Zweites Buch* (*Second Book*), written in 1928. In the former he argued that Germany should abandon her former pursuit of economic power through colonies, instead 'turning our eyes towards the east'. This meant 'finally putting a stop to the colonial and trade policy of the pre-war period and passing over to the territorial policy of the future'.[134] New German communities would eventually be settled on land carved out of Poland and Russia, and Germany would also have self-sufficiency in raw materials and food, together with guaranteed outlets for her manufactured goods. Such goals would involve conflict but this was another key ingredient of Hitler's thinking. He said in 1923 that 'All of nature is one great struggle between strength and weakness, an eternal victory of the strong over the weak'.[135]

These ideas have sometimes been dismissed as the vague fantasies of an immature fringe politician. This is a mistake, on two counts. First, there were many on the conservative right who took them seriously in the late 1920s and early 1930s because Lebensraum fitted closely into the pan-German concepts already apparent before 1914 in Imperial Germany. Hitler therefore found ready converts among the so-called respectable sectors of big business, the armaments industry and the military High Command. Many non-Nazis recognized the flow of the argument and were willing to take it seriously. Second, the eventual shaping of German hegemony in Europe bears a close resemblance to the original prototype, even if it was to be implemented by the SS rather than Hitler's state channels. *Mein Kampf* need not be considered the 'blueprint' for Hitler's future projects, as suggested by Trevor-Roper, but it is surely more than the 'daydreaming' attributed to it by A.J.P. Taylor.

The development of Hitler's economic policy, 1933–45: an outline

There appear to have been four main phases in the emergence of an economic policy, although these did not follow on logically from each other.

The first, lasting from 1933 until 1936, has been called a period of 'partial fascism'. The state moved into a programme of job creation to reduce the levels of unemployment while, at the same time, seeking to control wages and eliminate trade union powers. In these respects there is some similarity to Mussolini's corporativism. But in other respects the government's economic policy was highly pragmatic, especially while it was under the direction of Schacht (President of the Reichsbank from March 1933 and Economics Minister from June 1934). He gave priority to developing a favourable trade balance by means of a series of bilateral trade agreements with the Balkans and South American states. These underdeveloped areas provided Germany with essential raw materials in return for German investment and credits for German industrial products. The complexities of foreign exchange were dealt with by the New Plan (September 1934), which regulated imports and the allocation of foreign exchange to key sectors of the German economy. Overall, Schacht was convinced that it was essential to raise the level of exports if Hitler's objective of increased military expenditure were to be realized.

By 1936 Hitler had begun to show impatience with Schacht's somewhat cautious approach and opted openly for 'military and political rearmament', to be promoted by 'economic rearmament and mobilization'. The second economic phase therefore opened with the introduction of the 'Four-Year Plan'. The basic purpose of the Four-Year Plan was to achieve self-sufficiency or autarky, in both industry and agriculture, through increased productivity and the development of substitutes for oil and other key items. This became even more important when, in 1937, Hitler made clear his decision to prepare for war at the meeting with his chiefs of staff recorded in the Hossbach Memorandum. Goering was placed in control of the Four-Year Plan Office; this completely undermined Schacht's position so that the latter felt compelled to resign his post in November 1937. The Plan resulted in a steady increase in military expenditure, from 1.9 billion marks in 1936 to 5.8 billion in 1937, 18.4 billion in 1938 and 32.3 billion in 1939. There were, however, deficiencies. Although some progress was made in the manufacture of substitutes, targets were not met for the production of rubber and synthetic fuels; synthetic petrol, for example, met only 18 per cent of Germany's needs and it was still necessary to import one-third of all the raw materials needed by industry.

Ready or not, the Nazi economy entered its third phase in 1939. The outbreak of war saw the implementation of a military strategy known as Blitzkrieg, or 'lightning war'. The intention was to secure victory as rapidly as possible through preliminary aerial attacks, followed by the advance of panzer divisions of tanks and armoured vehicles. Blitzkrieg was, however, also an economic strategy. It was the means whereby Germany could achieve military victory over its neighbours without mobilizing its economic resources to the full. This lasted until the end of 1941 and saw the collapse and absorption of the economies of Poland, Denmark, Norway, the Low Countries and France. The invasion of the Soviet Union, however, brought the fourth phase – Total War. The German economy was now pushed to its limit. War production came under the control of Albert Speer and the Central Planning Board. The result was a more rapid increase in armaments, despite the heavy Allied bombing of German cities between 1943 and 1944. Yet, even at this point, Germany was massively outproduced by the two industrial giants – the Soviet Union and the United States. This was a major factor in the eventual destruction of the Third Reich.

Comments on Hitler's economic policy 1933–9

Traditional views on Nazi pre-war economic policies showed the following interlinked arguments. Almost as soon as he came to power Hitler took steps to reverse the later economic strategies of the Weimar Republic. This, in turn, was made possible by the creation of a new totalitarian regime that could simplify the process of implementing the new measures better suited to Germany's future role of dominance in Europe. By 1939, the Nazi economy had broadly achieved its key objectives of increasing Germany's national income, expanding the military base and reducing unemployment. At the same time, the majority of the population were probably better off than they had been in 1933.

Although there may well be elements of truth in these statements, they have recently been challenged and reinterpreted. In the first place, how new were Hitler's initial economic measures? During the 1950s it was widely argued that the Nazi regime imposed something new on Germany which contrasted with the dependence of the Weimar Republic on western capitalism and loans from the United States. The purpose of Schacht's New Plan was to create an alternative to the consumer-based capitalism that had been severely undermined by the Great Depression, focusing instead on central planning as a means of increasing industrial output and reducing unemployment. But this idea that there was a clean break in 1933 has now been questioned. Tough measures had already been implemented during the Weimar Republic, especially by Chancellor Brüning between 1930 and 1932.[136] Schacht's New Plan maintained Brüning's currency reform, trade restrictions, self-sufficiency and cuts on government welfare expenditure. It has even been argued that Schacht gained the credit for the successes achieved as a direct result of the policies of Brüning and his successors, Chancellors Papen and Schleicher. By 1933 the German economy had reached its lowest point and its imminent upturn coincided with Hitler's rise to power. Hence, Frei maintains, 'the Nazis benefited from being able to fall back on the investment plans of preceding governments' and were able to 'make a change in economic trends which had become apparent since 1932'.[137] Of course, the Schacht period was followed by a new departure which did break the economic links with the Weimar Republic. The limited emphasis of the New Plan was followed by the more ambitious objectives of the Four-Year Plan, which were that German armed forces were to be 'operational within four years' and the economy 'must be fit for war within four years'.[138] Yet this could not have been accomplished without the preliminary preparations based on the policies of those who could not have known where these would lead.

As to the substitution of a simpler and more direct 'totalitarian'-style economic management, the effectiveness of this had also been questioned – for very much the same reasons that Nazi administration is now regarded as an overlapping and confusing 'polycracy'. The basis of the criticism is that the multi-layering of agencies and the lack of proper delineation between them generated conflict and hampered efficiency. There was, for example, extensive rivalry between the Four-Year Plan Office, the Ministry of Economics, the War Ministry and the Plenipotentiary for Economics. It is true that a later wave of interpretation has questioned the extent of 'polycracy-based' criticisms of Nazi economic management; both Tooze and Overy, for example, for example, refer to these as an 'exaggeration'.[139] Even so, the point remains that Hitler used the foundations provided by the later leaders of the Weimar Republic to establish short-term economic security while, at the same time, developing an alternative structure to transform long-term economic priorities. There was, in other words, a greater break between Goering and Schacht than there had been between Schacht and Brüning.

How successful had the New Plan and the Four-Year Plan been by 1939? Before the outbreak of the Second World War it was widely argued that Hitler had performed something of an economic miracle. For example, the Cambridge economist Guillebaud maintained that Hitler's achievement of 'full employment', with many of the most important industries 'working to capacity' and the 'stabilization of wages and prices' was 'unique in economic history down to the present time'.[140] Even after the war, some historians held to the theme that Hitler had stimulated economic recovery from a previously low base. Jarman wrote in the 1950s that 'as each year passed the German factories grew busier' and that 'a mighty nation was at work'.[141] Since the 1980s judgements have been more critical. Buccheim, for example, argued in 2001 that the growth achieved up to 1938/9 'deformed the structure of the German economy' and 'carried in itself the seed of eventual decline'. Far from representing a healthy recovery, Nazi economic policy 'appears to have been directed against the development of a normal growth pattern'.[142] Others have been less negative about the state of the German economy after four years of Nazi management. According to Overy, the economy was 'certainly not facing a conventional economic crisis in 1938–9',[143] while Klein maintained that Hitler deliberately limited expenditure on rearmament to about 15 per cent of the GDP.[144]

What light do statistics throw on these arguments? Some seem to support the more positive interpretations of Nazi economic policy. Unemployment, for example, fell from 5.6 million in 1932 to 4.8 million in 1933, 2.7 million in 1934, 2.2 million in 1935, 1.6 million in 1936, 0.9 million in 1937 and 0.4 million in 1938. The figure for 1939 was as low as 119,000, leading Guillebaud to comment on Germany's 'extreme shortage of labour'.[145] This was more rapid than the reduction of unemployment in other major economies like the United States, France and Britain (which still had 1.8 million on the dole in 1938). During the same period wages gradually increased from a low in 1933 of 70 per cent of their 1928 to 75 per cent by 1934, 80 per cent by 1936 and 85 per cent by 1938. The national income, meanwhile, rose from forty-four billion marks in 1933 to eighty billion in 1938; this was particularly impressive since the 1938 figure was greater than the seventy-two billion of 1928, the peak year of the Weimar economy. There are, however, more negative perspectives. Buccheim's argument above rightly emphasizes the distorted nature of Germany's economic growth during the 1930s. Unemployment was reduced by a strong element of coercion and by the construction of major public works such as the autobahn; heavy industry was developed at the expense of light and consumer industries; and imports were heavily curtailed, except for raw materials from the Balkans to feed the developing war machine, thus creating a serious trade imbalance. The ways in which these themes affected the consumer population are dealt with separately in this book. In any case, the figures were clouded by the Reich's territorial expansion between 1938 and March 1939 to add the new and prosperous areas of Austria, the Sudetenland and Bohemia.

We can, therefore, draw the following conclusions for economic performance between 1933 and 1939. First, unemployment had virtually disappeared – but with a strong element of compulsion. Second, national income had increased – but had created serious distortions in the relationship between heavy and consumer industries to the detriment of the latter. And third, Germany's imports had been restricted in proportion to its exports – but at the expense of healthy and diversified trading relations with other countries. Such imbalances would have been difficult for a democratic state to impose on its population. Nazi Germany, however, possessed the political means to refashion its economic infrastructure and to create its own balance for the specific purpose of preparing for war. But what was the most effective way for totalitarian Germany to accomplish this?

Comments on Hitler's economic policy 1939–45

The Nazi economy between 1939 and 1945 was dominated by the two strategies of Blitzkrieg and Total War. Both are perceived to have had roots in the pre-war period but the relationship between them has been interpreted in two fundamentally different ways.

One argument places the emphasis on a largely pragmatic approach by the Nazi regime. In 1936 Hitler had reasoned that the relative success of Schacht's New Plan enabled him to move towards a more deliberate phase or rearmament in the Four-Year Plan and a decision, shown in the 1937 Hossbach Memorandum, to prepare for war. Yet, some historians have argued that Hitler acted under constraints and could not consider total mobilization and Total War. Klein, for example, maintains that he still depended on the support of the German consumer and therefore had to settle for a compromise economy which would proceed with a measured degree of rearmament but also allow a moderate level of consumer growth.[146] According to Sauer, this balance meant the creation of a 'plunder economy' since the only way Germany could expand through limited mobilization was by steadily increasing the economic base through a series of rapid and specifically targeted conquests. Hence Hitler 'committed himself to starting a war in the near future'.[147] The solution was Blitzkrieg, by which Hitler rapidly conquered Poland in 1939, much of western Europe in 1940 and further areas in eastern Europe and the Soviet Union in 1941. In each case the emphasis had been on maximum economic gain from less than total military expenditure. Unfortunately, the argument continues, this balance was upset by the switch to Total War in 1943. This was far from a logical step since it undermined the previous delicate balance between consumer and military needs. The basic reason for the change was the failure to defeat the Soviet Union, the survival of Great Britain and the entry of the United States into the war. From engaging in a series of rapid military and economic gains Germany was now in a struggle for survival against the vastly superior economic power base of the Allies.

The alternative argument is the opposite of this. Total War was not the result of the failure of the favoured policy of Blitzkrieg; rather, Blitzkrieg was the premature and incomplete anticipation of the real intention – Total War. From the start Hitler had the more ambitious aim of equipping Germany with an economic base capable of achieving Lebensraum and, according to Berghahn, 'a German-dominated empire conquered by force'.[148] This approach acknowledges the importance of Schacht's preparations before 1936 in providing trading networks with the Balkans as a first step to German hegemony there, in the construction of autobahns, and in the controls on wages to develop a disciplined workforce. Such measures were to be the first step in the long-term preparation for Total War. But 1935 and 1936 brought an economic crisis in the form of a food shortage that affected the whole of the German workforce. Hitler therefore took what he considered the only way out: to impose further constraints on the workforce while, at the same time, accelerating rearmament to achieve Lebensraum and long-term economic salvation. According to the Hossbach Memorandum, the Four-Year Plan was therefore a commitment to Total War by the years 1943–5. Unfortunately for Hitler, the outbreak of war with Britain and France was premature, which meant that the economy could at this stage support only Blitzkrieg strategies. Blitzkrieg was therefore an emergency response – or, in the words of Overy, 'total war by default'.[149] The German economy had not been sufficiently enlarged to engage in Total War until after 1941, by which time the powers and resources against Germany were overwhelming. Overy maintains that Germany would have been 'much better prepared' for a war fought at the time originally anticipated, since it would 'have had rockets, inter-continental bombers, perhaps even atomic weapons'.[150]

As with most other general controversies about Hitler, it is very difficult to reconcile differences over long-term aims and policies. But this can be partially altered by changing the perspective – or the question – by refocusing the arguments on intention to the question of how Nazi economic policies contributed to Germany's eventually defeat. Both interpretations provide an explanation for the disruption of Germany's war effort. The first points to the inability of Germany to adapt as successfully as its enemies to Total War, after making the most of its limited resources by the use of Blitzkrieg. In moving to Total War after 1941, Hitler was taking on a commitment that was simply too large for Germany's economy to sustain. The emphasis of the second interpretation is that Germany was fighting Total War before she was ready to do so. Germany lost because she did not have the time she needed to complete long-term preparations for conflict against the United States as well as against Britain and the Soviet Union. By the first approach, Hitler was attempting the impossible, against all the logical constraints that had brought his earlier success; by the second, Hitler had overreached Germany's capacity before his preparations were complete.

Why Germany was initially victorious and eventually defeated is therefore easier to explain than why Hitler took the decisions that placed Germany in the way of victory and defeat. Initial victory was due largely to the successful military use of a rearmed but limited economic base, while eventual defeat resulted from military decisions that distorted the economic base. In the early years Hitler moved rapidly against limited targets in Eastern and Western Europe and, although he failed to knock Britain out of the war, the United States and the Soviet Union were still uninvolved by early 1941. Latterly, he stretched Germany's resources in a three-front war: in Eastern Europe, Western and Southern Europe, and North Africa and the Atlantic. By 1942 he was unable to match the combined resources and efficiency of his three opponents: Russia, the United States and Britain. It is always tempting to use 'what if?' approaches when considering Hitler's policies, strategies and mistakes. But such counterfactual arguments are always inadequate when dealing with actual outcomes. The German economy was overwhelmed by the task it confronted in the military situation of 1943–5 and a variety of explanations should be considered, even if these are apparently contradictory.

The social impact of economic policies 1933–45

1933–9

Although the general economic trend in the pre-war years would appear at first sight to have had positive implications for the German people, there were in fact several negative side-effects. The fall in unemployment from 5.6 million in 1932 to 119,000 in 1939, for example, was accelerated by rearmament and the increased use of conscripted and forced labour, both of which meant the creation of a workforce which had come increasingly under direct state control. Although, as we have seen, wages increased from 70 per cent of their 1928 level in 1933 to 85 per cent by 1939, there had been a far greater increase in the cost of living over the same period – 71 per cent of the 1928 level in 1933 to 90 per cent in 1939. Two deductions can be made from this. Not only was the workforce earning less in 1939 than it had been in 1928; but those in employment had been marginally better off in 1933 than they were in 1939. It is also significant that these wages were earned during a working week that had been extended over the period 1933–9 by over seven hours.

Much was made by the government of the increased attention being given to the increase in consumer goods during the period of national economic recovery. It is true that in Germany the level of production rose by 69 per cent and that Germans became the world's largest per-capita owners of radio sets; progress was also made in developing the comparatively cheap Volkswagen. But the overall production of consumer items was low by comparison with that of industrial goods, which increased during the same period by 389 per cent. In other words, in return for their lower wages in real terms, workers were producing far more in terms of heavy industrial goods and armaments than they were consumables. Nor could this growing difference be offset by imports, since the general flow of trade was dictated by the search for industrial autarky, not for consumer affluence. Goering affirmed that guns would make the German people 'strong', while luxuries would only make them 'fat'. As for those consumables emphasized by the regime, radio sets were of vital importance in the spread of propaganda, while the Volkswagen was used as a long-term incentive for hard work and regular saving; in the end, however, very few cars were actually delivered and there was no equivalent in Germany to the huge increase in vehicle ownership in the United States, Britain and France.

Different sectors of the German population were affected in different ways by the performance of the economy between 1933 and 1939. The largest single group – the industrial workers – certainly benefited from the decrease in unemployment from 6 million in 1932 to 0.4 million in 1938. It has, however, been shown that the trend was already downwards before Hitler came to power in January 1933. In addition, the collective influence of working-class organizations was steadily eroded, the trade union movement coming under a general ban from May 1933. The gap was filled by a pro-Nazi German Labour Front (DAF) under Robert Ley. Two other organizations were established: Schönheit der Arbeit (Beauty of Labour) and Kraft durch Freude (Strength through Joy), which had the overall effect of regulating leisure as well as working hours and increasing the possibilities for exploitation by employers.

Germany's rural population comprised three sections, all pro-Nazi at the outset of the regime. The peasants, or small landowners, were upheld by Nazi ideology as the backbone of the German race, but there was a tendency to paint an idealized and highly unrealistic picture. The result was a series of damaging attempts by the government to freeze the peasantry into an unchanging class. The Reich Entailed Farm Law of 1933 severely limited the subdivision and sale of peasant plots, which inevitably prevented consolidation, mechanization and more effective use of fertilizers. The second group, agricultural workers, made very few substantial gains. Many continued to experience grinding poverty and migrated in desperation to the towns at a rate of 2.5 per cent per annum (compared with 1.5 per cent per annum before 1933). The third category, the wealthy landlords, were the only real beneficiaries of Nazi rule. The rapid increase in land values enabled them to retain their economic prominence, which partially offset the loss of some of their political influence.

The business sector consisted of two main groups. The small businessperson, usually from the middle class, was attracted at an early stage by Nazi promises to protect the 'small man' from the burden of monopolies. This group did benefit initially, mainly from much tighter control over the labour force. On the whole, however, the NSDAP preferred to cultivate the support of big business, which increased its ownership of industry from 40 per cent of the total in 1933 to 70 per cent by 1937; this was accomplished mostly through the absorption of smaller enterprises. It is true that the state exercised greater influence and control during the period of the Four-Year Plan. The new Hermann Goering Works, for example, became a major state-owned steel producer. But some of the great names in private enterprise rapidly increased their profits by up to 150 per cent between 1938 and 1942. Great industrialists also collaborated closely with the government over the war effort and worse: several, for example, supplied Auschwitz with equipment for the gas chambers. This co-operation between the government and big business has led some historians to see the Nazi regime as a bastion of capitalism. It would, however, be more appropriate to argue that Hitler decided at the outset to avoid confrontation with capitalism, even if, in the process, it meant subverting a number of earlier economic principles.

1939–45

In the early phases of the war, attempts were made to ameliorate the impact on the civilian population. Measures were taken that seem to provide strong evidence for Blitzkrieg being an economic as well as a military strategy; what has been called 'a peacetime economy at war' meant that there were several initial compromises to maintain civilian morale. There was, for example, no immediate and substantial increase in armaments production, since the peacetime levels of the Four-Year Plan were sufficient for the military Blitzkrieg against Poland and western Europe, and even the opening attack on the Soviet Union. The plunder of conquered territories removed the necessity of finding additional revenues from the

German population, who were spared sudden increases in taxation. It has been estimated that Reich drew from its occupied neighbours the equivalent of 1,000 per cent of its own 1938 revenues; much of the population also benefited materially from the expropriation of Jewish assets and property.[151] During the first three years of the war, Germans were also spared increases in compulsory contributions to labour and levels could be maintained as in peacetime because of the influx of foreign labour from Poland, the Low Countries and France. Overall, it seemed that the Nazi regime was doing what it could to remove any economic grounds for social discontent.

Latterly, however, the whole experience of German civilians changed dramatically. At the Berlin Sportpalast in February 1943 Goebbels demanded, and received, support for a war 'more total and more radical than we can even imagine it today'.[152] The economy was managed more tightly by Todt and Speer in order to meet the challenge of a reviving Soviet Union in the east and new Anglo-American offensives in the west. The full horrors of war brought considerable suffering to a population that had been partially protected from, if not entirely inured to, hardship during the earlier phase of Blitzkrieg. By 1945 civilian deaths had reached a total of 3.6 million (compared to 3.25 million military casualties) and almost all of Germany's cities had been shattered by Allied bombing, the worst affected being Hamburg, Dresden and Berlin. Hunger, even starvation, was widespread and there was a massive displacement of peoples from occupied areas in the east as a result of the redrawing of boundaries. The population was particularly harshly treated by invaders from the east, women being raped in their hundreds of thousands. One legacy of all this has been the controversy over the argument for German 'victimhood'.[153] On the one hand, such a notion has been weakened by the widespread initial support for Hitler, the benefits that accrued from his early military successes and the atrocities committed against the peoples of eastern Europe. On the other, there is acknowledgement of the catastrophe of 1945, the Führer's abandonment of the German people to their fate, and a post-war vacuum that makes it difficult to commemorate many of the German dead with anything resembling pride in their sacrifice. Where the controversy becomes most direct and confrontational is over any attempt to compare the German victimhood in total defeat with the Jewish victimhood in the Holocaust. This is, however, a minority approach, taken largely by the post-war far right.

Rejected by the Volksgemeinschaft

The Nazi purpose for the *Volksgemeinschaft* was to reconcile what Peukert calls 'a society of fractured traditions, social classes and environments'.[154] In place of embittered Germans from competing economic groups, there would be healthy, vigorous and productive Aryans who would be ready for their ultimate role of Lebensraum, or external expansion, and conquest. This stereotype proved attractive to most of the population and therefore ensured their loyalty to a regime that appeared to value them so highly. They were to be prepared for this by propaganda and indoctrination, carefully targeted social benefits and a new work ethic implicit in work and leisure organizations like the RAD, SdA and KdF.

But there was another side. Although inclusive to Aryans, the *Volksgemeinschaft* excluded 'community aliens' who threatened its ideal. Some individuals were removed because they had genetic 'impairments' that threatened to 'contaminate' Aryan 'purity'; this was generally carried out with as little publicity as possible, usually in secret. Others were rejected for 'endangering' popular cohesion as criminals, 'asocials' or political opponents. These were processed through the Nazi judicial system; again, this was carried out on an individual basis, although with sufficient publicity to provide a deterrent for the rest of the population.

But by far the largest exclusions were whole groups who did not meet the requirements of the *Volksgemeinschaft* for racial reasons. These became targets of obsessive hatred.

Rejected on genetic grounds

Among the earliest exclusions from the Volksgemeinschaft were 'the physically malformed, mentally disturbed, and intellectually retarded'.[155] Although race was not necessarily involved, genetic problems affecting individuals were seen as a threat to the race and community as a whole. In addition to diluting the 'purity' of the Aryan race, they used up resources and care required by the rest of the population. Dr Heilig, a representative of the Nazi Physicians' League, argued in a 1934 pamphlet that 'the useless dissipation of costly medications drawn from the public store cannot be justified'.[156] The Nazis also tried to undermine Christian-based morality by means of constant propaganda against the genetically disabled in key areas of the school curriculum. One example of this is Problem 95 in an arithmetic book: 'The construction of an insane asylum requires 6 million RM. How many thousand housing units @ 15,000 RM could be built for the amount spent on insane asylums?'[157]

At the same time, the regime had to balance what it perceived as the interest of the community with the need to avoid alienating the population. This meant that measures actually taken were either firmly based on 'legal' statutes or conducted in secrecy. The former included the Law for the Prevention of the Hereditarily Diseased, under which 0.5 per cent of the population was sterilized between 1934 and 1939; the three largest categories of victims were the 'feebleminded', schizophrenics and epileptics. Sometimes sterilization was combined with abortion and all marriages from 1935 had to have permission from public health offices. More drastic – and secretive – action was implemented in wartime, the most notorious of which was the T-4 'euthanasia' programme, named after the centre of the operation based at 4 Tiergarten Strasse in Berlin. Initially this was targeted at children who had been diagnosed with mental or physical disabilities attributed to heredity. The whole process was carried out covertly and medically disguised as death through other factors rather than as a result of the injections, poison or gas actually administered in special wards or chambers. The adult euthanasia programme was authorized in the summer of 1939 and began to operate in 1940, under partial cover of the war with Poland. This was done by the *Einsatzgruppen* advancing behind the military campaigns in Poland and was extended to parts of Germany such as Pomerania. Within months six hospitals were being equipped with gassing installations disguised as showers and crematoria, based on the original model at Brandenburg hospital. This part of the operation continued until Hitler ordered it to be stopped in August 1941, by which time up to 80,000 victims had been killed in the gas chambers. The new system was based on decentralized killing in hospitals through the use of poisons – more in line with the methods originally used against children.

The emphasis on circumspection was due partly to the fear that the German population would find the spread of 'euthanasia' unacceptable. The lessons drawn from the opposition shown by the Catholic Church and other organizations were to be applied also to the use of more controlled and secretive measures of racial genocide in the extermination camps in Poland.

Rejected as criminal, social and political 'enemies'

Another category of people rejected by the Volksgemeinschaft were 'asocials'.[158] These were all considered 'alien to the community' (*gemeinschaftsfremd*) and were subjected to more publicized persecution than were those with genetic disabilities. Among 'asocials' were alcoholics, prostitutes, 'idlers', 'grumblers' and vagabonds, all of whom were seen as a threat to the moral fibre and 'purity' of the community. Four other groups were considered especially dangerous.

One was a category generally described as 'habitual criminals', offenders against persons or property deemed by the law to incorrigible. Repeat offenders were severely dealt with under the Habitual Criminals Law of November 1933, the worst being sentenced to 'security confinement'. During the war, the focus switched from confinement to extermination: Hitler justified this on the grounds that 'penitentiaries do not have the function to preserve the criminals for a possible rebellion'.[159] Hence most of those originally sentenced to security confinement were transferred to camps (such as Mauthausen for men and Ravensbrück or Auschwitz for women), where many were worked to death. Political opponents were considered equally dangerous. Usually members of banned left-wing parties, such as the Communists or Social Democrats, many had been interned as early as 1933 in concentration camps like Dachau. Before the end of the Nazi period it had become increasingly common for such 'offenders' to be caught by the rise in the number of capital offences (from three in 1933 to forty-six before the end of the war)[160] or to be condemned to the harshest labour conditions in concentration and extermination camps. There they were identified by red triangles, to distinguish them from the 'habitual criminals' who wore green triangles.

Another major category targeted by the state was homosexuality. The main reasons for this were a perceived 'affront' to masculinity through 'unnatural behaviour', the loss of future children to the Reich, and a threat to 'public morality'. Active measures against homosexuals began in May 1933 and were intensified with the involvement of the SS with the Reich Central Office for the Combating of Homosexuality, set up in 1936. Again, the war was a catalyst for still more radical action: most identified as homosexuals after 1939 – especially in the army – were sent to camps where they were identified by pink triangles and suffered fates similar to criminals and political offenders. Lesbians, who had initially been excluded from active harassment, were increasingly persecuted during the late 1930s, on the grounds that they threatened the gender role expected by the Nazi regime. Finally, the regime took increasingly severe measures against religious opponents, although the full rigour of the courts was reserved for those regarded as a political or security threat. Usually Protestant and Catholic clergy were protected from the harshest measures by the respect in which they were held by the population at large. This did not, however, apply to smaller religious groups, especially the Jehovah's Witnesses,[161] who were less likely than most Catholics or Protestants to adapt to life in Nazi Germany: they refused, for example, to use the Hitler salute or serve in the army. They were regarded as exiles from the *Volksgemeinschaft* through their own choice and tried in special courts. Where possible the charges against them were increased by association with delinquency or political activity: many, for example, were accused of being implicated in Communist conspiracies.

Rejected as race 'enemies'

For the first few decades after 1945 race was seen by most historians as the rationale for the internal developments and the external drive of the Third Reich. After a period when there was increasing questioning as to whether its influence was as important as pragmatism and naked power, there has been swing back towards emphasizing the impetus of race in the whole Nazi system. Kershaw, for example, argues that 'Perhaps the most significant shift in perspective, compared with the position in the early or mid-1980s, is the seriousness with which Nazi racial ideology is now viewed as a key motivating force for action.'[162] Barkai goes so far as to say that 'Auschwitz was latent in the anti-Semitic obsessions of Hitler and his Party from the beginning in the way in which the embryo is in the egg or fruit within the bud'.[163]

Fundamental to all Hitler's policies was his absolute belief in the superiority of the 'Aryan' race and the need to prepare the German people for its role as the master of Europe. He categorized humankind into three separate groups: 'founders' of culture, 'bearers' of culture and 'destroyers' of culture. The Aryans, of course, formed the highest group. According to the Nazi race theorists, the essential characteristics of the typical Aryan included a tall and slim build, a narrow face and nose, a prominent chin, fresh complexion, and gold or blond hair. It is ironical that one of the few Nazi leaders to fit this description – Heydrich – was obsessed with what he considered to be the 'taint' of a Jewish forebear. Hitler aimed gradually to 'purify' the German race so that the majority of people would eventually conform to this ideal appearance. This would be achieved by eliminating miscegenation and by special breeding programmes undertaken by the SS. Race therefore became a vital part of all indoctrination, the purpose being, in von Shirach's words, to create 'the perfect and complete human animal – the superman!' The main obstacle to this was what Hitler called 'subman', who threatened to 'pollute' the Aryan race. The main victims of this mentality were, above all, Slavs, Gypsies and Jews.

The Slavs, frequently referred to in *Mein Kampf*, comprised the majority of the peoples of eastern Europe, including Russians, Poles, Czechs, Slovaks, Ukrainians, Bulgarians, Serbs, Croats and other smaller groups. The Treaties of Versailles and St. Germain left comparatively few Slavs within Germany and Austria, which meant that Slavs were seen as an 'external' rather than an 'internal' threat. This was partly because their population growth was more rapid than that of Germany and partly because their territorial possessions (substantially increased between 1919 and 1920) acted as a bulwark against the future eastward expansion 'needed' by a 'healthy' Aryan race. For most of the 1930s there were few measures within Germany affecting Slavs, while German foreign policy pursued a cautious and pragmatic approach, especially to Poland and Russia. It was in the climate of war that the anti-Slav component of Nazi racism was implemented, although not against *all* Slavs. Some, especially Poles, Russians and Serbs, received barbaric treatment as enemies. Others like Bulgarians, Croats and Slovaks were treated, albeit with suspicion, as allies. Nazi dealings with the Slavs after 1939, whether as invading conquerors or as controlling partners, also set loose a flood of policies against two racial groups both within the Reich and in the Slav areas outside. These were the Gypsies and the Jews.

The Nazi case against the Gypsies (more accurately called Sinti and Roma) was that they had 'polluted' blood that had originally been Aryan during the course of their westward migration from the Punjab, which had involved centuries of contact with the 'inferior races' of eastern Europe. They were considered a major threat to the population of Germany because of their itinerant lifestyle and sexual contacts. To deal with this the Reich Central Office for the Fight Against the Gypsy Nuisance was set up in 1936, the emphasis being on containing Gypsies within officially designated sites. This was followed in December 1938 by Himmler's decree for 'Fighting the Gypsy Plague' which imposed systematic registration and measures to prevent miscegenation. The most extreme changes, however, accompanied German military expansion into Slavic eastern Europe, especially from 1941. Gypsies were deported from Germany and Austria into occupied eastern territories and incarcerated in Chelmo, Treblinka and a new Gypsy enclosure (BIIe) at Auschwitz-Birkenau set up in September 1942. The process was accelerated by Himmler's Auschwitz Decree on Gypsies

(December 1942) and Eichmann's efforts to bring the Gypsies within the scope of the 'Final Solution' targeted at the Jews. This meant that between 1.25 and 1.5 million Gypsies perished in the gas chambers, an atrocity that 'has been largely invisible in current historiography about Nazi genocide'.[164]

It was the persecution of the Jews that provided the Nazi regime with its dynamic. In part, German anti-Semitism was the culmination of centuries of discrimination throughout Europe. This had reared its head again after 1880 with violence in Vienna and Berlin, blatant discrimination in the French army and a series of pogroms in Tsarist Russia. H.S. Chamberlain wrote in 1901 that 'The entrance of the Jew into European History' had meant 'the entrance of an alien element – alien to that which Europe had already achieved, alien to all it was still destined to achieve'.[165] Anti-Semitism could therefore be seen as a tidal force: its high-water mark at the end of the nineteenth century brought Hitler in with its flotsam.

Hitler's own views on Jews were the main driving force behind the whole Nazi movement: anti-Semitic policies were therefore a sublimation of his personal obsession. *Mein Kampf* is full of the most inflammatory references of the Jew as a 'parasite' and 'polluter', contaminating art and literature and reducing men to his own 'base nature'. In one of his speeches he fantasized about hanging the Jews of Munich from lampposts until their 'bodies rotted'. There is no doubting the elemental force of his hatred. At the same time, there was also a calculated use of the techniques of scapegoating; the paradox here was that anti-Semitism as an irrational force could be used rationally to strengthen the Volksgemeinschaft. There would be numerous occasions on which the regime called for sacrifice. This would elicit two sentiments – a positive effort to meet the demand and negative resentment against those who made the sacrifice necessary. The former could be used by the regime, while the latter needed to be deflected away from the regime. It made sense to target a minority group picked out by the Führer from the taint of many centuries. The methods used to generate hatred were varied. One was the spread of the vilest misinformation, based on Hitler's earlier technique of the 'big lie': hence Streicher's *Der Stürmer* alleged ritual killing of Christian children by Jews. Another was Hitler's oratorical device of blaming Jews for all perceived threats, ranging from the economic crisis of 1935–6 to the hostility of Britain and France to German designs on Polish territory in 1939. A third was the carefully orchestrated 'spontaneity' of Kristallnacht, publicized by Goebbels as the 'righteous indignation of the German people'.

Nazi measures against the Jews unfolded in three main stages, each more radical than the last. The first, between 1933 and 1938, saw extensive legislation that imposed a series of limits on the activities of Jews. In April 1933 Jews were excluded from the civil service, prevented from working in hospitals and removed from the judiciary. Two measures were introduced in 1935, collectively known as the Nuremberg Laws. The Law for the Protection of German Blood and Honour banned marriage or sexual relations between Germans and Jews, while the Reich Citizenship Law stripped Jews of their German citizenship and removed their civil rights under the law. Between them, these were the most comprehensive anti-Semitic measures in modern history. Yet, at this stage, there were still some constraints on Nazi action. President Hindenburg managed to keep civil service jobs for Jews who had fought or lost relatives in the First World War. In addition, Frick issued a memorandum from the Ministry of the Interior instructing authorities not to *exceed* the instructions on the Jews. In some instances, authorities were embarrassed by the excesses of militants like Julius Streicher, with his virulent tabloid *Der Stürmer*. On the occasion of the 1936 Olympic Games Hitler ordered the removal of all anti-Jewish notices from Berlin: he was clearly playing safe so as not to alienate the establishment or international opinion, while at the same time secretly preparing more comprehensive measures for the future.

From 1938 anti-Semitism became more violent and all remaining constraints on persecution were swept aside in the second phase. In July 1938 Jews were banned from participating in commerce, their last preserve. The authorities also attempted to identify and control the movement of Jews by decrees on compulsory 'Jewish' names, identity cards and passports. The law no longer offered any protection, as was all too evident on the night of 9–10 November 1938. Kristallnacht, orchestrated by Goebbels, saw the destruction of 7,000 Jewish businesses and most of Germany's synagogues. This was led by the SA in retaliation for the assassination by a Polish Jew of an official in the German embassy in Paris. The violence of the mobs caused some irritation at the top levels of the administration, which preferred a more systematic and less messy approach – such as the confiscation of Jewish assets. At Hitler's instigation several possibilities were now examined for removing the Jewish population of Germany altogether, including a scheme for its resettlement on the island of Madagascar.

But Hitler soon came to the conclusion that emigration was not feasible. Between 1941 and 1945 his anti-Jewish obsessions were sublimated in the most extreme measures seen in the whole of human history. The catalyst for this was war, specifically the conquest of Poland in 1939 and the invasion of the Soviet Union in 1941. Between 1939 and 1941 German Jews were brought under the same restrictions as those in Poland: they were made to identify themselves with Star of David armbands (blue and white in Poland and yellow and black in Germany) and were confined to urban ghettos. This was a crucial stage in the move to genocide, initiated by mass shootings by the SS Einsatzgruppen and Wehrmacht detachments, and taken over by the gas chambers in the extermination camps. The official turning point here was the Wannsee Conference in January 1942, although this merely provided official sanction for decisions already taken. Goering instructed Heydrich to convene a conference to find a 'total solution of the Jewish question in the German sphere of influence in Europe'. The details were organized by Eichmann and attended by a combination of government and NSDAP officials and officers from the SS and Gestapo. The latter included General Muller (head of the Gestapo), and General Hofmann (Race and Settlement Main Office). The meeting was used to give unanimous approval for the use of gas chambers to 'evacuate' (a euphemism for 'exterminate') the whole of European Jewry. It was clear indication that the SS had already set the pace and were now pulling the government and party with them. Growing conflict between the three sectors may have been apparent elsewhere but there was no question as to the supremacy of the SS in implementing the Holocaust, initially through mass shootings and then through extermination camps at Chelmo, Auschwitz-Birkenau, Belzec, Sobibor, Treblinka and Maidenek. Exterminations began in earnest from mid-1942 and a total of between three and four million Jews went to the gas chambers. Organized by Eichmann, the whole process was conducted with industrial efficiency and leading German firms competed for contracts to manufacture the equipment for the gas chambers and crematoria. Yet the Nazis were constantly aware of the need to maintain secrecy for fear of a public backlash. The details were not brought to light until early in 1945 as the Russians liberated the camps in Poland and the Allies those in the west.

GERMAN FOREIGN POLICY, 1919–39

The foreign policy of the Weimar Republic, 1919–33

By far the most important influence behind German foreign policy before the rise of Hitler was the Treaty of Versailles. Since this was fundamental to the mainstream of European diplomacy, its terms and significance have already been examined (see pp. 12–13).

The Treaty of Versailles caused great bitterness in Germany. There it was condemned by the entire range of political opinion, from far left to extreme right. It was seen by Hugo Preuss, a prominent politician and legal expert, as a severe blow to the new republic; he referred to the 'criminal madness of the Versailles Diktat'[166] and claimed that the new constitution 'was born with this curse upon it'. It was hardly surprising, therefore, that the major objective of the republic's foreign policy was to lift the burden of Versailles and seek a revised settlement. The question, of course, was how could this be accomplished?

One of the earliest strategies was that devised by Joseph Wirth, Chancellor for two brief periods in 1921 and 1922. This was the policy of 'fulfilment', a strange approach which, according to Hiden, was

> a necessary expedient based on the premise that to show determined good faith in trying to carry out the peace terms properly would not only demonstrate how impossible a task this was, but would therefore also induce the Allied powers to be more lenient in interpreting the treaty.[167]

In other words, let the treaty discredit and destroy itself through its very harshness. The British government was not unsympathetic, but the French were determined that the treaty should be applied to the letter. Hence, when Germany defaulted on a reparations payment of a specific number of telegraph poles, French troops entered and occupied the Ruhr in 1923. The policy of 'fulfilment' was immediately replaced by one of passive resistance called for by the Chancellor, Wilhelm Cuno. Relations between Germany and the Western powers had therefore reached a dangerous low.

Elsewhere, Wirth had been more successful. He opened up diplomatic relations with Europe's other isolated power, Bolshevik Russia. Representatives of Germany and Russia used the international conference at Genoa (1922) as a front for their own Treaty of Rapallo. This established diplomatic relations between the two states and laid the foundations for commercial contacts and economic co-operation. Rapallo was a diplomatic triumph for the Weimar Republic in eastern Europe, but clearly something had to be done to improve relations with the West.

This was to be the work of Gustav Stresemann. Chancellor in 1923 and Foreign Minister between 1923 and 1929, he pursued a skilful combination of aims. He intended, on the one hand, to rebuild cordial relations with other states and to remove the underlying international tensions which Europe had experienced in the early 1920s. He even saw Germany as 'the bridge which would bring East and West together in the development of Europe'. For his promotion of détente and his condemnation of war, Stresemann has sometimes been called a 'good European'. On the other hand, he was also a patriot who was as convinced as anyone that the Treaty of Versailles must eventually be revised. Much of his diplomacy was therefore double-edged. He once observed: 'We must get the stranglehold off our neck. On that account, German policy, as Metternich said of Austria, no doubt after 1809, will have to be one of finesse.'[168] More specifically, he had three objectives. One was 'the solution of the Reparations question in a sense tolerable for Germany'. A second was the 'protection of Germans abroad, those 10 to 12 millions of our kindred who now live under a foreign yoke in foreign lands'. Third, he hoped eventually for 'the readjustment of our eastern frontiers'.[169] The other face of the 'good European' was, therefore, the 'good German'.

There are three particularly important examples of Stresemann's policy of reconciliation between Germany and the rest of Europe. These were Germany's accession to the Locarno Pact (1925), her membership of the League of Nations (1926) and her involvement in the

Kellogg–Briand Pact of 1928. These all seemed to indicate that Germany was now a reformed and rehabilitated power. Yet, at the same time, Stresemann was pursuing covert policies which benefited Germany at the expense of the rest of Europe and which were clearly revisionist in intention. Gatzke refers to Stresemann's 'appeasement abroad' and 'rearmament at home'. A good example of the latter was the 1926 Treaty of Berlin between Germany and Russia. This extended the earlier relationship established by the Treaty of Rapallo. Both powers now agreed to remain neutral if either were involved in a war with a third country. Even more significant, however, was Germany's use of her special relationship with Russia as a means of evading the rearmament restrictions imposed by the Treaty of Versailles. The German army (Reichswehr), under von Seeckt, derived a great deal from secret training and manoeuvres on Russian soil. Stresemann's attitude to Germany's secret rearmament ranged, in the words of Gatzke, 'from passive acceptance to active assistance'.[170] This was because co-operation needed, in Stresemann's view, to be accompanied by an increase in self-confidence and strength. Hence, in Stresemann's words, 'The main asset [of a strong foreign policy] is material power – army and navy.'[171]

What was the extent of Stresemann's success? Between his death in 1929 and the accession of Hitler in 1933, Germany experienced several positive developments. The Allied powers removed in 1930 all the occupying troops still in the Rhineland and, in 1932, the Lausanne Conference judged it expedient to alter radically the method by which Germany should pay reparations. It might, therefore, be thought that revisionism had made substantial inroads into the Versailles Settlement. Yet, during this same period, the Weimar Republic's foreign policy experienced a profound crisis. The Great Depression upset the republic's political stability and caused a swing to the parties of the right. These had always opposed Stresemann's policies of détente and collaboration with the West. Hitler, especially, increased the intensity of his attacks on the republic, reviving the myth that the German army had been 'stabbed in the back' in 1918 and that the republic had always been dominated by the 'November Criminals', the 'traitors' of the First World War. The way was therefore open for the more intensive pursuit of revisionism by a regime which took full advantage of the head start provided by the Stresemann era but which rejected Stresemann's moderation.

Hitler's foreign policy, 1933–9

Hitler assumed responsibility for German foreign policy in January 1933. Although he had a considerable number of preconceived ideas, he decided that his initial strategy should be cautious and moderate. The main reason for this was Germany's still vulnerable position in Europe. The country was regarded by the Western powers as a defeated state, under the constraints of the Treaty of Versailles. Furthermore, the German government still had to contend with the manifest distrust shown by France and with the extensive system of alliances constructed by France in eastern Europe. Germany had not yet developed a counter-alliance, unless the pact with Russia, renewed in 1931, is included. Fascist Italy, perhaps the most likely prospect for an alliance with Germany, was at this stage hostile to Germany's designs on Austria, since Mussolini had not yet abandoned the possibility of expanding Italy's frontiers into the Alps. Between 1933 and 1935, therefore, Hitler had little option but to make conciliatory diplomatic gestures and to lull the suspicions of the rest of Europe. At the same time, he clearly intended to revive Germany's military power; the problem, he told his generals, was that this 'building of the armed forces' was also 'the most dangerous time'.[172] He must therefore avoid any possibility of retaliation.

An example of Hitler's early diplomacy was his attitude to the Geneva Disarmament Conference (1932–3) and its immediate follow-up. The politicians of the Weimar Republic, especially Stresemann, had shown interest in the case for a general reduction of armaments throughout Europe, since this would help offset the one-sidedness of the Versailles provisions. Hitler, however, was less interested in this type of approach for, as Craig points out, he intended to exploit Germany's grievance over arms, not deprive her of it.[173] He certainly wanted to avoid any future limitations on German rearmament but without being blatantly provocative. His opportunity came when the British Prime Minister, MacDonald, proposed a reduction of French troops from 500,000 to 200,000 and an increase in German troops to parity with the French. This was far below Hitler's expectations; he knew, however, that the French would reject the proposal and was therefore able to project a moderate image in supporting MacDonald. When the French did decline the offer, Hitler withdrew from the Disarmament Conference and then from the League of Nations. Realizing that this might provoke some sort of retaliation, he decided to cover his tracks with bilateral agreements which could later be broken. In 1934, therefore, he drew up a Non-Aggression Pact with Poland. This was partly to break the French system of alliances in eastern Europe and partly to allay the suspicions of western Europe that he had long-term designs on Polish territory. In reality, of course, he had no intention of keeping to the pact. He declared, privately, 'All our agreements with Poland have a purely temporary significance.'[174] For the time being, however, he decided to conceal his hand.

Hitler's pretended moderation encountered a setback in 1934 when the Austrian Nazis assassinated Chancellor Dollfuss in an abortive attempt to seize power and achieve a political union with Germany. Hitler was seriously embarrassed by this development which put a brake on the possibility of closer relations between Germany and Italy. He was therefore obliged to play down the activities of the Austrian Nazis, since he was not yet strong enough to use such opportunities to further a more aggressive course. Much would depend on the success of his rearmament policy. What stage had this reached by 1935?

There had never been any question of Hitler abiding by the disarmament provisions of the Treaty of Versailles. When he came to power in 1933 he inherited ten divisions; by the middle of 1934 he had increased the total to 240,000 men, more than twice the number allowed by Versailles. By 1935 there was no longer any point in pretending. On 11 March he formally announced the existence of a German airforce. On 16 March he issued a decree introducing conscription and warning that the military provisions of Versailles would no longer be observed. The reaction of the other powers posed a major diplomatic problem which Hitler needed to resolve. The League of Nations formally censured Germany's unilateral decision to rearm and, in April 1935, Britain, France and Italy formed the Stresa Front. In the following month, France responded of her own accord by drawing up a mutual assistance pact with the Soviet Union. It seemed that Germany had reached the critical phase of almost total isolation.

The period 1935–7, however, provided Hitler with a series of opportunities. He was able to end German isolation, put pressure on Britain and France and bring together a formidable diplomatic combination in central Europe. He was greatly assisted in accomplishing all this by favourable external trends and events.

The first of these was the reluctance of the British government to become involved in continental obligations, which meant that it was always receptive to a deal on armaments levels. In June 1935 Hitler secured an Anglo-German Naval Pact by which he undertook not to build a German fleet beyond 35 per cent of the total British strength. This was another example of Hitler's preference for bilateral agreements and it ruined any chance that the Stresa Front might be able to put concerted pressure on Germany: France and Italy were both furious with Britain's co-operation with Hitler. But the real windfall for Hitler was the involvement of Italy, from 1935 onwards, in Ethiopia (see pp. 152–4). This had several beneficial results for Germany. Imperial expansion diverted Italian attention away from Austria, Hitler's target to the south. It also had considerable diplomatic repercussions as Britain and France antagonized Italy by applying economic sanctions. Above all, Britain now saw Italy as a potentially hostile power and became more apprehensive than ever about commitments in Europe; she needed to be free to deal, if necessary, with Italian threats in the Mediterranean or Africa. Hitler therefore gambled that Britain would not be prepared to back any military action by France to prevent any further breaches of the Treaty of Versailles. He decided to remilitarize the Rhineland ahead of his original target. This he accomplished in March 1936 with only 22,000 troops, against the advice of his generals who feared instant retaliation. His judgement proved correct. The British government, anxious not to become involved, took no action and persuaded the French government to do likewise.

From this stage onwards Hitler was able to construct a new network of partners and satellites. Italy, involved in the Ethiopian adventure and the Spanish Civil War, was no longer a rival in central Europe and gravitated towards Germany in the 'Rome–Berlin Axis' of 1936. At the same time, Hitler extended the scope of his diplomacy to outflank France. He assisted Franco to replace the Spanish Republic with a far-right regime deeply hostile to France. Russia, France's partner since 1935, was the target of the Anti-Comintern Pact, drawn up in November 1936 between Germany and Japan and eventually including Italy. Meanwhile, Germany was also implementing the Four-Year Plan and a policy of autarky which involved the economic penetration of Romania, Yugoslavia, Bulgaria and Greece. By the end of 1937, Hitler's position was sufficiently secure for him to consider adopting a more openly aggressive policy.

Therefore, in November 1937, Hitler summoned to a special conference the War Minister (Blomberg), the Commander-in-Chief of the Navy (Raedar), the Commander-in-Chief of the Army (Fritsch), the Commander-in-Chief of the Airforce (Goering) and the Foreign Minister (Neurath). The sixth person present was Colonel Hossbach, whose unofficial record of the meeting is generally known as the Hossbach Memorandum. According to this document, Hitler revealed the underlying purpose of his foreign policy and his hopes for the future, including schemes for the enlargement of Germany. Hitler added that there was some urgency because his plans would be resisted by Britain and France, and Germany's military superiority could not be expected to last beyond the period 1943–5. The Hossbach Memorandum, therefore, clearly indicates a change in the tempo of Hitler's diplomacy. It has been argued that Hitler was now willing to run high risks to attain his objectives and that he was prepared, if necessary, to launch a series of swift military campaigns. His new approach came as something of a shock to some of his subordinates, who inevitably tried to point out the dangers involved. Hitler's response to this was to reorganize the structure of the army and to replace Blomberg, Fritsch and Neurath. He was clearly determined to remove any obstruction to the next phase of his foreign policy.

Two targets were particularly prominent in 1938: Austria and Czechoslovakia. In March he accomplished the long-intended Anschluss and, in defiance of the Treaty of Versailles, incorporated Austria directly into the Reich. The result was a radical change in the balance of power in central and south-eastern Europe. Germany now had a joint border with Italy, completely outflanked Czechoslovakia and had gained direct access to Hungary and the Balkans. Hitler had also scored a major personal triumph: once again he had ignored warnings that his action would provoke foreign intervention and once again he had been proved right. Indeed, the ease with which the Anschluss had been accomplished led inexorably to the next undertaking. This was the removal of the German-populated

Sudetenland from Czechoslovakia and its incorporation into the Reich. Again, this has been seen as a 'virtuoso performance'.[175] Hitler used a variety of expedients; these included the use of Henlein's Sudeten Nazis as an internal pressure group, and the serious differences between the provinces of Bohemia and Slovakia. According to Noakes and Pridham, 'Hitler now proceeded to use the ethnic diversity of the country as a lever with which to break it up into its ethnic components.'[176] Above all, he exploited the unwillingness of Britain and France to take direct action in support of Czechoslovakia. The result was the Munich Agreement (29 September 1938) which allowed Hitler to annex the Sudetenland to the Reich. In return Chamberlain, the British Prime Minister, secured a promise that Britain and Germany would 'never go to war with one another again'. The whole episode showed the bankruptcy of collective security, of Franco-Soviet co-operation and of the British policy of appeasement. The Munich Agreement, conversely, built up Hitler's image within Germany and convinced him absolutely of his ability to accomplish the objectives outlined in the Hossbach Memorandum.

There is a school of thought that Hitler saw Munich as something of a failure – that he had allowed himself to be talked into making a diplomatic agreement instead of going ahead with the military option which he had threatened throughout the crisis. He certainly made up for this during the course of 1939. Once again working on an internal crisis, he engineered the break-up of Czechoslovakia and, in March, incorporated Bohemia and Moravia into the Reich. Having accomplished his objectives in central Europe, Hitler turned his attention eastwards, gaining Memel from Lithuania. He was now determined to complete the union of all Germans within the Reich, recover the last vestiges of territory lost at Versailles, and begin the process of Lebensraum.

This meant that his next victim was Poland. Hitler swiftly stepped up the pressure by demanding Danzig and the Polish Corridor, only to meet determined resistance from the Polish Foreign Minister, Józef Beck. By this stage, Poland was bolstered by an Anglo-French guarantee. This had been delivered in March and was a clear indication that the Western powers had finally come to recognize the futility of appeasement. Hitler, however, was utterly confident that he could continue to outwit Britain and France. He was convinced that the British government was bluffing and that France would not go to war alone against Germany. In any case, he made his own position more secure by drawing up in May 1939 the Pact of Steel with Italy (see p. 155) and in August the Non-Aggression Pact with the Soviet Union. The latter was a major diplomatic turnabout which made a nonsense of any undertaking by the West to protect Poland. Hitler still expected to avoid a conflict with Britain by seeming to negotiate further with the Polish government and, through a series of manufactured border incidents, providing evidence of Polish 'aggression'. But his invasion of Poland on 1 September 1939 provoked declarations of war from both Britain and France, much to Hitler's surprise. He was also let down at the last minute by his most important ally: Mussolini felt obliged to inform Hitler that Italy was insufficiently equipped at this stage to undertake direct military action. Despite these unexpected obstacles, Hitler was supremely confident of success and proceeded to demonstrate the awesome power of the new German army operating a Blitzkrieg strategy.

Aims of Hitler's foreign policy

While the statesmen of the Weimar Republic were trying in the 1920s to achieve a revision of the Versailles Settlement and, at the same time, effect a reconciliation with the other powers, Hitler was already devising more elaborate schemes, to which he added substantially in the 1930s and early 1940s. There are three major sources for discerning Hitler's ideas. The first, of course, is *Mein Kampf*, written in Landsberg prison, and subsequently published; it achieved a mass circulation and was read by millions of Germans. The second is *Hitler's Second Book*, which dealt explicitly with foreign policy but remained unpublished in his lifetime. The third source is a series of spoken remarks made by Hitler and edited by Dr Henry Picker as Hitler's *Tischgespräche* (*Table Talk*). Because of the undisciplined and often rambling nature of these works, it is difficult to put together a carefully structured outline of his policy. The basic aims, however, seem clear enough.

He maintained that all previous governments had been restricted in their foreign policy by the notion of the 'fixed frontier'. Even the conservatives and neo-Bismarckians were wrong to aim at recreating the territorial arrangements of 1914, for 'the German borders of the year 1914 were borders which presented something incomplete'. As an alternative to the 'border policy' of the 'national bourgeois' world, the Nazis would follow a 'territorial one', the whole purpose of which would be 'to secure the space necessary to the life of our people'. The limited policies of Bismarck had, perhaps, been necessary to establish and build up the 'power structure' for the future. But Bismarck's successors had denied Germany her natural process of expansion and had pursued an 'insane' policy of alliance with Austria–Hungary and maritime conflict with Britain. Now the mistakes of history should be rectified, Lebensraum could be achieved, and the 'inferior races' could be deprived of the territory to which their low productivity and potential gave them no natural right. 'According to an eternal law of Nature, the right to the land belongs to the one who conquers the land because the old boundaries did not yield sufficient space for the growth of the population.' Returning to the theme of struggle which had permeated *Mein Kampf*, Hitler affirmed: 'Every healthy, vigorous people sees nothing sinful in territorial acquisition, but something quite in keeping with its nature.' The intended direction of this expansion was made abundantly clear in *Mein Kampf*: 'We put a stop to the eternal movement of the Germanic people to Europe's South and West and we turn our eyes to the land in the East.' More specifically, 'In speaking of new territory in Europe, we can, above all, have in mind only Russia and its subjugated border states.'[177]

Did these ideas gradually evolve into an overall programme, a blueprint which Hitler intended to follow? This question has produced one of the major historical controversies within the theme of Nazi foreign policy.

On the one hand, some historians emphasize the fundamental logic of Hitler's designs and acknowledge that he did develop a definite programme and set of intentions. These so-called 'programmists' and 'intentionalists' owe much to the pioneering work of Trevor-Roper, who maintained that *Mein Kampf* was 'a complete blueprint of his intended achievements'.[178] More recently, it has been argued, by Hillgruber, that Hitler pursued his aims systematically 'without, however, forfeiting any of his tactical flexibility'.[179] Similar views are expressed by Jäckel, who claims that Hitler's 'programme of foreign policy' can be divided into three phases:

> During the first phase, Germany had to achieve internal consolidation and rearmament and to conclude agreements with Britain and Italy. During the second phase Germany had to defeat France in a preliminary engagement. Then the great war of conquest against Russia could take place during the third and final phase.[180]

Jäckel also maintains that there is 'ample documentary evidence to prove that he always kept this outline in mind'. There is an alternative 'programme', pointed to by other historians but overlapping that deduced by Jäckel. Hitler's first priority was to destroy the Versailles

Settlement and rearm Germany. This would be followed by the creation of an enlarged Reich which would incorporate all of Europe's German population. This, in turn, would be the prelude to the achievement of Lebensraum from conquered territory in Poland and Russia.

Historians of the 'intentionalist' school are in broad agreement on Hitler's formulation of a programme or series of objectives. There is, however, a sub-debate between what might be termed the 'continentalists' and the 'globalists'.[181] The former maintain that Hitler's objective was the conquest of Lebensraum in the east. According to Jäckel, 'Hitler's main aim in foreign policy was a war of conquest against the Soviet Union'.[182] But a number of historians also claim that Hitler had an ambition that transcended the defeat of Russia and the achievement of Lebensraum: namely, world conquest. During the 1970s and 1980s these included Hillgruber, Hildebrand, Hauner and Thies. Hillgruber argued that Hitler's policy geographically was 'designed to span the globe; ideologically, too, the doctrines of universal antisemitism and social Darwinism, fundamental to his programme, were intended to embrace the whole of mankind'.[183] In 1976 Thies put forward a powerful argument that 'Hitler's "ultimate goals", as they were conceived and developed in their global framework, can be dated as far back as 1919 and 1920. They were thus formed much earlier than the determination of his "short-term goals" when he was writing *Mein Kampf* in the years from 1924 to 1926.'[184] After that, 'Hitler never gave up the idea of conquering the world with Europe's help'. His ultimate target was the United States. Anticipating a transatlantic war, he made advance preparation for the introduction of special long range bombers capable of bombing New York; these were the Messerschmitt 261/4 (actually an Me 261 with four engines).[185] This aircraft was planned and tested but not put into production, although the project was kept going until September 1944 despite the failure of Hitler's armies in eastern Europe. Goering, meanwhile, had been convinced by Hitler as far back as 1938, pointing to the results of a possible victory over the United States: 'Then Germany becomes the biggest world power; then all the global markets belong to Germany.'[186]

Thies also maintained that 'the controversy over "New Lebensraum in the East" versus "Global Supremacy" had not yet been resolved'.[187] This is as true now as it ever was: indeed, the debate has been given a revived impetus, reflected by the translation of Thies's work into English in 2012.[188] This was largely on the initiative of Berghahn, who argues that 'the Nazi ambitions went well beyond the murderous conquest of *Lebensraum* in the East'.[189]

There is a school of thought which denies that Hitler pursued a particular programme in his foreign policy. Rather, he was profoundly influenced by the needs of the moment. This case has been put most forcefully by A.J.P. Taylor, who argues that Hitler's projects, as outlined in the Hossbach Memorandum, were 'in large part daydreaming, unrelated to what followed in real life'. In his opinion, 'Hitler was gambling on some twist of fortune which would present him with success in foreign affairs, just as a miracle had made him Chancellor in 1933.'[190] There has been qualified support for this line of thought, although for different reasons. Mommsen, for example, argues that Hitler did little to shape his foreign policy and that his whole approach was spontaneous – a series of responses to specific developments: 'in reality the regime's foreign policy ambitions were many and varied, without any clear aims and only linked by their ultimate goal: hindsight alone gives them some air of consistency'.[191] Broszat, too, points to the lack of any fundamental design and maintains that Lebensraum was basically an expression of the need to sustain a dynamic momentum.

Some historians have remained cautious or unconvinced by either scenario, pointing to Hitler's aims as too general to constitute 'planning'. Bullock maintained in 1967 that there are elements in Hitler's foreign policy of both planning and disorganized spontaneity. After all, Hitler had 'only one programme: power, first his own power in Germany, and then the expansion of German power in Europe'.[192] Elsewhere, he argued that 'he was at once both fanatical and cynical'.[193] Kershaw suggested in 1997 a different perspective. Hitler's 'ideological aims' were important 'in deciding the contours of German foreign policy'. Yet, these aims 'fused' in the formulation of policy 'so inseparably with strategic power-political considerations' and 'economic interest' that 'it is impossible to distinguish between them analytically'.[194] This makes it fairly clear that Kershaw regards the programmist approach as inappropriate in Hitler's case. Most recently, Kitchen's conclusion in 2008 was that Hitler was a 'daring gambler', driven by 'certain obsessions', also a 'master tactician'. 'He did not have a blueprint for foreign policy, but he was driven by a fanatical anti-Communism, a virulent racism, a determination to carve out Lebensraum in the east and by the conviction that war was an end in itself.'[195]

Another major debate on Hitler's foreign policy is whether there is an underlying continuity with early periods. The original argument was that there was a fundamental break, both with the foreign policy of the Weimar Republic and with that of the Kaiser's Second Reich. But this earlier consensus was shattered during the late 1960s by Fischer who, in *Germany's Aims in the First World War*,[196] claimed that Germany deliberately engineered the conflict in order to pursue expansionist aims which were really a prelude to those of Hitler. These aims had included: economic dominance over Belgium, Holland and France; hegemony over Courland, Livonia, Estonia, Lithuania and Poland, as well as over Bulgaria, Romania and Turkey; unification with Austria and the creation of a Greater Germany; control over the eastern Mediterranean; and rule over a dismantled Russia. Clearly, in the light of such a programme, Hitler's objectives would appear far from new; they could more appropriately be called a continuation than a radical departure. In addition, there were precedents for the *völkisch* emphasis of Hitler's expansionist policies in a number of pan-German and Lebensraum groups in pre-1914 Germany.

Of course, such plans were never implemented. The Second Reich lost the First World War and was itself replaced by the more moderate Weimar Republic. Here, surely, would be a case for denying continuity. Yet certain trends can be detected linking the Weimar Republic and the Third Reich. In the first place, there was considerable continuity of military and diplomatic personnel which lasted until Hitler's radical changes in 1938. The Weimar Republic had contained, within the Foreign Ministry, men like Neurath and Bülow, who also served Hitler for the first five years of the Third Reich. Much the same applied to Germany's ambassadors abroad, drawn as they were largely from the former aristocracy. This continuity of personnel at first lessened the likelihood of any sudden and dramatic switch of policy. In any case, it could be argued, Hitler was able to continue with the objectives of the republic as long as he concentrated on whittling away the Versailles Settlement. Indeed, by 1938 he had accomplished the targets of the republic's revisionists: Germany had regained full sovereignty over all internal territories, including the Saar and Rhineland; the restrictions on armaments had been ignored since 1935; and the Germans of Austria and the Sudetenland had been incorporated into the Reich.

In retrospect, however, it is obvious that the continuity between the diplomacy of the Weimar Republic and the Third Reich can be misleading. The crucial point which showed that Nazi foreign policy was as revolutionary as its domestic counterpart was that Hitler saw revisionism merely as a step towards projects which were well beyond the ambitions of the republic's statesmen. Although the republic's politicians had a strong element of opportunism, even ruthlessness, they did not share Hitler's social Darwinism and racialist vision. They also respected the traditions of European diplomacy and, under Stresemann, contributed much to international co-operation. One of Hitler's aims was to smash the multilateral agreements, like the Locarno Pact, which had been carefully built up during the 1920s. As for the continuity of personnel, it suited Hitler to retain the appointments made by the republic, so that he could give his regime a façade of moderation and respectability during the period of maximum vulnerability. As soon as he had accomplished safe levels of rearmament he instituted radical changes, in both his policy and his appointments. The turning-point was clearly the Hossbach Memorandum of 1937 and its follow-up. The developments of 1939, too, went far beyond any republican revisionism. According to Noakes and Pridham, 'It is in the policy pursued in Poland after 1939 and in Russia after 1941 that the distinction between Nazism and conservative German nationalism emerges clearly for the first time.'[197]

Finally, to what extent was Hitler's foreign policy influenced by events within Germany? Recent historians have argued strongly that there is a direct correlation between Germany's economic problems and performance and the pursuit of an expansionist policy in Europe. Sauer, for example, maintains that Blitzkrieg was an economic as well as a military strategy. It enabled Germany to rearm without causing German consumers excessive suffering and thereby depriving the regime of their support.[198] The practical effect was the deliberate dismantling of neighbouring states in order to strengthen the German economic base. Kershaw sees the relationship between the economy and militarism as more problematic. Hitler's Four-Year Plan and his Hossbach Memorandum were responses to the economic crisis of 1935–6 and locked Germany into a course of rearmament – and war.[199] The process was less deliberate than Sauer maintains, but no less inexorable. It could also be argued that Hitler accelerated the pace of his foreign policy in order to divert German public opinion from domestic problems, especially economic. This was a well-worn device, used both in the Second Reich and in Mussolini's Italy.

There is a certain logic to all of the views outlined in this section, but they need to be carefully integrated into an overall argument consisting of four components. First, Hitler was not uniquely responsible for creating an entirely personal foreign policy. As Fischer has shown, he inherited the main hegemonist aims from the Second Reich. Nevertheless, second, he played an important part in renovating these within the context of a more forceful ideology based on a racial and *völkisch* vision, contained in *Mein Kampf* and the *Second Book*. He therefore personalized and amended certain historical concepts, and it would be quite wrong to suggest that these were not seriously intended. In this respect, there is much to commend the approach of the 'intentionalists', although whether we can go so far as to accept that Hitler had a 'programme' – continental or global – is more doubtful. Third, Hitler implemented his ideas in his move towards war during the late 1930s partly as a result of domestic issues, especially the shaping of the German economy: the balance between guns and butter required a Blitzkrieg approach to conquest. Hence, the Four-Year Plan stepped up rearmament and the Hossbach Memorandum set an agenda for conflict. By 1938 these internal forces had locked Germany into a course which was likely to lead to war. Only at this point can Taylor's thesis be included. With growing confidence provided by his military preparations, Hitler became increasingly opportunistic, playing the diplomatic system with some skill and achieving what he wanted over the Anschluss and the Sudetenland. Why this course resulted in war has generated another controversy.

Hitler and the outbreak of the Second World War

The Nuremberg Judgement maintained that the Second World War was the outcome of Nazi policy and of Hitler's determination 'not to depart from the course he had set for himself'.[200] This raises the fundamental question: was the conflict really Hitler's war?

The majority opinion is that it was. The previous section provided an outline of the various arguments about Hitler's plans for European and world mastery, which are clearly relevant to the debate on the origins of the Second World War. There has also been much emphasis on what Hitler himself had to say about struggle and war. *Mein Kampf*, the *Second Book* and *Tischgespräche* all focus on militarism and unlimited expansion, together with the notion that struggle and war were fundamental human activities and needs. 'War is the most natural, the most ordinary thing. War is a constant; war is everywhere. There is no beginning, there is no conclusion of peace. War is life. All struggle is war. War is the primal condition.' The logical conclusion, therefore, is that Hitler wanted war, not only to achieve the objectives of his foreign policy, but to purify and strengthen the Aryan race. Hitler's responsibility for the outbreak of war is emphasized by a variety of British, German and American historians. Sontag, for example, argues that Hitler's policy in 1939 was, 'like the annexation of Austria and the Sudeten districts of Czechoslovakia, merely preliminary to the task of winning "living space"'.[201] Trevor-Roper believes that 'The Second World War was Hitler's personal war in many senses. He intended it, he prepared for it, he chose the moment for launching it.'[202] Fest affirmed the orthodoxy that 'who caused the war is a question that cannot be seriously raised'.[203] Much the same conclusion has been arrived at by Hillgruber, Hildebrand and Weinberg.

The alternative view, held by A.J.P. Taylor, relates to his argument that Hitler lacked any specific programme or long-term objectives, as outlined in the previous section. Instead of pursuing policies which led inevitably to war, Taylor argues, Hitler was, by and large, continuing those of the Second Reich and the Weimar Republic. He goes further: 'Hitler was no more wicked and unscrupulous than many other contemporary statesmen', although 'in wicked acts he outdid them all'. Hitler's diplomacy was based on short-term expedients and he doubted that a major conflict would be the outcome. Part of the Hossbach Memorandum made it clear that 'He was convinced of Britain's non-participation, and therefore he did not believe in the probability of belligerent action by France against Germany.' According to Taylor, the Hossbach Memorandum contained no plans for war

> and would never have been supposed to do so, unless it had been displayed at Nuremberg. The memorandum tells us, what we know already, that Hitler (like every other German statesman) intended Germany to become the dominant power in Europe. It also tells us that he speculated how this might happen. His speculations were mistaken. They bear hardly any relation to the actual outbreak of war in 1939.[204]

He also maintains that Germany was not really ready for war in 1939 – the levels of armaments confirm that Germany had not developed an advantage over Britain and France.

There has been considerable criticism of the Taylor thesis, both from historians convinced that Hitler did have long-term objectives which included war (for example, Trevor-Roper) and those who, although less convinced about this, feel that Taylor's approach is too narrow. One method of criticism is to remove the debate from the predominantly diplomatic ground which Taylor preferred to occupy and focus, instead, on the economy. Mason, for example, argues that Taylor's view

> leads to an overwhelming concentration on the sequence of diplomatic events, [his judgements] rest very largely upon the diplomatic documents [and that] these documents were primarily the work of conservative German diplomats, who, in dealing with their specific problems, were able to cover up or ignore the distinctive language and concepts

> of National Socialism. This helps to nurture the illusion that the foreign policy of the Third Reich was much the same as that of the Weimar Republic.[205]

Instead, Mason argues, Hitler deliberately chose war in 1939 as a way out of the difficulties faced by the German economy.

There is, finally, an approach which would apportion at least part of the responsibility for the outbreak of war to the other powers. In this case, however, responsibility is associated less with 'guilt' than with 'misinterpretation', 'inconsistency' and 'default'. It has been argued that Hitler's progress towards war was unintentionally accelerated by Western leaders, paradoxically, because of their very hatred of war. Daladier and Chamberlain, who found war morally repugnant, assumed that the rationale of all diplomacy was the pursuit of peace. Chamberlain, in particular, made the crucial mistake of assuming that even Hitler had fixed objectives and that if these were conceded to him, the causes of international tension would be removed. Hitler, of course, was greatly encouraged by the pressure exerted on the smaller states by the British and French governments and mistook forbearance in the interests of peace for weakness and diplomatic capitulation. This explains the increasingly aggressive stance which he adopted during the Sudeten Crisis of 1938. By 1939 Chamberlain had at last got the true measure of Hitler and decided to extend guarantees to Poland. This sudden switch appeared to be a desperate turn within a bankrupt policy and clearly failed to convince Hitler of Chamberlain's seriousness. Liddell Hart compared the pre-war crises with allowing someone to stoke up a boiler until the pressure rose to danger level and then closing the safety valve. It could certainly be said that the Western powers let Hitler accomplish so many of his objectives before 1939 that they precipitated conflict by eventually trying to stand firm. On the one hand, according to Henig, one cannot argue

> that firmer action before 1939 would have prevented war. It might have precipitated it earlier. Evidence seems to suggest fairly clearly that Hitler was determined to fight in October 1938 to gain Sudeten Czech territory. It might have been better, from a military point of view, for Britain and France to have fought then rather than later. This would not have prevented war but it might well have localized it.[206]

GERMANY AT WAR, 1939–45

German involvement in the Second World War is often divided into two distinct phases. The first was the period of Blitzkrieg or 'lightning war'. This saw a series of rapid military victories over Poland, western Europe and the Balkans, as well as initial success against Russia, bringing most of Europe under German control. The main reasons for the Blitzkrieg strategy are dealt with on pp. 218–19. The second period was one of Total War (1942–5). By this time Blitzkrieg had clearly failed to defeat Britain and the Soviet Union and proved helpless against the United States. During this second phase, Germany was slowly but inexorably ground down by the overwhelmingly greater industrial capacity of the Allies, who were much more effectively geared to fight a prolonged war. In retrospect, it is surprising not that Germany lost the war but that she survived so long.

Blitzkrieg and the expansion of the Third Reich, 1939–41

German armies invaded Poland on 1 September 1939, secured by the Non-Aggression Pact from possible retaliation by the Soviet Union. Although Britain and France had both declared war on Germany in support of Poland, they were unable to take direct military action; for them the period 1939–40 was one of inactivity, generally known as the 'phoney war'. The German attack on Poland was the last to be planned entirely by the German generals. It was highly professional and was the first completely mechanized invasion in history, comprising armoured vehicles, tanks and preliminary air attacks on selected targets. The Polish cavalry was routed and Warsaw was taken after a converging drive from East Prussia, Pomerania, Silesia and Slovakia. When Stalin intervened on 17 September to claim the territory set aside for Russia by the Non-Aggression Pact, Poland's fate was sealed. She was partitioned for the fourth time in her history and ceased to exist as an independent state.

The strategy of Blitzkrieg was applied next to the West, with even more spectacular success. The first targets were Denmark and Norway, chosen to consolidate Germany's position before the major assault on France, long considered by Hitler to be Germany's 'natural enemy'. Norway was especially important as it was a major outlet for Swedish iron-ore supplies and had enormous potential for North Atlantic naval bases. Besides, it dominated Germany's submarine route past the Shetlands and could well be used by Britain unless quickly taken. The task, accomplished in April 1940, demonstrated a new version of Blitzkrieg: namely, combined land and sea operations. It seemed that the German war machine was irresistible and there was clear evidence of a sense of defeatism in the Low Countries and France – Hitler's next victims. The Netherlands, Belgium and Luxembourg all fell to a renewed German onslaught in May 1940. This, however, was only the preliminary to Hitler's major objective – the conquest of France. Again, this was accomplished by a variation of Blitzkrieg. This time von Kleist's panzer divisions punched a hole through the Ardennes, supposedly impassable and therefore lightly defended. Guderian's forces then overwhelmed the French Ninth Army. In the subsequent race to the Channel ports, the Germans captured most of Flanders, and the British army was evacuated at Dunkirk. The German offensive then flowed southwards, culminating by the end of June in the capture of Paris and the capitulation of France.

Why was France defeated so easily? It used to be thought that the French armies were overwhelmed by superior numbers. More recent estimates have shown that this was not the case. Against the 103 German divisions on the western front, France mustered 99 which were also supported by British contingents. The Allies had a definite superiority in tanks (3,000 against 2,700), in warships (107 against 13) and in artillery pieces (11,200 against 7,710). The only real deficiency of the Allies was in air power, where the Luftwaffe had the advantage. The real reason for Germany's success has to be sought, therefore, in vastly superior strategic thinking. Hitler's campaign was based on the '*Sichelschnitt*' (sickle cut) through the northern plains of France via the Ardennes, as explained above. According to Noakes and Pridham, 'It was perhaps the most brilliant military plan of modern times.'[207] The French, by contrast, were stuck in the mould of their First World War strategy. They assumed that any conflict with Germany would again be defensive and slow moving, a belief which was symbolized by the vast and ultimately useless Maginot Line, constructed at enormous expense between the wars.

By June 1940 Hitler had achieved in the West all his objectives but one – a satisfactory settlement with Britain. Hitler did not intend, at this stage, to undertake a fight to the finish with Britain: his first priority was the quest for Lebensraum in eastern Europe. In any case it might be possible to produce honourable peace terms. His interpretation of recent history was that Britain had always distanced itself from Europe unless it could rely upon a particular power to act as its 'continental sword'. The collapse of France had now removed this sword.

It would make sense, therefore, for Britain to resume its traditional position of neutrality and isolation. Hitler did everything possible to encourage this. He made a series of statements that he had no hostile intentions against Britain and that he certainly never intended to seek to destroy the British Empire.[208] When his peace approaches were contemptuously rejected by Churchill, the new British Prime Minister, Hitler considered that he had no option but to give the directive for the invasion of Britain. This would be the most ambitious Blitzkrieg to date, starting with an all-out preliminary air offensive, followed by a massive landing operation which would be codenamed 'Operation Sealion'.

The events of 1940–1 were to prove the first setback in Hitler's war. This was due in part to a lack of total commitment to the task which he had undertaken. He overestimated the possibility of reconciliation with Britain on the one hand while, on the other, underestimating the British capacity for resistance. The result was that Hitler seriously misused Germany's resources and undermined the whole purpose of Blitzkrieg. In the first place, he mismanaged the invasion plan. According to Craig, Goering's direction of the preliminary campaign to knock out resistance from the RAF was amateurish: he frittered away Germany's strength in the air by hitting too wide a variety of targets and not concentrating on British airfields.[209] Hitler's decision to go for British cities also contributed to the survival of the RAF in the early and crucial stage, making possible its eventual victory in the Battle of Britain. The RAF also had the advantage of more effective aircraft in the Spitfire and Hurricane, more experienced pilots, and a better warning system. Once the RAF had confirmed its superiority in the air by 1941, Hitler was forced to postpone Operation Sealion.

But, despite the failure of Hitler's plans, Britain posed no direct threat to Germany in 1941. It did not possess sufficient resources to engage in a major continental war and, in 1941, suffered a number of reverses which built Hitler's confidence to a new peak. The opportunity was, in a sense, unsought. Mussolini had made a series of disastrous mistakes in North Africa, Greece and Yugoslavia, resulting in temporary incursions by British troops. In order to consolidate Germany's southern flank and to rescue Mussolini from defeat, Hitler despatched Rommel to North Africa and German panzer divisions to the Balkans in 1941. Within weeks the British were forced back into Egypt and had to evacuate Greece and the Greek islands in the Mediterranean.

These reverses did not, however, make the defeat of Britain any more imminent. Hitler had already decided to approach the problem from a different angle and to unleash another Blitzkrieg, this time against Russia. In retrospect, this decision seems to be the ultimate in folly. Yet, at the time, it must have had a certain compelling logic. Ideologically, of course, Hitler had a long-standing urge to smash what he regarded as the centre of international Bolshevism and world Jewry – in his eyes synonymous evils. At the same time, Germany would at last achieve Lebensraum in eastern Europe, a design frequently mentioned in *Mein Kampf* and the *Second Book.* The defeat of Russia would also enable him to dominate the Eurasian land mass and accumulate sufficient strength to accomplish the next stage in his quest for world supremacy. Operation Barbarossa was therefore the culmination of all his previous policies – indeed, their logical fulfilment – even though it was introduced against the advice of his High Command.

One question is frequently asked about this decision. Why did Hitler open up a second front, thereby bringing into action a new enemy, before disposing of Britain? This could be seen as a monumental blunder, one which eventually cost Hitler the war. After all, he had once argued in 1939 that 'we can oppose Russia only when we are free in the West'.[210] On the other hand, it has been argued that he took the decision to invade Russia precisely because he had not managed to defeat Britain. According to Weinberg, this was 'Hitler's answer to the challenge of England – as it had been Napoleon's'.[211] By means of another swift and decisive campaign Hitler was certain that he could deprive Britain of any lingering hope that she might in future be able to use a 'continental sword'. There would also be wider advantages. As early as 31 July 1940 Hitler told his army chiefs: 'If Britain's hope in Russia is destroyed, her hope in America will disappear also, because the elimination of Russia will enormously increase Japan's power in the Far East.'[212]

But there is another possibility: that Operation Barbarossa was a pre-emptive strike against the Soviet Union which was becoming a looming military threat. Stalin had taken the decision during the 1930s to prepare for an offensive war at a time of his choosing and had accordingly stockpiled huge quantities of weapons. If this was the case, and recent historical research suggests that it was a major factor in Stalin's Five-Year Plans, then Hitler must have deduced Stalin's intention, or even picked up some of the details through German intelligence. It must have seemed to Hitler that by 1941 the gap was growing rapidly between the military strength of the two powers. Stalin would clearly attack eventually and the best chance Germany had of taking on the Soviet Union was by getting in first, especially since Stalin was prepared to go to great lengths to avoid a war until he was ready. Besides, Hitler's hands were free at the time: France had been smashed and Britain, although undefeated, was unable to bring the war to the continent. The most appropriate time for another major campaign was therefore 1941.

On 18 December 1940, Hitler therefore issued Directive no. 21 for Operation Barbarossa and ordered that 'The German armed forces must be prepared to crush Soviet Russia in a quick campaign even before the end of the war against England.' The invasion was delayed until June 1941 to enable Hitler to rescue Mussolini in the Balkans and North Africa. When it came it was to be a Blitzkrieg on an unprecedented scale, consisting of 4 million men, 3,300 tanks and 5,000 aircraft. At first the Germans encountered little resistance and advanced more rapidly than had any previous invasion force in history. Russian resistance folded and, by September 1941, the Germans held a line extending from the outskirts of Leningrad to the Black Sea. Hitler now intended to capture the rest of European Russia at least as far as the Urals.

By the end of 1941 Hitler had reached the peak of his power in Europe. Blitzkrieg had been applied in a succession of waves, each more extensive than the last. Poland had been crushed in the initial assault of 1939, followed in 1940 by western Europe. His attempt to apply it to Britain had failed, but the second Blitzkrieg in the east produced even more stunning results than the first. There was, however, one major shortcoming, which was ultimately to prove fatal to the Third Reich. Operation Barbarossa had not fulfilled the objective of finishing off the Soviet Union by the end of 1941, a serious failure since Blitzkrieg depended on instant victory. Thus, although Hitler's mastery over Europe seemed formidable, the tide was about to turn against Germany. From 1942 onwards Hitler's lightning wars were transformed into a more prolonged and destructive war of attrition – Total War.

Europe under Nazi rule, 1939–45

After his conquests, Hitler constructed a Reich which was intended to last a thousand years. To ensure this, he considered it essential to build a 'New Order' by which Germany would effectively dominate Europe. The two main elements of Hitler's scheme were, according to Rich, the purification of the Germanic race and the extension of Germany's frontiers in search of Lebensraum in the east.[213] Taken together, these brought about the greatest upheaval in Europe since the collapse of the Roman Empire.

Map 5 shows the extent of Hitler's domination of Europe by 1942 (see p. 250). The details of this are dealt with, country by country, in Chapters 6 and 7, but it would be useful here to draw the various threads together. The first area to be incorporated was Austria, by the Anschluss of 1938 (see p. 318). This was followed by the dismantling of Czechoslovakia, with the absorption of the Sudetenland in 1938 and Bohemia in 1939, the latter as a German protectorate under Heydrich. Slovakia was allowed to become a puppet state under the leadership of Tiso (see pp. 372–4) until direct military occupation by the Germans after the 1944 rebellion.

The situation in south-eastern Europe was highly complex, involving a combination of Italian rule, German 'rescue missions', puppet regimes and outright conquest. On the whole, Hitler was content initially to allow Italian domination of the Balkans and the eastern Mediterranean. Albania, for example, came under Mussolini's rule in 1939. His attempt to subdue Greece, however, failed and in 1941 the Germans had to take over and partition the country. Yugoslavia was also crushed and divided, the southern part being allocated to Italy, Serbia coming under German military occupation and Croatia establishing another puppet government, this time under Pavelic. The other states of the area were more careful or fortunate. Hungary allied herself to Germany until 1944, when Horthy was replaced by Szálasi's pro-Nazi Arrow Cross regime (see p. 32). Bulgaria's alliance with Germany was transformed into almost total Nazi control over Prince Cyril in 1943. Romania's connection with the Reich was similarly strengthened by Antonescu (see pp. 349–51). The greatest single problem for Hitler in southern Europe was the collapse of Italy in 1943 and the need to pour German troops into the north to prop up Mussolini's new Salò Republic. Between 1943 and 1945 Axis co-operation and alliances throughout the region were therefore replaced by total German domination.

Western Europe came under Nazi rule in 1940. Denmark experienced least upheaval; she retained her parliamentary monarchy until 1943, although under German 'protection'. Norway was jointly administered by a German commissioner, Terboven, and a Norwegian collaborator, Quisling (see pp. 377–8). The Netherlands were ruled by Reichs Commissioner Seyss-Inquart, who had previously been Governor of Austria, and Belgium by General von Falkenhausen. Luxembourg was, by 1942, incorporated directly into the Reich, along with the Belgian districts of Eupen and Malmédy and the French provinces of Alsace and Lorraine. Finally, France herself was divided after being conquered in 1940. Two-thirds, including Paris and the Atlantic coast, were placed under General von Stülpnagel. The rest was allowed to establish a puppet state under Pétain and Laval, based in Vichy (see pp. 385–6).

The greatest changes came in eastern Europe. Poland was conquered, plundered and destroyed in 1939. This was followed by an attack on the Baltic states (see pp. 336–7) and on Russia. Part of Poland – West Prussia, Southern Silesia and Posen – was incorporated directly into the Reich. The rest formed the General Government of Occupied Polish Territories under the brutal administration of Hans Frank. The second wave of German conquests (1941–2) brought further reorganization, this time in Russia. Two vast new territories were set up, under Rosenberg. The first was Ostland, comprising the Baltic states and White Russia, the second the Ukraine. There were plans for two more, Muscovy and the Caucasus, which would have accounted for Russia up to the Urals. The whole of eastern Europe, therefore, was set aside for future German expansion in accordance with Hitler's designs in *Mein Kampf* and the *Second Book*.

All areas under Nazi rule were intended for maximum exploitation by the Third Reich. The basic justification for Lebensraum in eastern Europe was that the low productivity and cultural achievements of the 'inferior races' deprived them of a right to separate statehood and territory. Hitler considered that the Slavs possessed far more land than their history warranted; Frank observed that the Poles 'have no historical mission whatever in this part of the world'.[214] Russia was to be set aside for the resettlement of up to 100 million Germans once the rapid population increase, projected by Hitler, had begun. Meanwhile, the peoples of the occupied countries of both eastern and western Europe would be used to enhance Germany's war effort. A severe shortage of labour had by 1942 become apparent within the Reich. Albert Speer, Minister for Armaments and War Production from 1942, managed to increase economic growth and the production of war *matériel* by deliberately promoting foreign labour, both voluntary and forced. By 1944 there were at least 7.5 million foreign civilians working in Germany. A constant supply of labour was ensured by mass deportations. In some cases slave workers were provided by the Plenipotentiary for Labour, Sauckel, for use by the Reich's industrial and armaments firms. According to evidence produced at the Nuremberg Trial in 1945, eastern workers like the Tartars and Kirghiz 'collapsed like flies from bad housing, the poor quality and insufficient quantity of food, overwork and insufficient rest'. Western workers were also badly treated. Krupp of Essen kept its French workers 'in dog kennels, urinals and in old baking houses. The dog kennels were three feet high, nine feet long, six feet wide. Five men slept in each of them.'[215] While people were exploited, the national wealth of the occupied states was systematically plundered. Gold and foreign holdings were removed from all the banks, and industrial produce was requisitioned on a massive scale. It has been estimated that France provided Germany with 60 billion marks and 74 per cent of her steel, while Belgium and the Netherlands lost two-thirds of their national incomes.[216]

The Nazi occupation of Europe was carried out with an unprecedented contempt for the subject peoples. This was due primarily to the racial emphasis of Hitler's rule. There were two distinct aspects here. One was a search for racial purity for the German people. This was entrusted to the SS; Himmler was made head of the RKFDV (the Reich Commissariat for the Strengthening of German Nationhood). One of the results was the large-scale kidnapping of foreign children who fitted the Aryan stereotype. At the other end of the scale were Europe's 'lower orders', including Poles and Russians, considered to be fit only for forced labour. According to Bormann, in 1942, 'The Slavs are to work for us. In so far as we don't need them, they may die. Therefore compulsory vaccination and German health services are superfluous.'[217] At the bottom of Hitler's descending racial scheme came the Jews.

Contempt for the subject peoples bred an unimaginable brutality, evidence of which came to light in 1945 and 1946. Terror was made systematic through the extension of the SS and the SD and through basic legislation. Two examples of the latter, both in 1941, were the 'Commissar and Jurisdiction Decrees' for Russia, and the 'Night and Fog Decree' for the West. The authorities were provided with unlimited powers to uphold security, including the use of torture, arbitrary arrest and summary execution. Large-scale atrocities against the subject peoples were all too common. Three examples will suffice. In 1941, 100,000 civilians in Kharkov were forced to work all day digging a huge pit and were then machine-gunned into it. The reason was that the German authorities felt that they were a threat to the levels of available foodstocks. In 1942 all the men of the town of Lidice, in Bohemia, were executed and the children and women sent to concentration camps. This was in retaliation for the assassination of Heydrich, the Governor of Bohemia. A similar event occurred in 1944 when the inhabitants of Oradour-sur-Glâne, in southern France, were herded into the local church and barns and burned alive as a punishment for resistance activity. It was later discovered to be the wrong village. Vast numbers of people died in various camps, including over four million Soviet prisoners-of-war. Many camps, especially in Poland, became extermination factories as part of Hitler's scheme for altering the racial composition of Europe. Auschwitz, for example, killed over one million Jews, Treblinka 700,000, Belzec 600,000, Sobibor 250,000, Maidenek 200,000 and Kulmhof 152,000. Among the most horrific of all the Nazi activities were the appalling medical experiments carried out without anaesthetic by the likes of Josef Mengele at Auschwitz. As Foot writes, these 'did not advance human knowledge in any useful way whatever; unless it is useful to know how nasty man can be to man'.[218]

The very awfulness of Nazi occupation implies a high degree of efficiency. In one respect this is true; the regime took human extermination to unprecedented levels. There were, however, severe administrative problems which prevented Hitler from coming even close to establishing uniform control over Europe. There was no overall plan, merely a series of local *ad hoc* expedients, usually lacking any central co-ordination or control. The basic problem was Hitler's own withdrawal from active administration to involve himself in the conduct of the war from the remoteness of Wolfsschanze in East Prussia. As in Germany itself numerous administrative conflicts developed from the chaos of the conquered areas. Four examples can be cited. The first was France where there was an increasingly complex overlap of authority. The second was Norway, which saw a major conflict between Terboven and Quisling. Third, Poland was the scene of a bitter clash between the new Governor, Hans Frank, and Reich officials like Goering and Himmler, both of whom tried to interfere with policy decisions and administrative detail. Finally, Rosenberg had much the same problem in his attempt to run the Ukraine. As he did with all political disputes, Hitler tended to ignore complaints and allow his subordinates to settle things among themselves. Overall, Hitler's policy towards the east was applied haphazardly and with an almost total lack of underlying discipline. At a conference held in July 1941, Hitler argued for initial caution and for concealing the true intention of Nazism in Russia for as long as possible in order to ease and hasten the conquest: 'we do not want to make any people into enemies prematurely and unnecessarily'. Germany's conduct towards the conquered area, he continued, should be 'first to dominate it, second to administer it, and third, to exploit it'. As events turned out in Russia and elsewhere in Europe, the occupying forces, while ruthless, frequently lacked discipline and purpose, therefore going directly against Hitler's own instructions. The result was administrative confusion and the alienation of huge sections of the population. In Russia the Great Patriotic War was in part provoked by unnecessary German excesses, while in other countries the occupying authorities had to deal with an ever increasing problem of resistance movements.

Total war and the contraction of the Third Reich, 1942–5

From the beginning of 1942 there were indications that the character of Hitler's war was changing. In declaring war on the United States he involved Germany against the world's greatest industrial power, while military reverses in Russia and North Africa severely tested the German economy for the first time.

The initiative for involving Germany in a conflict against the United States came from Berlin, the reverse of Washington's decision to enter the First World War. This is generally seen as one of the most irrational of Hitler's acts, and was taken without consultation with his military staff. Hitler displayed total ignorance of the United States, believing the whole nation to be deeply corrupted by its ethnic mixture and 'permanently on the brink of revolution'. But why provoke a new conflict? Why not dispose of Britain and Russia first? There is a case for saying that Hitler extended the war in order to redress the failure of the previous stage, just as the attack on Russia had been supposed to hasten the end of Britain's involvement. It is possible that Hitler's reasoning was that the United States could be expected to enter the struggle eventually – clearly this would be another major problem for Germany. On the other hand, this would also upgrade the alliance between Germany and Japan since the latter would attack British and American interests in the Far East and the Pacific. This would be of vital importance, for it would divert US attention from Europe for long enough to enable Hitler to complete the destruction of Russia and to force a settlement on Britain. There would therefore be no repetition of 1918, when US troops had broken the deadlock on the western front and tipped the balance in favour of the Allies. It was crucial to ensure that Japan did not withdraw from the war prematurely. Hence, according to Jäckel, 'Japan had to do more than enter the war. It had to be kept from pulling out before victory had been won in Europe.'[219] This was a serious miscalculation by Hitler. President Roosevelt made the decision to concentrate as much on the war in Europe as on Japan, for fear that Russia and Britain might be defeated, leaving the USA to face Germany alone. All Hitler had succeeded in doing, therefore, was to strengthen the war effort against him on the periphery – at sea and in North Africa – at the same time as his life and death struggle in Russia.

During the course of 1942 and 1943 the Wehrmacht suffered a series of reverses which turned the tide of the Second World War. The worst disasters occurred in Russia, with the surrender of Paulus at Stalingrad in one of the most crucial battles in modern history. But there were also crises in North Africa, with the defeat of Rommel at El Alamein. Indeed, the commitment in North Africa had a crucial effect on the campaign in Russia since it prevented Hitler from pouring in sufficient reinforcements to counter the Russian recovery. It also gave the Western Allies a change to attack Hitler's 'fortress of Europe' via its most vulnerable point of access. The result was to be the collapse of Mussolini's regime, the withdrawal of most of Italy from the war and the need for Hitler to deploy, in support of Mussolini's Salò Republic, divisions which were desperately needed in Russia.

Meanwhile, Germany was also failing to win control over the sea and air. At first, Hitler's emphasis was on creating a large surface fleet to challenge Britain's world naval supremacy. Eventually, however, he was converted by his naval commanders to a more specialized form of warfare based on U-boat attacks on merchant shipping in the Atlantic. But, despite heavy losses inflicted on Allied ships, Hitler had, in effect, lost the battle for the Atlantic by late 1943. This was of vital importance since Hitler was unable to prevent a massive influx of supplies from the United States to Britain under Lend–Lease. He also failed to disrupt the supply route via Murmansk through which the Western Allies made a significant contribution to the Russian war effort.

Aerial warfare affected Germany more directly. The failure of Operation Sealion was due largely to the victory of the RAF in the Battle of Britain and to a rapid increase in British aircraft production. With the entry of the United States into the war came heavier saturated bombing of German targets. This was conducted round the clock, by the United States Air Force during the day and the RAF at night. A deliberate attempt was made to destroy German cities, and hence German morale, and also to knock out key industrial centres. The former included Hamburg, Cologne, Essen, Dortmund, Berlin and Dresden. The main industrial targets were ballbearing plants, armaments factories and communications networks. Two arguments have been advanced as to whether this bombing made a significant difference to the outcome of the war. One is that the Armaments Minister, Albert Speer, pulled together the German economy in 1944 for a final effort; this counteracted the effect of Allied bombing, as German armaments production increased during the period of heaviest destruction. Thus, criticism is often levelled against Bomber Command for, in effect, conducting a war on civilians. On the other hand, it could be argued that, although the attacks of 1944 may not have led to a dramatic decrease in production, they did, nevertheless, prevent the sort of increase which might otherwise have occurred. In addition, catastrophic damage was inflicted by the Allies on Germany's transport and communications network; this was far more important than the destruction of cities in breaking the Nazi war effort.

By 1944 Hitler's 'Fortress of Europe', won by Blitzkrieg, was being breached from three main directions. The first battering ram was applied by the Red Army, which conquered eastern Europe during the second half of 1944 and the early months of 1945. Meanwhile, the Western Allies were hammering at Mussolini's Salò Republic and, in June 1944, opened up a third front with the invasion of France. Hitler now became increasingly irrational, living on false hopes and drawing comfort from the example of Frederick the Great, the eighteenth-century Prussian king who had held off, in the Seven Years War, a combination of Russia, Austria and France. Hitler firmly believed that sooner or later Russia and the Western Allies could be induced to attack each other. 'All of the coalitions in history have disintegrated sooner or later. The only thing is to wait for the right moment.'[220]

He did manage two last-minute successes. He defeated, in September 1944, a British airborne invasion at Arnhem which attempted to capture the bridgeheads of the lower Rhine. He also came close in December 1944 to breaking through the Allied lines at the Ardennes in what is usually called the Battle of the Bulge. But these did no more than slow down the Anglo-American advance. The Western Allies now conformed to Eisenhower's strategy of a slow and methodical thrust on Germany across the whole front rather than the British preference for a quick advance on Berlin. The result was that the Russians reached Berlin first. Hitler committed suicide on 30 April 1945 after entrusting the succession to Commander-in-Chief Admiral von Dönitz. On 7 May the German High Command surrendered: 'The Third Reich had outlasted its founder by just one week.'[221]

Hitler as a war leader

How effective was Hitler as a military leader? We have seen that there were occasions on which Hitler had considerable success, usually in pushing the High Command in a direction where it was reluctant to move. He was especially adept at the use of Blitzkrieg tactics against Poland in 1939 and against the Low Countries and France in 1940. On the other hand, Hitler also made major blunders in military organization and strategy. Perhaps the best evidence for this is provided by four men who served under him and were directly involved in the war effort: all were highly critical. One was Hitler's official war diarist, Percy Ernst Schramm, who subsequently published a detailed account of Hitler's personal life and military leadership, based on first-hand observation. The other three were generals in the High Command: Manstein, Halder and Jodl. Halder, who replaced Beck as Chief of General Staff in 1938, wrote a totally condemnatory tract in 1949 entitled *Hitler as War Lord*. Jodl produced a memorandum in 1946, shortly before being executed at Nuremberg for war crimes. Even allowing for the fact that each of these men had reason to distance himself from Hitler, the combined weight of criticism is formidable.

On the question of Hitler's direction of the war, Halder observed that the Führer destroyed the High Command as the apex of military organization. 'He may have had a gift for mass political leadership. He had none for the leadership of a military staff.'[222] Indeed, his divide-and-rule policy 'destroyed a well organized system of military command which no true leader would ever have given up'. According to Jodl, Hitler allowed little influence and 'resented any form of counsel regarding the major decisions of the war. He did not care to hear any other points of view.' Instead, he had 'an almost mystical conviction of his own infallibility as a leader of the nation and of the nation and of the war'. Schramm maintained that Hitler constantly interfered in military operations. He 'violated the tried and proven principle that subordinate commanders must be allowed a certain limited freedom because they are in a better position to evaluate the prevailing circumstances in their sector of the front and might be able, through swift action, to deal with a sudden crisis'. Overall, Schramm added, 'Hitler had already made himself dictator of state and society during peacetime. The war consolidated his dictatorship over the military.'[223]

Consequently, Hitler can be blamed personally for all the main strategic blunders. Schramm argued that Hitler's early success was based on huge risks which, even in retrospect, could be considered irresponsible. As the situation deteriorated he was incapable of taking a balanced decision and never saw the need for organized military retreat; he was 'unable to bring himself to make militarily necessary decisions such as the evacuation of untenable outposts'.[224] This can be supported by reference to a range of decisions in the latter phase of the war, from his refusal to let Paulus pull out of Stalingrad to his determination to hold all German outposts in France against enveloping Allied attacks. Hitler found the defensive role utterly distasteful. Instead of an orderly contraction of all his front lines, he adopted what Schramm called a 'wave break doctrine', whereby positions had to be held even after the enemy had swept past and isolated them; they could always be used as advance posts during the German recovery which Hitler hoped would occur as a result of his determination and willpower. Eventually he lost all sense of perspective. According to Halder, 'The delicate interplay between yielding pliancy and iron determination which is the essence of the art of generalship was impossible to this man, who could be termed the very incarnation of brute will.'[225] Almost exactly the same conclusion was arrived at by Manstein: 'Ultimately, to the concept of the art of war, he opposed that of crude force, and the full effectiveness of this force was supposed to be guaranteed by the strength of will behind it.'[226] Halder drew comparisons between Hitler and men of greater reason and more limited and practical objectives in what he regarded as the true

7 Adolf Hitler, c.1940 (© Popperfoto/Getty)

German military tradition: he cited, especially, von Moltke and Bismarck. He concluded of Hitler, 'this demoniac man was no soldier leader in the German sense. And above all he was not a great General.'[227]

THE HOLOCAUST

It has taken nearly over half a century for the Holocaust to be given its true perspective. Major changes have now occurred in its interpretation, which this book aims to reflect. The growth of interest has been phenomenal: more books are now published each year on the Holocaust than on any other historical subject: about 300 in English alone, compared with approximately fifty on another stalwart, the Third Reich.[228]

There are several reasons for the limitations of earlier perceptions. They were probably heavily influenced by priorities during and immediately after the war. It is now known that the Allies knew a great deal about what was happening in the extermination camps – but they did not divulge it since this would have endangered their code-breaking operations.[229] It has also been shown that the methods used by the International Military Tribunal at Nuremberg hindered a full understanding of the scope of the Holocaust through its use of 'illustrative minimum' evidence to secure safe convictions.[230] Then, over a longer period, knowledge about the Holocaust was limited by the impact of the Cold War and the need for West Germany's co-operation in defence agreements against the Soviet Union. Similarly, the Soviet emphasis was on the brutality of capitalism generally rather than the targeting of a minority for which it had little sympathy itself. The late 1980s, however, saw the end of the Communist regimes in eastern Europe, with their perceived threat to the West and their suppression of information about the war years. As a result, more details have emerged on the Holocaust as a European as well as a German problem. Although Germany has fully accepted primary responsibility, there has also been more emphasis on the collaborative nature of the Holocaust, possibly encouraged by the search for reconciliation within the context of an expanding European Union.[231] For the first time, Europe has tried to grasp the enormity of an event which stands out even in that continent's proclivity for violence and barbarism. In the words of Diner: 'Today the Holocaust stands at the negative core of European self-understanding.'[232]

Outline 1939–45

Indeed, the Holocaust was the climax of a long history of anti-Semitism in most European countries, refined to its very essence in Nazi Germany after 1933. But it was in the period from 1939 onwards that anti-Semitism entered the phase of genocide. During the course of that year there were three indicators for the future. The first was a threat made by Hitler in a speech to the Reichstag on 30 January in which declared that a world war would bring the 'annihilation of the Jewish race in Europe'.[233]

Second, his regime took the first step towards achieving this by invading Poland on 1 September. Then, three months later, authorization was given for the gassing of mental patients within Germany.

Although there was, as yet, no immediate acceleration of actual killing, several intermediate measures were taken to make this possible when the time came. Decrees were issued in November 1939 making the wearing of the Star of David compulsory for all Jews in the *Generalgouvernement*. This was accompanied by the establishment of ghettos in Poland: the first, in October 1939, was soon to be followed by Lodz in the following February and Warsaw in October. 1940 also saw the development of plans to construct new types of camps in German-occupied Poland. Auschwitz was authorized by Himmler in April 1940 and this, in turn, provided the model for others which followed from 1941.

But the real accelerator of genocidal policy was the German invasion of the Soviet Union in June 1941. As the Wehrmacht and Waffen SS penetrated the Baltic states, Belorussia, the Ukraine and Russia itself, mass shootings of Jewish civilians were carried out by Einsatzgruppen of the SS and police units of the Wehrmacht. But this approach soon ran into difficulties. It diverted personnel and resources from the task of finishing off the Red Army and it adversely affected the morale of German troops. It was also difficult to keep the killings secret from the German population, a condition to which Himmler attached some importance. Hence the Reich now moved to another method – the use of gas chambers and high-temperature crematoria.

A key development in the transition was the Wannsee Conference; held on 20 January 1942, this was organized by Eichmann, presided over by Heydrich, and attended by five high-ranking SS officials, along with representatives of seven ministries of state and party offices. There had been a six-month delay since Goering's original order to Heydrich to prepare a 'Final Solution' to the 'Jewish question' and problems experienced in the meantime had raised questions about the effectiveness of the Einsatzgruppen. The Wannsee Conference therefore confirmed a process which had already started – the move to industrialized rather than military genocide.

Between 1941 and 1942 new extermination camps were opened at Birkenau (attached to Auschwitz), Belzec, Sobibor, Treblinka and Maidanek, all fitted with gas chambers; similar facilities were provided to some of the concentration camps in Germany itself. The mass deportation of German Jews began in October 1941, followed by the clearing of all Polish ghettos between 1942 and 1943. Developments in central and eastern Europe had a direct impact on German-occupied western Europe, as Jews were transported to the camps from occupied France, Belgium and the Netherlands. The Nazi regime also applied pressure to Germany's allies – Slovakia, Hungary, Romania and Italy – to co-operate with extermination programme; Northern Italy was occupied in 1943 and Hungary in March 1944. Figure 7 provides a summary of the numbers of Jews killed in the Holocaust.[234] The totals include lowest and highest figures, recent estimates for the Soviet Union having been revised upwards.

What is generally considered to have been the most horrific series of events in human history has inevitably generated controversy, particularly on the issues of why it occurred and who was involved.

Origins and development of the Holocaust

One particular issue periodically raises its head: denial either that the Holocaust took place at all or that it took a particular form. The vast majority of historians accept that the evidence for the Holocaust is overwhelming. But a small minority has questioned the whole basics of the Holocaust, including the extensive use of gas chambers. Their views have come under counter-attacks from historians like Lipstadt,[235] who seek to 'expose falsehood and hate'.[236]

A more genuine historical debate is whether the Holocaust was the logical fulfilment of the Nazi policy of anti-Semitism or the result not of careful planning but rather of the failure of alternative strategies. In considering whether the extermination of the Jews was always intended, or whether it emerged institutionally, few historians have seriously attempted to deny the ultimate responsibility of Hitler. The disagreement between them has arisen over the means by which his anti-Semitism was converted into the 'Final Solution'.

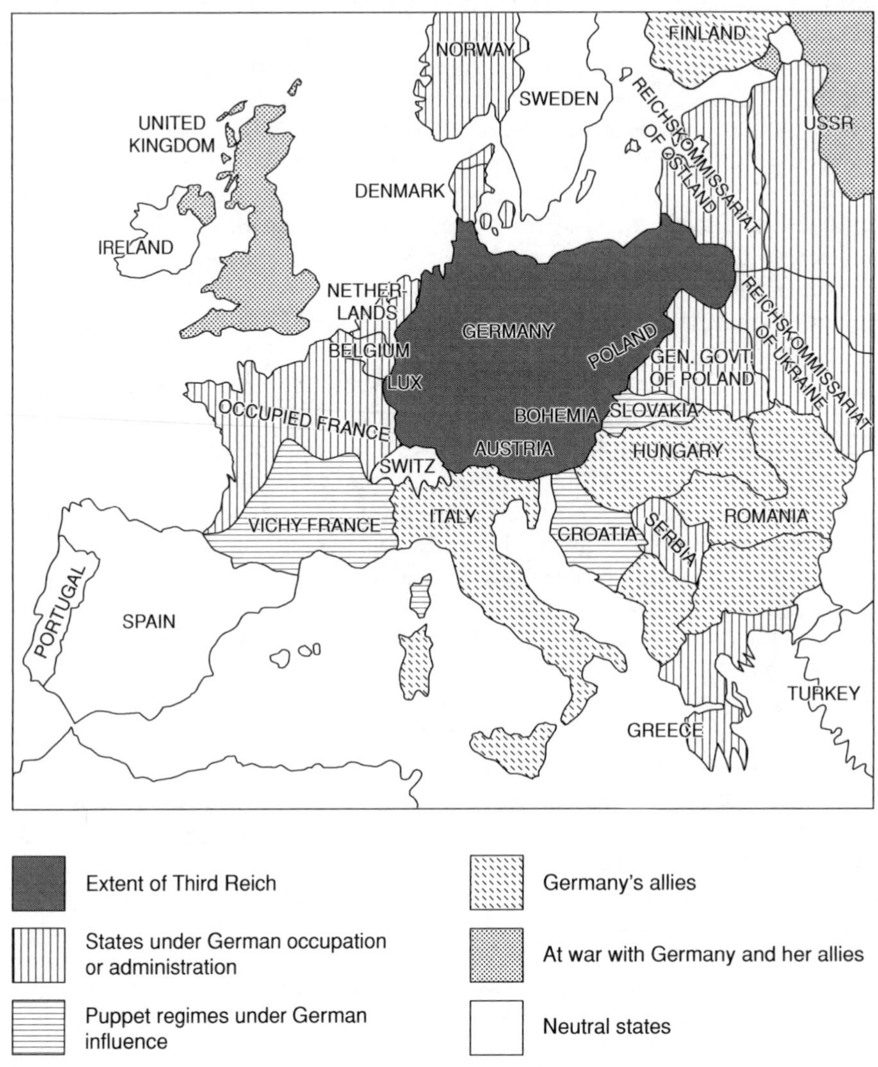

Map 5 Europe under Nazi influence by 1942

Some historians, collectively described as 'intentionalists', maintain that the Holocaust can be attributed to Hitler's Führer state as one of the functions of a personalized totalitarian regime. Fleming, Jäckel, Hillgruber and others argue that Hitler implemented the decision in the summer of 1941. The reason was that the collapse of Russia in the wake of the German invasion seemed inevitable and this was the perfect chance to achieve a long-held ambition. Goering therefore ordered Heydrich to bring about 'a complete solution of the Jewish question within the German sphere of influence in Europe'. Although no document has ever been found linking this order directly to Hitler, it makes no logical sense to deny his ultimate authorship. Dawidowicz places this in a more general context, arguing that there was a gradual escalation of persecution from the nineteenth century, through to Hitler's ideas in the 1920s, then to implementation in the 1930s, and ultimately to extermination.

Most recently – and forcefully – Goldhagen has argued that there are four clear precursors in Hitler's thought and speeches for the Holocaust. First, 'Hitler expressed his obsessive eliminationist racist antisemitism from his earliest days in public life': this can be seen explicitly in *Mein Kampf*. Second, on coming to power, Hitler 'turned the eliminationist antisemitism into unprecedented radical measures'. Third, in 1939 he 'repeated many times his prophecy, indeed his promise: the war would provide him with the opportunity to exterminate European Jewry'. This, finally, he proceeded to do 'when the moment was ripe'. Hence, Goldhagen concludes, 'The genocide was the outgrowth not of Hitler's moods, not of local initiative, not of the impersonal hand of structural obstacles, but of Hitler's ideal to eliminate all Jewish power.'[237]

Some historians have given the Holocaust a more 'structuralist' or 'functionalist' approach, attributing it to a sequence of administrative actions rather than to an overall design by the Führer. Originally put by Hilberg in the early 1960s,[238] this has since been taken further by Mommsen and Broszat. The structuralist case is that mass extermination was not the 'solution' originally intended: rather, it was adopted after the failure of plans to resettle Jews in Madagascar and Siberia. The latter was actually started after the invasion of Russia in 1941 but was then blocked by the growing Russian resistance to the German advance. Since Poland and the western areas of the Soviet Union contained the largest concentrations of Jewish people in the world, the Nazi conquest was being impeded. The regime therefore sought a new and swifter solution, which was also to become the 'Final Solution', first through the mass killings by the Einsatzgruppen, then in the newly constructed extermination camps. According to Broszat, therefore, 'the liquidation of the Jews began not solely as the result of an ostensible will for extermination but also as a "way out" of a blind alley into which the Nazis had manoeuvred themselves'.[239] As for 'the widespread assumption' that genocide 'rested on a clear directive from Hitler', Mommsen argues that this is based on 'a misunderstanding of the decision-making process in the Führer's headquarters' and that 'the idea that Hitler set the genocide policy in motion by means of a direct instruction can be completely rejected'.[240]

The intentionalist–structuralist debate on the Holocaust is part of the broader one on the nature of the Nazi state, already covered earlier in this book. It is no coincidence that the intentionalists also argue that the structure of dictatorship in Germany depended on the personality of Hitler himself and that he deliberately exploited any weaknesses and contradictions within it to his own advantage. He would therefore have chosen the time, the method and the institutions for the implementation of a scheme of extermination which had always existed in his mind. The structuralists, by contrast, see consistency in the weakness of Hitler's response to institutional chaos and the disorganized way in which the Holocaust was finally implemented. This makes it possible to conclude that the Holocaust was the administrative response to the failure of earlier policies.

Perhaps the gap between the two arguments is greater than it need be: both can be employed in a substantial overlap. Out of power, Hitler initially thought in terms of genocide – but, once in power, moderated this in order to broaden his support. This explains why he limited early measures to the Nuremberg Laws and even ordered the removal of discriminatory public notices at the time of the 1936 Berlin Olympics.

It is true that there was a violent acceleration in Kristallnacht (1938). Nevertheless, there was no inexorable move towards extermination. Furthermore, during the first two years of the war, Hitler hoped for a possible peace with Britain and did not at this stage wish to antagonize the United States. Even for the period of mass killing there is scope for a 'moderate functionalist' approach. Bartov, for example, sees the 'mechanics of decision-making and organization' as functionalist, while intentionalism can be applied to the involvement of the higher Nazi echelons – including the 'legitimizing' role of Hitler himself.[241] Browning agrees that Hitler 'signalled his expectations' and that subsequent implementation was by a form of 'consensus' politics. At the same time, he reasserts the central importance of Himmler, as the main interpreter of Hitler's wishes.[242] This would fit other interpretations as to the growing importance of the SS in the Nazi system – at least until late 1944 and 1945 when Himmler's fall from favour coincided with the declining importance of the SS. Overall, Browning considers that there is now a greater consensus on the main themes of the Holocaust's origins. There is, for example, less support for any 'big bang theory' and more for 'prolonged' and 'incremental' stages; at the same time, some stages were more 'pivotal' or 'decisive' than others.

Of particular importance in the development of the Holocaust was the Second World War. Although it may not, as the intentionalist argument implies, have provided the original motive for the killing of millions of Jews, it certainly intensified and accelerated the process; almost all recent studies of the Holocaust have emphasized the role of the war in this way. Bartov applies the connection more broadly: 'we now recognize that most cases of genocide and "ethnic cleansing" in the twentieth century were carried out within the context of destructive and bitter wars'.[243] Of course, the Holocaust would still have been inconceivable without an underlying intent: it would have been a step too far as a progression from nothing. The Nazi regime at peace had already given anti-Semitism a 'legal' structure, imposing a range of restrictions on the Jewish population of the Reich. There had also been an undercurrent of extreme violence in both attitudes and public outbursts, exemplified by the propaganda promoted by Streicher and the organized 'spontaneity' of Kristallnacht. At war, however, the same regime was able to bring to bear all the forces which had previously been under at least some form of constraint.

In *ideological* terms, war provided the opportunity to give literal meaning to Hitler's concept of 'struggle', so that overcoming 'race enemies' eventually became more important than defeating the Allies. The *military* dimension brought conquest and the exposure of populations to the SS and Wehrmacht, while the invasion of Russia had implications also for countries already conquered in the West; according to Diner, 'From the eastern killing fields in 1941, the disposition for genocide moved westward, paradoxically reversing the direction of German expansion.'[244] The military impetus was followed up by *organizational* changes which gave new direction to genocidal policies. Within the Reich the war increased the power of the SS at the expense of the Nazi state; externally, this became increasingly influential in the network of satellite states carved out of Germany's conquests between 1939 and 1941. Under the auspices of the SS, the processes of Lebensraum and genocide became ever more closely linked. Reorganization also affected Germany's allies, as pressure was brought to bear from 1943 onwards for the settlement of Jewish 'questions' in a manner devised by the SS structure. This was made possible by *technological* factors. Victory in war had brought German control over the railway network over central, western and – above all – eastern Europe. The extermination camps established in Poland were linked by rail to all parts of Nazi-occupied Europe, while the actual methods of destruction involved firms, like IG Farben, which had long been part of Germany's industrial infrastructure.

Compliance and complicity

An issue which has attracted increasing interest – and controversy – is the extent to which the measures of Holocaust were imposed by the Nazi regime on populations which had no say in the matter and, in most cases, very little knowledge of what was actually happening. This can be subdivided into the reactions of the German people within the Third Reich, and the reactions of peoples and regimes conquered by – or allied to – the Reich. In each case it needs to be asked whether people were *compliant*, in the sense of being obedient to a higher authority without necessarily co-operating with it, or *complicit* – in other words playing a more direct and active role within a structure provided by that authority or, in some cases, even by themselves. Again, we will find that the prevailing conditions of war were of paramount importance.

The German people?

German responsibility for the Holocaust has rarely been questioned, except by a small minority of historians and far-right activists who challenge its very existence. For most observers, the key issue is the precise meaning of 'German responsibility'. Was it the Nazi regime pursuing its objectives largely in isolation of the people it ruled? Or was there a broader responsibility through the participation of those people? As with debates on other aspects of Nazi Germany, there have been considerable swings of interpretation during the post-war period.

Traditional views certainly emphasize support for Hitler as a populist leader, which was strongly associated with an unconditional German surrender to authority. But the very strength of that authority meant that limits could be placed on popular participation in the regime's most extreme policies – and certainly on any opposition to them. Although support for racism and anti-Semitism may have been widespread, widespread acceptance of extermination did not necessarily follow. The Nazi regime had extensive control over policy and information relating to the Holocaust, which it chose to withhold from the majority of the population. Himmler, for example, gave explicit instructions for secrecy: he said of the extermination policy to an assembly of SS officials in 1943: 'Among ourselves, we can talk openly about it, though we can never speak a word of it in public . . . That is a page of glory in our history that never has been and never can be written'.[245] From this, it seems, knowledge of the exterminations, especially of the gas chambers, was withheld from the general public and confined, on a strictly need-to-know basis, to those who were actually involved. Although some rumours – even evidence – may have emerged in the process, would they have been widely believed? And if they had, how many would have been brave enough to defy the repressive organs of the SS and Gestapo? In these circumstances how could the majority of German people have been held directly responsible for the exterminations?

More recent views have, however, spread the extent of involvement and responsibility. But the question remains as to how far this should go. Dülffer endorses the view that the Holocaust was above all due to Hitler. 'But to recognize this is not to exculpate the hundreds of thousands of others who were involved in carrying out the Final Solution.'[246] All the German functionaries involved in the process should, therefore, also be held responsible. Goldhagen goes well beyond this. Hitler's ideal, he maintains, 'was broadly shared in Germany'.[247] The bureaucracy was heavily implicated and there was widespread collaboration with the SS from the civil service, business corporations and the army. This deprived Jews of their basic rights and assets, isolated them and eventually killed them. The whole process was made possible by the underlying strength of German anti-Semitism; this is dealt with further on p. 226. Such views have certainly had their impact. Although the true extent of knowledge about popular acceptance of the Holocaust will probably now never be known, it is now accepted that it was more extensive than was originally believed.

Nevertheless, the pendulum has partially returned. Goldhagen has come under some criticism for providing a monocausal explanation based on the especially deep-rooted nature of anti-Semitism in Germany. Other countries had experienced similar hatreds at the turn of the nineteenth century, including France, Austria and, above all, Tsarist Russia – which had produced the most brutal and destructive pogroms in Europe at the time. Germany, by contrast, had shown some progress in assimilating its Jews during the nineteenth century and especially under the Weimar Republic between 1918 and 1933. Why, therefore, should Germans have been overwhelmingly susceptible to eliminationist fanaticism? One point is particularly significant here. Rosenfeld argues that Goldhagen underestimates the importance of gas chambers by maintaining that the Holocaust would have continued even without them. Rosenfeld adds that, 'as a means of killing that minimised contact between victim and perpetrator', gas chambers 'should not have been necessary for a people thirsting to kill Jews en masse'.[248] Bearing in mind both the revelations of Goldhagen, and the strictures of his critics, a combined approach is preferable. On the one hand, the knowledge that the German population had of the Holocaust was wider than previously thought, especially through the complicity of the army and central or local administration. On the other hand, such knowledge and compliance were within the structures imposed upon the German people by the Nazi regime, not fired by a uniquely anti-Semitic German population.

Other regimes and peoples?

As we have already seen, there was considerable variation in the overall pattern of Germany's wartime control. Austria and the Czech lands had already been integrated into the Reich before the outbreak of war in 1939. Subsequent conquests between 1940 and 1941 had included Denmark, Norway, Belgium, Netherlands and France in the west; Poland, the Baltic States, Ukraine and part of Russia in the east; and Yugoslavia and Greece to the south. There were also collaborationist regimes and allies in Italy, Vichy France, Hungary, Romania, Slovakia and Croatia. Italy's involvement in the Holocaust is dealt with in Chapter 4 and the impact on the Soviet Union in Chapter 3.

The traditional view is that the Nazi regime imposed the Holocaust on other countries in Europe through its wartime control over them. In many cases the non-Jewish population suffered from appalling mistreatment as well, particularly in Poland. In this sense, the pre-war regimes were forced to radicalize their policies against the Jews under the impact of their own occupation. There have, however, been some changes in emphasis, with more evidence of popular involvement in the killing of Jews in some of these areas. This applies especially to eastern Europe, where political changes since 1989 have facilitated the growth of free research.

An overall perspective might now be as follows. Many countries had their own inter-war experience of anti-Semitism, particularly those which had experienced authoritarian dictatorship. When these countries came under German control or influence there was more local involvement than previously thought, leading to the possible extension of the epithet 'willing executioners' beyond Germany. On the other hand, it was the Nazi regime which provided both the opportunity and the structure for the killing of the Jews of these countries, under the powerful influence of wartime conditions. Most of Germany's occupied states or allies came somewhere between these two influences. There was, however, no uniform balance: each of the following specific examples was different.

Austria had been integrated into the Reich from 1938 and had therefore come under all the Nazi controls. Its people suffered as much as other parts of Germany from the impact of war and the SS were particularly active there. Yet Austria had a long-standing background of anti-Semitism, especially at the turn of the century. Karl Lueger, Georg von Schönerer and the Archduke Franz Ferdinand had all pursued a strong anti-Jewish agenda which had been among the earlier influences on the young Hitler; in this respect, therefore, Nazism had roots within Austria as well as Germany.

The other areas incorporated directly into the Reich were Bohemia and Moravia. Here there was far less evidence of earlier anti-Semitism. Jews had been assimilated in the Czech lands during and after the eighteenth-century Enlightenment, especially in Prague. During the period of the Czechoslovak Republic (1918–39) Jews had played an important part in the country's politics, culture and economy. Where anti-Semitism did appear, it was as a response to the Sudeten crisis of 1938, in which Sudeten Germans and some Czechs turned on the Jews as the instigators of their conflict with each other. Even so, the vast majority of the population of the Czech lands deplored what they regarded as imported anti-Semitic influences. From March 1939, however, they had no choice. With the German takeover, Bohemia and Moravia came to be seen as a prototype for the Nazi treatment of Jewish issues. There was some collaboration from the protectorate's state president, Hácha, but the more circumspect approach of Prime Minister Eliáš delayed the introduction of Nuremberg Laws in Bohemia for as long as possible.[249] Eventually they had to be enforced by full Nazification under Reichsprotektor von Neurath. This was intensified in 1941, with the arrival of Heydrich, who promptly ordered the execution of Eliáš for treason. Heydrich's assassination by members of the Czech resistance brought a reign of terror to the area which made the identification and deportation of Jews a priority. Meanwhile, Slovakia, the eastern portion of the former democracy, had been allowed to set up an autonomous state under the leadership of Cardinal Tiso. At first this co-operated with the Nazi regime, starting the deportation of its Jews early in 1942. Then, after the German defeat at Stalingrad, followed by the growing threat of Soviet advance, these initiatives were suspended and more direct measures were implemented by the Reich. Even so, Slovakia had a much weaker case than either Bohemia or Moravia for denying complicity in the Holocaust.

Poland, the first country to be conquered by the Nazi regime, has been the subject of greater controversy. On the one hand, Poland was one of the main victims of Nazi brutality. Its statehood was obliterated and, unlike Romania and Hungary, there was no continuity with the regime of the 1930s. Some historians, like Chodakiewicz, point to equality of victimhood between Poles and Jews, both of whom were despised by the Nazis as 'inferior races'.[250] This approach is part of a broader case frequently put for Polish non-collaboration with the Nazi regime. Against this there is at least some evidence of Polish co-operation with the Nazi system against the Jews. A pogrom was conducted at Jedwabne in 1941 by Polish civilians; according to J.T. Gross, the killings were not organized by the Germans, who had just taken over from Soviet occupation. Instead of showing resistance or non-collaboration, Polish society 'did not stand up particularly well' to either totalitarian regime.[251] There were twenty other similar incidents in north-eastern Poland, including Radzitów; the population accepted the harshest measures against Jews, regarding them as complicit in the former occupation by the Soviet regime. The Polish Police (or Blue Police) collaborated with the Nazi authorities, as did the *Baudienst* units who assisted Germans in clearing ghettos and performed other duties. Recent Polish historiography has revealed a willingness to come to terms with the possibility that Poles were both 'victimizers and victims'.[252] Yet, allowing for these two perspectives, the overall balance is tilted nearer to forced – or non-compliance than it is to complicity. There was less actual co-operation with Nazi measures against the Jews than in most other areas under German occupation and certainly less than in Germany's allies: Hungary, Romania and Slovakia.

Did Hungarian anti-Semitism have indigenous roots? Or was it imposed on a reluctant population under German influence? Probably a combination of both applies. During the period of the Dual Monarchy, Hungary had experienced less politicized anti-Semitism than Austria. But when the Treaty of Trianon had shorn away all the Slav territories, leaving Hungary as a bleeding Magyar rump, the Jewish minority suddenly became more obvious – and targetable. The first moves towards anti-Semitic legislation came in 1938, intensified in 1939 and 1941. Although their Nuremberg style was clearly influenced by Nazi Germany, the regime which introduced them was still independent; it therefore *allowed* itself to be influenced. Whether this applies also to the Holocaust in Hungary is more controversial. On the one hand, Braham maintains that the momentum for the killing of Hungary's Jews came inexorably from Germany. There is certainly evidence to support this. The Luther Memorandum from the German Foreign Ministry (October 1942) demanded more speed in the elimination of Jews from public life and their evacuation to the east, while Goebbels recorded in his diary in April 1943 that 'The Jewish question is being solved least satisfactorily by the Hungarians.'[253] The most important changes in the plight of the Jews occurred after German occupation of Hungary in March 1944 when, according to Braham, Eichmann 'finally had a chance to test his well-oiled death apparatus on a massive and grandiose scale in a lightning operation'.[254] Ránki, however, adopts a different approach. She maintains that 'Hungarian institutions participated fully in the deportation of the Jews' and that 'Hungarian society accommodated the "Final Solution" *because* they were immersed in decades of state-sponsored and social antisemitism'; this, together with 'antisemitic and extreme right-wing government policies *inevitably* led to the Holocaust in Hungary'.[255] There was also willing bottom-up complicity with the top-down directives. According to Ránki, 'the German occupational regime could clearly function only if it could rely absolutely upon the Hungarian civil service'.[256] It is not difficult to see why such contrasting views are possible. As will be seen in Chapter 7, Hungary herself oscillated between periods of sturdy autonomy, when there was some reluctance to follow German orders, and more direct co-operation with the Nazi regime. Prime ministers favouring an independent line were Teleki (1939–41), Kállay (1942–4) and Lakatos (August to October 1944), while those who co-operated actively with Germany were Imrédy (1938–9), Bárdossy (1941–2) and Sztójay (March to August 1944). President Horthy, who had also exercised some constraint, was replaced in October by the more fanatical Szálasi, who presided over the most destructive period of the Hungarian Holocaust.

Romania experienced a similar combination of internal and imported influences although, unlike Hungary, it was never subject to Nazi occupation. Anti-Semitism was ingrained in Romania's past: Jews had been denied full statehood in the 1866 Constitution and there had been a strong reluctance to grant basic rights to the Jewish minority in the new territories acquired in 1919. Anti-Semitic policies accelerated after 1929, with the growing influence of fascist elements on the regime of King Carol II (1930–40). Yet Romania's wartime experience was complex – resulting in the most instinctively anti-Semitic of the non-Nazi dictatorships doing less than some of its neighbours (certainly Hungary) to implement the Holocaust along Nazi lines. On the one hand, Romania was under less pressure than some of the other regimes and therefore had more room for manoeuvre. Under Antonescu Romania was, according to Ioanid, 'a fascist dictatorship and a totalitarian state'.[257] There was an enthusiastic application of anti-Jewish measures, involving deportations, summary executions, forced labour and starvation. But, after the defeat of Romanian armies on the Russian front in 1943, there was a growing gap between Romania and Germany and less co-operation with German officials than in Hungary. Yet, given the huge overall figure of Romanian Jews, Romania's involvement in the Holocaust was extensive – whatever form it took.

The Jewish response to persecution

Most studies in racism and anti-Semitism focus on the motivation of the persecutors. Attention is now being given to the reaction of the persecuted. One view is that there was little resistance – and for a reason. According to Hilberg, the Jews tried to avoid provoking the Nazis into still more radical measures: 'They hoped that somehow the German drive would spend itself.' Furthermore,

> This hope was founded on a two-thousand-year-old experience. In exile the Jews had always been a minority; they had always been in danger; but they had learned that they could avert danger and survive destruction by placating and appeasing their enemies.[258]

Other explanations have also been put forward.[259] It was, for example, more difficult for most Jews to resist than it was for other sectors of the population. Unlike partisans, they tended to be concentrated in ghettos and had no access to wooded areas for concealment. They also lived among a largely hostile population in most countries in central and eastern Europe. Internally there were tactical and ideological differences among those who wanted to resist, some being Zionist, others pro-communist.

Yet we should not conclude from this that there was no attempt to contest Nazi measures; on the contrary, there were several. There were, for example, numerous self-help organizations. Comprising lawyers, doctors and artists, these were intended to evade the discriminatory legislation where possible and to minimize its effects. These were also linked to the Reich Association of German Jews which tried periodic public appeals: in 1935, for example, it complained to the Minister of War about the exclusion of Jewish servicemen from the German armed forces. Jewish lawyers also complained to the League of Nations about discrimination in Upper Silesia, still officially under League supervision as a plebiscite area. In this instance the government backed down and withdrew some of its measures (although it reinstated them when the League's supervision ended in 1937). More radical opponents were prominent in the illegal groups organized by the Communists and Social Democrats. These, according to confidential Gestapo reports, contained disproportionately large numbers of Jews. It is unlikely that such reports would have distorted this point, since they were intended to collate information, not to spread propaganda.

In a sense such Jewish activities were counterproductive. Winterfelt argues that the various organizations impeded the full realization of the extent of anti-Semitism. The only real alternative was emigration, which the response actually discouraged. 'Instead of trying to make life for Jews under Nazi tyranny as pleasant as possible, everything, and every possible Pfennig, should have been invested in attempting to get Jews out of the country.'[260] There is some support for this: the United States allowed an immigration quota of 25,000 per annum, which was never filled before 1939.[261] On the other hand, different figures show that there was a major concerted effort to leave Germany: 130,000, or 20 per cent of the Jewish population, emigrated between 1933 and 1937, while a further 118,000 followed them after Kristallnacht, leaving something like 164,000. This occurred despite the upheaval and dislocation, and the loss of up to 96 per cent of emigrants' financial assets. Housden therefore puts a different case to that of Winterfelt: 'If emigration amounted to opposition through escape, the vast majority of the Jews did oppose the Third Reich.'[262]

Perhaps not surprisingly, historical controversy intensifies over the period of the Holocaust between 1941 and 1945. One debate concerns the extent of the Jewish administrative co-operation with the authorities. As the Germans occupied eastern Europe they established Jewish authorities, or *Judenräte*, in areas of heavy Jewish population. In the Ghetto of Lodz,

	Jewish population (million)	*Number of Jews killed (million)*		*% of Jewish population killed*
* Poland	3.300	2.350–2.900	Latvia	89
* Soviet Union	2.1–4.7	0.700–2.200	Poland	88
+ Romania	0.85	0.200–0.420	Lithuania	87
R Bohemia }			Yugoslavia	87
* Moravia }	0.360	0.233–0.300	Germany	83
+ Slovakia }			Bohemia }	
R Germany	0.240	0.160–0.200	Moravia }	83
+*Hungary	0.403	0.180–0.200	Slovakia }	
* Lithuania	0.155	0.135	Netherlands	80
* France	0.300	0.060–0.130	Greece	80
* Netherlands	0.150	0.104–0.120	Austria	67
* Latvia	0.095	0.085	Hungary	50
* Yugoslavia	0.075	0.055–0.065	Romania	49
* Greece	0.075	0.057–0.060	Soviet Union	48
R Austria	0.060	0.040	Belgium	48
* Belgium	0.100	0.025–0.040	France	43
+*Italy	0.075	0.009–0.015	Italy	26
+ Bulgaria	0.050	0.007	Bulgaria	14

R Reich before September 1939
* *Conquered and under German occupation*
\+ *Allied to Germany*
+* *Allies eventually occupied*

Table 1 Numbers of Jews killed in the Holocaust

Source: *Nazism 1919–1945, Volume Three: Foreign Policy, War and Racial Extermination: A Documentary Reader*, Edited by J. Noakes and G. Pridham, new edition, 2001, ISBN 978 8 85989 602 1, p. 629. Used by kind permission of University of Exeter Press.

for example, the *Judenräte* organized labour rotas, enforced discipline and prepared people for the resettlement ordered by the Nazis. Hilberg argues that the *Judenräte* aimed to avoid provoking the German authorities by making themselves indispensable to the German war economy and they certainly did a great deal to help the German administration, the resources of which were heavily stretched. 'The Jewish and German policies, at first glance opposites, were in reality pointed in the same direction.'[263] In some cases, Jewish officials even knew the secret of the exterminations but decided to remain silent. While accepting the humanitarian motive behind this, some historians, like Robinson, see it nevertheless as 'collaboration.'[264] Against this, it is strongly arguable that without such co-operation the plight of the victims would have been even worse. The same applies to those *Judenräte* in Upper Silesia which tried to stamp out opposition to the Nazis and sometimes handed offenders over to the Gestapo. But, according to Trunk, 'Under the system of collective responsibility, any act of a single person could lead to collective punishment of the whole ghetto community, whose doom would then be sealed.'[265] What the *Judenräte* were doing, therefore, was governing humanely. The fact that their authority was delegated to them by an inhumane system does not make them complicit.

Much has also been written about compliance within the death camps, especially over the apparent docility with which millions of Jews went to the gas chambers. One argument is the sheer extent of the deception applied by the Nazi authorities. Deportees were led to believe that they were being taken to the camps to be resettled. The next, and cruellest, deception was that those selected for the gas chambers were told that they were to be showered and deloused before taking on new trades allocated to them: they would therefore have been preparing themselves for a revival of the type of existence they had experienced in the ghettos. In these instances the SS and the German administration became expert at avoiding any trouble by building up hopes.

Even in such terrible circumstances, however, there were examples of Jewish resistance. In 1942 Jewish inmates in Sachsenhausen rioted in protest against a decision to move them to the east. This was the only instance in Germany but there were also examples in 1943 at Treblinka, with 750 escapes, and at Sobibor, with 300 breakouts. Meanwhile, in Berlin, the Herbert Baum Group co-ordinated Jewish opposition, distributed anti-Nazi propaganda and made common cause with the Communists. There were twenty-four examples of armed uprisings in ghettos in Poland and Lithuania. In addition to Warsaw, there were, for example, uprisings in Cracow, Czestochowa, Lvov, Tuczyn, Vilnius and Bialystok. Cox also points out that 'Jews served in disproportionately high numbers in the partisan armies', including 30,000 with Soviet partisans, 1,600 in Slovakia, 7,000 with Tito, and, in Belorussia, a host led by the Bielski brothers; in France, meanwhile about one in six Maquis was Jewish.[266] Even this contribution is probably an underestimate, since the identity of Jews was often subsumed into larger groups (Russian, Polish, Lithuanian, Yugoslav or French) keen to emphasize a national identity.

Personality and evil

Finally, there is the disturbing question of how so many people could allow themselves to be involved in acts of evil. There can be no question that the participants were unaware of the real nature of what they were doing, whether in the Einsatzgruppen or in the camps. Even Rudolf Hoess, the commandant of Auschwitz, maintained that 'Our system is so terrible that no-one in the world will believe it to be possible'.[267] But how could this 'terrible system' have had so many practitioners? One possibility is that a minority of sadists enforced a system which others knowingly followed through fear of retribution if they disobeyed orders. The impetus here is evil as a positive force, released by psychopathic behaviour. The main example would be the influence of Streicher, who derived sexual gratification from the persecution and torture of helpless people. There is no doubt that thousands of similar characters were attracted to membership of the SS by similar prospects. But it is equally certain that they were a small minority among all those involved in the Holocaust. There must be a better explanation.

The alternative, according to Hannah Arendt, is that the process of extermination was dealt with 'neither by fanatics nor by natural murderers nor by sadists. It was manned solely and exclusively by normal human beings of the type of Heinrich Himmler.'[268] Far from being sadistic, Himmler was squeamish about the details of mass murder and issued official instructions that SS officials were not to torment the inmates of the camps. In 1943 an SS *Untersturmführer* was sentenced to death for succumbing to the temptation to 'commit atrocities unworthy of a German or an SS commander'.[269] Rudolf Hoess always maintained that he was doing to the best of his ability the job allocated to him and that, at the same time, he remained 'completely normal': 'Even while I was carrying out the task of extermination I led a normal family life. I never grew indifferent to human suffering.'[270]

By this route we arrive at a preposterous conclusion. Among the sadists handling the extermination programme were 'normal' family men, who presided over them and tried to do their duty like decent German citizens. The extermination programme was seen as an arduous duty to be carried out. It involved the denial of the preferences of the participant, not their sublimation. But this was the clue. Denial of preference was initially directed by external discipline. External discipline led to internal self-discipline as the participant adapted to a new routine. Routine brought familiarity with the task which, in turn, reduced the chance of rejecting it. Yet in all this some absolute values could remain. These were parallel to and yet entirely cut off from the genocidal tasks being carried out. Hence, men like Hoess, who remained a practising Catholic while commandant at Auschwitz, literally led double lives, neither of which intruded on the other. We are left with the image of evil, in the words of Arendt, as being essentially 'banal'. In its ordinariness it can affect any group of people at any time. This is a far more frightening concept than a system dominated by psychopaths.

Yet, for all that, evil can operate as banality only in the most extraordinary situations. The context was provided both by modern technology and a bureaucratic mentality: according to Baumann, modernization 'contains all the technical elements which proved necessary in the execution of genocidal tasks',[271] while Mommsen maintains that modernity produced 'a purely technocratic and bureaucratic mentality' as well as a 'pseudo-moral justification' for genocide.[272] This, however, has been questioned by Housden. Taking the specific example of Hans Frank, Housden believes that this Nazi official did not conceive of himself 'as a cog in a much wider machine'. It was quite the reverse. 'He was seduced and thrilled into expecting much more than this for himself. He wanted more in terms of intellectual prestige, national respect, financial wealth, historical importance, even sexual delight.' Hence Housden departs from the Arendt explanation; Hans Frank, at least, was more an example of the 'vanity of evil' than of the 'banality of evil'.

REFLECTIONS ON HITLER'S DICTATORSHIP

This chapter has examined a variety of theories and standpoints about Hitler and the Nazi regime. These have included a number of debates involving 'intentionalism' versus 'functionalism'; paradoxes such as 'chaos' and 'consent'; and political, social, economic and racial perspectives in the contexts of *Gleichschaltung*, *Volksgemeinschaft*, *Lebensraum*, *Blitzkrieg* and Total War. It is now time for a considered overall conclusion. Of all the questions which have been asked about Hitler and Nazi Germany, one always returns. How could it have happened that Hitler was *able* to take control over Germany and in due course of Europe?

Three broad approaches have been advanced by way of an answer. First, Germany was part of a collective experience of upheaval affecting much of Europe after the First World War, the roots of which went back beyond the turn of the century. Second, Germany followed her own special path, or *Sonderweg*, which led uniquely to the Nazi era. Third, Hitler's individual leadership shaped Germany's experience between 1933 and 1945 in the way that nothing else could have done. All three of these clearly have a part to play and have already been considered at various points in this chapter. But, in the final analysis, what weight should they be given against each other?

Nazi Germany as part of a collective experience?

Chapter 1 provided a background to the problems experienced by many European societies after 1918 – Germany included. One of these was the dislocation caused by the First World War on all states, especially those which had been defeated or deprived of territory and resources in the peace settlement. Another was the effect of economic crisis, whether inflation or depression, and the concomitant impact on social structures. This, in turn, put severe pressures on the functioning of democratic institutions and alienated large sections of the population from their previous party loyalties. Meanwhile, Germany – like other countries – was affected by modernist influences,[273] contained in end-of-the-century theories of biological engineering, or demographic studies of population trends in eastern Europe. Social engineering was another facet which was widely influential, as far afield as the Soviet Union and the United States.

More negatively, anti-Semitism had been widespread at the turn of the century, especially in Austria (where Hitler had been influenced by Schönerer and Lueger) and Russia, which experienced the greatest levels of violence against Jews. Racial theories were also broad currency, advanced by works such as Gobineau's *Essai sur l'inégalité des races humaines*, published as far back as 1855. Add to this the revolution in communications and there was huge potential for radical change at all levels – and in many parts of Europe.

All of these developments are, of course, crucial to understanding the broad setting in which Germany found herself. But some interpretations remain predominantly at this level, focusing on Hitler's Germany as part of a broader phenomenon or as a reaction to developments elsewhere; such a perspective is too limited.

The most obvious example is the Marxist interpretation of the Nazi period which was prevalent in the German Democratic Republic until its demise in 1989. This saw Hitler and the Nazi regime as the logical consequence of a capitalist process. He was merely the pawn of the most extreme forms of finance capital within Germany. Their political infrastructure had manipulated him into power in 1933 and then used him to destroy labour organizations and the working class. Far from losing control over Hitler, capitalism continued along an increasingly aggressive course in pursuit of financial hegemony in Europe, then the world. By this analysis, therefore, Hitler had no independent input: he was part of a larger process. The analysis itself is doubly flawed: it is based on a preconceived formula of historical change which, in turn, provided ideological justification for the political system which replaced Nazism in East Germany.

Another approach may be less heavily structured or influenced by ideology – but it does have an underlying motivation. Some historians have attempted to place Nazi Germany in a more collective balance of culpability. Although their studies are detailed and often complex, their aim is to draw equivalence between what happened in Nazi Germany and developments elsewhere, especially in the Soviet Union. This has been done at two levels.

The first can be considered a serious academic approach. During the Historical Controversy (*Historikerstreit*), which took place in Germany in 1986–7 about the possible rehabilitation of Hitler and the regime, both Nolte and Hillgruber sought to draw comparisons with the Soviet system of Stalin to avoid singling out Germany for special historical blame. Nazism itself was a reaction to Bolshevism and the Soviet Gulag system both preceded and *led to* Auschwitz.[274] According to Hillgruber, the murder of Jews in Nazi Germany 'cannot qualitatively be judged different' to Stalin's murder of Ukrainian peasants.[275] It has also been argued that a persistently condemnatory approach to the German experience serves only to demonize the subject and to obfuscate the search for really meaningful explanations.

The problem here is that the most extreme development of the entire period, the Holocaust, becomes reactive to something else. Certainly it can be compared with the Soviet gulag but should not lose its uniqueness in the process. It is, after all, the most extreme and – arguably – the most logical outcome of the Third Reich.

The other level seeks more obvious exoneration of Hitler and Nazism. Some historians have sought to absolve Hitler from responsibility for the outbreak of war or from association with the Holocaust. Irving, for example, showed 'a gradual progression from partial exoneration, through rehabilitation, to the virtual elevation of Hitler to a level of historical and moral greatness'.[276] His work also led to eventual denial of the gas chambers, and to placing the killing of Jews on a par with other events of the war such as the Allied bombing of Dresden.

Some forms of analysis are by their very nature generic – and are valid within certain limitations. One such is the 'totalitarian' approach, which emphasizes that Hitler, Stalin and Mussolini were all part of the phenomenon of the totalitarian state associated with Fascism and Communism; these were identifiable by certain common characteristics. This does a great deal to explain the category and characteristics of the Hitler dictatorship (see Chapter 2) and in providing comparisons with Stalin (Chapter 9). But it is primarily a starting point to explain terminology, to establish criteria and to introduce a structure for analysis. It is not a device for explaining the origins of any specific regime. This also applies to the generic explanations of Fascism; we can surmise what Fascism was, where it came from, who supported it and what it stood for – but not why Nazism took hold so completely in Germany.

Germany's 'special path'?

In some respects Nazism grew from uniquely German roots as well as from more widespread influences. Many of Hitler's ideas on race came from the writings of racially orientated German scientists or hygienists such as Haeckel, Schallmayer and Ploetz. Although less violent than in Russia and less politicized than in Austria-Hungary, anti-Semitism had its most extreme theoretical justification in Germany, expressed in the numerous tracts produced by the likes of Hentschel, Lanz and Dinter.[277] These were to have a direct influence on Hitler's more extreme description of the Jews in *Mein Kampf*. Hence, according to Burleigh and Wippermann, 'Hitler's racism was neither original nor without contradictions, either in parts or as a whole.'[278]

Germany also experienced a particular form of social fracturing which someone like Hitler was able to exploit. Unification had been carried through in 1866 and 1870–1 by force of arms and the subsequent Kaiserreich (1871–1918) had been a distinctive mixture of autocratic rule and democratic participation. The ruling classes – the Junkers and the new industrialists – felt threatened by the ever-increasing numbers of urban workers, while the middle classes were increasingly destabilized. This goes some way towards explaining the emergence of support for extreme parties like the Communists and Nazis during the declining years of the Weimar Republic. As for the Third Reich's expansionism, this had to some extent been anticipated by Germany's policy before 1914 and during the First World War. Recent social studies have also shown the huge personal popularity of Hitler among the German people, in contrast to the more manufactured cult of Stalin in the Soviet Union. Part of this was a feeling that Hitler was able to provide tradition with a new direction.

All of these are crucial to explain how Hitler was able to attach his ideas and appeal to various levels of the German experience. But just how far should we take the connection between Nazism and the uniqueness of the German past? Here are three examples of the 'special path' or *Sonderweg* approach. To be fair, these are taken from much more extensive arguments which do not necessarily represent the entire book. But they do stand out in their particular context as following the *Sonderweg*.

The first is the 'surrender of Germans to authority' argument, advanced by A.J.P. Taylor in a survey of German history from Luther to Hitler, first published in 1945. He maintains that the National Socialist dictatorship had a 'deeper foundation' and that

> During the preceding eighty years the Germans had sacrificed to the Reich all their liberties; they demanded as reward the enslavement of others. No German recognized the Czechs and Poles as equals. Therefore every German desired the achievement which only total war could give.[279]

Others, too, have argued that the failure of the 1848 revolutions was of crucial importance in depriving Germany of a liberal base.

Second, 'the straight line of German history' is presented by Shirer, who argues that the subjection of Germany to Prussia was the crucial factor and was to have 'disastrous' consequences.

> From 1871 to 1933 and even to Hitler's end in 1945, the course of German history as a consequence was to run, with the exception of the interim of the Weimar Republic, in a straight line and with utter logic.[280]

Similarly, there was a direct cultural line.

> German culture which became dominant in the nineteenth century and which coincided with the rise of Prussian Germany, continuing with Bismarck through Hitler, rests primarily on Fichte and Hegel, to begin with, and then on Treitschke, Nietzsche, Richard Wagner, and a host of lesser lights . . . They succeeded in establishing a spiritual break with the West.[281]

As for *Mein Kampf*, 'It offered, though few saw this at the time, a continuation of German history.'[282]

The third example is much more recent and forms only a small part of a widely respected work. It has, nevertheless, been contentious. In 1996 Goldhagen maintained that German racism was endemic – to the extent that it defined the Holocaust. He pointed to 'the development in Germany well before the Nazis came to power of a virulent and violent "eliminationist" variant of antisemitism'. Indeed, 'When the Nazis did assume power, they found themselves the masters of a society already imbued with notions about the Jews that were ready to be mobilized for the most extreme form of "elimination" imaginable.'[283]

All of these imply that Germany was a ready arena for someone like Hitler to make a special impact, and that in various ways the German people had surrendered to something which had made them particularly vulnerable to him – whether this surrender was to 'authority' or to 'Prussia' or to 'virulent anti-Semitism'. While not denying that there were powerful elements of authoritarianism, Prussianization and anti-Semitism in Germany, can we really say that these were so powerful as to prepare the German people to be 'Hitlerized'? After all, the democratic Weimar constitution was based very much on the institutions of the Kaiserreich and, although these were badly flawed, neither could be described as a 'surrender' to authoritarianism. Similarly Prussia's domination of Germany should not consequentially be associated with authoritarian control. The Weimar Republic did little to change Prussia's status yet it should not be forgotten that the state government of Prussia remained democratic (based on a coalition between the Centre Party and the SPD) for some time after the Republic government had lurched to the right. If anywhere set a bad example for the rest of Germany between 1919 and 1933, it was Bavaria not Prussia. Finally, to give a generic description to virulent anti-Semitism is to overlook the advances made in reducing constraints on the Jews in Germany, both in the nineteenth century and in Weimar Germany. We should also remember that the increase in the popular vote for the Nazis between 1930 and 1932 was due to factors other than anti-Semitism. The most intense racist feelings therefore *followed* rather than preceded the rise of Nazism.

The uniqueness of Hitler's impact?

It makes most sense to acknowledge the supreme importance of Hitler within the context of Germany's experience in a radicalized and embattled Europe. It is impossible to conceive of Nazi Germany without Hitler, whereas a more traditionally authoritarian regime could well have occurred: indeed, the assumption of the conservative right in Germany is that that was where it *was* heading under Hindenburg. Yet what actually happened was that a peripheral extreme was suddenly thrust into the centre by a previously marginalized man who was released by the fracturing of constraints. Hitler took full advantage of the situation in which he found himself in order to effect a total change. For this reason, he should be considered revolutionary; Lukacs calls him 'the greatest revolutionary of the twentieth century', although he adds that this is not intended to be 'approbatory'.[284] It was Hitler who developed Nazism, whereas neither Lenin nor Stalin can be given the full credit for Communism, nor even Mussolini for Italian Fascism. One of the important effects of Goldhagen's work is to revive the centrality of ideology in the Nazi system after its earlier dilution by the 'intentionalist'–'functionalist' debate. Hitler's aims, as expressed in *Mein Kampf*, are now taken much more seriously than the 'daydreaming' once attributed to them by A.J.P. Taylor. The whole process of Nazification, the 'Reconstituting society as the *Volksgemeinschaft* was', according to Eley, 'an ineluctably ideological process'.[285] Similarly, a new style of foreign policy, based on ignoring established frontiers in the pursuit of Lebensraum, revolutionized international relations in a way which entirely transcended the more limited Weltpolitik of the Kaiserreich. As for anti-Semitism, Hitler extended its earlier punitive role into something intended to be redemptive and eliminationist, thereby revolutionizing Germany's internal priorities. He was impatient with the limited 'pogrom' approach to anti-Semitism and wanted to convert prejudice and hatred into extermination. This was unique even in German history. How, it might be asked, could the Holocaust have happened without Hitler? Or the paraphernalia and race mystique of the SS?

Also of decisive importance were Hitler's opportunism and strategy. He it was who moved the Nazi Party away from an earlier course and more into line with the needs of the moment – until it was safe to resume its revolutionary impetus. His emphasis on a strategy of 'legality' and of winning over the upper and middle classes brought him into conflict with the Strasser in the late 1920s, while in 1934 he found it necessary to cull the radical activists under Röhm. In both cases his judgement proved correct and consolidation provided a basis for revolution at a later date. Above all, his charismatic leadership held both the nation and his subordinates. There was never an alternative. His cult may have been orchestrated by Goebbels – but the latter remained devoted to him to the end, without aspirations of his own to the leadership. The details of the racial mystique and much of the organization behind eliminationist anti-Semitism may have been provided by Himmler – but, until April 1945, the Reichsführer SS was never anything but a loyal subordinate to the Führer.

Of course the whole system was at times chaotic and the case has been strongly made for its endemic inefficiency. The particular strength of the functionalist argument has been to correct the automatic connection between ruthlessness and efficiency. But this does not necessarily weaken the personal nature of Hitler's dictatorship. The regime may have been operated by others, whether at central or at local levels. But all actions were justified in terms of the 'Will of the Führer' and 'Working towards the Führer'. It was still the state Hitler wanted, even if he was not always fully in control of the methods it used. Functionalism therefore presents a case for how it worked, rather than for what it wanted. This is where intentionalism prevails – because it recognized the overriding influence of Hitler's ideas as the drive behind the regime.

So far the argument has been put for the overriding importance of Hitler's particular influence in Germany. Yet it is possible to go too far in this direction and to overstate the case. We should not go to the other extreme and place the entire explanation for the Nazi experience on the person of Hitler. For in that direction lies the abnegation of all other reasons in the impression that the German people were deluded by promises, then intimidated by terror and finally left in ignorance of the eliminationist nature of his rule. This will not do – for three reasons. First, as the intentionalists show, Hitler's ideas were plain for all to see. Second, historians emphasizing social factors in the Third Reich have demonstrated the widespread nature of personal support for Hitler. Third, there were occasions on which Hitler could have been removed from the scene: with a more severe sentence after the Munich Putsch, by President Hindenburg, and through intervention by the army. That none of these happened was a reflection on what Germany had become in its acceptance of Hitler's regime. But if any of these *had* happened could Germany have experienced the same Third Reich – or an alternative one? And would the outcome have been the same?

The approach which makes the most sense is to combine the three perspectives considered – but in the reverse order of their importance. This means placing Hitler firmly as the key factor into the background of a Germany in crisis within a more generally volatile Europe. Burleigh's laconic description is relevant here: he describes his recent biography of Hitler as

> an account of the longer-term, and more subtle moral breakdown and transformation of an advanced industrial society, whose consequences astute observers, with an instinct for these things, could predict someways before they happened. But encouraged by irresponsible and self-interested sections of the elite . . . the mass propelled itself against charity, reason and scepticism, investing its faith in the otherwise farcical figure of Hitler, whose own miserable existence gained meaning as he discovered that his rage against the world was capable of indefinite generalisation.[286]

This contrasts with Shirer's 'line', which is perhaps more relevant to modern Russian history. Lukacs, for example, argues that Hitler's place in German history is 'more extraordinary' than that of 'Stalin's in the history of Russia'. After all, 'There was no Ivan the Terrible (whose rule, in many ways, resembled Stalin's) in the history of Germany. Stalin fits more into the pattern of Russian history than Hitler fits into that of Germany.'[287]

Chapter 6

Dictatorship in Spain

On paper, Spain had certain assets which could well have equipped her for democracy rather than the dictatorship to which she twice succumbed between the world wars. For example, the 1867 constitution had given her a parliament with two chambers, one of which was elected from 1890 by universal male suffrage. In practice, however, the political and social fabric faced desperate problems which eventually resulted in the collapse of the parliamentary system in 1923.

One problem was a series of external disasters. Spain became the first power to lose her imperial role, suffering in the process humiliating naval and military defeats. Cuba had risen in revolt in 1895 and Spain had been defeated by the United States in the War of 1898. More serious still was a crisis in northern Morocco, which Spain had been trying to conquer since 1909. Spanish troops were pinned down by indigenous resistance movements and General Silvestre was defeated by the Riffians in 1921 at Anual, losing 12,000 of his contingent of 20,000. Military disasters were accompanied by internal instability which involved the growth of powerful opposition to central government from the left and from the regions. The former consisted of a strong trade-union movement, as well as anarchist organizations influenced by the nineteenth-century philosopher Bakunin. Left-wing radicalism frequently overlapped with demands for the independence of regions such as Catalonia. Although the central government succeeded in suppressing this rebellion, it was unable to restore full confidence in its rule and resorted increasingly to graft and corruption. In the view of Thomas, 'By 1923 the Spanish parliamentary system was bruised almost to death.'[1]

DICTATORSHIP TO REPUBLIC, 1923–31

Primo de Rivera, 1923–30

The result was that the Spanish king, Alfonso XIII, acquiesced in a military coup in 1923 by Miguel Primo de Rivera, a general who, according to Payne, was neither an intellectual nor a politician but who had become 'impatient with constitutions', preferring 'order and simplicity'.[2] He was well-meaning but unsophisticated; depending on intuition rather than reason, he convinced himself that he was most in touch with the needs and aspirations of the Spanish people. 'Your president is vigilant', he proclaimed, 'while you are asleep'. He liked to be portrayed as an Atlas who, 'with his stout shoulders unshakeably avoided the collapse of the lofty roof of our beloved fatherland'.[3] He also saw himself as strengthening the Christian base of society and as a sentinel against the threat of communism. The best means of serving Spain, in his view, was to dispense with party politics. He was much influenced by political developments in Italy and was once introduced by Alfonso XIII on

8 General Miguel Primo de Rivera, photo taken in 1928 (© Universal History Archive/Getty)

a trip abroad as 'my Mussolini'. His regime was not, however, based on ideology. Instead, it was largely pragmatic. He tried at first to manage with a cabinet of military officers but came to the conclusion by 1926 that a broader-based and more systematic government was necessary. He therefore introduced a 'National Assembly', a corporative chamber intended to represent different classes and interest groups. He also developed a new party, the *Unión Patriótica,* to mobilize popular support for the authoritarian system. 'This', he claimed 'is a national movement which signifies, above all, faith in the destinies of Spain and in the grandeur and virtues of our race'.[4] As it turned out, the whole political system was too diffuse: it was neither one thing nor the other. It was not sufficiently democratic to heed the demands for alternative policies, nor was it sufficiently authoritarian to prevent these demands being made. During the six years he was in power, Rivera pursued bold policies, sometimes with notable success. He avoided the humiliation experienced by previous governments in dealing with Morocco and managed to subdue the protectorate by 1926. Internal problems were more complex. He considered that Spain's most urgent need was stability, to be achieved partly by reviving traditional virtues and partly through a process of modernization. He therefore strengthened Spain's infrastructure through the extension of public works. Unfortunately, his policies were handicapped by inadequate financing. One possible means of raising the necessary revenue was a complete overhaul of the taxation system, but this was fiercely resisted by the upper classes and the bankers. He resorted then to the alternative expedient of borrowing and, in his later years, made extensive use of the 'extraordinary budget'. He aimed also at more direct government intervention in economic activity, hoping to create new industries and bring about protection through higher tariffs. There were signs of economic improvement during the 1920s. According to Rial, however, his economic policies 'produced only a short-lived, unevenly distributed spurt'.[5] In any case, Carr maintains, whatever prosperity there was 'was to a large extent the result of favourable outside circumstances for which the regime could take no credit'.[6] It has also been pointed out that any economic reform was not accompanied by much needed social changes. There was, for example, no improvement in the conditions of either industrial or agricultural workers. Rivera was not blind to the need for social reform but he was too heavily committed to the wealthier classes, upon whom he depended for support.

Rivera's dictatorship ended in January 1930, the result of overwhelming economic and political difficulties. Spain experienced a slump in share prices in the stock markets and an erosion of the currency. The whole basis of economic growth was threatened so that Rivera had to stop using the extraordinary budget and batten down the hatches. This signalled the end of prosperity, but the regime was not strong enough to withstand the backlash. Rivera had been unable to provide a permanent legitimacy for his government and he fell as a result of an attack from the left and the withdrawal of support from the right. The offensive was launched by Spanish republicans, the press, universities and the socialists, while the conservatives saw nothing to gain by prolonging Rivera's regime. The upper classes, fearing the impact of economic decline, hoped that a change of government would regenerate confidence. Above all, the army was alienated by Rivera's attempts to reform the promotion system and eliminate some of the more blatant privileges. Disturbed by this overall lack of confidence, the King requested and received Rivera's resignation in January 1930. The dictator was in poor health in any case and died only two months later.

Interpretations of Primo de Rivera's regime

Most historians now agree about the type of regime introduced by Primo de Rivera. Despite the misleading impression created by the titles of some of their books,[7] they do not consider it as fascist. According to Blinkhorn, Primo de Rivera's rule did not rest on a mass movement; 'it lacked a totalitarian vision' and the regime 'was not a fascist one'.[8] Like Salazar, Rivera was hostile to the whole concept of the totalitarian state, for its paganism and hostility to Christian-based civilization. Instead, as Ben-Ami states, there were closer parallels with the contemporary authoritarian systems of Poland under Piłsudski and Portugal under Salazar, and with the later system of Metaxas in Greece. Rivera's *Unión Patriótica* was an official party of national unity but with measured mobilization of support rather than a mass movement like those created by the totalitarian right; in this respect, it was similar to Salazar's *União Nacional.* Both leaders were suspicious of indigenous fascist organisations, regarding them as agents of instability and internal chaos. Ultimately, Rivera's power base was paradoxical. On the one hand, it depended on the official support of the monarchy and the goodwill of the political, social and military elites. On the other, it transcended the narrowness of the more traditional *caudillo* form of dictatorship by its claim to a wider base of popular support and a single national party. The problem was that the regime could last only as long as it was tolerated by monarchy and aristocracy and became vulnerable as soon as these expressed disillusionment with Rivera's more radical experiments. The essential difference between Rivera and the fascist leaders was that the former had to work within an existing system, even if he was trying to redefine it. Fascism, by contrast, frequently worked outside traditional institutions even where, as in Italy it acknowledged a role for the monarchy, earlier political organs and the Catholic Church. Withdrawal of royal support therefore brought about the collapse of Rivera in Spain, whereas it *followed* the collapse of the mainstream of Mussolini's Fascism in Italy.

Where, therefore, does Rivera's dictatorship stand in twentieth-century Spain? Two very different approaches are possible here.

One is that the regime was an isolated phenomenon, a break in the more complex developments of the 1920s and 1930s. Before 1923 the monarchy had become imperilled by the crisis in Morocco and by the growing instability brought by political and social antagonism, exacerbated by economic instability. Between 1923 and 1930 Rivera managed to avoid the collapse of the monarchy by urgently needed reforms and a settlement in Morocco. Yet, as we have seen, these achievements were flawed and their eventual limitations meant that the Rivera period was an interlude between two periods of crisis. This meant that the revolution that had been building up before 1923 was merely postponed until after 1930. Rivera's place in Spanish history was therefore strictly limited in that he had comparatively little impact on the future.

A contrasting interpretation is that Rivera's dictatorship played an integral role in the overall development of Spain in the twentieth century. Ben-Ami, for example, sees his regime as 'a most significant turning point in modern Spanish history',[9] a view endorsed by Blinkhorn[10] and Rial.[11] This could produce two logical, but different – approaches to Rivera's importance. One is that Rivera had a direct impact on the future through his modernizing policies – limited though these were in practice. But it required the greater determination and ruthlessness of the new right of Francisco Franco to push Spain into the next phase of development; in this sense, Rivera prepared the way for Franco, although the latter went much further than the former would have wanted. The other approach – and the one now most favoured by recent historians – is that Rivera's influence was one by default.[12] Ben-Ami argues that that Rivera 'had shattered the foundations of the old regime without enthroning a new state, thus leaving behind him a dangerous vacuum of power'.[13] Rial similarly maintains that 'the dictatorship was no mere "parenthesis" in political evolution, but a revolutionary break in continuity well beyond the country's subsequent ability to accommodate'.[14] Certainly, Rivera's military reforms had fundamentally destabilized the army, which, in turn, set in motion a series of unintended changes. In the short term the backlash against Rivera brought down the Spanish monarchy as well. Rivera's successor, General Berenguer, tried to promote a new system of authoritarian reform. But the republicans who had been so successful against Rivera in 1929 and 1930 were not likely now to be satisfied with a few compromises and promises. Instead they took full advantage of the restoration of parliament and party politics, winning a majority in the municipalities in elections of 1931. This was taken as a vote of no-confidence in the monarchy. Fearing revolution if he tried to keep himself in power, Alfonso XIII voluntarily left Spain, expecting, no doubt, no doubt, to be recalled when the political scene had quietened down. He was replaced immediately by the Second Spanish Republic.

The demise of the Rivera regime not only pulled down the monarchy; in the longer term it helped prepare the way for a more radical right-wing dictatorship. When the Second Republic, in turn, faced crisis and collapse, it was to be replaced not, as Alfonso had hoped, by a restored monarchy, but by a right-wing dictatorship which was more radical and ruthless than anything Rivera had anticipated. But this could be installed only by overcoming a newly empowered – but divided – republic. This meant a prolonged and bitter civil war.

REPUBLIC TO DICTATORSHIP, 1931–9

The Second Republic lasted eight years: from 1931 to 1939. From 1936 onwards it was confronted by an all-out assault from General Franco, who eventually installed himself as *caudillo*.

The Second Republic to 1936

The opening years of the republic (1931–3) were dominated by the left, first under Zamora and then Azaña. The early governments introduced a series of major reforms, intended to alter the political and social structure of Spain. Early measures included the introduction of an eight-hour working day, together with benefits (covering maternity, retirement and accident insurance) and paid holidays. These were followed by military changes which sought to control the power of the army by requiring officers to swear loyalty to the republic. There were also attempts to reduce the top-heavy officer corps in the army through early retirement. The momentum increased as the 1931 Constitution introduced universal suffrage at the age of twenty-three and a single-chamber parliament, or Cortes, abolished the nobility and, in Article 26, took extensive measures against the Church. The republicans regarded the Church as a reactionary force which had become resistant to any progressive ideas and which therefore needed drastic change. The main measures introduced by Article 26 were the right of the state to dissolve religious orders (which now had to register officially), the secularization of education and the forcible introduction of the type of social reform like the legalization of divorce, which had been resisted by the Church. The Associations Law (May 1932) completed the measures against the Church, preventing members of religious orders from engaging in trade or industry, abolishing Church schools and nationalizing Church property. Meanwhile the 1932 statute granted a degree of autonomy to Catalonia, which now had its own parliament, president and government, as well as control over such functions as education, taxation and police. Finally, the Law of Agrarian Reform (1932) tried to narrow the gap between the landless peasantry and the enormously wealthy landlords, allowing the state to purchase unworked lands of over fifty-six acres in certain parts of Castile, Andalusia and Extremadura. Overall, this was the most extensive package of reforms Spain had ever experienced.

Unfortunately, everything went wrong; nearly all the changes aroused bitter opposition from Spain's various vested interests. In part, this was a throwback to the end of the monarchy. Salvadó has argued that the 'pillars of the old regime', who had deserted the King 'out of sheer expediency', were now able to 'act as a constraint upon change'.[15] A portion of the army resented the pruning of its ranks. The Church went on to the defensive, finding a champion in Gill Robles, who set up in February 1933 a coalition of right-wing Catholic groups (the Spanish Confederation of Right-Wing Autonomous Groups, or CEDA). The landlords did everything in their power to resist the legislation on land, which was never applied effectively anyway. Azaña therefore failed to benefit Spain's lower orders and succeeded only in terrifying the privileged. Azaña's government fell after being defeated in a general election on 19 November 1933. This meant a swing to the right with a series of coalition governments. These proceeded to dismantle the previous reforms, or at least did everything possible to render them unworkable. This policy, in turn, provoked action from the left in industrial areas – such as the Asturias revolt of 1934, which was bloodily suppressed. The government also removed from circulation any left-wing leaders, irrespective of whether they had been responsible for the violence. Even so, chronic instability characterized the whole period. By the time that the Assembly was dissolved in January 1936 the republic had experienced twenty-six governmental crises, where seventy-two ministers had served during a period of four and a half years.[16]

There followed one of the most famous elections in modern history, as much of Spain polarized into two political camps. The left-wing parties (Communists, Socialists, Liberals, Republicans and Anarchists) combined to form the Popular Front – later known as the Republicans. This was countered on the right by the National Front – or Nationalists, who consisted of monarchists (especially the Carlists of Navarre), conservatives and the CEDA. Outside these blocs were the centre, the Basques and a new far-right organization known as the Falange, under Jose Antonio Primo de Rivera. The result of the election was close, with a victory for the Popular Front (with 4.2 million votes) over the National Front (3.8 million). The Popular Front secured 258 of the 473 seats in the Cortes.

As Azaña formed a new government, the Nationalists looked on sullenly and awaited an opportunity to seize power. Azaña proceeded to reintroduce the earlier reforms. He also removed Franco, whom he regarded as the major threat in the army, by posting him to the Canary Islands as military governor. Unfortunately, the second Azaña administration did

9 General Francisco Franco, 1892–1975 (David King Collection)

nothing to allay the fears of the right that he was drifting towards communism. Indeed, all his policies were interpreted as openly provocative. The right therefore opted for action and the army hatched a plot to overthrow the republic. General Franco, who had returned from the Canaries, led seasoned Spanish contingents from Morocco into the south of Spain, while General Mola advanced from the north with support from Navarre. The republic was to be snuffed out by the two converging forces.

Outline of the Spanish Civil War 1936–9

The purpose of this section is to give a brief survey of the overall context and main events of the Spanish Civil War. Further details are provided in the separate sections indicated.

The two sides now confronting each other are usually called the Republicans (or Republic, or Loyalists) and the Nationalists (or Insurgents, or Right). These labels cover a range of adherents which, in the case of the Republicans, was especially wide; they comprised members of the Popular Front – republicans, socialists, liberals, communists (pro- and anti-Moscow), anarchists and regional minorities. The Nationalists included disillusioned military officers, monarchists (especially Carlists), conservatives, pro-Catholic parties and, finally, the Falange. The leaders, especially Franco and Azaña, are dealt with in separate sections. The areas and groups in Spain who supported each side – including classes, army, clergy and others are analysed on pp. 274–84. The issues involved in the war – both general and specific, are covered on pp. 271–2 and the reasons for Franco's eventual victory – and the Republic's defeat on pp. 285–9.

At first the Nationalist offensive moved slowly. General Emilio Mola gradually established a grip on northern Spain, except some of the Basque lands, and made Burgos the capital of the new Nationalist government – the Junta of National Defence – in direct defiance of Republican Madrid. Meanwhile, Franco invaded from Morocco. In August 1936 the two Nationalist zones linked up along the Portuguese frontier with the capture of Badajoz. The Republicans, however, still controlled the far north, part of the south, almost all of the east and, of course, Madrid in the centre. Franco made an unsuccessful attempt to grab Madrid and then laid siege to the city from November 1936; the Republicans held out but transferred their capital to Valencia on the east coast. The Nationalists failed to cut the road between the two cities.

Meanwhile, foreign interest in the war was growing rapidly. Germany and Italy stepped up their supplies to Franco. France was at first openly sympathetic to the Republicans but was manoeuvred by Britain into a more neutral stance through the establishment of the Non-Intervention Committee, which tried to end the war by denying arms to both sides. All the major powers initially paid lip service to the principle of the Committee, but Germany and

Italy eventually defied its provisions by openly increasing the flow of war *matériel* to the Nationalists. Although the Soviet Union provided some assistance to the Republicans, the disparity between the two sides was considerable. This showed in 1937 when Franco was able to mop up Republican territory in the south, including Malaga. In the far north, meanwhile, occurred an event that provoked an international outcry – the German bombing of the Basque town of Guernica. By October 1937 the Nationalist domination of northern Spain was completed by the conquest of the Asturias.

The Republicans were not finished, however; they had major – if temporary – successes at Guadalajara (March 1937) and Teruel (December 1937). But Franco doggedly persevered, assisted by further Italian and German reinforcements. By 1938 the Nationalists had split the Republic into two areas, isolating Catalonia in the north-east from what was left of Republican Castile. They now concentrated on the region along the Ebro River before launching an assault on Catalonia in December 1938. It was now only a matter of time before the Republic was completely destroyed, especially since the international situation had become even more unfavourable to it. Britain and France, prepared to appease Hitler over Czechoslovakia, were clearly in no mood to confront him over his assistance to Franco. Russia, meanwhile, ended her commitment to the Republic, which was therefore deprived of all foreign help. The Nationalists were free to bomb and starve into submission the three key Republican cities – Barcelona (which fell in January 1939), Valencia and Madrid (March 1939). By 1 April 1939 Franco's government had been recognized by much of Europe, by democracies as well as dictatorships. The regime now controlled a country that had experienced appalling destruction and hardship but Franco retained his position by keeping Spain neutral during the Second World War. His grip on Spain tightened during the post-war period and was ended only by his death in 1975.

SIDES AND ISSUES IN THE SPANISH CIVIL WAR

The sides

The Spanish Civil War is often seen as a fundamental divide between right and left – the first major struggle between fascism and communism. This view is now generally seen as an oversimplification and the result of the propaganda used by each side about the other. The recent tendency is to examine all the complex issues behind the confrontation. Hence, according to Preston, 'the Spanish Civil War was not one but many wars'.[17] The basic argument of this section is that, on the one hand, there were fundamental differences between the two sides, often expressed in powerful ideological terms. On the other hand, there were also many cross-currents in Spain which tended to complicate the major issues. The Civil War was, in fact, fought between broad coalitions – of the right (Nationalists) and left (Republicans).

The Nationalists

The Nationalist aims were the more coherent, largely because of the overwhelming influence of Franco. He projected the whole war as a fight against the godless left which he thought was trying to subvert the whole of Spanish society. In this respect, Franco emphasized the defensive nature of the uprising. He also caught the imagination of the Church by his talk of a crusade, and was careful to associate his army closely with the Catholic religion, even to the extent of making the receiving of communion compulsory among his troops. In place of the corrupt 'communist republic', with its malfunctioning and bickering parties, its declining moral standards and growing secularization, Franco promised to revive Spain's glorious traditions. These included military power, firm personal leadership and overriding religious zeal.

The factions of the right all shared Franco's repugnance of the far left, but they disagreed on long-term objectives. The Carlists (officially the *Comunión Tradicionalista*), for example, hoped that Franco's appeal to tradition would include the eventual return of the monarchy. Heavily based in Navarre with a preference for increased clerical state powers, the Carlists were also strongly linked with the Catholic Church. Their military contributions were particularly important in the opening phases of the war, up to 100,000 Carlist troops fighting in Mola's campaigns in northern Spain. The more moderate right wished to retain at least part of the constitutional structure, while the more radical right – the Falange – aimed to create a classless and corporatist system influenced by the Italian model. The Falange experienced a rapid increase in support in 1936 – benefiting from its skills in propaganda and the appeal of its uniforms, especially the blue shirts. Originally under the leadership of José Antonio Primo de Rivera (until his execution by the Republicans in November 1936) the Falange retained a powerful activist influence over the other groups throughout the Civil War.

Franco steered carefully between these various positions and was able to represent them all. In April 1937 he introduced a decree to unify the different groups of the right into a loose party known as the FET-JONS. Although this has often been described as 'fascist', some historians, including Preston, Eisenwein and Shubert, have argued that, while fascism did provide the 'structural foundation of the new state system' it does not follow 'that Franco himself can be regarded as a fascist dictator'.[18] He was not himself inclined to fascism, although he admired the organization of the fascist regimes. He aimed to combine the fascist, traditionalist and conservative elements of the Spanish right without allowing any of them to disrupt the overall balance that his personal leadership imposed. This is one of the key reasons for the Nationalists being a more homogeneous political and military coalition than the Republicans. It also, perhaps, explains why and how Franco was able to distance himself from fascism after the eventual failure of the fascist regimes elsewhere in the Second World War. To him it was simply a matter of adjusting the overall balance of the coalition under his rule.

The Republicans

The Republicans were more complex than the Nationalists, with a greater range of organizations, aims and methods. They also had a number of leaders associated with the struggle against the right: moderate Republicans like Zamora (president of the republic to 1936) and Azaña (president 1936–9), together with leftists like Prieto and Caballero, regarded with equal abhorrence an enemy that would impose terror by means of a permanent military junta. Depending on the ideological views of the Republicans concerned, the result of a Nationalist victory would be the end of liberal democracy or the total exploitation of labour in the interests of the capitalist classes. The immediate task was therefore to defend the republic and what it had so far achieved. Azaña said in 1937: 'We are waging war because it is being waged on us.'[19] The Republicans were, however, at a major disadvantage in that they were by no means agreed about what was worth preserving.

The moderate Republicans hoped to keep the existing institutions and to move closer towards the western democratic system once Franco's military threat had been removed. It has been argued that had the Republican war effort been led by moderates there would have been a much stronger likelihood of sympathy from the democracies. The radical left, however, wanted more fundamental radical changes, including the establishment of a workers' state. At this point there was a serious division within the Republican camp, as the radical left were unable to agree on a strategy for further change. One section, comprising the CNT (*Confederación Nacional del Trabajo* or anarchosyndicalists), left-wing socialists and Anti-Stalinist communists – the POUM (*Partido Obrero de Unificación Marxista*) – all felt that the real effort should go into extending the scope of the revolution through rapid collectivization and the creation of workers' militias. This would strengthen the republic to defeat the right. Hence, according to the anarchist Berneri, 'we shall not win the war by confining the problem to the strictly military conditions of victory but by associating these with its political and social conditions'. There was therefore a strong emphasis on social reforms such as the collectivization of industry and agriculture; most of the changes here were in Catalonia. Against this was the view of the Spanish Communist Party (*Partido Comunista de España*, PCE), on orders from Moscow, that absolute priority must be given to the defeat of Franco. According to the Party Secretary, 'we cannot achieve the revolution unless we win the war; the first thing is to win the war'.[20] To give priority to the revolution would only alienate the rest of the left and risk destroying the Popular Front altogether. Ironically, the mass mobilization of support which this needed was never fully realized, as the Republic eventually lost the propaganda war. The PCE had gained the upper hand from 1937, largely under the influence of Soviet involvement on the side of the Republic.

Internal support for the sides

How did the various groups within Spain respond to the two sides? Examples particularly worth examining are the institutions (particularly the Church and army), the regions and the social classes.

Institutions

By far the most influential of these was the Catholic Church. Only a small minority supported the Republic. This included some of the lower clergy, partly to preserve democracy and partly for social reasons. A number of individual Catholics opposed the Nationalists, for which they were executed. Others, however, suffered at the hands of anti-clerical mobs in Republican zones, which killed about 7,000 members of the clergy and holy orders. This influenced many who had not initially been fully persuaded to support the Nationalists.

Much of the Church establishment threw in its lot with the Nationalists, including archbishops, bishops, most priests, and holy orders, especially the Dominicans and Jesuits. There were several main reasons for this. One was the opportunity to win back the position of the Church generally and reverse the long-term decline of church attendance and the secularization of what had once been Europe's most Catholic country. Both had been apparent in industrial cities and among agricultural workers in southern areas. More specifically, the Church leadership hoped to reverse the Republic's anti-clerical legislation of 1931. The Catholic opposition to the Republic was further strengthened as result of the massacre of clergy and members of religious orders in Republican areas in the opening months of the war in 1936. The Church increasingly looked to Franco for a way out of its current crisis and as the best protection against what was seen as the atheistic left.

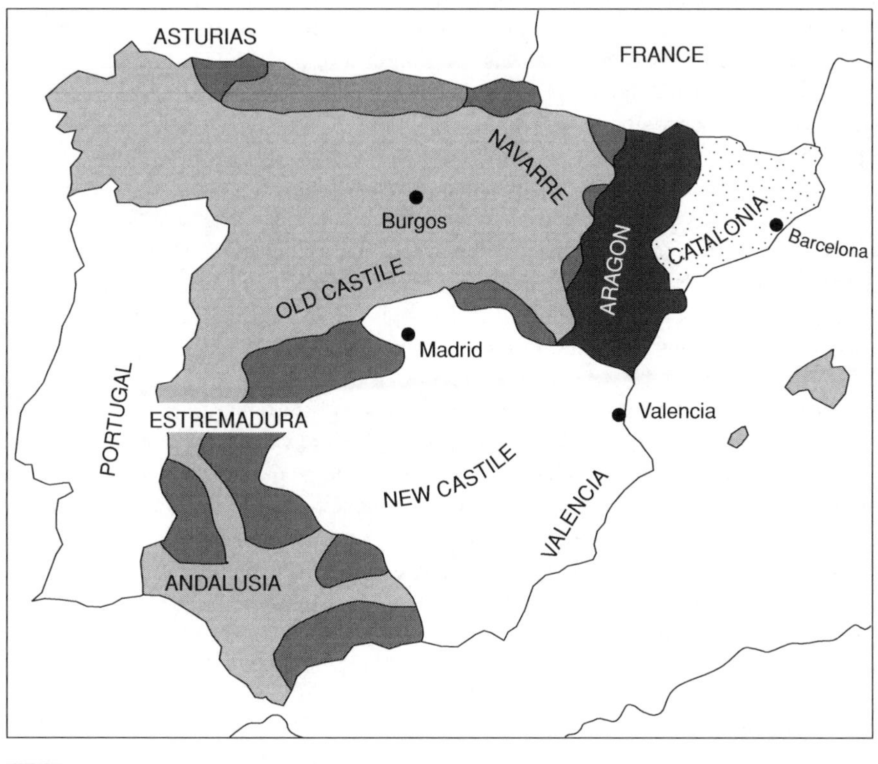

Map 6 The Spanish Civil War 1936–9

The initiative was taken by the Pope Pius XI, who maintained that it was the left, not the far right, that posed the main threat to religion in Europe. 'The first, the greatest and now the general peril is certainly communism in all its forms and degrees.' He considered Spain to be especially at risk. 'Satanic preparation has relighted . . . in neighbouring Spain that hatred and savage persecution.' Hence 'our benediction, above any mundane and political consideration, goes in a special manner to all those who assume the difficult and dangerous task of defending and restoring the rights to honour God and religion'. As for Franco himself, 'We send from our hearts the apostolic blessing, propitiator of divine favours'.[21] The Spanish bishops, meanwhile, fully justified Franco's rebellion on the grounds that it was reasonable in the defence of Christianity. They even quoted the Catholic Church's leading medieval theologian, St. Thomas Aquinas. This powerful ideological undertone would seem to justify Gallo's view that this was 'the last of the European religious wars'. Given the status of the Church, its long-term decline, and the anticlerical legislation of the Republic, it is hardly surprising that the Church supported the Nationalists. According to Lannon, 'The Church could not be anything but anti-Republican in real terms', while the popular front 'could not easily regard the Church as anything but an enemy'.[22] A variety of actions indicated the extent of the Church's commitment. Pastoral and collective letters were sent to clergy in Spain and the outside world justifying support for Nationalists; blessings were given to Nationalist troops and for their campaigns; and there was a steady increase of propaganda against Republic and its supporters, especially the Soviet Union. There was even justification for Franco's purges at the end of the war and massacres during its course.

The other main institution was the Spanish army which, it is sometimes supposed, rose as one against the Republic. If this had been so the Republic would have collapsed within weeks. The reality was more complex, as the army contained a mixture of liberal and reactionary influences. Most of the senior officers remained loyal to the Republic, as they had been appointed in the first place partly because of their political support for the regime. The vast majority of the middle-ranking officers, by contrast, took part in the 1936 uprising. They opposed the reforms of Azaña, especially the effort to reduce the size of the officer corps through early retirement. They also came to believe that Azaña was a 'pervert who nourished hatred for the virile virtues of the army, which he intended to destroy, leaving Spain helpless and prey to freemasonry and Marxism'.[23] The role of the army was therefore to save the state, whose government, according to General Kindelan, was 'in the gutter', and act as 'the guardian of the values and historical constants of the nation'.[24] The army also intended to prevent decentralization and the growth of regionalism, for this would eventually lead to the disintegration of Spain as a military power.

The regions

Map 6 on p. 275 shows the areas under Nationalist and Republican control during the various phases of the Spanish Civil War. In 1936 the Nationalists claimed the allegiance of Galicia, León and Navarre (all in northern Spain), large areas of Extremadura and Old Castile, much of Andalusia, the Balearics in the Mediterranean and the Canaries in the Atlantic. The original areas under Republican control were the Asturias, much of Aragon (in the north), parts of Extremadura and New Castile (including Madrid), Valencia, Murcia and parts of Andalusia. The overall trend of the war was the Nationalist north–south offensive, which gradually overcame the Republican east–west defensive.

Two regions need special explanation – Catalonia and the Basque country. Both supported the Republic against the Nationalists, but for pragmatic rather than ideological reasons. There was also a limit to their support – which was never unconditional. Their main concern was to prevent the establishment of a right-wing dictatorship, but they had no desire, either, to see the revival of a strengthened centralized system of the left base on Madrid. Catalonia's commitment was not to the Republic as such. Rather, it saw the Republic as the only means of preserving the autonomy granted in the 1932 Catalan Statute. Franco, it was well known, intended to reimpose a unitary state, while Catalonia aimed at independence. Although it was never in a position to secede from Spain, it formed its own *Generalitat* and army. Increasingly it was seen by the Republican government in Madrid as an ally rather than a province, particularly in view of the complex state of its internal affairs. During the course of the Civil War Catalonia resisted bravely; Barcelona was bombed by the Nationalists and eventually conquered in 1939. Like Catalonia, the Basques also felt that the Republic would be more likely to uphold the autonomy granted in the statute of October 1933. Despite a considerable range of political viewpoints there was an internal alliance between PNV (Basque National Party) and other parties, including socialists and communists. The Basque government managed to prevent the extreme anticlericalism seen in other areas and also prepared their own defences rather than become fully integrated into the Republic. Independence remained the key Basque objective – although through co-operation with Republicans. But, like the Catalans, they suffered at the hands of Franco. At the outset the Basque country was surrounded by Nationalist-held territory. The Nationalists therefore considered it an enemy and launched a major offensive in 1937: this included the bombing of Guernica – which became a great symbol of 'fascist' brutality – and the capture of Bilbao.

Social classes

To what extent did the sides in the Civil War reflect class divisions? The general trend is obvious. According to Carr, 'Where they were free to choose, the working classes chose the Republic and the upper classes were, with few exceptions, fanatic Nationalists'.[25] The middle classes are more difficult to assess but it seems that the young intellectuals and members of the professions were inclined to the Republic, their elder peers to Franco. Preston argues that the greatest divide was in the rural areas between the landlords and the exploited peasants; this applied especially in Andalusia and Extremadura. The wealthy landlords did whatever possible to destroy the reforming legislation of 1931 and showed a callous indifference to the plight of the poorest peasantry. It is hardly surprising, therefore, that where they could the peasantry and estate owners aligned themselves respectively with the Republicans and Nationalists.

Despite the self-evident political allegiance on the basis of class differences, there were some less predictable cross-currents. One was the generational divide, which affected many families in a tragic way: younger members were more likely to commit themselves to the Republic, their elders to Franco. Another cross-current was loyalty to regional patriotism or to the Catholic Church, both which might displace the priority of class loyalty. Finally, the accident of where they lived decided for many people which side they supported. As in any civil war, it was taken for granted that the population of occupied zones would act as cannon fodder for the victors.

Issues between the sides

The sides in any war – and especially civil war – simplify opposing positions and press ideas to extremes. To do otherwise would be considered an incomplete war effort and an obstacle to the pursuit of ultimate victory. Two generalizations are often made about the two sides in the Spanish Civil War.

A struggle between 'fascism' and 'communism'?

The Nationalist case was that the Republic was an alien intrusion, subjecting traditional Spain to the full threat of communism. This had first become apparent through the measures taken by the Second Republic from 1931 onwards; the dangers had then intensified with the assistance given to the Republicans by Stalin and the Soviet Union from the end of 1936. According to the rebels, the shadow of communism covered everything in the Republican sphere. This was also the perspective of the right wing outside Spain. In Britain, the author Florence Farmborough spoke for many in 1938 when she idealised Franco's 'National Crusade against the Red Ministers of the corrupt Spanish Government who, dupes of Soviet Russia, were undermining the foundations of his country's well-being'.[26] Franco, she said, was to be admired for his devotion to 'the Reconquest of Spain from the Red Infidel'.[27]

The Republicans, by contrast, saw the Nationalist uprising as a military threat to the progress already made by the Second Republic. What made it particularly dangerous was its identification with the foreign ideologies and structures of Italy and Germany and their imposition on conquered areas with external military support. It was therefore an easy step to describe the new right as 'fascist' and as a departure from earlier Spanish dictatorships like that of Miguel Primo de Rivera.

These were obvious oversimplifications, produced as defensive propaganda. There may have been *elements* of truth in both cases. A substantial part of the support for the Republic *did* come from communist activists (whether from the PCE or POUM) and the influence of the Soviet Union *did* grow as the western democracies made it clear that the Republic could not rely on their support. Similarly, organizations within the Nationalists (like the Falange) *were* influenced by Mussolini, and Franco's movement as a whole *was* directly aligned with fascism externally. Yet, in both cases, the elements of fascism and communism were only partial. Neither side adopted the overall label – nor liked it being used by its opponents. We have already seen that Franco kept fascist influences under control within the broader context of the FET-JONS. The Republicans, perhaps, were more under communist control than the Nationalists were under fascism. But even here communist policies and organization were far from uniformly accepted by the rest. Disagreements over strategy and priorities suggest that communism was no more the *overriding* defining character for the Republic than fascism was for the Nationalists.

There was also a strong international perspective. The 1930s were a decade in which extremes were seen to be developing on both right and left, as democracy shrivelled in some parts of Europe and withdrew into a defensive mode in others. The Spanish Civil War came to be seen, in E.H. Carr's description, as a European war fought in Spain, and politicians were quick to add the labels of 'fascism' and 'communism' to the two extremes. In Britain, especially, these were used freely and indiscriminately. Baldwin, for example, referred to the 'mumps and measles' of fascism and communism. He saw what was happening in Spain as a clear example of such polarization and as full of warnings for the future. 'We English hate fascism, but we loathe bolshevism as much. So if there is somewhere where fascists and Bolsheviks can kill each other, so much the better.'[28]

A struggle between 'Christianity' and 'atheism'?

This was another issue that attracted extreme interpretations at the time. The original military revolt was not undertaken as a religious cause. But the Nationalists found it useful to claim to be defending Spanish Christianity against the forces of atheism since this appeared to legitimize their actions during the course of the war. For their part, the Republicans made no claim to be supporting any atheist offensive – or even to be acting in its defence. Instead, their aim was to make Spain a secular state and to control what they saw as the excessive power of the Catholic Church. Atheism, it is true, was an influence, especially from the communist left, but it was never official Republican policy.

In a radio broadcast in August 1936, Mola announced that one of the objectives of the Nationalist offensive in the north was to 'build a great, strong, powerful State that is set to be crowned by a Cross'.[29] Franco also made an early announcement that he would defend the Church, along with '*Patria*, religion and the family'.[30] He was supported by the papacy, which associated what was happening in Republican Spain – especially the perceived domination by communism – with atheism. The case was also put by Spanish Church leaders: the Bishop of Salamanca referred to the Nationalist effort as 'a crusade against communism to save religion, the fatherland and the family'.[31] The same theme was taken up in Britain and elsewhere by the *Tablet*, which declared that Franco was 'saving Europe from the New Barbarism'.[32] In its justification for foreign support for Franco, the *Daily Mail* painted a lurid picture: 'Like Lucifer before the Fall, Stalin may mobilise the powers of Darkness, but the German Michael is also fast preparing to take the field.'[33]

The Republicans rejected any accusation that they were trying to eliminate Christianity. Rather, their aim was to bring the Church into line with a society that had already become more secular. Why, for example, should the Church continue to have so much control over education, or over the official ban on divorce, when the vast majority of Catholics in Spain never attended church services other than for baptisms, weddings or funerals? The left-wing press in Britain welcomed the promise of 'an absolute freedom of religious thought',[34] reflecting Azaña's response to criticism of the 1931 reforms: 'Do not tell me that this is contrary to freedom. It is a matter of public health.' The Republic was therefore trying to remove not the Church itself – less still Christianity – but an embedded obstacle to modernizing reform.

The Republic's measures against the Church were, however, open to considerable criticism. The treatment of the Catholic Church was more radical than anywhere else in Europe except the Soviet Union. Its status was more secure in Italy under the 1929 Lateran Treaty; in Germany under the 1933 Concordat; in authoritarian dictatorships like Austria, Poland and Portugal; and in western democracies like the United Kingdom, France and the United States. There was also an outcry throughout Europe at the massacre of clergy and members of religious orders in Republican areas during the opening months of the war in 1936. The victims included 13 bishops, 4,184 priests, 2,365 members of male religious orders and 283 nuns.[35] Yet criticism by the Nationalists and their supporters was overstated in several ways. Any balanced assessment shows that reforms of 1931 were at least partially needed, even if these were taken too far. The Nationalist case was, in part at least, opportunist propaganda, supported by an institution with an embedded aversion to growing secular influences in Spain. Generalizations about the influence of communism on the Republicans (largely true) were extended automatically to the threat of atheism against the Church and Christianity (largely untrue). There is no evidence that the Republican half of Spain was anti-Christian to the point of fighting for atheism. It was more a case of wanting to control the clerical influence on a society that the Republican half had accepted as secular. It is therefore vital to distinguish between secularism and atheism, especially if the latter was associated with other ideological connotations. The Nationalists and their supporters automatically connected atheism with communism and the Soviet Union. But such influences did not represent the majority of Republican supporters' viewpoints: as we have seen, communism was more an organizational than an ideological influence.

THE OUTSIDE WORLD AND THE SPANISH CIVIL WAR

Outline

The European powers reacted quickly to the outbreak of civil war in the wake of Franco's uprising. Baldwin's government in Britain chose neutrality and put pressure on Blum, the French prime minister, to do the same; Roosevelt's administration in the United States supported Britain's line. At first, the Soviet Union made no definite decision, but Stalin soon changed his mind, opting to back the beleaguered Republic, as did the Latin American republic of Mexico. Hitler's Germany, Mussolini's Italy and Salazar's Portugal expressed early support for the Nationalists. Many other regimes in Europe and Latin America tried to keep clear of the conflict, although there was, among them, a greater volume of sympathy for the Nationalists than for the Republic.

By the end of 1936 there was a flow of weapons and advisers to the Nationalists from Italy and Germany, which was sustained throughout the war. Portugal co-operated fully with Franco, allowing transit facilities and handing back Republican refugees, while avoiding any direct military involvement in the war. The Soviet Union, meanwhile, had started arms deliveries to the Republic. Although substantial, these were to prove more precarious and the provision had virtually stopped by 1938. The western democracies, led by Britain, set up the Non-Intervention Committee (NIC) almost as soon as the war had started, with the aim of trying to prevent the supply of arms and war *matériel* to either side. At first all the powers subscribed to this, although Germany, Italy and the Soviet Union proceeded to ignore and bypass its provisions. Britain, France and the United States, however, continued to abide by them.

The Spanish Civil War had a huge impact on peoples as well as on governments. Most democracies were divided over whether their citizens supported the Nationalists or the Republicans. The former tended to gain the sympathy of the political right, of spokesmen for the Catholic Church and of business interests, especially oil corporations. The Republic, on the other hand was more likely to attract the support of the political left, particularly in Britain and France. Many individuals ignored their governments' official policy of non-intervention to volunteer for service in the International Brigades (p. 282). The Brigades even contained men and women prepared to defy their government's open backing for the Nationalists. It is, therefore, hardly surprising that Europe was influenced by unprecedented amounts of propaganda.

The powers and the Republicans

The Republic hoped at the outset for sympathy, even assistance, from its fellow democracies in Europe – especially France – to enable it to face up to the impending threat of another military dictatorship. This was not forthcoming.

In Britain, for example, there was extensive sympathy for the Nationalists from the ruling classes, who expected Franco to impose a pro-British dictatorship – somewhat like Salazar's in Portugal. In ideological terms, the real enemy was considered to be communism, not fascism, and therefore Stalin, not Franco. The British government still hoped to come to terms with Germany and also to revive Anglo-Italian friendship. There was no question of direct support for the Nationalists but, equally, there appeared to be a strong case against risking a general war for the sake of bolstering up a Republic that was inclining increasingly to the left. On 26 July 1936, therefore, Prime Minister Baldwin instructed Foreign Secretary Eden that: 'On no account, French or other, must you bring us into the fight on the side of the Russians.'[36] France, however, was reluctant to become involved, even though Blum's Popular Front government was more sympathetic than Baldwin to the Republic. Blum and Daladier feared the impact of any French involvement on France internally: it would alienate important groups like the Catholic Church and would stir up extremes greater than those in Britain. There was also growing concern that the large number of strikes, exacerbated by France's delayed recovery from the Depression, might turn political, even revolutionary. Above all, the French government feared the prospect of diplomatic isolation in Europe if it supported the Spanish Republic unilaterally. Therefore Blum and Daladier were susceptible to British pressure on them to ban all arms sales to the Republic and to persuade other countries to keep out of the conflict.

This was to be the purpose of the Non-Intervention Committee, an initiative led by Britain and – because of Blum's dilemma – followed by France. By the end of August 1936 the idea of non-intervention had gained the support of twenty-seven European states, including Germany, Italy and the Soviet Union. The Committee itself was set up in September 1936 in London, presided over by the Earl of Plymouth. Its self-proclaimed purpose was to 'abstain from all interference, either direct or indirect, in the internal affairs' of Spain and to prevent 'the exporting, re-exporting and delivery to Spain, Spanish possessions or the Spanish zone in Morocco, of all types of arms, munitions and war materiel'.[37] It quickly became apparent that the NIC could not enforce these provisions, as Germany and Italy had no intention of carrying out principles. The Spanish Republic, increasingly disillusioned by failures to deal with the large arms supplies to the Nationalists, did what it could to undermine the NIC by seeking Soviet help and recruiting the International Brigades. The British and French governments were fully aware of the problems, although Eden argued that 'even a leaking ship serves its purpose'. By the time it had been disbanded in April 1939 its reputation lay in tatters and little has been done to revive it since. Eisenwein and Shubert, for example, argue that 'the NIC fell short in almost every other respect of fulfilling its original mandate. Not only did it fail to halt foreign intervention in Spain, but its existence fatally undermined the hope that international conflicts could be effectively resolved through collective negotiation.'[38] Salvadó goes even further: 'The NIC's blatant inefficiency was largely the consequence of being, in reality, a piece of humbug, an instrument of British diplomacy.'[39]

The Republic's main ally was Stalin, although at first he prevaricated. His initial concern was that the rise of Hitler in Germany necessitated improved relations between the Soviet Union, Britain and France. Soviet assistance to Spain along the lines proposed by Comintern policy could well undermine the Treaty of Mutual Assistance between the Soviet Union and France in 1936 and destroy the policy of collective security to which Stalin still held. But, for several reasons, Stalin soon changed his policy. He was alarmed by the growing evidence of German and Italian support for Franco – and encouraged by the willingness of the Republic to hand over its gold reserves to Gosbank in October 1936. He developed new objectives, which Payne describes as geostrategic and internal.[40] Strategically he intended to reduce the German threat in Europe by developing closer connections with Britain and France; this meant trying to persuade the latter to reverse their policies towards Spain and to be more open to a popular-front approach. Internally, Stalin hoped to develop, under Soviet influence and Spanish Communist Party control, a more effective Spanish resistance to the Nationalists. This would involve reducing the influence of the POUM and Anarcho-Syndicalists and enforcing a more disciplined approach. Stalin might, of course, have had a more opportunist and pragmatic motive: by supporting the Republic he would strengthen its resistance, thereby prolonging German involvement and diverting Hitler's attention from eastern Europe.

The Soviet Union sent the first arms shipments to the Republic in October 1936. Total contributions to the Republican war effort amounted to 627 aircraft, 331 tanks, 60 armoured cars, 1,170 artillery pieces, small arms and ammunition, along with Soviet advisers, engineers and pilots. Officers from the NKVD increased Soviet influence over the Republic's political organization and military strategy. But Soviet assistance ceased well before the end of the war. Stalin had always been unwilling to commit Russia too heavily in case he should leave Russia vulnerable to invasion by Germany. In any case, his involvement in Spain was partly intended to stiffen the West against fascism but, once it became clear that appeasement was the order of the day, he lost interest. Munich finally convinced Stalin that he should withdraw altogether, leaving the Republic vulnerable to the final Nationalist offensive in 1939.

The greatest initial advantage of the Republic was that it had the world's fourth largest gold reserve – sufficient, it might be thought, to finance military operations against Franco. Added to this was government control over the main cities and industrial areas. But the Republic soon met serious difficulties in paying through normal banking channels for arms shipments. The main reason for this was the reluctance of bankers to defy government orders on neutrality. Eventually the Soviet Union agreed to make necessary provision. The price, however, was to transfer Spain's gold reserves to Moscow; Stalin refused point-blank to provide the Republic with the credit being made available to Franco by Hitler and Mussolini. In September 1936 707 tonnes of ingots and coins were moved from Madrid to Cartagena to prevent them from being captured by the Nationalists who were besieging the capital; the consignments, worth a total of $805 million, were then transferred by sea to Odessa, before eventually arriving in Moscow in November. Most of it was used up in financing Soviet equipment to Republic, although a portion found its way to France, where it was impounded.

The Republicans also received military help from the International Brigades. Organized by Comintern, these provided a total of between 35,000 and 40,000 volunteers from France (which provided the largest number), Britain, Canada, Yugoslavia, Hungary, Czechoslovakia, Sweden, Switzerland, Austria, Germany, Italy and fifty-three other countries.[41] The greatest concentrations took part in the battles for Teruel and Aragón (December 1937 to April 1938). They also served in the defence of Madrid – although their exploits may have been exaggerated by Francoists and anti-Republicans abroad to give the impression that only outside help was keeping the Republic afloat. In September 1938 the Republic's Prime Minister, Negrin, announced at the League of Nations General Assembly the withdrawal of all foreign troops, hoping that the Nationalists would do the same. After the departure of the Brigades in October, Mussolini responded by pulling out 10,000 Italians. But the vast majority remained, seeing the Nationalists through to victory in 1939.

The powers and the Nationalists

As we have seen, some of the powers, including Britain, France and the United States, were ambivalent about the Nationalists. But three states specifically supported their rebellion and campaign against the Republic: Portugal, Germany and Italy.

Salazar supported Franco for ideological and strategic reasons. There were strong connections between what the Nationalists stood for and the beliefs of Salazar himself – social conservatism, the role of the Catholic Church and, above all, anti-Communism. Indeed, the future of the Salazar regime was at stake, for a Communist victory in Spain would then lead to pressure for intervention in Portugal. At the same time, Salazar was unwilling to commit to a full military alliance, since this would put a strain on the Portuguese economy and would threaten Portugal's connection with Britain, thereby endangering the security of Portugal's Atlantic islands. He therefore made a limited but significant contribution to Franco's enterprise. 10,000 *Viriatos* (volunteers paid by Portuguese government) fought alongside the Nationalists and the Portuguese authorities were instructed to return Republican refugees from Andalusia and Extremadura. Portugal was one of the main offenders in evading the restrictions of the NIC, although Foreign Minister Monteiro did much to reassure the British government that Franco's victory 'would not necessarily mean an Italian- or German-type military victory'.[42] Portugal was also of crucial strategic importance, especially in the earlier period, allowing the Nationalists to link the northern and southern offensives, secure in the knowledge that they had a friendly neighbour to their west. Access to Portugal's roads, railways and, above all, ports, compensated for the Nationalist restrictions in the Republican-dominated east of Spain. According to Salvadó, Portugal was 'the perfect conduit through which foreign aid could be delivered'.[43]

Mussolini also had good reason to support the Nationalists. Strongly in favour of the dictatorship of Primo de Rivera, he deplored Spain's swing to the left in 1931 with the formation of the Second Republic. He became involved in some nefarious dealings with anti-Republic rightists in 1934, although not at that stage as part of a deliberate plot to overthrow the Republic. But when an opportunity came in July 1936 to assist Franco's crossing from Morocco and Mola's advance in northern Spain, Mussolini despatched the first consignment of aircraft. He formalized the connection with Franco in the Secret Pact of Friendship in November 1936. Mussolini's intervention seemed to make sense, after Italy's imperial expansion in Libya and Ethiopia, as part of his new ambition to make the Mediterranean an Italian sea and to threaten Britain's sea routes. Meanwhile, Mussolini could depend on establishing closer relations with Germany even, perhaps, to the extent of being able to claim the role of 'senior fascist'. Finally, his propaganda against Republican Spain and communism would be sure to weaken the Anglo-French position in Europe and undermine their attempt to maintain sanctions on Italy over the invasion of Ethiopia. To fulfil these extensive ambitions Mussolini was prepared to provide Franco with considerable assistance. He sent 78,000 ground troops, most in the CTV (*Corpo di Truppe Voluntarie*), half of whom were actually members of the Italian regular army, while equipment included[44] 950 tanks, 763 aircraft, 1,672 tons of bombs and 1,930 cannon.

Hitler had initially shown indifference to Spain as all his expansionist ambitions lay in the east. The only real significance of the west was the traditional enmity with France; there had been no significant mention in *Mein Kampf* of any ambitions involving Spain. Everything, however, changed with Franco's uprising. Hitler provided 16,000 military advisers, the latest aircraft and the services of the Condor Legion, 140 aircraft (Heinkel 51s and Junkers 52s), 48 tanks and 60 anti-aircraft guns.[45] Total contributions in manpower amounted to about 19,000 – usually 5,500 at a time but rotated to ensure that their training and experience were spread as widely as possible. Hitler's response was more pragmatic, opportunist – and cautious – than Mussolini's. His aims were to cause problems within France by splitting the left bloc, while establishing a pro-German Nationalist regime in Spain would ensure that France would be confronted from three directions by hostile right-wing regimes. He intended to use the connections between the Spanish Republic and the Soviet Union to exploit the fear of communism and to prevent the tightening of any connection between France and Russia. There were also advantages in encouraging Italy to become more fully involved in Spain, since this made it easier for Hitler to carry out the Anschluss with Austria in 1938 and to encourage Italy to join the Anti-Comintern Pact and the Pact of Steel. In addition, Hitler was persuaded by the economic reasons put to him by the Four Year Plan

Office for supporting the Nationalists: Germany would be provided with direct access to Spain's minerals as these came under Nationalist control, especially iron-ore, copper, pyrites, mercury, lead, zinc and wolfram (tungsten). Previously on a par with Britain as an importer of strategic materials, Germany was now able to establish a commanding lead, adversely affecting the rate of Britain's rearmament. Finally, Hitler was influenced by the arguments of Goering that involvement in the Spanish Civil War would provide an opportunity to 'try out my young air force' and to establish whether the 'materiel' was 'fit for purpose'.[46]

In terms of manpower, the total contributions to the Nationalist war effort were therefore 10,000 Portuguese, 78,000 Italians and 19,000 Germans. In addition there was support from volunteers from other countries. These included up to 1,500 Irish Catholics under O'Duffy, 300 French volunteers from the *Croix de Feu*, White Russians who had fought against the Bolsheviks in the Russian Civil War, and right-wing volunteers from eastern Europe. At first the Nationalists faced a massive problem in financing all this aid, as all of Spain's gold reserves were in Republican hands, but Italy and Germany soon offset this in a series of financial agreements. According to Vinas, these were 'the principal way in which the Burgos [Nationalist] government could manage to make the international payments necessary to strengthen the war sector of its economy'.[47] Italy provided aid worth a total of $263 million, while Germany contributed arms worth $215 million. Altogether Franco may well have received as much as $570 million from abroad. A significant amount of business was also done by multinational companies in the western democracies. Whealey cites as examples the Texas Oil Company, Texaco, Shell, Standard of New Jersey and the Atlantic Refining Company. Clearly the expectation and hope of major financiers was for a Nationalist victory.

A prelude to the Second World War?

A common generalization is that the Spanish Civil War was directly related to the Second World War. This has, however, been challenged by an alternative view – that its connection was more with the First.

Two quotations exemplify the first approach. Liddell Hart maintained that the second Great War of the twentieth century began in Spain in July 1936,[48] and, according to Whealey, the Spanish Civil War was 'an opening round of the great power struggle now called World War II'.[49] There is extensive support for this argument. The Spanish Civil War helped bring on general war by providing opportunities for both Hitler and Mussolini. Their further pressure was encouraged by the absence of any resistance from the western powers. Eisenwein and Shubert argue that by 'turning a blind eye' to the political implications of foreign intervention in Spain, the non-intervention policy of Britain and France 'contributed to the uninterrupted rise of fascism elsewhere in Europe'.[50] Germany benefited most directly: 'Hitler welcomed the Duce's imperialist concentration on the southwest, because that meant Austria by 1938 was free for the Führer's taking.' The Spanish war also 'helped divert France, Britain and the USSR in the fall of 1938 from uniting to defend Czechoslovakia against German territorial demands'.[51]

There are, however, some inconsistencies in trying to establish a *direct* connection between the Spanish Civil War and the Second World War. One is the way in which the latter actually broke out. The immediate reason was Hitler's refusal to heed the Anglo-French Guarantee to Poland (March 1939), which was actually a reversal of the appeasement they had followed during the civil war. Another was the reversal of Stalin's foreign policy: his Non-Aggression Pact with Germany was a total abandonment of the Comintern 'popular front' against fascism that had prevailed in Spain. And, of course, the economic impact of the Spanish conflict on Italy actually delayed Mussolini's entry into the Second World War – despite the apparently bellicose Pact of Steel with Germany in 1939. Finally, there were mixed lessons learned from the Spanish war in terms of strategy and weaponry: for every successful application of military experience gained between 1936 and 1939, there were several mistakes or missed opportunities when it came to a broader conflict.

Some historians have therefore reset the context of the Spanish Civil War and the Second World War. A.J.P. Taylor maintained as early as 1961 that the Spanish Civil War had no significant effect on the European powers. In 2004, Payne argued that 'The Spanish war was a clear-cut revolutionary/counterrevolutionary contest between left and right, with the fascist totalitarian powers supporting the right and the Soviet totalitarian power supporting the left'. But, he continued, this was not the way in which the Second World War broke out. This followed the Nazi–Soviet Pact (August 1939) which allowed the Soviet Union 'to conquer a sizable swath of Eastern Europe while Germany was left free to conquer as much of the rest of the continent as it could'.[52] If anything, the Spanish situation resembled more 'a post-World War I crisis than a crisis of the era of World War II'.[53] This view certainly deals with the inconsistencies mentioned in the actual outbreak of the war: the change of Soviet and western policy which, between them, brought about the situation in which war occurred. It also provides more continuity between the Spanish conflict and the past, an area ignored by some international perspectives. Payne's argument that the 'revolutionary breakdown of institutions' and the development of full-scale civil wars was characteristic of the period after the First World War is exemplified by the situations in Germany, Hungary and Finland, while there were no other equivalents in the 1930s.

It could, however, be argued that there was an alternative connection between the Spanish Civil War and the Second World War – one that was *in*direct, even paradoxical. The latter conflict was accelerated by the inconsistent nature of western and Soviet policies arising in part out of lessons deduced from the situation in Spain. The Anglo-French switch from appeasement to guarantees in March 1939 was due directly to failure of the Munich Agreement, but also to the indirect and cumulative impact of Spanish Civil War. Similarly, the sudden change in Stalin's policy in August 1939 related to his distrust of western resolve which, he felt, had been amply demonstrated over the Anglo-French attitude to the Spanish Republic. But both Stalin and Hitler made the same mistake – wrongly deducing from the Spanish Civil War that appeasement had become irreversible. While it would be an oversimplification to see the Spanish Civil War as the prologue to the Second World War, to cut the connection altogether would be to underestimate the volatility caused by lessons wrongly learned from the period 1936–9.

THE OUTCOME AND IMPACT OF THE SPANISH CIVIL WAR

Why did the Nationalists win – and the Republic lose – the war?

The outcome of the Spanish Civil War was decisive in many ways. Like the Russian Civil War, it produced major changes: in this case, it swept away the Second Republic, along with the reforms introduced from 1931 onwards, and substituted a Nationalist dictatorship with a starkly different set of beliefs and objectives. This section offers explanations as to why the Nationalists won and the Republic lost. Although the answers have already been inferred, a more integrated comparison is now needed, connecting the propositions that the Nationalists won *because* the Republicans lost while the Republican defeat was the *result* of Nationalist victory.

As we have seen, both sides were coalitions of different groups. Neither coalition was naturally cohesive and both had a range of views and objectives. But there were certain obvious differences. The Nationalists covered a narrower political spectrum – from the moderate right to the far right, whereas the Republicans had support from the centre to the far left (which was itself fragmented). The Nationalist coalition depended more on attack and rebellion, favouring a more disciplined form of structure and leadership. The Republic already had an official government and therefore the more complex task of defending what had so far been achieved. It also had to live with numerous existing rivalries and, in the interest of getting external help from somewhere – anywhere – it took on new ones. There was therefore a clear contrast between the more centralized and structured system of Nationalist control and the fractured command of the Republicans.

One of Franco's main priorities was to create unity among his supporters. He managed to overcome internal disputes and to balance the different Nationalist groups. He satisfied the Carlists by leaving open the question of the monarchy and by catering for their demand for legislation that favoured the Catholic Church. These moves, admittedly, were not to the liking of the more radical Falangists, but they were pacified by being allowed to direct propaganda and to influence those characteristics of a mass movement that Franco was prepared to allow; they were also pleased by his close relations with Italy and Germany. The army, bereft of any real ideas of its own, depended completely on Franco to maintain its position and influence. He was able to impose a more uniform approach on the Carlists, Falange and conservative factions within a new political party, the FET-JONS, established in 1937, which linked the Falange with the earlier *Juntas de Ofensiva Nacional Sindicalista*. At the same time, he prevented any of the constituents from becoming predominant. He also maintained military control: some Carlists, for example, wanted to establish a distinctively corporatist regime along traditional lines with clerical influences – and also a separate military academy. Franco reacted by exiling the faction's leader, Fal, who subsequently left for Portugal.

The Republic suffered from more permanent divisions which undermined its war effort and military capacity; indeed, it has been argued that it experienced 'a civil war within the civil war'. There was, for example, a three-sided conflict between liberal constitutionalists; authoritarian socialists or communists (PCE); and far-left anarchists (CNT) and Anti-Stalinist communists (POUM). The ideological range was considerable, the two extremes being western democratic theories on the one hand and the revolutionary left on the other. The latter, in turn, was divided over the primary objective of the war, in complete contrast with the unity of the Nationalist strategy. One Republican approach was to maintain the Popular Front and put all the effort into the defeat of Franco; this was backed by most socialists, Marxists and pro-Stalin communists. The alternative emphasis was that of the CNT and the POUM; these wanted to progress with the 'revolution' in the belief that compromising on this would weaken the war effort. The disagreements were sometimes violently expressed: fighting, for example, broke out in Barcelona in 1937 between anarchists, socialists and communists. Republican Spain was also affected by disunity caused by importing conflicts from the Soviet Union which had resulted from the Stalin–Trotsky rivalry and the terror of the show trials. Overall, the Soviet Union interfered far more in Republican politics than did Italy and Germany in Nationalist Spain.

All this had implications for the way in which the war was won – and lost – amongst the wider population. The Republic increasingly lost support in both urban and rural areas. This was partly a matter of the difficulty of challenging the spread of Nationalist control and partly popular disillusionment with Republican disagreements over how to implement collectivization. In the Nationalist zones, therefore, former Republican supporters focused on survival, realizing that they had more to lose from Nationalist brutality than they could gain from supporting dwindling Republican aspirations.

As in any war, leadership was crucial. For the Nationalists, Franco combined the main forms in his person, becoming *Generalísimo* of the army in September 1936 and 'Head of Government of the Spanish State' in October 1936. Throughout the period of the war, Franco also took the title of *Caudillo* – indicating a perceived connection with the warrior-leaders of medieval times. In Casanova's words, his was 'a single military command and a centralised political apparatus'.[54] Jackson describes Franco as 'an authoritarian leader of immense contradictory forces within his camp', who made 'good use of the diplomatic and administrative talent at his disposal',[55] while Gallo sees him as 'competent and determined'.[56] Although Franco had shortcomings, he showed remarkable determination and commitment to his principles; these, according to Crozier, were 'Duty, Discipline and Order'.[57] His basic programme was single-minded and simplistic, assuming the nature of a crusade which was fired by bigoted passion. The Republicans had no equivalent, their leadership being more fragmented and regionalized. The Republic's democratic system had been retained sufficiently to separate out the offices of president and prime minister, which were filled by different persons, as were the regional governments of Catalonia and the Basque country. There was no overall figure remotely comparable to Franco. Instead, different leaders represented divergent groups and interests. Azaña, a Republican, was Prime Minister (1931–3 and 1936), before becoming President in 1936. Largo Caballero, leader of the *Partido Socialista Obrero Español* and of the trade union organization UGT, was President of Republic between 1936 and 1937. Martínez Barrio, formerly Prime Minister in 1933, was the speaker of the Cortes throughout the war. Negrín, a socialist leader, succeeded Caballero as President from 1937 to 1939; he, especially, felt obliged to strengthen his alliance with the PCE communists because of their deep involvement in the military and the dependence of the Republic on Soviet aid. The Republic therefore had an overall lack of united control; furthermore, none of these politicians were military leaders and had to involve themselves in difficult negotiations with the various split commands of the Republican militias.

Another significant reason for the victory of the Nationalists was their superior military structure and organization. The Nationalists inherited an army, which they geared up for revolt, whereas the Republicans had to build one to defend the status quo. Not surprisingly, the Nationalists had a professional corps (including seasoned Moroccans), whereas the Republicans initially had to depend on militias. The main difficulty was that the Republican militias had to be converted into a People's Army through 'militarization', even though the militia system was actually preferred by Anarchists, POUM and left socialists. Militarization involved a unified command, which Anarchists and POUM disliked, fearing overall communist control. The Nationalists had no such problems, as Franco imposed rigorous military discipline on all his forces. He also developed a far more efficient military administration. Carr maintains that 'Its notable achievements notwithstanding, the Popular Army, as a military machine that could be deployed by a unified command, was inferior to the Nationalist Army'.[58]

The Republic had its fair share of loyal generals but a severe shortage of middle-ranking officers, which meant that it was necessary to promote numerous inexperienced NCOs to this vitally important level. Beevor points out that 'The new breed of republican commander emerging at this time was young, aggressive, ruthless and personally brave, but as utterly conventional and unimaginative as the old officers of the metropolitan army'.[59] Examples include Modesto, Lister and Tagüeña. The Nationalist army was trained or re-trained from the outset, important contributions to this being provided by the Germans, especially the Condor Legion. The Nationalists also had a more systematic method, their twenty-eight military academies turning out a total of 30,000 trained officers. A serious disadvantage of the Republican militia system – and its successors – was that all strategy was discussed at length, which reduced efficiency and encouraged insubordination. In fact the failings of the Republican high command has been seen by Beevor as the single most important factor in the outcome of the war.[60] Their offensives against the Nationalists were too conventional and overdependence on their propaganda value seriously undermined their flexibility. This was largely the result of reliance on obsolete tactics directly imported from Russia, where the more flexible Marshal Tukhachevsky had already been purged. Hence, during the late 1930s, 'The exhortation of the new republican brigades may have been revolutionary in language, but the manoeuvring was Tsarist'.[61] As for Nationalist battle strategy, Franco was imaginative but solid. His great strength was his cautious and thorough preparation. He would never start an offensive unless he was certain he could see it through to the end. He was often criticized by his allies abroad for his slowness but, in the end, he got results.

As we have already seen, the Spanish Civil War involved an international dimension. This worked very much in favour of the Nationalists and against the Republic. The involvement of the powers in the Nationalist struggle was generally *constructive* whereas the Republic experienced, on balance, a more *obstructive* intervention. The Republic was up against an international climate which had the unfortunate combination of non-intervention and appeasement. Non-intervention was applied against the Republic, but was rendered ineffectual against the Nationalists because of the pursuit of appeasement to avoid any possibility of a drift to war with Germany. Admittedly, Soviet intervention provided some considerable help to the Republic at a time when the latter was deprived of the assistance it had hoped to receive from the western democracies. But the quality was well below that of the Germans and Italians to the Nationalists, in both quantity and quality. The Nationalists benefited at three main stages of the war, managing as a direct result of external contributions to overcome Republican defences or attempted offensives. The first was the transporting of Spanish troops from Morocco into southern Spain in Italian and German aircraft, enabling Franco to conquer Andalusia in 1936. The second was the boost given to Nationalist morale, after a series of Republican victories in 1937, by a sudden increase in Italian equipment. And the third was another massive flow of armaments in 1939 which made it possible for Franco to crush Catalonia, now starved of Soviet aid. The Nationalists could also depend on also had regular supplies through south-western Spain and Morocco or, more particularly, through Portugal. The Republic, on the other hand, suffered disruption to deliveries to the west coast of Spain (which it controlled) because of the threat of Italian submarines in the Mediterranean to Soviet supply ships. This meant that Soviet deliveries to the Republic had to be made by northern routes. But, since the northern ports of Spain were soon closed by the Nationalists, the arms consignments had to be smuggled through French ports and across the French frontier. This became increasingly difficult as the Nationalists increased their stranglehold on northern Spain in 1938–9 – so that eventually the Soviet Union gave up the attempt.

Financial arrangements also benefited the Nationalists. Any initial advantage the Republic may have had through its control of Spain's gold reserves was dissipated when these were shipped off to the Soviet Union. There they disappeared, some used to secure arms on the international markets, some appropriated to boost Soviet foreign exchange for its own purposes. At all events, the gold reserves were all used up and the Soviet Union provided no further aid beyond 1938. The Nationalists were treated more leniently. Both Germany and Italy advanced war material on the basis of longer-term loans and concessions, usually based on the supply of strategic minerals (like tungsten) from the areas under Nationalist control. Ultimately, of course, Franco was relieved of the necessity of paying back Italy and Germany for their contributions since he managed to avoid defeat in the Second World War while they did not. A significant amount of business was also done by multinational companies in the western democracies. Whealey cites as examples the Texas Oil Company, Texaco, Shell, Standard of New Jersey and the Atlantic Refining Company. Their role was vital: according to Whealey, 'without oil, the Generalissimo's machines would have ground to a halt'. They also deprived the Republic of its last chance of survival: 'Multinational corporations in the sterling dollar countries . . . helped to crush the Spanish Republicans' hopes.'[62]

The relative length of foreign involvement in the war was crucial. Franco benefited from Italian and German help from beginning to end, mainly because both of his suppliers continued to see the advantage of assisting him. For Mussolini it was a matter of maintaining his prestige in Europe and in relation to Germany. To Hitler the advantage was in reminding the western democracies of what might happen should the conflict in Spain become more generalized: this meant playing on the Anglo-French policy of appeasement. The Republic, by contrast, was starved of Soviet assistance during the last year of the conflict because of a change in Stalin's foreign policy. Abandoning any hope of reviving collective security with Britain and France, he reversed the popular front policy of Comintern and, instead, sought an accommodation with Germany that eventually resulted in the Nazi-Soviet Non-Aggression Pact in August 1939.

Overall, the Nationalists succeeded in their rebellion and military action against the Republic. The key factors were their greater cohesion, the unitary leadership provided by Franco, the momentum provided by a more effective military strategy, and the higher levels of assistance from outside Spain. The Republic lost its struggle for the reverse reasons, suffering from internal divisions, inappropriate and obsolete military strategies, a divided leadership and command, and generally hostile attitudes in Europe. Above all, the momentum continued to run in favour of the Nationalists, ensuring by 1938 that there was no hope for the Republic's survival.

What impact did the war have on the Spanish people?

It is a truism that civil war is the most vicious form of conflict, especially in its impact on civilians. The Spanish war was widely known for the suffering it caused, partly because the attention of Europe was upon it. For substantial parts of the population it meant exposure to extreme terror and a struggle for survival.

Terror occurred in both camps: the 'Red Terror' applied by the Republic and the 'White Terror' by the Nationalists. The Red Terror looked back to some of the actions of the Cheka and NKVD in Soviet Russia, while the more extensive White Terror anticipated some of the worst examples in Fascist Italy and Nazi Germany. In Spain the two forms confronted each other for the first time, involving civilians and captives of war in purges, summary executions, torture and massacres. Estimates of the total number of victims vary: Beevor puts the casualties of the Red Terror at 38,000 and those of the White Terror at between 80,000 and 200,000.[63]

The Republican wave of terror took place mainly in 1936, targeted at suspected rebels or sympathizers with the rebel cause. Revolutionary tribunals presided over the summary shooting of 'fascists' and Russian-style *checas* were set up to deal with suspected Nationalist spies. Part of the 'Red Terror' also meant mobs running riot in the streets or the countryside, killing members of the clergy and religious orders. This was defended at the time as the inevitable result of accumulated historic resentments and fears of an imminent return of clerical oppression. The anarchists, especially, saw the Catholic Church as 'the psychological operations branch of the [Nationalist] state'.[64] The result was extreme brutality as feelings ran completely out of control and 13 bishops, 4,184 priests, 2,365 members of male orders and 283 nuns were slaughtered in dreadful circumstances – mostly in 1936. On the whole, the extent of the Red Terror diminished as the war progressed. This was partly the result of a more deliberate focus on propaganda against the activities of the Nationalists and, more bluntly, because the area under the Republic's control shrank steadily. Towards the end of the war there were as many instances of summary killings through Republican in-fighting as there were executions of Nationalist supporters.

Nationalist terror, by contrast, intensified throughout the Civil War. In all areas conquered by Franco's forces, civilians suspected of left-wing leanings, especially trade unionists and middle-class professionals (including lawyers and journalists) were taken before committees that included a landowner, a civil-guard commander, a Falangist, and sometimes a priest.[65] Especially targeted were known communists or anarchists – or anyone who might become involved in future resistance to the Nationalist takeover. There were new waves of killings in recent acquisitions and a second wave to establish permanent rule within established Nationalist areas. The process involved summary executions and massacres all over Nationalist Spain, including cities like Seville, Pamplona, Burgos, Córdoba, Málaga and Valladolid. Particularly notorious was the massacre of hundreds of prisoners in the bull ring at Badajoz. The execution of captured Republicans was often upheld by the Church as a 'purge' of 'atheist influences'.

If the momentum of killing differed between the two sides, there was also a contrast in official attitudes. The Republican leadership was generally less tolerant of mass killings. Azaña, for example, threatened to resign in protest against the mob killing of Nationalist prisoners in Madrid in 1936 and there is no evidence that systematic purges were supported by the likes of Largo Caballero. With the Nationalists, the reverse was the case. Franco exhorted his squads to greater efforts against the left (often sanctioned by the authorities of the Church) as a necessary part of a crusade. This culture seeped down from the top. Eisenwein and Shubert identify one particularly significant difference. 'Repression on the right was above all distinguished by the fact that the greater part of it was systematically carried out under the ubiquitous gaze of the recognized authorities.'[66] While the Republic either disowned or tried to excuse the atrocities committed in its name, the Nationalists justified theirs as a cleansing process. In this respect Franco was certainly as brutal as Mussolini and, some have argued, comparable to Hitler. The question arises as to why the Republic was not more affected by the waves of terror in the Soviet Union. After all, the purges carried out under Lenin and Stalin were the real Red Terror in Europe, arguably exceeding in sheer quantity anything carried out by the far right – with the single exception of the Holocaust. The answer has to be that the Republic never gave itself up to Stalin's *diktats* and despite the growing extent of Soviet military influence, retained at least some democratic control over its political system. If anything rivalled the Red Terror of Stalin, it was the White Terror of Franco.

The everyday life of most Spaniards was more directly affected by Nationalist activities than by the Republic. Here Franco was able to use the initiative and momentum of the White Terror to enforce compliance and to influence civilian behaviour into accepting the inevitability of permanent Nationalist rule as each area was conquered. To most people the priorities were to avoid the attention of officials and to get on with the business of survival. In most cases this was a habit which continued well into Franco's post-war regime, so that the population's response to being terrorized was to become brutalized and accept the situation. Unlike the countries that later experienced German occupation, resistance in Spain never achieved the support of anything but a small and brave minority.

There are two reasons for this. First, patriotism – a key concept in any war – can be more easily redefined in a civil conflict than after an external invasion. Franco applied the full force of the Spanish past in a propaganda offensive against the stereotyped enemy within, who was atheistic, communistic and effete. The ideas of the Republic were more complex and open to interpretation. What, after all, was the 'freedom' that many Republican victims extolled with their last breath before the execution squads? Was it the type that promoted social equality or freedom of expression? In which case, how could the differing approaches of the communists, socialists, anarchists and liberals be reconciled? While they lived in the Republican zone people could accept – and even defend – these different approaches. But, once the Nationalists took over, their subjects lost the libertarian logic of resistance. Instead the Nationalists could impose the more compelling logic of the nation state. How could the Republic hope to oppose this? The second reason was that the Nationalists were able to stifle libertarian opposition through the reinstatement of traditional Catholic power. Franco ensured that the Church resumed control over all ceremonies involving the population. The open profession of Catholic faith was also necessary for any appointment to public office and education was returned to the influence of the Church with the permanent abolition of all anticlerical legislation introduced by the Republic in 1931. How could the population defy Franco's systematic penetration of its consciousness with supposedly Spanish virtues? Franco even attached to his government an influential Catholic group, *Opus Dei*, which, in the longer term, became an influence for reform. It is difficult to quantify the extent to which Spaniards were won over to Catholic revival. Some civilians may well have seen the restoration of Catholic influence as the forgiving side of coercion; failure to accept, or at least to go through the motions of accepting, this might expose them to the alternative of terror.

The Nationalists had another carrot (at least until 1939) to convince the Spanish people not to defy the stick of terror. Most of the areas under their rule experienced higher standards of living. According to Eisenwein and Shubert, 'Material comforts . . . made life in the Nationalist zone considerably more palatable than it was in Republican Spain'.[67] There were fewer food shortages and considerably less rationing than in the Republican areas, especially in besieged Madrid. The continual expansion of Nationalist control ensured ever greater access to agricultural production. Of particular importance was the credit obtained for war material from Germany, Italy and multinational companies. This meant that Franco could separate the financing of the war from his domestic policies, which resulted in a greater material security for the population in the Nationalist zone. But this advantage ended with the arrival of peace in 1939. In Spain's 'Hunger Years', which overlapped the first half of the Second World War, some 200,000 people starved to death. This was largely the result of Franco's new economic policy of autarky, a direct imitation of the Nazi approach. The worst of the civilian suffering therefore occurred *after* the end of the Republic. According to Sánchez, 'It was social revenge at its crudest, and the result was that even employed adults went hungry and their children starved'.[68]

To summarize, the Nationalists had the momentum in the war, which meant that more and more areas of Spain came under their control. This had two main implications. First, the Nationalists were more systematic in their elimination of 'enemies' of all kinds. Hence there were far greater numbers of Republican victims than there were targets of the Republicans. The terrorized population in the conquered areas were therefore forced into acceptance of the new Nationalist regime. Second, life in the conquered areas improved for the population who made this transition. Most civilians did comply, especially in the absence of any stigma of collaboration with an *external* enemy. A new wave of terror after the war ensured the destruction of any remaining political democracy or social reform and, instead, an unqualified commitment to a rigidly defined traditionalism.

FRANCO'S REGIME, 1939–75

Franco owed an enormous debt to the fascist states who put him in power. It might therefore be thought that his future should inevitably have been linked with theirs and that their fate should also have been his. Yet, by 1945 both Nazi Germany and Fascist Italy lay in ruins and their leaders were dead. Franco, by contrast, was still firmly in control and managed to impose his will on Spain until his death thirty years later.

Franco's regime after 1939 began with a period of consolidation and revenge, together with inward-looking economic policies based on autarky. This overlapped a difficult decision made by Franco to maintain Spanish neutrality during the Second World War – which ensured that he was not overthrown in 1945 by western intervention. For the remainder of the 1940s, however, Franco failed to bring Spain out of international isolation and pressed on with his measures of domestic control. During the 1950s, there was some relaxation in both areas, while the period 1959–73 saw a number of extensive social and economic changes – part of what has been identified as 'late Francoism' (*Tardofranquismo*).

The Second World War and Franco's foreign policy to 1975

1939–45: Franco's 'neutrality'

Spain never became totally involved in the Second World War, thereby avoiding the catastrophic military defeat suffered by Italy and Germany. There was never any doubt about Franco's sympathies for the Axis cause. General Aranda said on 5 June 1939 that 'Franco is deeply and firmly convinced that his path lies by the side of Italy and Germany. He openly detests the French and does not love the British'. In August 1940 Franco assured Mussolini of his intention 'to hasten our preparations with a view to entering the war at a propitious moment'.[69] But when, in 1940, Hitler met Franco at Hendaye in the Pyrenees he found the Caudillo evasive and uncooperative. Why?

One possibility was that Franco followed a stalling policy, which some historians have seen as 'masterly inaction'. The purpose of this was to play for time and, if necessary, to avoid committing Spain to support for the Axis alliance. Another was that Franco was motivated entirely by necessity. He had no option but to remain neutral. The Spanish economy had been ruined by the Civil War and the disruption of international commerce caused by the Second World War was sufficient to make immediate recovery impossible. The army was run-down and war-weary and there was a strong possibility that Britain and the United States would seize Spain's Atlantic islands the moment an alliance was made with either Italy or Germany. Franco was therefore grateful when his neighbour and fellow-dictator, Salazar, urged him to remain neutral.

More recently, a third reason has emerged for Franco's neutrality; bearing in mind Franco's enthusiasm for the Axis powers and their cause, this seems more likely than the other two. The argument is that Franco did not enter the war because he could not get what he wanted as a *price* for his participation. He needed two things: sufficient gains to make it worth his while to join the Axis, along with assistance from both Germany and Italy to make his participation possible and realistic. Franco sought territory in north Africa at the expense of France, which would be the fulfilment of his pre-Civil War objectives and career. But he would need German co-operation and assistance for this, not least because he was restricted by the exhaustion of the Spanish army in 1939. The question that arises here was who made the decision that determined Spain's neutrality: Franco – or Hitler? Franco subsequently took refuge behind the 'masterly inactivity' explanation, but it seems more likely that Hitler was simply not prepared to pay Franco's price. Franco had assumed that Hitler was desperate for Spain's co-operation in seizing Gibraltar, which would effectively close the Mediterranean to the British navy. However, he overestimated the importance of this to Hitler, given that Germany would have to support a second ally suffering from post-war weakness – the first of course being Mussolini's Italy. In any case, Hitler had his own aims in north Africa, which did not involve handing over former French territory to Spain.

The outcome, therefore, was that Spain remained officially neutral. Until, that is, June 1941, when Franco changed his policy from 'non-belligerence' to one of 'moral belligerence'. This meant that Spain kept out of the war against the western powers (Britain and the United States) while accepting involvement in the 'crusade against communism' and the Soviet Union. Franco's Foreign Minister, Suñer, maintained that 'Russia is to blame for our civil war' and that 'the extermination of Russia is a demand of history'.[70] Hence Franco sent 18,000 volunteers in the Blue Division to assist the German invasion. By 1943, however, it had become evident that Hitler was bogged down at Stalingrad; Franco cut his losses and withdrew his remaining troops from the Russian front. He was therefore the one European dictator who managed to pull out of the Russian flame without burning his fingers. In fact, he was able to extricate himself from all hostilities so that the western Allies, much as they disliked Franco's regime, had no reason to overthrow it during their onslaught on the Axis powers.

1945–75: from isolation to acceptance?

All the same, Spain was isolated in the late 1940s, which meant that Franco's foreign policy was based on the search for diplomatic recognition. At first this was provided only by Salazar's Portugal and Peron's Argentina, the latter agreeing to provide grain and meat on special terms. The rest of the world was hostile. The 'Big Three' at Potsdam opposed any possible bid by Franco's Spain to join the United Nations since his government did not 'in view of its origins, its nature, its record and its close association with the aggressor states, possess the qualifications necessary to justify such membership'.[71] A United Nations communiqué endorsed this view in December 1946, referring to Spain as a 'Fascist regime patterned on and established largely as a result of aid from Hitler's Nazi Germany and Mussolini's Fascist Italy'.[72] Nor were individual European countries likely to be receptive, most of them having recently elected left-wing governments. For a while Franco shrugged off this ostracism as a deliberate conspiracy that showed just how necessary his authoritarian regime was. 'Spaniards know what they can expect from abroad, and as history teaches them, ill-will against Spain is not something which began today or yesterday.'[73]

Gradually the situation began to improve as Spain became less obnoxious in the eyes of the western states. The main reason was the escalation of the Cold War with the perceived threat of world communism sponsored by the Soviet Union and China. The Berlin blockade (1948–9) and the Korean War (1950–3) both gave Franco an opportunity to end Spain's isolation and he played his diplomatic role with some skill. The result was the 1953 Madrid Pact between Spain and the United States. This provided Spain with $600 million in military aid and $500 million in economic assistance, in return for the American use of three air bases, naval facilities, pipelines and communications.[74] According to Gallo, this agreement was 'a triumph for the regime'; while Grugel and Rees go so far as to say that the regime's 'alliance with the US' was 'to be its salvation'.[75] Although the United States would have preferred to see Spain as a member of NATO, this was prevented by opposition from Norway, Denmark, the Netherlands, Belgium and Britain, even though these had agreed to the admission of Salazar's Portugal as a founding member. Nevertheless, President Eisenhower's visit to Madrid in 1959 symbolized the end of Spanish isolation in fact, even if it took longer for the rest of world to come to terms with this.

Meanwhile, another important development took place during the mid-1950s. At the very time that Salazar had announced his intention to stand firm against proposals from Britain and France for a new wave of decolonization – and to maintain Portugal's 'historic mission' of empire – Franco did the opposite for Spain. During his earlier years Franco had served in Morocco and had condemned Primo de Rivera's plans for withdrawal in the 1920s. It might be thought that he would now use the remaining Spanish empire as a rallying cry to unite public opinion behind him, perhaps as a more pragmatic version of Salazar's vision for Portugal. But he did not. With surprising haste he conferred independence on Spanish Morocco and the Spanish Sahara, although not on the Canary Islands which were an integral part of Spain. To a large extent this decision was based on a realistic assessment of Spain's position in the world: it could no longer aspire to be one of the major powers and needed, instead, to come to terms with the west.

Further progress was made during the 1960s, although this was slower than in the domestic sphere. Again, the main development was in relations with the United States. The Madrid Pact was renewed in 1963, when it stated that any threat to Spain would be a 'common concern' to the United States. Although preoccupied with the war in Vietnam, President Johnson (1963–9) maintained positive relations with Spain, while President Nixon (1969–74) drew up a new five-year agreement with Franco. Relations also improved with West Germany and the new French Fifth Republic. Even so, Spain was still not regarded as a desirable partner in international organizations. She was not admitted to NATO or the EEC until, in the decade after Franco's death, she had proved herself capable of sustaining basic democracy. A different perspective to this is offered by Buchanan. Spain, he argues, was able to 'sit comfortably' in southern Europe between 1970 and 1974, along with Salazar's Portugal and the Colonels' junta in Greece. Besides, 'It is easy to forget that . . . "democratic" Europe was still small, constricted and in many respects under threat'.[76] Democracy was limited to comparatively few countries (the six members of the EEC plus Scandinavia, Britain, Austria and Switzerland), most of which had experienced some form of political instability. Hence 'for much of the later Franco period the benefits and resilience of West European democracy were much less evident than hindsight might allow'.[77] The real difference came at the end of the Franco period, when the gap suddenly widened and Spain was threatened with renewed isolation by the collapse of fellow right-wing regimes in Portugal and Greece.

Franco's domestic policies 1939–75

The domestic sphere saw a period of repression and tight controls during the 1940s, followed by some easing in the 1950s and the 'transformation' brought by *Tardofranquismo* during the 1960s and early 1970s.

1939–59: Francoist repression and its easing

Immediately after the Civil War Franco introduced the most appalling repression, intensifying in peace the absolute power he had established in war. By the Law of 8 August 1939 he gave himself total control over state policy and administration, including supreme power of legislation without ratification by any legislative or judicial procedures. Franco was further strengthened by rivalries among his supporters, which allowed his systematic manoeuvring between different groups. Comparison has been made with Hitler who also promoted discord between individual officials. But in the case of Franco, it was the various *organizations* that differed; he preferred heterogeneity and conservatism to homogeneity based on radicalism. He imposed his own uniformity, using methods that were violent and at times as summary and horrific as those employed in the three major dictatorships. The continuation of wartime terror involved the army since 'The defence of internal peace and order constitutes the sacred mission of a nation's armed forces and this is the mission we have carried out'.[78] He therefore authorized the use of military tribunals until 1943, which employed three-minute trials and imposed mass executions. There was an increase in the number of concentration camps and in the incidence of confessions under torture. According to Carr, 'the firing squad and prison replaced the dungeons and fires of the Inquisition'.[79] There was also a systematic network of informers among the civilian population and the capture of documents during the war made possible the identification of 'enemies', like trade union members, for reprisals.

Given time, most regimes, however repulsive, begin to relax their grip. By the late 1940s Franco had begun to reduce the degree of terror and try to make Spain less abhorrent to western states. By the Law of Succession (1947), he defined Spain as a 'Catholic, social and representative state'.[80] The economy, however, remained a major problem. After the Civil War the method chosen for reconstruction was autarky, or self-sufficiency, involving heavy government intervention in wage levels, import quotas and the regulation of industry – the main priority. The predictable consequence was terrible hardship, which included poverty, widespread starvation and the spread of accompanying diseases such as tuberculosis. Franco used tough words to justify his policy: 'We do not want an easy, comfortable life . . . we want a hard life, the difficult life of a virile people.'[81] A gradual economic growth followed, averaging 4.35 per cent per annum between 1951 and 1959. This was, however, beset with serious problems which revealed the utter inadequacy of autarky. According to Carr, 'Autarky had ceased to be a stimulus; it had become a straitjacket'.[82] Industrial growth, for example, led to an increased demand for imports, which in turn put a strain on Spain's balance of trade.

By the end of the decade Spain faced an economic crisis and a need for urgent change. There had also been a tentative emergence of opposition; this was no longer related to Civil War confrontation but to the problems of Franco's post-war regime. Reformist in their aims, these included intellectual and artistic dissent, working-class movements and strikes, and student revolts. Even the establishment realized the need for administrative reform and the Catholic-dominated organization *Opus Dei* introduced proposals for economic change. Much was now at stake.

1959–73: 'Tardofranquismo'

Considerable importance has recently been attached to the period 1960–74 in Spanish history. According to Townson, it has hitherto been 'unjustifiably neglected'. He argues that 'Over the last 15 years of the Franco dictatorship, between 1960 and 1975, Spain underwent the greatest period of economic upheaval in its history, while experiencing vast social and cultural changes'. There were also political developments despite the 'ossified nature of the political system'.[83]

Certainly, the government recognized the necessity of creating a more balanced economy by reducing controls and depending more openly on market forces. In 1959 it introduced a Stabilization Plan to bring the economy into line with others in the West. Despite its name its intention was to move away from the previous policy of Autarky, as was the purpose of its successors, the Development Plans (1964–73). The measures included deflation, restrictions of the money supply, reductions in budgetary expenditure, wage controls, the promotion of foreign investment and the reduction of trade restrictions.[84] Initial hardship was followed between 1961 and 1966 by a so-called 'economic miracle'. Between 1959 and 1974 the Spanish economy grew by 6.9 per cent per annum, after Japan, the second highest rate in the developed world. Industry during the same period averaged an annual growth of 10 per cent.[85] Abandoning autarky promoted two vitally important foreign-exchange earners which helped stimulate growth. One of these was tourism: the total number of foreign visitors to Spain increased from six million in 1959 to twenty-one million in 1969 and thirty-four million in 1972. The other boost was a Spanish workforce abroad of 1.5 million which sent its earnings back to the mother country – sufficient to cover half of Spain's foreign debt.[86] The government, of course, ascribed all the new-found prosperity to the Stabilization Plan and its successors. This is an oversimplification since Spain was one of many European countries experiencing a sudden economic surge. Yet it could be argued that the economic plans ended the isolation on which autarky had previously been predicated and made possible the flow of more benign influences into Spain.

The same applied to social, cultural and religious developments during the 1960s. Tourism had a particularly important impact on Spain. Pack argues that it 'provided compelling evidence of its acceptance by democratic Europe'[87] while encouraging 'a tolerance and even an embrace of foreign attitudes and behaviours'.[88] Overall, 'Tourism became a central turbine driving Europeanization'.[89] Meanwhile, sectors of the population were learning how to be critical of the regime without bringing down upon themselves the full wrath of a still tightly-controlled political system. Cultural changes included a substantial increase in the numbers of students at university, while the expenditure on education as a whole for the first time exceeded that on the military. The political structure, however, was still largely unaffected by the changes sweeping through the economy and society: while he was willing to reform inefficient and corrupt administrative structures, Franco stopped short of any move towards a representative democracy. It remained his view that progress had to be disciplined, not unleashed. Still, his basic aim was no longer to terrorize the population but rather, to neutralize and depoliticize it, encouraging it to make the most of the economic boom that Spain was experiencing during the 1960s.

Extensive changes were therefore made during the period of *Tardofranquismo*. There were, however, remaining shortcomings. The existence of such a large Spanish workforce abroad was an indication of one of the main shortcomings of the economy – the lack of full employment. Other persistent problems were the depressed condition of agriculture and the iniquitous system of taxation that prevented the state from extracting sufficient revenue from the sectors of society that benefited most from the boom. The result was that the gap between rich and poor increased as the new-found wealth was inadequately distributed. Nor had the political structure been properly addressed. Although still illegal, opposition welled up through the system in form of working-class activism and student unrest. A more radical form was Basque separatism, the violent tactics of ETA provoking the government into issuing the 1975 Anti-Terrorist Law. Even the Church, once a loyal ally, now distanced itself from the regime. By the 1970s part of the upper clergy finally withdrew support from Franco, leaving his regime with a weakened religious sanction. To make matters worse, Spain was experiencing the economic problems common to other parts of Europe in the wake of the 1973 oil crisis. This threatened to cut away one of Franco's main boasts – that he had presided over unprecedented economic growth.

Would the regime, after all, abandon reform and return to its old practices? This was always a possibility, considering that, politically, it was still a dictatorship – and one beset with the growing problems symptomatic of what Carr has called the 'Agony of Francoism' between 1969 and 1975. Could it continue to evolve? Or would it end suddenly in revolution – or counter-revolution? Franco's own solution was to ease the way for the return of the monarchy by grooming Prince Juan Carlos for future authority. Others in the Francoist regime wanted to push more specifically towards a constitutionalist system. The counterpart to these proposals 'from above' was increasing pressure for the return of full democracy 'from below'. Franco himself held the balance – but he did not have the time to complete the transition to his own satisfaction.

The end of Franco

On 17 October 1975 Franco collapsed during a cabinet meeting. Doctors were summoned to the palace and performed a tracheotomy to enable him to breathe. Rumours soon circulated that Franco was dying, but these were officially denied. Indeed, the surgeons made every effort to prolong Franco's life. They succeeded until 20 November, by which time he was permanently on a respirator and kidney machine, and his stomach had been removed. It was almost as if the establishment dared not let him die for fear of the uncertainty that would follow. His end was in distinct contrast to the exhibition of Mussolini's corpse slung up from a petrol station in Milan in 1945, to Hitler's suicide in his Berlin bunker a few months later, and the discovery of Stalin lying on the floor after a stroke in 1953.

Spain's transition to a post-Francoist state was far more rapid and extensive than anything Franco had envisaged. But his nominee to lead this transition was all too conscious of the collapse of right-wing regimes elsewhere in southern Europe and he had no desire to repeat the destabilizing experiment with the left-wing politics in neighbouring Portugal. Juan Carlos aimed for a democracy based on constitutional monarchy rather than another authoritarian regime with a hereditary dictator. With the co-operation of most political groups, he presided over the 1977 Law of Political Reform, which prepared for the legalizing of political parties and a general election based on universal suffrage. This took place in June 1977, less than two years after Franco's death but forty-one years since the previous election.

REFLECTIONS ON FRANCO'S WAR AND REGIME

A summary of Franco's career

Franco's career falls into three main phases.

First, all his experience before 1936 was gained in the Spanish Foreign Legion and the Spanish army. Serving in both Morocco and Spain, he achieved the rank of general in 1926 and, in 1928, director of the military academy of Zaragoza. He was treated somewhat inconsistently during the Second Republic, alternating between demotion and being given specific commands; he was, for example, in charge of suppressing the revolt of the Asturias in 1934. He was not a politician and possessed few political skills, although hostility to the Second Republic forced him into establishing connections with political leaders of the right. Hence his instinct and training were for military action, while his experience in diplomacy and political leadership were acquired through necessity. This was in complete contrast to the other main dictators of the period – Hitler, Stalin and Mussolini – none of whom were military leaders, although all had pretensions to be military strategists. The main parallel might be professional soldiers like Piłsudski of Poland and Metaxas of Greece, although even they were unusual in the list of dictators.

Second, Franco's rise to power between 1936 and 1939 came from a military rebellion and victory in a bloody civil war. He was unique, among all the European dictators covered by this book, in achieving this precise combination. Other patterns varied. Piłsudski came to power through a bloodless military coup and without a subsequent civil war. Lenin established himself by a coup but the civil war that followed was partly in defence of the new regime and partly to enforce Bolshevik control; throughout the process, he remained a political not a military leader. Metaxas *was* a military man, but was appointed to power; his subsequent dictatorship did not involve civil war. Others differed even more from Franco. In Mussolini's case the *threat* of rebellion was sufficient to coerce the existing government into concede power and ended with Mussolini accepting the premiership in formal court dress. The civil war in Italy followed the overthrow of Mussolini in 1943. Stalin manoeuvred himself into a position to inherit a regime after eliminating the candidacy of others. He consolidated his power through purges, not by civil war. Finally, Hitler was elected to power by a malfunctioning democratic system which he subsequently converted into a personalized regime that launched wars on others. Franco's seizure of power was therefore most *directly* connected with civil war, enabling him to use his main strengths – the mobilization and leadership of military forces and the control of competing groups within the Nationalists.

Third, Franco's dictatorship, which lasted between 1939 and 1975, had a unique combination of features. The regime was never party-based in any populist sense: its emphasis was on control rather than mass mobilization. The party (FET-JONS) was used to contain the different elements supporting Franco, and to curb the mobilizing tendencies of the Falange. Whether or not Franco was fascist has already been considered. It seems that he saw the organizational and expansionist 'advantages' of fascism but was dubious about its radicalism. He was, of course, closely involved with Fascist Italy and Nazi Germany but, after their defeat, distanced himself from their ideology. More controversial is whether Franco's regime could be called 'totalitarian'. It could certainly be argued that Franco was the closest of all the authoritarian dictators, as defined on pp. 24–5, to being totalitarian. The brutality of his regime and the effectiveness of its control over the population is, for some, sufficient reason to use the term. And yet the dynamic of Franco's system was traditionalist rather than radical or revolutionary, which prevents the description of 'totalitarian' from being convincing. We have already seen the problems that can exist in the distinction between 'totalitarian' and 'authoritarian' (pp. 24–5). This applies especially at the borderlines between the two, as exemplified by Franco's Spain and Mussolini's Italy. Franco's regime was unquestionably more ruthless internally than Mussolini's. Yet Mussolini produced a new ideology and generated populist support. Franco's control and authority remained intact until 1975, whereas Mussolini's evaporated in 1943. On the other hand, Italy was invaded externally, which meant that fascism within could be eliminated in a late civil war; Spain was not invaded and the influence of fascism there faded of its own accord.

Comparing the borderlines suggests that Franco's dictatorship was a 'strong authoritarianism', while Mussolini's was a 'weak totalitarianism'. Alternatively, Franco could be adjudged as 'militarily authoritarian' between 1936 and 1939, 'functionally – but not ideologically – totalitarian' between 1939 and 1949; 'defensively post-totalitarian-authoritarian' during the 1950s, 'flexibly authoritarian' between 1959 and 1969, and aware of the need to find a 'post-authoritarian' settlement from 1969.

Interpretations of Franco's war and regime

Previous sections in this chapter have already suggested interpretations for specific areas of Franco's involvement in the overthrow of the Spanish Republic and in establishing a dictatorship to replace it. More general conclusions can now be drawn.

An overview of Franco's place in modern Spanish history

Early twentieth-century Spain was liable to periodic crisis resulting from a conflict between change and reaction, between modernizing and traditionalist influences. The extent of this conflict varied. Sometimes it was intense, as with the sudden reversal of the policies of Primo de Rivera by the radical reforms of the Second Republic, followed by the appearance of an extreme authoritarianism under Franco. Alternatively, the confrontation could become less intense as one side gradually succeeded in imposing its will; this was shown by the gradual easing of the intensity of Franco's dictatorship from 1949 and, again during the 1960s; the process ended with the peaceful re-emergence of liberal democracy and the death of Francoism.

Franco's role in this overall pattern has been interpreted in two different ways. On the one hand, his involvement in modern Spain has been seen as positive, a necessary counter to the negative and destructive side-effects of modernization. Authoritarianism was therefore necessary to control these until such time as its grip could be gradually relaxed. The other interpretation reverses the emphasis. Modernization and reform were an inevitable manifestation of progress. In trying to disrupt these Franco was imposing an arbitrary system to uphold – at all costs – traditional obstacles to change.

A 'positive' view of Franco's role

Sympathetic explanations of Franco's aims and methods are based on the necessity of meeting the threats to Spain in the 1930s. Franco identified three in particular. One was the swing to the left in Republican Spain through the acceleration of liberal democracy. The difficulty of adjusting to this had already been recognized by Primo de Rivera, who had deliberately restricted the role of parliamentary institutions and the 'corrupting' influence of party politics. Any swing to the left also meant a greater exposure to the negative influences of socialism, anarchism and, above all, communism. The second major threat was the undermining of the Catholic Church by the Republic's campaign for secularization, which seemed to overlap an attack on Christianity itself. And third, in addition to the threats to Spain's traditional forms of authority and belief, there was also an assault on its unitary nationhood by the devolution of powers to two of its regions.

The extent of Spain's peril has been used to explain Franco's intervention. To some, it provided full justification for the various stages involved. Franco compensated for the failure of Primo de Rivera's earlier dictatorship through a successful military uprising and the single-minded and ruthless pursuit of victory. The fall of Primo de Rivera showed that no other approach was now possible. The new regime of Franco, established in 1939, saw further measures to eradicate any remaining threats. To Francoist supporters these were a necessity to complete the task undertaken during the Civil War; to his less convinced apologists the measures were excessive – but did not destroy the legitimacy of what Franco had achieved. Externally, Franco did exactly the right thing in outwitting the Axis to keep Spain neutral during the Second World War: he was praised for looking beyond any prospect of winning prestige, or fulfilling any obligations to repay Italy and Germany for their support. Instead, he maintained the primacy of *Spain's* interests. After 1945 he managed Spain's diplomatic isolation with some skill, persuading some of the members of NATO that his anti-communist stance was relevant to them in the Cold War; in particular, he increased Spain's credibility by enlisting the support of the United States. He also had the wisdom gradually to relax the tightness of his control on Spain, which led to a burst of reform and prosperity in the era of *Tardofranquismo*. As for the succession, he had always had a return to monarchy in mind, ultimately seeing himself, in addition to all his other titles, as interim regent. In this respect, Franco's dictatorship was seen as *custodial*.

How has Franco's regime been evaluated by historians? Some opt for a mixed judgement which is neither unfavourable nor entirely favourable.[90] Others, while strongly critical of the extremes of Franco's measures, focus as much on the responsibility of the Second Republic's defective policies for its own demise. But more explicitly sympathetic to Franco is Crozier,[91] whose biography of Franco was published in 1967, when the late Francoist period had eight more years to run. Crozier lacked the benefit of hindsight from the perspective of the rapid changes after 1975. Nevertheless, while reserving judgement over the future, he had plenty to say about Franco's role in the past, insisting that it was important to place him within the context of Spanish history. Crozier argues that 'No amount of criticism on philosophical or doctrinal grounds can obscure the central fact of Franco's achievement in giving Spain more than a quarter of a century of stability and material progress.'[92] He also stressed the Communist danger in Spain before the Civil War, which greatly increased after it had started. 'Franco's victory removed it.'[93] Franco also prevented a permanent threat from the far right: he 'broke the fascists when they had outlived their usefulness' and also 'gradually liberalized his regime'.[94] Finally, Crozier's biography makes generalizations about the Spanish character in Franco's favour. If 'Franco's attitude towards his enemies was ruthless and vindictive' it was 'a typically Spanish attitude'. This was because 'The Spaniards are a deeply Manichean people, singularly unqualified for democracy.'[95] More recently, controversy was caused by the 2011 entry on Franco in the *Dictionary of Spanish Biography* (*Diccionario biográfico español*). Its author, Suárez, was criticized for being too favourable to Franco[96] – as much for what Suárez underplays as for any direct partiality; for example, he fails to mention the many thousands of people killed during the Francoist era and considers the use of terms such as 'totalitarian' and 'dictatorship' inappropriate. The former charge is particularly serious, especially in the context of increasing awareness of Francoist atrocities. The refusal of Suarez to use certain descriptions is more understandable, given the debate that now exists over terminology. Even so, Casanova considers that the entry 'is simply recreating the old propaganda in favour of Franco'.

A 'negative' view of Franco's role

Critics of Franco focus on his deliberate stifling of reform and liberty – and the extreme brutality by which he forced Spain back into the traditional mould from which she was seeking to break free. The changes made in Spain after 1931 meant, above all, modernization and progress. One example was the growth of liberal democracy after the overthrow of the dictatorship of Primo de Rivera and of the monarchy itself. Furthermore, this seemed to be happening at the time when other states were falling to dictatorship. Constitutional changes were accompanied by improved conditions of labour, which were not inevitably connected to the far left – the influence of communism came with the impact of the Nationalist rebellion and civil war. Meanwhile, secularization was part of a long-term process in Spain – as it was elsewhere. Admittedly there were major difficulties in maintaining political stability, social equity and secular control. There were also pressures between right and left (and, of course, within the left itself), as well as traumatic reactions such as the Asturias revolt and anticlerical riots. But Franco oversimplified the threats arising from this instability and arrogated to himself the right to destroy the whole process, in a crusade against modernization in any form. He offered no innovative alternative, only a negative and immobilizing regime which he reinforced by a systematic terror more intense and prolonged than the Red Terror of his opponents. His supporters also fell for his dishonest approach to Spain's involvement in the Second World War. Far from deliberately keeping Spain neutral, he failed to convince Hitler that Spain as an ally was worth Germany's effort. Franco's demands were simply too high, and out of proportion with what he could deliver in turn. After the end of the Civil War, Franco showed the true extent of his ruthlessness by channelling his White Terror into a Spanish gulag system, while his economic policy of autarky created deprivation and starvation. There were, it is true, some concessions after 1959, but these were in response to internal and external pressures. Increased prosperity was also part of a more general economic improvement from which much of Europe, including Portugal, also benefited.

Most historical assessments are unequivocally hostile to Franco. Almost all historians argue, or strongly imply, that he distorted the trend of Spain's development. Trevor-Roper gave a particular example of this as early as 1972 when he maintained that Franco *caused* a Communist threat. This provides an effective response to arguments like Crozier's that Franco rescued Spain from communism. In fact, Franco aimed to save Spain not from communism but from liberal democracy. 'It is true that in the course of the struggle the Spanish Communists gradually rose to power on the republican side, just as the "Fascist" Falange rose to power on Franco's side. But that was the consequence, not the cause of the struggle.' Had the Republic been successful in the war, it 'might have emancipated itself from such temporary Communist allies as skilfully as General Franco emancipated himself from his temporary Fascist allies'.[97] The utter brutality of the regime is dwelt on at length by Franco's critics, who see little – if any – justification for this. It did not bring genuine peace because, according to Sánchez: 'peace was nothing but the regime's manipulation of Spaniards' fear of more violence'.[98] Preston, too, denounces any attempt to defend Franco. He argues that it is a basic misconception that Franco provided social peace, for this ignores his labour camps and executions, indications of his 'brutal efficiency'. In this respect, Preston insists, 'Franco stands comparison with the cruellest dictators of the century'.[99] Finally, Franco is condemned for his complete reversal of progressive change. In Casanova's words, the 'peace of Franco' meant that 'The reformist project of the Republic and all that this type of government meant was swept away . . . and the workers' movement and its ideas were systematically wiped out, in a progress that was more violent and long-lasting than that suffered by any of the other European movements opposed to Fascism'.

Conclusions?

There is no question as to the utter brutality of Franco's conduct of the war and imposition of his regime; nor of the sterility of his approach by contrast with the progressive aims of an admittedly flawed Republic. Previously this has been wholly or partially justified by the threat *of* Communism or the threat *to* Christianity and historic Spain. In its extreme form this was crude propaganda. But even Franco's apologists used these as at least a partial defence, along with observations on the nature of the Spanish people. Franco *was* brutal, but brutality was excusable, or at least understandable, as a part of the environment which produced it and as a defence against a worse evil. Such attitudes no longer make much sense. It is becoming as difficult to put a favourable side to Franco as it is to Hitler and Mussolini. This is because Spain and Europe have changed dramatically since Franco's death, sweeping away much of the basic approach on which Franco's apologists operated before 1975 – that there were two sides to the regime, with the future still to provide evidence for Franco's long-term success.

Any connection between Franco and post-1975 Spain is highly tenuous. The rapidity of Spain's adjustment to democracy was not the result of any long-term and steady control that was, if not benevolent, at least ultimately beneficial. It was due to decisions taken to depart from Franco, first in the policy of the new monarch, Juan Carlos, to pursue democracy and then by the failure of the new electorate to support the remnant of Franco's splintered party. Nor are there any special Spanish characteristics preventing Spain from full access to Europe. The period after 1975 proved that Spain is as suited to democracy as any other European state – given stability and favourable circumstances. Nor was there an inherent threat of communism in Spain. This was exaggerated by Franco, who then had the excuse to crush it. Any credit he gained for doing the west a 'service' was almost entirely the result of the Cold War climate; this, of course, was eventually weakened by détente, the end of the Cold War and the collapse of the Soviet Union. Finally, general changes in international perceptions further discredited Franco. These included the growing emphasis on human rights, increased social awareness within the Catholic Church and a greater worldwide intolerance towards dictatorship.

Franco's regime was therefore a brutal episode in modern Spanish history which has proved to be no more logical or necessary than Mussolini's to Italy, Hitler's to Germany or Stalin's to Russia. Yet Franco's excesses have not been subjected to any Spanish equivalent of destalinization or denazification. Instead, the governments of the early post-Franco years shied away from any policies that might revive any fundamental splits within Spain. The ultimate irony – and revenge on Franco – was that he lapsed into *irrelevance*. This happened so rapidly that initiatives have been taken in the new century to 'unearth Franco's legacy'.

'Unearthing' Franco's war and regime

There is a considerable contrast between the official monuments of the Franco regime in the Valley of the Fallen (which contains a mausoleum for both Franco and José Antonio Primo de Rivera) and the makeshift graves all over Spain for the hundreds of thousands of executed Republicans. For the last quarter of the twentieth century these resting places were left largely intact. Then, shortly after 2000, work was started on unearthing the Francoist past.[100] In this context, 'unearthing' has a double meaning. In one way it is a means of revealing Spain's recent past through a new type of research, based on archaeological exhumations and interviews to establish oral evidence. In turn, these build up to a second purpose – to ensure that there is a permanent reminder of the world of Franco that goes beyond the regime's own constructs and artefacts. But the whole process has revealed two conflicting strategies for handling the Francoist past.

During the transition to democracy form 1975 the whole Franco era, including the Civil War, was not heavily stressed in Spain. For a while there was, in effect, a 'pact of oblivion' which was observed by politicians from most political parties, including the PSOE (Socialist Party) and the PP (*Partido Popular*). Its purpose was to give the transition a chance by not reigniting old tensions and passions but rather by breaking the cycle of conflict between left and right. Moving away from Franco meant not taking action against his former supporters; there was more of an emphasis on 'forgiveness' than on 'justice'. As Jerez-Farrán and Amago point out, 'In Germany, France and Italy Fascist collaborators were publicly named, brought to justice, or censured, or they openly confessed or expressed regret, but this same auto-critical process did not and has not occurred in Spain'.[101] Perhaps this overstates the parallel. 'Collaborators' in Spain were not being unpatriotic, as in France, or supporting an occupying power; nor were they easily recognizable as 'fascist', as in Germany and Italy. Would Spanish 'fascists' be former members of the Falange – or would they be main upholders of Franco's regime? In Spain the past was seen as too intricate to disentangle in the way that happened with denazification in Germany or destalinization in Russia. There was the additional complication that many Spaniards considered that *Tardofranquismo* had at least been moving in the right direction and parallels have even been drawn with the loosening of previously rigid regimes by Gorbachev in the Soviet Union and de Klerk in South Africa. It was widely accepted that a calmer environment than Spain would allow the image of Franco to fade, thereby guaranteeing the permanence of Spain's new democracy.

But the amnesty has also had its critics, especially of the political influence behind its implementation: it has, for example, been described not so much as 'amnesty' as 'amnesia' – and by 'decree'. The 'pact of oblivion' certainly had deficiencies. For a while it seemed completely one-sided. All the war memorials were those of the victors. Did these celebrate the outcome of a 'righteous' war? And what of the defeated? Should they be forgotten? Such anomalies made it difficult to escape from the past. Instead, Spain began to show a revived consciousness of the Franco period – and a willingness to work through it in order to move on. There were several strong influences behind this trend. One was the revival of German self-examination, after reunification, to compensate for the secrecy and repression of the former East Germany. Another was the removal of the threat of a new conflict between left and right. The far right had become marginalized and its attempts at the occasional coup had been overcome. It was, therefore, no longer necessary to stress the potential dangers of opening up the Francoist past. Above all, the last two decades of the twentieth century experienced an exponential growth of historical research, throughout the western world, into Soviet Russia, Nazi Germany, the Holocaust and other key areas. The Spanish Civil War and the Franco era were bound to be affected. This has happened through a rapid increase in the number of monographs and more general works by Spanish, English and American historians – some of which have been used in rewriting this chapter. But the range of historical investigation has broadened to involve the wider public. In addition to the publication of memoirs and autobiographies written by men and women who lived through the Franco era, a great deal of oral evidence has been collected, based on recent interviews; these have established what Labanyi calls the 'politics of feeling'.[102] In 'denouncing an injustice', such testimony has 'a particular urgency'. Documentary films, too, provide 'a flashpoint in the memory war, arising from varying views on how the Spanish past should be remembered'.[103] Most widely publicized of all investigations were the exhumations of bodies from mass-burial sites since 2000, many reported on television;[104] by 2008 these amounted to over 4,000 bodies from 171 sites. Attention was therefore focused on dead as well as living victims of the Franco era.

Chapter 7

Dictatorship elsewhere

DICTATORSHIP IN SOUTH-WESTERN EUROPE

Introduction

During the twentieth century, the two countries of the Iberian Peninsula followed broadly parallel histories, although with some significant individual variations.

Spain, which has already been covered in Chapter 6, was a monarchy until 1931. Between 1923 and 1929 actual power was exercised by the dictatorship of General Primo de Rivera; when this ended in Rivera's fall, King Alfonso XIII followed soon afterwards. Spain became a republic until 1936, which was subsequently challenged and overthrown by a military rebellion which expanded into a full-scale Spanish Civil War. Between 1939 and 1975 Franco's dictatorship neither confirmed Spain as a republic nor restored the monarchy: his preference was for the latter and he always considered himself as a long-term regent. Towards the end of his regime he planned for his own powers to pass – undiluted – to a new king, but the 1975 incumbent, Juan Carlos, took his own decision that Spain should evolve into a permanent constitutional monarchy; this was subsequently accepted by a referendum. Portugal started the century as a monarchy before becoming a republic in 1910. During the 1920s power moved increasingly into the hands of Dr Antonio Salazar, who eventually became prime minister in 1928. He remained in this office until his retirement in 1968 after a stroke. His successor, Caetano, was overthrown during the 1974 revolution, after which the republic eventually became a westernized democracy. Both Spain and Portugal were subsequently able to strengthen the political and economic foundations of their new systems through their membership of the European Community, later the European Union.

Franco and Salazar had a considerable chronological overlap. Franco's regime was installed by 1939 and survived until his death in 1975; Salazar was fully in control between 1928 and 1968. This meant that while part of their incumbency was within the main period of the dictatorships considered in this book, most of it was outside – by between twenty-three and thirty-one years. In both cases the policies pursued after 1945 had their origins in the 1930s and early 1940s, although there was some late modification during the 1960s. Their styles of dictatorship raise comparisons over similar questions: were they radical or traditionalist, brutal or preventive, uniform or changing?

The role of war was particularly important in the development of both states. The pattern in Spain was neutrality in the First World War, colonial war in Morocco, Civil War (1936–9) and official neutrality in the Second World War. Portugal entered the First World War on the side of the Allies, experienced no equivalent to the Spanish Civil War, remained neutral in the Second World War, and became embroiled in colonial wars in defence of its colonies in Africa during the 1960s. The issue of colonies was also significant to Spain, although in different ways. Franco gained much of his military experience in the campaigns in Morocco, which he subsequently applied to establishing and maintaining his dictatorship; then, later in his career, he decided that Spain should join the process of decolonization. Salazar, by contrast, had no military experience but remained convinced that the African colonies were integral to Portugal's future. For this reason he resisted decolonization to the point where the whole dictatorship was threatened with collapse. Finally, their attitudes to the other powers had both similarities and differences. Germany and Italy developed military ties with Spain, and Franco depended on their assistance in the Spanish Civil War. Salazar maintained a close diplomatic relationship with the Axis powers, making it possible for their aid to reach the Nationalists. Both dictators feared and despised the Soviet Union and from 1941 contributed volunteers to Hitler's invasion. But their attitudes to Britain differed: Franco always saw her as a potential threat, while Salazar did what he could to maintain Portugal's reputation as Britain's 'oldest ally'. After 1945 neither Franco nor Salazar had a comfortable time in Europe, although Spain was the more ostracized and isolated – at least until the United States realized Spain's usefulness within the context of the Cold War.

Portugal

At the beginning of the twentieth century Portugal was ruled by an authoritarian monarchy. This was, however, overthrown in 1910, to be replaced by a republic which, in 1911, introduced a democratic constitution with a two-chamber parliament, direct suffrage, and an executive with limited powers. Overall, the new regime was by far the most progressive in Portugal's history. Unfortunately, it was also inherently unstable. The sophisticated political system proved inappropriate to a society which was one of the most backward in Europe and in which 70 per cent of the people were illiterate. As in many other parts of Europe democracy foundered on political instability. During the sixteen years of the republic's existence there were nine presidents, forty-four governments, twenty-five uprisings and three temporary dictatorships.[1] This catalogue makes Portugal, in the words of Payne, 'the most politically chaotic of any single European . . . state in the twentieth century'.[2]

Political crisis was intensified by economic disaster caused by a series of incompetent budgets, an increase in inflation and a deterioration in Portugal's balance of payments. By the mid-1920s all the influential sectors of society – the professional middle class, the army and the Church – had come to the conclusion that the republic would have to be replaced by a more stable regime. On 17 June 1926 it was therefore destroyed by General Gomes da Costa, who installed a *dictadura* (or dictatorship) in its place.

The Estado Novo

The new military rulers, however, proved equally unable to tackle Portugal's economic problems, as the cost of living soared to a level thirty times that of 1914. By 1928 the head of state, President Carmona, handed over complete responsibility for the Portuguese finances to a professor of economics at the University of Coimbra, Dr Antonio de Oliveira Salazar. In 1932 Salazar became Prime Minister, a position he held until incapacitated by a stroke thirty-six years later.

Throughout this lengthy period he remained in complete control, seeing himself as the only person who could reconcile the conflicting trends in Portuguese society or provide an alternative to Portugal's inefficient democracy. His power base was a formidable array of groups disillusioned by the anarchy of the republic. These included army officers who felt that the forces had been neglected, the Church who hated the republic's anticlerical policies, the upper bourgeoisie and banking interests who wanted economic stability, and, finally, right-wing intellectuals and monarchists. All trusted this remote academic far more than Portugal's more flashy military leaders.

What sort of person was Salazar? Bruce describes him as a 'devout and Right-wing Catholic, a quiet and an austere man, dressed usually in a rather ill-fitting dark suit'.[3] He had little personal charisma and avoided any hint of a personality cult; in this respect he was the very reverse of Mussolini. He did, however, have a strong character, and as early as 1928 affirmed: 'I know quite well what I want and where I am going . . . When the time comes for me to give orders I shall expect it [the country] to obey.'[4] His ideas were clearly and forcefully stated. He profoundly distrusted parliamentary democracy, for it had 'resulted in instability and disorder, or, what is worse, it has become a despotic domination of the nation by political parties'.[5] He therefore saw his role as establishing a paternalist regime, a government without parties. The individual should submit to this government without seeking to limit its powers. 'Let us place our liberty in the hands of authority; only authority knows how to administer and protect it.'[6] Salazar also sought to revive traditional virtues and loyalties and to develop a national pride based on the glorification of Portugal's history; for this reason his cult of empire assumed major importance. Overall, he tried to develop a state which, although based on tradition and in some ways an escape from the realities of the twentieth century, was nevertheless new in its organic development. Hence, he called his model the *Estado Novo*, the New State.

The basis of the *Estado Novo* was the 1933 constitution which replaced the multi-party system with a 'unitary and corporative republic'.[7] The new lower house – the National Assembly – was elected on a list system through a restricted franchise. It also had few powers over the government and could not initiate financial legislation. A one-party system was confirmed, with the National Union (UN) acting as 'a pressure group intended to bind all sections of the community in a corporative movement'.[8] This was the means whereby Salazar hoped to achieve harmony and discipline and to break the long-standing strife between labour and capital. It operated through the upper house of parliament – a corporative chamber – which was selected from various sections of the community, including industry, commerce, agriculture, the army and the Church. Industrial relations were regulated by the National Labour Statute of 1933 which forbade workers' strikes and employers' lockouts. The whole point of corporativism was to present a viable alternative to the

10 Antonio Salazar, 1889–1970, photo taken in 1964 (© Popperfoto/Getty)

liberal idea, which Salazar distrusted, without adopting the collective principle as embodied in communism, which he hated.

Salazar's *Estado Novo* had a mixed record in the period up to 1945. On the positive side, it undoubtedly provided greater political stability; the solid support from the wealthier sections of society brought to an end the pendulum of revolution alternating with counter-revolution. Above all, Salazar achieved a considerable amount in the financial sector. He produced a series of balanced budgets, stabilized the currency, reduced corruption and improved the process of tax collection. According to Gallagher, his methods 'were those of a careful accountant'.[9] On the other hand, the *Estado Novo* attempted few progressive reforms. Salazar was 'not an economic innovator' and balanced budgets became an obsession which served only to discourage foreign investment and loans. Industrial growth was minimal; the proportion of the workforce in industry increased hardly at all between 1920 and 1940. Agriculture, too, experienced neither fundamental changes in methods nor sustained efforts to improve irrigation. Above all, a real barrier to change was exerted by the social elite which upheld the regime. Social reform was held back by a rigid class system, something which concerned Salazar not at all. After all, he had once said quite openly: 'I consider more urgent the creation of élites than the necessity to teach people to read.'[10]

In his foreign policy Salazar had several priorities, which were sometimes difficult to harmonize. One was to retain the friendship of Britain, based on the Alliance of 1386 as renewed in 1643, 1654, 1660, 1661, 1703, 1815 and 1899. This carried no military commitments but it offered at least some protection for the Portuguese empire by making it unlikely that Britain would co-operate with powers that had designs on Portuguese territory. Salazar certainly preferred existing connections with Britain to any new obligations to Germany or Italy. He was also strongly averse to the Soviet Union, which he saw as an ideological threat to the Catholic Church and as an inveterate enemy to right-wing regimes; he therefore welcomed attempts by other European leaders to isolate Stalin while, at the same time, he avoided involving Portugal in the Anti-Comintern Pact.

Above all, Salazar was determined to remove any possible threat from Portugal's more powerful neighbour, Spain. He was particularly concerned that the Republicans should not win the Civil War, for this might tempt a future left-wing regime to intervene against the *Estado Novo*, perhaps even to the extent of incorporating Portugal into a federation with Spain. Hence Salazar depended on Franco's victory to maintain 'the immutable principle of the duality of the [Iberian] Peninsula'.[11] Portugal's involvement was limited – but significant nonetheless. Salazar gave moral support to the rebel forces under Franco; Portugal provided transit facilities for German arms bound for Nationalist-held areas in Spain; 18,000 Portuguese joined the Viriatos, a volunteer force; and Republican refugees seeking asylum in Portugal were handed over to Nationalist forces – and death. In March 1939 Salazar cemented relations with the new Nationalist regime in the Iberian Pact (or Treaty of Friendship and Non-Aggression). At the same time, Salazar avoided the temptation of an alliance with Italy or Germany, believing that 'in accordance with the true interests of the Portuguese nation its foreign policy is always to avoid, if possible, any entanglements in Europe'.[12] Nevertheless, he had to be careful not to antagonize either regime.

Salazar therefore had to resolve the problem of a vicious circle: he had to prevent friction with Britain over his backing for Franco – and with Nationalist Spain over his continued 'alliance' with Britain. Fortunately for Salazar, Franco was equally determined to play his own themes in foreign policy: to Salazar's relief, Franco proved quite capable of fending off the influence of the fascist powers and, although more ruthless than Salazar, Franco had a similarly traditionalist approach to ideology. Salazar therefore had to exert less pressure on Franco than he had thought. In turn, Britain relaxed when she saw that Salazar was keeping his distance from the 'fascist' powers on the continent and developing an 'Atlantic triangle' between Portugal, Britain and Brazil (which had introduced her own 'New State' under President Vargas in 1937). With his bilateral friendship with Franco, it seemed that, by 1939, Salazar had managed to 'square' the vicious circle and establish a form of diplomatic stability.

The Second World War

Everything now depended on whether Salazar could keep Portugal out of a major conflict which, from 1938 onwards, threatened Europe. He had no intention of ending the Anglo-Portuguese alliance but, at the same time, was determined that it should not interfere with Portuguese neutrality in mainland Europe. As in the 1930s, he had to steer a balance between any threat from Germany, British reactions and Spanish unpredictability. In many ways, Salazar disliked what Nazi Germany stood for and criticized the invasion of Poland in September 1939. In 1940 he told the Italian minister in Portugal: 'My main worry is that Germany may obtain a crushing military victory over the Allies.' If this happened, Hitler would 'Germanise Europe', carrying 'a neo-paganism of mystic and racist origin that is contrary to our Roman and Catholic traditions'.[13] He was particularly concerned about Hitler's conquest of France in June 1940 since this might encourage Franco's Spain to join the Axis powers to make swift and easy territorial gain – as Mussolini's Italy had done. It could also force Britain to retreat into peripheral defence and encourage her to annex Portugal's islands (the Azores, Madeira and Cape Verde) to maintain control over the Atlantic. If either – or both – of these scenarios were to happen, mainland Portugal might well be invaded and brought under Axis and Spanish control. Salazar therefore had to maintain his balancing act. He did so with some skill but also benefited from changing circumstances and events beyond his immediate influence.

The German threat was a real one. In 1940 Hitler and Grand Admiral Raeder developed a contingency plan to occupy Portugal's islands in the Atlantic and invade Portugal herself; this has been seen as a significant part of a more general scheme for German world dominance. But it was never actually implemented. Portugal was saved from German action by Hitler's growing preoccupation with bolstering up Mussolini in the Balkans and north Africa and with the faltering German campaign in the Soviet Union. Britain's reactions were also problematic: in May 1943 Churchill advocated British annexation of Portugal's Atlantic islands without any preliminary warning, until he was dissuaded from such a course by the rest of the war cabinet. Instead, he requested permission from Salazar to build a naval base in the Azores. As it became increasingly clear that the Axis would lose the war, Salazar agreed to Allied use of the Azores to defend the north Atlantic and later to defend the route taken by troops from North America for the invasion of France. This made Portugal more co-operative than any of the other neutrals in the war. Spain, meanwhile, posed less of a threat. Franco was determined not to involve Spain on the side of Italy and Germany, realizing that the danger that external war could well reverse his victory in a particularly gruelling civil war. Salazar encouraged Franco to keep to his resolution. In July 1940 a Protocol was signed to the 1939 Treaty, providing for joint consultation in the event of a threat to either Spain or Portugal. This removed the possibility of Franco considering Portugal a threat and therefore of unprovoked Spanish action against Portugal. According to Robinson, this agreement 'went some way to cementing a Peninsular Bloc, and therefore Iberian neutrality, provided no attack came from outside'.[14]

The war had a limited impact of on Portugal herself. The population never experienced direct rationing, and the hardship caused by the Allies' economic blockade on Europe was no worse in Portugal than in other neutral states. Salazar's refusal to enter the war meant the complete absence of bombing, although there were periodic German threats and attacks on Portuguese shipping – mainly as an inducement to keep open normal channels of trade. This was something that Salazar was determined to do, although to both sides in the war. Trade with Germany accounted for 19 per cent of Portugal's exports in 1941, increasing to 25 per cent in 1942.[15] There was, however, pressure from Britain to reduce trade with Germany in food and, more importantly, in strategic materials. Again, Salazar had to maintain a balance between meeting German demands for one of Portugal's main raw materials, wolfram (for tungsten), used in the armaments industry, and recognizing British counter-demands for its limitation. This was not dissimilar to Sweden's predicament over her continued trade with Germany in iron ore and ball-bearings, and proved increasingly uncomfortable. Salazar was eventually reprieved by the inevitability of Hitler's defeat and agreed to a total embargo on wolfram to Germany.

After the Second World War

Salazar felt isolated and vulnerable in the immediate post-war period. His formula for survival was, on the one hand, to insulate his dictatorship internally from Western ideas and influences while, on the other, contributing as much as possible on the international scene to make Portugal an indispensable link in Western security.

Salazar's domestic policies continued to be deeply conservative; Bruneau maintains that he 'intentionally isolated Portugal from the outside world'.[16] Salazar remained committed to old-fashioned budgetary financing, restricting the use of the foreign credit and investment that did so much to rebuild the shattered economies of the other states of western Europe. He continued to believe that rapid industrialization would weaken the social elites that underpinned his regime and would therefore destroy the cohesion of the *Estado Novo*. Although Salazar claimed that the Estado Novo had become politically more democratic, with elections 'as free as they are in the free land of England',[17] the number of voters rose only slowly as a proportion of the population as a whole. 14.6 per cent voted in the 1949 election and 14.8 per cent in 1965, compared with 10.6 per cent in 1938.[18] But since the opportunities for legitimate party politics were still strictly limited, any opposition that developed to the regime after the War tended to be conspiratorial or resistance-based. The Communist Party (PCP) was one of the strongest, although it went through periods of strength alternating with internal crisis. Salazar continued to emphasize the ever-growing danger of internal 'subversion'. The secret police, renamed the *Policia Internacional e Defensa do Estado* (PIDE), was expanded, while detention without trial and the use of torture became routine. One of its victims, Mário Soares (later to be Portugal's premier between 1976 and 1978), wrote that 'In Portugal the police cannot be wrong and therefore anyone held on a political charge is by definition guilty. Police enquiries actually suffice as proof, and defending lawyers may not interfere while they are being made.'[19]

In his foreign policy Salazar was, at first, greatly assisted by the climate of the Cold War, in which the United States and Britain were more concerned with what they perceived as the new left-wing dictatorships in Soviet-influenced eastern Europe than with the residual right-wing dictatorships of the Iberian Peninsula. Even so, there was a distinction in Western policy towards Portugal and Spain. Franco remained a pariah and, although left alone, was kept in isolation. Salazar, on the other hand, was included in the West's plans for future security, whatever reservations it might have about Salazar's continuing dictatorship. In 1949, therefore, Portugal was invited to join NATO as a founder member, while in 1951 her significance as an 'Atlantic' power was recognized in the Defence Agreement which formalized to right of the United States to continue to use the Lajes Base in the Azores. In 1955 Salazar managed to gain wider credibility for Portugal by the latter's inclusion in the United Nations Organization. He also improved relations with other European states by agreeing with de Gaulle's 'third force' policy and by supporting the principle of German reunification; in both cases his stance was rewarded during the 1960s with aid and arms.[20] It looked, therefore, as if Salazar had achieved some recognition and rehabilitation by the time his leadership ended in 1968.

Or had he? Another trend during the 1950s and 1960s was the growth of international criticism of Portugal. This was due less to internal or domestic factors (after all, Portugal was one of many dictatorships in the post-war era) than to her colonial policies, now perceived by most of the world as anachronistic. This antipathy increased with the eruption of resistance to Portuguese rule in Africa, while the cost of dealing with the rebellions had a profound effect on the *Estado Novo* itself. To this we now turn.

The empire and the Estado Novo, 1926–74

Throughout its entire existence, the *Estado Novo* had one particular source of strength – and weakness. This was Portugal's overseas empire which comprised: the Atlantic islands of Azores and Madeira; the African colonies of Guinea Bissau, the Cape Verde Islands, Principé, São Tomé, Cabinda, Angola and Mozambique; Goa, Damao and Diu in India; Macau in China; and East Timor in Indonesia. Some of these possessions were historic, the remnants of a larger empire that had been partially destroyed by the Dutch in the seventeenth century or lost through the independence of Brazil in the early nineteenth. Other areas – the hinterlands of the African colonies – were added in the late nineteenth century, the result of grudging agreements with Britain and Germany. The early twentieth century, however, saw a change in Portugal's basic colonial policy. The Portuguese republic, which replaced the monarchy in 1910, envisaged the movement of the African colonies towards autonomy and ultimate independence, as had happened with Brazil.

This long-term vision was, however, changed by Salazar, who switched the emphasis to Portugal's 'historic responsibilities' and the permanence of empire.[21] Before becoming Prime Minister, Salazar had, from 1930, served as Overseas Minister and had introduced the Colonial Act (1930), and, with his successor, Armindo Monteiro, the Organic Charter (1933). The Colonial Act simplified the overall administration by bringing the colonies under the direct control of Lisbon, while a new imperial mystique was also developed. According to Monteiro, Portugal was, through her empire, 'entitled to invoke the past, not as a remembrance of dead things, but as a source of inspiration for the future'. It also guaranteed Portugal a world role. Jorge Ameal emphasized that 'our sovereignty as a small European state spreads prodigiously over three continents and is summed up in the magnificent certainty that we are the third colonial power' [after Britain and France]. Portugal also had an historic obligation to 'civilize' and convert the peoples of Africa: 'in this heroic element is contained the most noble sentiment of our mission as a chosen people, since the task of civilizing must have, above all else, a spiritual content'.[22] The overseas empire, like any other, was also of economic importance, supplying Portugal with raw materials, providing markets for manufactures and opportunities for Portuguese emigrants. As far as the regime was concerned, the underlying rationale for empire would never need to be changed. There were, of course, possible threats to Portuguese colonies during the Second World War – but these seemed to have been settled by agreements made with Britain and the United States over the Azores and by the admission of Portugal to NATO as a founding member.

Salazar's problem came with the decision made by the *other* powers to decolonize. The process started with the British acknowledgement of Indian independence in 1947 and the Dutch and French retreat, in the face of military defeat, from Indonesia and Indochina respectively. During the next phase Britain, France and Belgium voluntarily decolonized in Africa in the late 1950s and early 1960s. Salazar's commitment to empire was so deep that that he resisted, with all his strength, pressures to follow suit in Angola, Mozambique and Guinea-Bissau. The government argued that the Portuguese public overwhelmingly valued the colonies, and that Angola and Mozambique were as much a part of Portugal as Minho or Alentejo. In any case, the Portuguese empire had always been an important counterweight to Spanish influence, while any Portuguese operations against 'terrorism' were an invaluable contribution to defending Africa and the free world from the influence of Communist China and the Soviet Union.[23]

When it came, the colonial conflict was therefore a shock to Portugal. The first disaster was the Indian capture of Goa, Damao and Diu, in 1961, a decision taken after Salazar's refusal in 1954 to enter discussions with Nehru with a view to voluntary decolonization, and now made possible by Britain's refusal to put pressure on a Commonwealth partner to exercise restraint. The situation then deteriorated in the African colonies as revolts erupted in Angola in 1961, Guinea Bissau and the Cape Verde Islands (1963) and Mozambique (1964). A series of guerrilla movements emerged; they were all committed to ejecting Portuguese rule and they received assistance from neighbouring recently-independent Black African states (like Guinea-Conakry, Congo-Brazzaville, Zambia and Tanzania), and Communist regimes in China and Cuba. Motions of support for the movements were regularly passed in the United Nations General Assembly.

It was no foregone conclusion that the *Estado Novo* had lost the colonial war by the time of its own fall in 1974. Bruce argues that 'there was no evident sign of any weakening in Portugal's determination to remain in her overseas provinces'.[24] According to Gallagher, the 'guerrillas were not in a position to inflict a military defeat, with the possible exception of those operating in the smallest mainland African territory'.[25] Certainly, the guerrillas faced limitations. Most of their activities were well away from the urban centres and were concentrated on the border areas with neighbours which were assisting their cause. In some cases the guerrillas themselves were divided between different organisations. In Angola the MPLA (Popular Movement for the Liberation of Angola) contested power with the UPA (Union of the Peoples of Angola) and UNITA (National Union for the Total Independence of Angola). In Mozambique the main organization, FRELIMO (Front for the Liberation of Mozambique), competed with COREMO (Revolutionary Committee for Mozambique).[26] To some extent, these divisions were due to tribal rivalries, cutting across national resistance within territories which had had artificial colonial frontiers imposed upon them. The Portuguese also had support from white regimes such as Rhodesia and South Africa and received weapons from some of their allies in NATO (especially the United States) which circumvented the embargo on providing equipment for use in Africa.[27] As a result, there were few signs of shortages in *matériel* during the course of the war down to 1974. There were even some signs of lessons being learned. Salazar's successor, Caetano, decided to introduce reforms within the colonies as well as in Portugal herself and, in particular, to develop the infrastructures of Angola and Mozambique. Yet it is equally clear that time

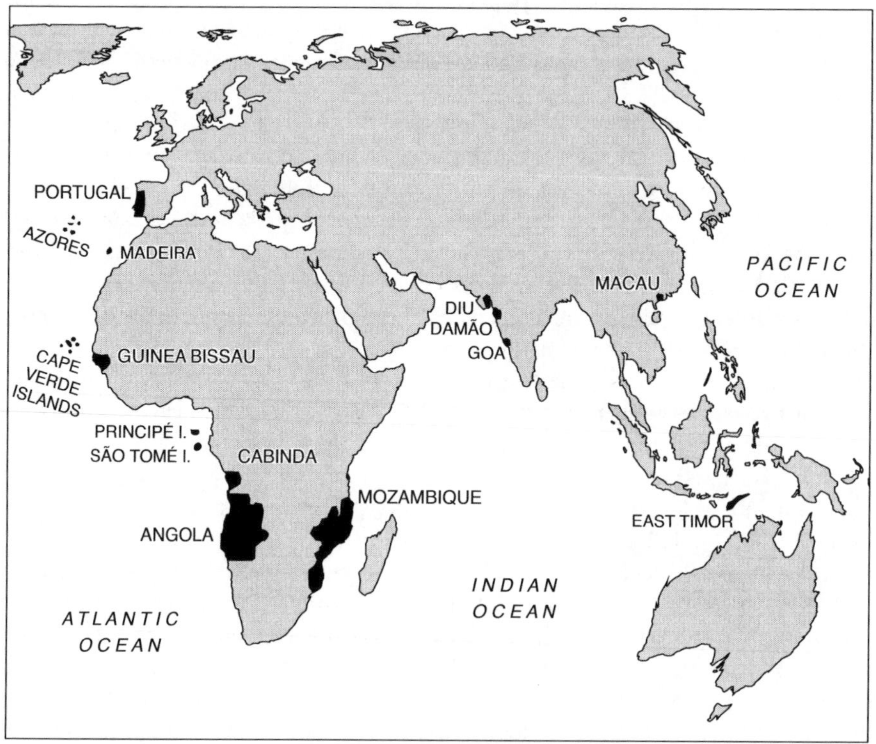

Map 7 The Portuguese overseas empire in the twentieth century

was on the side of those pursuing the 'liberation struggles'. Portugal may not have been facing imminent defeat in 1973 or 1974, but she had neither the resources nor the moral argument to win in the longer term. A small state with a dated, self-imposed mission could hardly expect to hold out indefinitely against the condemnation of most of the world.

Even so the withdrawal from empire or, as Gallagher puts it, the extrication of Portugal 'from the colonial morass she had got herself into',[28] came as a direct result of developments within Portugal rather than through military crisis overseas. The two were, of course, interconnected. The pressures of war accelerated a crisis in Portugal which was also the outcome of a series of changes developing for ten years or more. Most historians agree that the colonial war was the main catalyst in transforming Portugal: Birmingham, for example, argues that it 'brought more dramatic changes to Portugal's social culture than the world war had brought in 1943'.[29] Caetano's increase in military expenditure to over 45 per cent of Portugal's annual budget – to maintain 142,000 troops in Africa – accelerated the collapse of a temporary boom in the late 1960s and the slide into recession. This, in turn, caused an increase in unemployment and intensified opposition from trade unions and the political left.

The most direct impact of the colonial war was the destabilization of the Portuguese army which had not, after all, been directly involved in any other military conflict since the First World War. Even before 1960 Salazar had made the training academies more accessible to entrants outside the traditional elites from the upper levels of society; this dilution of the military elite increased during the 1960s. The prospect of prolonged and dangerous service overseas deterred many potential recruits so that, compared with the levels of 1958, admissions to the academies fell to 50 per cent and, by 1973, to 25 per cent. In an attempt to fill the gap, the government recruited university graduates who had completed their military service, allowing them more rapid promotion than officers who had come up through the academies.[30] Both segments of the officer corps became disillusioned with the regime: the traditional elite because it was threatened by what it saw as rising parvenus, and the new elements by a questioning of the very values of Salazar and Caetano. Both groups – and others, who were influenced by the Marxist texts they had studied in the academies' counter-revolutionary classes – began to question Portugal's inflexible strategies in Africa. They took their cue from General Spínola, who was convinced of the need for negotiation with the rebels and a policy to win 'hearts and minds' among the people.[31] In 1974 Spínola published his arguments for an alternative to continuing the conflict – a looser commonwealth instead of an integrated empire. On 25 April 1974 the government was overthrown as a result of a military coup planned by junior army officers with the support of Spínola.

By 1974, therefore, the *Estado Novo* had outlived its original purpose of stabilizing Portugal and, with its die-hard economic and colonial policies, now threatened whatever limited harmony it had achieved. Its founder had been incapacitated by a stroke in 1968. His successor, Caetano, had not been able to exert Salazar's unique blend of authority and reassurance and, although more inclined to reform, had attracted less support. Events in Africa had convinced a large part of the population that it was time for Portugal to distance herself from her tradition and past achievements and to accept modernization. This fundamental change of attitude enabled Portugal to progress, via the coup and revolution of 1974 – and subsequent political manoeuvring – from dictatorship and overseas empire to democracy and integration with Europe.

A 'fascist' regime?

Before – and after – its end in 1974 there was a debate as to whether the *Estado Novo* was a 'fascist' regime. Some historians have placed the emphasis on the system as a whole, considering the extent to which 'fascism' helped shape or colour Salazar's rule. Anderson, for example, maintains that the entire regime was 'inspired by fascism', and that Salazar 'made his corporate state totalitarian'.[32] In a detailed study of the opposition to Salazar, Raby argues that the regime undoubtedly exhibited several fundamental characteristics of fascism', albeit 'a weak, semi-peripheral fascism, appropriate to the position of a weak, semi-peripheral country'. Nevertheless, 'its origins, functions and structures' were 'similar to those of other fascist regimes'.[33] Mario Soares tended to use 'fascism' in a general sense as the worst manifestations of the regime as a whole. In his 1975 edition he wrote: 'In the time of Salazar and Caetano, Portugal was a refuge for the agents and survivors of international Fascism, a sort of paradise where they could settle all kinds of plots and plans without interference . . . In the world-wide organisations of reaction, the Portuguese dictatorship is sadly missed.'[34] He added: 'Fascism in Portugal was an insult to the world's conscience.'[35]

To some authorities, 'fascism' is not an appropriate term. Birmingham criticizes 'loose usage of the term "fascist"' since it 'fails to illuminate the specific nature of Portuguese government in the 1930s' and its 'contrasts of substance and style' with Spain and Italy.[36] Others acknowledge 'fascism' as a more specific part of the right-wing nature of the regime. Although it may have exerted some influence, it never succeeded in subverting the predominantly traditionalist nature of the power base. Pinto, for example, argues that 'The fascist were divided and merely junior partners in the large coalition that brought down Portuguese liberalism'.[37] Manifestations of fascism were confined to organizations like Preto's PNF and the Blue Shirts. But these did not flourish; 'pacts between the military élite and Salazar' joined 'conservative groups within the UN' to take often violent and repressive action against 'fascist groups'.[38] Indeed, the military dictatorship set up in 1926 saw gradual 'constitutionalisation' and 'civilianisation' which effectively blocked the influence of the fascists. Instead, the real influence lay with the authoritarian right, 'supported by powerful institutions such as the Church, most military officers, as well as landowning and industrial groups'.[39] Overall, 'The New State meant the hegemony of a traditionalist, catholic and anti-democratic right'.[40]

With this debate in mind, how should we identify the main features of Salazar's regime and what comparisons might be made with other European dictatorships?

PORTUGAL COMPARED WITH OTHER DICTATORSHIPS

Salazar's regime was certainly authoritarian and had many features in common with other dictatorships in Europe, including Austria under Dollfuss, Piłsudski's Poland, Horthy's Hungary, Franco's Spain, and the Baltic states; there were even some influences from Fascist Italy and Nazi Germany. All the distinguishing features of the Estado Novo were from the right of the political spectrum. It was based on the supreme power of Salazar himself; an American diplomat reported in 1936 that Salazar could 'make any decision without necessity for consultation with any other individual in Portugal'.[41] His dictatorship was ensured, like those of most other regimes of the right, by a reduction in the powers of the legislature so that no legal enactments could occur without his personal approval. His position was further underpinned by the establishment of a one-party state and a ban on all forms of political opposition. This was ensured by a secret police force, initially the Policia de Vigilancia e Defesa do Estado (PVDE), later the Policia Internacional e de Defesa do Estado (PIDE). The nation was associated with the glories of imperialism, in defence of which military expenditure was given priority. All of these were characteristic of authoritarian regimes elsewhere. His introduction of corporative institutions also owed much to right-wing ideas before 1914, possibly to the same stream which influenced Mussolini. Griffin considers it to be one of the 'para-fascist regimes' which learned to adapt to 'the era of the masses' and sought a 'façade of legitimation'.[42] Above all, Salazar, in common with almost all inter-war dictators, had a deep and profound hatred of communism.

Yet we should not deduce from this that Portugal was one of the regimes of the extreme right between the wars. On the whole, Salazar was much more conservative and less radical than the so-called totalitarian regimes of Germany and Italy. According to Gallagher,

> Although Salazar, like Mussolini and Hitler, set about creating a strong state to fulfil his goals, it was not required to be as drastic as theirs in its regulatory or coercive methods; the aim was merely to strengthen existing social values and modes of behaviour rather than pioneer a radically new social order.[43]

In part, this was due to Portugal's internal instability; according to De Meneses, this meant that 'the Portuguese dictator had to make continuous concessions to those who supported his rule', which meant that any ideology had to reflect 'the virtues of stability and order' rather than those of change.[44] This contrast between Portugal, on the one hand,

and Germany and Italy, on the other, was apparent in a number of ways. There was, for example, a clear ideological difference. Salazar said in 1934 that he feared that totalitarianism might 'bring about an absolutism worse than that which preceded the liberal regimes'. In particular, 'Such a state would be essentially pagan, incompatible by its nature with the character of our Christian civilization and leading sooner or later to revolution.'[45] His ideological base was traditional and Catholic – more in line with Franco than with Hitler or Mussolini. His personal power was also more discreet and less ostentatious than that of most of his contemporaries. Salazar had no wish to develop a personality cult – he even ended the official use of the term *dictadura*. The one-party state in Portugal was based on a different premise to those in Germany and Italy. The Uniao Nacional (UN) was not intended as a radical means of reshaping political views and of mobilizing political opinion. Rather, it was a device to create consensus, or to demobilize politics altogether. It is true that opponents of the regime were firmly dealt with: repression was effective, but the PIDE made less use of terror than any other secret police system in Europe and Portugal had no death penalty. Minorities were not persecuted as they were elsewhere. Anti-Semitism did not become a feature of Salazar's regime, despite attempts of the Blueshirts to make it so, and Portugal even provided sanctuary for some of the Jewish exiles from Germany. As for expansionism, Salazar always emphasized that Portugal had 'no need of wars, usurpations or conquests'.[46] Unlike the vast majority of right-wing regimes, Portugal was already a satiated power and wanted nothing more than to preserve those territories won in the past. This made the whole notion of empire a traditionalist and conservative one. In the economic sphere, the corporate state meant far less state involvement than in Italy. There was also no drive for industrial expansion, since this did not suit the traditional nature of the Portuguese economy. The purpose of social policy was to conserve existing values; education was therefore not intended to radicalize, which explains why not a great deal was done to extend its range.

Portugal was therefore one of the milder dictatorships of the inter-war period. This, and the cautious foreign policy of Salazar, enabled it to outlive the others on the right, with the single exception of Spain. Its successful longevity served, however, to delay the movement to democracy and to open it to charges that Portugal, along with Spain, provided Europe's last gasp of fascism.

DICTATORSHIP IN CENTRAL AND EASTERN EUROPE

Introduction

At the beginning of the twentieth century over three-quarters of the total area of Europe was ruled by three empires: Turkey, Austria-Hungary and Russia. By 1914 the Balkan provinces of Turkey had splintered into six independent states; their treatment after the First World War and subsequent problems are dealt with on p. 361. Central and eastern Europe underwent a similar transformation in 1918 as a result of the defeat of Tsarist Russia and the disintegration of Austria-Hungary. From the territory of these two empires no fewer than eight 'successor states' were established as a result of the Treaty of Brest-Litovsk and the Paris Settlement. The former (dealt with in Chapter 2) destroyed Russian sovereignty over Finland, Poland and the three Baltic states of Estonia, Latvia and Lithuania. The Paris Settlement, comprising the Treaties of St Germain (1919) and Trianon (1920), acknowledged the collapse of the Habsburg monarchy and the establishment of Austria, Hungary and Czechoslovakia.

The Paris Settlement ensured that Austria and Hungary were now merely the German and Magyar rumps of the old empire. The provinces of Bohemia, Moravia and Slovakia were converted into the state of Czechoslovakia. Galicia was ceded to Poland, Transylvania to Romania, Croatia and Bosnia-Herzegovina to Yugoslavia, and South Tyrol and Trentino to Italy. These provisions have been the subject of vigorous debate ever since and three arguments seem to represent the full range of opinion. At one extreme, the new Czech leader, Masaryk, welcomed the changes which had 'shorn nationalism of its negative character by setting oppressed peoples on their feet'. At the other extreme, some observers looked nostalgically back to the days of the multinational empire of the Habsburgs. One of these was Eyck, the German historian, who saw the 'dismemberment of the Austro-Hungarian state' as 'a basic error'.[47] More recently, A.J.P. Taylor pointed to the transitory nature of the empire, but also to the difficulty of managing without it: 'The dynastic Empire sustained central Europe, as a plaster cast sustains a broken limb; though it had to be destroyed before movement was possible, its removal did not make movement successful or even easy.'[48]

An analysis of the problems confronting the 'successor states' should enable the reader to weigh the relative merits of these views. It should also explain why this part of Europe should have become the scene of a series of domestic crises, which promoted dictatorship, and of international confrontations, which precipitated general war.

The first of these problems was the ethnic composition of the 'successor states'. In theory, the Paris Settlement was eminently reasonable; President Wilson's principle of 'national self-determination' ensured that the Slav peoples all received their own homelands, whether in Czechoslovakia, Poland or Yugoslavia. In practice, however, the settlement discriminated against both Austria and Hungary by so drawing the new boundaries that large minorities of Germans and Magyars were separated from their respective homelands. Hence 3.1 million Sudeten Germans came under Czech rule, as did the Hungarian population of Slovakia. The justification was that the Sudetenland was an industrial area which was indispensable to the economic viability of Czechoslovakia. In any case, to have left the province with Austria would have created a geographic impossibility and the Allies could hardly transfer it to Germany. There was therefore a tendency among the peacemakers to shrug off such anomalies; King Albert of the Belgians asked, 'What would you have? They did what they could.'[49] Unfortunately, the policy of favouring the Slavs at the expense of non-Slavs did not always work, for there was serious friction between the various subgroups who were brought together as co-nationals. Slovaks, for example, accused Czechs of monopolizing power, and some historians consider that the nationalist tensions which existed in the Danube area were worse after the dissolution of the empire than they had ever been before.

Ethnic conflicts were compounded by economic difficulties resulting initially from the manner in which the resources of the empire were carved up. The 'successor states' received disproportionate shares of the industries and agricultural land of Austria-Hungary. Czechoslovakia, for example, inherited only 27 per cent of the empire's population but nearly 80 per cent of its heavy industry, sufficient to enable it to compete successfully with many Western industrial states. Hungary was less fortunate. Although it received between 80 and 90 per cent of the specialized engineering and wood-processing plants, these had access to 89 per cent less iron ore and 85 per cent less timber. There was also a serious disruption in what had been a free-trade area of some 55 million inhabitants in which certain areas had specialized. In the textile industry, for example, most of the spinning was concentrated in Austria and the weaving in Bohemia. From 1919, however, each of the newly independent states was forced to build up those areas of its economy which had previously been undeveloped, the purpose being to create a more balanced agricultural and industrial base. Therefore, Austria had to build up her weaving and Bohemia her spinning. This, in turn, precipitated a round of tariff increases in order to protect infant industries from competition from neighbours; in their struggle for survival, many of the 'successor states' had to accept the principle of self-sufficiency even if it meant tariff wars and reduced exports. For a short period, in the second half of the 1920s, most governments managed a respectable rate of economic growth. This, however, was reversed, from 1929 onwards, by the onset of the Great Depression.

Political instability was due, in part, to economic crisis, in part to institutional defects. A great deal of thought had gone into the preparation of the constitutions of the 'successor states' in 1918 and 1919 and all the most advanced features of Western democratic thought had been enshrined in the new regimes, including universal suffrage, proportional representation and strict legislative control over the executive. One of the great disappointments of the inter-war period was that these constitutions failed to work properly in any country in central and eastern Europe, with the single exception of Czechoslovakia. In most cases there was a steady slide towards authoritarian regimes. In 1926 Piłsudski installed himself as Polish leader after a military coup, as did Smetona in Lithuania in the same year. By 1934 Austria had moved to the right under Dollfuss, while Estonia had succumbed to Päts and Latvia to Ulmanis. Hungary experienced more drastic changes, which resembled violent swings of the pendulum: within the space of twenty-six years it was ruled by a radical left-wing 'dictatorship of the proletariat' under Béla Kun, a conservative–authoritarian regime under Horthy, and a far-right, pro-Nazi dictatorship under Szálasi. None of these states had experience of the subtleties of a constitutional democracy, since they had previously experienced only the autocracy of Tsarist Russia or the milder but authoritarian monarchy of the Habsburgs. It was, therefore, unduly optimistic to expect a country like Poland or Austria to operate the type of constitution which baffled even the experienced politicians of the French Third Republic.

The fourth problem was even more serious than the ethnic conflicts, economic difficulties and institutional defects. Feuds developed between the 'successor states' which soon interacted with the rivalries between the major powers in the area. The motives varied. Hungary followed a revisionist course, spurred on by an irredentist policy which aimed to reclaim her lost Magyar territories from Slav neighbours. Austria, deprived of her role as a major power, sought an Anschluss, or union, with Germany, while Poland aimed to expand her frontiers to those of 1772, at the expense of the Soviet Union and Lithuania. The Baltic states had to focus their attention on basic survival. After 1920 these policies resulted in the emergence of two blocs. One, which consisted of Austria and Hungary, sought to revise the Paris Settlement, and gravitated rapidly towards Italy and Germany. This trend was completed by the Anschluss and Hungary's membership of Hitler's Anti-Comintern Pact. The second bloc comprised Poland, Czechoslovakia, Yugoslavia and Romania. These states formed close diplomatic links with each other and, during the 1920s, could depend on French guarantees against the aggression of other powers. During the 1930s, however, French influence collapsed in central and eastern Europe. As a result, this 'Little Entente' was undermined as various states hastened to make their own additional arrangements with Germany. Czechoslovakia tried to hold out against German influence, but she was set upon in 1938 by Germany, Hungary and Poland, all intent on claiming their fellow-nationals in the Sudetenland and Southern Slovakia. The failure of the West to support Czechoslovakia was a catalyst for Soviet aggression. In August 1939 Stalin sought to wipe out the memory of Brest-Litovsk by agreeing with Hitler the partition of Poland and the division of eastern Europe into German and Soviet spheres of influence. This pact enabled Hitler to launch his Blitzkrieg on Poland and, in so doing, to complete the destruction of the Paris Settlement.

Austria

In 1919 Austria was the German remnant of the Austro-Hungarian monarchy. It contained a population of a mere eight million people, of whom over one-third lived in Vienna. This transition from a major power to a state not much larger than Switzerland was so sudden that it caused 'a terrifying array of problems',[50] both internal and external. By 1933 the search for solutions in a democratic context had clearly failed and Austria drifted into a period of authoritarian government under Dollfuss (1932–4) and Schuschnigg (1934–8), which was ended by the absorption of Austria into Germany and the imposition of the Nazi dictatorship.

Austria's political problems were intensified by a loss of identity; Austrians had never wanted to be a separate entity, preferring instead Anschluss, or union with Germany. According to Bauer, one of the leaders of the Austrian Social Democrats, 'If we stay independent, then . . . we shall live the life of a dwarf-state.'[51] In the event, Austrians had no choice, for Anschluss was explicitly forbidden by the Treaties of Versailles and St Germain. But they developed no real commitment to the separate identity thus forced upon them. The 1920s saw the steady decline of democracy; although the 1920 constitution provided for a federal republic and a strong legislature, it was rendered unworkable by the constant rivalry between the left-wing Social Democrats, under Bauer and Renner, and the conservative Christian Socialists under Bishop Seipel. Initially in coalition until 1922, the two had drifted apart and the Christian Socialists dominated most of the governments of the 1920s and 1930s. Unable to achieve a majority in parliament, the Christian Socialists were constantly looking over their shoulders at the Social Democrats, whom they accused of trying to introduce a programme of 'Austro-Marxism'. Indeed, fear of the socialist left eventually induced the Christian Socialists to rely on a paramilitary force called the Heimwehr, the activities of which became increasingly sinister.

The main catalyst for the change from democracy to dictatorship was economic crisis which, according to Stadler, prevented 'a reasonably intelligent, civilized and industrious nation from settling down and making a success of their new state'.[52] Much of the blame has been placed on the terms of the 1919 Treaty of St Germain; according to the Austrian delegation, 'what remains of Austria could not live'.[53] Austria was now able to produce only one-quarter of her food and was obliged to import most of her coal and raw materials. By 1922 the situation had deteriorated badly, with rampant inflation and hunger riots. Chancellor Seipel offered a series of solutions in the form of international loans and careful budgetary controls and, for a while, Austria experienced a small boom. This did not, however, reverse the permanent trade deficit and was, in any case, wiped out by the Great Depression. In 1931 the entire Austrian banking system, Kredit Anstalt, collapsed under the strain which, in turn, resulted in the withdrawal of all foreign investment. Industrial production declined in 1932 to 61 per cent of its 1929 level, while the unemployment rate rose, in the same period, from 9.9 per cent to 21.4 per cent.[54]

Austria now entered an authoritarian phase as her leaders, unable to do much about the financial and economic crisis, sought to minimize the symptoms of political instability. The Christian Socialist leader, Dollfuss, became Minister of Agriculture in 1931 and Chancellor in 1932. This 'physically tiny and excessively vain man'[55] was a devout Catholic and implacable opponent of the left, determined to rid the country of 'godless Marxism'. Highly critical of 'so-called democracy', he aimed to establish a 'Social Christian German state of Austria, on a corporative basis, under strong authoritarian leadership'.[56] His subsequent measures certainly showed the seriousness of his intentions. In 1933 he severely weakened the Austrian parliament and made it possible to rule by executive decree. He then turned on the parties and movements, apart from the Christian Socialists. His measures against the Social Democrats (to 'remove the rubbish accumulated under the Republic'[57]) precipitated the 1934 civil war, from which Dollfuss emerged victorious. Meanwhile, under the influence of Mussolini, he had set up a mass party, the Fatherland Front, and went on in 1934 to introduce a corporative system similar to that in Italy. His own power increased dramatically as, in imitation of Mussolini, he accumulated for himself no fewer than five cabinet posts. His personal rule was abruptly terminated by his assassination in 1934, but the system was maintained in its essentials by his successor, Schuschnigg, until the latter's replacement by Nazi rule in 1938.

The main issue from 1935 onwards was the future of Austria in relation to Germany. To some extent, the obstacle to voluntary Anschluss was the Austrian leadership itself. Both Dollfuss and Schuschnigg were fully in favour of union with Germany, but within the traditional model of Austro-German dualism rather than under the more recent Prussian domination. Schuschnigg, especially, distrusted German militarism, the influence of Hitler and, of course, the intentions of the Austrian Nazis whom he saw as an enemy in the midst. He therefore pursued a policy of maintaining Austrian independence for the moment by manoeuvring diplomatically between Hitler and Mussolini and avoiding direct dependence on either Italy or Germany. Italy, however, soon lost the will to counter German influence in Austria as her own attention was diverted to the campaign in Ethiopia and the war in Spain. There was little, therefore, to prevent German ascendancy in Austria. The 1936 Austro-German Treaty tightened the link and, in 1938, Hitler summoned Schuschnigg to Germany, charging him with having broken this pact. Convinced that Hitler was trying to find an excuse to take over Austria, Schuschnigg announced a national plebiscite for a 'free', independent and united Austria. Hitler, however, moved too quickly for Schuschnigg. The Austrian Nazis caused so much internal unrest that Schuschnigg was forced to resign before the plebiscite could be held. He was succeeded as Chancellor by the Nazi leader, Seyss-Inquart, who promptly requested German intervention. There was no resistance to the German invasion and Hitler was given a rousing welcome in Vienna. The plebiscite held on 10 April 1938 returned a vote of 99.75 per cent in favour of the Anschluss as carried out by Seyss-Inquart and the German government.

Under the supervision of Bürckel, Reich Commissioner for the 'reunification of Austria and the German Reich', the whole face of Austria was now changed. The name itself disappeared: Österreich became Ostmark, eliminating any suggestion that Austria had ever been an empire in its own right. In May 1939 Ostmark was subdivided into seven *Gaue*, each under a Gauleiter; unlike Germany itself, Ostmark had party officials who doubled up as Reich governors, thereby avoiding the administrative conflict between party and state officials elsewhere. By 1942 even the appellation Ostmark was removed, to be replaced by the 'Alps and Danube Reich Regions'. Any opposition was purged by the Gestapo and the SS, and special courts were set up to deal with political cases. The entire economy was subordinated to the German war effort and the gold reserves were appropriated. The Austrian army was fully integrated into the Wehrmacht and all officers and soldiers were obliged to take the oath of personal allegiance to the Führer. Although substantial parts of the population played an active role in the institutions of the Reich there was, nevertheless an increase in disillusionment and opposition, especially after 1943. Resistance was attempted by a variety of groups, including communists, socialists, Catholics, factory workers and intellectuals; three movements of particular importance were the Austrian Freedom Movement, the Austrian Freedom Front and the Anti-Fascist Freedom Movement for Austria. When the

Anschluss ended in 1945 Austria accepted a future as a small non-aligned state and not part of a German monolith.

Was there an 'Austro-Fascist' regime?

Throughout the period Austria experienced a complex pattern of right-wing influences which calls for some explanation. The first major movement was the *Heimwehr*, a radical mass movement which was, however, increasingly used by the political right, the Christian Socialists. As the regime became, under Dollfuss, more rigidly authoritarian, it developed, in the Fatherland Front, its own mass base, which overlapped many of the activities of the Heimwehr. The relationship between these components in the governments of Dollfuss and Schuschnigg have been the subject of two very different interpretations.

On the one hand, Lewis maintains that the Christian Social Party destroyed the democratic republic and established, from 1934 onwards, an 'Austro-fascist' regime. The whole purpose of the dictatorship of Dollfuss was to eradicate the left in Austria, rather than to establish control over all parts of the political spectrum. 'Parliamentary democracy in Austria was destroyed in order to wipe out the Social Democratic movement, not to protect the country against fascism. The result was a form of fascism itself: Austro-fascism.'[58] The regime, or *Ständestaat*, had many of the hallmarks of fascism: the Christian Socialists had a strong populist tradition which 'fostered a distinct form of fascist thought which contributed to the creation of the *Ständestaat*';[59] the parliamentary system was replaced by a series of councils, a typical example of corporatism; and the Heimwehr played an integral part in the Christian Socialists' control rather than being a competitor. In other words, fascism was operating at the centre of the Austrian state rather than on its fringes.

The reverse is usually asserted. Payne and others maintain that the dictatorship of Dollfuss and Schuschnigg was traditional rather than fascist. Indeed, part of their motive was to prevent more radical groups like the Heimwehr from seizing the initiative. Hence, in Payne's view, 'the non-fascist forces of the right were able to organize a pre-emptive authoritarian government of their own'.[60] The main inspirations for Dollfuss were the authoritarian regimes and styles of leadership shown by Primo de Rivera in Spain and Piłsudski in Poland. The corporatist constitution of 1934 was similar to that introduced in Portugal in 1933 and had very little to do with Italian influences. Similarly, the emphasis of Dollfuss was always Catholic and Western, and he frequently criticized the racist values of Nazi Germany. It is true that some fascist trappings were introduced, such as the *Sturmkorps* set up in 1937; although this has been likened to the SS, it was closer to Assault Guards formed in pre-Franco Spain. Any youth movements were rooted firmly in Catholicism and there was no reference to militarism, expansion or 'new man'.

11 Dr Engelbert Dollfuss (left), 1892–1934 (© Popperfoto/Getty)

There is, of course, a third possibility, best described by Kitchen: 'Dollfuss's state was semi-fascist, clearly modelled on the example of Italy, but he had no mass support and his regime was only superficially similar to full fascism.'[61] Features similar to fascism were the regime's 'outright rejection of the liberal democratic tradition'[62] as well as its 'militant anti-Marxism' which involved measures against Communist Party and Social Democrats and the reorganization of the workforce. Nevertheless, Austria fell short of Italy and Germany. There were, for example, no revolutionary leanings, and those groups aimed at achieving mass appeal were largely a failure. Above all, neither militarism nor imperialist expansion was ever part of the programme of Dollfuss or Schuschnigg and neither leader introduced rearmament or compulsory conscription along Italian lines. Kitchen concludes: 'Austro-fascism was thus not the fully-fledged fascism of Italy or Germany';[63] Austria did not become 'fully fascist' until the imposition of German control after the Anschluss of 1938.

Austria: victim or perpetrator?

When they occupied and zoned Germany in 1945 the Allies did the same to Austria. But their attitude to Austria's involvement was not entirely clear-cut. On the one hand, they declared that Austria was 'the first free country to fall victim to Hitlerite aggression'.[64] On the other hand, their Moscow Declaration (November 1943) reminded Austria that 'she has a responsibility which she cannot evade for participation in the war on the side of Hitlerite Germany'.[65] There was also considerable emphasis on denazification, which created so much resentment in the early post-war years that the Austrian government 'reinforced the myth of collective suffering' by selecting documents 'designed to convince the Allies of patriotic hostility to the Anschluss regime'.[66] Overall, it has been asserted, post-war public opinion in Austria showed residual support for at least some of the elements of Nazi rule, as well as remnants of anti-Semitism. There was, according to Bukey, 'little incentive for ordinary Austrians . . . to reexamine their prejudices, especially after blame for their own suffering and for the Holocaust had been projected onto the shoulders of the Germans'.[67] The question has, therefore, been raised as to whether Austria was a 'victim' of Nazi Germany or a 'co-perpetrator' with it.

The case for Austria's victimhood is based on several propositions. Kindermann, for example, argues that there was a fundamental difference between Germany, where Nazism had risen 'from within', and Austria, where it had been imposed 'from without'. Hitler, who had a long-standing hatred of Austria, did what he could to destabilize the regime in the 1930s, accusing it of drifting away from Germany towards 'Switzerlandization' and falling increasingly under the influence of 'the Vatican, Habsburg monarchists and Jews'. Hence he exhorted the Austrian Nazis into 'terror campaigns unprecedented in Austrian history'. These provoked the Austrian authorities into taking counter-measures, which were the 'beginning of Europe's first state-organised resistance to Nazi imperialism'. In the process, 'Austria's leaders developed a new concept of the Austria state which rejected *Anschluss*'. But, although other parts of Europe praised this successful stand against German aggression in 1934, 'no effective international measures were introduced to protect Austria's long-term independence', eventually allowing Hitler's military occupation in 1938. Before that happened, Austria had shown more determination to resist than other potential victims of Nazi aggression. Even after the occupation 'there was no Austrian Vichy-type government'; rather, the previous state was expunged, which meant that 'there was in those years no Austria as such capable of forming a collective will or of cooperating with anybody'. From this arises the argument that collusion with the Nazi regime can only have been on an 'individual basis' and not from the 'state and people of Austria after that state had been destroyed'.[68] Even individuals were never committed to Germany: only a minority of those who had enthusiastically welcomed Hitler were Nazis.

There is no questioning the antipathy felt by the pre-Anschluss regime to Nazi Germany. Dollfuss and Schuschnigg were both strongly committed to avoiding Anschluss, Dollfuss actually forfeiting his life. But this does not automatically negate the impact of Austrian public opinion. Two elements are significant here: the spontaneity and extent of Austrians' support for the Reich and actions taken by them to demonstrate that support. It is not enough just to attribute to electoral manipulation the overwhelming Austrian approval of the Anschluss in 1938. Enthusiasm was widespread and genuine. The Catholic Church urged a 'yes' vote on the grounds that Nazism had repulsed 'the danger of godless Bolshevism that destroys all'. Even Renner, the Austrian Republic's first Chancellor, was in favour: 'As a Social Democrat and therefore as a proponent of nations' right to self-determination . . . I will vote yes.'[69] As Steininger argues, 'Who among the Catholics and socialists would still vote "no" in the face of such "recommendations"?'[70]

This, along with subsequent developments, opens up an alternative perspective – that in addition to collective victimhood, there was something rather more than individual co-operation. The enormous popularity of Hitler had entirely evaded both Dollfuss and Schuschnigg. The overwhelming plebiscite result confirmed the enthusiasm of the cheering crowds welcoming the German invasion in April 1938, something quite unique in the history of the Nazi occupations. Nor were the radical steps subsequently taken to integrate Austria into the Reich entirely German-controlled. Native-born Austrians were assigned the major positions in the new Ostmark administration. They were also disproportionately represented in the SS and Wehrmacht, operating both inside and outside Austria (14 per cent from only 8 per cent of the Reich's population). So too were the most notorious of the commandants of the extermination camps in Poland, including Erbel at Treblinka and Stangl at Sobibor. Other Austrians heavily involved in the deportation and extermination of the Jews included Seyss-Inquart and Kaltenbrunner, while '80 percent of Adolf Eichmann's men were from Austria'. Even the Einsatzgruppen contained 'a conspicuously large number of Austrians'.[71] According to calculations eventually made by Wiesenthal, Austrians were directly responsible for the deaths of no fewer than three million Jews.[72] Much the same applied to spontaneous outbreaks of anti-Semitism. According to Steininger, 'In no city of the Reich were pogroms so spontaneous, so general and so brutal as in Vienna or Innsbruck.'[73] Writing in 2008, Steininger added that Austrians 'were not only victims but also perpetrators'.[74] Historians are now more ready to pursue this line than in earlier decades, as are politicians – Austria's Chancellor, Vranitzky, had made a very similar statement in 1991.

Hungary

Between the wars Hungary experienced a more complete range of regimes than any of the other 'successor states'. The collapse of the Habsburg monarchy in 1918 was followed by the establishment of a democratic republic under Károlyi. This, in turn, was replaced in 1919 by the Soviet Republic of Béla Kun, one of the very few communist dictatorships established outside Russia between the wars. This, however, soon succumbed to a counter-revolution which was based on reactionary terror. This was stabilized by Admiral Horthy, who established a more permanent right-wing regime between 1920 and 1944; although there was some alternation between moderate and radical governments, there was little evidence of direct fascist influence. Then, in 1944, Horthy was overthrown by the Germans and a Nazi-style dictatorship under Szálasi was installed; during this period the whole regime was radicalized and became particularly brutal. With the defeat of Germany in 1945 Hungary came under a second and, this time, more durable communist administration.

Hungary's political experience was therefore similar to the swing of a pendulum: it moved from the centre violently to the left, through the conservative right to the extreme right, before returning to the far left. In the process, it experienced dictatorship under communism, traditional conservatism and radical Nazism. More than any other country in Europe, it provided a microcosm of the different movements and regimes experienced by inter-war Europe.

The different styles of dictatorship

Hungary seceded from the Austro-Hungarian Empire once it had become clear that the defeat of the Central powers was inevitable. In October 1918, a new Hungarian National Council was set up under Károlyi, which was intended as a progressive and democratic parliamentary system based on universal suffrage, secret ballot, freedom of the press and land reform. This experiment was never given a chance to work. Hungary was invaded by Czech and Romanian detachments seeking to extend the boundaries of states, and the Western Allies denounced Károlyi for his refusal to allow his territory to be used as a base for operations against Soviet Russia. Károlyi was even denounced as a Bolshevik; this was a major blunder which served only to bring about the very communist regime which the Allies had hoped to avoid.

For Károlyi, under severe external pressure, now felt impelled to bring the communists into collaboration with his own Social Democrats and even thought in terms of seeking assistance from Russia to support the new regime against its numerous enemies. In March 1919 he resigned in desperation and a new, far-left coalition was set up, dominated by Béla Kun, who, according to Molnár, behaved like a less ambitious Lenin.[75] A new Revolutionary Governing Council heralded the formation of a Soviet Republic and introduced a string of new institutions and policies, including a 'Red Army', revolutionary tribunals, a network of councils and extensive nationalization. Béla Kun made no secret of the narrow base of his power. He had, he said, set up 'a dictatorship of an active minority on behalf of the by and large passive proletariat'. He also considered it necessary to 'act in a strong and merciless fashion . . . at least until such time that the revolution spreads to the [other] European countries'.[76]

Despite the fears of some of the western states, the Kun regime was not a mere 'lunatic fringe'. It had the strong support of progressive intellectuals and the new government included the composer Bartók, the film director Korda and the physicist von Kármán.[77] It did, however, pursue a radical-left programme. The state took over the larger landed estates for redistribution to the peasantry; nationalized industrial concerns with over twenty workers; requisitioned essential items; and prepared the way for the establishment of councils for workers, peasants and soldiers. The ultimate aim was a close connection and alliance with Soviet Russia.[78] But the regime collapsed after only 133 days for a combination of internal and external reasons. Internally, the government lacked extensive popular support. According to Ignotus, 'by any reliable estimate, Kun's brand of nation-redeeming only appealed to a minute fraction of the working classes'.[79] It also failed to win over the peasantry by refusing to redistribute, to their private ownership, the land confiscated from the nobility; the unpopular agricultural reforms concentrated, instead, on trying to create over-large collective farms. In many ways the regime was too doctrinaire and neglected to exploit national sentiment: in some areas, statues of national heroes were actually removed. Instead, there was popular resentment of the Jewish influence within the regime, adding to an already strong presence of anti-Semitism in Hungary. All this meant that Kun struggled increasingly to maintain his authority, especially since he had no centralized party machine with which to enforce his new measures.[80] Internal instability turned into a crisis as a result of external threats. The invading Romanians broke through the Hungarian lines and half-hearted attempts by the Allies to mediate failed to prevent them from reaching Budapest. In any case, the end of Kun's regime came as a relief to those who feared the spread of Communism through central Europe. Kun was forced into exile, eventually in the Soviet Union where, ironically, he perished during Stalin's purges.

The swing to the left was now followed by a lurch to the right. The 'Red Terror' was replaced by an infinitely more savage 'White Terror' as 'officers' detachments' prowled those parts of the country not occupied by the Romanians, slaughtering workers and Jews and torturing to death any suspected members of the Béla Kun regime. This appalling phase of Hungarian history was ended in 1920 with the emergence of Admiral Horthy as the head of state, or Regent. A convinced anti-communist, Horthy constructed an authoritarian system which rested on the traditional power bases: the landed gentry, the industrial capitalists and the government bureaucrats. It was not, however, totalitarian; he retained the Hungarian constitution and allowed most of the parties to function, although with carefully restricted powers. Of all the 'dictatorships' covered in this book, the Horthy regime was probably the most borderline; indeed, it might be possible, for the 1920s, to dispense with the term altogether.

The lengthy period of Horthy's rule is usually divided into two distinct phases: the moderate conservatism of the 1920s and the more complex zigzags between caution and radicalism which characterized the 1930s.

After the bloodbath of the 'White Terror', Horthy concentrated on providing the new regime with an aura of legitimacy. He chose as his Prime Minister Count Bethlen, a leading aristocrat who had the confidence of the capitalists and landowners. Bethlen was suspicious of democracy as applied in those countries which had not, as yet, acquired political maturity and sophistication, and hoped to reach a position halfway between 'unbridled freedom and unrestrained dictatorship'.[81] He considered it safest to return to the limited democracy of pre-war Hungary and was willing to allow many components of a constitutional system. But his concessions were cosmetic rather than functional; his franchise, for example, drastically reduced the size of the electorate. He should, nevertheless, receive some credit for a period of relative political stability and economic progress. By 1929 industry had recovered from its dreadful performance of the early 1920s and had exceeded the production figures of 1913.

The Bethlen era was ended by the Great Depression which hit Hungary as seriously as any country in Europe. The industrial growth of the late 1920s had depended heavily on foreign capital investment which was withdrawn following the collapse of the banking system in central Europe. To make matters worse, Hungary's agriculture suffered disastrously under the strain of low prices and foreign tariffs against food exports. The overall result was large-scale poverty and, in some areas, people starved to death. Bethlen, unable to cope with the inevitable outbursts of discontent, resigned in 1930. Horthy was now faced with a dilemma about the style of rule which he should adopt. He ultimately opted for an increased personal role. But he experienced difficulties with his choice of prime ministers.

Basically, there were two types of premier: those who were in the conservative tradition of Bethlen, and those who had radical, even fascist, leanings. Horthy manoeuvred uncertainly between the two styles. Between 1932 and 1936 Hungary was governed by Gömbös, a radical and, according to Pamlényi, 'an uncompromising advocate of arbitrary, totalitarian forms of government'. His real aim was the 'realization of a less concealed, total form of fascist rule free of parliamentary trappings'.[82] His death in 1936 was followed by a zigzag sequence of conservatives like Daranyi (1936–8) and Teleki (1939–41) and radicals such as Imrédy. It seemed that Horthy was unable to decide which style of right-wing rule was more appropriate to Hungary's needs.

Much the same could be said of his foreign policy. The basic influence behind Hungarian diplomacy was a powerful revisionist urge resulting from the Treaty of Trianon (1920). This had deprived Hungary of two-thirds of its territory and consigned 3.3 million Hungarians to Yugoslavia, Romania and Czechoslovakia. According to Sinor, Hungary was a 'mutilated, dismembered, disarmed country, surrounded by strong and hostile neighbours'.[83] The immediate priority was to emerge from isolation. The first major development was the 1927 Treaty of Friendship with Italy, and it seemed that Mussolini was the obvious ally for the future. Then, after 1933, Hitler emerged as a real alternative. The Horthy regime oscillated between distancing itself from Germany (because of its fear of German expansionism) and collaborating with Hitler in the hope of smashing the Trianon settlement. After much dithering, Prime Minister Imrédy settled for the latter course and, by the First Vienna Award (1938), Hungary benefited territorially from Hitler's destruction of Czechoslovakia.

At the same time, a succession of premiers thought that they could prevent Hungary from being sucked into Germany's European war. Teleki went so far as to refuse German troops access via Hungary to Poland's southern frontier, and he even provided asylum for Polish refugees from Hitler's Blitzkrieg. But again irredentism or perhaps territorial greed prevailed. With German support, Hungary acquired, in the Second Vienna Award, some 17,000 square miles of Romania, together with 2.5 million people. Inevitably, Hitler expected in return a commitment from Hungary and this was fulfilled when, in 1941, Premier Bardossy provided Hungarian troops for the invasion of Yugoslavia and the Soviet Union. At first it seemed that Hungary would have no cause to regret her deeper involvement, for the Axis powers appeared invincible in 1941. By 1943, however, all illusions had been destroyed in the shattering defeat inflicted on the Hungarians by the Soviet army at Voronezh, to the north of Stalingrad. Horthy tried to extricate Hungary from the war by opening negotiations with the Allies. Hitler's response, in March 1944, was the occupation of Hungary and the enforcement of the full rigours of Nazi policies, including the deportation of Hungarian Jews to the extermination camps in Poland, with the full co-operation of the new prime minister, Sztójay. Horthy, in desperation, signed an armistice with the Soviet Union in October 1944. He was immediately arrested by the Germans and confined to Dachau and Buchenwald. After the end of the war he found refuge in Portugal where he lived for the rest of his life. He escaped extradition and trial for 'war crimes' largely through Stalin's intervention: 'Leave him alone; after all, he did ask for an armistice.'[84]

Horthy was succeeded by one of the most fanatical regimes of the whole period – a fascist dictatorship under Szálasi. The latter became prime minister in October 1944 and also replaced Horthy as head of state, with the new title of Nation Leader. His authority was based on Nazi support and his power exercised through his Arrow Cross party, a blatantly Nazi-style movement. He formulated a programme of 'Hungarism' or the construction of a Greater Hungary which would cover the entire Danube basin. He was also committed to the introduction of a corporate state, the nationalization of industry and the mechanization of agriculture. But Szálasi achieved none of his. He lost control over the Arrow Cross which created chaos, torturing and murdering tens of thousands of people, including workers, intellectuals, civil servants, workers and, above all, Jews. A large proportion of the Jewish population had already been deported to Germany under the general organization and surveillance of Eichmann. The extreme anti-Semitism of the Arrow Cross meant that the Nazi occupiers received total co-operation in completing the extermination programme through forced marches to camps, extermination in the provinces and massacres of helpless people massed in the Budapest ghetto. But, faced with the steady advance of the Soviet forces, the regime could not survive beyond the winter of 1944–5. Szálasi eventually met the fate which Horthy escaped. Like his contemporaries, Bárdossy, Imrédy and Sztójay, he was put on trial in Hungary, condemned to death and executed.

Resistance to the regime, which developed only after the end of Horthy's rule, had little time to develop and therefore showed less consistent defiance to the German occupation than in some of the other states in eastern Europe and the Balkans. The crucial factor in the defeat of the Nazis and the overthrow of the post-Horthy regime was the arrival of the Red Army, which also played an important part in the development of a new system. By 1945 Hungary had established, as in 1919, a coalition government dominated by the Communists. This time, however, the regime did not collapse, as it had behind it the full support of the Soviet Union. The Communists had also learned, from the failure of Béla Kun's 'dictatorship of the proletariat', and realized the importance of patriotism and organizational efficiency as well as ideology. Gradually, however, the other parties were undermined and then eliminated so that, by 1948, Hungary was a one-party state. This remained the case until liberalization occurred in 1989.

Reasons for Hungary's instability

The most important catalyst behind this experience of so many different styles of dictatorship was the break-up of the traditional Hungarian state. Many Western politicians and intellectuals warned of the effects of depriving Hungary of so much territory by the Treaty of Trianon – and they were proved right. The overall impact was massive dislocation and a huge sense of collective grievance. This was the more unbearable since Hungary had achieved autonomy and nationhood by the Ausgleich of 1867. In accommodating the minority Slav populations, the powers reduced pre-war Hungary by almost two-thirds. Over eighty years after Trianon, a modern Hungarian historian can still write:

> The sheer magnitude of the losses, which cannot be compared to anything but those occasioned by the Ottoman conquest in the sixteenth century, combined with the dubious arguments that were supposed to justify them, are sufficient to explain the bitterness they engendered.[85]

Like Austria, Hungary became a 'dwarf state'. Unlike Austria, it had no large ethnic neighbour with which it could now identify: there was never any possibility of a Hungarian Anschluss.

All parts of the population were affected. The working classes faced the prospect of mass unemployment through the loss of key industries to Hungary's newly emergent or enlarged neighbours. This meant that they were susceptible to radicalization, initially by the communist left, later by the fascist right, especially by the Arrow Cross. The latter process was accelerated by the severe impact of the Great Depression on an economy which

12 Admiral Miklós Horthy, 1868–1957 (© Popperfoto/Getty)

was already struggling to come to terms with its dislocation. The middle classes were doubly damaged. They were hit by the decline of industry and commerce and also by the impact on the machinery of government. The pre-1914 civil service in Budapest had been among the largest in Europe. Although it was no longer strictly necessary, every effort was made after 1919 to maintain it at its existing size. The result was that employment was bought at the cost of lower salaries and the creeping impoverishment of state employees. The upper levels of society faced a further crisis. They too resented the settlement which deprived many of them of their estates and reduced their landed wealth. But there was also a deep fear of the way in which the settlement threatened to radicalize the working and middle classes. There was therefore a powerful reason to pursue conservative policies in an attempt to preserve what was left of traditional Hungary; the extent of the threat meant that Horthy's conservatism merged with reaction and, as measures became more extreme under Gömbös, some of the methods associated with fascism began to appear. This explains the zigzag between moderate and radical governments in the 1930s.

The tragedy of Hungary was that it was impossible to pursue consistent political moderation. Even the intelligentsia suffered a sense of cultural alienation by a process which seemed to cut Hungary off from its past. A form of cultural irredentism helped make the Hungarian equivalent to German *völkisch* influences not only influential but respectable. These were adapted by extremists within Hungary's 101 far-right parties and eventually converted into the equivalent of German Lebensraum in the form of Szálasi's 'Hungarism'. Hungarian irredentism was diluted only by the savage experience of Nazi domination, war and post-war communist rule. Modern Hungary has resumed its democratic course within its restricted frontiers. It is, however, ironical that two of the three states given Hungarian territory in 1919 have since broken up.

Poland

The First World War proved to be the turning-point in modern Polish history. It smashed the three empires which held it captive (Russia, Germany and Austria-Hungary) and created a power vacuum which a new state in eastern Europe could fill. The core of independent Poland was the former province removed from Russia by the Treaty of Brest-Litovsk (1918). To this was added territory from Germany by the Treaty of Versailles (1919) and from Austria and Hungary by the Treaties of St Germain and Trianon (1919 and 1920). The Polish government, however, considered the eastern frontier to be too restrictive; hence, in

1919, Poland launched an attack on the Soviet Union and captured much of the Ukraine, including Kiev. The Soviet army soon recovered and drove the invaders back to Warsaw, which was subsequently besieged. Poland now appeared to be in dire peril but, with French assistance, managed to rout the Russians and reoccupy western Ukraine, possession of which was confirmed by the Treaty of Riga (1921). To this substantial slice of territory was added Vilna, seized from Lithuania, and parts of Upper Silesia. Overall, Poland, with an area of 150,000 square miles and a population of twenty-seven million, was one of Europe's more important states.

Unfortunately, the new Second Republic was confronted by a series of desperate problems. The first was the mixed composition of its population. Poles comprised only two-thirds of the total; the rest included four million Ukrainians, three million Jews, one million Germans, one million Belorussians, and small numbers of Russians, Lithuanians and Tartars.[86] The second problem was political instability. The constitution proved inappropriate to the ethnic structure since it provided for a centralized rather than a federal state. In theory, Poland was an advanced democracy, with guarantees of individual freedoms. Unfortunately, proportional representation encouraged the growth of small parties and prevented the formation of stable governments; altogether, there were fifteen cabinets between November 1918 and May 1926, an average lifespan of only five months. The whole situation was aggravated by a major economic crisis in which inflation led to the Polish mark sinking to a level of fifteen million to the dollar. This inevitably hindered the task of reconstruction, promoting shortages and unemployment. This unstable period came to a dramatic end when, in May 1926, General Piłsudski led several regiments of the Polish army into Warsaw. He replaced the democratic government with an authoritarian regime which lasted, beyond his own death in 1935, until the eventual liquidation of Poland in 1939.

Piłsudski was already something of a national hero. He had organized the Polish legions which had fought for the country's independence in the First World War. He had then become head of state between 1919 and 1922, leading the Polish offensive against Russia and organizing the defence of Warsaw in 1920. He had voluntarily stepped aside in 1922 into semi-retirement. Between 1922 and 1926, however, he watched with disgust the deteriorating political scene. At first he was not disposed to take drastic action because 'If I were to break the law I would be opening the door to all sorts of adventurers to make coups and putsches.'[87] Eventually, however, he became convinced that direct action was unavoidable. His solution was a call for national unity and a common moral sense, to be promoted by a grouping called Sanacja.

Piłsudski's achievements related mainly to the restoration of the Polish state after a century and a half of foreign rule. He strengthened the executive through his changes of 1926 and the constitution of 1935 (which he did not live to see), and made the administration more professional and efficient. He revived the morale of the army and, through a skilful foreign policy, strengthened Poland's standing in Europe. On the other hand, his regime witnessed serious financial and economic problems. The Great Depression had a particularly devastating effect on Polish agriculture and, as elsewhere, caused a sudden spurt in industrial unemployment. Piłsudski resorted to an unimaginative policy of financial constraints and drastic deflation. But this only aggravated the problem, and even by 1939 Poland's per capita output was 15 per cent below that of 1913. 'Thus,' observes Aldcroft, 'Poland had little to show economically for 20 years of independent statehood.'[88]

Piłsudski also showed serious flaws in his character. His rule became increasingly irksome as he himself became increasingly petty. Rothschild argues that Piłsudski's best years were behind him and that he had become 'prematurely cantankerous, embittered and rigid'.[89] Overall, it could be said, he completely lost the will to temper discipline and constraint with progressive reform; his emphasis on continuity therefore precluded any possibility of meaningful change. Piłsudski was one of the few dictators to die before the general upheaval of 1939–40. The authoritarian regime which he had established continued for the next four years, but it became less personal and more ideological. The reason for this was that, cantankerous though he had been, Piłsudski proved irreplaceable; the likes of Slawek, Rydz Śmigły and Beck lacked his popularity and charisma. Faced with ever growing pressure from the right, the Sanacja after Piłsudski was forced to collaborate with Poland's semi-fascist movements, since it lacked Piłsudski's confidence to defy them.[90] Whether Poland would eventually have become a fascist state is open to speculation, but it is interesting to note that its movement in that direction was due to the lack of leadership rather than to any personality cult. Polish 'fascism' therefore served to conceal mediocrity rather than to project personal power.

Piłsudski and his successors were faced with the problem of upholding the security of the new Polish state. This was given some urgency by the resentment of all her neighbours against Poland's territorial gains. At first Piłsudski sought safety in an alliance with France and Romania in 1921. Gradually, however, the will of France to assist Poland grew weaker. In 1925 France signed the Locarno Pact which, alongside Britain, Italy, Belgium and Germany, guaranteed the 1919 frontiers in western Europe but not in the east. By the early 1930s Piłsudski felt that he could no longer depend upon France and therefore sought accommodation with the powers which threatened Poland; he formed non-aggression pacts with Russia in 1932 and Germany in 1934. After Piłsudski's death, however, Poland slid towards destruction. There was a dreadful inevitability about the whole process: given Hitler's policy of Lebensraum and Stalin's determination to wipe out the memory of Brest-Litovsk, Poland did not stand a chance. According to Syrop, 'It is clear now that once Hitler and Stalin had jointly decided to wipe Poland off the map, no Polish policy and no power on earth could avert disaster.'[91]

Foreign Minister Beck showed courage in defying Hitler's demands for a Polish corridor and was bolstered by the Anglo-French Guarantee of March 1939. He clearly felt that Poland stood a chance of holding off Germany, as Piłsudski had fended off Russia in 1920. This time, however, Poland was crushed by Hitler's Blitzkrieg. The Polish cavalry, which had triumphed over Soviet infantry, was now shot to pieces by German tanks and aircraft. By mid-September the western half of Poland had been conquered by the Nazi war machine. The Polish government transferred to the east, only to be trapped by Soviet troops who were moving into position to take up the territory agreed in the Nazi–Soviet Non-Aggression Pact. Poland was therefore at the mercy of her two historic enemies. Stalin proceeded to impose communist institutions in the east, while the German zone was divided in two. The north-west and Silesia were absorbed directly into the Third Reich and were immediately Germanized; Gauleiter Forster said that his intention was 'to remove every manifestation of Polonism within the next few years'.[92] The rest was placed under Governor-General Hans Frank, who stated that no Polish state would ever be revived. The German occupation of Poland was to prove more destructive and horrifying than that in any other conquered territory, especially after the annexation of the Soviet sphere from 1941. Six million people died out of a total population of thirty-five million. Many of these were Jews, who perished in extermination camps set up at Auschwitz-Birkenau, Maidenek, Sobibor, Belzec and Treblinka. In retaliation against the uprisings, German demolition squads systematically pulled Warsaw apart, the only occupied capital where this happened.

The devastation did not destroy the Polish national spirit and three resistance organizations had come into existence by mid-1941. The first was a government in exile under Sikorski which established an army abroad and integrated Polish servicemen into the American and British forces. The second was the underground Home Army (AK), the third the Polish Workers' Movement (PPR), a communist organization led by Gomułka. At first there was co-operation between Sikorski and the Soviet Union but, as the Soviet victory over Germany became increasingly likely, Stalin did everything possible to weaken Sikorski and the AK. His task was made easier by the Yalta and Potsdam conferences of 1945. The Western Allies were, of course, unhappy about Poland falling under Soviet influence, but they were unable to prevent it. Hence, when recreated, Poland eventually became one of Stalin's satellite states, with a regime which was far more systematically pervasive than Piłsudski's had ever been. It was not until 1989 that the monopoly of the Communist Party was broken.

Problems limiting achievements or achievements despite problems?

'Problems' and 'achievements' form the two poles attracting two different types of historical interpretation. Broadly, one of these stresses that Poland's achievements were limited by her problems and deficiencies, while the other emphasizes the importance of Poland's achievements in the *face* of these problems.

Most historians have placed heavy emphasis on Poland's difficulties, some of which were inherited, others self-imposed. Both were sufficiently severe to impose serious limitations on what the Second Republic was able to achieve between 1918 and 1939. Polonsky's view is typical: 'Independence . . . presented the Poles with daunting and, in the end, insuperable problems'.[93] Political instability affected the opening years and Piłsudski's takeover in 1926 provided only a temporary respite. The 1935 Constitution was intended to provide a more permanent solution but, according to Roos, it 'rendered poor service to the Polish nation in the years from 1935 to 1939'. This was because Piłsudski died before he could take on the presidency 'meant for him' which, instead, fell into the hands of less talented incumbents.[94] Meanwhile, the Republic struggled to come to terms with Poland's considerable economic problems. Prażmowska maintains that proposals for industrialization 'proved too difficult to realise' as 'successive governments were not able to build a strong industrial infrastructure'.[95] Land reform was 'disappointing' as too little was released and Ukrainians were excluded from the redistribution scheme. This 'exacerbated relations' between them and the Poles.[96] Indeed, ethnic tensions aggravated all other problems. Minorities comprised over a third of Poland's population. Jews had been largely unassimilated and remained targets for far-right Polish groups like the Falanga, while four million Ukrainians deeply resented their inclusion as a result of the Russo-Polish War (1920–1). There has also been widespread criticism by historians of the Second Republic's deliberate Polonization which ignored provisions in the Treaty of Riga and the constitutions of 1921 and 1935.[97] Security and defence were compromised by the over-confidence resulting from Poland's victory over Soviet Russia in 1921. This had relied heavily on cavalry and Poland did too little to build in any quantity her high-quality aircraft and tanks. In the 1930s, especially, she failed to modernize at the same rate as either of her main threats – Russia and Germany. Poland also moved away from her close diplomatic connection with France, despite the latter's aim to 'broaden her alliances, tying Poland into a regional bloc including Czechoslovakia, Romania, Hungary and even possibly the Soviet Union'.[98] Instead, Poland opted for improvements in relations with Germany: Beck co-operated with Hitler in 1938, benefiting territorially from the dismemberment of Czechoslovakia. During the crisis of 1939 Poland returned – too late – to dependence on France, only to be forced into reopening talks with Germany over Danzig. Bearing in mind this range of problems and crises, there is a great deal of support for the case put by Davies: 'If the Second Republic had not been foully murdered in 1939 by external agents, there is little doubt that it would soon have sickened from internal causes.' There is less agreement with his deduction from this that the Second Republic 'was indeed destined for destruction'.[99]

While acknowledging the serious nature of the problems affecting inter-war Poland, some historians have avoided seeing these as overwhelming. Roos, for example, argues that 'the "September catastrophe" was no criterion of the country's inner vitality'.[100] The main advocate of this course is Stachura, whose revisionist approach has questioned many of the previous criticisms of the Second Republic. Although there were parliamentary problems they have 'unduly overshadowed historians' overall assessments of the republic.'[101] The Sanacja was generally 'beneficial to Poland', as was Marshal Piłsudski, who was a 'statesman of international eminence'.[102] Stachura has also switched the previous view that Poland exploited her minorities to a newer emphasis on the regrettable lack of their co-operation. 'Faced with German revanchism, Ukrainian subversion and widespread Jewish hostility, the republic's treatment of its ethnic minorities . . . was, in fact, generally even-handed, equitable and restrained.'[103] Indeed, the Polish government was faced with constant provocation and opposition: 'far too many of the minorities were determined not to reciprocate the flexible Polish attitude, even when one concession after another was granted'.[104] As regards her stability in a Europe containing two hostile neighbours – what other course could Poland have taken? Victory over the Russians in 1921 provided initial security and established Poland's reputation as a military power that forestalled Germany's aggression for over a decade. Eventually, however, Poland was badly let down by the West: the Locarno Treaties of 1926 contained no provisions for the protection of Polish frontiers and the Anglo-French Guarantees to Poland in March 1939 could not be followed by military aid in face of the German invasion in September. But for the external violation of Poland, 'there is no good reason' to believe that Poland could not have continued to resolve her internal crises as these 'had been resolved in the past'.[105]

Revisionism is always a welcome redress to earlier assessments since it changes the vantage point. But it is nearly always accompanied by the occasional overemphasis or passing dismissal. In this case, recent coverage of Poland's ethnic minorities, especially the Jews and Ukrainians, remains controversial. Perhaps the importance of Ukrainian additions to Poland in 1920–1 has been understated. Timely and influential though it was, Poland's victory in 1921 led to her being targeted in August 1939: one of the key reasons for Stalin's participation in the Nazi–Soviet Non-Aggression Pact was the recovery of Polish conquests in the Ukraine. This condemned Poland to obliteration. But it is surely legitimate to ask, if this had *not* happened, how long Poland could have survived before losing control of its conquests of 1921.

The nature of the Polish right wing

Poland is rightly seen as the victim of the aggression of Europe's two leading dictatorships in 1939. At the same time, however, Poland had itself become a dictatorship and had spawned a number of far-right parties. In this respect it followed an experience similar to that of Austria and Portugal. As in these countries, a distinction needs to be made between a conservative authoritarian establishment and semi-fascist minority groups which wanted to radicalize the right.

Piłsudski is normally associated with authoritarian dictatorship. He said: 'We live in a legislative chaos. Our State inherited the laws and prescriptions of three States, and these have been added to.'[106] This provided the justification for his assumption of power in 1926. He was in no sense a radical. His aim was to reconcile, not to radicalize. According to Rothschild, the purpose of the Sanacja was to form a 'non-political phalanx of all classes and parties supposedly prepared to elevate general state interests above particular partisan and social ones'.[107] This new order would be kept together by Piłsudski himself. Ironically, he did not resume the presidency in 1926, serving, instead, in the humbler capacity of Foreign Minister with two brief spells as premier. Yet no one doubted that ultimate power lay in his hands: 'I am a strong man and I like to decide all matters by myself.'[108] To emphasize this point, he reduced the power of the legislature, arguing that 'The Chicanes of Parliament retard indispensable solutions.' He saw Western-style party political manoeuvres as highly destructive in Poland, since they had produced a parliament which was in reality a 'House of Prostitutes'. He therefore broke the back of the party system and surrounded himself with loyal followers. Yet his dictatorship was never complete; his aim was not to set up a totalitarian state and a new political consciousness, but rather to depoliticize Poland and to create unity through heightened moral awareness. According to Lukowski and Zawadzki, therefore, 'The Sanacja under Piłsudski was a secular authoritarian system of government of a non-fascist type'.[109] His successors were somewhat less restrained than Piłsudski and, in the words of Payne, 'accentuated state control and authoritarianism'.[110] Between 1935 and 1939 the authoritarian regime was becoming more involved in regulating the economy and mobilizing popular support behind a new government organization, the Camp of National Unity, or OZN. This took on several outward appearances of proto-fascism.

Even so, the post-Piłsudski governments were less radical than most other non-fascist dictatorships in Europe. More open to far-right influences were the minority movements such as the National Democrat Party; strongest in western Poland, this was violently anti-Semitic, strongly nationalistic and sympathetic to both Fascist Italy and Nazi Germany, even though the latter was widely perceived as the national enemy. From this developed the even more extreme National Party (OWP) and Camp of National Radicalism (ONR). But the most explicitly fascist group was the Falanga, which was strongly influenced by the Spanish Falangist movement; it also had similarities to Codreanu's Legion and Iron Guard in Romania.

As elsewhere, the traditionalist authorities were not prepared to tolerate the excesses of these minority groups and at various stages during the 1930s resorted to banning them. Even though they stood no chance of coming to power they did, nevertheless, provide a core for that section of the Polish population which was prepared to collaborate with the Nazis, especially in implementing their anti-Semitic policies.

Estonia, Latvia and Lithuania

The Baltic enclaves Estonia, Latvia and Lithuania, originally provinces of Tsarist Russia, had been occupied by Germany in the First World War. Like Poland, they filled the power vacuum left by the defeat of both Germany and Russia. By 1920, the last foreign troops had been withdrawn and the newly independent republics could concentrate on internal consolidation.

In this they appeared to be assisted by liberal constitutions guaranteeing individual freedoms, rights for ethnic minorities, proportional representation and powerful parliaments. Unfortunately, in the Baltic republics, as elsewhere, these principles proved extremely difficult to operate. One of the main problems was the proliferation of parties competing for power; in 1925, for example, the Latvian parliament (Saeima) contained no fewer than twenty-six parties. The result was political instability, as Estonia saw seventeen governments in fourteen years, Latvia sixteen in the same period and Lithuania eleven in seven years. All this occurred at a time when political continuity was particularly important to tackle a wide range of economic and social problems, especially land reform and industrialization.

The first move to the right occurred in Lithuania in 1926. After a prolonged economic depression many prominent Lithuanians questioned the relevance of democratic institutions. The most important of these was Smetona, who seized power with the help of the military and established an authoritarian regime similar to that of Piłsudski in Poland. Democracy lasted somewhat longer in the other two states but was wrecked eventually by the Great Depression which caused a decline in exports, an increase in unemployment, and misery in the rural areas. In 1934 they followed Lithuania's example. Dictatorships were set up by Päts in Estonia and Ulmanis in Latvia.

The three regimes had much in common. All imposed the usual measures associated with dictatorship, including restrictions on political parties, the strengthening of presidential powers and dependence on the army. Smetona went further than either of his contemporaries, transforming Lithuania into a one-party state and developing the aura of a personality cult – he was known as Leader of the People (*Tautos Vadas*). But none of the regimes had an ideological base. Indeed, all were as suspicious of the extreme right as they were of the radical left. The fascist movements which developed in the Baltic states (the Thunder Cross of Latvia, the Estonian Freedom Fighters and the Lithuanian Iron Wolf) were regarded as a major danger, to be disciplined or even banned.

The three Baltic dictators have attracted far less condemnation than the others. Vardis argues that 'As dictatorships go . . . their rule was the mildest in Europe',[111] while Hope classifies them as 'benign rather than malignant'.[112] The repressive measures were by no means complete and left considerable room for manoeuvre. The press, for example, was less constrained than elsewhere and was still able to convey left-wing views. There was no attempt to introduce a complete corporate system and private enterprise continued to flourish. The Baltic peoples recovered reasonably well from the worst impact of the Depression and certainly enjoyed a higher standard of living than their contemporaries in the Soviet Union. By the late 1930s two of the three, Estonia and Latvia, showed signs of returning to a more obvious democratic base. Payne maintains that 'Both of these regimes exercised policies of very moderate authoritarianism and may well have had the support of the majority of the population.'[113] Yet, in 1939, the independence of all three Baltic republics was snuffed out. Two contrasting explanations have been provided for this.

One is that the three states were, like Poland, condemned by their geo-political position in Europe, strategically placed as they were between Germany and the Soviet Union. Dallin argues that their demise was as near as possible inevitable and that 'whatever these countries did or failed to do was ultimately immaterial'.[114] It could certainly be argued that the situation which brought the states into existence at the end of the First World War was unique and never to be repeated – the almost simultaneous collapse of major powers in the region. But it was hardly to be expected that this power vacuum would remain or that Russia would countenance the permanent loss of her Baltic territories. Hence, the fate of the republics was decided when the Nazi–Soviet Non-Aggression Pact of August 1939 allocated Estonia and Latvia to Stalin, and Lithuania to Hitler.

An alternative view is that the Baltic states did too little to help themselves. They failed to set up an effective security system or to co-operate sufficiently to mobilize the 500,000 men available. Any attempts which were made at alliance were unsatisfactory. A pact was drawn up in 1921 but Latvia and Estonia refused to admit Lithuania because they were afraid of being drawn into a border conflict between Lithuania and Poland. The 1934 Treaty of Friendship and Co-operation did include Lithuania but provided only for consultation on foreign policy and not on military planning. By 1939 there were three divergent approaches: Latvia wanted to remain strictly neutral, Estonia was primarily anti-Russian and Lithuania anti-German. Anderson has argued:

> It would be idle to pretend that the Baltic states were a factor of first importance in European affairs; nevertheless, placed as they were between Russia, Poland and Germany, if united, they could have played a respectable role in north-eastern Europe. Their fate during the months that followed, then, would probably have been somewhat different.[115]

The Baltic States were particularly unfortunate in being occupied by *two* of the totalitarian dictatorships: first by the Soviet Union (1940–1), then by Nazi Germany (1941–4) and finally by the Soviet Union again from 1944. The process was initiated by the Nazi–Soviet Non-Aggression Pact, followed a few months later by pacts forced on the Baltic States to allow the Red Army to be stationed on their territory. Stalin then systematically tightened his grip, assisted by Hitler's transfer of Lithuania to the Soviet sphere in exchange for a further slice of Poland for Germany. In 1940 Estonia, Latvia and Lithuania were brought under direct rule as various examples of Sovietization followed. These included the collectivization of some farms, measures to control the press and all publications through a single State Publishing House, the banning of over 10,000 books and the imposition of tight controls on writers, musicians and artists. The NKVD arrested a wide variety of suspects and introduced a milder version of the Terror that had already swept through the Soviet Union. The numbers of people killed or uprooted in the first full year of Soviet occupation were 60,000 in Estonia, 34,250 in Latvia and 75,000 in Lithuania.[116] Plans had been drawn up by June 1941 for the deportation of many more – including higher civil servants, local government officials, trade unionists, businessmen, clergymen and army officers.[117] These were, however, interrupted by Hitler's invasion of the Soviet Union on 22 June 1941. Lithuania and Latvia were rapidly conquered and, although the Russians held out longer in Estonia, Tallinn fell in late August. 'The speed of the initial German thrust through the Baltic states surpassed that of most German offensives during the Second World War.'[118] Indeed, the advance covered 480 kilometres in seventeen days.

The whole area came under direct German rule after the appointment of Rosenberg (himself a German from the Baltic) as Reich Minister for the Occupied Eastern Territories. Even before the invasion Rosenberg had drawn up instructions for the future rule of the Baltic States which would include 'measures to establish a German Protectorate there, so that it will be possible in the future to annex these territories to the German Reich. The suitable elements among the population must be assimilated and the undesirable elements exterminated'.[119] In practice, however, German control frequently fell short of original intentions. The excessive overlapping of jurisdictions and functions in many cases mirrored what was happening in Germany itself, whether between party and administration or Wehrmacht and SS. Ultimately the Baltic States were merged into *Reichskommissariat Ostland*, and Rosenberg gradually gave way to Lohse, previously *Gauleiter* of Schleswig-Holstein. There was also a problem with racial strategies. The deportations envisaged never materialized and most civilians escaped the mass upheaval imposed on them by the Soviet

Union. Hiden and Salmon make a significant comparison between Nazi and Soviet rule. 'For the majority populations of the Baltic countries, the best that could be said of German rule between 1941 and 1944 was that it was less harsh than the periods of Soviet rule which preceded and followed it, and less brutal than the treatment meted out by Germany to the other subject nationalities of eastern Europe.'[120]

A significant exception to this was the Jewish population of the Baltic States. Large enclaves existed in Vilnius, where Jews constituted 28 per cent of the total population, Riga (9 per cent) and Kaunas (26 per cent); they were also spread widely through the rural areas, except in Estonia. The Nazi plans for this minority exceeded anything envisaged by the Soviet occupiers for the majority – nothing less than mass extermination. This was started by *Einsatzgruppe A*, the most effective of the four killing units, which shot 125,000 Jews within four months in 1941. Other Jews were transferred to concentration camps near Riga or further afield in Poland. From the outset, groups of civilians in Lithuania and Latvia collaborated with occupiers, either in pogroms against the Jews or as volunteers in the police forces acting with German units. One of major factors in the hatred for Jews was that they had been seen as the main collaborators with the Soviet occupation, with which a disproportionate number of Jews had served. It was one of the nastiest examples of indigenous antipathy erupting into mass slaughter – and quite at odds with the relative harmony between Jews and other peoples promoted by the Baltic governments between the wars.

The Nazi dictatorship ended in 1944 with the fall of Tallinn and Riga to the Red Army but the price was the re-imposition of Stalinism and the transformation of the Baltic States into Soviet Socialist Republics. The Baltic republics were, therefore, the only creations of the Brest-Litovsk and Paris settlements not to be revived after the end of the Second World War. A second and more intensive wave of Sovietization followed, with a return to collectivization, industrialization and rigid controls. Deportations to Siberia were resumed: between 1944 and 1952 80,000 Estonians were sent to labour camps in Siberia, along with 136,000 Latvians and 250,000 Lithuanians.[121] Although an order for their release was eventually issued by Khrushchev, most of the exiles had already died in captivity.

Despite examples of co-operation with Soviet changes and Nazi racial policies, there was also a long record of defiance from some Baltic groups against the rule of both totalitarian regimes. Against the first Soviet occupation it was initially passive and symbolic, accompanied by a leaflet campaign. Then resistance groups emerged, like the Lithuanian Activist Front (LAF), which planned for a provisional government and raised a force against the deportations announced by the Soviet regime on the very eve of the German attack. Subsequent Soviet propaganda wrongly maintained that this was resistance against the German forces: in fact, the invaders were cautiously welcomed as the lesser of two evils. If, however, the Germans expected gratitude from the Baltic peoples for 'liberating' them from Soviet rule, they were soon to be disappointed. Within a year disillusionment had set in at the absence of any real return to autonomy, at the controls exerted over the local economies and at the demands for contributions to German manpower for the war against the Soviet Union. Examples of defiant groups were the Supreme Committee for the Liberation of Lithuania, the Latvian Central Council and, in Estonia, the Republic National Committee. Most resistance was political, with guerrilla activities confined mainly to Lithuania, where small units linked up with Belorussian fighters and Jewish escapees. Despite being weakened by previous campaigns and measures taken by security clamp-downs, resistance of many different kinds continued from 1944 well into the second Soviet era.

Throughout the war the Baltic peoples hoped for some sort of assistance from, or mediation by, the West. But the harsh truth was that the area was of little strategic importance to either Britain or the United States, neither of which risked alienating their Soviet ally in 1944 by an unrealistic challenge to Stalin's claims. There were no Baltic governments in exile and no resistance contacts with London. Even Churchill was prepared to concede the area to the Soviet sphere of influence in acknowledgement of 'the tremendous victories of the Russian armies'.[122] Estonia, Latvia and Lithuania therefore had to wait until the collapse of the Soviet Union at the end of 1991 before their statehood could be re-established. By 2004 their realignment was complete as they had switched their membership from the Warsaw Pact to NATO and from the Soviet Union to the European Union.

DICTATORSHIP IN THE BALKANS AND TURKEY

Introduction

The one common link between all the Balkan peoples was their historic subjugation to the Turks; all of the states of south-eastern Europe were originally part of the Ottoman Empire. Greece became independent in 1830, followed by Serbia and Romania after the Crimean War, Bulgaria in 1878 and Albania in 1912. The First World War saw a division of loyalties. Bulgaria allied herself to Germany, Austria-Hungary and Turkey (known collectively as the Central powers). Serbia and Albania were invaded and occupied by the Central powers, while Romania and Greece opted to join the Allies. Following the defeat of the Central Powers in 1918 Bulgaria lost Eastern Thrace and part of Macedonia by the Treaty of Neuilly (1920), while Turkey forfeited her dominions in the Middle East and parts of Anatolia by the Treaty of Sèvres (1920) before undergoing major internal changes after the revolution of Mustapha Kemal Atatürk. By 1923 Turkey had recovered its Anatolian losses by the Treaty of Lausanne – largely at the expense of Greece, which had tried to exploit Turkey's predicament. Romania emerged from the war considerably enlarged by Hungarian territory ceded by the Treaty of Trianon (1919), while Serbia was united with territory removed from Austria by the Treaty of St. Germain (1919) and Hungary to form the Kingdom of the Serbs, Croats and Slovenes; later this was renamed Yugoslavia. The 'peacemakers' hoped that this settlement would provide secure frontiers in a troubled area and, at the same time, enable the different countries to benefit from parliamentary regimes and progressive policies.

Appearances were, however, deceptive and this initial optimism was not fulfilled. The Balkan states faced massive economic, social and political problems which led inexorably to dictatorship.

The first failures occurred in the agricultural policies of the various governments. The immediate post-war priority was to redistribute land to the peasantry but, in every case, the reform programme was either incomplete or did not affect a high enough proportion of the population. There remained a large and discontented rural proletariat which placed intolerable pressure on the land and aggravated the problem of low productivity. The other half of the economy, industry, also experienced difficulties. The most serious were inadequate domestic sources of investment, which made most of the Balkan states prey to external influence; Albania, for example, came to depend too heavily on Italy, while Romania and Bulgaria found themselves ensnared by Germany.

Although it is hazardous to generalize about an area as complex as the Balkans, there does seem to have been an identifiable political trend. At first the Balkan states operated as democracies, with radical governments (like that of Stambuliski in Bulgaria) attempting radical reforms. There followed a drift to the right as the parliamentary system was undermined by bickering parties and a rapid sequence of weak governments. The eventual outcome was a series of authoritarian regimes. Albania was the first to succumb as Ahmed

Zogu proclaimed himself President in 1924 and King Zog in 1928. Yugoslavia, too, came under a royal dictatorship, in the form of Alexander I, from 1929. Romania's equivalent was King Carol (1903–40) and Bulgaria was ruled with an iron hand by King Boris from 1935. Greece experienced a more ideologically based dictatorship under General Metaxas (1936–41).

All of these regimes found themselves caught up in hectic diplomacy and bitter rivalry. Before the First World War the Balkans had been the 'powder keg' of Europe, always threatening to transform a local crisis into a general conflagration between the major powers. After 1918 the area of greatest potential danger shifted to central Europe but the south-east remained unstable and volatile as some of the defeated states sought to reconstitute their former power. Bulgaria and Hungary, in particular, advanced revisionist claims against their neighbours. The latter, fully conscious of the resentment of Bulgaria and Hungary, sought security in two major multilateral agreements. The first was the Little Entente (1920–1) in which Romania, Yugoslavia and Czechoslovakia sought to isolate Hungary and to prevent the possibility of a Habsburg restoration. The second was the Balkan Pact of 1934, comprising Romania, Yugoslavia, Turkey and Greece and directed, among other objectives, towards the containment of Bulgaria. There was also a considerable amount of bilateral diplomacy between individual Balkan states. The overall result was that, by 1939, a precarious balance of power had been achieved in which uneasy détente had come to replace active confrontation. What happened was that this balance was destroyed by the involvement of the great powers, and the Balkan states were sucked one by one into the Second World War.

This happened at a time when the Balkan states were having to deal with internal ethnic difficulties. In some cases, two or more groups had been competing for power throughout the 1920s and 1930s, as with the Serbs and Croats in Yugoslavia or the Ghegs and Tosks in Albania. Most countries had substantial minorities who felt oppressed, excluded or ignored – the Slovenes, Macedonians and Bosnians in Yugoslavia and the Magyars and Ukrainians in Romania. By 1940 there were already clear fault-lines which greatly facilitated the process of external intervention and the forceful redrawing of national boundaries or, as in the case of Yugoslavia, the fragmentation of the existing state. In all Balkan states there were also large Jewish communities. These were increasingly targeted by far-right groups who were integral to the rise of Balkan fascism and pressurized governments to co-operate with the Nazi implementation of the Holocaust.

A final point is worth a mention. The politics of the right were particularly complex in the Balkans, especially the relationship between conservatism and fascism in the formation of dictatorships. Each state had a different experience. In Yugoslavia the conflict was regionalized: conservatism was centred on Serbia, while fascism became strongly established in Croatia as a radical opposition. Eventually there were to be two dictatorships. In Romania the conservative right and the fascist right clashed continuously. Although fascism was eventually eliminated as an organized movement, the conflict had pulled conservatism so far to the right that it even secured the approval of Hitler. In Bulgaria the conservative right remained in control throughout the 1930s and was hardly challenged by fascism. In Greece some have claimed that traditionalism and fascism came together in the person of Metaxas. All of these issues will be looked at further in the following sections.

Albania

The main developments in Albania between the wars were the internal dominance of Ahmed Zogu, later proclaimed King Zog, and the ever growing influence of Fascist Italy, resulting in 1939 in direct rule.

Albania established itself as an independent state in 1912, after the First Balkan War. Almost immediately it encountered external threats to its very existence. During the First World War, for example, it was occupied by no fewer than seven armies, while both Greece and Italy had expectations of Albanian territory as a reward for having joined the Allies. Their claims to territory so delayed international consideration of the future of this tiny state that the Albanians impatiently took matters into their own hands. Setting up a Regency Council and a Committee of National Defence, they managed to evict an Italian occupation force of 20,000 men. By 1920 Albania was a fully independent state and a member of the League of Nations. Indeed, a report commissioned by the League was full of optimism about Albania's future: 'It seems clear that the essential elements of a prosperous Albania exist' and that 'it possesses all the conditions necessary for the formation of a politically and economically independent state'.[123]

Unfortunately Albania was to suffer from serious instability which led to political chaos and dictatorship. The problem was partly socio-economic: inadequate development and the long-standing conflict in the south between the Muslim landowning aristocracy and the Christian agricultural workers. It was also political. Albania was torn by the rivalry between Bishop Noli and Ahmed Zogu, the former much influenced by Western ideas, the latter entirely indigenous. At first they served in the same government but, in 1922, Noli withdrew to form an opposition. In 1924 Zogu did badly in an election and considered his position so perilous that he fled to neighbouring Yugoslavia. Noli, who now replaced him, attempted to introduce a series of reforms but his government lacked internal unity and effective leadership. In 1924, therefore, Zogu was able to make a sudden comeback. Invading Albania with his followers, a thousand Yugoslav volunteers and forty officers of the White Russian army, he overthrew Noli and had himself proclaimed President. He took immediate action to consolidate his power and, in 1928, elevated his title to 'Zog I, King of the Albanians'. He was backed by a new constitution which remained in existence until 1939.

13 King Zog, 1895–1961, photo taken on 6 April 1939 (© Popperfoto/Gettty)

Ahmed Zogu is described by his most recent biographer, Tomes, as 'a slender, soft-spoken gentleman' with a 'cultivated urbanity, neat moustache and ever-present cigarette-holder'.[124] Like Mustafa Kemal Atatürk, with whom he is sometimes compared, Zog was a Muslim modernizer; his aim was 'to civilise my people and make them as far as possible adopt Western habits and customs'. Unlike Atatürk, however, he struggled to make any permanent impression; indeed Atatürk accused Zog in 1928 of 'performing an operetta'.[125] Zog resented this attitude, especially since he had been an admirer of the Turkish revolution, and was never able to improve the strained relations between Albanian monarchy and the Turkish republic. He did, however, persevere in bringing under central control Albania's two main ethnic groups – the Ghegs in the north and Tosks in the south. For this, he considered that a monarchy was the most suitable form of government and borrowed ideas from Bonaparte, especially from the latter's imperial phase after 1802. The official line on this was expressed in the Tirana *Telegraph*: 'the republican form of government has proved to be . . . incompatible with the essential political needs of the country.'[126] His role was based partly on the development of personality cult: he presided over parades and stage-managed jamborees where the participants saluted him with hand on heart, the palm facing downwards. According to Tomes, these 'clearly owed much to fascist models'.[127] He was also ruthless in playing off the tribal and religious groups against each other and in using informers and assassins against possible political opponents. Yet he claimed 'legality' as the basis for all his changes – although the interpretation of 'legality' was always dubious. He got the Assembly to offer him the kingship. He also reduced the legislature to a manageable single chamber with only fifty-six members, all of whom were elected from nominations by loyal local government officials and not drawn from the now-banned political parties. The King controlled the parliamentary agenda and introduced most legislation himself. He secured a Penal Law for Political Offences to target any political opponents or troublesome intellectuals, while his censorship measures were rigid and pervasive. And yet, at first, he rarely lost sight of his westernizing ambitions, especially the improvement of transport, education and health. He attempted, through land reform, to force estate owners to sell a portion of their land to their tenants, who would pay by means of loans from a new agricultural bank. Unfortunately, the administrative system was inadequate when it came to enforcing these reforms and his attention was diverted by one crisis after another from 1931, including ill health and a second attempt on his life.

Zog was also confronted by the need to guarantee economic security. This, in turn, provided a link between domestic and foreign policy. Zog identified Albania's main need as foreign aid, and Italy as the most likely source. He therefore signed a series of agreements with Mussolini. The first, in 1925, allowed the Italians to finance a new National Bank and a Company for the Economic Development of Albania. In return, Mussolini expected to be given increased control over Albania's military security and foreign affairs. Zog went further down this perilous road in the 1926 Treaty of 'Friendship and Security' and the 1927 defensive military alliance. By 1933 he was uncomfortably aware of Albania's dependence on Italy and openly defied the Italian dictator by refusing his demands for a customs union. Mussolini, however, won his point because, by 1935, Albania was in urgent need of further Italian loans to wipe out the large budgetary deficit which had accumulated during this brief period of conflict. The process of Italian colonization was well advanced by 1939. It remained only to transform this into direct political control. Feeling the need to keep up with the hectic pace of Hitler's foreign adventures, Mussolini invaded Albania on 7 April 1939 and overthrew the Zog regime. Albania came under the direct rule of Victor Emmanuel III, and the diplomatic corps and army were united with those of Italy. This arrangement continued until the surrender of Italy in September 1943. From this date Germany was the occupying power, a transition which marked an increase in the number of savage atrocities.

Historians are universally critical of Zog's rule in Albania, although there is some disagreement as to whether his failure was total. On the negative side, Pollo and Puto argue that 'Zogu's return meant the establishment of a totally reactionary dictatorship in Albania'. It is true that order was restored, but 'it was the worst possible kind of stability'.[128] Logoreci, too, maintains that the monarchy was a 'pitiful incongruity' which made Albania 'the laughing stock of Europe',[129] while Stavrianos believes that any reforms attempted were only 'skin deep'.[130] Representing the Albanian Communist view, Frasheri accuses Zog of playing a 'demagogical game' that 'aimed at creating an illusion among the dissatisfied strata of the population of the country'.[131] The regime was 'on the way of making of Albania a fully bourgeois state': the 1929 civil code was 'based on the principle of the bourgeois laws' and the 1931 commercial law was 'drafted after the codes of laws of the capitalist states of Europe'. Falling increasingly under the influence of Mussolini, Zog showed 'complete capitulation to fascist Italy'.[132] This combination provoked a popular opposition based on Communist leadership – which occurred throughout the country, especially Tirana, 'with outstanding speed'.[133] A more balanced approach is a re-evaluation by Fischer.[134] Zog's main success was ensuring that 'central government was recognized in all parts of the country. Here Zog must be considered successful'. In the process, he managed to give Albania 'a certain political stability', which, in turn, provided 'an environment ideal for the growth of an Albanian national consciousness'.[135] On the other hand, he went into decline during the 1930s, showing 'limited constructive talent' and an inability 'to grasp economics' or 'the magnitude of the peasant problem'. In fact, he 'clearly failed in his attempts to create economic stability in Albania'.[136] He was also unable 'to choose competent advisers'.[137] Yet, throughout the time he was in power, 'Zog was not a tyrant for he was without the means and possibly without the inclination to be overtly oppressive'.[138] It is, therefore, misleading to compare Zog directly with most other dictators in Europe. Indeed, Tomes maintains that 'the new Arab kingdoms of Iraq and Saudi Arabia presented most points of similarity' and that 'he might also be likened to a host of more modern rulers of post-imperial countries in Africa and Asia'.[139]

Bulgaria

Bulgaria was the only Balkan state to have allied itself during the First World War to the Central powers. As one of the defeated combatants, Bulgaria was treated severely by the Allies, losing Western Thrace to Greece, the Dobruja to Romania and several key frontier areas to Yugoslavia. The Treaty of Neuilly (1919) also ended military conscription, reduced Bulgaria's army to 33,000 and imposed an indemnity of 450 million dollars, payable over thirty-eight years. Bulgaria's leaders, therefore, faced considerable problems in adjusting to the country's loss of territory, prestige and status; this was reflected in the wide variety of regimes experienced between the wars. Bulgaria's first government, under Stambuliski, was radical and reformist. After this had been overthrown in 1923, Bulgaria reverted to a more traditional style of politics. This, however, proved so chaotic that another coup, this time in 1934, set up a right-wing regime which was gradually converted by King Boris into a royal dictatorship. After a period of German influence, Bulgaria emerged from the Second World War with all the components of a pro-Moscow communist system.

Between 1919 and 1923 the Prime Minister of Bulgaria was Stambuliski, leader of the Bulgarian Peasant Party (BANU). Representing Bulgaria at the Paris Conference, he had to sign the Treaty of Neuilly, for which he was never forgiven by the various interests within his country. He nevertheless concentrated on Bulgaria's rehabilitation, seeking to collaborate with Bulgaria's neighbours – Greece, Romania and the new Kingdom of the Serbs, Croats and Slovenes. He also had ambitious schemes to transform Bulgaria into a 'model agricultural state',[140] in which land would be redistributed to benefit the poorer peasants, while men between the ages of twenty and forty were required to contribute a period of manual labour. These policies led to 80 per cent of the rural masses owning plots and a substantial

14 King Boris of Bulgaria, *r.*1918–43 (© Popperfoto/Getty)

improvement in infrastructure through the construction of bridges, roads and canals, the laying of railway lines and the draining of swamps.[141] Meanwhile, Stambuliski hoped to achieve an international *Green Entente* with fellow-Balkan states, along with Hungary, Poland and Czechoslovakia. He appeared unassailable when, in the 1923 elections, the BANU won an overwhelming majority in the legislature. At this stage, however, his premiership began to unravel. He was confronted by numerous enemies which included communists on the far left, liberals in the centre, and the army which was concerned about Stambuliski's leftist leanings. Most lethal of all was the Internal Macedonian Revolutionary Organisation (IMRO) which resented any foreign policy based on reconciliation rather than the recovery of Bulgarian losses to Serbia; they were particularly incensed by attempts made by the government to control their activities. The combination of opponents proved too much, even for a popularly supported government. In June 1923 Stambuliski was ousted by a military coup. He was handed over to a vengeful IMRO, at whose hands he met a horrifying end: he was tortured, mutilated and finally shot, his head being sent to Sofia in a biscuit tin.

Stambuliski was succeeded by a bewildering array of short-lived regimes, assailed by changing combinations of enemies. The following examples give an idea of the complexity of Bulgaria's politics between 1923 and 1935. The first government consisted of a coalition, the Democratic Alliance, under Tsankov. Although initially moderate, this became increasingly repressive. Reacting to communist attempts to seize power and assassinate the king, Tsankov's government conducted an active campaign against left-wing parties which, by 1925, had been virtually eliminated. In 1926 Tsankov was replaced by Liapchev, who relaxed the controls of Tsankov and reintroduced a measure of democracy. One remaining problem, however, was that Liapchev was himself a Macedonian and refused to deal with the disruptive activities of IMRO both inside and outside Bulgaria. His government was also destabilized by the impact of the Great Depression and the gradual erosion of support for his Democratic Alliance. He was therefore defeated in 1931 by the People's Bloc, a new coalition of centre-left parties (including several splinters from Stambuliski's BANU), which claimed to represent the peasant majority in Bulgaria. Soon, however, the People's Bloc was under attack from a revived Communist far left and a new National Social Movement, a fascist organisation set up on the far right by former premier Tsankov. The People's Bloc also squandered the opportunity to introduce new agrarian reforms, giving priority instead to internecine party-political rivalries.

The whole discredited edifice of party-based governments collapsed in 1934. Bulgaria's history from this point was dominated by dictatorships, although these too were of different types. The first resulted from a military coup carried out in May 1934 by Velchev and Gheorgiev, colonels in the Bulgarian army. They were motivated by disillusionment with constitutional democracy, the growing isolation of Bulgaria abroad (especially with the 1934 Balkan Entente between Romania, Yugoslavia, Greece and Turkey) and Bulgaria's unsavoury reputation as a breeding ground for terrorism. The new regime managed to destroy the organisation of IMRO and set itself an ambitious target – to centralize the state and establish a corporatist system through the Directorate for Social Renewal. It was not, however, securely based. Stavrianos has called it 'dictatorial but not fascist'.[142] It did not have the ideological base of fascism; the premier, Gheorgiev, had little upon which to conduct a personality cult; and there was no base of popular support. It also drew attention to itself by its republican and anti-monarchist elements.

By process of elimination, the next and final stage in Bulgaria's inter-war political development was royal dictatorship. King Boris III intervened against military rule in April 1935 to restore 'orderly and peaceful life'.[143] According to Ristelhueber, he showed 'a combination of flexibility and subtlety'.[144] In 1935 he issued a manifesto which announced major changes. There would, he insisted, be 'no going back' to the unstable era of party politics; hence, all political parties were banned. In 1937 he drew up a new constitution which guaranteed the place of a legislature in the Bulgarian system but placed tight conditions on the purpose and conduct of elections. It was possible, for example, to elect only candidates who had no party attachment and voting was made into something of an ordeal as a result of heavy police surveillance. In defence of Boris, it has been argued that he did much to reduce the level of political extremism and terrorist violence. For example, he banned fascist movements such as the Home Defence, the National League of Fascists, the Ratnitsi, or Warriors, and the Bulgarian National Legions. On the other hand, Bulgaria became, in effect, a police state in which terror now came from above. Boris also sought to pull Bulgaria out of the grips of the Depression. But the cost was almost total dependence on Nazi Germany which was by 1939 taking 68 per cent of all Bulgaria's exports and providing 66 per cent of her imports. This, in turn, pulled Bulgaria directly into the Axis's political and diplomatic orbit.

Like most other states in eastern Europe and the Balkans, Bulgaria sought at first not to become involved in Hitler's war. Then, in 1941, Boris allowed the Germans to use his country as a base for operations against Greece and Yugoslavia, in return for territory to be extracted from these two victims. By 1943, however, Boris's commitment to the Axis cause was being questioned and he died in suspicious circumstances in August 1943 after an interview with Hitler. His place was taken by Prince Cyril who acted as regent for the six-year-old king, Simeon. Cyril strengthened the links with Germany, effectively transforming Bulgaria from an autonomous dictatorship into a puppet regime under full Nazi control. This was eventually disposed of in 1944 as a result partly of internal resistance from the Fatherland Front under the leadership of Dimitrov and partly of the Russian invasion. By 1946 it had become clear that Bulgaria would be a communist state with close links with the Soviet Union. It was not until 1989 that this was liberalized sufficiently to allow for opposition groups.

Yugoslavia

Yugoslavia was one of the most heterogeneous of the smaller states of Europe. Its original core was the pre-war kingdom of Serbia, to which was added a significant number of territories in 1918. These included provinces of the former Austro-Hungarian monarchy, like Croatia, Slavonia, Dalmatia, Carniola, Styria, Carinthia, Istria, Baranja, Backa, the Banat, Prekomurje, Medjurmurje and Bosnia-Herzegovina. Small but important frontier areas were received by the Treaty of Neuilly from Bulgaria and, finally, the previously independent state of Montenegro was added in the south. The result of these gains was a considerable ethnic mix. The new nation had a total of twelve linguistic groups, of which three were predominant. These were the Serbs, Croats and Slovenes which, between them, accounted for ten million out of the total population of twelve million.[145] The generous boundary changes meant that there were also significant numbers of Germans, Magyars, Albanians and Turks.

This conglomerate was at first called the 'Kingdom of the Serbs, Croats and Slovenes'. It adopted a new constitution in 1921 which provided for a parliamentary monarchy under King Alexander, recognized the existence of political parties and based the electoral system on proportional representation. This constitution could not, however, provide a guarantee of permanent stability. The country faced two sets of serious problems, economic and political. Serbia had been devastated during the First World War and had experienced, proportionately, one of the heaviest population losses in Europe. Post-war recovery was made extremely difficult by the impoverishment of the peasantry, and the persistent threat of economic instability served only to destabilize the political scene. This, in any case, was threatening enough. The main problem was the mutual distrust, often hatred, between the Serbs and Croats. The former were Orthodox in religion and socially conservative; the latter tended to be Catholic and more open to progressive Western influences. The main area of conflict between them was the type of regime to be established. The Serbs wanted a centralized state (in effect a Greater Serbia), which they won in the 1921 constitution. The Croats, by contrast, aimed at a decentralized federation and did everything possible to undermine the predominantly Serb governments of the 1920s. A major crisis occurred in 1928 when the Croatian leader, Radich, was assassinated in the parliament, the Skupshtina.[146] In the riots that followed there were open demands for an end to the power of Serbia and for the creation of a 'free Croatia'.

At this point King Alexander seized the initiative and imposed the sort of royal dictatorship which was to set the pattern for other Balkan states. He moved rapidly to close the parliament and abolish the 1921 constitution. He was motivated by an impatience with party bickering, which he found repugnant; he had, in any case, developed a profound suspicion of Western democratic systems from his earlier contacts with the court of Imperial Russia. According to Dedijer, he was 'autocratic by temperament',[147] and unable to share power: he frequently screamed at his ministers. He saw himself as the saviour of his state, which he decided to rename Yugoslavia. In his proclamation of 6 January 1929 he observed, 'I am sure that all, Serbs, Croats and Slovenes, will loyally support my efforts, whose sole aim will be to establish as rapidly as possible such administration and organization of the state as will best conform with the general needs of the people and the interests of the state.'[148] To accomplish this he scrapped the old local government boundaries and set up nine new units, or *banovine*, which were superimposed across the old ethnic areas. He failed, however, to draw the sting of the problem. In 1931 the numerous Croatian exiles appealed to the League of Nations, making allegations that Alexander had imposed a reign of terror in Croatia and was making systematic use of brutality and torture.

In fact, Alexander tried to modify his rule by granting in 1931 a new constitution which officially ended the period of dictatorship. Two views have been put forward to explain his action. One is that this was a phased return to normality after a period of tough discipline. An alternative view is that the new concessions were 'merely a fig leaf for the royal dictatorship, which continued as before'.[149] Several points seem to support the second argument. The 1931 constitution greatly reduced the power of the parliament, maintained the structure of the police state, introduced an Italian-style electoral system, and abolished the secret ballot. Far from leading Yugoslavia back to democracy, Alexander only narrowed the base of his regime. In the process, he alienated not only the Croats but a large number of the more progressive Serbs. At the same time, he faced a growing economic crisis which included a trade deficit, a collapse of agricultural prices and the end of foreign investments and credits. The picture looked bleak indeed when, in October 1934, Alexander was assassinated, while on a visit to Marseilles, by a Macedonian terrorist.

He was succeeded by his son Peter, who, at eleven, was too young to rule. The regent was Prince Paul, who, according to Stavrianos, was 'ill suited for his task, being a dilettante and more interested in his art collection'.[150] Paul delegated most of his powers to his Prime Minister, Milan Stoyadinovich, who inclined towards fascism and built up a mass movement of green-shirted youths. Stoyadinovich also projected himself as the *Vojda*, or leader, but failed the ultimate test of maintaining law and order. The threat from Croatia grew increasingly serious until, in 1939, Stoyadinovich was replaced by Tsvetkovich, who had a more moderate and less repressive answer to Croatian separatism. By the *Sporazum* of August 1939 Croatia was given a measure of autonomy which included its own assembly.

Among the reasons for this concession were developments elsewhere in Europe. Hitler, for example, had shown the utmost ruthlessness in Czechoslovakia, turning the Slovaks against the Czechs and promoting internal dissolution to make possible external invasion and German occupation. The Yugoslav government wanted to avoid the same thing happening between Croatia and Serbia. The solution seemed to be to remove the sort of irritants which had encouraged the Slovaks to connive at the destruction of their partnership with the Czechs. To make doubly sure that the Czech experience would not be repeated, Yugoslavia maintained and intensified her already close relations with the Axis powers. This process had been under way since the early 1930s and had involved a shift of original policy. During the 1920s Yugoslavia had depended on French support to offset the threat of Italy over the Fiume issue. Then, during the last year of his life, King Alexander had taken the initiative of moving closer to Germany. During the regency of Paul, Yugoslavia became increasingly dependent on German economic aid, as was shown by the trade agreements of 1934 and 1936. By 1939 Yugoslavia seemed a willing enough client state to Germany, although extremely wary of Hitler's habit of exploiting the resentment of ethnic minorities. It seemed, therefore, that the safest course of action was to keep close links with Germany, somehow satisfy the Croats, and sit tight.

By 1941 Paul had become sufficiently confident to follow a more active policy. He was now convinced that the Axis powers would win the war and that the best guarantee of Yugoslavia's external security would be to join the Tripartite Pact between Germany, Italy and Japan. This, however, had drastic consequences. Paul's regime was overthown in a wave of anti-Axis feeling, intensified by fears that Yugoslavia was about to be forced into war on the orders of Hitler. In fact, the immediate threat now came from Italy. Mussolini used the internal chaos in Yugoslavia as an opportunity to launch an invasion from Albania, which Italy had already occupied in 1939. Mussolini had always expressed the most profound contempt for Yugoslavia, regarding this new country as an 'artificial contrivance of Versailles'.[151] The Italian offensive, however, was not entirely successful, and needed German assistance. Eventually the Yugoslav state was dismembered (see Map 8). Slovenia in the north was partitioned between Germany and Italy, the southern provinces were added to Bulgaria and Italian Albania, Serbia passed under German administration, and Croatia became a pro-Nazi puppet regime under its own *Führer* (*poglavnik*) – Pavelic. The collapse of Yugoslavia was accompanied by serious disorder and appalling massacres as old ethnic scores were settled. No other state in Europe must have appeared so unlikely ever to be resurrected in the future.

Yet Yugoslavia became the centre of the most effective partisan activity in Europe. According to Dedijer, this was the 'first massive uprising in Hitler's "Fortress of Europe", one of the high points in the history of struggle against tyranny'.[152] The two main branches of resistance were the right-wing and predominantly Serbian-based Chetniks, under Mihailovich, and the communist partisans under Josip Broz, better known as Tito – himself a Croatian. Of the two resistance movements, Tito's partisans were the more successful. Tito followed a non-doctrinaire strategy and tried to attract as wide a range of support as possible. He employed highly effective hit-and-run tactics and made maximum use of Yugoslavia's mountainous terrain. He devised a political programme which was likely to appeal to all parts of Yugoslavia, with emphasis on federalism and self-determination. The partisans were, it is true, helped by Hitler's constant need to drain off German troops from Yugoslavia to fight on the Russian front; they also received direct aid from the Red Army in 1944 and 1945. But it is usually acknowledged that the prime credit for the liberation of Yugoslavia should go to the partisans. Yugoslavia was, in effect, one of the very few occupied states to free itself.

This was of enormous importance in Yugoslavia's post-war history. Tito carried out his promises, by introducing a federal structure, but also determined that Yugoslavia should never again fall under the influence of a great power. His independent line resulted in Yugoslavia being excluded from the Soviet orbit in 1949 and Yugoslavia eventually emerged as one of Europe's very few neutral states and as a key member of the world's 'non-aligned movement'.

Interpretations of forces behind the collapse of Yugoslavia

Most historians see a direct connection between the collapse of the first Yugoslavia and the internal problems developing during the 1920s and 1930s within one of Europe's most heterogeneous states. These problems meant that the rival groups turned against each other once external pressure was applied by the great powers, greatly facilitating the country's conquest and partition.

Internal crises occurred from the very beginning of the 'Kingdom of the Serbs, Croats and Slovenes' and became increasingly serious. Dragnich argues that 'In the idealism of the moment, too many things were taken for granted'.[153] Insufficient attention was paid to the political, religious and cultural differences ingrained in the background of the different groups: Slovenia and Croatia had previously been part of Austria-Hungary and the other areas had been ruled by the Ottoman Empire – until Serbia's independence in 1878, Bosnia-Herzegovina's transfer to Austria-Hungary in 1908, and Macedonia's conquest by Bulgaria in 1912 and Serbia in 1913. Yugoslavia's political difficulties originated from the 'frailty of democratic traditions'.[154] Although the 1921 Constitution provided for a constitutional monarchy, the parliament was destabilized by a multiplicity of parties representing regional interests and never producing a working majority for either of the two largest parties – the Radicals of Serbia and the Croatian Peasant Party. This rivalry was caused by bitter resentment of the Serbs by the Croats and Slovenes. 'Virtually all the communities in the new state disagreed over one issue: Should the regime be centralized or should it be a decentralized federation?'[155] Radich and the Croatian Peasant Party pursued a policy of

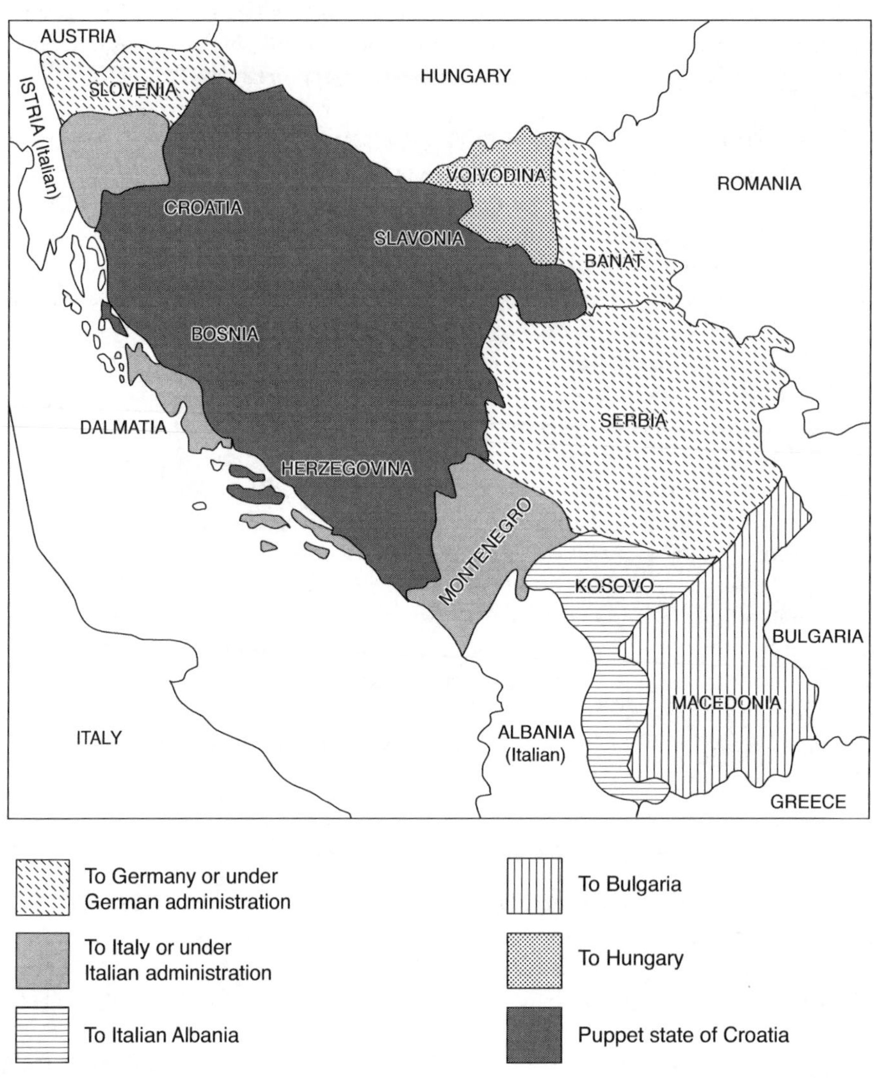

Map 8 The dismemberment of Yugoslavia 1941

separatism, to which the Slovenes also aspired. This meant that 'The "three-tribe" nation thus stood divided from the very beginning.'[156]

Political complications were exacerbated by other manifestations of Yugoslavia's multiple heritage, especially different legal codes and currencies. This meant that 'The merging of these multiple systems was slow, and the kingdom, from the beginning, lagged well behind the rest of Europe in embracing twentieth-century methods'.[157] The peasant base of Serbia 'retarded the process of urbanization and development of the middle class'. Industrial development was 'stunted', favouring Slovenia and Croatia at the expense of Serbia, Montenegro and Macedonia.[158] Not surprisingly, 'profound tendencies toward the disintegration of the new state existed within it from the beginning'.[159]

The attempts by Alexander's dictatorship to end regional rivalries failed, although some measures, like the new name of Yugoslavia, were welcomed by the Croats and Slovenes. But, although he genuinely tried to foster a multi-ethnic state, increasingly Alexander used Yugoslavism as the justification for his own power and, in any case, reaffirmed the underlying policy of centralism to which the Slovenes and Croats had always objected; to them, it made little difference that Serbian centralism had become Yugoslav centralism. It seemed that some progress was made in 1939, when an agreement instigated by Paul gave Croatia a measure of autonomy. But the *Sporazum* came too late. According to Ristić, it 'could not bridge the gap between the two peoples so long kept apart by foreign conquests and later by both Serbian and Croatian political careerists'.[160] It did not resolve the bitterness between Serbs and Croats, threatened to stir up the other groups excluded from the agreement, and provided no internal unity in the face of external aggression. As a result the external aggressors, especially Germany, were able to use internal animosities to impose a new structure on occupied Yugoslavia.

Plausible though this line of argument seems, it has been subject to some criticism. Other historians have argued that Yugoslavia was actually destroyed by pressure from *without*. The implosion from within *followed* the conquest and dismantling of a country which might otherwise have survived as a national entity, despite the considerable internal problems that it was having to confront. Bennett's argument is that 'The first Yugoslavia was not an unmitigated disaster doomed to end in the slaughter of the Second World War. That it did has more to do with foreign intervention . . . than any innate desire of Serbs and Croats to wipe each other out.'[161] After all, there were promising indicators in 1939. According to Cipek, the *Sporazum* was possibly the 'first step towards solving the national question'. It would have needed extending since Bosnian Muslims and Slovenes would also have wanted self-determination; yet such a process could have been accomplished within a new national structure. But 'The federalisation of Yugoslavia, which seemed inevitable after 1939, was interrupted by the Second World War.'[162] What subsequently happened was that German and Italian occupation made the Ustasha more popular with the Croatian public, who had become thoroughly radicalized.

Another element to the argument against the inevitability of Yugoslavia's internal collapse is provided by Allcock, who questions some of the general assumptions already covered. Yugoslavia was by no means unique in experiencing internal political instability. According to Allcock, 'the fragility of democracy was a general feature of European politics at this time'.[163] Certainly, the counterpart to divisions within Yugoslavia was discord within other Balkan states, Hungary and Poland. Even Czechoslovakia, the only creation of 1919 that survived as a democracy, was subject to conflicts between its ethnic components. What really counted in their longer-term future was the attitude of the major powers. Allcock criticizes Italy, Germany, the Soviet Union, the United States, France and Britain. Mussolini's constant interference in Albania eventually spread northwards and eastwards into Yugoslavia and Greece. Germany's search for economic autarky through the exploitation of the less developed areas of south-eastern Europe made Yugoslavia a particularly attractive target. Russia, meanwhile, exerted a destabilizing influence through unpredictable policies, especially the Nazi–Soviet Non-Aggression Pact of 1939. The United States proved inconsistent: highly influential in setting up of the new Europe after the First World War, its non-membership of the League of Nations and withdrawal into isolation meant that it played little part in the further development of post-war Europe, let alone the Balkans or Yugoslavia. Britain and – increasingly – France neglected Yugoslavia and other areas, largely because of their own preoccupations. As a result, the Balkans 'were left to stew in their own juices'.[164] Hence, Allcock concludes, the state of Yugoslavia was 'ended by eternal invasion and not by its own divisions. It is only under these conditions that internal fascism was able to become a significant force within Yugoslavia'.[165]

Conservatism and Fascism in Yugoslavia

We have seen that dictatorship emerged in two main forms in Yugoslavia. One was the conservative type which sought to maintain the new status quo, mainly in favour of Serbia. The other was the radical style which sought separate national fulfilment – this took the form of proto-fascism in Croatia.

Before the First World War, Serbia had been an expansionist state, gaining territory as a result of the Balkan Wars of 1912 and 1913. The peace settlement, however, fulfilled any remaining irredentism and gave Serbia the task of coming to terms with all the other ethnic groups attached to it in the new state of Yugoslavia. This automatically led to the search for a new balance. The monarchy, itself Serbian, was therefore anxious to avoid radicalism. This meant that the dictatorships of Alexander and Paul were essentially conservative – similar in some respects to that of Boris of Bulgaria. There were more radical elements in Serbia, such as the Zbor under Ljotic, but the authorities were always wary of them because of their potential for disruption.

The real manifestation of the radical right occurred in the province which deeply resented its close association with Serbia. Croatian nationalism came to be connected with the far right because it was radicalized by its hatred of Serbian traditionalism. Pavelic's Ustashi aimed at nothing less than the complete independence of Croatia with expanded frontiers to include Croatia, Dalmatia and Bosnia. The Ustashi were also racial and *völkisch* in their ideas: they were deeply anti-Semitic and exclusive, claiming that the Croats were 'Western' and 'Gothic' not 'Eastern' and 'Slavic'.[166] They were also one of the most violent of all the terrorist movements, organizing assassinations and sabotage during the 1930s. They even set a modern precedent in collaborating with a foreign organization, the IMRO, to assassinate the head of state in 1934.

All of these influences were crucial to the pattern of Pavelic's dictatorship in the puppet state of Croatia set up in 1940. The Ustashi became a radical mass movement, recruiting especially from the urban population. Croatia was, of course, a one-party state under the leadership of the *poglavnik*, who adopted all the paraphernalia of fascism. Above all, it used terror on a massive scale to convert, expel or exterminate the various minorities in Croatia, especially Serbs and Jews. Of all the regimes outside Germany and Italy, Ustashi Croatia was probably the most genuinely fascist. It was also the most ruthless and arguably the most totalitarian. In both the Serbian and Croatian cases, however, the developments were strongly influenced by external ideologies and methods, adopted as a means to achieve frustrated internal ethnic aspirations.

Romania

Romania entered the First World War in August 1916 and was rapidly defeated by Austria-Hungary, but, on the latter's collapse, ended up as one of the main beneficiaries of the peace settlement. By the Treaty of Trianon Romania received 31.5 per cent of the area of the former kingdom of Hungary and emerged as the largest of the Balkan states.[167]

The political scene, however, was to prove extremely unstable. The first stage was a coalition government between the Nationalist Party of Transylvania and the Peasant Party of Wallachia, under the leadership of Vaida. This was committed to a policy of economic and social reform. It failed, however, to gain the approval of King Ferdinand, who dismissed the entire government in a royal coup in 1920, substituting a more authoritarian regime under Averescu. This, in turn, was replaced in 1922 by a liberal government under Bratianu, which had some major achievements to its credit; a new constitution was drawn up in 1923, based on Western democratic principles. Unfortunately, the reforming impetus broke down and, in 1928, the government was resoundingly defeated by the main opposition, the National Peasants. The new Prime Minister, Maniu, hoped to revive a policy of social and economic reform. This time, however, good intentions were destroyed by the impact of the Depression and the emergence of another royal dictator.

Ferdinand died in 1927, leaving the succession open. The main claimant was Carol who had, however, been excluded from the throne earlier because of widespread disapproval of his sexual activities. The National Peasant government now pursued an ultimately fatal policy. Hoping to win Carol's permanent support and wanting to demonstrate that it was not morally prudish, it assisted Carol's return to Bucharest. Soon after his coronation, however, Carol dismissed Maniu and his cabinet. He was convinced that the only solution to Romania's political and economic problems was a regime based on 'dynastic authoritarianism'.[168] He expressed strong reservations about parliamentary systems and openly admired Mussolini's regime. He therefore proceeded to install a series of puppet governments and, in 1938, abolished the 1923 constitution, introducing, instead, an imitation of Mussolini's corporate state. He also replaced the traditional party structure with his own 'Front of National Rebirth'.

Meanwhile, Romania had seen the emergence of an indigenous fascist movement. This originated, in 1927, with the formation by Codreanu of the League, or Legion, of the Archangel Michael. In 1930 it developed a paramilitary organization known as the Iron Guard. The 'Guardists' were violently anti-Semitic and typically fascist in offering a 'third way' between middle-class capitalism and communism. Codreanu also stressed the importance of mass enthusiasm. Describing a campaign in 1930 he said, 'We looked like crusaders. And crusaders we wanted to be, knights who in the name of the cross were fighting the godless Jewish powers to liberate Romania.'[169] At first King Carol was prepared to ally himself with the fascist right and even to make use of its mass base. Soon, however, he found it an encumbrance and a threat to internal security. In 1938, therefore, he took the drastic step of banning the Iron Guard, along with Romania's political parties. Codreanu was prosecuted for treason and sentenced to serve ten years in prison. There, along with other imprisoned Legionaries, he was strangled by the guards. The whole episode provides an example of the bitter distrust between the reactionary right, in the form of royal absolutism, and the radical right, in the form of fascism.

Subsequent events were even more tortuous. King Carol had to abdicate in 1940, in utter humiliation. The immediate reason was that Romania was forced to give up territory to three aggressive neighbours: Bessarabia and Northern Bukovina to Russia, Northern Transylvania to Hungary, and Southern Dobrudja to Bulgaria. Carol was succeeded by Michael, who tried to prevent the complete disintegration of Romania by entrusting power to a military dictatorship under General Antonescu. At first Antonescu was prepared to collaborate with the revived Iron Guard, now under Sima. Indeed, he went so far as to proclaim a National Legionary State with himself as Leader, or *Conducator*. Before long, however, the Iron Guard once again became troublesome, seeking total power and a more extreme regime. Antonescu therefore purged the Guard, dismissed Sima and destroyed, once and for all, the influence of homegrown fascism in Romania.

At the same time, Antonescu strengthened links with Germany. Romania played a significant part in the invasion of Russia and was largely responsible for the conquest of the Crimea. Then, at Stalingrad, the Romanian army was shattered, and with it Antonescu's reputation. By 1944 Romania was under threat of Soviet attack. Michael tried at the last minute to win the support of the Western Allies by sacking Antonescu and installing, in turn, Generals Senatescu and Radescu. In the process, he deliberately distanced Romania from Germany, thereby reversing Antonescu's policy.

Michael's initiative was doomed. The Western Allies had already secretly consigned Romania to the Soviet sphere of influence, in return for a Soviet guarantee of the security of Greece. Under Soviet influence a new National Democratic Front was established, coming increasingly under the control of the Communists. The previous leaders were dealt with one by one: Antonescu, for example, was tried and executed as a war criminal in 1946, and Michael was forced to abdicate in 1947. Finally, in 1948, a new constitution was drawn up, based on that of the USSR. The country remained under a neo-Stalinist regime until the overthrow of Nicolae Ceauşescu in December 1989.

The Romanian right wing

The right wing in Romanian politics was especially complex, giving rise to three conservative dictatorships – under Ferdinand, Carol and Antonescu – and a number of fascist movements, the most prominent of which was the Iron Guard.

The reason for this complexity lies in a combination of continuity with the period before 1914 and the transformation of Romania in 1919. There had already been social dislocation in the form of a massive peasant rebellion in 1907, along with ethnic disturbances and outbreaks of anti-Semitism. These had been sufficient to incite the sort of conservative reaction which was common throughout the Balkans. But, more than anywhere else in the area except Yugoslavia, it was the impact of the First World War which helped shape the form of Romania's subsequent politics and dictatorship.

These changes have been described by Livezeanu as a 'national revolution' in which conservative responses became more extreme. Hence, 'the postwar "status quo" represented a profoundly revolutionized state of affairs, "conservation" of which demanded more than traditional conservative measures'.[170] There were bound to be problems in converting the old state of 138,000 square kilometres and 7.8 million people into a new nation of 295,000 square kilometres and 14.7 million people, especially since over 30 per cent of population were minorities (Hungarians, Ukrainians, Bulgarians, Germans, Gypsies and Jews) which reduced the overall proportion of Romanians. This made it extremely difficult to practise progressive parliamentary politics, which made it very likely that there would be a right-wing reaction. This, in turn, was influenced by the far right, which fed off the social discord resulting from Romania's enlargement. It was all part of a vicious circle.

The reactionary right and the radical right had a stormy relationship, with the regimes of Carol, Michael and Antonescu alternating between tolerating and banning the Legion and Iron Guard. But the cumulative influence of the Legion had a ratchet effect on the official regime, forcing it to institute increasingly ruthless forms of dictatorship. They were, however, distinctively different. Fascism, especially in the form of the Legion and Iron Guard, was visionary in its extremism, whereas the conservative regimes were largely

15 Ion Antonescu, 1882–1946 (© Popperfoto/Getty)

pragmatic, using ideas when it suited them but preferring not to be permanently committed to them.

During the 1930s Romanian fascism consisted of several movements and layers which varied in intensity from proto-fascism to the genuine article. By far the most important, however, was the Iron Guard, which had a powerful appeal to younger sections of the population, including students, workers, peasants, lawyers, civil servants and teachers. Ioanid maintains that the main characteristics of Romanian fascism were anti-communism, nationalism and imperialism, anti-Semitism and racism, the 'myth of the state', 'mysticism', 'social diversion' and 'false anti-capitalism'.[171] These were all typical of both Italian Fascism and German Nazism, although the proportions that made up the combination differed in each case. Codreanu made his preferences clear: 'I am against the large Western democracies' and 'I am for a Romanian foreign policy aligned to Rome and Berlin'.[172] Above all, he emphasized eternal struggle and perpetual war against the enemies of the *Tara*, or Fatherland. The Romanians he considered biologically distinct from other ethnic groups and therefore 'superior' to minorities such as Hungarians and Jews. The latter were a particular target and Romanian fascists fully supported demands for their extermination. From 1937 Codreanu also spoke increasingly of the expansion of Romania into the south-western Ukraine ('Transnistria') and for the establishment of a Danubian–Carpathian federation under Romanian rule.

Some of this cut little ice with those in power: the monarchy, the army officers and traditionalist politicians. They were less concerned about mobilization of opinion than about the accumulation of power and about dealing with opponents; increasingly, Codreanu came to be seen as a dangerous radical who would destabilize the regime. Although some observers claim that Carol was a 'monarcho-fascist', this term is not particularly appropriate. Carol was never inclined to any systematic ideology and remained traditional and conservative in his policies. This also applied to Michael and the *Conducator*, Antonescu. Yet, when the latter did finally succeed in destroying the Legion, he ruled, in Payne's words, as 'a right radical nationalist dictator with the support of the military'.[173]

Strangely, this was preferred by Hitler since Antonescu offered more security as a Romanian satellite. This was understandable because Hitler's main concern in 1941 was the military use of Romania rather than its complete ideological conversion. Hence, a conservative regime which had been radicalized by its contact with fascism was an ideal balance. In any case this radicalized conservatism proved to be one of the most extreme of all the European states in its policies towards the Jews. The extent of Romania's involvement in the Holocaust is dealt with on p. 256.

Greece

Greece was the oldest of the Balkan states, winning her independence from the Ottoman Empire in 1830. Her territory had been greatly extended by the Treaty of Sèvres (1920), by which she received from Turkey Eastern Thrace, many of the Aegean islands and the administration of Smyrna. From Bulgaria she gained Western Thrace (see Map 9). Yet, despite being one of the victors in the First World War, Greece deteriorated into prolonged chaos during the 1920s and 1930s, eventually succumbing to the dictatorship of Metaxas.

Her problems were both external and internal. The external crisis was the more immediate and urgent. The Greek government found its territorial gains from Turkey difficult to digest. In 1920 the Ottoman Sultan was overthrown and a dynamic leader, Mustapha Kemal, set up a new Turkish republic with its capital in Ankara. Kemal's main objective was to destroy the Treaty of Sèvres and, in particular, to drive the Greeks out of Turkish territory. The Greek government found itself isolated diplomatically from its former allies, and fought a disastrous war in Turkey. The Greek army was badly equipped and had severe problems of communication. By 1922 the Greeks were defeated and, by the Treaty of Lausanne (1923), were obliged to give up Eastern Thrace. The whole episode was a triumph for rejuvenated Turkish nationalism over Greek pretensions to imperialism.

Foreign problems acted as a catalyst for internal political instability as Greece experienced numerous changes of regime between 1920 and 1935. At first the conflict was between a discredited monarchy and the republicans, but the abdication of King Constantine in 1922 did little to guarantee peace as his successor, George II, also had to renounce the throne. Party politics in the new republic, formed in 1924, became so chaotic and boisterous that the military decided to intervene, with General Pangalos imposing a brief dictatorship in 1926. Democracy had a second chance when Venizelos was elected to power in 1928, but the parliamentary system was destabilized by the disastrous impact of the Depression on the Greek economy, especially on shipping and tourism. Greece reverted in the early 1930s to a series of short and unstable regimes, punctuated by attempted coups and counter-coups. This sorry state of affairs continued until 1935 when General Kondyles forced the Greek parliament to abolish the republic. He then arranged a plebiscite which produced a suspiciously large majority in favour of the return of the monarchy – in the person of George II. The new king dispensed with the services of Kondyles but, in 1936, appointed an even more authoritarian premier in the form of General Metaxas, who dominated Greece for the next four years.

Metaxas tried to maintain an independent foreign policy and to avoid becoming a mere puppet of the Axis powers. He was initially more suspicious of Italy than of Germany, largely because of Mussolini's aggressive designs on Corfu (see Chapter 4). Then, in 1939, he came to the conclusion that Germany, too, needed watching: Hitler's designs on Czech and Polish territory caused a wave of apprehension even in states which sympathized ideologically with Nazism. Hence, shortly after the Italian invasion of Albania, the Greek government, along with Romania, accepted an Anglo-French guarantee of security of the kind which had already been extended to Poland. The hollowness of this promise was, however, demonstrated in September 1939, when nothing could be done to prevent the German invasion of Poland. Metaxas decided that his only course of action was to keep Greece neutral no matter what happened elsewhere in Europe.

Metaxas referred to the new Greece as the '4th August regime' after the date on which the constitution was amended to reduce the parliamentary role. His power lacked any party base, his own group (*Eleftherophrones*) comprising only six members of parliament. Instead, his authority depended on the king himself, even though he contrived to reduce the latter's involvement in the details of government. His fundamental antipathy to party politics led to the atrophy of a western-style parliamentary system and his ultimate intention was to introduce a corporate system that would cover the political sphere as well as the economy and society. On the positive side, he did introduce reforming laws on working hours, minimum pay, health insurance and paid holidays. These were motivated partly by genuine concern about deplorable existing levels and partly to justify his new powers by winning popular support. But any improvements were accompanied by increased controls through a combination of propaganda and coercion. The former promoted orchestrated mass demonstrations and an extreme personality cult, while the latter took the form of a repressive police state. The political police was placed under the leadership of Maniadakes and was charged with eliminating opposition (especially communists), upholding and reforming moral and political values, monitoring education and controlling the media. Whether these measures were based on traditional and conservative, or on new and fascist, influences will be considered in the next section. We can, however, say that attempts to mobilize public opinion behind Metaxas had limited results. According to Petrakis, 'the efforts of the propaganda machine to present an image of a charismatic leader failed to turn artificial enthusiasm into genuine belief'.[174] Metaxas never managed to achieve the sort of popularity he wanted, even though he was much more concerned about this than, say, Salazar. Petrakis refers to his 'insecurities, fears and doubts as to the Greek people's love for him'.[175] Opposition and outright hatred were especially strong in outlying areas like Crete, the Peloponnese and Macedonia, or where there were substantial ethnic minorities. Indeed, the fact that he is remembered at all owes less to his internal governance than to his brief management of the crisis caused by external invasion.

The most positive perspective on Metaxas is his defiance of Mussolini's ultimatum of 28 October 1940. There was greater popular acclamation for Metaxas's response – *Ochi!* (No!) – than there had been for any of the internal actions of the pre-war regime. Metaxas then showed effective leadership and organized a successful military counter-offensive against the Italians. He emphasized that Greece 'has a debt to herself to remain worthy of her history'.[176] The Italians suffered a series of defeats, the worst at Metsovo. By the end of 1940 Greece had succeeded in liberating herself. The death of Metaxas in January 1941 came as a major blow, leaving a gap in the country's leadership. The successful war with Italy might have contributed towards a partial rehabilitation of his reputation – but any positive effect was soon to be wiped out by the German invasion. This came in April 1941 as Hitler launched an onslaught to rescue Mussolini from total humiliation. Despite help from British troops, the Greek mainland and islands were rapidly conquered. Protected by the British, the king withdrew to Egypt, as his country was partitioned between Germany, Italy and Bulgaria, and administered by puppet regimes under Tsolakoglou, Lotothetopoulos and Rhalles. These were all ideologically sympathetic to Nazism but, unlike Metaxas, lacked the Hellenic drive that placed Greek nationalism above all other considerations.

They also failed to gain from the Greek people the sort of collaboration received from the puppet regimes of Hungary, Croatia, Romania and Bulgaria. Part of the reason was that the Greek population suffered more severely than almost any other: 7 per cent of all Greeks died under German occupation and 30 per cent of the national wealth was removed. Greeks, it has been argued, were driven to resistance.[177] Certainly there was massive support for the National Liberation Front (EAM) and its National Popular Liberation Army (ELAS). These organizations scored a number of notable successes against the occupying forces and, by 1944, were setting up administrations in newly liberated areas. The Greek effort was

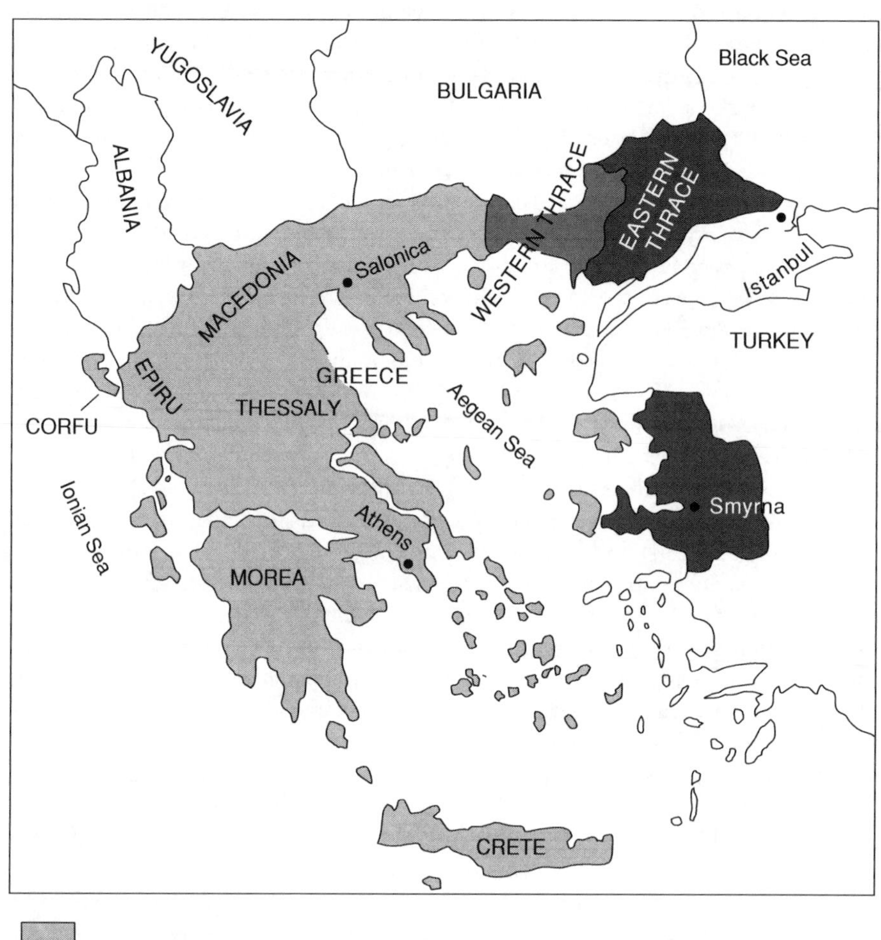

Map 9 Greece after the First World War

assisted not by the Russians, as elsewhere in the Balkans, but by the British, who made a series of landings from 1943 onwards.

The anti-German Greek government in exile returned to Athens in October 1944, but the eviction of the Nazis did not mean the end of Greece's internal problems. Between 1946 and 1949 the country lapsed into civil war as the various ex-resistance groups competed for power. The main threat was from the Greek communists, supported by Greece's neighbours and the Soviet Union. Eventually the communist insurgency was overcome by a pro-Western government, largely with American political and economic support under the label of the Truman Doctrine. The origins of this conflict can be seen in the Metaxas

16 General Ioannis Metaxas, 1871–1941 (© Popperfoto/Getty)

era, in the war with Germany, and in the relations between the West and the Soviet Union. Between 1936 and 1941 the Metaxas's authoritarianism undermined the base of Communism in Greece; then, in 1941 the German occupation destroyed the base of Greek authoritarianism. As part of the Greek resistance from 1941 to 1944 Communism re-established its earlier vitality and contributed substantially to the national struggle against Germany. By 1945, however, it had diverged from pro-western visions of the future in its preference for the Soviet model that was being imposed in other parts of the Balkans. Consequently, the Greek Civil War was one of the earlier flashpoints of the broader Cold War. The victors in the Civil War owed much to Metaxas and, after an unstable parliamentary interlude, influenced the future military dictatorship between 1967 and 1974. According to Clogg, the police and army officers who had served Metaxas formed the 'nucleus' of the 'anti-Communist alliance' after 1943, while 'the twelve colonels who established the military dictatorship in April 1967 had been officer cadets under Metaxas'.[178] The colonels' regime survived until 1974, when it was discredited by defeat by Turkey in the Cyprus War and forced to restore a parliamentary system to Greece.

Metaxas: conservative or fascist?

There has been some debate about the style of regime introduced by Metaxas. According to Hondros, the Metaxas regime was 'a royal bureaucratic dictatorship'.[179] Payne argues, 'Though the regime used the fascist salute and sometimes employed the term totalitarian, it was neither generically fascist nor structurally totalitarian [but rather] a primarily bureaucratic form of authoritarianism.'[180] Against these views, Kofas maintains that the regime of Metaxas had a powerful 'quasi-fascist' element.[181]

There is a strong case for the traditionalist nature of Metaxas's dictatorship. His anti-liberalism was autocratic rather than totalitarian, as was his dislike of parliamentary politics which, he thought, would 'throw us into the embrace of communism'.[182] He was also elitist in his support of a pyramid class structure with a nobility at the apex. Nor did he have any revolutionary doctrine as such. The ideas of Metaxas, like those of Franco and Salazar, were based on reviving his country's historic role: 'We owe it therefore to revert backwards in order to rediscover ourselves.'[183] Although his regime was inspired by nationalism, this was not associated with militarism. This meant that the irredentism of the early 1920s was not reactivated in the late 1930s and Metaxas did not seek closer connections with the Axis powers as a means of preying on Greece's neighbours. It is true that there was a brutal system of police interrogation and that political opponents were ruthlessly dealt with. In this sense, there was a real terror. But this was not accompanied by systematic targeting of minorities. Indeed, the condition of the Jews improved during his administration; he even forbade discrimination against them and criticized those regimes where anti-Semitism was practised. The Metaxas regime had little difficulty in gaining recognition from the political establishment at home and abroad. It was not in conflict with the traditional Greek monarchy and was also acceptable to Britain and France, who guaranteed Greek security in 1939. Finally, Metaxas himself denied that he was a fascist. He told a British official that 'Portugal under Dr Salazar, not the Germany of Hitler or the Italy of Mussolini, provided the nearest analogy.'[184]

On the other hand, Metaxas went further than the other Balkan leaders in the style of his leadership and the totality of his vision. He fostered a personality cult, proclaiming himself Leader (*Archigos*), 'First Peasant' and 'First Worker'. He aimed to replace constitutional democracy with an entirely new system, the keynote of which would be the suppression of individualism to the interests of the state; his programme would therefore be radical rather than conservative. The spirit behind his changes would be historic and racial: he aimed to revive the glories of the Greek past. He spoke of the three phases of Greek civilization. The first was the Golden Age of Pericles in the fifth century BC, the second was medieval Byzantium. The third would be the emergence of a racially pure Hellenic order under Metaxas himself. He began his dictatorship with a proclamation of martial law and a ban on normal political activity: 'There are no more parties in Greece . . . The old parliamentary system has vanished for ever.' He also imposed a censorship which was so severe that it applied even to blank spaces in newspapers. Gradually he constructed a network of terror and indoctrination which was clearly influenced by the Third Reich; the Athens police headquarters displayed pictures of Hitler and Goebbels, and Greek security was based heavily on the SS and Gestapo. *Mein Kampf* was widely read and became a major influence behind the National Organization of Youth (EDN), which, according to Kofas, provided the regime with a 'fascist base'.

This is perhaps taking things too far. The view of Close is that what Metaxas really aimed at was to maximize the efficiency of the state machinery, which was not unnatural since he had risen through the ranks of the army and been in a family with strong civil service traditions.[185] Hence, his authoritarianism was exercised through intensifying traditional methods rather than inventing new ones. It is true that he borrowed ideas from Nazism, but these were in the quest for efficiency rather than for ideological change. In any case, fascism was associated with Italy which, after Mussolini's invasion of Corfu in 1923, was seen, along with Turkey, as the principal national enemy. Vatikiotis is also doubtful that Metaxas had any real commitment to fascism. After all, 'he considered himself an enlightened despot and a patriot who defended his country's independence and honour'.[186] His 'new state' showed 'a minimal oversimplified political ideology vaguely akin to that of European (Mediterranean) fascism'.[187] The conclusion might therefore be that Metaxas was attracted by the style of power rather than the ideology behind it: although he used elements of fascism, he was not overtly or even latently a fascist.

Turkey

At one stage, Turkey had governed all the areas so far considered in the Balkans, along with a swathe of territory across North Africa and the Middle East. By 1912, however, she had lost almost all of the Balkans. Bosnia-Herzegovina had been annexed by Austria-Hungary in 1908, and the other provinces had become independent: Greece in 1830, Romania between 1862 and 1878, and Bulgaria, Serbia and Montenegro in 1878. By 1913 four of these had considerably enlarged their territories, confining Turkey to a small enclave beyond Constantinople. The African territories of the Ottoman Empire had, meanwhile, been annexed by France, Britain and, most recently, Italy. This left Turkey only the Arab areas of the Middle East by 1914.

Territorial shrinkage had been accompanied by a struggle for internal regeneration. Some of the Sultans did provide much-needed reforms, such as the 1876 Constitution. There were, however, lapses into corruption and repression, which provoked uprisings in the Balkans. By 1908 the situation had become so serious that the Young Turk revolt forced the Sultanate to restore the 1876 Constitution. Then, from 1913 real power fell to the revolutionaries, who were now calling themselves the Committee of Union and Progress (CUP). Although they allowed elections in 1913, the other parties were severely disadvantaged. As a result, Turkey became a one-party dictatorship – the only example in pre-1914 Europe. In effect, it was governed by the triumvirate of Enver, Talât and Cemal. It had no overriding ideology as such, apart from the desire to modernize and preserve, attempting to restore and expand the most secular and positive influences of the Tanzimat period. But its association in the First World War with the Central Powers (Germany, Austria-Hungary and Bulgaria) brought Turkey military defeat. On 30 October 1918, Turkey was forced to sign an armistice with the Allies, a few days after the CUP liquidated itself and its regime.

Then followed a period of both chaos and recovery. By the Treaty of Sèvres (20 August 1920), the Allies ended Turkey's rule over the Arab provinces, granted autonomy to the Kurds, authorized the Greek occupation of Smyrna for five years, and removed Eastern Thrace, the Aegean Islands, Rhodes and the Dodecanese. British intervention forced Sultan Mohammed VI to sign the Treaty. This, however, provoked a Nationalist uprising against both the Treaty and the Sultanate. Under the leadership of Mustafa Kemal the Nationalist Turks resisted the intervention of the Italians and, above all, the Greeks, who invaded Smyrna. By September 1922 the Greeks had been decisively defeated by Kemal's forces. The following September the Allies agreed by the Treaty of Lausanne to modify the territorial provisions of Sèvres. Eastern Thrace was restored to Turkey, providing a more substantial presence in Europe, and the Greeks were deprived of their entitlement to Smyrna.

These developments were accompanied by major political changes. In November 1922, the Sultanate itself was abolished, and a new Turkish Republic was proclaimed in October 1923, with its new capital in Angora (renamed Ankara in 1930). Constantinople (renamed Istanbul in 1930) remained the commercial and financial centre of the new republic but the overall centre of gravity was now very much in Anatolia. This was paradoxical, since the main influences were now unquestionably from Europe.

The regime of Mustafa Kemal Atatürk, 1923–38

Mustafa Kemal was President of the Turkish Republic from the time of its formation until his death in 1938. He was influenced by a combination of ideas from the earlier Young Turk and Tanzimat reformers but with a heavy admixture of western influences as selected, interpreted and filtered by his Republican People's Party (RPP). He was determined to transform his country by sweeping aside the forces of reaction and resistance. Indeed, 'Surviving in the world of modern civilization depends upon changing ourselves.'[188] He wanted to bring Turkey within the mainstream of western European development rather than continue to emphasize the previous Islamic and Middle Eastern base.

Kemal's 1931 Manifesto presented an official ideology with six components; these were symbolized by the six-arrow emblem (the *Altı Ok*) adopted by the RPP. The first, and overriding, influence was Secularism. The Islamic religion was officially separated from the state – and from all social activities performed by the state. Kemal argued that 'The Turkish Revolution . . . means replacing an age-old political unity based on religion with one based on another tie, that of nationality.'[189] He started by abolishing the Caliphate and Seriat and then proceeded on the principle that all Turkey's laws 'should be based on secular grounds only'.[190] Hence, when the new Civil Code was introduced in 1926, it was based on the Swiss Civil Code of 1912. Other changes proved more controversial. The Hat Law of 1925 banned the use of the traditional fez and discouraged the wearing of the veil by women; these were in the interests of freeing people from inhibitions imposed upon them in the past by religious practices. Similarly, the change to Latin script from 1927 onwards was designed to cut the connections with the more Arabic influences of Islam. All education was reformed by the Law of the Unification of Education, which established the Ministry of Education in 1924, and ended classes in religion from 1928 onwards. In 1935, even the official day of rest was changed – from the Islamic Friday to the western Sunday.

The other five principles were all closely related to Secularism. The second was Republicanism, especially French and American, although it was applied in an authoritarian rather than democratic format, tolerating opposition only in a strictly limited sense. The third was Nationalism. The basis of Turkish nationhood was changed from religious and ethnic to linguistic and cultural; it involved limiting the nation state to the post-war Anatolian base and the abandonment of the earlier pan-Islamic ideals. If anything, it was now more receptive to the West than it was to other regimes and cultures in the Middle East. The fourth, Populism, concerned the social composition of Turkey. According to Kemal, 'Our people is composed, not of social classes with conflicting interests, but of classes whose coexistence is indispensable one to the other.'[191] All classes would be developed by the Republic, with the ultimate aim of achieving harmony between them. Kemal was aware of both the crisis caused by class conflict in the west – and the development of alternatives in socialism and communism which acknowledged this class conflict as a prerequisite. He therefore tried to avoid both the western and communist versions. This was also apparent in the fifth principle, Revolution. According to Kemal, 'The aim of a people's organization as a party is not the realization of certain classes over against those of other classes. The aim is rather to mobilize the entire nation, called People.'[192] The emphasis was very much on change from above on 'radical change executed with order and method'.[193] Finally, the purpose of the sixth, Etatism, was to legitimize the state's close involvement in social – and particularly economic – change. The 1936 labour code, for example, prevented the formation of trade unions based on class lines, and banned both strikes by workers and lock-outs by employers.

Politically, Turkey under Kemal was a one-party state – except for brief periods in 1924–5 and 1930. Kemal did not promise a democratic system as a priority; nor did he rule one out in the future. Yet his was a more subtle exercise of authoritarian rule than existed elsewhere. In theory at least, his authority was constrained in a number of ways. Three examples can be provided of this. First, he was chosen as President by the National Assembly, in contrast to the alternative expedients, used elsewhere, of popular mandate or self-perpetuated rule. Second, his Prime Minister chose the cabinet of ministers, which in turn was subject to the approval of the National Assembly. And third, although the President could veto legislation passed by the National Assembly, this veto could be rescinded by a majority within the Assembly.

In practice, however, his authoritarian powers were considerable. Some of these came through the control of his Republican People's Party over the Assembly. Mustafa Kemal was, for example, the party's President-General, with the powers to appoint the other two members of the Council of the Presidency-General. Candidates for election to the National Assembly and local government bodies were chosen by the Party, which also influenced the process of indirect election through electoral colleges. Hence, as long as the President controlled the Party as President-General, he had little to fear from the assembly. In addition, the army was always there as a back-up; even though it never did play a direct role in his regime, it was comforting to know that Kemal could always rely on the support of Çakmak, the Chief of General Staff between 1924 and 1944. And then, of course, Kemal's personal reputation was immense: both as the founder of the modern Turkish state and as the enunciator of the principles behind it. He was known informally as *Büyük Önder* (Great Leader); his formal title, from 1934, was *Atatürk* (Father of the Turks). In addition, he was known as 'saviour' and 'teacher'. He was also given extensive coverage in the history of the Turkish Republic, which became compulsory in the school curriculum. In short, a strong personality cult developed, although it should be said that this was more spontaneous and less contrived than in Mussolini's Italy or Stalin's Russia.

What was the extent of Atatürk's achievement? There is no question as to the scope of his intended modernization. It covered everything from fundamental changes to the political structure right down to detailed regulations concerning the wearing of headgear. In sweeping away the Sultanate and Caliphate he transformed Turkey from an early-modern Islamic empire into a twentieth-century secular republic. He did more than anyone before – or since – to reorientate Turkey away from the Middle East towards the West and Europe, where many of his reforms were received with as much enthusiasm as within Turkey itself. Yet it has to be said that their immediate effect on the great mass of the Turkish population was limited. Zürcher summarizes the problem as follows:

> A farmer or shepherd from Anatolia had never worn a fez, so he wasn't especially bothered about its abolition. His wife wore no veil anyway, so the fact that its use was discouraged did not mean anything to him or her. He could not read or write, so the nature of the script was immaterial to him.[194]

There was a more positive impact in the towns than in the countryside, but in both economic growth was knocked back by the Depression. Elements of policy, such as etatism, were therefore heavily diluted by harsh realities.

Atatürk's foreign policy showed considerable skill. His initial contribution was a military one and, as we have seen, ended both Greek and Italian expansionist ambitions at Turkey's expense. Without his leadership it is difficult to see how the post-war chaos could have been ended or the territorial settlement of Sèvres revised by the Treaty of Lausanne. Then, from 1923 onwards, he maintained good relations with both the Western democracies, despite differences with Britain over the Mosul region in Iraq and with France over the repayment of debts incurred by the Ottoman regime. Meanwhile Turkey's relations with the Soviet Union improved dramatically, with a ten-year treaty signed in 1935 and acceptance of Soviet advice on economic issues. Atatürk also took Turkey into the League of Nations in 1936 and, in the growing crisis caused by the revisionist challenges, supported the West and the USSR against Germany and Italy. The abolition of the Sultanate may have ended Turkey's claims to be a great power – but Atatürk used this to enhance Turkey's diplomatic importance.

What kind of regime?

It is not difficult to put the case for Atatürk as a revolutionary. As we have seen, he transformed the base of Turkey, completely eclipsing the efforts of earlier reformers. By comparison, the Young Turks were unsuccessful in their endeavours; Quataert argued that the Revolution of 1908 'appears as a Middle-East turning point that failed to turn' and that it 'offered a largely unrealized potential for social change'.[195] Atatürk therefore succeeded where they had failed. Thomson summarized the views of many historians when he argued that 'His policy was no less radical than Lenin's in Russia'; he took Turkey through 'a great social revolution', conducting it 'from the center by a dictatorial government'.[196]

While recognizing the extent of his transformation, we should not, however, overlook evidence of at least partial continuity between Atatürk's regime and the past. Brooker, Zürcher and Davison all pointed to the influence of both the Tanzimat era and the Young Turk intellectuals. Indeed, the Tanzimat period was a 'seed-time in which ideas which later came to fruition under the Republic first took root'.[197] A few examples will suffice. During the Tanzimat, the army had already been westernized, particularly in 1869, providing also a future training ground for a renovated bureaucracy. The administration had been divided into ministries or departments and provincial administration completely overhauled by the *vilayet* law of 1864. A number of clauses from the 1924 Constitution were modelled closely on their equivalents in the 1876 Constitution, including the concept of *Vatan* – or Fatherland – equality before the law, guaranteed individual rights and civil liberties, and the theory of responsible government. Davison therefore believes that 'The Republic is, in historical terms, the child of the Second Constitutional Period (1908–18), the step-child of the era of Abdülhamid II (1878–1908), and the grandchild of the era of reforms (1826–78)'.[198]

How confident can we be that Atatürk's regime was actually a dictatorship? Despite its acceptance of certain democratic influences from the West, it does seem to fulfil the criteria of a developing authoritarian regime. Between 1922 and 1925 a revolutionary change of power was accompanied by a brief 'pluralist phase',[199] and expectations that a multi-party system would follow. From 1925 onwards, however, it became clear that power would be monopolized by the Republican People's Party. This power was used to impose – from above – a series of radical changes which were considered by the leadership to be integral to the country's future. In the process, opposition was eliminated by the Law on the Maintenance of Order, introduced in 1925 and renewed in 1929, and by trials and tribunals. The purges of 1925–6 involved about twenty executions, some on the basis of tenuous evidence, and tough measures were taken against minority groups such as the Kurds in south-eastern Anatolia. Zürcher certainly considers the regime 'authoritarian' and goes so far as to attribute to it a number of 'totalitarian tendencies',[200] in its actions against organizations like the Freemasons or Turkish Women's Union and against left-wing newspapers. Others have found similarities with Mussolini's Italy, especially in the role of nationalism, of the legitimacy of a one-party system, of the personality cult and of a populist type of corporativism. There were, however, more differences than similarities between Kemalism and Fascism. The latter was a popular movement, orchestrated by Mussolini; Kemal, by contrast, introduced his changes on a largely indifferent population. Nor did Kemal have any expansionist programme; if anything his whole rationale was an acceptance of the collapse of a past empire rather than on an attempt to create a future one. With that in mind, together with Kemal's affinity with western ideas, it would clearly be wrong to consider Turkey to be in any way fascist. Perhaps Payne's description makes the most sense: 'It became a prototype of the modernizing and westernizing developmental dictatorship in a non-Western country.'[201]

Turkey after Atatürk

Atatürk died in November 1938 after suffering from cyrrhosis of the liver, the result of years of excessive alcohol consumption.[202] His death came as a shock to the Turkish people, since the nature of his illness had – understandably – been concealed from them. After a brief contest for the succession, the presidency went to Ismet Inönü, Atatürk's former prime minister. This continuity ensured that internal stability did not disintegrate in the testing times ahead.

The most immediate threat came from outside Turkey. At first Inönü maintained Atatürk's diplomacy, and further tightened relations with Britain, France and the Soviet Union. 1939, however, brought two blows – Italy's invasion of Albania in April and, more seriously, the Nazi–Soviet Non-Aggression Pact in August. In October 1939 Inönü signed a treaty with Britain and France with a view to 'collaborate effectively' in the event of a threat to the Mediterranean. This could have been instrumental in bringing Turkey into the war against Germany and Italy but Inönü made strenuous efforts to prevent this from happening. In 1941 he even made a treaty of friendship with Hitler, while at the same time Turkey remained militarily neutral. Churchill and Roosevelt both tried to involve Turkey, especially after the German defeat at Stalingrad. But Inönü stalled for over a year and only entered the war on the side of the Allies in February 1945 in order 'to qualify as a founding member of the United Nations'.[203] This had no practical significance, as Turkey took no part in any of the campaigns of the last few months of the war. In staying out of the war, Inönü maintained the existing regime *beyond* the war, thus emulating the achievements of Salazar and Franco and avoiding the Greek descent into chaos and civil war. At the same time, Turkey was received with less enthusiasm by the West after the war. According to Zürcher, 'Turkey's policies during the war have often been seen as immoral and as reneging on the treaty of 1939.'[204] The prevailing atmosphere of the Cold War, however, prevented Turkey from being isolated and she finally committed herself by joining NATO in 1951.

Atatürk had often hinted at the possibility of Turkey becoming a democratic state in the longer term. After the Second World War this began to happen. Constitutional amendments introduced in 1945 allowed for more direct elections to the National Assembly and also introduced voting by secret ballot. In 1946 an official opposition was set up, in the form of the Democratic Party; in the 1946 election this won 65 of the 465 seats. In 1950, following further reforms to political parties, the Democratic Party won a majority and came to power. From that time onwards Turkey became a parliamentary democracy, although this was interrupted by periods of military rule in 1960–1, 1971–3 and 1980–3. Since the last of these Turkey maintained a broadly democratic course, although concerns were expressed about periodic abuses of the rights of minority groups. This was particularly significant in Turkey's application to join the European Union.

DICTATORSHIPS BEYOND EUROPE

Introduction

Although the scope of this book is 'European' (including the Asiatic regions of Russia and Turkey), it is worth adding a brief section on dictatorships in other parts of the world. The intention is to examine the extent to which leaders and ideologies of European regimes *influenced* those in Latin America, Asia and Africa. The main period covered is 1918–45, with further selected developments after the Second World War.

As with Europe, there is a basic problem of definition. A more general approach is adopted by Brooker, who defines a dictatorship as 'a regime that is not a democracy nor a monarchy'.[205] This does not necessarily apply to Europe, for two reasons. One is that several European monarchs were involved in the process of dictatorship – including Alexander in Yugoslavia, Boris in Bulgaria and Carol in Romania. Second, it is not impossible to include democracy in certain types of dictatorship, especially if the latter is totalitarian. Booker's approach is therefore more applicable to the non-European world, for which it was clearly intended. Here democracy and dictatorship have more obvious boundaries, especially in Latin America, while monarchies tend to be more traditional and connected with a non-European or pre-European past.

These preliminary observations still leave a considerable variety of extra-European dictatorships: personal, military, 'developmental', nationalist, fascist, communist, traditionalist, corporatist, or a mixture of several of these. The key question to be considered is whether these were of indigenous origin and the extent to which they were influenced by Europe. It will also be necessary to distinguish between regimes and movements and to establish whether the two were integrated or antagonistic.

Latin America and the Caribbean

It has been argued that European authoritarian systems have been most widely copied in Latin America. Yet there were significant, indigenous influences from the struggle for independence against Spanish and Portuguese rule in the early nineteenth century, to say nothing of the subsequent periods of political consolidation and inter-state military conflict. By the inter-war period Latin America had already developed its own distinctive political frameworks and structures, with a long tradition of dictatorship. But the developments already considered in Europe could not have failed to make some impact. The question is – how much?

The style of dictatorship occurring most frequently in Latin America and the Caribbean was that imposed by the *caudillos*. Some of these derived their power from a military coup, while other regimes started more or less constitutionally – before later degenerating into dictatorship. These were usually short on ideology, copying from sources they identified as useful, but taking strong action against any ideology they considered dangerous: this applied mostly to communism, but also included several fascist movements. European influences were more marked in the form of techniques for propaganda, publicity and personality cult. A few examples of *caudillos* were: Legula (1919–30) and Benavides (1933–9) in Peru; Machado (1925–33) in Cuba; Ubico (1931–44) in Guatemala; Terra (1931–8) in Uruguay; Morinigo (1940–8) in Paraguay; Trujillo (1930–61) in the Dominican Republic; Vargas (1930–4 and 1937–45) in Brazil; and Batista, who seized power in Cuba in 1933. Two *caudillos* of the inter-war period were particularly harsh. Martinez subjected El Salvador between 1931 and 1944 to a reign of terror, eliminating opponents and arranging for the massacre of communists and 20,000 recalcitrant peasants. Similarly, Gómez used fear to maintain his control over Venezuela in the periods 1922–9 and 1931–5, spending twice as much on his secret police as on Venezuela's education. After 1945 the best-known *caudillo* regimes were those of: Francois Duvalier (1957–71) and Jean-Claude Duvalier (1971–86) in Haiti; Stroessner (1954–89) in Paraguay; Videla (1976–81) and Galtieri (1981–2) in Argentina; and Pinochet (1973–90) in Chile. All were brutal – using tactics of torture and terror to control the population, and depending on military support.

Several Latin American dictatorships of the inter-war period had links, however tenuous, with right-wing regimes in Europe. Machado was an ardent admirer of Mussolini, although there were no obvious Italian Fascist components in his rule in Cuba (1925–33). Uriburu of Argentina envisaged a political reorganization in line with fascism and corporatism while, in Peru, Cerro based his rule on a fascist-type party – the Revolutionary Union which had a section of Blackshirts; this, however, faded rapidly during the mid-1930s. Morinigo, who seized absolute power in Paraguay in 1940, surrounded himself with pro-fascist officers and retained his own preference for fascism until after the end of the war. Even so, the extent and scale of his commitment to fascism remained dubious. But the two most likely candidates as neo-fascist dictators were Vargas and Peron. The former seized power in Brazil in 1930 and retained dictatorial power until 1945; he was subsequently elected for a second spell as president between 1950 and 1954. Although he was in many ways a traditional *caudillo*, Vargas's regime was more complex than that. He was influenced by various European models of the right, especially by those of Portugal and Italy. His Estado Novo was inspired by Salazar's regime of the same name, with the addition of components from Mussolini's corporatism. But it is doubtful that the description sometimes applied to Vargas as a 'fascist' is justified. For one thing, his regime lacked the element of aggressive and expansionist nationalism that characterized Mussolini's rule. For another, Vargas found himself in conflict with those movements within Brazil that *were* fascist. He even committed Brazil to the Allied side in the second half of the Second World War. Similar reservations could also be applied to using the label to the dictatorship of Peron; despite his corporatist policies, mass mobilization of public support and sympathies with Mussolini (and even Hitler), Peron had no comparable militarist, racist or expansionist aims for Argentina.

Yet if Latin America lacked any authentically fascist *regimes*, there were several examples of fascist and national socialist *movements* although, in these, indigenous influences were at least as strong as European. One was the National Socialist Movement (MNS or *Nacis*) which developed in Chile during the 1930s. Another was the Gold Shirts of Mexico, which emerged in the same decade, as did the Revolutionary Union in Peru (with its appendage the Blackshirts), and a Falangist organization (FSB) in Bolivia. Perhaps the most fruitful territory for fascist-influenced movements was Brazil which produced at least ten such movements, the largest of which was the Brazilian Integralist Action. Many such movements, however, clashed with the ruling regimes which had less radical political agendas. Some were suppressed after attempting a takeover, as happened to the MNS and Gold Shirts; others, like the Integralists, were banned after the introduction of a new constitution. Nowhere in Latin America was there any equivalent to a fascist party-based government; even the widespread European pattern of fascism or Falangism as a component within a right-wing regime was not the norm in Latin American dictatorships. Indeed, many regimes regarded fascism with deep suspicion and followed a similar course to that taken by King Carol of Romania against Codreanu's Iron Guard.

There were far more communist parties than fascist movements. Almost every Latin American country produced one, most several. Some communist parties were tolerated legally and contested elections; others lived a twilight semi-secret existence or immersed themselves in labour and trade-union activity. But there were no instances of direct communist involvement in inter-war dictatorships in Latin America – if anything, communist parties played a part in *opposing* such regimes, as in Colombia and Peru. It was not until the post-war period that communist or communist-influenced regimes made an appearance in the region in, to give three examples, Nicaragua, Venezuela and – above all – Cuba. Against all the broad trends of twentieth-century Latin American history, Castro's left-wing dictatorship proved to be more durable and successful than any regime on the right. Seizing power from Batista in 1959, Castro announced his ideological conversion to Marxism-Leninism in 1961, although he also remained a nationalist. His regime survived attempts to overthrow it and Castro managed to preside over the longest-lasting dictatorship (1957–2008) anywhere and developed important ideological and strategic connections with Africa during the 1970s and 1980s.

Asia

Between the world wars Asia had a wide variety of regimes. These ranged from absolute monarchies and traditionalist Asiatic regimes to European colonies and emergent powers with a new European-style economic and military base.

The most deliberate graft of European influences on to an Asiatic structure can be seen in Japan. This started with the period of rapid modernization during the reign of the Emperor Meiji (1868–1912), who was strongly influenced by ideas and structures from the west, especially Britain, Germany, France and the United States. He introduced fundamental changes to the army, navy, economy, customs and political structures that included a new Diet or assembly. Further developments before and after 1900 included extensive militarization which led to Japanese expansion at the expense of China (1894–5), Russia (1904–5), Korea (1910) and – more intensively – against Manchuria and China in the 1930s. After 1930 Japan was particularly influenced by Italy and Germany, with whom she eventually combined in the anti-Comintern Pact and the Axis military alliance. The regime that entered the Second World War through a surprise attack on Pearl Harbor was widely seen in 1941 as a 'fascist dictatorship' and there is still a divergence of opinion among historians as to the suitability of either or both of these terms as descriptions of Japan before 1945.

Japan under Hirohito and Tojo was certainly regarded as 'fascist' by Marxist analysts, who adopt a generic term to describe an authoritarian regime in the throes of rapid industrialization and social upheaval. Other interpretations stress Japan's aggressive expansionism as a typically 'fascist' means of diverting attention from internal problems and crises against a common external enemy – the Chinese during the 1930s and the western powers from 1941. The Japanese variant has often been described as 'military' fascism, which in any case was strongly influenced far-right movements drawing their inspiration from Nazi Germany. Examples included the Cherry Blossom Society (set up in 1930 and strongly represented by officers in War Ministry and on the General Staff), the Great Japan Youth Party, and the Eastern Way Society. Historians arguing against applying the label 'fascism' to Japan point out that, although fairly numerous, such movements were small and lacked the dynamic mass-involvement characteristics of the fascist regimes in Europe. It is essential to distinguish between 'regimes' and 'movements': all genuine fascist regimes were based on mass movements, while not all such movements produced fascist regimes. Stanley G. Payne provides a particularly pithy summary: 'Japan had evolved a somewhat pluralistic authoritarian system which exhibited some of the characteristics of fascism, but it did not develop fascism's most distinctive and revolutionary aspects', adding that Japan had more in common with the Second German Reich than with the Third.[206]

There has also been some debate as to whether Japan was even a 'dictatorship'. Arguments in favour included the subordination of both country and society to militarism, control by a rigid style of leadership exercising authoritarian discipline, and the most brutal treatment of occupied areas (the Rape of Nanking, for example). Japanese mistreatment of civilians and prisoners of war has been compared with the excesses of the Waffen SS and Einsatzgruppen in the disregard for human life. Conversely, it has been argued that Hirohito's monarchical rule disqualified him from being considered a dictator. As we have already seen, however, this approach is too dismissive. In any case, Hirohito's authority existed, at least until 1940, alongside a constitution that allowed, and cabinets that were based on, party politics. After that, the Emperor continued to exert at least some moderating influence over Japan's wartime leadership. This unusual behaviour for a dictator won the monarchy – and its incumbent – a reprieve from the Allies after the defeat of Japan in 1945. The other possibility for the role of Japanese 'dictator', Tojo, exercised no personality cult and was at no time fully in control of the military. Finally, any *ideological* base for Japan's authoritarian rule was traditional, even if the *methods* of communication and control were modern and European. Although there were inevitable distortions, Japan was not, according to Ben-Ami Shillony, 'an ideological disciple of the Axis'. Indeed, society was in some ways 'freer than those of the Soviet Union or Kuomintang China', even though these 'ostensibly fought on the side of democracy'.[207]

Other areas used ideas that originated in Europe to establish ideological regimes based on adapted variants. These developed roots *before* 1945, especially during the inter-war period and global conflict of the Second World War. Three main examples can be cited. The first was China, where the search for a permanent replacement for the former Chinese Imperial regime gave rise to two movements – the Kuomintang (KMT) and the Chinese Communist Party (CCP). Some historians have seen strong fascist influences in the former, which was essentially a military-based regime using a panoply of European ideas. Others, however, deny that it was actually fascist and that there was the same basic problem as in Japan in dealing with mass organizations. In any case, the KMT under Chiang Kai-shek was preoccupied by two major priorities – defeating the external enemy – Japan – and overcoming the main internal threat to its existence – Mao Zedong's CCP. After losing the Chinese Civil War, Chiang withdrew in 1949 to Formosa, recently liberated from Japanese occupation, where, with some support from the United Sates, he presided over an authoritarian and anti-communist regime until his death. Meanwhile, mainland China had come under the control of a new variant of communism. In part this was of European origin and Mao acknowledged the importance of Lenin and the 'salvoes of the October Revolution'. He learned from the Bolsheviks the importance of organization and conspiracy which lay behind his view that 'A revolution is . . . an act of violence by which one class overthrows another'[208] and that 'The seizure of power by armed force . . . is the central task and highest form of revolution'.[209] To these inter-war influences, however, Mao added a distinctive twist, adapting Marxism-Leninism to the needs of an agricultural rather than an industrial society. His more pragmatic approach enabled Chinese Communism to develop in two stages – as an ultimately victorious adversary against the right-wing forces of the KMT and then as a new regime. At first the latter seemed to be less heavily centralized than the Soviet Union. In the longer term, however, there were to be close similarities with Stalinism. By the end of the 1950s Mao's China had all the all the hallmarks of a totalitarian regime with high degree of ruthlessness. His dissatisfaction with slow rate of agricultural and industrial growth led to extreme methods resulting, as with those of Stalin in the 1930s, in millions of deaths. He also unleashed the 'Great Proletarian Cultural Revolution', which included the most extreme personality cult seen up to that time. Only after his death did the whole system become more susceptible to reform and outside influences.

Two other areas also developed Communist dictatorships, with roots from before, during and immediately after the Second World War. This time there was an additional struggle against former colonial occupiers, from which emerged a variety of new regimes, ranging from extreme dictatorships, using totalitarian methods of control, to authoritarian states moving towards a limited system of democracy. The People's Republic of North Korea emerged from a war for liberation against Japan (to which Korea had been annexed in 1910). Communism was the main focus for opposition and Kim Il Sung was installed in power by invading Soviet armies in 1945. Although it later withdrew in 1948 the Soviet Union continued to support regime, as did Communist China after 1949. All the characteristics of totalitarian dictatorship emerged once the regime was guaranteed is existence by the stalemate of the Korean War (1950–3). 'Kimilsungism' emerged as a new form of personality cult which, according to some historians, eclipsed even that of Stalin and Mao Zedong; it had the added refinement of hereditary succession, the first seen in any Communist regime. Politically, the regime became increasingly repressive, while socially and economically it became almost totally isolated from the outside world. Meanwhile, Indo-China had also experienced major political changes, with the emergence of four new states from the former French empire – North and South Vietnam, Cambodia and Laos. Communist North Vietnam was established by Ho Chi Minh as an orthodox Marxist-Leninist collective leadership and united with South Vietnam in 1975. Utterly different was the rule of the Khmer Rouge in Cambodia. Pol Pot developed the most extreme dictatorship anywhere in the world, his variant of Marxism-Leninism killing or enslaving over one-third of the population of Cambodia, until the Vietnamese put paid to his activities by invading Cambodia in 1978 and removing the Khmer Rouge from power.

The post-war period produced a variety of other systems that have been described as dictatorships. These all had strongly indigenous roots, although some also contained European influences. One of these was Indonesia under Sukarno (1949–68) and Suharto (1967–98), which has been seen as a 'developmental' authoritarian system, aiming to weld together a diverse region with the fifth largest population in the world to a nationalist base strengthened by the anti-colonial struggle against the Japanese and Dutch in the 1940s and further reinforced by extensive anti-leftist purges in the 1950s and 1960s. Pakistan, meanwhile, had several periods under military rule, especially during its conflicts with India and the secession of Bangladesh (formally East Pakistan). Another repressive military regime developed in Burma and for two decades the country was virtually closed to the outside world. Two Middle-Eastern states developed more distinctively ideological systems; these were based on Ba'athist revivalist movements under strong personal control – whether the Assads in Syria or Saddam Hussein in Iraq. In some ways the most diverse developments have taken place in Iran, where the revolution of 1979 which replaced a long-standing pro-western military autocracy under the Shah with an anti-western populist theocracy under the Ayatollahs. The overall picture has been complicated still further by militant Islamist movements in parts of the Middle East.

Africa

Africa was the most recent area of emerging states since it was a continent experiencing colonization and independence later than America or Asia.

Some areas were independent – or had been given internal autonomy – before 1945. The oldest was Ethiopia, which dated back to the Middle Ages. After the overthrow of Italian occupation she was restored to her previous status as an absolute monarchy under Emperor Haile Selassie, although with certain adjustments. His was not a modern dictatorship and it clearly contained the seeds of transitional instability for the future. Other independent states included Liberia, established for emancipated slaves in 1822, and Egypt, where British occupation had ended in 1922. The Union of South Africa had been afforded dominion status within the British Empire in 1910. The South African regime has often been referred to as a dictatorship because of its limited franchise, based on racial criteria. But it is more accurately described as a severely restricted constitutional system: although repressive of the majority, it still had an elected parliament based on a multi-party system. It has also been referred to as 'fascist'. Again, this is technically incorrect, although there *were* direct influences from Nazi Germany on various individual movements before 1939 and during the Second World War: examples included the Greyshirts, Blackshirts and Ossewabrandwag (OB).

The rest of Africa did not achieve independence until after the Second World War – during the 1950s, 1960s and 1970s. Rule by colonial powers, however, varied considerably, as did the preparation for the future and the timescale envisaged. Some colonial regimes had a particularly bad record, in many cases akin to dictatorship. Germany was the most repressive of all the powers before 1914. Although a parliamentary system, if top-heavily ruled, Germany had no aspirations to transfer this system to the colonies, even in the distant future. Instead, there were examples of racism – and even genocide – against, for example, the Herero people of South West Africa. Between the wars Italy expanded her 'Roman Empire' in Northern and Eastern Africa, where Mussolini brought Libya, Somalia, Eritrea and Ethiopia under Fascist rule. There were mass killings in Libya and the use of mustard gas in the conquest of Ethiopia was condemned in the League of Nations. The Italians also attempted in the colonies to create an indigenous Fascist movement linked to Rome, although with mixed success. No colonial regime could claim an exemplary record, but the others were less extreme than this, if subject to their own lapses. In the British colonies, administration was based on adaptations of Westminster and Whitehall to the colonial scene. At first indigenous participation was restricted until, during the 1950s and 1960s, preparations were made for their independence as future democracies. The French and Portuguese systems envisaged a more direct connection between the colonies and the metropolitan power, until major contrasts emerged between Salazar's concept of the imperial future in the Estado Novo and the French decision to follow a course similar to Britain's.

When independence did eventually occur throughout Africa, there was a narrow boundary line between democracy and dictatorship. The transition between these was often easier than elsewhere. Most independent regimes started as democracies but some of these quickly turned into something else. Many became single-party states ruled by strong individuals who banned all opposition during at least part of their rule, while claiming democratic 'legitimacy'. Examples – by no means exhaustive – included Nkrumah in Ghana (1957–66), Banda in Malawi (1963–94), Sékou Touré in Guinea (1958–84) and Obote in Uganda (1962–72 and 1980–5). Many others were more borderline, retaining the basic constitution and multi-party system but accused of manipulating elections and intimidating opponents. Examples of military dictatorships, originating in a coup and subsequently suspending elections or banning opposition, were Sudan under Nimeiry (1969–85), Zaire (or Congo) under Mobutu and Kabila, and Liberia under Doe (1980–90). In a few cases dictatorship was based on widespread violence and extreme personality cult – the most notorious leaders being Amin in Uganda (1971–9) and Bokassa in the Central African Republic (1966–79).

Portugal exerted an influence disproportionate to her size in the broader period between the 1920s and 1970s. According to Gallagher, Salazar's style of dictatorship had a direct impact on the later regimes of Nasser in Egypt and Qadhafi in Libya. The indirect influence was even greater, as the collapse of the Portuguese empire in Africa provided a catalyst for revolution and the sudden spread of Marxism-Leninist *regimes*, as opposed to the already widespread existence of communist *movements*. Some of these, like Machel's Mozambique and Neto's Angola, retained at least some democratic features, while others – especially Mengistu's Ethiopia – accentuated the ideological base and added features of personalized and arbitrary power.

An even wider influence behind Africa's regimes was the imposition of colonial boundaries, which cut arbitrarily through ethnic, tribal or religious groupings. This increased the chances of internal instability and conflict, with some extreme cases as in Rwanda and Burundi, Nigeria, Congo and Angola. One solution to this problem was the initial abandonment of western-style democracy, based on party politics, and the justification instead for a single party of national unity. There is no question that this increased the number of what might technically be described as dictatorships. But the momentum for this slowed during the 1980s, with a general swing (with some notable exceptions) back to the style of democracy of the early post-colonial period. It was also widely predicted soon after independence that the colonial boundaries would eventually be transformed, by regional divisions or consolidation, into states corresponding more closely to the tribes of pre-colonial Africa. But half a century after independence this had not happened. Few boundaries had been altered and only one secessionist movement had succeeded – with the emergence of the new state of Southern Sudan. Other attempted changes, like Biafra, failed. Even the most diverse of the states managed to hold together – Angola, Congo, Zambia and above all Nigeria. A fundamental – and as yet unanswered – question arises from this. Have African states managed to overcome the centrifugal tendencies of tribalism and become genuine nations? Or have tribal influences been seriously exaggerated, as some historians believe? In either case, is the era of dictatorship coming to an end?

Chapter 8

Dictatorships vs democracies

By the beginning of 1939 a total of twelve European countries had avoided dictatorship. These were Czechoslovakia, Denmark, Norway, the Netherlands, Belgium, Luxembourg, France, Sweden, Switzerland, Eire, the United Kingdom and Finland. Although they shared with the dictatorships some sort of assembly elected by universal suffrage, they still had the full legitimacy of representative democracy.

At the end of 1940 only five of these twelve democracies remained. Seven others had been *destroyed* by German invasion – in addition to those dictatorships – Austria, Poland, the Baltic states, Albania, Yugoslavia and Greece – that had already succumbed to Germany, Russia or Italy. The first democracy to be overrun was Czechoslovakia, deprived of the Sudetenland in September 1938, then of Bohemia and Moravia in March 1939. In April 1940 Denmark and Norway were also occupied by Germany; they were followed, over the next two months, by Belgium, the Netherlands, Luxembourg and France. Most of these areas were placed under direct occupation: Bohemia and Moravia, Denmark, the Netherlands, Belgium, Luxembourg and most of France. Others became puppet dictatorships: Slovakia, Norway and Vichy France.

Three of the remaining five democracies were unoccupied and managed to keep out of the conflict that had engulfed the other seven. But, in the process, Sweden, Switzerland and Eire became vulnerable and *marginalized.*

The last two democracies – the United Kingdom and Finland – remained *defiant*, choosing to fight for their identity by combining with one of the major dictatorships against another.

This classification will be used to explain the experience of all twelve democracies and to analyse their reactions to the threats posed by Nazi Germany or the Soviet Union.

SEVEN DEMOCRACIES DESTROYED

Seven of the regimes that had still been democracies in 1939 had been invaded and occupied by 1940. In the process, they were subjected to control over their administration, economy and society. There were marked similarities – and differences – between the reactions of the different states to their subjection to dictatorship.

1. Czechoslovakia

Czechoslovakia was established at the end of the First World War from the northern Slav provinces of Austria-Hungary. She was treated generously by the Treaty of St. Germain (1919) to give her a stronger chance of survival, particularly with the inclusion of the industrial borderlands of the Austrian part of the Empire – the Sudetenland. The new state was rooted firmly in democracy and had an inter-war record of moderate politics. She also gave priority to her own defence by a combination of systematic armament and periodic treaties with other states. Examples of the latter included the Franco-Czechoslovak Treaty of 1920 and the 1935 Pact with the Soviet Union. Czechoslovakia remained the only example of a successful democracy in central-eastern Europe as all the other recent states – including Poland, the Baltic States, Romania and Bulgaria – drifted into dictatorship in the 1930s, as did the original core of the Habsburg monarchy, Austria and Hungary. Above all, Czechoslovakia contrasted with the authoritarian and turbulent experience of the other experiment in bringing Slav groups together into a new nation – Yugoslavia.

But there were also significant elements of vulnerability. Externally, the main pressure came from Nazi Germany, with Hitler's ambitions of reuniting all German minorities with the Fatherland – at the expense of Germany's neighbours. There were also claims from Poland and Hungary to territory they considered had been over-generously allocated to Czechoslovakia at their expense. Internally, the main domestic threats were Slovak aspirations for autonomy within the new state and resentment from substantial ethnic minorities like Hungarians, Germans and Ukrainians. These internal pressures worked in combination for the destruction of a perfectly viable and robust democratic regime. The main external blows came from Hitler, who in turn exploited the complexity of Czechoslovakia's ethnic diversity.

This involved a two-stage process. The first was the loss in September 1938 of the Sudetenland: the latter's substantial German population was used by Hitler to extort the Munich agreement from Britain and France. Although this may have benefited Britain by providing a year in which to rearm, it did Czechoslovakia no good at all. Russia was unable to fulfil the terms of its treaty with Czechoslovakia (1935) and Germany took over all of Czechoslovakia's main border defences. Whereas Czechoslovakia had stood a realistic chance of defending herself in 1938, she had none whatever early in 1939. Further conspiracy followed. The remainder of the Czechoslovak state fell victim to the separatist aspirations of a Slovak minority who were manipulated by Hitler for the benefit of the Reich. The state president, Hácha, tried to restore the full integrity of Czechoslovakia by dismissing some of the Slovak ministers. Hitler used this to pressurise Jozef Tiso into declaring himself president of an independent Slovakia. At the same time, Hácha was summoned to Berlin where he was obliged to sign away the sovereignty of Bohemia and Moravia, under the threat that the Germans would otherwise bomb the capital. On 15 March German troops entered Prague.

Divided and severely depleted, Czechoslovakia functioned from March 1939 as two components. One, comprising Bohemia and Moravia, was occupied and made a protectorate of the Reich. The other, Slovakia, was allowed nominal independence and became, in effect, a puppet state and ally of Germany.

Bohemia and Moravia

In the longer term Hitler hoped to 'purify' the country by deporting the Czechs to remote parts of the Soviet Union; several plans were actually drawn up to this effect during the war – but had to be deferred because of Germany's need for industrial labour. For the moment, a decree established the Protectorate of Bohemia and Moravia. In theory this was self-administered but all major issues were under the direct control of Berlin. The president and prime minister were subordinate to the newly-created Reich protector, the first of whom was von Neurath. His office contained departments paralleling the Czech ministries, while the district authorities were similarly supervised by German-appointed governors. The

Czechs tried to retain an element of democracy. A new National Assemblage and its core, the National Committee, replaced the existing parliament, comprising appointed members of all parties except the Communists. But this was forced inexorably into the political shade of the German Protectorate's administration, which exerted full control over the country's military capacity, including 1,600 aircraft and 2,175 artillery pieces,[1] and aimed restrictive measures against the middle classes and intellectuals. As yet, however, there was no systematic use of terror; this was partly because of constraints exercised by von Neurath, who argued that the country could be more effectively exploited with its co-operation.

Things changed when Heydrich replaced von Neurath as Protector in September 1941. Authorized by Hitler to follow a harsher policy, he immediately declared martial law. The prime minister, Eliáš, was sentenced to death for treasonable activities (for which there was little evidence) as were hundreds of other Czech leaders. Any pretence at autonomy was ended as the power of the Protector became absolute. In contrast to von Neurath, Heydrich imposed widespread terror: this was very much in keeping with his position as head of Reichssicherheitshauptamt (Reich Security Office). He also increased the intensity of anti-Semitic policies and converted part of Theresienstadt into a ghetto for Jews of the whole Protectorate as well as for further quotas from Germany and Austria. Terror was intensified in retaliation for the assassination of Heydrich by Kubiš and Gabčik in May 1942. New measures included widespread arrests and the summary executions of some 23,000 people.[2] Most notorious was the destruction of Lidice and Ležáky, the shooting of their men and the deportation of their women to concentration camps. These actions were widely publicized to act as a deterrent to further resistance. Greater stability followed during the administrations of Wilhelm Frick and Karl Frank but Bohemia and Moravia remained firmly in the Nazi grip until 1945.

The Czech reaction to Nazi occupation shows a certain ambivalence. On the one hand, resistance groups did emerge – and quite quickly. These included the military underground or Defence of the Nation (ON); the Political Centre (PU) which tried unsuccessfully to co-ordinate early political opposition to German rule; and moderate leftists (PVVZ). The three organizations formed the Central Committee for Home Resistance (UVOD), which became the main unit of resistance within Czechoslovakia. Meanwhile, the Communists (KSC) followed a separate programme that was dictated by Moscow and was therefore affected by the changing relations between Hitler and Stalin. On the other hand, the actual manifestation of resistance was limited, the assassination of Heydrich being the most spectacular act of defiance until the Prague revolt of 1945. Not surprisingly, there is a debate about what this actually means. Mastny believes that 'despite a few positive signs, the balance of the Czechs' response to Nazi rule was overwhelmingly negative'.[3] A different case has been put by Luža, who maintains that the Czechs did what they could and that 'behind the morale of resistance stood its realistic representation of the vital interests of the Czech people during the course of the war'.[4]

There is much to support Luža's view. What resistance there was had a strong democratic heritage and aimed at minimizing the sufferings of a population which had few prospects of freeing itself. Although the extent of Czech co-operation with the Germans was considerable – in politics, administration, the economy and the labour force – they also resorted to the opposition strategy they had used against the Habsburgs: public patriotic rallies and religious ceremonies. In some cases defiance was more active, as partisan units derailed trains and blew up railroads and bridges. Until 1945, however, most of this took place in Slovakia rather than in the Czech lands – for reasons that point more towards Mastny's argument. The Czechs had lost their earlier will to defend their democracy partly because they had been deprived of the military means to do so by the Anglo-French policy of appeasement in 1938. Munich had been a betrayal which had destroyed the means and the motive to resist. A willingness to fight had given way to a reluctance to shed blood in what would now be a futile conflict; after all, Hácha's capitulation to Germany in March 1939 had prevented the development of a popular will to resist.The argument among all sections of society was that co-operation was in the best interests of the population. Only a small minority joined the Czech underground, and even here many were dubious of the activists who were flown in from Britain to organize resistance. The harsh response to the assassination of Heydrich seemed to indicate that resistance was counterproductive anyway, given the strength of the occupying power. Finally, active Czech resistance was impeded by adverse geographical factors. Bohemia and Moravia were almost surrounded by the Reich and their open countryside made it far more difficult to defy German troops who benefited from the excellent communications infrastructure of a compact industrial state. It is not surprising that internal resistance remained ineffective until the end of the war, even though the German occupation and military control were clearly in disarray at the beginning of 1945.

Resistance abroad was an entirely different matter. Exiles from Bohemia and Moravia, along with some from Slovakia, fought in volunteer units with the Allies – both in the west (North Africa and France in 1944) and with the Red Army on the eastern front. A government in exile was set up in London under Beneš, easily the most important and highly regarded of the Czech leaders. His influence was enormous: according to his former personal secretary, 'nothing of political importance, insofar as it depended on the Czechoslovak government in exile, could be decided without Beneš, let alone against him'.[5] He was driven by a determination to undo Munich by re-establishing Czechoslovakia. Although he tried to maintain close relations with both east and west, he was particularly pro-Soviet: Moscow, at least, had been prepared to honour its obligations in 1938. He therefore signed an alliance with the Soviet Union and also sought accommodation with Czechoslovakia's communists. The government that was restored in 1945 was therefore a genuine coalition. Beneš succeeded in getting back most of Czechoslovakia but he had to pay a price – the cession of the tail, Ruthenia, to the Soviet Union. It could be argued that his policy resulted in the domination by the Soviet Union for the following four decades. But what was the alternative? The Red Army alone drove the Germans back in eastern Europe and at least Czechoslovakia did not suffer the major geographical shift experienced by Poland.

Czechoslovakia suffered less from the war and from German occupation than did most other parts of eastern Europe. Bohemia's co-operation and Slovakia's autonomy mean that there was far less bloodshed than, for example, in Poland. Indeed, alone among its neighbours Bohemia and Moravia experienced a net population increase in the war years. There were no military losses in the Second World War, compared with 200,000 in the First World War. There was also less bombing than elsewhere. Prague escaped the destruction experienced by the cities in Poland and the Reich (including Austria) and of many in occupied western Europe. The Jewish inhabitants of Czechoslovakia were the major exception: of a pre-war total of just over 100,000, some 70,000 died.[6]

Slovakia

At the same time as the German occupation of Bohemia in March 1939 Hitler put pressure on Slovakia to declare itself independent from Bohemia and Moravia by the Treaty of Protection of the Slovak State. Under the presidency of Monsignor Jozef Tiso, a cardinal in the Catholic Church, the new republic did appear to possess certain advantages. It had a fairly widespread support, particularly from the Catholic Church, and it gained a positive response to the new constitution of July 1939. Tiso hoped to maintain a considerable degree of independence from Germany and to promote conservative Christian values like those of Dollfuss and Schuschnigg in Austria or Salazar in Portugal. In many respects the early Slovak republic was therefore similar to those authoritarian corporatist and semi-clerical regimes rather than to the more radical system of Nazism. At first Germany paid every apparent respect to the new republic, hoping that it would become a model to the New Order in Europe. Accordingly, the Reich interfered as little as possible in Slovakia's internal affairs. As long as Tiso promised co-operation and 'to continue directing domestic political development in Slovakia in a spirit unqualifiedly positive and friendly towards Germany'.[7]

Increasingly, however, Tiso was pressurized by the radicals like Mach (head of propaganda) and Tuka, who were more openly pro-Nazi. A rift opened up between them and the more conservative members of the government as, despite Tiso's efforts, Slovakia came increasingly under Germany's influence. The armaments industry was subordinated to the Nazi war effort by the 1940 Treaty for the Organization for Total War, which placed twenty-six enterprises at the disposal of the Wehrmacht. Slovakia contributed over 50,000 men to the invasion of Russia in 1941, while the SS and Hitler Youth left their mark on the Slovak equivalents (the Hlinka Guards and the Hlinka Youth) organized by Mach. There was also increasing interference by German advisers in government agencies; von Killinger, an SA leader, became German minister in Bratislava and committed himself to ensuring that Slovakia's support for Germany was unqualified. He was determined 'to govern Slovakia in such a way that during the war she will be economically 100 per cent at our disposal and that she will be led politically in such a way that there cannot be the slightest doubt that she is absolutely keeping in line'.[8] Tiso tried to draw the line against full political subservience, especially if it affected the Catholic Church. In response, the radicalized sections of the Slovak state, including the Hlinka Guards, co-operated with Germany's approach. But Germany had to delay any full confrontation because of the invasion of Russia in June 1941. Von Killinger's successor from January 1941, Ludin, focused on propaganda and tightening German control over the economy. His measures were not without success as, by 1942, 99.6 per cent of mining and metallurgy were in German ownership.

The Nazis had a major say in the treatment of Slovakia's Jews. At first Tiso and the pro-Nazi radicals in his cabinet constructed a package of limited anti-Semitic policies such as the exclusion of Jews from business and the professions. Then Tuka and Mach seized the initiative and pursued a Nazi scheme for the resettlement of Slovak Jews in Poland. Although Tiso went along with this, he called a halt on the orders of the Pope and for two years resisted a resumption of the deportations, which had spilled over into exterminations at Auschwitz, Maidenek and Lublin. The fate of the Jews, however, was sealed when Slovakia was brought under direct military subordination in September 1944. Altogether the Final Solution was vigorously implemented in Slovakia – with or without the Slovak government's compliance – and a community of 100,000 was exterminated.

Whatever Tiso's claims to the contrary, the Slovak republic was closely tied to the fortunes of Germany. From 1943 onwards this made for extreme vulnerability. As the German military machine was breaking down in Russia, domestic resistance grew against Slovakia's involvement in a futile war. The banned parties collaborated in exile to form a Slovak National Council which was committed to ending the link with Germany and to reinstating Czechoslovakia, this time as a federation. By the Christmas Agreement of 1943 communist and democratic leaders formed the Slovak National Council (SNR) to act 'in agreement with the Czechoslovak government and the liberation movement abroad'.[9] Its main objective was to produce a national uprising in Slovakia, to be led by disaffected officers within the army. Encouraged by the advance of the Red Army into Poland, the Slovak National Council called for a popular uprising in September 1944 to replace Tiso's government. The insurgents succeeded in holding for several months a large part of central Slovakia but, by October, the rebellion had been crushed by the Germans, partly because the Soviet Union had failed to deliver the expected support. Suspicious of the rival influences within the SNR of democrats and communists, Stalin preferred to see it weakened by defeat. For their part, the western Allies were unable to intervene and, in any case, saw no reason to become involved in an area well away from their own sphere of operations. The Germans now installed, under Stefan Tiso (a relative of the previous president), a more subservient regime. This was described by Hoensch as 'a mere puppet of, and executioner for, the German occupation force'.

The German occupation was ended by the arrival of Soviet troops in April 1945. The Slovak republic was instantly liquidated and the former state of Czechoslovakia revived, with Beneš installed as its first post-war president. Jozef Tiso was tried for treason and collaboration with Nazism and hanged in Bratislava in 1947. But, under Soviet influence, the early broad-based and multi-party governments gave way from 1948 to a more exclusively communist regime which remained in existence until it was brought down by popular movements in 1989.

2. Denmark

Denmark had not been involved in the First World War but had benefited from its aftermath, with the acquisition of northern Schleswig after a plebiscite. Seeing no reason to change direction in the future, she continued a policy of neutrality, although recognizing that this was dependent on Germany's compliance. Thus the first and most significant element of Danish democracy was the hope for peaceful coexistence with its neighbours. The Danes posed no threat to anyone and based everything on the trust that no-one would threaten them. They also operated a political system which possessed all the components of an early twentieth-century liberal democracy, including government responsibility to a bicameral parliament (in this case, the *Rigsdag*, which comprised the *Folketing* and the *Rigsting*).

The inter-war period brought periodic domestic crisis and instability, although these were no worse than anywhere else. There were, for example, serious economic problems, exacerbated by the Great Depression. These were, however, offset by reforms like insurance provision for sickness, unemployment and old age. Political extremism, meanwhile, was confined to the Danish Nazis (DNSAP) on the far right and the Communists on the far left. In electoral terms neither was significant, the DNSAP achieving 1.8 per cent of the popular vote in 1939 and the Communists 2.4 per cent. Throughout the period the mainstream parties retained firm control – the Social Democrats, Radical Liberals, Liberals, Conservatives and Agrarians. Unsurprisingly, coalition governments were the norm, ensuring a fully-functioning democracy with no apparent leanings towards dictatorship. More problematic was Denmark's precarious position in Europe, especially its proximity to Germany. Possible causes of future conflict included Denmark's blocking German access to northern Europe and the Baltic, along with Germany's resentment at the loss of its co-nationals in northern Schleswig. This fatal combination of strategic location and internal issues had already accounted for Austria in 1938 and Czechoslovakia between 1938 and 1939. There were therefore weak spots within Denmark's apparent stability, as external threats reacted with internal problems that did not appear too serious per se. The DNSAP, together with the Danish Rally (Nationalt Samvirke), welcomed the prospect of Nazi involvement in Danish affairs, while the precarious balance of the economy meant that Denmark was forced to consider closer co-operation with Germany to preserve its normal pattern of trade. Although the government had increased the defence budget by 1939, Denmark remained in constant danger of invasion by a revived Germany.

When this came in April 1940 it was, nevertheless, a shock. Germany's preoccupation in eastern Europe gave the western states a sense of anti-climax and false security. Denmark had not been involved in the declaration of war on Germany in September 1939 and expected a limited ultimatum, at the most for bases or airfields. The Danish government might have been prepared to meet this to guarantee its survival as an independent state and free society. Instead, it was faced with a general invasion, military collapse within a few hours and general occupation.

Unlike Norway, where the government relocated in Britain, Denmark co-operated directly with the invaders. The King, Christian X, did much to sustain public morale and to lessen the blow of the occupation. He was helped by an initial German undertaking not to interfere in Denmark's internal affairs or to undermine Denmark's sovereignty. The Germans were prepared to make this concession since it meant that fewer resources would have to be poured into the occupation. This policy of 'protection' would also be a sign to the rest of Europe of the possible reward for co-operation with the New Order. But there were three points on which the Danes would not negotiate. There was to be no interference with parliamentary process of government, no Danish involvement in war, and no discriminatory laws against Denmark's Jewish population. A series of arguments over specific legal cases meant that these intentions were gradually eroded in a 'slippery slope' towards collaboration. The Germans insisted on the resignation of several ministers who spoke out against them and, in August 1940, the government of Scavenius accepted a demand for the removal of trade barriers between Germany and Denmark and the harmonization of German and Danish duties and indirect taxation.

These demands and concessions incurred hostile public reactions which, in turn, provoked stronger German counter-measures. Early opposition was expressed in the form of community singing of patriotic songs, while flying flags at half-mast was the response to particularly contentious German demands. The king often expressed his sympathy with public opinion, mingling with the crowds in the streets of Copenhagen. The German response gradually became more punitive. In 1941 the government had to comply with tougher penalties for sabotage and a ban on the Communist Party. There was also pressure to allow Danish volunteers to fight in Russia and for Denmark to join the Anti-Comintern Pact. More unrest and strikes followed. The German plenipotentiary Best tried to revive co-operation by allowing elections to the *Folketing*, hoping that the far right would exercise a restraining influence on the rest of the population. But 94 per cent of electorate voted for mainstream parties and only 3.3 per cent for the Danish Nazi Party and the NS. Youth organizations developed within the different political parties, opposing the ideological influence of national socialism and newspapers emerged with titles like *De Frie Danske* (*Free Danes*) and *Frit Danmark* (*Free Denmark*). Even so, most Danes hoped for some form of compromise which would allow the return of democratic government.

But this proved impossible. Hitler was becoming convinced that conciliation was no longer effective. In contrast to his original view that Denmark was a positive example to the rest of Europe, he now saw the country as a weak link in his Fortress Europe against the western Allies. The German occupation was therefore tightened. In August 1943 Best demanded a ban on all demonstrations and strikes and the death penalty for sabotage. When the Danish government refused to comply it was replaced by direct military power under General von Hannecken. The whole status of the occupation changed with the internment of many prominent politicians and the demobilization of Danish security forces. The king rejected Best's offer of a government based on limited nominations. Instead, he reversed his previous policies and now defied Germany to impose direct occupation. This was made inevitable by the uprising of August 1943 and by German measures to round up Denmark's Jewish population.

Official policies and public opinion therefore changed more dramatically in Denmark than in other occupied states. With the end of the government experiment in limited co-operation with German occupation, discreet opposition turned into more active defiance. From August 1943 the public were more inclined to support sabotage, which now became more extensive in Denmark than in Norway. Encouraged by the Normandy landings and the prospect of liberation, Danish partisans blew up railway lines, armaments factories and even the Gestapo headquarters. Meanwhile, a rash of strikes reduced the capacity of Germany to supply its defences against the Allied threat. Retaliatory measures, such as the declaration of emergency and interference with Copenhagen's power supplies, failed to intimidate the population. Now that Germany looked certain to lose the war, it had become clear the Danish public preferred direct occupation to being labelled a German ally. But the end was delayed until 5 May 1945, when the German surrender freed Denmark. A new government had already been agreed on 1 May, comprising both resistance members and politicians with parliamentary experience. The result was a more peaceful transition than that experienced by some of Denmark's neighbours.

Overall, Danish policy was not one of resistance; nor was it one of full collaboration. Denmark had not been permitted to be neutral; therefore the government had opted to avoid involvement in the war, to recognize the futility of military defiance and do as much as possible to maintain Danish sovereignty within the restrictions of conquest and occupation. In the process it maintained the support of a large proportion of public opinion – a near-impossible achievement in the complex condition of war. The cost of occupation was considerable: eight billion kroner, or 22 per cent of the Danish national income per annum,[10] and resistance cost up to 1,400 lives. Yet this was substantially less than in Denmark's occupied neighbours. The nature of the occupation also meant less physical destruction and far fewer Jewish casualties in the Holocaust: 472 Jews were arrested out of a total population of 7,000, the rest being smuggled out to Sweden.

3. Norway

As an independent state, Norway had, from 1905, been a typical example of Scandinavian political stability. The country had survived the Great Depression, through consensus rather than confrontational politics, a model of the effective operation of proportional representation. As in Denmark, extreme parties had fared badly: the far-right Nasjonal Samling won only 1.8 per cent of the popular vote in 1936, while the Communists were down to 0.3 per cent. Norway had also been strongly committed to peace and neutrality. In 1938 a neutrality pact had been signed with Denmark, Sweden, Finland and Iceland. Unfortunately, this was not based on strength: Norway's defences had deteriorated badly during the 1920s and 1930s. The Norwegian government tried to keep out of the Second World War but the Germans launched a surprise attack in April 1940, drawn by Norway's mineral resources and strategic domination of the North Atlantic. Norway may well have been the victim of a disagreement between Hitler and Admiral Raeder, commander-in-chief of the German navy. Hitler assumed that the north would be sorted out by the Nazi–Soviet Non-Aggression Pact. Raeder on the other hand was looking for ways to increase Germany's strategic naval power[11] and stressed that the Norwegian coast offered a safe haven for German warships and submarines. Hitler was eventually convinced and decided on German expansion into the area. When Norway insisted on defending her neutrality he launched a surprise attack, dealing with Denmark at the same time. Whereas the latter surrendered within hours, the Norwegian armed forces resisted until June.

Norway also declined the sort of co-operation with Germany agreed by Denmark. Hitler insisted that the king accept Quisling, leader of the Norwegian Nazi Party (Nasjonal Samling – NS), as head of government. When Haakon refused, withdrawing into temporary exile in London, the government came under German control. Quisling was appointed minister president in February 1942, although most actual power remained with Terboven, previously *Gauleiter* of Cologne and now appointed *Reichskommissar* for Norway. Quisling's ideas were influenced by Nazism, in particular by Alfred Rosenberg.[12] He had a vision of the regeneration of Norway under his own leadership as *Fører*; he developed a private army that was similar to the SA and SS; and he condemned parliamentary politics, probably as a result of his own disappointing showing in the 1936 elections. He was also strongly anti-Semitic and believed in the utmost importance of Nordic racial purity and supremacy. His initial hope was that Norway could work to promote peace and co-operation between Britain and Germany to form a great Nordic peace union. By 1940, however, he had become convinced that Britain had succumbed to Jewish influence and was therefore no longer worthy of such a destiny. He therefore threw in Norway's lot entirely with Germany: 'in the Greater German community we shall have a leading position in the working of the New Order.' He attempted to reshape Norwegian society as a whole and had some success in increasing young membership of the NS movement and in Nazifying local government. Under Quisling and Terboven, Norway was heavily exploited to meet the needs of Hitler's war effort in Europe. The Germans appropriated the funds of the Norwegian national bank, depleted the industrial stock and increased the national debt nine-fold.

Most of the population remained quiet, if sullen, but a variety of resistance activities did develop. Early examples showed a particular resentment against the measures of the Quisling government. In autumn 1940 there was a strike against the NS state-controlled central Sports Union to which all teams had to belong; in October the churches formed a common front against Nazism in a Christian Council, criticizing many of the decrees of the government; in December 1940 the Supreme Court resigned as a protest against incursions into the independence of courts; and spontaneous grassroots opposition emerged from the National Federation of Trade Unions (LO). Resistance intensified from 1942 with teachers' protests against regulations on the education of youth according to Nazi principles. Their stand was supported by religious organizations as bishops and pastors read letters of protest from the pulpit. Gradually civilian resistance became more organized in form of the Coordination Committee, which included representatives from trade unions, the professions, industry and agriculture. At first the effects were more damaging for the NS than a threat to the control exercised by the Germans: the most significant result was an increase in Terboven's power at the expense of Quisling's. But this tightening of the German grip served to focus Norwegian resistance in more specifically anti-German ways. A secret press, for example, had a growing impact on public opinion and escape routes opened up for refugees of different kinds.

17 Vidkun Quisling, 1887–1945
(© Popperfoto/Getty)

As in most other occupied states the strongest resistance was external, with the Norwegian armed forces serving abroad numbering 15,000. The Norwegian merchant navy also played an important role in the war against Germany. Those ships that had escaped German hands carried vital supplies across the Atlantic, assisted at the evacuation of Dunkirk in 1940, and carried troops for the Normandy landings in 1944. The XU, a military intelligence organization, worked closely with British intelligence, as did Milorg, an underground army set up in spring 1941. Despite German reprisals, commando groups carried out daring raids on German positions in Norway. All such activities were conducted on behalf of the government in exile – a constant declaration and reminder that Norway continued to see itself as undefeated and defiant.

But there was one major problem. Norway did not have the strength to liberate herself and the main impetus of the attacks of the western Allies was in the Mediterranean and France, not in Scandinavia. In 1944 Allies advised restraint within the resistance because they had decided against an invasion of Norway and backup would therefore be difficult. Norway therefore had to wait until the general capitulation announced by Dönitz on 7 May. This made Norway one of the last of the occupied countries to see the back of German troops. Within a week King Haakon returned Norway to her customary democratic system. The general election of October 1945 produced a coalition government which gave priority to reconstruction. It also dealt with the collaborators. Terboven had already committed suicide but Quisling was captured. He was put on trial and eventually executed for treason.

The name Quisling holds a particular place in the hall of infamy. It has been pointed out that Quisling's role was no worse than that of other collaborators elsewhere in Europe. Still, it is he rather than they 'who is remembered above all as the archetypal traitor',[13] even though his impact ceased abruptly at the end of the war. His NS party was entirely uprooted during the purges that followed the German withdrawal. In proportion to the population as a whole, more collaborators were dealt with than almost anywhere else (1,400 per 100,000 in Norway, compared with 1,200 in the Netherlands, 1,000 in Belgium and 300 in France and Denmark).[14] It was almost as if Norway acknowledged the extent of the indigenous roots of collaboration and saw Quisling as the source of its influence. The nearest equivalent to the hatred accorded to him is the French aversion to Pierre Laval.

4. The Netherlands

The Dutch Republic had been a major naval and colonial power before falling into decline in the eighteenth century. Briefly occupied by France during the revolutionary and Napoleonic wars, it had been reconstituted as an enlarged Kingdom of the Netherlands in 1815 before reverting to its previous size in 1830. It had remained neutral during the First World War and emerged with a democratic constitution based on universal suffrage: proportional representation was used for the first time in the election of 9 September 1918.

The Netherlands had a series of paradoxical experiences between the wars. Despite relative political stability, there was some political activism during the 1930s from both party fringes, including the NSB (Nationaal-Socialistische Beweging in Nederland), under Mussert, and the Red Front. Both, however, performed badly in the elections of 1937 and 1939 and posed no real challenge to Dutch democracy. More threatening were economic difficulties aggravated by inflation in Germany, which affected the Dutch guilder. Despite a period of recovery with the operation of the Dawes Plan in Germany, the Dutch were affected again by the Depression from 1929 onwards as unemployment increased from 18,000 to 100,000. A particular feature of the Dutch financial crisis was the government's insistence on retaining the gold standard long after other countries had abandoned it. While Britain began her recovery between 1931 and 1933, the Dutch economy suffered a decline in exports through inflated prices, with a consequent increase in unemployment. When the Dutch government finally reversed its policy in September 1936, a measure of recovery followed, although this was closely tied to Germany's rearmament – which employed large amounts of Dutch labour.

Economic issues, in turn, affected any defence programme. Throughout the period the Netherlands expected to remain neutral in any future conflict; the government had not been involved in the Anglo-French declaration of war on Germany in September 1939 and was encouraged by the military inactivity of the Phoney War over the following seven months. But there was only a real chance of Dutch neutrality if Germany's aspirations were the same as those in the First World War. Unfortunately, Hitler's plans were more ambitious those of the *Kaiserreich* – encompassing virtually every state in western and northern Europe. In these circumstances the Dutch had a particular difficulty – their close connection with the German economy. In bad times this meant that little funding was left over for rearmament. Even during the recovery of the late 1930s a substantial proportion of the Dutch workforce was still building German weapons and aircraft rather than for Dutch defence. Alarm signals sounded with the German remilitarization of the Rhineland in 1936, resulting in an increase in the defence budget from 93 million guilders in 1937 to 261 million in 1939. Even so, Dutch weapons were outdated, while there were no tanks and only 140 aircraft. It was all too little and too late – and with far too much assistance to a future enemy. It is true that there were strategic preparations for a Fortress Holland north of the Maas and Waal rivers, to be created by partial flooding. But these needed time to activate.

This was not available. On 10 May 1940 Germans launched a sudden attack, with no formal declaration of war. Four days later the Luftwaffe bombed Rotterdam following an ultimatum for the latter's surrender. This, too, was based on shock tactics as bombers headed out to sea on an apparent course for Britain, only to return and attack the key industrial city and port. Civilian areas were deliberately targeted, with heavy casualties and extensive destruction. After a German threat to destroy Utrecht, the Dutch High Command recognized the futility of further resistance and surrendered on 15 May. In the meantime Queen Wilhelmina and some of her ministers had left the country, eventually creating a government in exile in Britain.

What were Germany's plans for the Netherlands? Hitler saw the Dutch as racially close to the Germans and proposed a New Order in the *Reichskommissariat Niederlande*. This was to be the 'Westland' of German-occupied Western Europe, first in its expansion, then its defence.[15] Accordingly, Seyss-Inquart was appointed *Reichskommissar* of the Netherlands with instructions to make the area an integral part of the expanded Reich. Despite denying that Germany would seek to subvert Dutch beliefs and traditions, he issued orders banning Orangist insignia and royal street names. His officials also implemented a policy removing any non-Nazi institutions: for example, all parties were prohibited except for NSB. Seyss-Inquart was assisted by Rauter, another Austrian Nazi, who headed the SS in the Netherlands. Between them they squeezed everything they could out of the country. They aimed to integrate the former Dutch forces into the military police or the Netherlands Labour Service; they made it compulsory for every man between the ages of eighteen and forty-five to work in German factories; and they undermined the Dutch economy by confiscating all Dutch gold in October 1940 and debasing its silver in January 1941. Above all, the Germans introduced extreme anti-Semitic measures: from February 1941 Dutch Jews were deported to camps in Germany, especially Mauthausen. By the end of the war only 30,000 Jews remained of an original population of 140,000.

The Dutch people had less leadership than some of their neighbours in how they should react. Unlike Denmark, there was no steer from the former government, now in exile, or from the Dutch parliament, the States General, which did not meet throughout the war. At first, many felt that things would eventually improve under occupation – or at least that the time had come to make the best of the inevitable German victory in Europe. In his *Synthesis of War* Jan de Geer saw the hopelessness of defiance; after all, if France had also surrendered, what could the Netherlands do other than maintain good relations with Germany? Besides, where were the monarch and her government? For many, collaboration meant a more active role. The Germans saw Mussert as a local force for integration, giving him the title of *Leider* of the Netherlands in 1942; his NSB was the only legal party in the Netherlands and his version of the SS was upgraded into the *Standarte Westland* (Land of the West Brigade). Meanwhile, the Dutch Volunteer Legion was formed in 1941 to serve in Russia. Other units followed, including the *Landstorm* (Territorial Guard) in 1943, which played an active role against the Allied invasion from 1944. Altogether, 5,000 Dutch nationals belonged to the Waffen-SS and 54,000 to other organizations – out of a total population of nine million.

There were, however, examples of resistance. After the initial shock of the invasion and occupation, the Dutch population became increasingly defiant. Many doctors, architects, lawyers and teachers resigned in protest against the Nazification of the Dutch professions. There was an ever-growing readership for illegal newspapers and pamphlets, while *Radio Oranje* used BBC transmissions to maintain contacts with the Dutch resistance. The latter comprised numerous small groups, which were deliberately decentralized and had little contact with each other. They became adept at forging documents, producing counterfeit currency, printing illegal material and hiding refugees. Measures were also taken to assist the Jews. Communists organized a protest in February 1941 against their deportation; this eventually expanded into a strike in which all sectors of society participated. Jews were widely assisted by the Dutch population, who concealed them in roof spaces and attics. The German response was to issue emergency measures, which were retained until 1945. Meanwhile, the government in exile co-ordinated resistance and intelligence through the SOE in London, while Dutch volunteers served with the Allies and in those parts of the merchant marine that had escaped capture during the German invasion.

Despite the Normandy landings in June 1944, the liberation of the Netherlands took longer than expected. The initially rapid advance through France slowed as it reached the Low Countries and Germany, stalled by the German Ardennes Offensive and the British failure to capture Arnhem. The Dutch population had to endure the 'Hunger Winter' of 1944–5, which brought 30,000 deaths through starvation. Liberation came later than in other areas and Queen Wilhelmina's government did not return until after the general German surrender on 5 May 1945. As in France, Belgium, Norway and Denmark, collaborators were dealt with either summarily or by judicial process: Mussert was sentenced to death and shot in May 1946. Those involved in the German occupation were also scrutinized, Seyss-Inquart being sentenced to death at the Nuremberg tribunal in October 1946.

The impact of the war was as severe as anywhere in western Europe. The overall cost was 220,000 lives, the loss of 33 per cent of GDP, extensive damage to infrastructure from bombing by both the Germans and the Allies, and deliberate destruction caused during the German retreat in 1945. Particularly badly affected were homes, factories, bridges and railways.

But post-war recovery was swift, within the political structure of a restored democratic system and a more integrated economic structure.

5. Belgium

From the sixteenth century, the southern Netherlands had been ruled by one of the major powers – Spain, Austria and France. In 1815 it was joined with the Kingdom of the Netherlands, against which it revolted in 1830. Belgian independence had been achieved by 1839 but, despite international recognition of its neutrality, Belgium was invaded by German forces in August 1914 as part of the Schlieffen Plan to defeat France. In compensation for the considerable destruction suffered during the First World War, Belgium received reparations from Germany, along with the industrial area of Eupen-Malmédy. Her subsequent economic problems were similar to those of most other states of the inter-war period: with the impact of the Great Depression, unemployment reached 23.5 per cent in 1932 but dropped back to 15 per cent by 1937. Politically, it was one of Europe's more secure democracies, with a constitution operating on the principle of the separation but integration of legislative, executive and judicial powers. The bicameral system comprised the House of Representatives and Senate, the former elected every four years by men and women over the age of twenty-one. One possible source of friction was the distinction between the two main regions of Belgium – Flanders in the north and French-speaking Wallonia in the south. Both areas developed far-right parties, including the Rexists and the Flemish nationalist movement (VNV). These did not, however, threaten Belgium's basic political stability and the popularity of the extremists was in decline by 1939.

Despite the experience of the First World War, Belgium eventually opted to maintain its long-standing commitment to neutrality. In the process it left behind the 1920 Treaty of Mutual Guarantee with France, withdrew from the 1925 Locarno Pact and in 1937 accepted an undertaking that under no circumstances would Germany invade Belgium. In this respect, Belgium's aspirations were similar to those of the other small democracies – Denmark, the Netherlands, Norway and Switzerland. There was, however, additional reason for peaceful coexistence with Nazi Germany: the Maginot Line, constructed by the French between the wars, stopped before reaching the Ardennes, leaving the Belgian frontier with Germany unprotected. By 1939 Belgium had accepted the inevitability of increased rearmament, which was intensified after the declaration of war on Germany by Britain and France in September 1939. The Belgians had 650,000 troops available in 1940, more than either the British in France or the Dutch. But this advantage was nullified by the German Blitzkrieg in May. The Belgian air force was largely destroyed on the ground, while the recently constructed fortifications were useless in preventing the onslaught which was only part of a more general attack on France and the Netherlands. Nevertheless, Belgium held out for eighteen days, longer than either the Netherlands or Denmark.

But this had no effect on the occupation that followed. Belgium was placed under *Militärverwaltung*, or direct military rule, headed by Reeder and Falkenhausen until July 1944, then by Grohé until end of the war. The Germans exploited the differences between the two main parts of the population, expressing a clear preference for the Flemings over the Walloons, on the grounds that the former were more closely related to the Germans and therefore racially 'superior'. Most former magistrates, aldermen and burgomasters were replaced by Degrelle's Rexists, and by De Clerq's Flemish Nationalists. The military authorities also imposed an indemnity to pay for the occupation, rationed all essentials, curtailed press and academic freedoms, and deported 375,000 Belgian labourers to Germany. Anti-Semitic laws provided for the seizure of Jewish property and for the compulsory wearing of the Star of David. Altogether, 25,000 Jews were eventually transported to Auschwitz and other camps.

The policy of the Belgian leadership towards all this was less clear-cut than it was elsewhere. The Prime Minister, Pierlot, fled abroad, first to France, then to Britain, setting up a government in exile. Some of his fellow ministers followed his example, while others remained in Belgium. The role of the monarchy was especially contentious. In contrast to the Netherlands, King Leopold III decided not to go into exile and surrendered to the Germans on 28 May, for which he was criticized by Pierlot. Leopold remained in Belgium, under German supervision, although he was still supported by much of the population. There has always been more controversy about the role of the monarchy in Belgium than elsewhere. In Denmark the king stood for constitutionalism, accepted by the rest of the government until the national uprising in 1943. By contrast, the monarchs of Luxembourg, the Netherlands and Norway led regimes in exile. In Belgium, it is true, the monarch tried to intercede, with some success, in reducing the harshness of the occupation. But the real test came in the post-liberation atmosphere of 1945, when any record of co-operation with the Germans was treated with derision. Whereas he had been praised earlier in the occupation for remaining to carry out his responsibilities while his officials had fled abroad, he was eventually discredited as a collaborator. Although the population opted after the war to retain constitutional monarchy, Leopold himself was obliged to abdicate in 1950, in favour of his son, Baudouin.

The population at large showed a broad range of responses to the occupation. The Germans received extensive co-operation from the administration, once the key post-holders had been replaced by Nazi sympathizers. There was also some military collaboration, an example being Degrelle's *Légion Wallonie*, which co-operated with the SS in Belgium and also served on the eastern front. By contrast, although much of the population appreciated the difficulties faced by the monarch and the attempts he made to ameliorate conditions, there was widespread resentment of the occupation. Within Belgium itself opposition came from a variety of political groups, ranging from the communists through socialists and social democrats to conservatives. There was even dissent from some patriotic fascists, showing that the far right was not fully united. Saboteurs destroyed bridges and railway lines and the attack on German troops was at least as large – in proportion to the population – as in France. Allied pilots shot down over Belgium were assisted by escape routes and with false identity papers. Up to 20,000 Jews were also saved from the camps through concealment by civilians. Meanwhile, the government in exile created appropriate ministries to deal with the influx of refugees from Belgium. It conscripted all Belgians in other countries to fight with the British army, navy or RAF. Assistance also came from the Belgian Congo in form of volunteers and financial resources, while colonial forces played an important role against the Italians in Abyssinia.

Belgium was liberated by the Allies towards the end of 1944. But the Ardennes Offensive caused considerable suffering before the final expulsion of German troops in February 1945. By the end of the war some 40,000 civilians and soldiers had been killed, 12,000 political prisoners interned, and nearly 27,000 Jews exterminated in the death camps.[16] In addition, Belgium had had to pay about 65 per cent of its national income for the expense of the occupation and had endured major destruction, partly by Allied bombing in 1944 on German positions and industries, and partly by the German defence in 1944–5. Belgian recovery was assisted by measures taken towards the end of the war by the government in exile, including the introduction of a new currency and the signing in 1944 of a new economic agreement with representatives of Holland and Luxembourg; this was the effective beginning of Benelux. Further developments matched those in Netherlands and Luxembourg – the movement towards a new defence policy within NATO and economic integration in the EEC and European Union.

6. Luxembourg

With a population of 293,000, Luxembourg was the smallest of all the democracies covered in this chapter. The Grand Duchy leaned to the right and was strongly influenced by the Catholic Church. It was, nevertheless, a democratic state with universal suffrage, a legislature comprising the Council of State and the Chamber of Deputies, and a range of political parties: apart from the period 1925–6, most governments were dominated by the Liberals and Social Democrats. The main political threat came from the far left but a government attempt to ban the Communist Party was rejected by a referendum in 1937.

Luxembourg's main external threat came from Germany. This, however, seemed to have been contained by the post-war settlement in 1919, which also enabled the Grand Duchy to pursue a policy of neutrality as a member of the League of Nations. At the same time, it maintained friendly relations with the Weimar Republic and then with Nazi Germany. But the warning signs came with the German remilitarization of the Rhineland (1936) and occupation of Austria (1938) and Bohemia (1939). Luxembourg's main concern was its complete lack of any defences. By 1939 Germany had reinforced its gun emplacements along the border – until these commanded a view of the entire country. After a temporary reprieve during the Phoney War (September 1939 until April 1940), Luxembourg was swamped in May by the German invasion. 47,000 refugees blocked the roads westwards, while the Grand Duchess and her government fled, first to France and then to Britain, where they set up in exile.

Germany condemned Luxembourg to oblivion as a separate entity and a nation state. More extreme measures were taken than elsewhere in western Europe: these were concerned not just with pacification and occupation but with racial 'purification'. Himmler considered that the population had been 'polluted', with the result that Luxembourg came closer than any other western European country to being systematically 'cleansed', albeit on a much smaller scale than happened in eastern Europe. The German People's Movement (*Volksdeutsche Bewegung* or VDB) was used to convert or intimidate the population. Heavy restrictions were imposed on other ethnic influences and the French language was banned, as were French greetings and names. Meanwhile, the economy was completely absorbed and transfers enforced to supplement the labour force in Germany. Above all, much of the population was threatened with deportation. Jews were sent to their deaths in Germany, while two-thirds of the remaining Luxembourgers were intended for eventual deportation to the Ukraine as part of Himmler's measures against non-Aryans. Newcomer summarizes the overall impact of such measures: 'The brutal German policy of absorbing Luxembourg into the German state cost the Luxembourg citizenry the highest proportion of people sent to concentration camps, people imprisoned and people deported of all the countries of Europe.'[17]

The population was too small to try to resist the German invasion or absorption. Nevertheless, it opted from the start for other forms of non-cooperation and did not, like Denmark, try to develop a constitutional coexistence with Germany. When a plebiscite was arranged in October 1941, 97 per cent of the electorate opposed welcoming German rule. This result was ignored as Luxembourgers were made German nationals and 12,000 called up to the German army. The reaction to this was a general strike called in 1942 and over one-quarter of those enlisted failed to report. Only 2,000 joined the German army voluntarily, far fewer than those who served with the Allies, in the RAF and Royal Navy. Many also fought in the Belgian Brigade or with the Belgian resistance.

Wartime Luxembourg was particularly affected by two contrasting experiences. One was the intensity of the German occupation between 1940 and 1944. The other was the Ardennes Offensive between 1944 and 1945. The former had violated the integrity of Luxembourg but had prevented wholesale devastation. The latter incurred greater destruction but offered the prospect of liberation. The 'Battle of the Bulge' was one of the major battles of the Second World War and the largest ever fought on Luxembourg soil, causing desolation across half the country. It did, however, fatally weaken German resistance in the west; it also ensured that Luxembourg would be one of the first countries in western Europe to see the end of German rule.

7. France

France became a dictatorship as a direct result of military defeat by Germany in 1940 and the overthrow of the Third Republic. It is difficult to see how fascism could have come to power in any other way.

France did, of course, have several anti-democratic influences. It is sometimes seen as the seedbed of fascism with the convergence of ideas from the far left (Sorel) and far right (Maurras). There was also a strong undercurrent of nationalism, militarism and anti-Semitism, the Dreyfus case pulling all three together during the 1890s. In the 1930s, France was inclined towards appeasing right-wing dictatorships, especially Mussolini over Abyssinia and Hitler over the Sudetenland. Yet in no way could it be argued that France by 1940 was on the verge of becoming a dictatorship herself. There was no more of a threat to democracy from the far right within France than in Belgium, the Netherlands and Britain. Indeed, France managed to sustain democracy throughout the inter-war period. Although there were periods of political turbulence, these were navigated by broad-based governments of either the right or the left, including the Bloc National under Clemenceau (1919), the Cartel des Gauches under Herriot (1924), Poincaré's National Union (1926) and Blum's Popular Front (1936). As for appeasement, France always acted in conjunction with Britain. During the Spanish Civil War, the French governments were sympathetic towards the Republicans – but were warned by London that no British support would be forthcoming if France were to become embroiled. Similarly, Daladier was not unwilling to assist Czechoslovakia in 1938 but not without the support that Chamberlain was desperately anxious not to give.

What actually destroyed the democracy within the Third Republic was the most catastrophic military reverse in the whole of France's history. This resulted from the triumph of the German Blitzkrieg offensive over the French defensive system based on the Maginot Line. The rapidity of French defeat, which occurred in under six weeks, took everyone by surprise, Britain included. Prime Minister Reynaud, who had succeeded Daladier in March, resigned on 16 June. A new government, under Marshal Pétain, a hero of the First World War, secured an armistice on 22 June. This had echoes of the Treaty of Versailles imposed on Germany in 1919. For example, France was required to pay an indemnity and the costs of German occupation while, at the same time, having to reduce her army to 100,000. Altogether, France was forced to pay 60 per cent of her national income to Germany. Conquest was also followed by partition. Alsace-Lorraine was returned to the Reich; the departments of Pas-de-Calais and Nord were placed under military occupation; and other parts of north-eastern France were assigned to Germany – after their population had been 'rebalanced'. The bulk of France was divided into two main areas. The north, comprising the Atlantic coast and its interior, was placed under immediate German occupation, while a 'free zone' based on Vichy was established in the south. Nominally Vichy provided the government for all of France – but the northern part of the Pétain regime was entirely subordinate to the German occupation. Between the two areas rigid border controls were imposed and any access between them required official permission and papers. From late 1942 distinctions between the two areas were removed as the Germans occupied Vichy on the same terms as the rest of France.

The collaborationist regime therefore covered the whole of France in theory while, in practice, governing only the southern part based on Vichy. Its credibility was based almost entirely on the reputation and leadership of Marshal Pétain, who expected unconditional loyalty and obedience: 'You, the French people, must follow me without reservation on the paths of honour and national interest.' According to the anthem of the regime, the Marshal was 'France's saviour'. Furthermore, 'we, your men, we swear to serve you and follow in your footsteps. For Pétain is France, and France is Pétain'.[18] The message of Pétain was that France had to undergo an 'intellectual and moral revival'.[19] He focused on a 'National Revolution', the tone of which was unmistakably authoritarian, with the emphasis on 'work, family, country', rather than 'liberty, equality, fraternity'. The democratic past was denounced, especially the Third Republic, which was held to have brought France to defeat and ruin.

Pétain was served by a succession of subordinates. Laval was Foreign Minister until December 1940, when he was succeeded by Flandin who, in turn, gave way to Admiral Darlan. Laval proved the most resilient, returning as Prime Minister in April 1942. He believed in the vital importance of the closest co-operation with Germany, which would eventually create a New European Order, under German control but in partnership with France. Meanwhile this most virulently anti-Semitic of Vichy's leaders was a major influence behind the persecution of France's Jews and other minorities. He also drove the more extreme social changes sought by the National Revolution. He emphasized that France had been defeated because it had been 'feminized' by the Third Republic: women were blamed for the population stagnation which had placed France in military peril, the reason being their preference for employment and independence. Such influences had to be reversed by the restoration of male dominance and the emphasis on the family.

The ideological basis of the National Revolution is debatable. The policies of Vichy were largely traditional but also influenced by the radical right. In some respects, they were a combination of the two. Pétain always asserted the importance of Charles Maurras and Action française rather than of Nazi or Italian Fascist influences. There may well be something in this and the original contributions of France to fascism have already been noted. Any corporatism in the National Revolution therefore came largely from French origins, enhanced by traditional values which were strongly reasserted after the fall of the Third Republic and supported by Catholic Church. Yet there was also an ideological connection with Germany, which owed more to Laval than to Pétain. Laval maintained that 'parliamentary democracy has lost the war; it must disappear, ceding its place to an authoritarian, hierarchical, national and social regime'.[20] This was a clear indication of Laval's open sympathy with Nazi ideas. According to Ousby, 'The National Revolution was also, if not fascist, close enough to being fascist to tempt its architects into believing it would win France the respect of the Reich and, with that respect, a worthy place in the new European Order'.[21] The Vichy regime was certainly a dictatorship: the constitution and the leadership of Pétain could be described as authoritarian, with totalitarian influences injected by Germany through Laval.

How successful was the Vichy regime – at least in its early stages? There is some evidence to show that Pétain was popular in 1940, offering as he appeared to do a way out of total defeat and disaster. He remained more moderate than Laval and retained some links with the previous regime – such as the *Marseillaise*. He received strong backing from the Catholic Church, which had never been a strong supporter of the Third Republic and now saw Pétain's leadership as 'providential'. According to Christofferson, 'Vichy was the revenge of the Church, in many respects'.[22] Yet every apparent success in the regime's policies was cancelled by more obvious shortcomings. Women benefited from better provision for antenatal assistance but their role in society was adversely affected by a wave of official antifeminism. It was also impossible to enforce the laws restricting women's labour because of the shortage of men and the fact that over a million of the armed forces captured in 1940 remained in captivity in Germany until the end of the war. Although the National Revolution showed more interest in the culture and traditions of rural France and attempted to revive the economic influence of a self-sufficient peasantry, this conflicted with German aims to control agricultural production for its own uses. The working class also found itself worse off under Vichy, again because of German pressures. Pétain's Labour Charter of September 1941 had aimed to end class conflict but was overwhelmingly rejected by the workforce as a hollow system which imposed restrictions on the right to strike. As for the constitution, this was seen as too mystical, vague and anti-Third Republic. Instead, administration depended on the system of prefects which pre-dated that regime and, indeed, it predecessors. But this was, in itself, a problem because of the conflict between the local prefects and the central government. The latter was underpinned by the paramilitary Légion française, which took an oath of personal allegiance to Pétain, then by the fascist Milice, installed after the German takeover in 1943. 'Inevitably, it seems, the military state that Pétain believed was the answer to France's decline was based on nothing less than brute force.'[23]

There can be no question about the extent of persecution inflicted by the Vichy regime. The slogan of the National Revolution, 'Work, Family, Fatherland', unlike the earlier 'Liberty, Equality, Fraternity', excluded identifiable minorities like foreigners, Gypsies, Freemasons and, above all, Jews. The Germans actually received more co-operation from the Vichy government than from Paris, even though the latter was more directly under German control. This was demonstrated by a series of measures emanating from Vichy. In July 1940 citizenship was revoked for naturalized Jews, while in October laws were issued to intern foreign-born Jews in camps. All Jews were excluded from public office, teaching and most professions. By 1941 they were also being deprived of their property through a process of 'Aryanization' and the *Statuts des Juifs* (June 1941) took anti-Semitism to a new level. Most of these measures followed those introduced in Occupied France – without the need for any pressure on the Vichy authorities by the Germans. By the summer of 1942 the Vichy authorities were also assisting the transportation of Jews to death camps. Out of the total of 330,000 Jews in France in 1939, 75,000 were eventually rounded up and sent to Auschwitz, and smaller numbers to other camps.[24] Some 30,000 survived through rescue operations, 50,000 escaped from France and 150,000 survived without help.

There are several insights into the treatment of Jews in France under the occupation. One is the strength of anti-Semitism there even before the German conquest. This is emphasized by McMillan: 'Vichy's anti-Semitism was entirely home-grown and in certain respects even exceeded German requirements.' He also argues that Vichy showed a 'willingness to go much further than the previous regime, partly in order to curry favour with the Germans but more to try to lend substance to its claims to be an autonomous state, aspiring to exercise influence even in the occupied zone'.[25] On the other hand, the overall percentage of Jews who died in the camps was lower in France than elsewhere. This was because the pace of the rounding-up and deportation slowed substantially after 1942. Taking this into consideration, Christofferson argues that 'France's record of saving German Jews from extermination was one of the best of all European nations, far better, for example, than the Netherlands'.[26] Yet any such limitation was based less on humanitarian considerations than on Vichy's awareness from 1942 of its increasing subordination to Germany and its alienation from public opinion, which had accepted earlier anti-Semitic laws but not the deportations. The main thought of the government was for the consequences of a backlash, either of a German takeover or of a popular rebellion. In the end, Laval thought he had found the solution – of using co-operation with the Germans as a means of extracting concessions and prolonging Vichy's autonomy. This may have slowed the deportations but it did not prevent the flood of public opinion away from the regime.

The reason for this was the growing resistance to the regime and the threat from outside. Up to 1942 Vichy had kept at least the pretence of independence and had even possessed colonies in North Africa. These, however, were conquered by British and American troops and the Vichy government was deprived of any significant role. Many Frenchmen therefore switched their support to internal opposition movements. In Vichy the fight was no longer against old enemies like capitalists, communists or republicans. Instead, the target was now the collaborator. With this came the emphasis on the future liberation of France. The dominating nature of the Vichy regime actually provoked the growth of this new resistance. Kedward argues: 'Had Vichy been less authoritarian, less dogmatic, and less repressive this might have been avoided or at least delayed.'[27] He adds: 'Resistance was thus a political response to political provocation as well as patriotic response to a national crisis.'[28] The main groups which developed in the southern zone were *Combat* and *Libération*. By January 1943 these had been united into the *Mouvements Unis de la Resistance* (MUR). A similar process brought together a more complex pattern of resistance in the northern zone, where the earlier divergence between small groups like *Libération-Nord* and *Front National* gave way in March 1943 to the *Conseil National de la Résistance* (CNR). A key factor in the growing convergence was the reduction of aggressive competition between different interests. A specific example of this was the Communists. Initially compromised by the tortuous diplomacy between Hitler and Stalin between 1939 and 1941, they had not been able to agree with the other groups a stance against the German occupation. This, of course, changed with the German invasion of the Soviet Union in June 1941. In addition, the dissolution of Comintern meant that the Communist resistance could abandon the earlier priority of internal revolution and co-operate in the national task of evicting the external enemy. Other groups, too, modified their own specific aims in the pursuit of a more common objective.

Internal resistance needed external co-ordination and leadership. This was provided by de Gaulle, a junior general in the French army who left for exile in Britain and broadcast his intentions on the BBC on 18 June 1940. At first he had to struggle against the popularity of Pétain and his own obscurity as one of the lesser-known generals claiming to represent France. He also found it difficult to get on with Churchill and was thoroughly disliked by Roosevelt, who refused to recognize him as the future leader of France. For a while he had to struggle for leadership against General Giraud, preferred by the Americans. But, through strength of character and perseverance, de Gaulle eventually increased his credibility. He insisted that the Vichy government had no legitimacy since it had not been confirmed by the electorate: it was merely a client state of Germany. Eventually de Gaulle benefited from the declining credibility of Pétain and the Vichy regime, as well from the advance of the Allies across North Africa. His influence grew, even though, in theory, he shared the leadership of the resistance with Giraud after their reconciliation in 1943. De Gaulle was actually preferred by movements within France. His emissary, Moulin, established essential links between internal and external resistance, and forged closer co-operation between different groups and between north and south – in the United Movements of Resistances (MUR) and National Resistance Council (CNR). Moulin also persuaded most of groups, including Communists, to accept de Gaulle as the successor to Pétain and the alternative to Giraud. De Gaulle was therefore directly involved in both the liberation and the post-liberation government of France.

German defeat became increasingly likely as a result of events on the eastern front and in North Africa from 1942–3 onwards. At first the German response was to intensify their control through the direct occupation of southern sector in November 1942. This meant the end of Vichy's autonomy and tightened controls over the population through the creation of the Milice, the use of special courts martial to deal swiftly with any form of resistance or opposition, and the imposition of compulsory labour in Germany through the *Service du Travail Obligatoire* (STO), a major factor in the strengthening of the resistance. The beginning of the end for German rule in France came with the invasion by the Western Allies in 1944, the north falling in June and the south in August. Official collaboration under Pétain continued until the end of the war in May 1945. He and Laval were forced to go to Germany as the Vichy government in exile in August 1944 to avoid falling into the hands of the Allies in France. Meanwhile de Gaulle was allowed by the British and Americans to liberate Paris. He subsequently introduced a Provisional Government in August 1944, based on the *Commissaires de la République* who replaced the previous officials of Vichy. Different sectors of the resistance were integrated into the regular armed forces and special Courts of Justice dealt with collaborators. The new regime was recognized by both the United Kingdom and the United States, which France now joined as the third western allied power. As such, France participated in the post-war settlement and was included in the zoning arrangements for defeated Germany. President Roosevelt, however, remained convinced that de Gaulle was a possible danger. He pointed to certain authoritarian tendencies and warned that de Gaulle might set up another dictatorship.

Time was to show that de Gaulle avoided this trap, settling instead for a leadership that was paternalist but firmly rooted in democracy. France was returned to pre-war democratic values, shorn of Vichy and Pétainist traditionalist structures but with a stronger emphasis on authority and leadership embodied in de Gaulle himself. But it took time to discover this fully in the transition from the Fourth to Fifth Republics. De Gaulle's first presidency was short, ending with his resignation in January 1946. The Fourth Republic, with its constrained executive, weak presidency and strong prime minister, was not to his liking. Without him

France experienced some successes down to 1959, with movement into the EEC and membership of NATO. But there were also significant failures over Indo-China, Suez and Algeria. When he returned to power with strengthened presidential powers in 1959 he associated the new Fifth Republic with a distinctive Gaullist approach. On the one hand, he gave up French power through decolonization and Algerian independence. On the other, he reclaimed French sovereignty by partially withdrawing from NATO, imposing conditions on the EEC and developing an independent nuclear deterrent for France. Until his resignation in 1968 de Gaulle remained suspicious of both the United States and the United Kingdom while, at the same time, being the most willing of western leaders to improve relations with East Germany and the Soviet Union. The difficulties he had experienced as leader of the French resistance undoubtedly influenced his post-war policies and statesmanship.

THREE DEMOCRACIES MARGINALIZED

Three democracies managed to remain neutral during the Second World War, avoiding military occupation and retaining their own identity and political institutions. The cost, however, was high. They were affected by the conflict around them and, in their isolation, threatened with the constant prospect of invasion. Each found its own way of coming to terms with prolonged crisis.

1. Switzerland

Swiss democracy was a traditional federation of cantons overlaid with modern freedoms, although with one important exception: it was the only country in Europe to exclude women from the franchise. Its organic development was a compromise between the different linguistic groups, which was assisted by a growing rapport between French and German parts of Switzerland, in contrast to the obvious rift between them during the First World War. In the 1930s and early 1940s there was little support for Nazi Germany and political extremism did not flourish – whether on the right or the left. Ever since the end of the Napoleonic wars in 1815 Switzerland had also maintained a tradition of neutrality; despite occasional incursions by combatants in other conflicts, it suffered no actual invasion.

Switzerland's determination to protect the integrity of both federalism and neutrality did not, however, mean unconditional co-operation with its more powerful neighbours. At first it depended on frontier fortifications – although less elaborate than those of Czechoslovakia and France. But events of 1938–40 showed how vulnerable such static defences were against the might of the German Blitzkrieg. After the fall of France, Swiss military strategy changed from resisting the enemy at the frontier to falling back to the Alpine core within Switzerland. Preparations were made for a war of attrition from a *réduit national* (National Redoubt) – which would control the communications through Switzerland. The purpose was to emphasize how costly an invasion would be to any potential aggressor. According to Huber, chief of General Staff, 'In our situation there can only be one aim, to resist as long as possible'. He added 'We want to go down fighting, leaving the aggressor only a totally devastated country without material or human resources of any kind.'[29]

Although it had several times considered dealing with Switzerland, Germany had never followed through the invasion plan it had drawn up, Operation Tannenbaum. In part it was deterred by the Swiss *réduit* strategy, which would be so much more difficult to overcome than rolling across weakened and outdated fixed defences elsewhere. In any case, tempting as it might be to incorporate Switzerland into the Reich, little support could be expected from the German majority there. There was also a matter of priorities. Germany was already preoccupied – first with the invasion of western Europe, then with reversing Italian failures in the Balkans and north Africa, and finally expanding eastwards beyond Poland. There was never a sufficient hiatus to invade Switzerland since the maximum German expansion overlapped the beginning of the Soviet fight-back. Switzerland was also of questionable strategic importance. After the Anschluss, Germany bordered on its ally, Italy, and had direct access to the Balkans. Once France was conquered in 1940, Switzerland could therefore be left in isolation. It was easier to live with this – provided the Allies also respected Swiss neutrality – than to invest the considerable resources that would be necessary for Switzerland's conquest. Indeed, the Swiss would probably retaliate by blowing up the Gotthard rail tunnel, depriving Germany of its most direct means of providing Italy with coal supplies. In these circumstances, it is not hard to see why von Weizsäcker, at the German Foreign Office, called Switzerland 'an indigestible lump'.[30]

To an extent, therefore, Switzerland was saved from invasion by external circumstances. Nevertheless it remained highly vulnerable, surrounded by Axis powers and heavily dependent on Germany economically. This conditioned some of its policies, at least until 1944. Between September 1939 and August 1943 imports from Germany totalled 2.258 billion Swiss francs while exports to Germany were worth 1.972 billion. During the whole war period, the *Reichsbank* deposited 1.638 billion in Swiss banks; according to Steinberg, 'Switzerland, by acting as a reserve bank for the Germans, had done very handsomely out of the war'.[31] There was, however, a cost. Switzerland's trade with Britain suffered a sharp decline and there was pressure within Britain for punitive measures. In 1940 the British Foreign Office had to resist proposals by the Ministry of Economic Warfare to include Switzerland within the scope of the economic blockade. Pressure was put on Swiss companies following a sudden increase in Swiss exports to Germany in 1941. There were particularly strong British complaints about the more sensitive exports to the Axis. Lord Lovatt, for example, told the Swiss ambassador that exports for 'the equipment of the German war machine' were contributing to 'the loss of Allied soldiers, sailors and airmen in battle, and to the aerial attacks on this country'.[32] His pressure eventually succeeded, as Swiss exports to Germany dropped between1944 and 1945.

Despite these rough patches, relations between Switzerland and the Allies, especially Britain, were basically positive. Switzerland was held in higher esteem by Churchill than were the other neutrals – Sweden and Ireland. In October 1944 Stalin tried to persuade Churchill to send Allied troops through Switzerland to surprise Germany from the rear. Churchill refused to countenance the proposal, in contrast to the real consideration given in February 1940 by the Allied War Council to the occupation of central Sweden. In a minute to the Foreign Secretary, Churchill went so far as to say: 'Of all the neutrals, Switzerland has the greatest right to distinction.' He continued: 'She has been a democratic state, standing for freedom in self-defence among her mountains, and in thought, in spite of race, largely on our side.'[33] Despite the economic predicament imposed by their isolation, the Swiss remained largely pro-British – partly because they were also hostile to Germany, fiercely independent and committed to democratic traditions. An underlying sympathy for the Allied cause ensured that Switzerland was a reliable sanctuary for escaped prisoners-of-war. Admittedly, there were complaints about the occasional bombing mistakes made by the RAF and USAF through accidental incursions into Swiss territory, but these were far fewer than those issued against the Luftwaffe. The Swiss even took measures to prevent the latter, providing a constant source of irritation to the German government and periodically reigniting the argument for a German invasion.

Overall, Switzerland did manage to survive the considerable threats to its existence and integrity. But, in the process, she made substantial compromises. De Salis has aptly summarized her dilemma: 'The immediate threat of the Fascist and National Socialist ideologies and our entrenchment in our redoubt during the last war forced us to make a virtue of necessity and to concentrate passionately on the defence of our own particular and inviolate existence.'[34]

2. Sweden

During the seventeenth century Sweden had established herself as one the major powers of Europe, spreading her control over the Baltic and into Germany. By 1721 defeat by Russia in the Great Northern War had forced a more circumspect attitude to its neighbours. Subsequently she lost Finland to Russia in 1809 and was forced to acknowledge the independence of Norway in 1905. Military strength and expansion therefore gave way to the twin themes of constitutionalism and neutrality, which Sweden saw no reason to change during the twentieth century. A fully parliamentary system emerged in 1918, when elections based on universal suffrage were added to the bicameral *Riksdag* formed in 1867. Most governments were based on coalitions since no party – Conservatives, Liberals or Social Democrats – held a majority, especially during the 1920s and early 1930s. Parties of the extreme right and left fared badly: the *Nationalsocialistiska arbetarepartei* never achieved more than 0.7 per cent of the national vote – thereby failing to qualify for any seats in parliament,[35] while the Communists were divided and represented no real threat to their main rivals on the left, the Social Democrats.

Between 1914 and 1939 Sweden had a mixed record. Although one of Europe's seven neutrals during the First World War, she suffered from the British blockade against Germany which provoked severe rationing and food riots. A period of recovery and consolidation during the 1920s was followed by another downturn, with the Wall Street Crash, the Great Depression and rising unemployment. A second recovery was tied to a tightened economic link with Germany, in the form of iron-ore exports which were used to strengthen Germany's industrial growth and rearmament. The economic advantages to Sweden of this trade were sufficient to offset any opposition to the Nazi regime. More than ever, Sweden appeared to have committed herself to the path of neutrality, albeit with her defences strengthened by a new programme launched in 1936.

The Second World War was a greater challenge to Swedish security than the First. Two developments were of particular concern: the Russian attacks on Finland in the Winter War of 1939–40 and the German invasion of Norway in April 1940. Although public opinion was strongly behind its neighbours – and former provinces – the Swedish government decided on strict neutrality. Sweden's dilemma was magnified by the complexity of its strategic situation. The most direct threat to Sweden came from Germany – but only if Russia succeeded in taking over Finland. If Russia could be contained, in whatever way, Germany would be more likely to respect Swedish neutrality. If Finland's neutrality could not be sustained against the threat of Russia, then the best of a series of bad options would be to accept the inevitability of Germany's aid to Finland. Otherwise, if the USSR managed to conquer Finland it was quite possible that Germany would make a similar move on Sweden to prevent complete Soviet domination of the Baltic. At the same time, Sweden had to restrict her connections with Germany in order to avoid the possibility of retaliation from Britain, a very real possibility in 1939 and always a threat after 1940. The situation became especially difficult during the Continuation War between Finland and Russia, which overlapped Hitler's invasion of Russia in 1941 and growing British support for Stalin.

Sweden therefore had to perform a delicate balancing act which required a degree of opportunism and ruthlessness to maintain. This was in contrast with Denmark, which accepted German occupation to maintain its existence, and Norway, which tried to resist. Perhaps Sweden had more in common with Finland and Britain, where opportunism and ruthlessness were also key influences; except that these, unlike Sweden, *defied* their enemies and risked everything in the process. Instead, Sweden chose to come to terms with Nazi Germany over two key issues – transit arrangements and continued trade in strategic materials.

At first Sweden tried to reject German demands for automatic permission for rail transit across her territory. But the Swedish government feared German invasion if all such arrangements were rejected and persuaded the *Riksdag* to accept limited transit facilities. These applied initially to medical supplies, then to armaments and to troops on leave. But the agreement covered much more than was immediately apparent, allowing for the transport, to Norway and Finland, of a total of two million German troops and 75,000 railway wagonloads of armaments.[36] After the outbreak of the Continuation War between Finland and Russia, permission was also given for the movement of the Engelbrecht Division across Sweden in June 1941. Sweden complied, not least to save democratic process. The reasoning was also that Germany looked like winning the war – so what was the alternative? The economic situation was equally sensitive. Geographically, Sweden was vulnerable to German control over the Baltic – at least in the early stages of the war. This meant that the Allies could not guarantee any effective protection for Swedish commerce, any disruption of which would have a profound effect on the Swedish economy. This, in turn, would have two side-effects. One would be the growth of internal social unrest. The other would be the reduction of resources to spend on rearmament to reinforce Swedish neutrality. Concessions to Germany therefore appeared to be an essential component of Swedish neutrality.

Until, that is, Germany's changing prospects induced a rethink by the Swedish government. From 1943 onwards there was an increasing possibility that Germany would lose the war. The main implication of this was a shift from co-operation with Germany to a closer relationship with the Allies. This had to be gradual as Sweden was still committed to remaining outside the war. Eventually, however, Allied pressure told. From 1943 Sweden reduced its iron exports to Germany and, in 1944, ended its transit agreements over the transport of German troops. In 1944 there was strong pressure from the Allies to cut further the supplies to Germany, especially iron ore and ball bearings, and to close Swedish ports to German shipping. The last two years of the war also saw a change in Swedish policy towards Norway and Denmark. Sweden feared the possibility of chaos in the event of German withdrawal. Denmark and Norway requested military help but Sweden wanted to maintain its neutrality and not be drawn into the war at a late stage or provoke a German occupation. Instead, Sweden assisted the training of Norwegian and Danish 'police' to maintain internal order and stability – but not troops to fight against the Germans. There was, nevertheless, unofficial contact at lower military levels and from February 1945 the Norwegian police reserve camp in Sweden started to train recruits to the Norwegian resistance, providing instruction in sabotage and use of weapons. There were also positive features to Sweden's adjustment: one was that she became a refugee haven. Sweden welcomed Jews fleeing the Holocaust, including 7,500 from Denmark in October 1943. She provided for a total of 193,000 refugees by the end of 1944, including 80,000 Finns, 43,000 Norwegians and 18,000 Danes.[37]

Her strategic position gave Sweden a unique opportunity for survival while, at the same time, making it difficult to exercise genuine neutrality. She managed a successful – but tainted – legacy, the proportions of the mixture depending on the viewpoint of the beholder. The Swedish establishment remained sensitive about the way other countries perceived Sweden's role, opting on the whole for the case based on 'small state realism'. Gilmour has summarized the main tenets of this as: 'national independence'; the 'welfare and survival of the Swedish people'; the strength of 'German military hegemony over Sweden'; and making concessions only 'where they were essential'. Finally, 'neutrality was bent but not broken' and, throughout the war, 'national unity was paramount'.[38] Alternative views were apparent from the beginning. Churchill was especially critical of Sweden's relations with Germany, while being prepared to overlook similar concessions made in Switzerland's continued trade with the Germans. Kenney wrote in 1946: 'The Swedes who were most guilty of what was in effect a pro-German policy will soon be claiming that Swedish neutrality gave the Allies the victory!'[39] More recently, individual Swedes have challenged the usual orthodoxy; in 1991 Boëthius maintained that: 'One country that did not lift a finger to stop the Nazis' war and conquests was Sweden.'[40] The controversy will doubtless continue but 'small state realism' continues to provide a strong case. Gilmour's angle is that 'Sweden prudently looked after its own interests and spurned the tutelage of the self-interested and evidently untrustworthy combatants'.[41]

3. Eire

Ireland had been partitioned in 1922, with all except part of Ulster becoming independent as the Irish Free State (known as Eire from 1937 onwards). Technically it was still a dominion within the British Empire. Yet it was the only part of the empire not to join the war against the Axis powers. The Irish *Taoiseach* (prime minister), de Valera, announced in February 1939 that he was determined 'to preserve our neutrality in the event of war'.[42] This remained unchanged after the fall of the democracies in western Europe. In July 1940 he told the *New York Times* that 'We do not wish to become the base for attack by any power upon any other power. We do not have the slightest intention of abandoning our neutrality'.[43]

The most obvious reason for this decision was Ireland's weakness. By contrast with the other neutrals – Switzerland and Sweden – Ireland could not realistically have hoped to defend itself. Its army was limited to just under 7,500 regulars, clearly intended to maintain internal order. The air force consisted of four fighters and the navy of two patrol boats. Why, therefore, should Ireland make the ultimate sacrifice of its very existence by allying with Britain – especially since the struggle for independence from Britain was still very much within the national memory? Besides, there was still a complication over the future: the partition of Ireland meant that the six out of the nine counties of the historic province of Ulster remained in the United Kingdom. Fighting alongside Britain would involve an alliance which would, in turn, amount to the recognition of the separation of the north from the main part of Ireland. What could Ireland possibly add to Britain's struggle with Germany? The Royal Navy would safeguard the Atlantic approaches with or without Ireland's involvement and could, in the process, manage without a lease-back of the treaty ports of Cóbh, Castletown Bere and Lough Swilly (retained by Britain in 1921 but given up in 1938). Finally, it was clear in the early stages of the war that Hitler wanted to patch up the differences between Germany and Britain. If this did happen, Ireland's involvement would have been unnecessary as well as futile.

What kind of neutrality did Ireland pursue? For several reasons, it could never be absolute. Unlike Switzerland and Sweden, no special treaties were involved. Nor was there a commitment to any anti-British cause, as had often been demanded during the First World

War by radical republicans; all resistance to Britain had been ended by the compromise of the Irish Free State. The worst scenario would be the occupation of Ireland by Germany in the wake of a conquest of Britain. Not surprisingly, there was a clear preference for the survival of Britain and a return to the status quo. Hence Irish neutrality was often described as 'biased' towards Britain. There were practical examples of this. Information was passed on to Britain from Irish intelligence sources and there was some co-operation between Britain's MI5 and the Irish G2. Allied pilots crashing in Ireland were immediately released, while German pilots were interned for the rest of the war. Irish fire brigades were used to assist Belfast in the spring of a 1941 after German bombing raid. According to de Valera, 'any help we can give in the present time we will give them wholeheartedly, believing that were the circumstances reversed, they would also give us their help wholeheartedly'.[44] And, most striking of all, 124,500 men and 58,000 women went to join the workforce in Northern Ireland and Great Britain during the war and 38,500 volunteers joined the armed forces. Such concessions have been explained in two very different ways. George Bernard Shaw maintained that neutrality was a 'crack-brained idea', but that 'de Valera got away with it'.[45] A more positive view has been advanced by the historian J.P. Duggan: 'Through it all de Valera managed to give the Irish people the only type of neutrality that was attainable.'[46]

Internal reactions to neutrality showed a similar divergence of opinion. Most members of parliament and ministers within the government saw de Valera's approach as the only one possible. This applied also to part of public opinion; increasingly, however, public sympathy increased for the Allies, along with reservations about neutrality. This was reflected in – or led by – writers and the press. Samuel Beckett preferred France at war to Ireland at peace.[47] Writers like the novelist Frank O'Connor wrote in 1942 that Ireland was 'a non-entity state entirely divorced from the rest of the world'.[48] There was a sense of cultural isolation against which many emergent writers now fought: a war for the Irish mind seemed to parallel the controversy over neutrality in the political war. A small minority, however, wanted further distance from Britain, or even more active measures against it. Some were drawn to listen to the 'Germany calling' broadcasts of William Joyce (Lord Haw Haw) and there was a revival of IRA bombing campaigns in Britain.

External reactions tended to be strongly critical. Churchill complained of the 'so-called neutrality of so-called Eire'.[49] In particular, 'The fact that we cannot use the South and West coasts of Ireland to refuel our flotillas and aircraft, and thus protect the trade by which Ireland as well as Britain lives' was 'a most grievous burden and one which should never have been placed on our shoulders, broad though they be'.[50] During the latter stage of the war there were increased fears about security risks posed by Irish members of the British workforce, while travel was stopped between Britain and Ireland in March 1944. This was announced by Churchill in the House of Commons as 'the first step in a policy designed to isolate Great Britain from Southern Ireland and to isolate Southern Ireland from the outer world during the critical period which is now approaching'.[51] Once the war had ended, Churchill gave vent to his real feelings about Ireland. Criticizing Ireland's refusal to give the British access to airfield and ports, he added: 'This was indeed a deadly moment in our life, and if it had not been for the loyalty and friendship of Northern Ireland, we should have been forced to come to close quarters with Mr de Valera, or perish for ever from the earth.'[52] In contrast to Britain, the United States showed sympathy with Ireland's right to neutrality. There had been considerable historic support for Ireland's cause against Britain, strengthened, of course, by the considerable Irish presence in the United States. From the time of the American entry into the war, however, opinion shifted firmly in favour of Ireland contributing more to the war effort. The US government became especially critical of the number of foreign missions in Ireland, accusing Ireland of pursuing a neutrality that favoured the Axis powers. In February 1944 the US Ambassador to Ireland demanded 'the removal of these Axis representatives, whose presence in Ireland must inevitably be regarded as constituting a danger to the lives of American soldiers and to the success of Allied military operations'.[53] The Soviet reaction was the most critical of all. Foreign Minister Gromyko vetoed Ireland's accession to the United Nations in 1946 on the grounds that Ireland's relations with fascist regimes was 'hardly calculated to help her to admission' of that body.[54]

One of the advantages of neutrality was that the countries concerned had every reason to maintain a normally functioning democratic system. In most respects this applied as much to Eire as it did to Switzerland and Sweden. For example, a general election was held in 1944 at the height of the crisis in relations with the United States. De Valera was returned with an absolute majority for Fianna Fáil, ending the previous coalition government. This seemed to show the extent of public support for de Valera's policy towards the United States. On the other hand, his government imposed rigid censorship, even banning 'unneutral' comments about the war and the participants. By the Offences Against the State Act prisoners could be interned without trial, a measure aimed mainly against the IRA whom de Valera suspected of trying to drag Ireland into the war on the side of Germany. This action was, however, no more severe than measures taken during the period of civil war in the early 1920s.

Neutrality did not guarantee Ireland an absence from hardship. It is true that she did not suffer Britain's losses in the Blitz: any destruction was limited to strategic targets or accidental bombing, as was the case in Switzerland. The worst example was an attack on part of Dublin in May 1941 which killed thirty-four people and destroyed or wrecked 325 houses. There were also severe shortages, especially of white bread, grain, tea, coal, gas, paraffin, electricity and petrol. Fuel rationing had an impact on train and tram services which was at times more serious than in the United Kingdom. These problems continued into the post-war period, exacerbated by the wet summer of 1946 and the cold winter of 1946–7. Eire's recovery was only gradual, taking at least as long as in those democracies that had been involved in the war.

TWO DEMOCRACIES DEFIANT

Only two of the democracies that remained intact after June 1940 continued openly to defy the dictatorships that had come to dominate Europe. Yet Britain and Finland were never able to co-ordinate their efforts and, from 1941, were in constant danger of going to war against each other. This was because the dictatorship each engaged as an enemy was the partner of the other. Hence Finland collaborated with Germany against the Soviet Union which, in turn, was Britain's ally against Germany.

1. The United Kingdom

The United Kingdom of Great Britain and Northern Ireland had a mixed record of defending democracy in Europe in the ten years before the outbreak of war. Like most countries, it was more concerned with its own survival in a world of economic crisis and hostile political developments. This was complicated during the 1930s by a policy of appeasement. But a change occurred after 1939 with a greater determination to resist aggression and to provide leadership for others to do the same. Time was to show that Britain was to be better at defiance than she had been at persuasion which, by 1939, had come to be accepted as an inappropriate strategy for dealing with fascism and Nazism.

Looking back, from a post-war perspective, British democracy seemed strangely incomplete, a result of its gradual evolution without radical changes or written constitution. The franchise had developed more slowly than in many other European states. It was not until 1927 that all women over the age of twenty-one received the vote; only Switzerland left this later. Britain was also the only democracy in Europe not to adopt proportional representation. She had a bicameral parliamentary system which had become unbalanced because of the reduction of the powers of the House of Lords by the 1911 Parliament Act without any changes in the second chamber's composition. There was a smaller range of parties in parliament than anywhere else. A particular feature was the unprecedented domination of the political system by one party, the Conservatives, who amassed vast majorities in the 1918, 1931 and 1935 elections. This was due to the temporary inability of the electoral system to accommodate three large parties; as yet, Labour had not fully risen and the Liberals had not fully declined. Yet somehow British democracy found correctives for its own distortions, with Lib–Lab pacts producing Labour governments in 1924 and 1929–31, and a Labour leader, Ramsay MacDonald, heading a National Government dominated by Conservatives from 1931. It is true that the 1930s saw street violence between extremist groups (the Communists and Mosley's British Union of Fascists), described by MP Geoffrey Lloyd in 1934 as 'a deeply shocking scene for an Englishman to see in London'. Yet there was nothing at the end of the 1930s to indicate that Britain was in any danger of political revolution or of the drift towards dictatorship that had happened in large swathes of Europe. There were also extreme social problems, aggravated by the decline of Britain's staple industries, with a rise in unemployment and consequent poverty, squalor, dole queues and hunger marches. But the large majority of the population was unaffected by this misery, benefiting from Britain's new industries, consumer prosperity and diversions offered by the cinema.

Britain's role in Europe underwent two main periods between 1918 and 1945. The first has been characterized as one of moderation and constraint, with Collective Security in the 1920s and early 1930s followed by Appeasement from 1935. The second, between September 1939 and May 1945, was open defiance and a refusal to negotiate or compromise with the enemy.

Until 1939 British policy sent out mixed messages, although its intention was to avoid war while seeking to restrain likely aggressors. The dictatorships were, however, unreceptive, taking advantage of the diplomacy of moderate pressure and persuasion. Sanctions were applied only lightly to Italy after the invasion of Abyssinia in 1935, while the British-inspired Non-Intervention Committee actively discouraged help to Republican Spain, even while Italy and Germany were directly assisting Franco's Nationalists. Baldwin actually warned the French Prime Minister, Blum, that if France assisted the Spanish Republic and thereby provoked a war with Italy, Britain would not be involved on the side of France. There was no response from Baldwin to Germany's remilitarization of the Rhineland 1936 or from Chamberlain to the Anschluss March 1938. Appeasement reached a climax over the Sudeten crisis of September 1938, when the Munich Agreement signed away the Sudetenland to Germany. Chamberlain, it has been argued, lost the opportunity to stand up to Germany alongside France and the Soviet Union. The abandonment of appeasement through the guarantee to Poland came too late to prevent further aggression by Hitler who, in any case, went on to form the Nazi–Soviet Non-Aggression Pact. The Anglo-French position was therefore much weaker in September 1939 than it had been twelve months earlier.

Nevertheless, Britain's eventual contribution to the defeat of Italy and Germany cannot be overestimated. Admittedly the early period was profoundly discouraging, with the fall of France in June 1940 and the evacuation of all British troops from the continent. But Britain's survival between 1940 and 1941 prolonged the war long enough to ensure that Germany was crushed by other powers with much greater industrial strength. Britain kept the war going in the vital year between the fall of France in June 1940 and Hitler's invasion of Russia in June 1941. Thereafter Britain greatly assisted the war effort of the Soviet Union. Supremacy at sea ensured the supplies to Russia via the Arctic convoys to Murmansk, while Montgomery's campaign against Rommel in north Africa was a major distraction during Hitler's failing assault on the Soviet Union. In this respect, two turning points occurred at about the same time. More directly, Britain established a base for the United States. From 1943 joint bombing campaigns targeted German industries and cities, while Anglo-American operations saw the defeat of Rommel in North Africa, the invasion of Italy (1943), the Normandy landings (1944) and the subsequent campaigns on the western front. The British government was also directly responsible for co-ordinating the war effort with external powers, especially the United States, the Soviet Union and the countries of the British Empire and Commonwealth. It also linked up with resistance movements or governments in exile from Czechoslovakia, Norway, the Low Countries and France.

What impact did the war have on the style of democracy in Britain between 1939 and 1945? It has been suggested that Britain became a totalitarian state during the period of the war. This view should not, however, be pressed too far. The purpose of any measures taken was to mobilize a democratic system to fight a totalitarian one. It was a response to an emergency rather than an attempt to change the basis of normality: if anything it comes closer to the original Roman meaning of 'dictatorship' as a temporary set of emergency powers. Even here there were constraints and limits which, nevertheless, allowed an overall effectiveness in some ways greater than in Nazi Germany.

The governments of Chamberlain and Churchill exerted controls over the population much more quickly that had happened in the First World War. Conscription was introduced immediately in September 1939 by the National Service Act. By 1942 all men and women between eighteen and sixty could be called up for appropriate service: men between eighteen and forty were eligible for military service, while women were directed to the labour force, especially munitions. The Emergency Powers (Defence) Act, particularly Regulation 58A, empowered the Ministry of Labour to take whatever actions were needed. Government regulations also covered the *protection* of the civilian population as well as its *mobilization*. Arrangements were made for the evacuation of children from cities, for the construction of bomb-shelters and the enforcement of blackouts, and the rationing of essential commodities and some forms of food. Controls were imposed on freedom of expression by the Ministry of Information. Although the motive was to ensure security, the measures were often heavy-handed. The decision to close down the *Daily Worker* in January 1941 was criticized by other papers, including the *Daily Mirror*, while the poster campaign against loose talk lacked subtlety. According to George Orwell, 'the Government has done extraordinarily little to preserve morale; it has merely drawn on existing measures of goodwill'.[55] This was clearly not a system that was comfortable with exerting control over the way in which people thought or behaved.

Did political democracy disappear during the war years? It is true that compromises were made in the defeat of Hitler and that many normal democratic operations were suspended. For example, no general elections were held during the war in Europe, making the election of 1935 the last for ten years. This was the longest gap between general elections in Britain since the seventeenth century. Yet it was not intended as a measure *against* parliament; rather, it was an inter-party truce drawn up on 26 September 1939 not to 'nominate Candidates for the Parliamentary vacancies that now exist, or may occur, against the Candidate nominated by the Party holding the seat at the time of the vacancy occurring'.[56] This was enacted by regular amendments to the 1716 Septennial Act. It could be argued that the massive ten-year majority it gave the Conservatives was harmful to constitutional democracy. But there were mitigating factors. The parliamentary committee system partially offset the gravitation of power to the executive: an opposition front bench was elected by an administrative committee to monitor and question the activities of the government. In any case, MPs from other parties, like Attlee and Bevin, served in Churchill's coalition. Initially, the Conservatives held fifty-two ministerial posts in the coalition, to Labour's sixteen, a reflection of the relative strength of the parties in parliament at the time. By 1945 Labour's share had risen to twenty-seven. It was easier in wartime to pursue policies supported by both Labour and the Conservatives as the welfare of the population demanded that they sink their normal ideological differences for the sake of the common good. Nor did such arrangements have any permanent impact on democracy. Far from being damaged by the absence of a general election for ten years, Labour went on to win a landslide in 1945.

Economically, Britain managed to reach a peak of efficiency which eluded Germany – without resorting to the coercive measures and forced labour used by Nazi Germany and the Soviet Union. In 1943 armaments accounted for 55.3 per cent of all national expenditure, compared with 7.4 per cent in 1938.[57] Britain adapted more efficiently than Germany to abnormal economic pressures imposed between 1939 and 1945 – but without a totalitarian base. This is partly historic: Broadberry and Howlett argue that, despite its rapid industrial advance, Germany had 'a much smaller service sector, which failed to reap economies of specialization, and hence achieved lower productivity than its British counterpart'. Hence we should not be 'mesmerized by the success of Germany's rapid industrialization from the mid-nineteenth century on the basis of protectionism, state intervention, and universal banks. Britain's slower, more market-oriented development made for a more flexible economy which was better able to stand the strains of total war'.[58]

Britain's resilience and capacity for survival owed much to the leadership and the considerable popularity of Churchill himself. He was the only politician to inspire genuine support across party boundaries: this was shown by a vote of confidence in his leadership in July 1942, which he won by 476 votes to 25. Labour backed him in a way that had never been possible with Chamberlain. There have, admittedly, been questions about some of his decisions. Did he delay too long in opening up a second front in Western Europe, thereby handing the Soviet Union too much control in 1945 and condemning eastern Europe to nearly half a century of Soviet repression? The counter-argument is that his methods suited Britain's means. It took time to co-ordinate with Roosevelt the most effective strategy to deal with Germany. In any case, Churchill was more aware of the potential threat from Stalin in the future than Roosevelt. It is also apparent that Churchill's realism was accompanied by examples of ruthlessness. Giving preferential treatment to the defence of British airfields may have left London open to attack from the Luftwaffe – yet this helped win the Battle of Britain at the most crucial stage in the war. His strategy of saturation bombing against the civilian population of Germany has also been questioned – but at the time this was the most effective way of engaging in Total War against Germany. Above all, Churchill had the ability to inspire loyalty and trust on an unprecedented scale, making the most of the media of the time, whether on the radio or in reports of his famous war speeches in the House of Commons. Overall, he outperformed Britain's three other great wartime premiers – the Younger Pitt, Palmerston and Lloyd George, although his election defeat in 1945 showed that he, like Palmerston and Lloyd George, was most valued *as* a wartime leader.

The war's long-term political impact on Britain was surprisingly limited, leading to no immediate constitutional changes. The next amendment to the franchise did not take place until 1969, while the House of Lords had their delaying power further reduced in 1949 and their membership slightly altered by the introduction of life peers in 1959. None of these were due directly to the war. There was still no written constitution or bill of rights or an elected second chamber. Yet there were differences from the pre-war period. The main one was a reversion to a two-party system with the collapse of the Liberals in the 1945 general election. The next half-century saw alternating periods of party ascendancy (Labour 1945–51, 1963–70 and 1997–2010, the Conservatives 1951–63, 1970–4 and 1979–97). There were only two periods of stalemate: 1977–9 which involved an agreement between Labour and the Liberals, and 2010–15 which saw a coalition between the Conservatives and Liberal Democrats. Again, this pattern can in no way be attributed to the impact of the war. Despite being a major combatant, Britain experienced the sort of continuity which affected the neutral democracies (Sweden, Switzerland and Eire) which also experienced political refinements rather than the dramatic post-war changes of Czechoslovakia or France.

Of much greater importance was the social impact of the war, which highlighted changed perceptions of how the democratic process should be *used* rather than how it should actually operate. Most historians see the war as an accelerator of social change in Britain. Bruce, for example, argues that it was 'the decisive event in the evolution of the Welfare State . . . The war speeded changes and left a country markedly different and . . . markedly more humane and civilised than that of 1939'.[59] This was because the war had revealed the disparity in the standards of health care and provision, resulting in government measures to expand medical services, improve maternity care and provide free school meals, orange juice, milk and vitamins. The social landmark of the Second World War was the Beveridge Report, published in 1942. This identified the five major social deficiencies as 'giants': these were Want, Disease, Ignorance, Squalor and Idleness. The intention was to transform the pre-war system of Social Insurance, based on Want, into a new Social Security designed to cover all five. A series of measures followed in 1944, including White Papers on Health and Employment and a new Education Act. Churchill's coalition government therefore used the pressures of war – and the exceptional levels of political power these provided – to plan the types of social change that had eluded Britain after the First World War. The actual implementation of the new Welfare State was the work of Attlee's government after 1945 after the resumption of party politics and the Labour landslide.

The Second World War also exerted powerful economic pressures on Britain, although in the longer term these were generally more negative than the social changes. It has to be said, however, that the Second World War completed a process begun by the First. After 1914 Britain lost its position as the centre of international finance and trade; after 1939/45 Britain's economic strength contracted still further. British imports from the empire grew, while its exports dropped. The gap was filled by the transfer of British investments abroad, especially to India and Canada. Even more significant was the extent of Britain's debt to the United States – first through the lend-lease programme and then, when this was cancelled, through the loans raised by post-war governments. The full extent of the shrinkage of Britain's part in the international economy was not immediately recognized as successive governments tried to revive Britain's role in international finance. This meant restoring the sterling area, despite Britain's greatly reduced economic base. Such misplaced optimism, along with attempts to prolong Imperial commitments and retain world-power status, has been given as a reason for the relative slowness of Britain's post-war economic growth by comparison with the swifter recovery of Germany, Japan and France.

There are still debates about specific elements of Britain's involvement in the war: the excessively cautious diplomacy of appeasement, for example, or the sudden switch in policy from March 1939, or the delay in opening up a second front. But there is general consensus over the rightness of the decision to defy Nazi Germany.[60] There are also arguments as to whether eventual victory belonged more to the perseverance of Britain or to the might of the United States and the Soviet Union. But persisting with defiance – regardless of the likely outcome – kept the war open for others to join. And the reason for a democracy to do this had never been clearer. Churchill could have spoken for Britain when he said that he had 'only one single purpose – the destruction of Hitler' and that his life was 'much simplified thereby'.[61]

2. Finland

Finland had been ruled by Sweden until 1809, when she was transferred to Russia as a semi-autonomous Grand Duchy. She took the opportunity presented by Russia's defeat in the First World War – and revolution – to declare independence on 6 December 1917. A complex situation followed, which contained many of the seeds for conflict between 1939 and 1945. Civil war broke out between Finnish Reds, who aspired to a republic, and the Finnish Civil Guards (or Whites), who formed the government in Vyborg and were in favour of a monarchy. The Reds were armed by the Bolsheviks, while the Whites, under the military leadership of Mannerheim, were supported by the Germans. This struggle directly overlapped the last few months of the war on the eastern front between Revolutionary Russia and Imperial Germany – until this was ended in March 1918 by the Treaty of Brest-Litovsk imposed on Russia by the victorious Germans. The Finnish civil war ended in May 1918 in the victory of the Whites under Mannerheim. Friedrich Karl, Prince of Hessen, was invited in October to become King of Finland. This, however, was frustrated by the surrender of Germany to the western Allies in November; instead, Finland became a republic under President Stahlberg, and a new constitution was adopted.

This was based on a single-chamber parliament, the *Eduskunta*, originally established in 1906 and elected by universal suffrage based on proportional representation (Finland was actually the first country in Europe to enfranchise women). The basis for these changes had already been established while Finland was still a Grand Duchy within the Russian Empire, although the damage subsequently done by Tsar Nicholas II's policy of Russification meant that the whole process now had to be reinvented. After becoming independent Finland also developed a wide range of political parties including, within the mainstream, Social Democrats, Agrarian Union, Liberals, Conservatives and Swedish People's Party. On the far right was Lapua or the IKL (Patriotic People's Movement), which was influential during the1930s but in decline by the outbreak of war. It was strongly disliked by Mannerheim and other leaders in the struggle for independence. On the far left, the pro-Moscow Communists were more popular during the 1920s, with 11 to 12 per cent of the popular vote; they were, however, prohibited in 1930. Unfortunately, political harmony was disturbed by the periodic threat of renewed civil war between right and left. Part of the problem was the residual resentment of the leftists against the revenge taken against them by the Whites at the end of the civil war – some 10,000 Reds and their families died in camps through neglect. The re-engagement in earlier conflicts provided the background for Finland's future attitude to the Soviet Union and Germany.

It also had a direct influence on Finland's foreign policy. Here the ideal was neutrality, unencumbered by commitments to major powers – *if*, of course, this could actually be achieved. One possibility was closer co-operation, even unity, with other Nordic states. But this was prevented by internal disputes and external differences between Norway, Sweden and Finland. Instead, hopes rested on Germany and Russia imposing checks and restraints on each other. Given the choice between the two powers, most Finns still hoped for the weakening of Russia and for her isolation from the mainstream of European diplomacy. It is, therefore, hard to overestimate the shock caused in August 1939 by the announcement of the Nazi–Soviet Non-Aggression Pact. Finnish fears would have been intensified by the Secret Protocol allocating spheres of influence to Nazi Germany and Soviet Russia, the latter cleared to exert future control over eastern Poland, Estonia, Latvia – and Finland. The danger to Finland escalated when Hitler and Stalin began to claim their allocations by sending German and Soviet troops into Poland in September.

By October 1939, the Soviet Union was exerting heavy pressure on Finland. In its concern for the security of land and sea approaches to Leningrad, it demanded control over Hanko, some of south coast of Finland, and parts of Karelia – in total 2,761 square kilometres. In return, it offered some territorial compensation to the north of Lake Ladoga. When subsequent negotiations between Finland and Russia collapsed in November 1939, Stalin was encouraged by the success of Germany's Blitzkrieg in Poland to try the same against Finland – after accusing Finland of violating the border with artillery fire. Following the Soviet invasion on 30 November the Finnish government launched an unsuccessful search for outside help. It then approached League of Nations, which responded by expelling the Soviet Union from membership. Although completely outnumbered, the Finns put up a strong resistance and inflicted heavy losses on the Russians in what soon became known as the Winter War. In a radio broadcast on 20 January 1940 Churchill enthused: 'superb, nay sublime in the jaws of peril, Finland shows what free men can do. They have exposed, for all the world to see, the military incapacity of the Red Army.'[62] Yet, despite moral support from Britain, France and Sweden and the vague possibility of 100,000 Allied troops being sent to Finland, no military help was forthcoming. Finland eventually had to agree in March 1940 to the Peace of Moscow. Losses to Russia included the whole of the Karelian isthmus, the shores of northern half of Lake Ladoga, and territory along the Fenno-Soviet border in the north. But at least Finland had survived.

The experience of the Winter War gradually pushed Finland towards an understanding with Germany, culminating in 1941 in a commitment that stopped just short of an alliance. There were several reasons for this. One was the depth of hostility to the peace settlement. Government control over the press and radio had given the illusion of successful campaigns against Soviet forces and had failed to prepare the public for the extent of Finland's losses. There were also increasing suspicions of Soviet attempts to influence Finland's internal affairs through, for example, the election of a pliable president. Militarily the new frontier imposed by the Peace of Moscow made it more difficult for Finland to defend herself against a surprise attack in the future. And, of course, Finland was cut off from direct contact with the west in April 1940 by the German occupation of Norway and Denmark. At the same time, Russia was tightening her pressure on the southern shore of the Baltic by adding Lithuania to her sphere of influence. Finland therefore reacted positively to new approaches from Germany, including secret diplomacy suggesting future German support for Finland against Russia. Indeed, an agreement was drawn up later in 1940 to allow the provision of supply bases in Lapland. But the real breakthrough occurred with the German invasion of Russia in June 1941, followed by the Wehrmacht's rapid advance towards Moscow and the siege of Leningrad. Despite Mannerheim's reservations and evident distaste, there was growing political support for a deal with Germany and for closer connections with Nazis. It was at this point, according to Upton, that Finland 'made the error, which is usually fatal for small powers, of backing the loser in a great power conflict'. Yet, Upton adds, 'the choice which Finland made in 1941, however mistaken it turned out to be, was an entirely natural one in view of the historical background and the recent course of Finnish-Russian relations'.[63]

Hitler was eager to form a full military alliance with Finland. On 22 June 1941 he announced that 'In alliance with their Finnish comrades, the victors of Narvik stand on the shores of the Arctic Ocean.'[64] Finland took the opportunity to win back some of the losses of the Winter War. But it had a different understanding of the 'Continuation War' that now followed. Whereas Hitler saw the association between Germany and Finland as an 'alliance' and 'brotherhood', the Finnish government preferred the concept of 'side-by-side' involvement against Russia – but neutrality in any broader conflict. It had not been anxious to re-engage Russia and had reacted to specifically to Soviet air attacks. From the outset it tried to avoid any impression of any alliance with Germany and never agreed to any such commitment being drawn up. Finland was also reluctant to become involved in the German siege of Leningrad because of the importance attached by Russia to the city. Instead, Mannerheim pursued more limited objectives in recovering Karelian losses in the Winter War. With the entry of the United States into the war, it was also crucial to maintain good relations with the west.

Ultimately, the gradual ascendancy of the Allies forced Finland into a change of attitude to Germany. In theory, Finland was at war with Britain from the end of 1941, although there was no direct military engagement: this was partly because the United States had no desire to open up a front in the eastern Baltic. As Germany looked increasingly likely to lose the war, Finland sought possible ways to disengage – but without suffering too many losses to the Soviet Union. Eventually Mannerheim, who had replaced Ryti as President, agreed in September 1944 to an Armistice, by which Finland would return to its 1940 frontiers and pay an indemnity to the Soviet Union of $300 million. It was also to disarm and drive out all German forces still in Finland. This task took until April 1945 to accomplish and involved extensive destruction in Lapland.

Finland's losses had been extensive, including 11 per cent of its area. Some 85,000 people had died during the Continuation War, about 2 per cent of Finland's total population (although this compared with wartime losses of 10 per cent of Germany's population and 12 per cent of the Soviet Union's). Unlike other states in eastern Europe, Finland managed to retain her previous democratic system and to avoid being converted into a Soviet satellite (although for four decades she remained under Soviet influence).

The United Kingdom vs Finland?

The attitudes of Britain towards Finland underwent a change during the period in which the two countries were involved in their respective wars against each other's fellow-combatants.

In the earliest stage, the Winter War (1939–40), there was clear sympathy within the United Kingdom for the Finns, but with a sense of frustrated helplessness. Any real possibility of help was prevented by the refusal of Sweden to allow transit for Allied troops, although it is by no means clear that this would actually have happened. Britain's priorities in the

Baltic area were the Norwegian coast, access to the Skagerrak and reducing Sweden's iron-ore provision to Germany. Besides, if Britain and France had not been able to give military assistance to Poland after September 1939, how could they hope to assist Finland three months later? There was also an important technicality. Neither Britain nor France had declared war on Russia in September 1939, even though Russia had also invaded Poland. How could it have made sense for Britain to antagonize Russia at this point and quite probably convert the Nazi–Soviet Non-Aggression Pact into a formal military alliance between Russia and Germany?

The situation changed in June 1941. Following Hitler's invasion of Russia, Britain and Finland were driven further apart. This was because Stalin, Churchill's new ally against Hitler, was Finland's enemy. How, therefore, could Britain now support Finland? Similarly, what could Finland now expect from Britain when there were links to be had with Germany instead? All Britain could do was to hope that Sweden would limit the transit possibilities for German troops to Finland and make it as difficult for the Germans as it had done earlier for the Allies. Churchill's overriding emphasis had always been to get the Soviet Union involved against Germany. Having secured Britain's first ally since the fall of France in June 1940, what sense would it have made to assist the Finns in their Continuation War against Russia?

There is, of course, still a question as to whether Finland *should* have sided with Germany. The immediate answer is probably not, considering the particularly odious nature of that dictatorship and the opportunism used by Finland to recover territory from a war already settled. On the other hand, there had been clear Soviet provocation since the Peace of Moscow, which enticed the Finnish government to look towards Germany, despite earlier reservations. There now appeared to be an opportunity to re-establish Finland's security, whatever compromise might be needed. Was this really so different to Britain's position? Churchill's greatness as a war leader was at least partly the result of *his* opportunism, timing and, if necessary, ruthlessness. His alliance with the Soviet Union represented a major shift of opinion: after all, he had once tried to persuade Lloyd George's coalition government (1918–22) to upgrade British support for anti-Bolshevik forces in revolutionary Russia. Ultimately it was a choice between two evils, the lesser of which was Stalin and Communism. Churchill expressed his justification for this in parliament: 'if Hitler invaded Hell, I would at least make a favourable reference to the Devil in the House of Commons.'[65] For the Finns, on the other hand, the threat of Russia was greater than that of Germany. In both cases, therefore, national survival was at stake.

But were Finnish expectations realistic? Could Finland really have hoped for long-term success in another war with Russia? Perhaps not, but the alternative was to accept the likelihood of German hegemony in the future without an accompanying advantage of Finnish security against Russia. It is true that this future did not materialize and that the eventual defeat of Germany undermined Finland's security for a generation, pulling it within its enemy's orbit of influence. Finland's policy was therefore a risk, undertaken in 1941, which had completely failed by 1945. Yet did this not have parallels with the risk taken by Britain in 1940 in keeping the war open against all apparent odds – and again, in backing the Soviet Union even despite the latter's reverses after June 1941? If anything, when these decisions were made, Britain's risk was the greater since its enemy, Germany, seemed to be in the ascendant, while Finland's decision was taken against a foe apparently on the wane.

Britain and Finland both behaved ambivalently in their relations with each other's opponent. In September and October 1941 the Soviet Union tried to persuade Britain to declare war on Finland. Churchill, however, refused on the grounds that this would force Finland into an alliance with Germany; at the same time, he urged Finland to limit her recent advances to restoring the 1939 frontier. Then, in November, he issued an ultimatum that Finland must cease hostilities against Russia immediately. When Finland demanded further time to complete the recovery of areas lost in the Winter War, Britain declared war in December 1941 – although Churchill never implemented this in practice. The United States made no such declaration and maintained diplomatic relations with Finland until 1944.

Finland also played an opportunist role. While making the most of German assistance in the Continuation War, she was unwilling to enter into a formal and irrevocable alliance. The test came in April 1944 when the Soviet Union demanded terms and Finland was assailed by a counter demand by Germany for just such an alliance. Finland's elder statesman and military leader, Mannerheim, suggested that President Ryti should give a personal guarantee to Germany on Finland's behalf, in the process avoiding any obligation by the Finnish Parliament to a formal pact. For a while this was successful and Germany continued to provide essential supplies to the Finns. By September, however, Germany had been significantly weakened and the Soviet demands on Finland became more insistent. In September Mannerheim, who had by now been sworn in by parliament as president, wrote to Hitler breaking off relations with Germany. He also prepared the way to ending the war with the Soviet Union and joining the Allies by agreeing to clear Finland of German troops.

Throughout the war period, there had been strong evidence of mutual sympathies between Finland and Britain – more so than between either and Sweden. Ultimately, however, what counted was their strategic position and opportunities for allies. Hard realities separated them, placing them on opposing sides. Britain was one of the victors against Germany – but only in alliance with the Soviet Union. The latter had also defeated Finland and brought it within its orbit of control at the end of the war. The distance between Britain and Finland remained as the outcome of the war prevented full reconciliation for nearly half a century. The Cold War from 1947 involved Britain and the Soviet Union in opposing camps – at least until 1989. While this lasted Finland remained, as far as Britain was concerned, in a twilight area, neither fully a part of the Soviet zone nor free to disengage from Soviet influence. This ambivalence was itself suspect to the west, which feared the possibility of 'Finlandization' in non-Communist Europe. The key events in changing this were the collapse of Communism and the Soviet Union in 1991 and the eventual accession of Finland to the European Union.

Chapter 9

Dictatorships compared

THE ROLE OF IDEOLOGY

The term 'ideology' is normally understood to mean an organized set of ideas and ideals intended to deal with problems and, perhaps, to institute sweeping change. The totalitarian ideologies had in common a desire to destroy the existing system and to recreate it according to an ideal form often called a Utopia. In fact, Friedrich and Brzezinski believe that 'totalitarian ideologies are typically Utopian in nature'.[1] Authoritarian regimes, by contrast, were usually unable to produce a distinctive ideology. Although they often aimed to change the existing political system, they were much more prepared to adapt to more traditional influences and ideas. Hence, they tended to be backward looking, even reactionary, in contrast to the revolutionary nature of totalitarian ideologies.

It is usual to categorize three inter-war ideologies as potentially totalitarian: Marxism–Leninism, Nazism and Fascism (see Chapter 2). Of these, Marxism–Leninism was the most coherent, based on a systematic doctrine derived from the ideas of Hegel, Marx and Engels, as redefined by Lenin and Stalin. It incorporated an economic theory (economic determinism), a series of historical laws (dialectical materialism) and a belief in eventual progress towards a higher form of human organization called the 'classless society'. Fascism and Nazism owed to nineteenth-century writers like Nietzsche, Gobineau and H.S. Chamberlain such concepts as racial inequality and the inevitability of struggle. But neither possessed the disciplined structure of Marxism–Leninism, partly because, in the words of Bracher, neither had 'the kind of classic bible that Marxism possessed'.[2] Hitler's ideas, for example, were expounded very loosely in *Mein Kampf*, which was little more than an autobiography, while Mussolini's most explicit doctrinal statement was confined to an article in *Enciclopedia Italiana*. Neither of these sources had the coherence and weight of Marx's *Das Kapital* or Lenin's *The State and Revolution*. Bracher goes so far as to call Nazism 'an eclectic "ragbag" ideology, drawn from a multitude of sources'.[3]

As for the lesser dictators, few even attempted a systematic statement of beliefs beyond a simple reformulation of traditional ideas. This applied to all authoritarian leaders, whether military men like Franco and Piłsudski or academics like Salazar. Some of the more radical, potentially totalitarian dictators, who came to power as Nazi puppets during the Second World War, did have a go at organizing their thoughts. A typical example was Szálasi of Hungary; but, as Weber points out, Szálasi's writing is unsystematic and 'steadfastly ignores grammar, style and sense'.[4] Marxism–Leninism, Nazism and Fascism had in common the desire to transform the previous system through revolution. All three involved the manipulation of history and the movement towards an ideal. There were, however, major differences in the nature of that ideal. The Marxist Utopia involved two distinct phases. The first was the 'dictatorship of the proletariat', which was intended to eliminate all obstacles to achieving the second, and very different, phase: the 'classless society'. Force and struggle were therefore a means to an end. This end was fundamentally different in that it would see the decline of organized coercion and the conclusion of the 'prehistoric phase' of human existence. According to Engels, there would be 'a leap from slavery into freedom; from darkness into light'.[5] In complete contrast Nazi and fascist utopias envisaged one state only – uninterrupted and unending movement towards total domination and power. Fascism has been described as a 'national-imperial mission ideology' which made a 'powerful state the highest value'.[6] This process, the opposite to the 'classless society', is sometimes called 'etatism'. It also involved the perpetual glorification of war and struggle for, in Mussolini's words, 'war is to the man what maternity is to the woman'.[7] Nazism also focused on struggle, although the vehicle was race rather than the state, Aryanism rather than etatism. According to Hitler, 'All of nature is one great struggle between strength and weakness, an eternal victory of the strong over the weak.'[8] The victims were to be the race enemies, for 'All eugenic progress can begin only by eliminating the inferior.' These ideas were to be sublimated in the most horrifying way in the gas chambers of Auschwitz-Birkenau.

Elsewhere the purpose of ideology was less to transform than to revive. It was therefore less forward-looking and more traditional, even nostalgic. History was regarded less as a transition to a higher phase, more as providing examples for imitation. The clearest example of this was Salazar's stress on 'Deus, Patria, Familia' ('God, Country, Family') and on the historic role of Portuguese imperialism 'to defend western and Christian civilisation'.[9] Franco, in turn, aimed quite consciously at reviving the virtues of the historic Spain destroyed, he considered, by the Second Republic; he regarded himself therefore as the political reincarnation of Philip II. Even the more radical 'Hungarism' of Szálasi and the 'Hellenism' of Metaxas were essentially glorifications of national pasts. In other states presidential or royal absolutism lacked any systematic ideas and based itself on pragmatic common sense and an appeal to patriotism.

Which of the main ideologies proved to be of the most practical use? Marxism–Leninism certainly appears the most elusive in its ultimate aim: the 'classless society' and the 'withering away' of the state could occur only after profound change in human nature. Nazism and fascism, by contrast, intended to exploit and accentuate the most basic human instincts – the struggles for survival and domination. And yet events proved Marxism–Leninism a more efficient tool than either fascism or Nazism for transforming society, the economy and political institutions. The reason was that the practical application of Marxism–Leninism by Stalin stopped well short of the ultimate ideal of the 'classless society' and concentrated on the organization and coercion necessary for the phase of the 'dictatorship of the proletariat'. Fascism and Nazism lacked the capacity for complete institutional reorganization and for the mobilization of the economy for Total War, even though the latter featured so strongly in their scheme. On balance, therefore, Stalin had at his disposal a more adaptable ideological weapon than had either Hitler or Mussolini.

The fate of the minor Fascisms and Communisms

Even allowing for the differences in the use and meaning of ideology in various parts of Europe, two things are still clear. First, the three regimes of Italy under Mussolini, Germany under Hitler, and Russia under Lenin and Stalin initially developed ideological systems for their *own* countries. Second, they went on to impose their ideologies on most of Europe in their subsequent expansionist drive. Included among their conquests were the lesser dictatorships and then the democracies that had managed to survive their own internal ideological challenges; these all dealt with in Chapters 7 and 8. An issue that now needs to be considered is whether the systems that followed their conquest were in any sense the fulfilment of a logical movement these countries were already showing towards either fascism or communism, or whether the changes were entirely due to external pressures and ultimate control, especially by Germany and Russia.

In the lesser dictatorships it tended to be the latter. The natural trend there had been to an authoritarian-conservative system based on a variety of influences. One of these may have been fascism – but in a diluted form which fell far short of dominating the regime itself. This applied to Austria, Poland, the Baltic States, Albania, Yugoslavia, Greece, Bulgaria and Romania. Those dictatorships which, like Spain and Portugal, remained neutral in 1939 and therefore undefeated in the Second World War, showed no later inclination to strengthen the grip of fascism over the other components of their regimes. There is a strong possibility that the same might have applied to the dictatorships in central and eastern Europe – but for the upheaval of war. In almost all cases fascist movements were minority groups, often strongly suspected by the regimes they aimed to control. What thrust the minority groups into positions of power was external wartime occupation or domination. In the dictatorships where it had previously been controlled, fascism suddenly became the key influence in German-occupied states, albeit with a strong Nazi twist. The one possible case where indigenous fascism did break through was in Yugoslavia; even here, however, Italian and German control were crucial in breaking the state power that was still resisting the Ustasha by 1939.

In the democracies that still existed before the outbreak of war, there was certainly a far-right presence, especially in France, Belgium, the Netherlands, Britain and the Nordic countries. Some, parties, like the DNSAP in Denmark, the *Nasjonal Samling* (NS) in Norway or the *Nationaal-Socialistische Beweging* in the Netherlands, were Nazi and racist as much as they were fascist and corporativist. Others, like the British Union of Fascists (BUP) inclined more to Italian patterns. All had attachments of paramilitary groups and street fighters. But they also had in common a poor electoral performance during the 1930s: the DNSAP, for example, achieved only 1.8 per cent of the Denmark's popular vote in 1939. Even the Depression did not make much of a difference to their political credibility. The elevation of the far right was in all cases the result of Nazi invasion and Germany's attempt to rule with the sympathetic political elements that were suddenly given a share of power. This was particularly the case in the Low Countries and Scandinavia (see Chapter 8). This was not, however, permanently successful and in almost all cases the Germans had had to resort to direct rule by 1942 and 1943. By 1944 and 1945 indigenous fascism was targeted by growing resistance from internal movements co-operating with the Allies for the removal of German rule and for the restoration of democracy. The domestic far right therefore became a casualty of the military defeat of the external occupier.

Turning to the far left: to what extent was communism the development of internal trends, and to what extent the result of external intervention? Early examples seem to show ideological and organizational influences from Soviet Russia and the International, rather than any direct imposition by military force. This applied in 1918–19 to the brief activities of the Spartacists in Germany, of the communists in the Po Valley in Italy, and, of course the brief revolution of Béla Kun in Hungary. Thereafter, however, communist movements were dealt a severe blow in all those states that became dictatorships, being banned by the regimes of much of central and eastern Europe. They were tolerated in most of the democracies (with the exception of Finland) but they did not prosper in terms of public support; in many cases, their electoral performance was no more successful than that of the far right. If fascism did not have the strength outside Italy and Germany to elevate itself to power, the same was even more the case with communism beyond Russia. The outbreak of war made matters worse, as the occupied dictatorships experienced a more efficient Nazi purge on remaining communist influences, while all communist parties were banned in the occupied democracies. The only exception was the Baltic States, where the Soviet occupation in 1939–41 revived communist groups which, however, were promptly expunged by the Nazi invasion of 1941.

Major changes began to occur from 1944 onwards. Fascist groups went into decline, reflecting the collapse of most of Fascist Italy and the expected defeat of Nazi Germany, while communist groups revived rapidly. A key factor in this was certainly the influence of the Soviet Union, as the Red Army drove the Germans out of central and eastern Europe and Stalin imposed tight ideological controls over the countries he occupied. But there was also an internal development, which did not apply to fascist groups. Communism was reborn in the resistance to German and Italian rule. Examples occurred all over occupied Europe, from France to Poland, Romania, Greece, Albania and, above all, Yugoslavia. Yet most new communist *regimes* (with the exceptions of Yugoslavia and Albania) came into being in a way defined by the Soviet Union, at first as coalitions with other parties of the left, then under a tightened monolithic political system. The regimes that emerged in eastern Europe from 1948 were very much on the totalitarian pattern than were the more chaotic fascist regimes operating under Nazi tutelage during the war.

LEADERSHIP

Of the three types of leadership categorized by Max Weber – traditional, rational-legal and charismatic – two are particularly appropriate for the period 1918–45. The totalitarian states were a prime example of charismatic leadership, while the authoritarian regimes had a more traditional style. Yet there were differences within the categories and examples of crossovers between them.

All the dictatorships covered by this book depended upon the leadership of a single commanding figure. In some cases these were surrounded by a leadership cult, defined by Rees as 'an established system of veneration of a political leader, to which all members of the society are expected to subscribe, a system that is omnipresent and ubiquitous and one that is expected to persist indefinitely'. It is 'a deliberately constructed and managed mechanism' which aims at 'the integration of the political system around the leader's persona'.[10] It can also offer 'salvation' in return for 'veneration', while the mystique is one of the key strengths of the ideology behind it. Hence it is not surprising that references have been made to 'secular religions' or the 'sacralization of politics'.

In Russia, the Lenin cult was largely posthumous, created by the Party Central Committee. The Stalin cult originated by association with Lenin, then from 1929 assumed its own persona as well as he became the chief (*vozhd*). This, in turn, was part of the broader cult infused into the Soviet system – comprising the ideology, the revolution, the party and the state. At first the cult of Stalin was subordinate to that of Lenin. Then the revolution was Sovietized and Stalin represented the next dynamic stage becoming, in the process, the 'great educator'. In theory Stalin was subject to collective leadership and the ideology of communism was supposed to prevent any excessive accumulation of personal power. In practice he elevated his authority to heights which were unprecedented even in a country with an almost uninterrupted history of autocracy. At the same time, his actual power was sometimes constrained by the problem of enforcing his orders in the localities.

The situation in Germany was somewhat different. Whereas the Stalin cult was an addition to the Soviet one, the Führer cult embodied the whole Nazi structure. Unlike Stalin, Hitler did not owe his status to any predecessor – ideological or revolutionary. He was able to present himself as the originator of that ideology and revolution, not as their best consolidator and successor. Hitler's public appearances also differed from those of Stalin. He presided over mass processions and rallies and his speeches were more forceful and less reasoned than Stalin's, whose delivery was slow and considered. In theory Hitler was in total command, with no conceivable constraints. According to Broszat,

> Hitler's power as Führer exceeded that of any monarch. The notion of 'divine right' was replaced by the claim that the Führer was the saviour appointed by Providence and at the same time the embodiment and medium of the unarticulated will of the people.[11]

In practice, however, Hitler *was* frequently isolated at the pinnacle of the party and state apparatus.

In Italy, the cult of the Duce was different again. It was certainly not based on the 'best successor' approach: like Hitler, Mussolini had no predecessor or line of acknowledged ideological forebears. But, unlike Hitler, he did not bring a dynamic and cohesive ideology, even though he tried to reconcile the conflicting strands of Fascism and to select moments for dynamic action. His cult therefore existed as a separate entity which overlapped into Fascism. His main strength was as a populist demagogue. Although he had a greater flair for oratory than Hitler, he lacked the latter's mystique. Mussolini's power was never as strong as Hitler's, even in theory. He remained, officially, the appointee of Victor Emmanuel and it was to the King, not to the Duce, that the army and state officials owed their ultimate allegiance.

The 'authoritarian' states also depended on the strong-man image, although any 'cults' existed at a lower level than in Russia, Germany or Italy. Spanish leaders liked the imagery of the 'sentinel', while Franco was also known as *Caudillo*. The basis behind his authority was certainly traditional and yet it overlapped at times into the charismatic. He was, for example, careful to claim victory in the Spanish Civil War as inspired by God and he received the plaudits of the establishment, especially of the Church. In the victory celebrations he was surrounded by 'the dual imagery of the victorious general and the holy saviour'.[12] Although more open to public appearance than Piłsudski or Salazar, on most occasions Franco never managed to transcend a rather dour image. In terms of appeal and performance on the balcony he was no Mussolini – and never aspired to be. In Portugal, Salazar was even more aloof and retiring: his was not the sort of personality that would want a cult let alone benefit from one. He was willing to leave ritual to other components of the system, especially to the Catholic Church, as befitted one whose beliefs were strongly influenced by the ideas of St Thomas Aquinas.

In Poland, Piłsudski's popularity assumed cultic proportions after his defeat of the Red Army at Warsaw in 1921. But this was not something that he deliberately fostered and he had no wish to assume a populist form of dictatorship. If anything, his cult increased after his death in 1935, partly to legitimize the regime of less popular successors like Rydz-Smigly and Beck. It could be argued, therefore, that Piłsudski had a personality cult 'thrust upon him'. None of the other 'leaders' (which included Smetona as *Tautos Vadas* and Metaxas as *Archigos*) found it necessary to develop the sort of cult which played so important a part in the totalitarian states. This was because they aimed to quieten the population, not to rouse it; this could be more successfully accomplished by a more remote type of authority. Much the same applied to the monarchs of the period. King Alexander of Yugoslavia, Carol of Romania and Boris of Bulgaria were all traditionalist in their outlook, preferring the deference which went with their office to adulation based on radical ideas or promises. A possible exception to this was King Zog of Albania, who sought to project himself as a unifier after a period of civil war.

There was one special case. Mustafa Kemal was the creator neither of a totalitarian regime nor of a new ideology: he was neither communist nor fascist. Yet he did have a cult of leadership which transcended anything seen in Europe outside Italy, Germany or Russia. He was known as 'saviour' and 'teacher', as *Büyük Önder* (Great Leader) and *Atatürk* (Father of the Turks). There were, however, good reasons for this. He committed himself personally to a radical programme of modernization which involved breaking with tradition and replacing inertia with dynamism. Atatürk personified this approach – but not to the extent that he represented an ideology. Hence it would not be appropriate to compare him with Lenin or Mussolini – as some have tried to do.

Under Stalin a few smaller cults were allowed to develop around subordinate figures at different levels. A similar pattern developed in eastern Europe after 1945. The power vacuums in the former authoritarian regimes were filled by new leaders in the Stalinist mould. The strongest cults over the next few decades attached to Tito in Yugoslavia and Hoxha in Albania (both of whom managed to separate themselves from Soviet tutelage). Others who made some attempt to elevate themselves to similar status were Gheorghiu-Dej and Ceauşescu in Romania, Bierut and Gomulka in Poland, Ulbricht in East Germany and Gottwald in Czechoslovakia. Although their cults were artificial and varied in their success, they reached proportions to which their predecessors either could not manage or did not want.

STATE, PARTY AND ARMY

The leaders we have just examined presided over a wide variety of political systems, with contrasting approaches to institutional change, party influence and military presence.

In the totalitarian regimes some effort was made to transform the political establishment, although the leadership went about it in different ways. Russia saw the most extensive changes, which involved the eradication of Tsarist institutions. The three constitutions of the period (1918, 1922 and 1936) provided for a system of soviets, dominated at all stages by the Communist Party. This was able to exercise total control through its Central Committee, which, in turn, was subdivided into the Orgburo, Politburo and Control Commission. The Nazi leadership also sought political change, although in practice it stopped short of the sort of transformation seen in the Soviet Union. Instead of sweeping away the old system altogether, Hitler carried out some drastic surgery on it; for example, he perpetuated the emergency powers of the executive by means of the Enabling Act and, by merging the presidency and chancellorship, destroyed the checks and balances within the constitution. The key changes came at the centre with the new Chancellery and special deputies, although these tended to overlap and conflict with more traditional officials and agencies. Mussolini's Italy followed the German rather than the Soviet pattern. The effect, however, was still less complete; the superstructure of the monarchy remained intact and was eventually to become the focal point of opposition to the regime. There was also a more chaotic replacement of some traditional institutions like the Chamber of Deputies by the Chamber of Fasces and Corporations and the superimposition of other components of the Corporate State.

Elsewhere the dictators were less ambitious. One of the characteristics of authoritarian regimes was to stabilize and restore rather than transform, even though constitutional amendments were often involved. Examples of the emphasis on tradition and order can be seen in Salazar's *Estado Novo* (1935) and in the constitutions in the various Balkan states which granted increased powers to their respective monarchs. In Yugoslavia King Alexander suspended the 1921 constitution, replacing it in 1931 with one which severely curtailed the democratic process. New and similarly restrictive arrangements were introduced in Bulgaria by King Boris (1937) and in Romania by King Carol the following year.

What importance did the dictators attach to a party base and to radicalizing the masses? Again, the approach in the totalitarian states varied. Russia used the 'vanguard' method, by which the Communist Party dominated the entire system. Rather than attempting to generate mass involvement, it operated through the principle of 'democratic centralism', whereby a small elite acted on behalf of the whole population. Membership of the Communist Party was strictly limited and, during the 1930s, Stalin was able, through his purges, to reduce this further. The Party also provided the channels of control between the centre and the different republics of the USSR, in effect cancelling out the principles of national self-determination accorded to the nationalities by the 1922 and 1936 constitutions. Although Stalin reduced the role of the party in the process of decision making, especially during the period of war, he was never able to replace it. During the destalinization campaign under Khrushchev, the party – not Stalin – was given the official credit for the changes made between 1929 and 1953.

The Nazi and Italian Fascist parties possessed more genuine mass bases, which did much to radicalize politics and promote right-wing revolutionary fervour. But penetration by the parties of state institutions was less complete than in Russia. In Germany different layers of personnel were allowed to develop, some based on traditional offices, others created for new party functionaries. Even though they were all theoretically within and under the Nazi Party, there were a great many overlapping and conflicting jurisdictions. In Italy the situation was more paradoxical. On the one hand, more effort was made to integrate party organs into the centre of the government system – with, for example, the Fascist Grand Council and the Chamber of Fasces and Corporations. On the other hand, institutions based on the party did not guarantee party unity or the security of the leadership – as Mussolini was to discover to his cost when a majority of the Grand Council demanded his dismissal in 1943.

Elsewhere the development of a one-party system was intended to neutralize, defuse and depoliticize rather than to create a resurgent mass. This, for example, was the motive behind Salazar's National Union (UN). This did 'not pursue a popular, mass basis'.[13] Salazar said that 'We need neither fawn on the working class to get their backing nor provoke their ire only to have them later shot for their excesses'.[14] Similarly, Rivera's Unión Patriótica (UP) was intended to replace competition between parties for the mass vote. Parties were banned altogether in Bulgaria in 1935, elections being conducted without their participation in 1937. In Romania, the 1938 Constitution replaced the multi-party system with a single Front of National Rebirth.

Some authoritarian regimes remained multi-party states but instituted heavy controls or promoted overriding blocs or fronts. In Austria, for example, Dollfuss developed the Fatherland Front and in Spain Franco formed a broad alliance in the National Front before banning the multiple-party system at the end of the Civil War. In theory, Piłsudski's coalition Sanacja, and Rydz Śmigły's Camp of National Unity (OZON), existed alongside other parties but some of these met with indifference from the electorate, over half of which boycotted the elections of 1935. Finally, Zog proclaimed a multi-party system in his 1928 Constitution but made sure that it was curtailed by unofficial measures and corruption.

Political power, especially in closed systems, is sometimes associated with the military – in the process either of its attainment or its retention. Between the wars this was more the case with authoritarian than with totalitarian regimes.

Direct military intervention by the army was not involved in the rise of the three major regimes. In Russia the Red Army evolved out of the Red Guard, a paramilitary group which seized power in October 1917. In Germany Hitler actually prevented the takeover of the army by the SA, while in Italy the armed forces remained under the command of the King. In a number of other states the army did exert a direct influence. In Turkey, for example, Mustafa Kemal came to power in 1922 as the direct result of a military coup, as did Primo de Rivera in 1923 and Franco from 1936. Piłsudski used the army to seize power in Poland in 1926, as did Smetona in Lithuania. In some case a military coup provided the opportunity for future changes carried out by others. In Portugal the military coup of General Gomes da Costa in 1926 cleared the way eventually for the rise of Salazar. Similarly, the coup of Colonel Velchev in Bulgaria in 1934 was utilized by Boris to establish a royal dictatorship in 1935 and the Kondyles revolt in Greece in 1935 prepared the ground for General Metaxas from 1935.

Irrespective of how it had come to power, no dictatorship could have survived without the support of the army. There was, however, a contrast between those regimes which tried to absorb the military and those which allowed the army to remain as an independent and privileged institution. The most complete transformation was achieved in Russia. The Bolshevik regime built an entirely new army and subordinated it to the Communist Party by means of commissars; under Stalin these were known as *zampolits* (deputy commanders for political affairs). At the head of the whole system was the GPUVS or the Main Political Administration of the Soviet Armed Forces. In Germany control over the army was accomplished more gradually. Hitler had to earn its support in 1934 in the Night of the Long Knives but, by 1938, felt sufficiently confident to reorganize the High Command. He subsequently used the Waffen SS to politicize the army and infuse it with Nazi ideology. Italy, never a good example of a totalitarian state, did not experience a comparable process. Mussolini, in fact, claimed that he did 'not intend to use the army as a political arm'. He also failed to produce an equivalent to the Waffen SS, which meant that there was nothing to prevent the officers from taking part in a plot to depose him in 1943. Elsewhere the army achieved or retained a high status. In Portugal it had a special relationship with Salazar, until, that is, it was destabilized by the experience of the African wars. In Spain it was directly elevated and protected by Franco, who was, of course, the Commander-in-Chief. The same applied in Poland, although Piłsudski was less able than Franco to adjust to a civilian role. These and other leaders did whatever was necessary to prevent the penetration of the armed forces by radical right-wing groups, realizing that a disaffected officer corps could engineer a military coup and thereby imperil the whole regime.

SOCIAL CONTROL

The individual exists within a society; the society is contained within a state. An important characteristic of a totalitarian state is that it aims to subordinate both the individual and society. According to Buchheim, 'Totalitarian rule attempts to encompass the whole person, the substance and spontaneity of his existence, including his conscience.'[15] In Russia, both Lenin and Stalin intended to create a 'new type of man', the purpose of society being to impart to him the new political values and culture as directed by the state. There was a similar emphasis, in both Germany and Italy, on a radical change of attitudes and beliefs. In the smaller states there was no place for social transformation. The intention, instead, was to restore the traditional social balance. One example was Salazar's Portugal, of which Bruce writes, 'the state was never to swallow up the groups – hence it was never to be "totalitarian" – it was simply to act as the co-ordinating agent of these groups'.[16] In Spain, Franco's regime, according to Payne, followed the 'intolerant, ultra-Catholic norms of Spanish history',[17] while the main influence on Piłsudski's Sanacja was Polish civic virtue, based very much on social tradition.

How completely did the totalitarian regimes reach the individual? One of the most important methods used was propaganda. According to Friedrich and Brzezinski, 'The nearly complete monopoly of mass communication is generally agreed to be one of the most striking characteristics of totalitarian dictatorship.'[18] Each state had its own means of achieving this monopoly. Within the Soviet Union state ownership prevailed, in contrast to private ownership under state licence, as sometimes existed in Italy and Germany. The Nazi and Fascist systems placed greater emphasis than the Soviet Union on the use of radio, probably because Hitler and Mussolini were more adept than Stalin at the use of the spoken word. All systems tried to manipulate culture, whether through Socialist Realism or Aryanism; as shown in Chapter 4, Italy was probably the least successful in this respect. All redesigned the structure and function of education, although in different ways. The Nazi and Fascist approach was to close minds in order to make them unreceptive to anything but carefully programmed propaganda. The result would be a simplification of the whole intellectual process. Soviet education was based, in theory, on expanding the intellect so that it could deal with the complexities of the dialectic and other elements of Marxist ideology. In practice, however, Soviet education under Stalin stultified the intellect by demanding the complete acceptance, as an act of faith, of the ideas passed down from the leadership.

Elsewhere the traditional process of education was adapted to be politically supportive of newly independent states, as in Poland and the Baltic States, but without heavy ideological content, as in Austria, Hungary and Portugal. Traditional systems were not radically altered; indeed, some were rendered even more traditional. According to Article 43 of the 1933 Portuguese Constitution (as redrafted in 1935), 'The education supplied by the state aims at . . . the formation . . . of all the civic and moral virtues, these being guided by the principles of Christian doctrine and morality traditional in the country.'[19] This was at the expense of effective progress: it has been estimated that 50 per cent of the Portuguese population were still illiterate by 1970.[20] The exception to all this was Turkey, which used major reforms in education to update, secularize and westernize.

For a while perceptions of the roles of women and the family were polarized between regimes dominated by communism on the one hand and, on the other, those that were fascist, corporative or conservative. Bolshevik Russia under Lenin and the brief communist regime in Hungary under Béla Kun attempted to remove the inequalities between men and women. By contrast, Mussolini's Italy, Hitler's Germany and the authoritarian regimes in Portugal, Spain, Austria, Horthy's Hungary, the Baltic States and the Balkans intensified the traditional differences between gender roles, emphasizing the family and home orientation of women. Much the same applied to perceptions of the family. Early communist systems sought to weaken the family as a 'bourgeois' institution that impeded ideological influences over the individual, while right-wing dictatorships integrated the family into the hierarchy of social and political control. During the 1930s, however, dictatorships of all kinds gradually converged in their more practical attitudes. Most needed the input of female labour to contribute to economic growth, which tended to undermine the emphasis on women in the home rather than in the employment market; at the same time, the Soviet Union allowed more diversification for women's roles, including a much wider use of women in the armed forces. Whereas Hitler and Mussolini had to make extensive compromises over the composition of their workforces, Stalin moved further towards Germany and Italy in reviving the importance of the family as a means of promoting population growth and as a means of guaranteeing social control and discipline. In all cases, adjustments to preferred theory had to be made in the light of economic and social experience.

Attitudes to religion varied widely. Communism was fundamentally hostile, seeing it as a rival ideology. Hence both Lenin and Stalin took a range of measures against religion in all its forms – Christianity, Islam, Judaism and Buddhism. Nazism was more adaptable to Christianity, although more radical towards Judaism. At first Hitler claimed to be supportive of traditional Christian values and gained considerable support among both Catholics and Protestants, doing a deal with the Church by the Concordat in 1933. Later, however, he clashed with the Church over the euthanasia programme and Nazism itself became more overtly paganistic, atheistic or pragmatic. Italian Fascism reached that stage only during the phase of the Salò Republic. Up to that point it did not challenge the Church's spiritual supremacy and, despite Mussolini's own atheistic views, hastened to an agreement with the Church in the Lateran treaty of 1929.

Elsewhere the Church was afforded special status. In Poland it grew in influence during the 1930s with the growth of lay organizations such as Catholic Action, the introduction of religious education and the development of a new Catholic intelligentsia. This was not uncritical towards the creeping authoritarianism in the 1930s but the regime found it less threatening than did the communist governments after 1945. In Portugal the government was more actively supportive of the Church. Even though the 1933 Constitution provided for the official separation of Church and state, nevertheless, Catholicism was still officially considered 'the traditional religion of the Portuguese nation'[21] and relations with the Vatican were formalized by the Concordat of 1940. Salazar's view was typical of that of most authoritarian regimes: 'The state will abstain from playing politics with the church in the knowledge that the church will abstain from playing politics with the state.'[22] Secularization was not normally part of an authoritarian approach, although here Turkey was the exception, Mustafa Kemal abolishing both the Caliphate and the Seriat.

It was in their treatment of minorities or sub-groups that the totalitarian regimes inflicted the worst degradation. In Germany minorities were seen as race enemies, who included hereditarily diseased people or those with disabilities, the Gipsies and, above all, the Jews. Fascism targeted Arabs in Libya, Africans in Ethiopia and, from 1938 onwards, Italian Jews. In the Soviet Union the focus was on class enemies – members of the 'reactionary' bourgeoisie or peasantry, above all the kulaks. In theory there was a difference with the Nazi and Fascist minorities, in that those identified in the Soviet Union were susceptible to rehabilitation But in practice class often overlapped with ethnicity, at least in Stalin's quotas for purging by the NKVD.

Other regimes were more variable in their treatment of minorities. Officially, Portugal followed an *assimilado* policy in the colonies, although in practice the 'culture bar' was superseded by the 'colour bar' normal to overseas empires. The Romanian government practised open discrimination against ethnic Hungarians, although Poland made more of an effort to absorb the Ukrainians and Belorussians included within enlarged frontiers from

1921. In Spain, Franco was much less sympathetic than the Second Republic to Basque and Catalan regionalism, making it clear that he favoured a unitary Spain. All areas became more inclined to anti-Semitic legislation during the 1930s, including Poland under Rydz-Smigly. Even Turkey saw discrimination against minorities who were seen as a potential threat, especially the Kurds and Armenians.

What was the attitude of the various regimes to popular mobilization? In the totalitarian states, rallies were frequent and officially orchestrated, usually with a dynamic and revolutionary emphasis: paramilitary parades were more apparent in Germany, military and party in the Soviet Union. In the authoritarian regimes such displays were of two main types. Either they were the fringe activities of bodies like the Arrow Cross, Iron Guard, or Heimwehr, seeking to influence the regime and causing tensions with it in the process. Or they were official state rallies, like those of Franco, to celebrate historic events or the triumph of tradition over revolution. Perhaps the main exception was the Portuguese Legion, set up in 1936, with an average membership of 120,000 between 1936 and 1945.

Organized leisure activities were more a feature of the totalitarian systems, especially Germany, with the KdF and SdA. Authoritarian regimes tended to leave this to traditional bodies, particularly the Church. Youth movements were widespread, although their main purpose in Russia, Germany and Italy was induction into the prevailing ideology and subordination to the party and leadership. The main examples were Komsomol and Pioneers in the USSR, the Pimpf, HJ, JM and BDM in Germany and the Balilla, Avanguardisti and Fascist Levy in Italy. Elsewhere attempts were made by militant groups to influence youth – but were often unwelcome or seen as deviant. In Spain and Portugal, however, the regime did become involved. Portugal developed a Student Vanguard in 1934, which was replaced in 1936 by Portuguese Youth (Mocidade Portuguesa), the purpose of which was to stimulate 'physical activities', the 'formation of character' and 'devotion to country'.[23] The treatment of women was based on more egalitarian principles in the Soviet Union than in Germany or Italy, although in all three regimes there were differences between theory and practice. Elsewhere attitudes were generally conservative – especially in Spain, Portugal, Greece and the Balkan countries – conditioned, however, by traditional social norms as well as by official government policy. The one major exception to this was Turkey, which made some progress in improving the status of women by removing Islamic constraints. In this way it was working in the opposite direction to Spain and Portugal.

Finally, all regimes attached considerable importance to the attitudes of the people towards them. But the type of attitude would depend on the regime's expectations. Where the system expected full-scale involvement and total commitment, then half-heartedness would be seen as a sign of dissent. On the other hand, where the expectation was a depoliticized individual, refraining from enthusiastic action could be seen as positive behaviour. The most extreme expectations were in the Soviet Union and applied to all sectors of society. The Nazi regime opened certain channels for communication and control but focused specific attention on suspected 'deviants' rather than on everyday opinion. Italy found it hard to enforce conformist behaviour with any consistency, as was shown by the large-scale evasion from the youth organizations. In the authoritarian states, opposition was sometimes ruthlessly targeted, especially in Spain and Portugal. Both regimes were very destructive to creative writing and journalism through a policy of pre-emptive censorship. Less draconian measures were adopted in Austria, Hungary, Poland and the Balkans. Yet none of the authoritarian regimes developed the sort of controls which were applied by the neo-Stalinist systems in eastern Europe after 1948.

SECURITY AND TERROR

Propaganda, indoctrination and social mobilization were invariably backed up by measures of state security and terror. Totalitarian regimes, indeed, made a permanent connection between the two processes. Authoritarian states, although never strong on indoctrination, maintained a watchful security and sometimes pursued a brutal form of repression.

Terror had two main purposes. One was ideological. Both Hitler and Stalin legitimized their rule by identifying enemies of the people: in Germany they were 'race enemies' and 'sub-humans', in the Soviet Union, 'class enemies' and 'poisonous weeds'. In both cases they were to be removed, although this involved different methods. The other purpose was to prevent the development of opposition either by deterrence and fear or by actual arrest, followed by detention or execution. Measures here might be summary or judicial. In extreme cases, purges were conducted to remove a carefully targeted section of society or even of the establishment itself.

The security forces in the totalitarian regimes involved some of the most notorious institutions ever devised. The German structure comprised the SA and the SS-Gestapo-SD complex, while Soviet security evolved through the Cheka, GPU, OGPU, NKVD, MGB, MVD and, after the death of Stalin, the KGB. Italy's system was far less extensive or extreme, based on the OVRA and Special Tribunal. Here terror was more apparent with the rise of Fascist *squadristi* than with more mature fascist institutions. The OVRA never achieved the same notoriety as the SS or NKVD; according to Friedrich and Brzezinski, it was 'less total, less frightful, and hence less "mature" than in Germany and the Soviet Union'.[24] Indeed, its staff numbered only 375 in 1940.[25] The Special Tribunal was sparing in its use of capital punishment: 42 death sentences were imposed from 1927 to 1943, 31 of which were carried out.[26]

Elsewhere, methods varied considerably. Some regimes had no organized terror as such: examples included Horthy's Hungary, the Baltic states, Austria under Dollfuss and Piłsudski's Poland. Others developed machinery for repression which was more efficient than Italy's. Franco extended police functions to the army, which carried out huge numbers of extra-judicial killings and acts of vengeance. The total number of executions in Spain was anything up to 200,000 and some 400,000 passed through Spanish prisons between 1939 and 1945. Although Portugal saw far fewer victims, Salazar's secret police was actually more widely known: the PVDE (Police of Vigilance and State Defence) was set up in 1933, to be replaced in 1945 by the PIDE (International Police for State Defence). These targeted suspected Communists and dissidents, using a network of spies and informers. Yet there were constraints. Salazar's view was that in a small country 'a relentless economy of terror proved more effective than mass terror or recurrent bouts of large-scale purging'.[27]

What was the role of legal systems in these developments? In most authoritarian regimes the legal structure remained intact but was heavily leaned on by the state. But it did act as a restraining influence, especially once enemies of the state had been identified by the secret police. It was more difficult for these accused to be removed anonymously. Going through the judicial system meant that the numbers were automatically controlled. The exception to this was Franco's Spain, where the tribunals were for a while under the emergency control of the army – in the wake of a bloody civil war.

The totalitarian regimes varied. Italy was more like the authoritarian structures in that the judicial system retained some control over the prosecution and processing of prisoners within Italy. The Special Tribunal retained a legal base and was manned by legal officials. In Russia, however, earlier attempts to set up an independent legal order 'did not really take root'.[28] According to Wachsmann, 'the bloody and arbitrary justice of the Bolsheviks did nothing to increase respect for legality'.[29] Jurists were often untrained and subordinated to local party leaders. Pressure was put upon them to deal with the enemies of the state as they deserved. During the height of the Terror in the late 1930s the NKVD took the lead in prosecutions and regular courts rarely took part in political cases. In Germany, the situation was more complex. On the one hand, Germany had a longer and more continuous legal tradition. Legal officials were more highly trained – and this remained the case during the period of the Third Reich. Unlike Stalin, Hitler conducted no mass purges of judges. This meant that 'the legal system in Nazi Germany was much more firmly entrenched than in the Soviet Union'.[30] Yet the ideological influence in Germany was what really counted and the judicial system was brought round to this as the result of the work of certain key figures like Roland Freisler. Similarly, there were no constraints on the euthanasia programme or exterminations on racial grounds. These were well outside the scope of the normal legal process, going beyond even the NKVD courts. As Wachsmann maintains, 'an established legal system and a professional body of trained jurists provided no secure barrier against a descent into terror.'[31]

A key element of terror is the application of purges. In the totalitarian regimes, these were most common in the Soviet Union and least common in Fascist Italy. The dynamics and purpose also differed. Bullock, for example, points out the different directions taken by Hitler and Stalin during the 1930s. 'While Hitler between 1934 and 1938 accepted the need to curb radical excesses and allow a period of accommodation and restraint, Stalin in the same years moved in the opposite direction.' This involved 'a renewal of the revolution from above, culminating in a reign of terror'.[32] Of the three totalitarian dictators, Stalin was the most obsessed about the security of his position: unlike Hitler and Mussolini, he had not been the original inspiration behind the new system and needed to place firmly upon himself the mantle of Lenin. Stalin was also confronted by a huge range of local initiatives and inertias which needed to be spurred into action or, alternatively, reined back. The extent of Soviet terror is therefore in part a sign of administrative malfunctioning. In Germany purges served a more restricted purpose. The Night of the Long Knives was Hitler's method of cutting off the radical wing of the Nazi movement in order to guarantee military support for the new regime. It was not, however, followed by a clean sweep through the rest of the party leadership. One can only speculate on whether this would have happened had the Third Reich outlived Hitler. Would Goering, Himmler, Bormann or Goebbels eventually have become a Stalin? The only real equivalent to a purge in the authoritarian states was the summary execution of Republican opponents in the wake of the Civil War: this was actually more extensive than any developments within Italy – but fell far short of the slaughter of perceived opponents within the USSR.

One of the most notorious features of the panoply of terror was the use of concentration and labour camps. In fact, both preceded the era of dictatorship. During its 1896 war with the United States, Spain used camps in Cuba for the *renconcentración* of potentially hostile peasants. The same method was used by the British in the Boer War, then by the Germans in South West Africa, who developed the *Konzentrationslager* for the Herero people of South West Africa, where forced labour was added to the regime. This combination of confinement and labour came to be applied ruthlessly by Mussolini's occupying forces in Libya and Ethiopia during the 1920s and 1930s. It remained, however, a colonial device and was not imported into Italy itself.

The camps in Nazi Germany and the Soviet Union were a new departure. Although the early Nazi camps, such as Dachau and Sachsenhausen, were intended as centres of labour for opponents and 'deviants', most of the network ended up with facilities for mass killing, while six were set up specifically for this purpose. The overall conception of the German system was the more horrifying because of their eventual connection with the deliberate extermination of 6 million people. There was no Soviet equivalent to the RHSA, to Auschwitz-Birkenau, to the gas chambers or ovens. Nevertheless, the Soviet Gulag was incomparably greater in size, consisting at its height of 476 labour camps and 2,000 colonies, whereas the total number of camps administered by the SS was about 16. The twin purposes were penal and economic. Dzerzhinski set the original agenda: 'The republic cannot be merciful toward criminals and cannot waste resources on them'; instead, 'we will have to work to organize forced labour (penal servitude) at camps for colonizing undeveloped areas that will be run with iron discipline'.[33] This was taken to unprecedented lengths by Stalin both as a device for terror and as one of the pillars of the planned economy.

What links Nazi Germany with the USSR is that 'both regimes legitimated themselves, in part by establishing categories of "enemies" or "sub humans", whom they persecuted and destroyed on a mass scale'.[34] In Germany it was people with disabilities, then race enemies and finally Jews. In the Soviet Union it was class enemies, including kulaks and 'saboteurs', along with certain ethnic minorities. In terms of overall numbers, many more victims were processed through the Gulag system than through the SS network: more people died in the Soviet camps than in those in Germany and Poland. These deaths, however, were the result of neglect and overwork rather than a policy of genocide. The Stalinist system always retained a theoretical emphasis on correction and rehabilitation while the Nazi ideology was ultimately geared to a policy of disposal.

ECONOMIES

Within the totalitarian states the government sought to impose overall economic control. Most was attempted in the Soviet Union, where, as in the political sphere, the previous system was largely destroyed. Stalin's method was the Five-Year Plan, co-ordinated by Gosplan, which, by 1938, had been subdivided into fifty-four departments. His basic intention was to impose upon all sectors of the economy the principle of collective ownership while, at the same time, preparing the Soviet Union to resist an invasion from the West. The fascist states, by contrast, aimed to adapt rather than destroy the previous system. Germany's programme was based on *Gleichschaltung*, Italy's on the corporate state. In both cases the emphasis was on state direction but with a degree of private enterprise; the state allied with big business rather than seeking to destroy it. The ultimate objectives of both Hitler and Mussolini were autarky and the pursuit of Lebensraum, the assumption being that only territorial expansion would enable the German and Italian economies to reflect the industriousness of their respective people.

Elsewhere, the smaller states varied in their economic policies. Some, like Spain, Austria, Portugal and Turkey, were clearly influenced by Mussolini's corporate state, although they avoided some of its Fascist connotations. Others struggled on with open economies based on private enterprise and minimal state direction; eventually, however, the impact of the Depression forced Bulgaria, Romania, Yugoslavia and Greece into making trade agreements with Germany. These, in turn, dragged them into the vortex of German diplomatic and political influence.

The key test of the success of the planned economies was their capacity for mobilization in wartime. The Soviet system of the 1930s has been reinterpreted. It was once thought to have made the most successful adjustment to the demands of Total War and that Soviet success against Nazi Germany from 1943 onwards was due to the full implementation of the Five-Year Plans. It now seems that the Soviet recovery was made possible by the suspension of economic planning – the very reverse of Stalin's original intention. Even so, it could be argued that Stalin had geared the Soviet economy directly to the demands of Total War; the problems were how best to generate the necessary resources and how to make the best use of them. The experience of the fascist states was very different. The Italian economy reacted badly to being stretched by conflict in the 1930s. The Ethiopian campaign and the Spanish Civil War brought it close to collapse, while the campaigns in the Balkans and North Africa finished it off. Germany was geared specifically to a war of conquest followed by the absorption of large areas to consolidate the economic base. But to be fully effective, this conquest had to be rapid. As long as Germany could depend upon a successful Blitzkrieg the economy functioned smoothly and efficiently. Faced with the prospect of Total War, however, Germany fell far behind the Soviet Union in armaments production. By the time that Speer had managed to introduce more radical measures it was already too late: Soviet troops were closing in on the Third Reich.

The economies of other European states were also geared at times for warfare. Poland had to finance its war with the Soviet Union between 1920 and 1921and then maintained one of the largest conventional armies in Europe. Portugal had to set aside a substantial proportion of its GDP to maintain its position in the colonies. This became increasingly difficult as the regimes of Salazar and Caetano were confronted by guerrilla resistance in Angola and Mozambique. Spain's economy was dictated by civil war and needed a period of urgent recuperation. Given these priorities, it made sense to keep out of the Second World War, a chance which Mussolini did not take on behalf of Italy, and one which was not offered to Poland or the Baltic states.

We have seen that a key feature of industrial growth in the totalitarian states was military mobilization. How did the consumer fare faced with this priority? Stalin's industrialization was conducted entirely at the expense of consumer industries, while Hitler's policies tried at least to accommodate consumer expectations. In the Soviet Union full employment was accompanied by declining living standards and an overlapping sector based on forced labour. Hitler never dared inflict on the German consumer the sort of demands taken for granted by Stalin in Russia. In some ways the German consumer was worse off under Hitler than in the Weimar Republic, experiencing lower wages and a longer working week. Yet for all that, the level of consumer goods did rise between 1933 and 1938 and German consumers were not fully affected by the impact of military conflict until the introduction of the Total War economy from 1941. Mussolini also tried to combine rearmament with maintaining a steady standard of living – but with somewhat less success. After the invasion of Ethiopia the prospects for consumer industry declined rapidly and consumers were called upon to make extra sacrifices during the second half of the 1930s. At the same time, Mussolini lacked the political power of Stalin to convert austerity into industrial recovery.

Elsewhere conditions of the consumer varied. In Portugal the *Estado Novo* of Salazar made very little difference to the workforce, which continued to experience some of the lowest living standards in Europe. Spain's economic recovery after 1945 was slow and based so heavily on that a consumer boom did not occur until the 1960s autarky. In Austria and Hungary the population had had higher consumer expectations, given the industrialization which had been taking place in the former Dual Monarchy. Both, however, were badly affected by the loss of industrial regions, affecting both the capacity to produce and the ability to purchase. Even the countries with increased territory, like Poland and Romania, did not experience significant improvements in the standard of living. Probably the most successful in terms of consumer gains was Turkey, where for Mustafa Kemal, consumerism was an important part of the introduction of a westernized lifestyle.

All of the totalitarian regimes were severely tested by the special problems posed by agriculture. Tight, centralized control was particularly difficult in an economic activity which was essentially local and which required the exercise of on-the-spot initiative. It might have been possible more or less to co-ordinate decision-making in the industrial sector, but how could the same process take into account the diverse and unpredictable conditions faced by agriculture? The Soviet experience was catastrophic. Stalin's enforced collectivization alienated huge sections of the peasantry, and his determination to use agriculture to subsidize industrial development created an imbalance which permanently crippled the Soviet economy. Mussolini's policies were similarly disastrous for Italy. Although he avoided a social upheaval by not seeking to alter the pattern of land ownership, he did cause serious disruption to agricultural productivity. By insisting that farmers should switch to crops like wheat to enable the government to win its 'Battle for Grain', he created an imbalance which post-war Italy has struggled to resolve. Hitler managed to avoid the direct disruption inflicted by Stalin and Mussolini. It could, however, be argued that his belief in a strong peasantry underlay his policy of Lebensraum: he envisaged the settlement of German rural communities across the whole of eastern Europe. Lebensraum, in turn, conditioned Hitler's whole economic and military strategy, with all the implications examined in Chapter 5.

Some of the smaller states experienced agricultural reforms in the early 1920s; Stambuliski, for example, sought to redistribute land among the peasantry of Bulgaria in what was really the reverse of Stalin's policy. But the onset of the Depression forced the authoritarian regimes to abandon virtually all attempts to direct agriculture. The smaller dictators valued the support of the landed gentry too much to risk incurring their wrath by interfering with the status quo. In this respect, as in many others, they considered that things were best left as they were.

IMPACT OF WAR

Trotsky once described war as 'the locomotive of history'. At no time was this more relevant than during the period covered by this book. The impact of the First World War was covered in Chapter 1. This was followed by the Russian Civil War (1918–21), the Russo-Polish War (1920–1), the Abyssinian War (1935–6), the Spanish Civil War (1936–9) and the Russo-Finnish War (1940–1).

What were the attitudes of the various regimes to war? To Lenin it was external to communist ideology: it was the means whereby capitalism would tear itself apart and enable communism to triumph through revolution. Stalin, however, changed this approach by preparing more deliberately for war and eventually making the Second World War the means by which communism was spread. Revolutions were imposed from above in the wake of military victory. His attitude was strongly affected by the Russian Civil War – one of the most brutal conflicts of the twentieth century. For Mussolini, war was intrinsic to the ideology of fascism, being the ultimate means by which the dynamic forces come to bear. For Hitler, war was essential for the formation of the racial empire: in effect, the *Kampf-gemeinschaft* would forge the Volksgemeinschaft through the process of *Lebensraum*.[35] In the authoritarian dictatorships war was seen more as a means of adjusting frontiers. Irredentist nationalism was probably the strongest force in this. Hungary was the most obvious example, which did develop something more akin to fascist expansionism in Szálasi's 'Hungarism' (p. 325), but it lacked the resources on its own to carry it out. Poland proved the most successful of the inter-war states in frontier adjustment, in contrast to Greece whose aspirations to Turkish territory had been ended by 1922. Portugal had no claims; although, proportionate to her GDP, she had one of the largest military budgets in Europe, this was used to defend an overseas empire which had been held over several centuries. If there was an ideology here it was one of imperial fulfilment.

But the war which affected almost all of the dictatorships was the Second World War, the impact of which lasted from 1939 to 1948. The main trend was the domination of the authoritarian regimes by the totalitarian ones. This was anticipated by Germany's absorption of Austria in 1938 and Italy's subjection of Albania in 1939. In September 1939 Poland was dismembered by Germany and USSR. The Baltic States were Sovietized by 1940, while Greece was conquered by Germany and Yugoslavia was partitioned between Germany and Italy. Four others were in alliance with Germany: Slovakia, Hungary, Romania and Bulgaria. Three – Spain, Portugal and Turkey – remained neutral. A second wave of domination occurred after the collapse of Nazi Germany as Poland, Hungary, Romania, Bulgaria, Albania and the eastern zone of Germany itself ended up under Soviet control – a development which brought a seamless transition from the Second World War to the Cold War.

The totalitarian regimes pursued objectives which shaped the way in which the War developed. Germany's main priority was always in the east – with the pursuit of Lebensraum and racial frontier. This meant that the conflict in the west became subsumed into the race war. As Horowitz argues,

> The Nazi onslaught into Poland and then Russia – from June 1941 to May 1942 – corresponded to a shift in German priorities if not policies . . . the war aims of the Nazis shifted from victory over the Allied powers to victory over the Jews.[36]

The Soviet experience was somewhat different. Although Stalin had produced a massive build-up of Soviet armaments during the 1930s, he was initially forced onto the defensive. The Soviet recovery, however, provided the main momentum from 1943 as the war turned from one of survival into one of expansion – the reverse of Germany's Lebensraum. Mussolini, meanwhile, had deflected committed Italy to a war beyond its resources in the Balkans in the vain hope of completing a new Roman Empire. This, too, shaped the outcome of the war as a whole as Germany was drawn into southern Europe by the need to salvage Mussolini's empire. This had not been part of Hitler's intended Lebensraum and it fatally weakened his campaigns in the east. It also provided the means for the Western Allies to open up another front and relieve at least some of the pressure on the Soviet Union.

To what extent did war act as a major catalyst to change regimes internally? It certainly radicalized Nazi Germany. The SS, for example, expanded rapidly in importance, to the point where it is arguable that it had assumed many of the functions of the state itself. By 1944 it was running the army through the Waffen SS, the extermination programme through the RSHA, and the eastern occupied territories. It was also in charge of the Reich's racial policy through the RKFDV and had assumed virtual control over the industrial sector. In contrast, the war seemed to traditionalize Stalin's Russia: the purges were suspended, the planning system was replaced and, with the emphasis on the Great Patriotic War, traditional themes were brought back into the Soviet system. According to Rees, 'The war, eclipsing the October Revolution, became the great event that legitimised the Soviet regime until its ultimate demise.'[37] Fascist Italy had already experienced war 1936–9 and Mussolini had tried, through it, to radicalize Fascism. The Second World War merely wound Fascism down – apart from a final flare of radicalism in the Salò Republic from 1943, a development, however, arising out of the imminence of defeat. In Spain the Civil War made the actions of Franco's regime more brutal but it forced what radical influences there were into a broader conservative coalition. Once he was safely in power Franco exercised the option to avoid further radicalization by keeping out of the Second World War while, at the same time, showing solidarity with Germany by providing volunteers for the German campaign in Russia. Elsewhere, regimes were changed by their association with the totalitarian states: Albania, Greece and Yugoslavia were conquered and reconstructed, while Hungary, Romania and Bulgaria became allies and swung more to the right as a result. The main effect of this was on policies towards their minorities, especially the Jews.

The peoples and nationalities of eastern Europe were massively affected by the Second World War as they became caught up in a huge theatre of war and subsequent reorganizations brought by conquest or defeat. Nazi Germany, for example, restructured the populations of Poland, Ukraine, Belorussia and the Baltic States as soon as it had conquered them. This involved bringing them under SS or government administration, creating new colonies for Aryan settlers and removing existing Jewish inhabitants. Some historians see the Holocaust as closely connected with the other racial and ethnic policies of a radicalized regime acting in a new and terrible way. The Soviet regime also brought massive disruption, through large-scale resettlements based on generalizations about ethnic reliability. There was no change of internal structure as such – unlike the vast new administrative system imposed by Nazi Germany. The USSR retained its existing format but included the Baltic States and Moldavia. What was new, however, was the extension of new Communist regimes – under Soviet influence – to East Germany, Poland, Czechoslovakia, Hungary, Romania and Bulgaria. All this involved frontier changes and the large-scale movement of peoples through transportation or expulsion.

Many of the dictatorships covered in this book were at some stage involved in mass killings and war crimes. In extreme cases these extended to genocide. Before the Second World War the worst example had been the massacre of 1.5 million Armenians in Turkey between 1915 and 1916. Between the wars, Italy had a particularly bad record in Libya and Ethiopia (pp. 135–7) and, in the context of the Second World War, colluded with atrocities against Serbs and Muslims in Yugoslavia. From 1941, the Wehrmacht and SS carried out mass killings of Polish, Ukrainian and Russian civilians and of Soviet prisoners of war. Above all, attempts were made to exterminate all Jews living in areas under German occupation, initially by Einsatzgruppen units, later after transportation to the death camps. The Soviet regime was also involved in war crimes on a huge scale, including the activities of the Cheka in the Russian Civil War, the deportation of ethnic minorities by the Red Army and NKVD, savage treatment of Polish or German prisoners of war, and reprisals against German civilians or suspected ethnic 'traitors' in Ukraine, Belorussia or the Baltic. Total casualties were on an even larger scale than those committed by the Nazis, although it is sometimes hard to draw the line between peacetime and wartime atrocities. Nor did the Soviet system produce anything equivalent to the gas chambers which were used on millions of Jewish civilians after being tested on Soviet prisoners of war. Outside the totalitarian states the most notorious atrocities were committed in the Ustasha-held area of Yugoslavia. In Bosnia-Herzegovina and Croatia some 300,000 Serbs were massacred, along with smaller numbers of Jews and Gipsies. This was unprecedented in the area: according to Pavkovic, 'no regime or movement in Yugoslavia had ever attempted to wipe out a whole national or ethnic group'.[38] The wartime expansion of Germany eastwards had a profound impact on anti-Semitism and race conflict, converting both into the Holocaust. There were two basic reasons for this. First, such a policy of elimination could be accomplished only within the context of Lebensraum which, in turn, was inconceivable without war. Second, this expansion brought direct contact with the areas of most concentrated Jewish population in Europe – and within the country regarded by Hitler as Germany's greatest ideological enemy. The invasion of the Soviet Union therefore brought to a climax the previous phases of exclusion, expulsion and ghettoization – and converted them into mass murder. The new priorities were transmitted back to Germany's treatment of European Jewry more generally. This actually had an effect on Germany's priorities for the war at large; indeed, it became *the* war as far as the Nazi leadership were concerned.

Other countries involved in the Holocaust have already been considered in Chapter 5. In all cases the Nazi regime imposed the overall structure for extermination – either following military conquest, as in Poland, Bohemia, the Baltic States and Yugoslavia, or as a result of heavy pressure on an ally (Romania, Bulgaria, Slovakia); in some cases this led to occupation, as in Italy or in Hungary in 1944. All of these areas had experienced a degree of anti-Semitism during the 1920s and 1930s – but this could not of itself have produced a Holocaust without the direct agency of the Nazi regime. Yet, as previously shown, the countries which had been ruled by – or were still under – authoritarian dictatorships showed at least a degree of co-operation with Nazi measures. These were less obvious in Poland, the Baltic States and Bulgaria than they were in Hungary and Romania. Nevertheless, it is only recently that any degree of complicity has been acknowledged. This is a reflection on the transition of eastern Europe from closed communist regimes, which were generally dismissive of any special significance for the Holocaust, to post-communist democracies.

Epilogue

Europe since 1945

The period between the two world wars saw an unprecedented variety of regimes. These can be classified in two ways. First, it is possible to make a three-way distinction between democracies, left-wing dictatorships (Russia) and right-wing dictatorships (Germany, Italy and many smaller states). The alternative division is between democracy and dictatorship, the latter subdividing into totalitarian regimes (Stalinist Russia, Nazi Germany and possibly Mussolini's Italy) and authoritarian states. This book has looked at both types of classification.

The post-war period saw major political changes and shifts in the meaning of dictatorship. At the millennium, two major phases were discernible.

1945–89

After 1945 the regimes of the far left were greatly strengthened while, elsewhere, parliamentary democracy was revived. The far right, by contrast, was gradually squeezed out of Europe altogether. The collapse of the right-wing dictatorships was a direct result of military defeat in the Second World War at the hands of the Western democracies and the Soviet Union. The scope and extent of this defeat utterly discredited fascism as a doctrine or as a vehicle for political activism. It is true that the word itself survives. It is normally used to describe small parties of the far right which aspire, so far unsuccessfully, to revive a totalitarian form of nationalism. It is also sometimes used as a term of abuse against regimes or governments more appropriately called reactionary or traditionalist. Between 1945 and the 1980s Europe saw only three manifestations of the far right, all of which were authoritarian rather than fascist. Spain and Portugal survived as dictatorships, against the general trend, because they had avoided involvement in the Second World War. Neither, however, was able to outlive its founder: Portugal moved towards democracy after the 1974 revolution, Spain more gradually under the guidance of King Juan Carlos. Greece presents a different case. Between 1967 and 1974 the colonels briefly recreated the Metaxas era, but their regime was eventually doomed by its isolation, ostracism and defeat in war.

As a result of the decline of the far right, Europe was initially polarized between parliamentary democracy and the communist left. The reason was that Western Europe felt vulnerable after the Second World War to the threat which it perceived from the new Soviet superpower and came to depend on a renewed connection with the United States in the form of NATO. The Soviet Union, in turn, tightened its control in eastern Europe by means of Comecon and the Warsaw Pact. The West saw itself as the 'free world' and the Soviet bloc as the remaining source of dictatorship threatening this freedom. At first the term 'totalitarian' was widely used to describe the Soviet bloc, although its appropriateness began to be questioned afer the decline of Stalinist influences (see Chapter 2).

SINCE 1989

This situation lasted well into the 1980s, when a change occurred. Imperceptible at first, this accelerated with breathtaking speed towards the end of the decade. Gorbachev dismantled much of the remaining neo-Stalinist apparatus in the Soviet Union, while the period 1989–91 saw a political transformation. Communist regimes were toppled in Poland, Czechoslovakia, Hungary, East Germany, Bulgaria and Romania. The Warsaw Pact was disbanded, the Cold War formally ended and the Soviet Union was replaced by sixteen independent states; those in Europe were Russia, Belarus, Ukraine, Moldova, Estonia, Latvia, Lithuania, Armenia, Georgia and Azerbaijan.

The implications were mixed. There was a great deal more scope for political instability as national identities were revived after decades of suppression by communism. The result was a proliferation of nationalist and right-wing movements throughout eastern Europe, and of ethnic conflicts which saw the break-up of Yugoslavia and the emergence of authoritarian regimes in Serbia, Belarus and, for a while, Ukraine. On the other hand, some of the new states looked to closer association with NATO and the European Union as a means of avoiding any possibility of a return to ideologically based dictatorship, whether of the communist left or of a reborn far right. The development of democracy in eastern Europe has also led to a revival of the term 'totalitarian' to describe the pre-1989 regimes – now consigned to the past, to be examined as history.

By the millennium, dictatorship was being seen in Europe as a thing of the past. Many political theorists were referring to the 'end of ideology' and, in view of the end of the Cold War and the growth of European integration, some were even anticipating the 'end of history'. The twenty-first century is likely to prove both assertions rash. The seeds of

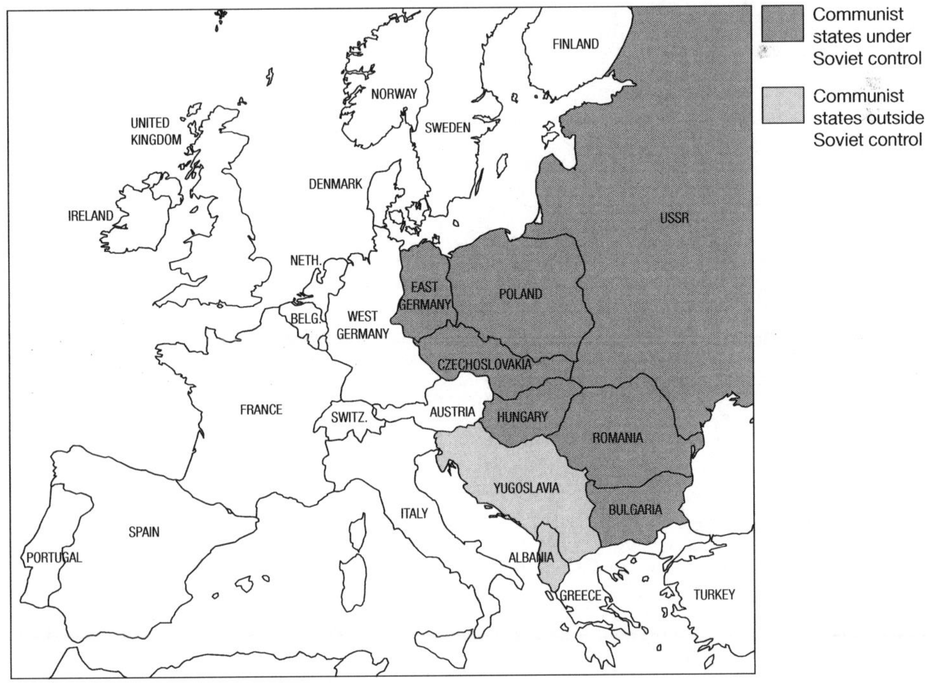

Map 10 Europe before 1989

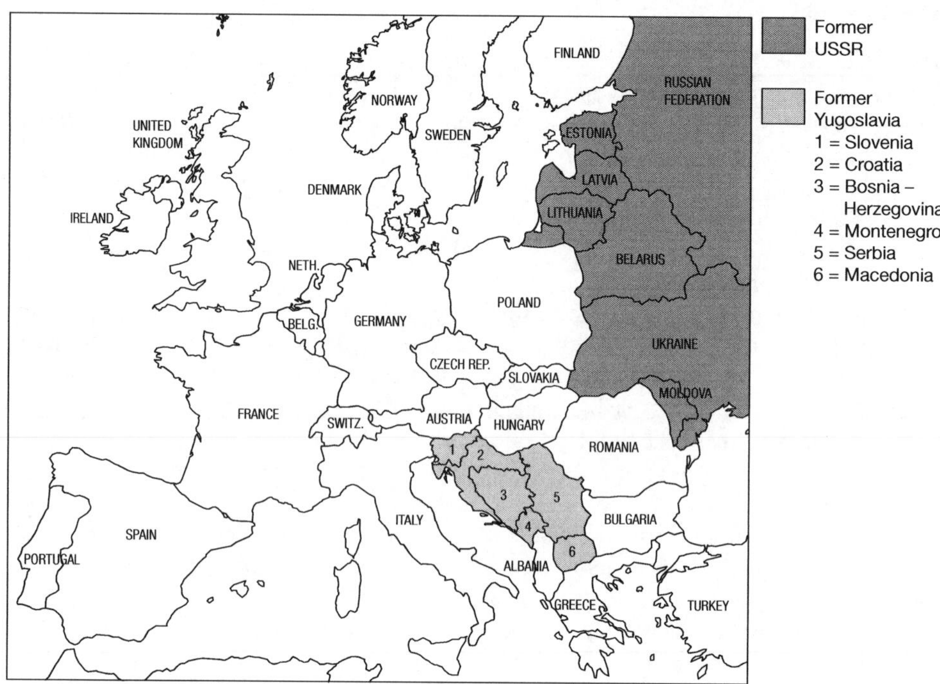

Map 11 Europe since 1991

many twentieth-century developments were sown in the 1890s. The 1990s could have been similarly productive and it remains to be seen whether dictatorship will be able to regenerate in the future.

Notes

1 The setting for dictatorship

1 See Z. Sternhell, 'Fascist Ideology', in W. Laqueur (ed.) *Fascism: A Reader's Guide* (Berkeley, CA 1976).
2 Quoted in A. Lyttelton (ed.) *Italian Fascisms from Pareto to Gentile* (London 1973), p. 211.
3 J.S. Hughes, *Contemporary Europe* (Englewood Cliffs, NJ 1961), Ch. 2.
4 K.D. Bracher, *The Age of Ideologies* (London 1984), Part II, Ch. 2.
5 S.G. Payne, *A History of Fascism* (London 1995), p. 79.
6 I. Kershaw, 'War and Political Violence in Twentieth-Century Europe', *Contemporary European History*, 2005, 14:1, pp. 107–123, at p. 113.
7 J.A.S. Grenville (ed.) *The Major International Treaties 1914–1973* (London 1974), Document: President Wilson's Fourteen Points, 8 January 1918.
8 A. Cobban, *The Nation State and National Self-determination* (London 1969), Part I, Ch. 4.
9 H. Kohn, *Political Ideologies of the Twentieth Century* (New York 1949), Ch. 13.
10 K.J. Newman, *European Democracy between the Wars* (trans. K. Morgan) (London 1970), Ch. 3.
11 D. Hoffmann, *Stalinist Values: The Cultural Norms of Soviet Modernity, 1917–1941* (Ithaca, NY 2003), p. 7.
12 R. Vinen, *A History in Fragments: Europe in the Twentieth Century* (London 2000), p. 184.
13 Hoffmann, op. cit., p. 9.
14 R. Ben-Ghiat, *Fascist Modernities* (Berkeley, CA 2001), p. 3.
15 Quoted in P. Fearon, *The Origins and Nature of the Great Slump 1929–1932* (London 1979).
16 M. Mazower, *Dark Continent: Europe's Twentieth Century* (London 1998).

2 Types of dictatorship

1 H. Buchheim, *Totalitarian Rule: Its Nature and Characteristics* (Middletown, CT 1968), Ch. 1.
2 J.J. Linz, *Totalitarian and Authoritarian Regimes* (London 2000), pp. 61–3.
3 M.R. Curtis, *Encyclopedia Americana*, s.v. 'Dictatorship'.
4 P. Brooker, *Twentieth-Century Dictatorships: The Ideological One-Party States* (New York 1995), pp. 1–6.
5 I. Kershaw and M. Lewin, *Stalinism and Nazism: Dictatorships in Comparison* (Cambridge 1997).
6 A. Perlmutter, *Modern Authoritarianism: A Comparative Institutional Analysis* (New Haven, CT 1984), p. 175.
7 For a basic definition of totalitarianism, see entry in J. Krieger et al., eds.: *The Oxford Companion to the Politics of the World*, second edition (Oxford 2001).

8 See C.J. Friedrich and Z.K. Brzezinski, *Totalitarian Dictatorship and Autocracy* (Cambridge, MA 1956).
9 Ibid., p. 9.
10 Ibid., p. 88.
11 See H. Arendt, *The Origins of Totalitarianism* (London 1986).
12 Friedrich and Brzezinski, op. cit., Ch. 2.
13 A. Gleeson, *Totalitarianism: The Inner History of the Cold War* (New York 1995), p. 3.
14 C.J. Friedrich, M. Curtis and B.R. Barber, *Totalitarianism in Perspective: Three Views* (London 1969), p. 55.
15 See J.L. Talmon, *The Origin of Totalitarian Democracy* (London 1952).
16 S. Tormey, *Making Sense of Tyranny: Interpretations of Totalitarianism* (Manchester 1995), p. 186.
17 Ibid., p. 188.
18 K.D. Bracher, *The Age of Ideologies* (London 1984), Part II, Ch. 1. See also the more recent emphasis on the 'sacralization of politics', especially in Emilio Gentile, *The Sacralization of Politics in Fascist Italy* (trans. Cambridge, MA 1996) and 'A Contribution to the Current Debate on Political Religions', *Journal of Contemporary History*, 2015, 50:2, pp. 168–187.
19 Friedrich and Brzezinski, op. cit., Ch. 2.
20 Ibid.
21 Ibid.
22 Bracher, op. cit., Part II, Ch. 1.
23 G.D. Obichkin et al., *V.I. Lenin: A Short Biography* (Moscow 1968), p. 33.
24 J.L.H. Keep, *The Debate on Soviet Power* (Oxford 1979), p. 173.
25 R. Pipes, 'The Origins of Bolshevism: The Intellectual Evolution of Young Lenin', in R. Pipes (ed.) *Revolutionary Russia* (London 1968).
26 T.H. Rigby, *The Changing Soviet System* (Aldershot 1990), p. 13.
27 Quoted in G.B. Smith, *Soviet Politics. Struggling with Change* (London 1992), p. 79.
28 Quoted in T.H. Rigby (ed.) *Stalin* (Englewood Cliffs, NJ 1966).
29 Quoted in L.G. Churchward, *Soviet Socialism: Social and Political Essays* (London 1987), p. 121.
30 G.P. Blum, *The Rise of Fascism in Europe* (Westport, CT 1998), p. 79.
31 R. Paxton, quoted in A.C. Pinto, 'Back to European Fascism', *Contemporary European History*, 2006, 15, pp. 103–115.
32 Quoted in I. Kershaw, *The Nazi Dictatorship* (4th edn, London 2000), p. 30.
33 Blum, op. cit., p. 4.
34 Ibid.
35 Quoted in D. Smith (ed.) *Left and Right in Twentieth Century Europe* (Harlow 1970), Ch. 1.
36 E. Nolte, *Three Faces of Fascism* (London 1964), p. 64).
37 Hildebrand, quoted in Kershaw, op. cit.
38 Blum, op. cit., p. 4.
39 See Z. Sternhell, 'Fascist Ideology', in W. Laqueur (ed.) *Fascism: A Reader's Guide* (Berkeley, CA 1976).
40 S.M. Lipset, *Political Man: The Social Bases of Politics* (New York 1960), Ch. 5.
41 Quoted in R.C. Macridis, *Contemporary Political Ideologies* (Boston, MA 1983), Ch. 9.
42 E. Weber, quoted in W. Laqueur (ed.) *Fascism: A Reader's Guide* (Harmondsworth 1979).
43 Kershaw, op. cit., p. 42.
44 Quoted in Kershaw, op. cit., p.42.
45 Ibid.
46 P.F. Sugar, 'Nationalism: The Victorious Ideology', in P.F. Sugar (ed.) *Western European Nationalism in the Twentieth Century* (Washington, DC 1995), p. 413.
47 K.R. Minogue, *Nationalism* (London 1969), p. 153.

3 Dictatorship in Russia

1 A. Ascher (ed.) *The Mensheviks in the Russian Revolution* (London 1976), Introduction.
2 Quoted in E.H. Carr, *The Bolshevik Revolution* (London 1950), Vol. I, Ch. 4.
3 E. Acton, *Rethinking the Russian Revolution* (London 1996), p. 183.
4 Quoted in A.E. Adams (ed.) *The Russian Revolution and Bolshevik Victory* (Lexington, MA 1974), extract by M. Fainsod.
5 Carr, op. cit., Vol. 1, Ch. 4.
6 Quoted in Adams, op. cit., extract by Fainsod.
7 Quoted in S.N. Silverman (ed.) *Lenin* (New York 1966), Ch. 2.
8 See G. Swain, *The Origins of the Russian Civil War* (London 1996); S. Smith, 'The Socialist-Revolutionaries and the Dilemma of Civil War', in V.N. Brovkin (ed.) *The Bolsheviks in Russian Society* (New Haven, CT 1997); L. Hertz, 'The Psychology of the White Movement', in Brovkin, op. cit.; E. Mawdsley, *The Russian Civil War* (London 1987).
9 The argument in this section is partly derived from Swain, op. cit.
10 Ibid., p. 252.
11 Ibid., p. 8.
12 Hertz, op. cit., p. 106.
13 P. Kenez, 'The Ideology of the White Movement', *Soviet Studies*, January 1980, xxxii, 1.
14 Mawdsley, op. cit., p. 283.
15 J.L.H. Keep (ed.) *The Debate on Soviet Power: Minutes of the All-Russian Central Executive Committee of Soviets* (Oxford 1979), Introduction.
16 J. Smith, *Red Nations: The Nationalities Experience in and after the USSR* (Cambridge 2013), p. 25.
17 Quoted in Ascher, op. cit., Introduction.
18 Figures adapted from Smith, op. cit., pp. 23–24.
19 Quoted in M. McCauley, *The Russian Revolution and the Soviet State, 1917–1921: Documents* (London 1975), pp. 184–186.
20 *A Short History of the Communist Party of the Soviet Union* (Moscow 1970 edition), pp. 134–135.
21 J. Rees, 'In Defence of October', in J. Rees, R. Service, S. Farber and R. Blackburn, *In Defence of October: A Debate on the Russian Revolution* (London 1997), p. 30.
22 R. Wade, *The Russian Revolution, 1917* (Cambridge 2000), p. 297.
23 Ibid., p. 298.
24 Keep, op. cit., Introduction.
25 R. Gregor (ed.) *Resolutions and Decisions of the Communist Party of the Soviet Union* (Toronto 1974), Vol. 2, Document 2.9.
26 R. Sakwa, *The Rise and Fall of the Soviet Union 1917–1991* (London 1999), Document 1.11, p. 16.
27 Quoted in G. Leggett, 'Lenin, Terror and the Political Police', *Survey*, Autumn 1975.
28 Ibid., p. 75.
29 Quoted in Carr, op. cit., Ch. 7.
30 Quoted in G. Leggett, *The Cheka: Lenin's Political Police* (Oxford 1981), Ch. 14.
31 R. Kowalski, *The Russian Revolution 1917–1921* (London 1997), Document 10.5, p. 155.
32 Quoted in D. Lane, *Politics and Society in the USSR* (London 1970), Ch. 3.
33 *A Short History of the Communist Party of the Soviet Union* (Moscow 1970), p. 172.
34 D. Volkogonov, *Lenin: Life and Legacy* (London 1994), p. 334.
35 R. Conquest, *Lenin* (London 1972), p. 104.
36 L. Trotsky, *History of the Bolshevik Revolution*, Vol. 1.
37 A. Kerensky, 'The Policy of the Provisional Government of 1917', *The Slavonic and East European Review*, July 1932, xi, 31.
38 Gregor, op. cit., Introduction.
39 C. Hill, *Lenin and the Russian Revolution* (London 1947), Ch. 8.

40 E. Mandel, 'Solzhenitsyn, Stalinism and the October Revolution', *New Left Review*, 1974, 86.
41 Leggett, op. cit., Epilogue.
42 S. Kotkin, *Stalin, Vol. 1: Paradoxes of Power, 1878–1928* (London 2014), p. 419.
43 E.H. Carr, 'The Russian Revolution and the West', *New Left Review*, 1978, iii.
44 Mandel, op. cit.
45 L. Schapiro, *1917: The Russian Revolution and the Origins of Present Day Communism* (Hounslow 1984), Epilogue.
46 Quoted in T.H. Rigby (ed.), *Stalin* (New York 1966).
47 M. McCauley, *Stalin and Stalinism* (Harlow 1983), Ch. 1.
48 P. Kenez: *A History of the Soviet Union from the Beginning to the End*, second edition (Cambridge 2006), p. 77.
49 Ibid.
50 L. Colletti, 'The Question of Stalin', *New Left Review*, 1970, 61.
51 Silverman, op. cit., Ch. 2.
52 Kotkin, op. cit., p. 739.
53 N. Krasso, 'Trotsky's Marxism', *New Left Review*, 1967, 44.
54 Quoted in E.H. Carr, *Socialism in One Country 1924–1926* (London 1958), Ch. 4.
55 Krasso, op. cit.
56 Quoted in E.H. Carr, *The Bolshevik Revolution*, op. cit., Vol. 1, Ch. 4.
57 Ibid.
58 J. Arch Getty, 'The Politics of Stalinism', in A. Nove (ed.) *The Stalin Phenomenon* (London 1993), p. 128.
59 Ibid., p. 129.
60 N. Rosenfeldt, 'The Secret Apparatus during the Stalin Era', in N.E. Rosenfeldt, B. Jensen and E. Kulavig (eds) *Mechanisms of Power in the Soviet Union* (London 2000), p. 41.
61 Ibid., p. 42.
62 I.V. Pavlova, 'The Strength and Weakness of Stalin's Power', in Rosenfeldt et al., op. cit., p. 38.
63 R.C. Tucker, *The Soviet Political Mind* (London 1972), Ch. 3.
64 I. Grey, *Stalin: Man of History* (Abacus ed. 1982), pp. 265–266.
65 R. Overy, *The Dictators: Hitler's Germany, Stalin's Russia* (London 2004), p. 13.
66 Kotkin, op. cit., p. 597.
67 A. Ulam, 'The Price of Sanity' in G.R. Urban (ed.) *Stalinism: Its Impact on Russia and the World* (London 1982).
68 I. Deutscher, *Stalin: A Political Biography* (London 1949), Ch. 9.
69 L. Viola, 'The Second Coming: Class Enemies in the Soviet Countryside, 1927–1935', in J. Arch Getty and R.T. Manning (eds) *Stalinist Terror: New Perspectives* (Cambridge 1993), pp. 69–70.
70 Arch Getty, op. cit., p. 132.
71 R. Thurston, 'The Stakhanovite Movement: Background to the Great Terror in the Factories, 1935–1938', in Arch Getty and Manning, op. cit., p. 160.
72 See R.R. Reese, 'The Red Army and the Great Purges', in Arch Getty and Manning, op. cit.
73 Ibid. p. 213.
74 See S. Fitzpatrick, 'How the Mice Buried the Cat: Scenes from the Great Purges of 1937 in the Russian Provinces', in C. Ward (ed.) *The Stalinist Dictatorship* (London 1998).
75 G.T. Rittersporn, 'The Omnipresent Conspiracy: On Soviet Imagery of Politics and Social Relations in the 1930s', in Arch Getty and Manning, op. cit., p. 114.
76 R.G. Sumy, 'Stalin and his Stalinism: Power and Authority in the Soviet Union, 1930–53', in I. Kershaw and M. Lewin (eds) *Stalinism and Nazism, Dictatorships in Comparison* (Cambridge 1997), p. 50.
77 A. Litvin and J. Keep, *Stalinism: Russian and Western Views at the Turn of the Millennium* (London 2005), p. 182.
78 K. McDermott, *Stalin* (Basingstoke 2006), p. 99.
79 E. Acton, *Russia*: *The Tsarist and Soviet Legacy*, second edition (Harlow 1995), p. 234.

80 Reese, op. cit., p. 199.
81 Ibid., p. 210.
82 Ibid., p. 213.
83 McDermott, op. cit., p. 107.
84 V. Brovkin, *Russia after Lenin: Politics, Culture and Society 1921–1929* (London 1998), p. 222.
85 M. Lewin, *Russian Peasants and Soviet Power: A Study of Collectivization* (New York 1968), pp. 516–517.
86 Arch Getty, op. cit., p. 140.
87 Quoted in M. Lynch, *Stalin and Khrushchev: The USSR 1924–64* (London 1990), p. 30.
88 R. Hutchings, *Soviet Economic Development* (Oxford 1967), Ch. 6.
89 See D.R. Shearer, *Industry, State and Society in Stalin's Russia 1926–1934* (Ithaca, NY 1996), p. 235.
90 Ibid., p. 236.
91 Quoted in Lane, op. cit., Document 15.
92 Ibid., Ch. 11.
93 N.S. Timasheff, 'The Family, the School and the Church', in C. Ward (ed.) *The Stalinist Dictatorship* (London 1998), p. 304.
94 S. Davies, *Popular Opinion in Stalin's Russia: Terror, Propaganda and Dissent, 1934–1941* (Cambridge 1997), p. 65.
95 Timasheff, op. cit., p. 305.
96 Sakwa, op. cit., Document 5.13, p. 195.
97 Ibid., p. 209, Document 5.22: The 1936 Constitution.
98 Davies, op. cit., pp. 59–60.
99 L. Viola, '*Bab'i Bunty* and Peasant Women's Protest during Collectivization', in C. Ward (ed.) *The Stalinist Dictatorship* (London 1998), p. 227.
100 Sakwa, op. cit., p. 209, Document 5.22.
101 Davies, op. cit., p. 75.
102 Ibid., p. 81.
103 Ibid., p. 82.
104 See Ward, op. cit., p. 193.
105 Quoted in R. Hingley, *Russian Writers and Soviet Society 1917–1978* (London 1979), Ch. 2.
106 Ibid., quoted in Ch. 9.
107 Quoted in McCauley, op. cit., Part II.
108 S. Fitzpatrick, 'Resistance and Conformity: Everyday Stalinism: Ordinary Lives in Extraordinary Times', in D.L. Hoffman (ed.), *Stalinism* (Oxford 2003), p. 174.
109 Ibid., p.176.
110 Ibid., p. 171.
111 L. Viola, 'Populist Resistance in the Stalinist 1930s', in L. Viola (ed.) *Contending with Stalinism: Soviet Power and Popular Resistance in the 1930s* (Ithaca, NY 2002), p. 1.
112 T. McDonald, 'A Peasant Rebellion in Stalin's Russia', in Viola, *Contending with Stalinism*, op. cit.
113 Sakwa, op. cit., Document 5.22, p. 208.
114 E. Mawdsley, *The Stalin Years: The Soviet Union 1929–1953*, second edition (Manchester 2003), pp. 69–70.
115 Quoted in A. Fontaine, *History of the Cold War from the October Revolution to the Korean War, 1917–1950* (trans. D.D. Paige) (London 1968), Ch. 1.
116 G.F. Kennan, *Soviet Foreign Policy 1917–1941* (Princeton, NJ 1960), Document 8.
117 Quoted in R.C. Tucker, 'The Emergence of Stalin's Foreign Policy', *Slavic Review*, December 1977, xxxvi, 4.
118 Quoted in A.Z. Rubinstein, *Soviet Foreign Policy since World War II* (Cambridge, MA 1981), Ch. 1.
119 Quoted in Tucker, 'The Emergence', op. cit.
120 Quoted in W. Laqueur, *Russia and Germany: A Century of Conflict* (London 1965), Ch. 11.

121 Quoted in T.J. Uldricks, 'Soviet Security Policy in the 1930s', in G. Gorodetsky (ed.) *Soviet Foreign Policy 1917–1991* (London 1994), p. 73.
122 Quoted in R. Hutchings, *Soviet Economic Development* (Oxford 1967), Ch. 6.
123 Quoted in Tucker, 'The Emergence', op. cit.
124 Ibid.
125 Ibid.
126 J. Haslam, *The Soviet Union and the Struggle for Collective Security in Europe, 1933–39* (New York 1984), pp. 52–53.
127 J.A.S. Grenville, *The Major International Treaties 1914–1973* (London 1974), pp. 195–196.
128 G. Roberts, *The Soviet Union and the Origins of the Second World War* (London 1995), p. 97.
129 *A Short History of the Communist Party of the Soviet Union* (Moscow 1970), p. 247.
130 See Laqueur, op. cit., Ch. 12.
131 Grey, op. cit., Ch. 24.
132 Quoted in A. Bullock, *Hitler: A Study in Tyranny* (London 1952), Ch. 12.
133 J. Sapir, 'The Economics of War in the Soviet Union during World War II', in Kershaw and Lewin, op. cit., p. 210.
134 See V. Suvorov, *Icebreaker: Who Started the Second World War?* (London 1990).
135 E. Radzinsky, *Stalin: The First In-Depth Biography Based on Explosive New Documents from Russia's Secret Archives* (trans. H.T. Willetts) (New York 1996), pp. 452–456.
136 Quoted in Radzinsky, op. cit., p. 454.
137 Quoted in ibid., p. 456.
138 See E. Mawdsley, 'Crossing the Rubicon: Soviet Plans for Offensive War in 1940–1941', in *The International History Review*, 2003, 25, pp. 815–865.
139 D.A. Volkogonov, *Stalin* (Moscow 1989).
140 McDermott, op. cit.
141 T.J. Uldricks, 'The Icebreaker Controversy: Did Stalin Plan to Attack Hitler?', *Slavic Review*, 1999, 58, pp. 626–643.
142 Litvin and Keep, op. cit., p. 198.
143 R. Sakwa (ed.), *The Rise and Fall of the Soviet Union 1917–1991*, Document 8.4: Khrushchev's Secret Speech (London 1999), p. 319.
144 P. Mezhiritsky, *On the Precipice: Stalin, the Red Army Leadership and the Road to Stalingrad, 1931–1942* (trans. S. Britton) (Solihull 2012), extracts from Chapter 31.
145 Grey, op. cit., p. 319.
146 B. Bonwetsch, 'Stalin, the Red Army and the "Great Patriotic War"', in Kershaw and Lewin, op. cit., p. 196.
147 Sakwa, op. cit., p. 255. Document 6.17: Stalin's Radio Broadcast of 3 July 1941.
148 See ibid., p. 193.
149 G. Fischer, *Soviet Opposition to Stalin* (Cambridge, MA 1952), p. 45.
150 Grey, op. cit., p. 422.
151 See D.A. Volkogonov, 'Stalin as Supreme Commander', in B. Wegner (ed.) *From Peace to War: Germany, Soviet Russia and the World, 1939–1941* (Oxford 1997).
152 Sapir, op. cit., p. 234.
153 Quoted in V.M. Kulish, 'Russia Strikes Back', in Purnell's *History of the 20th Century*, Vol. 5 (London 1968), p. 1936.
154 M. Harrison, *Accounting for War: Soviet Production, Employment and the Defence Burden, 1940–1945* (Cambridge 1996), p. 130.
155 See M. Von Hagen, 'From "Great Fatherland War" to the Second World War: New Perspectives and Future Prospects', in Kershaw and Lewin, op. cit.
156 V.S. Dunham, *In Stalin's Time: Middleclass Values in Soviet Fiction* (Durham and London 1990), p. 7.
157 J. Noakes and G. Pridham (eds), *Nazism 1919–1945: A Documentary Reader* (Exeter 1995 edition), Vol. 3, Document 640, p. 912.
158 Fontaine, op. cit., Ch. 8.

159 Estimates only approximate and take account of figures provided by J. Ellenstein, *The Stalin Phenomenon* (London 1976), Ch. 5.
160 *History of Soviet Society* (Moscow 1971), p. 273.
161 *A Short History of the Communist Part of the Soviet Union* (Moscow 1970), p. 271.
162 Mawdsley, op. cit., p. 72.
163 Deutscher, op. cit., p. 551.
164 See Grey, op. cit.
165 Extracts from P. Kenez, *A History of the Soviet Union from the Beginning to the End*, second edition (Cambridge 2006), pp. 172–173.
166 C. Ward, *Stalin's Russia* (London 1993), p. 188.
167 Ibid., p. 187.
168 Extracts from McDermott, op. cit., p. 142.
169 See McDermott, op. cit., p. 141.
170 Quoted in ibid., p. 141.
171 Quoted in C. Seton Watson, 'The Cold War – Its Origins', in J.L. Henderson (ed.) *Since 1945: Aspects of Contemporary World History* (London 1966).
172 Rubinstein, op. cit., Ch. 3.
173 C. Kennedy-Pipe, *Russia and the World 1917–1991* (London 1998), p. 211.
174 Ward, op. cit., p. 188.
175 Tucker, *The Soviet Political Mind*, op. cit., Ch. 6.
176 This subject is covered thoroughly in R.C. Tucker, 'The Rise of Stalin's Personality Cult', *American Historical Review*, 1979, 84:2, pp. 347–366.
177 Ulam, op. cit.
178 Grey, op. cit., extracts from Preface and Ch. 23.
179 McCauley, op. cit., Part III.

4 Dictatorship in Italy

1 Quoted in A. Cassels, *Fascist Italy* (London 1969), Ch. 4.
2 A.J.P. Taylor, *The Origins of the Second World War* (London 1961), Ch. 3.
3 A.J.P. Taylor, video of *Men of Our Time: Mussolini* (Granada Television 1987).
4 J. Pollard, *The Fascist Experience in Italy* (London 1998), p. 10.
5 Ibid., p. 18.
6 A. De Grand, *Italian Fascism: Its Origins and Development* (Lincoln, NE 1982), Ch. 1.
7 D. Mack Smith, *Italy: A Modern History* (Ann Arbor, MI 1959), Ch. 37.
8 See Z. Sternhell, *Neither Right nor Left: Fascist Ideology in France* (Berkeley, CA 1986).
9 See D. Roberts, 'How to Think about Fascism and Ideology', *Journal of Contemporary History*, 2000, 35.2, pp. 185–211.
10 A.J. Gregor, *Young Mussolini and the Intellectual Origins of Fascism* (Berkeley, CA 1979), Ch. 10.
11 See Cassells, op. cit., Ch. 2.
12 De Grand, op. cit., Ch. 2.
13 R. de Felice, *Interpretations of Fascism* (Cambridge, MA 1977), p. 56.
14 A. Lyttelton, 'Italian Fascism', in W. Laqueur (ed.) *Fascism: A Reader's Guide* (London 1976).
15 Pollard, op. cit., p. 32.
16 Ibid., quoted on p. 42.
17 Ibid., quoted on p. 41.
18 Ibid.
19 Quoted in J. Whittam, *Fascist Italy* (Manchester 1995), p. 2.
20 Quoted in L. Barzini, 'Benito Mussolini', *Encounter*, July 1964.
21 M. Gallo, *Mussolini's Italy* (New York 1973), Ch. 5.
22 C. Hibbert, 'Fallen Idol', *Spectator*, 19 June 1964; a review of Sir I. Kirkpatrick's *Mussolini: Study of a Demagogue*.
23 Sir I. Kirkpatrick, *Mussolini: Study of a Demagogue* (London 1964), Ch. 6.
24 See D. Mack Smith, *Mussolini* (London 1981).

25 P. Morgan, *Italian Fascism 1919–1945* (London 1995), p. 155.
26 B. Mussolini, 'The Political and Social Doctrine of Fascism', *International Conciliation*, January 1935, p. 306.
27 De Grand, op. cit., Ch. 10.
28 Quoted in Whittam, op. cit., p. 2.
29 From *Enciclopedia Italiana*, XIV, 1932, quoted in Pollard, op. cit., p. 119.
30 Quoted in Gallo, op. cit., Ch. 7.
31 Pollard, op. cit., p. 50.
32 S.G. Payne, *A History of Fascism* (London 1995), p. 114.
33 Quoted in Pollard, op. cit., p. 52.
34 Quoted in Payne, op. cit., p. 116.
35 Quoted in Whittam, op. cit., p. 43.
36 Ibid., quoted on p. 153.
37 Ibid.
38 Payne, op. cit., p. 118.
39 E. Tannenbaum, *Fascism in Italy: Society and Culture, 1922–1945* (London 1973), p. 73.
40 Payne, op. cit., p. 117.
41 Ibid., p. 119.
42 Lyttelton, op. cit.
43 See P. Melograni, 'The Cult of the Duce in Mussolini's Italy', in G.L. Mosse (ed.) *International Fascism: New Thoughts and New Approaches* (London 1979).
44 Quoted in Gallo, op. cit., Ch. 5.
45 See Emilio Gentile, *The Sacralization of Politics in Fascist Italy* (trans. Cambridge, MA 1996).
46 Ibid., p. 154.
47 Ibid., p. 159.
48 Ibid.
49 See S. Falasca-Zamponi, *Fascist Spectacle: The Aesthetics of Power in Mussolini's Italy* (Berkeley 2000), p. 26.
50 Ibid.
51 Ibid., p. 28.
52 Ibid., p. 36.
53 Ibid., p. 86.
54 Quoted in ibid., p. 86.
55 Quoted in R. Wolfson, *Years of Change* (London 1978), Ch. 11.
56 Pollard, op. cit., p. 67.
57 See Payne, op. cit., p. 224.
58 P.V. Cannistraro (ed.), *Historical Dictionary of Fascist Italy* (Westport, CT 1982), s.v. 'Cinema'.
59 See R.J.B. Bosworth, *The Italian Dictatorship: Problems and Perspectives in the Interpretation of Mussolini and Fascism* (London 1998), Ch. 7.
60 Quoted in Pollard, op. cit., p. 84.
61 Morgan, op. cit., p. 87.
62 Payne, op. cit., p. 117.
63 Ibid.
64 Whittam, op. cit., p. 56.
65 Pollard, op. cit., p. 65.
66 *Historical Dictionary of Fascist Italy*, s.v. 'Antisemitism'.
67 Gallo, op. cit., Ch. 13.
68 Quoted in Bosworth, op. cit., p. 102.
69 Pollard, op. cit., p. 127.
70 Ibid.
71 M. Van Creveld, 'Beyond the Finzi-Contini Garden. Mussolini's "Fascist Racism"', *Encounter*, February 1974.
72 *Historical Dictionary of Fascist Italy*, s.v. 'Antisemitism'.

73 Whittam, op. cit., p. 99.
74 Morgan, op. cit., p. 161.
75 *Historical Dictionary of Fascist Italy*, s.v. 'Antisemitism'.
76 B. Mussolini, *My Autobiography* (London 1928), p. 276.
77 Morgan, op. cit., p. 96.
78 Bosworth, op. cit., p. 145.
79 Quoted in Tannenbaum, op. cit., Ch. 7.
80 Quoted in P.C. Kent, *The Pope and the Duce* (New York 1981): overall argument summarized in Preface.
81 Quoted in G. Jackson (ed.), *Problems in European Civilization: The Spanish Civil War* (Lexington, MA 1967); extract by F.J. Taylor.
82 Cassels, op. cit., p. 58.
83 Pollard, op. cit., p. 84.
84 Tannenbaum, op. cit., p. 100.
85 De Grand, op. cit., Ch. 8.
86 Morgan, op. cit., p. 129.
87 *Historical Dictionary of Fascist Italy*, s.v. 'Industry'.
88 Quoted in Mack Smith, *Italy*, op. cit., Ch. 28.
89 See A. De Grand, *Fascist Italy and Nazi Germany: The 'Fascist' Style of Rule* (London 1995), p. 57.
90 Bosworth, op. cit., p. 264.
91 L. Caldwell, 'Reproducers of the Nation: Women and the Family in Fascist Policy', in G. Forgacs (ed.) *Rethinking Italian Fascism: Capitalism, Populism and Culture* (London 1986), p. 115.
92 See De Grand, *Fascist Italy and Nazi Germany*, op. cit., p. 59.
93 Bosworth, op. cit., p. 268.
94 V. De Grazia, *How Fascism Ruled Women: Italy 1922–1945* (Berkeley, CA 1992), p. 275.
95 Caldwell, op. cit., p.117.
96 De Grand, *Fascist Italy and Nazi Germany*, op. cit., p. 60.
97 Gregor, op. cit., Ch. 8.
98 Pollard, op. cit., p. 80.
99 Morgan, op. cit., p. 113.
100 C. Duggan, *Fascism and the Mafia* (New Haven, CT 1989), p. 264.
101 Tannenbaum, op. cit., Ch. 9.
102 G. Salvemini, *Prelude to World War II* (London 1953), p. 20.
103 A.P. Taylor, *The Origins of the Second World War* (Harmondsworth 1964), p. 85.
104 For a historiographical summary of this, see R. Mallett, *Mussolini and the Origins of the Second World War, 1939–1940* (Basingstoke 2003), Ch. 1.
105 M. Knox, *Mussolini Unleashed: Politics and Strategy in Italy's Last War, 1939–41* (Cambridge 1988).
106 A. Kallis, *Fascist Ideology, Territory and Expansionism in Italy and Germany, 1922–1945* (London 2000).
107 D. Rodogno, *Fascism's European Empire: Italian Occupation During the Second World War* (trans. Cambridge 2008).
108 See Mallet, op. cit.
109 Ibid., p. 8.
110 See S. Marks, 'Mussolini and Locarno: Fascist Foreign Policy in Microcosm', *Journal of Contemporary History*, 1979, 14, pp. 423–479.
111 See P.G. Edwards, 'Britain, Mussolini and the Locarno-Geneva System', *European Studies Review*, January 1980.
112 Quoted in R.B. Bosworth, 'The British Press, the Conservatives and Mussolini 1920–34', *Journal of Contemporary History*, April 1970.
113 R.B. Bosworth, *Mussolini* (London 2002), pp. 254–255.
114 R. Ben-Ghiat, *Fascist Modernities: Italy 1922–1945* (Berkeley, CA 2001), p. 125.
115 Mallett, op. cit., p. 8.

116 Ibid.
117 See ibid., p. 9.
118 P.M.H. Bell, *The Origins of the Second World War in Europe* (London 1996), p. 264.
119 Mallett, op. cit., p. 13.
120 H. Thomas, *The Spanish Civil War* (London 1961), Appendix 3.
121 Mallett, op. cit., p. 15.
122 Quoted in W. Shirer, *The Rise and Fall of the Third Reich* (London 1960), Ch. 9.
123 G. Ciano, *Diary 1937–38* (trans. A. Mayor) (London 1948), p. 29.
124 Bosworth, 'The British Press', op. cit.
125 Morgan, op. cit., p. 136.
126 R. de Felice, *Fascism: An Informal Introduction to its Theory and Practice* (New Brunswick, NJ 1976), quoted in D. Smyth, 'Duce Diplomatico', *Historical Journal*, 1978, 21, 4.
127 Ibid.
128 G. Carocci, *Italian Fascism* (trans. I. Quigly) (Harmondsworth 1974), Ch. 7.
129 De Grand, *Fascist Italy and Nazi Germany*, op. cit., p. 99.
130 D. Mack Smith, *Mussolini's Roman Empire* (London 1976), Preface.
131 M. Knox, *Mussolini Unleashed 1929–1941* (Cambridge 1982).
132 Whittam, op. cit., p. 122.
133 P. Kennedy, *The Rise and Fall of the Great Powers: Economic Change and Military Conflict from 1500 to 2000* (London 1988), p. 430.
134 Ibid., p. 458.
135 Morgan, op. cit., p. 177.
136 A. Kallis, *Fascist Ideology, Territory and Expansionism in Italy and Germany, 1922–1945* (London 2000), p. 59.
137 See ibid., pp. 51–52.
138 See D. Rodogno, *Fascism's European Empire: Italian Occupation During the Second World War* (trans. Cambridge 2008), p. 412.
139 Ibid., p. 413.
140 Mack Smith, *Mussolini's Roman Empire*, op. cit., Ch. 17.
141 Pollard, op. cit., p. 108.
142 Quoted in C. Leeds, *Italy under Mussolini* (London 1968), Ch. 5.
143 Pollard, op. cit., p. 109.
144 Quoted in *Historical Dictionary of Fascist Italy*, s.v. 'Italian Social Republic'.
145 Clark, op. cit., p. 309.
146 Pollard, op. cit., p. 114.
147 Ben-Ghiat, op. cit., p. 202.
148 See R. Battaglia, *The Story of the Italian Resistance* (London 1957).
149 G. Procacci, *History of the Italian People* (London 1970), p. 374.
150 See C. Pavone, *A Civil War: A History of the Italian Resistance*, translated by Peter Levy with the assistance of David Broder (London and New York 2013).
151 D. Mack Smith, *Italy: A Modern History* (Ann Arbor 1959), p. 491.
152 L. Barzini, 'Benito Mussolini', *Encounter*, July 1964.
153 Taylor, *Origins of the Second World War*, op. cit., p. 56.
154 W.W. Halperin, *Mussolini and Italian Fascism* (New York 1964), p. 4.
155 L. Fermi, *Mussolini* (Chicago 1961), p. 210.
156 Ibid., p. 212.
157 Mack Smith, *Mussolini*, op. cit., p. xiv.
158 Sir I. Kirkpatrick, *Study of a Demagogue* (London 1964) and J. Ridley, *Mussolini* (London 1997).
159 A.J. Gregor, *Young Mussolini and the Intellectual Origins of Fascism* (Berkeley, CA 1979), p. 237.
160 Roberts, op. cit., p. 208.
161 Ibid.
162 Ibid.
163 Taylor, *Origins of the Second World War*, op. cit., p. 56.

164 A. De Grand, 'Mussolini's Follies: Fascism in its Imperial and Racist Phase', *Contemporary European History*, 2004, 13:2, p. 128.
165 Ibid., p. 136.
166 R.J.B. Bosworth, *Mussolini's Italy* (London 2005), 570.
167 De Grand, *Fascist Italy and Nazi Germany*, op. cit., p. 147.
168 Halperin, op. cit., p. 4.
169 J. Ridley, *Mussolini* (London 1997), p. 201.
170 A.J. Gregor, *Giovanni Gentile: Philosopher of Fascism* (New Brunswick, NJ 2001), p. 102.
171 R. Kedward, 'Afterword: What Kind of Revisionism?' in D. Forgacs (ed.) *Rethinking Italian Fascism* (London 1986), p. 201.
172 Ibid., p. 201.
173 Bosworth, *Mussolini's Italy*, op. cit., p.568.
174 Quoted in De Grand, *Fascist Italy and Nazi Germany*, op. cit., p. 131.
175 Ibid., p. 138.
176 Quoted in ibid., p. 140.
177 Ibid., p 147.

5 Dictatorship in Germany

1 The concept of 'revolution', as applied to Germany in 1919, has sometimes been challenged, although consideration of the arguments would not be appropriate in a section which is here a background to another issue. For further details of the arguments on the 'German revolution', see S.J. Lee, *The Weimar Republic* (London 1998), Ch. 1.
2 Quoted in L. Snyder (ed.) *The Weimar Republic* (Princeton, NJ 1966), Reading No. 3.
3 Ibid., Readings to No. 18.
4 Ibid.
5 Quoted in A. Bullock, *Hitler: A Study in Tyranny* (London 1952), Ch. 2.
6 Quoted in J. Noakes and G. Pridham (eds) *Documents on Nazism 1919–1945* (London 1974), Ch. 1, Document 12.
7 I. Kershaw, *Hitler* (Harlow 1991), p. 29.
8 Noakes and Pridham, op. cit., Ch. 3, Document 4.
9 E. Davidson, *The Making of Adolf Hitler* (Columbia, MI 1997), p. 331.
10 Quoted in K. Sontheimer, 'The Weimar Republic and the Prospects of German Democracy', in E.J. Feuchtwanger (ed.) *Upheaval and Continuity* (London 1971).
11 E. Fraenkel, 'Historical Handicaps of German Parliamentarianism', in E. Fraenkel, *The Road to Dictatorship 1918–1933* (London 1970).
12 H. Mommsen, 'Government without Parties: Conservative Plans for Constitutional Revision at the End of the Weimar Republic', in L.E. Jones and J. Retallack (eds) *Between Reform, Reaction and Resistance: Studies in the History of German Conservatism from 1789 to 1945* (Providence, RI 1993), p. 350.
13 Quoted in S. Taylor, *Germany 1918–1933* (London 1983), Ch. 4.
14 J.W. Hiden, *The Weimar Republic* (Harlow 1974), p. 21.
15 A. Hitler, *Mein Kampf*, Vol. 2, Ch. 11.
16 Ibid., Vol. 1, Ch. 6.
17 P.D. Stachura, 'Who Were the Nazis? A Sociopolitical Analysis of the National Socialist Machtubernahme', *European Studies Review*, 1981, ii.
18 A. Bullock, *Hitler and Stalin: Parallel Lives* (2nd edn, London 1998), p. 158.
19 R.F. Hamilton, *Who Voted for Hitler?* (Princeton, NJ 1982).
20 H. Trevor-Roper, *The Last Days of Hitler* (London 1947), Ch. 1.
21 T. Childers, 'The Middle Classes and National Socialism', in D. Blackburn and R.J. Evans (eds) *The German Bourgeoisie* (London 1991), p. 326.
22 Stachura, op. cit.
23 D. Mühlburger, 'The Sociology of the NSDAP: The Question of Working Class Membership', *Journal of Contemporary History*, 1980, 15.
24 C. Fischer, *The Rise of the Nazis* (Manchester 1995), p. 108.

25 E. Eyck, *A History of the Weimar Republic* (Cambridge, MA 1962), Vol. 1, Ch. 10.
26 H. Boldt, 'Article 48 of the Weimar Constitution, Its Historical and Political Implications', in A. Nicholls (ed.) *German Democracy and the Triumph of Hitler: Essays in Recent German History* (London 1971).
27 J. Hiden, *Republican and Fascist Germany* (London 1996), p. 60.
28 H. Boldt, quoted in D.G. Williamson, *The Third Reich* (Harlow 1982), Ch. 3.
29 Noakes and Pridham, op. cit., Ch. 5, Document 7.
30 M. Broszat, *The Hitler State: The Foundation and Development of the Internal Structure of the Third Reich* (London 1981), Ch. 3.
31 Noakes and Pridham, op. cit., Ch. 7, Document 2.
32 Ibid., Ch. 8, Document 1.
33 Broszat, op. cit., Ch. 6.
34 Noakes and Pridham, op. cit., Ch. 8, Document 4.
35 Quoted in Sir J. Wheeler-Bennett, *The Nemesis of Power: The German Army in Politics 1918–1945* (London 1953), Part III, Ch. 2.
36 Quoted in J. Remak (ed.), *The Nazi Years* (Englewood Cliffs, NJ 1969), p. 52.
37 A. Kaes, M. Jay and E. Dimendberg, *The Weimar Republic Sourcebook* (Berkeley, CA 1994), Document 16, p. 49.
38 Remak, op. cit., pp. 52–53.
39 Ibid., p. 54.
40 J. Noakes and G. Pridham (eds), *Nazism 1919–1945: A Documentary Reader* (Exeter 1983–8), Vol. 1, p. 185.
41 K.D. Bracher, 'Stages of Totalitarian "Integration" (*Gleichschaltung*): The Consolidation of National Socialist Rule in 1933 and 1934', in H. Holborn (ed.) *Republic to Reich: The Making of the Nazi Revolution* (New York 1972), p. 116.
42 K.D. Bracher, *The German Dictatorship* (trans. London 1973), p. 244.
43 C. Leitz (ed.), *The Third Reich: The Essential Readings* (Oxford 1999), p. 27.
44 See K. Hildebrand, *The Third Reich* (trans. London 1984), Concluding Remarks.
45 Noakes and Pridham, *Nazism 1919–1945*, op. cit., Part III.
46 Information from Broszat, op. cit. and Noakes and Pridham, *Nazism 1919–1945*, op. cit.
47 See K.D. Bracher, *The German Dictatorship* (New York 1970).
48 See Hildebrand, op. cit.
49 See M. Broszat, *Hitler and the Collapse of the Weimar Republic* (Oxford 1987).
50 See extracts from H. Mommsen in Hildebrand, op. cit., p. 137.
51 See I. Kershaw, 'Working Towards the Führer: Reflections on the Nature of the Hitler Dictatorship', *Contemporary European History*, 1993, 2:2, pp. 103–118.
52 Information from Noakes and Pridham, *Nazism 1919–1945*, Ch. 10.
53 Ibid., Ch. 10, Document 8.
54 Ibid., Ch. 10, Document 30.
55 G.C. Browder, *The Gestapo and the SS Security Service in the Nazi Revolution* (New York 1996), p. 5.
56 Ibid., p. 6.
57 M. Kitchen, *The Third Reich: Charisma and Community* (Harlow 2008), p. 261.
58 Ibid., p. 262.
59 Ibid., pp. 260–261.
60 Quoted in Noakes and Pridham, *Nazism 1919–1945*, op. cit., Vol. 2, p. 500.
61 H. Höhne, *The Order of the Death's Head* (London 1972), p. 12.
62 Quoted in K.M. Mallman and G. Paul, 'Omniscient, Omnipotent, Omnipresent? Gestapo, Society and Resistance', in D. Crew (ed.) *Nazism and German Society 1933–1945* (London 1994), p. 169.
63 Ibid.
64 Ibid., pp. 169–170.
65 R. Gellately, *The Gestapo and German Society: Enforcing Racial Policy 1933–1945* (Oxford 1990), p. 212.
66 Mallman and Paul, op. cit., p. 174.
67 Hiden, *Republican and Fascist Germany*, op. cit., p. 181.

68 M. Burleigh, *The Third Reich: A New History* (London 2000), p. 183.
69 R.J. Evans, *The Third Reich in Power 1933–1939* (London 2005), p. 114.
70 E.A. Johnson, *Nazi Terror: Gestapo, Jews and Ordinary Citizens* (New York 1999), p. 483.
71 Quoted in Noakes and Pridham, *Nazism 1919–1945*, op. cit., p. 381.
72 Quoted in Bracher, *The German Dictatorship*, op. cit., Ch. 5.
73 Quoted in M.J. Thornton, *Nazism 1918–1945* (London 1966), Ch. 7.
74 Quoted in Bracher, *The German Dictatorship*, op. cit., Ch. 5.
75 Quoted in R. Grunberger, *A Social History of the Third Reich* (London 1971), Ch. 19.
76 T.L. Jarman, *The Rise and Fall of Nazi Germany* (New York 1961), p. 183.
77 D.J.K. Peukert, *Inside Nazi Germany: Conformity, Opposition and Racism in Everyday Life* (trans. London 1989), p. 153.
78 Ibid.
79 See E. Harvey, *Women and the Nazi East: Agents and Witnesses of Germanization* (New Haven and London 2003).
80 Quoted in D. Welch, *The Third Reich: Politics and Propaganda* (London 1993), p. 24.
81 Ibid., p. 26.
82 H. Boak, '"Our Last Hope": Women's Votes for Hitler – a Reappraisal', *German Studies Review*, 1989, XII:2, p. 303.
83 C. Koonz, *Mothers in the Fatherland: Women, the Family and Nazi Politics* (London 1988), p. 5.
84 Quoted in Williamson, op. cit., Document 7.
85 Quoted in Noakes and Pridham, *Nazism 1919–1945*, op. cit., Ch. 12.
86 Quoted in C. Haste, *Nazi Women: Hitler's Seduction of a Nation* (London 2001), Ch. 7.
87 J. Stephenson, 'Women, Motherhood and the Family in the Third Reich', in M. Burleigh (ed.) *Confronting the Nazi Past* (London 1996), p. 178.
88 Koonz, op. cit., p. 6.
89 Ibid., p. 14.
90 See Harvey, op. cit.
91 Ibid., p. 10.
92 Ibid., p. 299.
93 Quoted in Koonz, op. cit., p. 200.
94 Quoted in Grunberger, op. cit.
95 See Haste, op. cit., Ch. 7.
96 Koonz, op. cit., p. 17.
97 See Stephenson, op. cit., p. 107.
98 Quoted in Noakes and Pridham, *Nazism 1919–1945*, op. cit., Ch. 12.
99 P. Steinbach, 'The Conservative Resistance', in D.C. Large (ed.) *Contending with Hitler: Varieties of German Resistance in the Third Reich* (Cambridge 1991), p. 90.
100 Quoted in Grunberger, op. cit., Ch. 29.
101 Ibid.
102 Burleigh, *The Third Reich*, op. cit., p. 253.
103 Ibid., p. 254.
104 Quoted in Burleigh, *The Third Reich*, op. cit., p. 256.
105 Kershaw, op. cit., Ch. 7.
106 Quoted in Kitchen, op. cit., p. 115.
107 Ibid.
108 Quoted in F. Spotts, *Hitler and the Power of Aesthetics* (London 2002), p. 43.
109 R.G. Waite, *The Psychopathic God: Adolf Hitler* (New York 1993), pp. 5–6.
110 Peukert, op. cit., p. 69.
111 Quoted in Crew, op. cit., pp. 4–5.
112 Ibid., p. 6.
113 Quoted in Peukert, op. cit., p. 69.
114 O. Bartov, 'The Missing Years: German Workers, German Soldiers', in Crew, op. cit., p. 46.

115 See Mallman and Paul, op. cit., pp. 180–189.
116 See D.J. Goldhagen, *Hitler's Willing Executioners: Ordinary Germans and the Holocaust* (London 1997), especially Ch. 15.
117 I. Kershaw, *Popular Opinion and Political Dissent in the Third Reich* (Oxford 1983), p. 373.
118 Quoted in ibid., p. 126.
119 Details from D.J.K. Peukert, 'Youth in the Third Reich', in R. Bessel (ed.) *Life in the Third Reich* (Oxford 1986), pp. 30–36.
120 Quoted in D.J.K. Peukert, *Inside Nazi Germany: Conformity, Opposition and Racism in Everyday Life* (trans. London 1987; Harmondsworth 1989), p. 160.
121 Quoted in Peukert, 'Youth in the Third Reich', op. cit., p. 29.
122 See Peukert, *Inside Nazi Germany*, op. cit., p. 161.
123 Quoted in M. Housden, *Resistance and Conformity in the Third Reich* (London 1997), p. 58.
124 Ibid., p. 53.
125 Quoted in J. Laver, *Nazi Germany 1933–1945* (London 1991), p. 79.
126 Quoted in Remak, op. cit., p. 93.
127 Quoted in Housden, op. cit., p. 61.
128 T.S. Hamerow, *On the Road to the Wolf's Lair: German Resistance to Hitler* (Cambridge, MA 1999), p. 162.
129 M. Broszat, 'A Social and Historical Typology of the German Opposition to Hitler', in Large, op. cit., p. 28.
130 Ibid.
131 K. Kweit, 'Resistance and Opposition: The Example of the German Jews', in Large, op. cit., p. 67.
132 Peukert, *Inside Nazi Germany*, op. cit., p. 248.
133 Bracher, op. cit., Ch. 7.
134 Hitler, *Mein Kampf*, quoted in J. Laver (ed.) *Nazi Germany* (London 1991), p. 82.
135 Quoted in Remak, op. cit., pp. 32–33.
136 These are dealt with in S.J. Lee, *The Weimar Republic*, second edition (London 2010), pp. 151–156.
137 N. Frei, *National Socialist Rule in Germany: The Führer State 1933–1945* (trans. Oxford 1993), p. 71.
138 Noakes and Pridham, *Nazism 1919–1945*, op. cit., Vol. 2, p. 287.
139 See A. Tooze, *The Wages of Destruction: The Making and Breaking of the Nazi Economy* (London 2006) and R.J. Overy, '"Domestic Crisis" and War in 1939', in Leitz, op. cit., p. 115.
140 C.W. Guillebaud, *Economic Recovery in Germany* (London, 1939), p. 218.
141 Jarman, op. cit., p. 179.
142 C. Buccheim, 'The Nazi Boom: A, Economic Cul-de-Sac', in H. Mommsen (ed.), *The Third Reich Between Vision and Reality: New Perspectives on German History 1918–1945* (Oxford 2001), pp. 79–82.
143 Overy, op. cit., p. 108.
144 B.H. Klein, 'Germany's Economic Preparations for War', in H.W. Koch (ed.), *Aspects of the Third Reich* (London 1985), p. 360.
145 Guillebaud, op. cit., p. 218.
146 See extract in R.G.L. Waite (ed.), *Hitler and Nazi Germany* (New York 1965).
147 Ibid.
148 V.R. Berghahn, *Modern Germany: Society, Economy and Politics in the Twentieth Century* (Cambridge 1987), p. 149.
149 Quoted in G. Layton, *Germany: The Third Reich 1933–45* (London 1992), p. 72.
150 Ibid.
151 Kitchen, op. cit., p. 150.
152 Noakes and Pridham, *Nazism 1919–1945*, op. cit., Vol. 3, p. 665.
153 See H. Schmitz (ed.), *A Nation of Victims? Representation of German Wartime Suffering from 1945 to the Present* (Amsterdam and New York 2007).

154 Peukert, *Inside Nazi Germany*, op. cit., p. 208. See also T.W. Mason, *Social Policy in the Third Reich: The Working Class and the National Community* (Oxford 1993), pp. 279–280.
155 H. Friedlander, 'The Exclusion and Murder of the Disabled', in R. Gellately and N. Stoltzfus (eds) *Social Outsiders in Nazi Germany* (Princeton, NJ 2001), p. 146.
156 Quoted R. Proctor, *Racial Hygiene: Medicine under the Nazis* (Cambridge, MA 1988), p. 183.
157 Ibid., p. 183.
158 See L. Pine, *Nazi Family Policy 1933–1945* (Oxford 1997), p. 119.
159 Quoted in N. Wachsmann, 'From Indefinite Confinement to Extermination: "Habitual Criminals" in the Third Reich', in R. Gellately and N. Stoltzfus (eds) *Social Outsiders in Nazi Germany* (Princeton, NJ 2001), p. 177.
160 Ibid.
161 See N. Wachsmann, *Hitler's Prisons: Legal Terror in Nazi Germany* (New Haven 2004), pp. 125–128.
162 I. Kershaw, *The Nazi Dictatorship*, fourth edition (London 2000), p. 263.
163 A. Barkai, 'The German *Volksgemeinschaft* from the Persecution of the Jews to the "Final Solution"', in Burleigh, *Confronting the Nazi Past*, op. cit., p. 89.
164 S.H. Milton, '"Gypsies" as Social Outsiders in Nazi Germany', in R. Gellately and N. Stoltzfus eds., *Social Outsiders in Nazi Germany* (Princeton, NJ 2001), p. 212.
165 Quoted in Remak, op. cit., p. 5.
166 J.C.G. Röhl, *From Bismarck to Hitler* (Harlow 1970), Ch. 5, Document 1.
167 Hiden, *Republican and Fascist Germany*, op. cit., Ch. 4.
168 Röhl, op. cit, Ch. 5, Document 7.
169 Ibid.
170 H.W. Gatzke, *Stresemann and the Rearmament of Germany* (Baltimore, MD 1954), Ch. 6.
171 Quoted in ibid.
172 Quoted in H. Holborn, *A History of Modern Germany*, Vol. 3, 1840–1945 (London 1969), Ch. 12.
173 G.A. Craig, *Germany 1866–1945* (Oxford 1978), Ch. 19.
174 Ibid.
175 Ibid.
176 Noakes and Pridham, *Nazism 1919–1945*, op. cit., Ch. 18.
177 Quotations in this paragraph are from Hitler's *Mein Kampf* and his *Second Book*. Material and quotations are also from H. Von Maltitz, *The Evolution of Hitler's Germany* (New York 1973), Ch. 3.
178 Quoted in Williamson, op. cit., Ch. 9.
179 A. Hillgruber, *Germany and the Two World Wars* (trans. W.C. Kirby) (Cambridge, MA 1981), Ch. 5.
180 E. Jäckel, *Hitler in History* (Hanover 1984), Ch. 2.
181 See Kershaw, op. cit., for summary of debate and for quoted extracts.
182 Jäckel, op. cit., Ch. 4.
183 A. Hillgruber, 'England's Place in Hitler's Plans for World Dominion', *Journal of Contemporary History*, 1974, 9.
184 J. Thies, *Hitler's Plans for Global Domination: Nazi Architecture and Ultimate War Aims* (originally published 1976, trans I. Cooke and M. Friedrich) (New York 2012), p. 195.
185 Ibid., p.143.
186 Ibid., p. 147.
187 Ibid., p. 7.
188 Ibid.
189 V.R. Berghahn, 'Foreword', in ibid., p. xiii.
190 Quotations from A.J.P. Taylor, *The Origins of the Second World War* (London 1961), Ch. 7.

191 Quoted in K.H. Jarausch, 'From Second to Third Reich: The Problem of Continuity in German Foreign Policy', *Central European History*, 1979, 12.
192 A. Bullock, contribution to *Hitler and the Origins of the Second World War, Proceedings of the British Academy* (Oxford 1967), Ch. 8.
193 Bullock, op. cit., liii.
194 I. Kershaw, 'Nazi Foreign Policy: Hitler's "Programme" or "Expansion without Object"?', in P. Finney (ed.) *The Origins of the Second World War* (London 1997), p. 143.
195 Kitchen, op. cit., p. 302.
196 See F. Fischer, *Germany's Aims in the First World War* (London 1967).
197 Noakes and Pridham, *Nazism 1919–1945*, op. cit., Ch. 16.
198 See extract in Waite, op. cit.
199 I. Kershaw, lecture at Aston University, 1997.
200 J.L. Snell (ed.), *The Outbreak of the Second World War* (Boston 1962), extract from the Nuremberg Judgement.
201 R.J. Sontag, 'The Last Months of Peace, 1939', *Foreign Affairs*, 1957, xxv.
202 H. Trevor-Roper, 'A.J.P. Taylor, 'Hitler and the War', *Encounter*, 1961, xvii.
203 J. Fest, *Hitler* (London 1974), Interpolation Three.
204 Quotations from A.J.P. Taylor, op. cit., Ch. 7.
205 T.W. Mason, 'Some Origins of the Second World War', *Past and Present*, 1964.
206 R. Henig, *The Origins of the Second World War* (London 1985), Section III.
207 Noakes and Pridham, *Nazism 1919–1945*, op. cit., Ch. 19.
208 Williamson, op. cit., Ch. 10.
209 Craig, op. cit., Ch. 20.
210 Quoted in W.L. Shirer, *The Rise and Fall of the Third Reich* (London 1960), Ch. 19.
211 Quoted in Williamson, op. cit., Ch. 10.
212 Quoted in Hildebrand, op. cit., Ch. 1.
213 N. Rich, *Hitler's War Aims: The Establishment of the New Order* (London 1974), Vol. II.
214 Quoted in K. Syrop, *Poland: Between the Hammer and the Anvil* (London 1968), Ch. 16.
215 Shirer, op. cit., Ch. 27.
216 Thornton, op. cit., Ch. 9.
217 Ibid.
218 M.R.D. Foot, 'Nazi Wartime Atrocities', in Purnell's *History of the Twentieth Century*, Vol. 5 (London 1968).
219 Jäckel, op. cit., Ch. 4.
220 Quoted in T.L. Jarman, *The Rise and Fall of Nazi Germany* (London 1955), Ch. 15.
221 Bullock, *Hitler*, op. cit., Ch. 14.
222 F. Halder, *Hitler as War Lord* (trans. P. Findley) (London 1950).
223 P.E. Schramm, *Hitler: The Man and the Military Leader* (London 1972), Ch. 2.
224 Ibid.
225 Halder, op. cit.
226 Quoted in P. Stern, Hitler: *The Führer and the People* (London 1975), Ch. 22.
227 Halder, op. cit.
228 G. Weeks, 'Understanding the Holocaust: The Past and Future of Holocaust Studies', *Contemporary European History*, 2006, 15:1, pp. 117–129.
229 See R. Breitman, *Official Secrets: What the Nazis Planned, What the British and Americans Knew* (New York 1968).
230 See D. Bloxham, *Genocide on Trial: War Crimes Trials and the Formation of Holocaust History and Memory* (Oxford 2001).
231 B. Niven, 'Remembering the Holocaust: Representation, Neglect and Instrumentalization', *European History Quarterly*, 2006, 36:2, pp. 279–291, at p. 281.
232 D. Diner, 'The Destruction of Narrativity: The Holocaust in Historical Discourse', in M. Postone and E. Santner (eds) *Catastrophe and Meaning: The Holocaust and the Twentieth Century* (Chicago 2003), p. 68.
233 Noakes and Pridham, *Nazism 1919–1945*, op. cit., p. 1049.

234 Information adapted from ibid.
235 See D. Lipstadt, *Denying the Holocaust: The Growing Assault on Truth and Memory* (New York 1993).
236 Ibid., p. 222.
237 D.J. Goldhagen, *Hitler's Willing Executioners: Ordinary Germans and the Holocaust* (London 1997), p. 162.
238 See R. Hilberg, *The Destruction of the European Jews* (Chicago 1961).
239 M. Broszat, in D. Cesarini (ed.), *The Final Solution: Origins and Implementation* (London 1994), p. 7.
240 M. Mommsen, 'The Realization of the Unthinkable', in G. Hirschfield (ed.), *The Policies of Genocide* (London 1986), pp. 35–36.
241 O. Bartov (ed.), *The Holocaust: Origins, Implementation, Aftermath* (London 2003), p. 5.
242 C. Browning, 'The Origins of the Final Solution', in J.C. Friedman (ed.) *The Routledge History of The Holocaust* (Abingdon 2011), pp. 163–164.
243 Ibid., p. 7.
244 Diner, op. cit., p. 75.
245 Quoted in Remak, op. cit., p. 159.
246 J. Dülffer, *Nazi Germany 1933–1945: Faith and Annihilation* (London 1996), p. 179.
247 Goldhagen, op. cit., p. 162.
248 G.D. Rosenfeld, 'The Controversy That Isn't The Debate over Daniel J. Goldhagen's *Hitler's Willing Executioners* in Comparative Perspective', *Contemporary European History*, 1999, 8:2, pp. 249–273, at p. 262.
249 See L. Rothkirchen, *The Jews of Bohemia and Moravia: Facing the Holocaust* (Lincoln, NE 2005), Ch. 5.
250 See J. Connelly, 'Poles and Jews in the Second World War: The Revisions of Jan T. Gross', *Contemporary European History*, 2002, pp. 641–658.
251 J.T. Gross, *Neighbours: The Destruction of the Jewish Community in Jedwabne, Poland* (Princeton, NJ 2001), Ch. 5.
252 Connelly, op. cit., p. 656. See also N. Aleksiun, 'Polish Historiography of the Holocaust – Between Silence and Public Debate', *German History*, 2004, 22:3, pp. 406–432.
253 Quoted in T. Cole, *Holocaust City: The Making of a Jewish Ghetto* (London 2003), p. 53.
254 Quoted in ibid., p. 65.
255 Quoted in ibid., p. 61.
256 Quoted in ibid., p. 66.
257 R. Ioanid, *The Holocaust in Romania* (Chicago 2000), p. 293.
258 Hilberg, op. cit., pp. 666–667.
259 See G. Corni, *Hitler's Ghettoes. Voices from a Beleaguered Society 1939–1944* (trans. N.R. Iannelli) (London 2003), Ch. 11.
260 Quoted in A. Barkai, *From Boycott to Annihilation* (London 1989), p. 141.
261 Koonz, op. cit., p. 363.
262 M. Housden, *Resistance and Conformity in the Third Reich* (London 1997), p. 125.
263 R. Hilberg, 'The "Judenrat": Conscious or Unconscious Tool?', in *Patterns of Jewish Leadership in Nazi Europe 1933–45: Proceedings of the Yad Vashem International Conference* (Jerusalem 1977).
264 J. Robinson, 'Some Basic Issues that Faced the Jewish Councils', in I. Trunk, *Judenrat: The Jewish Councils in Eastern Europe under Nazi Occupation* (London 1972), p. xxxi.
265 I. Trunk, 'The Attitudes of the Judenrats to the Problems of Armed Resistance against the Nazis', in *Jewish Resistance to the Holocaust: Proceedings of the Conference on Manifestations of Jewish Resistance, Jerusalem, April 7–11, 1968* [Prepared under the supervision of Meir Grubsztein. Translated into English by Varda Esther Bar-on and others] (Jersualem 1971).
266 J.M. Cox, 'Jewish Resistance against Nazism', in J.C. Friedman (ed.) *The Routledge History of The Holocaust* (Abingdon 2011), p. 334.

267 Quoted in R. Breitman, 'The "Final Solution"', in G. Martel, *Modern Germany Reconsidered* (London 1992), p. 197.
268 Quoted in Höhne, op. cit., p. 352.
269 Quoted in ibid., p. 353.
270 Quoted in Noakes and Pridham, *Nazism 1919–1945*, op. cit.
271 Quoted in M. Housden, *Hans Frank: Lebensraum and the Holocaust* (London 2005), p. 251.
272 Ibid.
273 Housden, *Lebensraum and the Holocaust*, op. cit., pp. 192–193.
274 J. Lukacs, *The Hitler of History* (New York 1998), p. 34.
275 Ibid., p. 236.
276 Ibid., p. 26.
277 See M. Burleigh and W. Wippermann, *The Racial State: Germany 1933–1945* (Cambridge 1991).
278 Ibid., p. 42.
279 A.J.P. Taylor, *The Course of German History* (London 1945), p. 213.
280 Shirer, op. cit., p. 126.
281 Ibid., p.129.
282 Ibid., p.148.
283 Goldhagen, op. cit., p. 23.
284 Lukacs, op. cit., p. 258.
285 G. Eley (ed.), *The 'Goldhagen Effect'* (Ann Arbor, MI 2000), p. 23.
286 Burleigh, *The Third Reich*, op. cit., p. 3.
287 Lukacs, op. cit., p. 222.

6 Dictatorship in Spain

1 H. Thomas, *The Spanish Civil War* (London 1961), Ch. 2.
2 S.G. Payne, *Falange: A History of Spanish Fascism* (Stanford, CA 1961), Ch. 1.
3 Quoted in S. Ben-Ami, 'Dictatorship of Primo de Rivera: A Political Reassessment', *Journal of Contemporary History*, 1977, 12:1, pp. 65–84.
4 Quoted in ibid.
5 J.H. Rial, *Revolution from Above: The Primo de Rivera Dictatorship in Spain, 1923–1930* (London and Toronto 1986), p. 230.
6 R. Carr, *Modern Spain 1875–1980* (Oxford 1980), Ch. 7.
7 For example, S. Ben-Ami, *Fascism from Above: The Dictatorship of Primo de Rivera in Spain 1923–1930* (Oxford 1983).
8 M. Blinkhorn, Conservatism, Traditionalism and Fascism in Spain, 1898–1937', in M. Blinkhorn (ed.) *Fascists and Conservatives* (London 1990).
9 Ben-Ami, *Fascism from Above*, op. cit.
10 Blinkhorn, op. cit.
11 Rial, op. cit.
12 See Ben-Ami, *Fascism from Above*, op. cit., pp. 398–402.
13 Ibid., p. 399.
14 Rial, op. cit., p. 233.
15 F.J.R. Salvadó, *The Spanish Civil War: Origins, Course and Outcomes* (Basingstoke 2005), p. 28.
16 Thomas, op. cit., Ch. 10.
17 P. Preston, 'War of Words: The Spanish Civil War and the Historians', in P. Preston (ed.) *Revolution and War in Spain 1931–1939* (London 1984).
18 G. Eisenwein and A. Shubert, *Spain at War: The Spanish Civil War in Context 1931–1939* (London 1995), p. 173, footnote 11.
19 Quoted in J. Casanova, *The Spanish Republic and the Civil War* (trans. Cambridge 2010), p. 236.
20 Quoted in R. Carr and J.P. Fusi, *Spain: Dictatorship to Democracy* (London 1979), p. 26.

21 Quoted in F.J. Taylor, *The United States and the Spanish Civil War* (New York 1956).
22 F. Lannon, 'The Church's Crusade against the Republic' in Preston, *Revolution and War in Spain*, op. cit., p. 53.
23 Quoted in M. Alpert, 'Soldiers, Politics and War', in Preston, *Revolution and War in Spain*, op. cit.
24 Quoted in Carr, op. cit., Ch. 5.
25 Ibid., Ch. 9.
26 F. Farmborough, *Life and People in National Spain* (London 1938), p. 14.
27 Ibid., p. 20.
28 Quoted by R.A.C. Parker in W.J. Mommsen and L. Kettenacker (eds) *The Fascist Challenge and the Policy of Appeasement* (London 1983), p. 38.
29 Quoted in Casanova, op. cit., p. 295.
30 B. Shelmerdine, *British Representations of the Spanish Civil War* (Manchester and New York 2006).
31 Quoted in ibid., p. 82.
32 Quoted in ibid., p. 82.
33 Quoted in ibid., p. 83.
34 Ibid., p. 86.
35 Lannon, op. cit., p. 53.
36 Quoted in Salvadó, op. cit., p. 65.
37 Quoted in Casanova, op. cit., p. 216.
38 Eisenwein and Shubert, op. cit., p. 192.
39 Salvadó, op. cit., p. 72.
40 See S.G. Payne, *The Spanish Civil War, the Soviet Union and Communism* (New Haven and London 2004), pp. 295–297.
41 Information on International Brigades from Thomas, op. cit., Appendix III.
42 Quoted in Casanova, op. cit., p. 219.
43 Salvadó, op. cit., p. 65.
44 Thomas, op. cit., Appendix Three.
45 Casanova, op. cit., p. 226.
46 Quoted in ibid., p. 217.
47 A. Vinas, 'The Financing of the Spanish Civil War' in Preston, *Revolution and War in Spain*, op. cit.
48 Hart quoted in R.H. Whealey, *Hitler and Spain: The Nazi Role in the Spanish Civil War 1936–1939* (Lexington, Kentucky 1989), p. 142.
49 Ibid., p. 142.
50 Eisenwein and Shubert, op. cit., p. 206.
51 Whealey, op. cit., p. 135.
52 S.G. Payne, *The Spanish Civil War, the Soviet Union and Communism* (New Haven and London 2004), p. 313.
53 Ibid., pp. 313–314.
54 Casanova, op. cit., p. 278.
55 G. Jackson, *The Spanish Republic and the Civil War 1931–39* (Princeton, NJ 1965), Ch. 24.
56 M. Gallo, *Spain under Franco* (trans. J. Stewart) (London 1973), Introduction.
57 B. Crozier, *Franco: A Biographical History* (London 1967), Part IV, Ch. 6.
58 Carr, op. cit., Ch. 9.
59 A. Beevor, *The Battle for Spain: The Spanish Civil War 1936–1939* (London 2006), p. 219.
60 Beevor, cited in Casanova, op. cit., p. 337.
61 Beevor, op. cit., p. 219.
62 R. Whealey, 'How Franco Financed his War – Reconsidered', *Journal of Contemporary History*, 1977, 12.
63 Beevor, op. cit., pp. 97 and 105.
64 Ibid., p. 91.
65 Ibid., p. 99.

66 Eisenwein and Shubert, op. cit., p. 179.
67 Ibid., p. 184.
68 A.C. Sanchez, *Fear and Progress: Ordinary Lives in Franco's Spain 1939–1975* (Chichester 2010), p. 9.
69 Quoted in Gallo, op. cit., Part I, Ch. 2.
70 Quoted in R. Carr, *Spain 1808–1975* (Oxford 1966), Ch. 18.
71 Quoted in Gallo, op. cit., Part II, Ch. 2.
72 Ibid., Part II, Ch. 3.
73 Quoted in J.D.W. Trythall, *Franco: A Biography* (London 1970), Ch. 8.
74 C. Powell, 'The United States and Spain', in N. Townson (ed.) *Spain Transformed: The Late Franco Dictatorship, 1959–75* (Basingstoke 2007), p. 228.
75 J. Grugel and T. Rees, *Franco's Spain* (London 1997), p. 178.
76 T. Buchanan: 'How "Different" Was Spain? The Later Franco Regime in International Context', in Townson, op. cit., p. 87.
77 Ibid., p. 88.
78 Quoted in S. Ellwood, *Franco* (Harlow 1994), p. 109.
79 Carr, *Spain 1808–1975*, op. cit., Ch. 18.
80 Townson, op. cit., Introduction, p. 3.
81 Carr, *Spain 1808–1975*, op. cit., Ch. 20.
82 Ibid.
83 Townson, op. cit., Introduction.
84 Carr, *Spain 1808–1975*, op. cit., Ch. 20.
85 Townson, op. cit., Introduction.
86 Ibid., p. 12.
87 S.D. Pack, 'Tourism and Political Change in Franco's Spain', in Townson, op. cit., p. 47.
88 Ibid., pp. 56–57.
89 Ibid., p. 56.
90 See E. Malefakis, 'A Bifurcated Regime?' in Townson, op. cit., p. 253.
91 Crozier, op. cit.
92 Ibid., p. 506.
93 Ibid. p. 509.
94 Ibid. p. 511.
95 Ibid, p. 311.
96 See J. Treglown, *Franco's Crypt: Spanish Culture and Memory Since 1936* (London 2013). Also G. Tremlett, an article in the *Guardian*, 31 May 2011.
97 H. Trevor-Roper, 'Franco's Spain Twenty Years Later', in G. Jackson (ed.) *The Spanish Civil War* (Chicago 1972), p. 198.
98 A.C. Sanchez, *Fear and Progress: Ordinary Lives in Franco's Spain 1939–1975* (Chichester 2010), p. 9.
99 Carr, *Spain 1808–1975*, op. cit., Ch. 18.
100 See C. Jerez-Farrán and S. Amago (eds), *Unearthing Franco's Legacy: Mass Graves and the Recovery of Historical memory in Spain* (Notre Dame, IN 2010).
101 Ibid., p. 18.
102 See J. Labanyi, 'Testimonies of Repression' in ibid., pp. 192–205.
103 A.E. Hardcastle: '"El documental es un arma cargada de pasado": Representation in Documentary and Testimony', in ibid., p. 148.
104 Ibid., p. 4.

7 Dictatorship elsewhere

1 N. Bruce, *Portugal: The Last Empire* (London 1975), Ch. 1.
2 S.G. Payne, 'Epilogue', in L.S. Graham and H.M. Makler (eds) *Contemporary Portugal: The Revolution and its Antecedents* (Austin, TX 1979), p. 345.
3 Bruce, op. cit., Ch. 1.

4 Quoted in T. Gallagher, *Portugal: A Twentieth-Century Interpretation* (Manchester 1983).
5 Quoted in H. Kay, *Salazar and Modern Portugal* (London 1970), Ch. 5.
6 Quoted in ibid.
7 Gallagher, op. cit., Ch. 4.
8 Kay, op. cit., Ch. 4.
9 Gallagher, op. cit., Ch. 3.
10 Quoted in ibid., Ch. 5
11 Quoted in R.A.H. Robinson, *Contemporary Portugal: A History* (London 1979), p. 86.
12 Quoted in ibid., Ch. 3.
13 Quoted in ibid., p. 87.
14 Ibid., p. 88.
15 G.A. Stone, *Spain, Portugal and the Great Powers, 1931–1941* (Basingstoke 2005), p. 171.
16 T.C. Bruneau, *Politics and Nationhood: Post-Revolutionary Portugal* (New York 1974), Ch. 1.
17 Quoted in Robinson, op. cit., p. 67.
18 Robinson, op. cit., p. 68.
19 M. Soares, *Portugal's Struggle for Liberty* (trans. London 1975), p. 49.
20 Robinson, op. cit., p. 94.
21 Soares, op. cit., pp. 169–170.
22 J.E. Duffy, *Portuguese Africa* (Cambridge, MA 1959), Ch. 9.
23 Summarized from Soares, op. cit., p. 177.
24 Bruce, op. cit., p. 63.
25 Gallagher, op. cit., p. 178
26 See Bruce, op. cit., pp. 69–84.
27 See Soares, op. cit., pp. 189–190.
28 Gallagher, op. cit., p. 178.
29 D. Birmingham, *A Concise History of Portugal* (Cambridge 1993), p. 169.
30 See J.M. Anderson, *The History of Portugal* (Westport, CT 2000), p. 158.
31 Ibid., p. 159.
32 Ibid., p. 154.
33 D.L. Raby, *Fascism and Resistance in Portugal: Communists, Liberals and Military Dissidents in the Opposition to Salazar, 1941–1974* (Manchester 1988), pp. 5–6.
34 Soares, op. cit., p. 12.
35 Ibid., p. 12.
36 Birmingham, op. cit., pp. 158–159.
37 A.C. Pinto, *The Blue Shirts: Portuguese Fascists and the New State* (New York 2000), p. 236.
38 Ibid., p. 237.
39 Ibid., p. 238.
40 Ibid., p. 238.
41 Quoted in T. Gallagher, 'Conservatism, Dictatorship and Fascism in Portugal, 1914–45', in M. Blinkhorn (ed.) *Fascists and Conservatives* (London 1990), p. 166.
42 R. Griffin, *The Nature of Fascism* (London 1991), pp. 122–123.
43 Quoted in Gallagher, 'Conservatism, Dictatorship and Fascism', op. cit., p. 167.
44 F.R. De Meneses, 'The Origins and Nature of Authoritarian Rule in Portugal, 1919–1945', *Contemporary European History*, 2003, 11:1, pp. 153–154.
45 Quoted in Gallagher, 'Conservatism, Dictatorship and Fascism', op. cit., p. 163.
46 Quoted in ibid., pp. 164–165.
47 E. Eyck, *A History of the Weimar Republic* (Cambridge, MA and London 1962–4), Vol. I, Ch. 4.
48 A.J.P. Taylor, *The Habsburg Monarchy* (London 1948), Epilogue.
49 Quoted in S. Marks, *The Illusion of Peace* (London 1976), Ch. 1.
50 E. Barker, *Austria 1918–1972* (London 1973), Part I.
51 Quoted in K.R. Stadler, *Austria* (London 1971), Ch. 4.

52 Ibid.
53 Quoted in ibid.
54 Barker, op. cit., Ch. 9.
55 Stadler, op. cit., Ch. 4.
56 Barker, op. cit., Ch. 9.
57 Ibid.
58 J. Lewis, 'Conservatives and Fascists in Austria, 1918–34', in Blinkhorn, op. cit., p. 114.
59 Ibid., p. 103.
60 Payne, *A History of Fascism*, op. cit., p. 250.
61 M. Kitchen, *The Coming of Austrian Fascism* (London and Montreal 1980), p. 274.
62 Ibid., p. 277.
63 Ibid., p. 279.
64 Quoted in E.B. Bukey, *Hitler's Austria: Popular Sentiment in the Nazi Era, 1938–1945* (Chapel Hill and London 2000), Epilogue.
65 Quoted in R. Steininger, *Austria, Germany and the Cold War: From the* Anschluss *to the State Treaty 1938–1955* (London 2008), p. 22.
66 Bukey, op. cit., Epilogue.
67 Ibid.
68 Quotations from G.-K. Kindermann, *Hitler's Defeat in Austria 1933–1934: Europe's First Containment of Nazi Expansionism* (trans. S. Brough and D. Taylor) (London 1984), pp. xvi–xxv.
69 Steininger, op. cit., p. 15.
70 Ibid.
71 Ibid., p. 15.
72 Ibid.
73 Ibid.
74 Ibid., p. 14.
75 M. Molnár, *A Concise History of Hungary* (trans. A Magyar) (Cambridge 2001), p. 259.
76 A.C. Janos, *The Politics of Backwardness in Hungary 1825–1945* (Princeton, NJ 1982), Ch. 4.
77 P.F. Sugar (ed.), *A History of Hungary* (London 1990), p. 305.
78 R.J. Crampton, *Eastern Europe in the Twentieth Century – and After* (London 1997), Ch. 5.
79 P. Ignotus, *Hungary* (London 1972), p. 147.
80 Crampton, op. cit., Ch. 5.
81 Janos, op. cit., Ch. 4.
82 E. Pamlényi (ed.), *A History of Hungary* (London 1975), Ch. 9.
83 D. Sinor, *A History of Hungary* (London 1959), Ch. 32.
84 Quoted in Ignotus, op. cit., Ch. 9.
85 L. Kontler, *A History of Hungary* (London 2002), p. 344.
86 K. Syrop, *Poland: Between the Hammer and the Anvil* (London 1968), Ch. 14.
87 J. Rothschild, *Pilsudski's Coup d'Etat* (New York 1966), Conclusion.
88 Z. Landau and J. Tomaszewski, *The Polish Economy in the Twentieth Century* (London 1985), in D.H. Aldcroft, Editor's Introduction. Details to be added.
89 Rothschild, op. cit.
90 See J. Holzer, 'The Political Right in Poland, 1918–39', *Journal of Contemporary History*, 1977, 12.
91 Syrop, op. cit, Ch. 15.
92 Ibid., Ch. 16.
93 A. Polonsky, *Politics in Independent Poland, 1921–1939: The Crisis of Constitutional Government* (Oxford 1972), p. 506.
94 H. Roos, *A History of Modern Poland: From the Foundation of the State in the First World War to the Present Day* (trans. J.R. Foster) (London 1961), p. 141.
95 A.J. Prażmowska, *A History of Poland* (Basingstoke 2004), p. 168.
96 Ibid., p. 169.
97 See Roos, op. cit., pp. 132–133.

98 Prażmowska, op. cit., p. 171.
99 See N. Davies, *God's Playground: A History of Poland. Volume II: 1795 to the Present* (Oxford 1981), pp. 426, 431, 434.
100 Roos, op. cit., p. 169.
101 P.D. Stachura, *Poland Between the Wars, 1918–1939* (London 1998), p. 183.
102 Ibid., p. 184.
103 Ibid., p. 184.
104 Ibid., p. 184.
105 Ibid., p. 185.
106 Quoted in E.J. Patterson, *Pilsudski: Marshal of Poland* (Bristol 1935), p. 117.
107 Rothschild, op. cit., Conclusion.
108 Syrop, op. cit., Ch. 15.
109 J. Lukowski and H. Zawadzki, *A Concise History of Poland* (Cambridge 2006), p. 245.
110 Payne, op. cit., p. 322.
111 V.S. Vardis, 'The Rise of Authoritarian Rule in the Baltic States', in V.S. Vardis and R.J. Misiunas (eds) *The Baltic States in Peace and War* (University Park, PA 1978).
112 N. Hope, 'Interwar Statehood: Symbol and Reality', in G. Smith (ed.) *The Baltic States* (New York 1994), p. 63.
113 Payne, op. cit., p. 325.
114 B. Meissner, 'The Baltic Question in World Politics', in Vardis and Misiunas, op. cit. Also A. Dallin, 'The Baltic States between Nazi Germany and Soviet Russia', in Vardis and Misiunas, op. cit.
115 E. Anderson, 'The Baltic Entente: Phantom or Reality', in Vardis and Misiunas, op. cit.
116 R. Misiunas and R. Taagepera, *The Baltic States: Years of Dependence 1940–1990* (London 1993), p. 42.
117 J. Hiden and P. Salmon, *The Baltic Nations and Europe: Estonia, Latvia & Lithuania in the Twentieth Century* (London 1991), p. 115.
118 Misiunas and Taagepera, op. cit., pp. 45–46.
119 Hiden and Salmon, op. cit., p. 116.
120 Ibid., p. 119.
121 Ibid., p. 131.
122 D. Kirby, 'Morality or Expediency in British-Soviet Relations, 1941–42', in Vardis and Misiunas, op. cit., p. 172.
123 L.S. Stavrianos, *The Balkans since 1453* (New York 1958), Ch. 36.
124 J. Tomes, 'The Throne of Zog: Monarchy in Albania 1929–1939', in *History Today*, 2001, 51.
125 Quoted in ibid.
126 Quoted in B.J. Fischer, *King Zog and the Struggle for Stability in Albania* (New York 1984), p. 139.
127 Tomes, op. cit.
128 S. Pollo and A. Puto, *The History of Albania* (trans. C. Wiseman and G. Cole) (London 1981), Ch. 9.
129 A. Logoreci, *The Albanians* (London 1977), Ch. 3.
130 Stavrianos, op. cit., Ch. 36.
131 K. Frasheri, *The History of Albania* (Tirana 1964), p. 243.
132 Ibid., p. 255.
133 Ibid., p. 255.
134 Fischer, op. cit.
135 Ibid., p. 305.
136 Ibid., p. 304.
137 Ibid., p. 303.
138 Ibid., p. 304.
139 Tomes, op. cit.
140 B. Jelavich, *A History of the Balkans*, Vol. 2, *Twentieth Century* (Cambridge 1983).
141 See T. Gallagher, *Outcast Europe: The Balkans, 1789–1989 from the Ottomans to Milosevic* (London 2001), p. 97.

142 Stavrianos, op. cit., Ch. 33.
143 M. Biondich, *The Balkans, Revolution, War and Political Violence since 1878* (Oxford 2011), p. 114.
144 R. Ristelhueber, *A History of the Balkan Peoples* (trans. S.D. Spector) (New York 1971).
145 F. Singleton, *Twentieth-Century Yugoslavia* (London 1976), Ch. 5.
146 Stavrianos, op. cit., Ch. 32.
147 V. Dedijer, ‘Yugoslavia between Centralism and Federalism’, in V. Dedijer (ed.) *History of Yugoslavia* (New York 1974).
148 R.W. Seton-Watson and R.G.D. Laffan, ‘Yugoslavia between the Wars’, in S. Clissold (ed.) *Short History of Yugoslavia* (Cambridge 1966).
149 Stavrianos, op. cit., Ch. 32.
150 Ibid.
151 Quoted in V. Dedijer, ‘The Subjugation and Dismemberment of Yugoslavia’ in Dedijer, op. cit.
152 Ibid.
153 A.N. Dragnich, *The First Yugoslavia: The Search for a Viable Political System* (Stanford, CA 1983), p. 146.
154 B. Prpa-Jovanovi , ‘The Making of Yugoslavia’, in J. Udovi ki and J. Ridgeway (eds) *Burn this House: The Making and Unmaking of Yugoslavia* (Durham and London 2000), p. 50.
155 Ibid., p. 50.
156 Ibid., p. 53.
157 Ibid., p. 50.
158 Ibid.
159 Ibid.
160 D.N. Risti , *Yugoslavia's Revolution of 1941* (London 1966).
161 C. Bennett, *Yugoslavia's Bloody Collapse: Causes, Course and Consequences* (London 1995) p. 33.
162 T. Cipek: ‘The Croats and Yugoslavism’ in D. Djoki (ed.) *Yugoslavism: Histories of a Failed Idea 1918–1992* (London 2003), p. 78.
163 J.B. Allcock, *Explaining Yugoslavia* (London 2000), p. 231.
164 Ibid., p. 236.
165 Ibid., p. 236.
166 Payne, op. cit., p. 405.
167 Stavrianos, op. cit., Ch. 32.
168 S. Fischer-Galati, *Twentieth-Century Rumania* (New York 1970).
169 F.L. Carsten, *The Rise of Fascism* (London 1967), Ch. 5.
170 J. Livezeanu, ‘Fascists and Conservatives in Romania: Two Generations of Nationalists’, in Blinkhorn, op. cit., p. 220.
171 R. Ioanid, *The Sword of the Archangel: Fascist Ideology in Romania* (trans. P. Heinegg) (New York 1990), Ch. 4.
172 Quoted in Gallagher, *Outcast Europe*, op. cit., p. 103.
173 Payne, op. cit., p. 396.
174 M. Petrakis, *The Metaxas Myth: Dictatorship and Propaganda in Greece* (London and New York 2006), p. 183.
175 Ibid., p. 184.
176 Quoted in Jelavich, op. cit., Ch. 6.
177 Stavrianos, op. cit.
178 R. Clogg, *Greece 1940–1949: Occupation, Resistance, Civil War* (Basingstoke 2002), p. 53.
179 J.L. Hondros, *Occupation and Resistance: The Greek Agony, 1941–4* (New York 1983), p. 26.
180 Payne, op. cit., p. 319.
181 J.V. Kofas, *Authoritarianism in Greece: The Metaxas Regime* (New York 1983).
182 Quoted in ibid.
183 Quoted in Payne, op. cit., p. 319.

184 Kofas, op. cit., p. 186.
185 D. Close, 'Conservatism, Authoritarianism and Fascism in Greece, 1914–45', in Blinkhorn, op. cit.
186 P.J. Vatikiotis, *Popular Autocracy in Greece 1936–41: A Political Biography of General Ioannis Metaxas* (London and Portland 1998), p. 204.
187 Ibid., p. 14.
188 Quoted in N. Berkes, *The Development of Secularism in Turkey* (London 1964; 1988 edition), p. 464.
189 Quoted in ibid., p. 470.
190 Ibid, p. 470.
191 Quoted in Berkes, op. cit., p. 462.
192 Quoted in Berkes, op. cit., p. 463.
193 Quoted in P. Brooker, *Twentieth-Century Dictatorships: The Ideological One-Party States* (New York 1995), p. 246.
194 E. J. Zürcher, *Turkey: A Modern History* (London 1993), p. 202.
195 D. Quataert, *Social Disintegration and Popular Resistance in the Ottoman Empire, 1881–1908* (New York 1983), Conclusion, pp. 154–155.
196 D. Thomson, *Europe Since Napoleon* (London 1962), pp. 550–551.
197 R.H. Davison, *Essays in Ottoman and Turkish History, 1774–1923: The Impact of the West* (Austin, TX 1990), p. 244.
198 Ibid., p. 259.
199 See Zürcher, op. cit., p. 180.
200 Ibid., p. 187.
201 Payne, op. cit., p. 144.
202 Zürcher, op. cit., p. 191.
203 Ibid., p. 213.
204 Ibid., p. 214.
205 P. Brooker, *Defiant Dictatorships: Communist and Middle-Eastern Dictatorships in a Democratic Age* (New York 1997), p. 1.
206 Details to be added (London 2005 edition), p. 336.
207 Ibid., p. 337.
208 *Quotations from Chairman Mao Tse Tung* (Peking 1966), p. 11.
209 Ibid., p. 18.

8 Dictatorships vs democracies

1 G. Rhode, 'The Protectorate of Bohemia and Moravia 1939–1945' in V.S. Mamatey and R. Luža (eds) *A History of the Czechoslovak Republic 1918–1948* (Princeton, NJ 1973), p. 301.
2 J. Korbel, *Twentieth-Century Czechoslovakia: The Meanings of Its History* (New York 1977), p. 163.
3 V. Mastny, *The Czechs under Nazi Rule: The Failure of National Resistance, 1939–1942* (New York and London 1971), p. 225.
4 R. Luža, 'The Czech Resistance Movement', in Mamatey and Luža, op. cit., p. 301.
5 E. Taborsky, 'Politics in Exile 1939–1945', in Mamatey and Luža, op. cit., p. 323.
6 Figures from G. Rhode, 'The Protectorate of Bohemia and Moravia 1939–1945', in Mamatey and Luža, op. cit., p. 321.
7 Quoted in J.K. Hoensch, 'The Slovak Republic, 1939–1945', in Mamatey and Luža, op. cit., p. 279.
8 Ibid., p. 285.
9 A. Josko, 'The Slovak Resistance Movement', in Mamatey and Luža, op. cit., p. 372.
10 B. Nokleby, 'Adjusting to Allied Victory', in H.S. Nissen (ed.) *Scandinavia during the Second World War* (Minneapolis 1983), p. 318.
11 See M. Häikiö, 'The Race for Northern Europe, September 1939–June 1940', in Nissen, op. cit., p. 74.

12 For Quisling's political philosophy see P.M. Hayes, *Quisling: The Career and Political Ideas of Vidkun Quisling* (Newton Abbot 1971).
13 P.M. Hayes, *Quisling* (London 1971), Ch. 7. See also O.K. Hoidal, *Quisling: A Study in Treason* (Oslo 1989).
14 H.F. Dahl, *Quisling: A Study in Treachery* (trans. A.-M. Stanton-Ife) (Cambridge 1999), p. 416.
15 See G. Hirschfeld, 'Collaboration and Attenism in the Netherlands 1940–41', in W. Laqueur (ed.) *The Second World War: Essays in Military and Political History* (London 1982), pp. 101–118.
16 V. Mallinson, *Belgium* (London 1969), p. 122.
17 J. Newcomer, *The Grand Duchy of Luxembourg: The Evolution of Nationhood 963 A.D. to 1983* (New York and London 1984), pp. 264–265.
18 I. Ousby, *Occupation: The Ordeal of France 1940–1944* (London 1999), p. 89.
19 T.R. Christofferson and M.S. Christofferson, *France during World War II: From Defeat to Liberation* (New York 2006), p. 36.
20 Ibid., p. 37.
21 Ousby, op. cit., p. 79.
22 Christofferson and Christofferson, op. cit., p. 46.
23 Ibid., p. 65.
24 Ibid., pp. 112–113.
25 J.F. McMillan, *Twentieth-Century France: Politics and Society 1898–1991* (London 1992), p. 138.
26 Christofferson and Christofferson, op. cit., p. 113.
27 H.R. Kedward, *Resistance in Vichy France* (Oxford 1978), p. 230.
28 Ibid.
29 J. Steinberg, *Why Switzerland?* (Cambridge 1996), p. 68.
30 Ibid., p. 68.
31 Ibid., p. 69.
32 Ibid., p. 69.
33 Quoted in J. Wraight, *The Swiss and the British* (Michael Russell 1987), p. 323.
34 J.-R. De Salis, *Switzerland and Europe: Essays and Reflections* (London 1971), p. 71.
35 N. Kent, *A Concise History of Sweden* (Cambridge 2008), p. 231.
36 H.S. Nissen, 'Adjusting to German Domination', in Nissen, op. cit., p. 107.
37 B. Nokleby, 'Adjusting to Allied Victory', in Nissen, op. cit., p. 317.
38 J. Gilmour, *Sweden, the Swastika and Stalin: The Swedish Experience in the Second World War* (Edinburgh 2011), pp. 270–271.
39 R. Kenney, *The Northern Tangle: Scandinavia and the Post-War World* (London 1946), p. 234.
40 Quoted in Gilmour, op. cit., pp. 270–271.
41 Ibid., p. 287.
42 J. Lydon, *The Making of Ireland* (London and New York 1998), p. 377.
43 E. Arnold, 'Irish Neutrality between Vichy France and de Gaulle 1940–1945', in G. Morgan and G. Hughes (eds) *Southern Ireland and the Liberation of France* (Bern 2008), p. 33.
44 Lydon, op. cit., p. 381.
45 C.J. Carter, *The Shamrock and the Swastika* (Palo Alto, CA 1977), p. 234.
46 J.P. Duggan, *Neutral Ireland and the Third Reich* (Dublin 1985), p. 10.
47 See C. Wills, *That Neutral Island: A Cultural History of Ireland During the Second World War* (London 2007), p. 8.
48 Ibid., p. 8.
49 Duggan, op. cit., p. 9.
50 Lydon, op. cit., p. 378.
51 Wills, op. cit., p. 384.
52 Ibid., p. 391.
53 Ibid., p. 385.
54 Lydon, op. cit., p. 382.

55 Quoted in R. Pope, *War and Society in Britain 1899–1948* (London 1991), p. 40.
56 Quoted in A.R. Ball, *British Political Parties: The Emergence of a Modern Party System* (London 1981), p. 138.
57 S. Broadberry and P. Howlett, 'Blood, Sweat and Tears: British Mobilization for World War II' in R. Chickering, S. Förster and B. Greiner (eds) *A World at Total War* (Cambridge 2005), p. 158.
58 Ibid., p. 174.
59 M. Bruce, *The Coming of the Welfare State* (London 1961), p. 326.
60 See D. Dutton, 'Unity and Disunity: The Price of Victory', in K. Robbins (ed.) *The British Isles 1901–1951* (Oxford 2002).
61 Quoted in P. Clarke, *Hope and Glory: Britain 1900–2000* (London 2004), p. 208.
62 Quoted in F. Singleton, *A Short History of Finland* (Cambridge 1989), p. 130.
63 A.F. Upton, *Finland 1939–1940* (London 1974), p. 157.
64 Quoted in Singleton, op. cit., p. 135.
65 Quoted in A. Farmer, *Britain: Foreign and Imperial Affairs 1939–64* (London 1994), p. 16.

9 Dictatorships compared

1 C.J. Friedrich and Z.K. Brzezinski, *Totalitarian Dictatorship and Autocracy* (Cambridge, MA 1956), Ch. 7.
2 K.D. Bracher, *The Age of Ideologies* (London 1984), Part II, Ch. 4.
3 Ibid.
4 E. Weber, *Varieties of Fascism* (New York 1964), Reading 3, Introduction.
5 Quoted in R.C. Macridis, *Contemporary Political Ideologies* (Boston, MA 1983), Ch. 5.
6 Bracher, op. cit., Part II, Ch. 3.
7 Quoted in H. Kohn, *Political Ideologies of the Twentieth Century* (New York 1966), Ch. 10.
8 Quoted in J. Remak, *The Nazi Years* (Englewood Cliffs, NJ 1969), Ch. 3.
9 T. Gallagher, *Portugal: A Twentieth-century Interpretation* (Manchester 1983).
10 E.A. Rees, 'Leader Cults: Varieties, Preconditions and Functions', in E.A. Rees (ed.) *The Leader Cult in Communist Dictatorships* (Basingstoke 2004), p. 4.
11 M. Broszat, *The Hitler State: The Foundation and Development of the Internal Structure of the Third Reich* (London 1981), Ch. 6.
12 S. Ellwood, *Franco* (Harlow 1994), p. 114.
13 A.C. Pinto, *Salazar's Dictatorship and European Fascism* (New York 1995), p. 178.
14 Salazar, quoted in Pinto, op. cit., p. 178.
15 H. Buchheim, *Totalitarian Rule: Its Nature and Characteristics* (Middletown, CT 1968), Ch. 1.
16 N. Bruce, *Portugal: The Last Empire* (London 1975), Ch. 2.
17 S.G. Payne, *Franco's Spain* (London 1968), Ch. 2.
18 Friedrich and Brzezinski, op. cit., Ch. 11.
19 Quoted in R. Robinson, *Contemporary Portugal* (London 1979), p. 61.
20 D.P. Machado, *The Structure of Portuguese Society* (New York 1991), p. 88.
21 Quoted in Robinson, op. cit., p. 62.
22 Ibid., p. 63.
23 Ibid., p. 58.
24 Friedrich and Brzezinski, op. cit., Ch. 11.
25 R.J.B. Bosworth, *Mussolini* (London 2002), p. 222.
26 Ibid.
27 Robinson, op. cit., p. 56.
28 N. Wachsmann, *Hitler's Prisons: Legal Terror in Nazi Germany* (New Haven, CT 2004), p. 363.
29 Ibid., p. 363.
30 Ibid., p. 364.

31 Ibid.
32 A. Bullock, *Hitler and Stalin: Parallel Lives* (London 1991), Ch. 12.
33 Quoted in G.M. Ivanova, *Labor Camp Socialism: The Gulag in the Soviet Totalitarian System* (Armonk, NY 2000), p. 186.
34 A. Appelbaum, *Gulag: A History of the Soviet Camps* (London 2003), p. 20.
35 See O. Bartov, *Germany's War and the Holocaust* (Ithaca, NY 2003), p. 4.
36 I.L. Horowitz, 'Foreword', in I. Ehrenburg and V. Grossman, *The Complete Black Book of Russian Jewry* (New Brunswick, NJ 2000), p. vii.
37 Rees, op. cit., p. 4.
38 A. Pavkovic, *The Fragmentation of Yugoslavia: Nationalism and War in the Balkans* (2nd edn, London 2000), p. 43.

Select bibliography

The notes section listed the works which have been used in compiling this book. This final section is intended to select from these some titles to introduce the reader to further study.

GENERAL ISSUES (INTERNATIONAL RELATIONS, INSTITUTIONS AND IDEOLOGIES)

The following introductions to the period can be strongly recommended: H. James, *Europe Reborn: A History, 1914–2000* (Harlow 2003); M. Kitchen, *Europe Between the Wars* (Harlow 2003); M. Mazower, *Dark Continent: Europe's Twentieth Century* (London 1998); M. Pugh (ed.), *A Companion to Modern History, 1871–1945* (Oxford 1997); R. Conquest, *Reflections on a Ravaged Century* (New York 2000); and R. Vinen, *A History in Fragments: Europe in the Twentieth Century* (London 2000).

The various foreign policies are covered in the context of the individual states. The most accessible collection of documents on international relations covering the whole period is J.A.S. Grenville (ed.), *The Major International Treaties 1914–1973* (London 1974). Now under increasing pressure but still invigorating is A.J.P. Taylor, *The Origins of the Second World War* (London 1961). The debate this caused has been updated in P. Finney (ed.), *The Origins of the Second World War* (London 1997). Also recommended are R. Henig, *Versailles and After* (London 1984); R. Henig, *The Origins of the Second World War* (London 1985); S. Marks, *The Illusion of Peace, International Relations in Europe 1918–1983* (London 1976); and M. Trachtenberg, *Reparation in World Politics* (London 1980).

On institutions and ideologies, I found the following particularly informative and enlightening: K.J. Newman, *European Democracy between the Wars* (trans. E. Morgan) (London 1970); S. Tormey, *Making Sense of Tyranny: Interpretations of Totalitarianism* (Manchester 1995); H. Buchheim, *Totalitarian Rule: Its Nature and Characteristics* (Middletown, CT 1968); K.D. Bracher, *The Age of Ideologies* (London 1984); R.C. Macridis, *Contemporary Political Ideologies* (Boston 1983); C.J. Friedrich and Z.R. Brzezinski, *Totalitarian Dictatorship and Autocracy* (Cambridge, MA 1956); A. Perlmutter, *Modern Authoritarianism: A Comparative Institutional Analysis* (New Haven, CT 1984); J.J. Linz, Totalitarian and Authoritarian Regimes (London 2000); J.L. Talmon, *The Origins of Totalitarian Democracy* (London 1952); C.J. Friedrich, M. Curtis and B.R. Barber, *Totalitarianism in Perspective: Three Views* (London 1969); A. Gleeson, *Totalitarianism: The Inner History of the Cold War* (New York 1995); and A. Perlmutter, *Modern Authoritarianism: A Comparative Institutional Analysis* (New Haven, CT 1984).

Works specifically on communism and Soviet institutions include: I. Deutscher, *Marxism in Outline* (London 1972), J.S. Reshetar, Jr, *The Soviet Polity: Government and Politics in the USSR* (New York 1989); L. Gozman and A. Etkind, *The Psychology of Post-Totalitarianism in Russia* (Enfield 1992); M. Jaworskyj, *Soviet Political Thought: An Anthology* (Baltimore, MD 1967); R.A. Medvedev, *On Socialist Democracy* (trans. E. de Kadt) (Nottingham 1977); L. Cooper, *Power and Politics in the Soviet Union* (London 1992); E.A. Rees (ed.), *The Leader*

Cult in Communist Dictatorships (Basingstoke 2004); and R. Sakwa, *Soviet Politics in Perspective* (London 1998).

Fascism is dealt with in: G.L. Mosse (ed.), *International Fascism* (London and Beverly Hills 1979); E. Nolte, *Three Faces of Fascism* (New York 1963); M. Kitchen, *Fascism* (London 1976); F. Carsten, *The Rise of Fascism* (London 1967); S.J. Woolf (ed.), *Fascism in Europe* (London 1981); S.G. Payne, *A History of Fascism* (London 1995); Z. Sternhell, *Neither Right nor Left: Fascist Ideology in France* (Berkeley, CA 1986); M. Blinkhorn, *Fascism and the Right in Europe, 1919–1945* (Harlow 2000); and G.P. Blum, *The Rise of Fascism in Europe* (Westport, CT 1998).

DICTATORSHIP IN RUSSIA

Since the late 1980s there have been fundamental changes in the interpretation of the Lenin and Stalin periods. The second, third and fourth editions of this book have aimed to show how these have developed and to contrast new with original views. In the process, I have used some of the material from three of my other books. These are: S.J. Lee, *Stalin and the Soviet Union* (London 1999); S.J. Lee, *Lenin and Revolutionary Russia* (London 2003); and S.J. Lee, *Russia and the USSR 1855–1991* (London 2006).

The traditional works are still of enormous value to the student and general reader. On the Lenin era these include: E.H. Carr, *The Bolshevik Revolution 1917–23* (3 vols, London 1950), E.H. Carr, *The Russian Revolution from Lenin to Stalin 1917–1929* (London 1979); C. Hill, *Lenin and the Russian Revolution* (London 1974); L. Schapiro, *1917: The Russian Revolution and the Origins of Present Day Communism* (Hounslow 1984); L. Fischer, *The Life of Lenin* (London 1965); S.N. Silverman (ed.), *Lenin* (New York 1966); R. Conquest, *Lenin* (London 1972); A.E. Adams (ed.) *The Russian Revolution and Bolshevik Victory* (Lexington, MA 1974). Two more detailed works are: A. Ascher (ed.), *The Mensheviks in the Russian Revolution* (London 1976); and G. Leggett, *The Cheka: Lenin's Political Police* (Oxford 1981). Earlier works on Stalin and Stalinism include: I. Deutscher, *Stalin: A Political Biography* (Oxford 1949); A.B. Ulam, *Stalin: The Man and his Era* (London 1973); I. Grey, *Stalin; Man of History* (1882 edition, Abacus 1982); R.C. Tucker, *Stalin as Revolutionary* (London 1973); R. Hingley, *Joseph Stalin: Man and Legend* (London 1974); T.H. Rigby (ed.), *Stalin* (New York 1966); A. Nove, *Stalinism and After* (London 1975); M. McCauley, *Stalin and Stalinism* (Harlow 1983); E.H. Carr, *Socialism in One Country 1924–1926* (London 1958); J. Ellenstein, *The Stalin Phenomenon* (London 1976); and G.R. Urban (ed.), *Stalinism: Its Impact on Russia and the World* (London 1982). More specific material can be found in: M. Lewin, *Russian Peasants and Soviet Power: A Study of Collectivization* (New York 1968); R. Conquest, *The Great Terror* (London 1968); R. Hutchings, *Soviet Economic Development* (Oxford 1967); D. Lane, *Politics and Society in the USSR* (London 1970); R. Hingley, Russian *Writers and Soviet Society 1917–1978* (London 1979); R.C. Tucker, *The Soviet Political Mind* (London 1972); G. Fischer, *Soviet Opposition to Stalin* (Cambridge, MA 1952); G.F. Kennan, *Soviet Foreign Policy 1917–1941* (Princeton, NJ 1960); W. Laqueur, *Russia and Germany: A Century of Conflict* (London 1965); J. Haslam, *The Soviet Union and the Struggle for Collective Security in Europe, 1933–39* (New York 1984); and A.Z. Rubinstein, *Soviet Foreign Policy since World War II* (Cambridge, MA 1981).

Later works have provided some fascinating contrasts and have been heavily drawn upon for the more recent editions of this book. On the Lenin period they include: E. Acton, *Rethinking the Russian Revolution* (London 1996); I.D. Thatcher (ed.), *Reinterpreting Revolutionary Russia* (Basingstoke 2006); R. Wade, *The Russian Revolution, 1917* (Cambridge 2000); G. Swain, *The Origins of the Russian Civil War* (London 1996); E. Mawdsley, *The Russian Civil War* (London 1987); V.N. Brovkin (ed.), *The Bolsheviks in Russian Society* (New Haven, CT 1997); J. Rees, R. Service, S. Farber and R. Blackburn, *In Defence of October: A Debate on the Russian Revolution* (London 1997); and D. Volkogonov, *Lenin: Life and Legacy* (London 1994).

The most recent biography of Stalin is S. Kotkin, *Stalin, Vol. 1: Paradoxes of Power, 1878–1928* (London 2014). Other works on Stalin and Stalinism published since 1990 include: K. McDermott, *Stalin: Revolutionary in an Era of War* (Basingstoke 2006); C. Ward, *Stalin's Russia* (London 1993); C. Ward (ed.), *The Stalinist Dictatorship* (London 1998); H. Kuromiya, *Stalin* (Harlow 2005); S. Davies and J. Harris (eds), *Stalin: A New History* (Cambridge 2005); R. Service, *Stalin: A Biography* (London 2004); E. Mawdsley, *The Stalin Years: The Soviet Union 1929–1953* (second edition, Manchester 2003); E. Radzinsky, *Stalin: The First In-Depth Biography Based on Explosive New Documents from Russia's Secret Archives* (trans. H.T. Willetts) (New York 1996); D. Volkogonov, *Stalin: Triumph and Tragedy* (trans. London 1991); A. Nove (ed.), *The Stalin Phenomenon* (London 1993); D.L. Hoffman (ed.), *Stalinism* (Oxford 2003); and A. Litvin and J. Keep, *Stalinism: Russian and Western Views at the Turn of the Millennium* (London 2005).

Among the many recent works on the Stalinist politics, terror, economy and society are: J. Channon (ed.), *Politics, Society and Stalinism in the USSR* (London 1998); J. Arch Getty and R.T. Manning (eds), *Stalinist Terror: New Perspectives* (Cambridge 1993); G.M. Ivanova, *Labor Camp Socialism: The Gulag in the Soviet Totalitarian System* (trans. Armonk, NY 2000); A. Appelbaum, *Gulag: A History of the Soviet Camps* (London 2003); V. Brovkin, *Russia after Lenin: Politics, Culture and Society 1921–1929* (London 1998); D.R. Shearer, *Industry, State and Society in Stalin's Russia 1926–1934* (Ithaca, NY 1996); S. Davies, *Popular Opinion in Stalin's Russia: Terror, Propaganda and Dissent, 1934–1941* (Cambridge 1997); L. Viola (ed.), *Contending with Stalinism: Soviet Power and Popular Resistance in the 1930s* (Ithaca, NY 2002); and V.S. Dunham, *In Stalin's Time: Middleclass Values in Soviet Fiction* (Durham and London 1990); D.L. Hoffmann, *Stalinist Values: The Cultural Norms of Soviet Modernity, 1917–1941* (London 1999); and M. Harrison, *Accounting for War – Soviet Production, Employment and the Defence Burden, 1940–1945* (Cambridge 1996). Recent publications on foreign policy include: G. Gorodetsky (ed.), *Soviet Foreign Policy 1917–1991* (London 1994); G. Roberts, *The Soviet Union and the Origins of the Second World War* (London 1995); V. Suvorov, *Icebreaker: Who Started the Second World War?* (London 1990); P. Mezhiritsky, *On the Precipice: Stalin, the Red Army Leadership and the Road to Stalingrad, 1931–1942* (trans. S. Britton) (Solihull 2012); and B. Wegner (ed.), *From Peace to War: Germany, Soviet Russia and the World, 1939–1941* (Oxford 1997).

The general context of the Soviet Union under both Lenin and Stalin is covered in: E. Acton, *Russia: The Tsarist and Soviet Legacy* (second edition, Harlow 1995); P. Kenez: *A History of the Soviet Union from the Beginning to the End* (second edition, Cambridge 2006); N.E. Rosenfeldt, B. Jensen and E. Kulavig (eds.) *Mechanisms of Power in the Soviet Union* (London 2000); and J. Smith, *Red Nations: The Nationalities Experience in and after the USSR* (Cambridge 2013). Comparisons are drawn between the Stalin and Hitler regimes in: A. Bullock, *Hitler and Stalin: Parallel Lives* (London 1991); R. Overy, *The Dictators: Hitler's Germany, Stalin's Russia* (London, 2004); and I. Kershaw and M. Lewin (eds), *Stalinism and Nazism, Dictatorships in Comparison* (Cambridge 1997).

Finally, compilations of primary sources can be found in: R. Sakwa (ed.), *The Rise and Fall of the Soviet Union 1917–1991* (London 1999); R. Kowalski, *The Russian Revolution 1917–1921* (London 1997); M. McCauley, *The Russian Revolution and the Soviet State, 1917–1921: Documents* (London, 1975); P. Boobbyer, *The Stalin Era* (London 2000); and R. Gregor (ed.), *Resolutions and Decisions of the Communist Party of the Soviet Union* (Toronto 1974). The official Soviet views of the Lenin and Stalin periods (written after the destalinization of the 1950s) are contained in: *A Short History of the CPSU* (Moscow 1970); and *History of Soviet Society* (Moscow 1971).

DICTATORSHIP IN ITALY

Although less immediately noticeable than in the case of Russia, there have also been some changes in the interpretation of Fascist Italy.

Among the most valuable works reflecting scholarship before 1990 are: P.V. Cannistraro (ed.), *Historical Dictionary of Fascist Italy* (Westport, CT 1982); L. Fermi, *Mussolini* (Chicago 1961); A. Cassels, *Fascist Italy* (London 1969); D. Mack Smith, *Italy: A Modern History* (Ann Arbor 1959); D. Mack Smith, *Mussolini* (London 1981); M. Gallo, *Mussolini's Italy* (New York 1973); A.J. Gregor, *Young Mussolini and the Intellectual Origins of Fascism* (Berkeley, CA 1979); Sir I. Kirkpatrick, *Study of a Demagogue* (London 1964); C. Leeds, *Italy under Mussolini* (London 1968); R. Macgregor-Hastie, *The Day of the Lion* (New York 1963); C. Hibbert, *Mussolini* (Harmondsworth 1975), R. Collier, *Duce! The Rise and Fall of Mussolini* (London 1971); A. De Grand, *Italian Fascism: Its Origins and Development* (Lincoln, NE 1982); W.W. Halperin, *Mussolini and Italian Fascism* (New York 1964); G. Carocci, *Italian Fascism* (trans. I. Quigly) (Harmondsworth 1974); A.J. Gregor, *Italian Fascism and Developmental Dictatorship* (Princeton, NJ 1979); R. De Felice, *Fascism, An Informal Introduction to its Theory and Practice* (New Brunswick, NJ 1976); D. Mack Smith, *Mussolini's Roman Empire* (London 1976); M. Knox, *Mussolini Unleashed: Politics and Strategy in Italy's Last War, 1939–41* (Cambridge 1988); R. Battaglia, *The Story of the Italian Resistance* (London 1957); C. Duggan, *Fascism and the Mafia* (New Haven, CT 1989); and P.C. Kent, *The Pope and the Duce* (New York 1981).

The following works, published since 1990, have been used to update the historiography of the period for the third and fourth editions of this book: G. Forgacs (ed.), *Rethinking Italian Fascism: Capitalism, Populism and Culture* (London 1986); J. Whittam, *Fascist Italy* (Manchester 1995); J. Pollard, *The Fascist Experience in Italy* (London 1998); P. Morgan, *Italian Fascism 1919–1945* (London 1995); S.G. Payne, *A History of Fascism* (London 1995); R.J.B. Bosworth, *The Italian Dictatorship: Problems and Perspectives in the Interpretation of Mussolini and Fascism* (London 1998); R.J.B. Bosworth, *Mussolini* (London 2002); R.J.B. Bosworth, *Mussolini's Italy* (London 2005); J. Ridley, *Mussolini* (London 1997); R. Ben-Ghiat, *Fascist Modernities: Italy 1922–1945* (Berkeley, CA 2001); A. Gillette, *Racial Theories in Fascist Italy* (London 2002); A.J. Gregor, *Giovanni Gentile: Philosopher of Fascism* (New Brunswick, NJ 2001); Emilio Gentile, *The Sacralization of Politics in Fascist Italy* (trans. Cambridge, MA 1996); S. Falasca-Zamponi, *Fascist Spectacle: The Aesthetics of Power in Mussolini's Italy* (Berkeley 2000); D. Thompson, *State Control in Fascist Italy: Culture and Conformity 1925–43* (Manchester 1991); V. De Grazia, *How Fascism Ruled Women: Italy 1922–1945* (Berkeley, CA 1992); A. Kallis, *Fascist Ideology, Territory and Expansionism in Italy and Germany, 1922–1945* (London 2000); A. De Grand, *Fascist Italy and Nazi Germany: The Fascist Style of Rule* (London 1995); R. Mallett, *Mussolini and the Origins of the Second World War, 1939–1940* (Basingstoke 2003); D. Rodogno, *Fascism's European Empire: Italian Occupation During the Second World War* (trans. Cambridge 2008); and C. Pavone, *A Civil War: A History of the Italian Resistance*, translated by Peter Levy with the assistance of David Broder; introduced by Stanislao G. Pugliese (London and New York 2013).

DICTATORSHIP IN GERMANY

As with the chapter on dictatorship in Russia I have made substantial overlaps with one of my books in the *Questions and Analysis* series. S.J. Lee, *Hitler and Nazi Germany* (London 1998), especially the second edition of 2010, in an attempt to provide a synthesis between traditional and post-1990 interpretations. There has therefore been some interplay between the various editions of the two books.

By far the most detailed collection of primary sources is J. Noakes and G. Pridham (eds), *Documents on Nazism 1919–1945* (London 1974). Others include: A. Kaes, M. Jay and E. Dimendberg, *The Weimar Republic Sourcebook* (Berkeley, CA 1994); L. Snyder, *The Weimar Republic* (Princeton, NJ 1966); J. Remak (ed.), *The Nazi Years* (Englewood Cliffs, NJ 1969); J.W. Hiden, *The Weimar Republic* (Harlow 1974); and D.G. Williamson, *The Third Reich* (Harlow 1982).

The best known of the long-established texts are: A. Bullock, *Hitler: A Study in Tyranny* (London 1952); W.L. Shirer, *The Rise and Fall of the Third Reich* (London 1960); J. Fest, *Hitler* (London 1974); N. Stone, *Hitler* (London 1980); R.G.L. Waite (ed.), *Hitler and Nazi Germany* (New York 1965); M.J. Thornton, *Nazism 1918–1945* (London 1966); and A. Nicholls, *Weimar and the Rise of Hitler* (London 1968); H. Holborn (ed.), *Republic to Reich: The Making of the Nazi Revolution* (New York 1972); M. Broszat, *Hitler and the Collapse of the Weimar Republic* (Oxford 1987); P. Stern, *Hitler: The Führer and the People* (London 1975); and T.L. Jarman, *The Rise and Fall of Nazi Germany* (New York 1961). Especially recommended as overall interpretations of the Nazi era are: M. Broszat, *The Hitler State* (London 1981); K.D. Bracher, *The German Dictatorship* (trans. London 1973); K. Hildebrand, *The Third Reich* (trans. London 1984); E. Jäckel, *Hitler in History* (Hanover 1984); A. Hillgruber, *Germany and the Two World Wars* (Cambridge, MA 1981); J. Hiden and J. Farquharson, *Explaining Hitler's Germany: Historians and the Third Reich* (London 1983); H.W. Koch (ed.), *Aspects of the Third Reich* (London 1985); and I. Kershaw, *The Nazi Dictatorship: Problems and Perspectives of Interpretation* (London 1985).

More recent works on Hitler and the Third Reich are: A. Bullock, *Hitler and Stalin: Parallel Lives* (London 1991); R. Overy, *The Dictators: Hitler's Germany, Stalin's Russia* (London 2004); I. Kershaw, *The Nazi Dictatorship* (fourth edition, London 2000); I. Kershaw, *Hitler 1889–1936: Hubris* (London 1998); I. Kershaw, *Hitler 1936–1945: Nemesis* (London 2000); I. Kershaw and M. Lewin (eds), *Stalinism and Nazism, Dictatorships in Comparison* (Cambridge 1997); M. Burleigh, *The Third Reich: A New History* (London 2000); R.J. Evans, *The Coming of the Third Reich* (London 2003); R.J. Evans, *The Third Reich in Power 1933–1939* (London 2005); E. Davidson, *The Making of Adolf Hitler* (Columbia, MO 1997); N. Frei, *National Socialist Rule in Germany: The Führer State 1933–1945* (trans. Oxford 1993); M. Kitchen, *The Third Reich: Charisma and Community* (Harlow 2008); C. Leitz (ed.), *The Third Reich: The Essential Readings* (Oxford 1999 edition); H. Mommsen (ed.), *The Third Reich Between Vision and Reality: New Perspectives on German History 1918–1945* (Oxford 2001); M. Burleigh (ed.), *Confronting the Nazi Past* (London 1996); J. Lukacs, *The Hitler of History* (New York 1998); G. Martel, *Modern Germany Reconsidered* (London 1992).

There is a huge variety of publications on various aspects of the Nazi regime. The SS, Gestapo and the police state are dealt with in: H. Höhne, *The Order of the Death's Head* (London 1972); G.C. Browder, *The Gestapo and the SS Security Service in the Nazi Revolution* (New York 1996); R. Gellately, *The Gestapo and German Society: Enforcing Racial Policy 1933–1945* (Oxford 1990); E.A. Johnson, *Nazi Terror: Gestapo, Jews and Ordinary Citizens* (New York 1999); and N. Wachsmann, *Hitler's Prisons: Legal Terror in Nazi Germany* (New Haven 2004). Indoctrination is one of the main themes of: F. Spotts, *Hitler and the Power of Aesthetics* (London 2002); R.G. Waite, *The Psychopathic God: Adolf Hitler* (New York 1993); D. Welch, *The Third Reich: Politics and Propaganda* (London 1993); J. Dülffer, *Nazi Germany 1933–1945: Faith and Annihilation* (trans. London 1996). Recommended for coverage of Nazi economic and social policies, and the Volksgemeinschaft are: V.R. Berghahn, *Modern Germany: Society, Economy and Politics in the Twentieth Century* (Cambridge 1987); D.F. Crew (ed.), *Nazism and German Society 1933–1945* (London 1994); R. Grunberger, *A Social History of the Third Reich* (London 1971); R. Bessel (ed.), *Life in the Third Reich* (Oxford 1986); D.J.K. Peukert, *Inside Nazi Germany* (Harmondsworth 1989); D. Crew (ed.), *Nazism and German Society 1933–1945* (London 1994); T.W. Mason, *Social Policy in the Third Reich: The Working Class and the National Community* (Oxford 1993); G. Rempel, *Hitler's Children: The Hitler Youth and the SS* (Chapel Hill, NC 1989); R. Gellately and N. Stoltzfus (eds), *Social Outsiders in Nazi Germany* (Princeton, NJ 2001); R. Proctor, *Racial Hygiene: Medicine under the Nazis* (Cambridge, MA 1988); and M. Burleigh and W. Wippermann, *The Racial State: Germany 1933–1945* (Cambridge 1991). Women and the family have received detailed attention in: C. Koonz, *Mothers in the Fatherland: Women, the Family and Nazi Politics* (London 1988); C. Haste, *Nazi Women: Hitler's Seduction of a Nation* (London 2001);

L. Pine, *Nazi Family Policy 1933–1945* (Oxford 1997); and E. Harvey, *Women and the Nazi East: Agents and Witnesses of Germanization* (New Haven and London 2003). Support, opposition and resistance are included in: D.J.K. Peukert, *Inside Nazi Germany: Conformity, Opposition and Racism in Everyday Life* (trans. London 1987; Harmondsworth 1989); D.C. Large (ed.), *Contending with Hitler: Varieties of German Resistance in the Third Reich* (Cambridge 1991); I. Kershaw, *Popular Opinion and Political Dissent in the Third Reich* (Oxford 1983); M. Housden, *Resistance and Conformity in the Third Reich* (London 1997); T.S. Hamerow, *On the Road to the Wolf's Lair: German Resistance to Hitler* (Cambridge, MA 1999); and L.E. Jones and J. Retallack (eds), *Between Reform, Reaction and Resistance: Studies in the History of German Conservatism from 1789 to 1945* (Providence, RI 1993). Foreign policy and war are covered in: A. Hillgruber, *Germany and the Two World Wars* (trans. W.C. Kirby) (Cambridge, MA 1981); E. Jäckel, *Hitler in History* (Hanover 1984); J. Thies, *Hitler's Plans for Global Domination. Nazi Architecture and Ultimate War Aims* (originally published 1976, trans I. Cooke and M. Friedrich; New York 2012); P. Finney (ed.), *The Origins of the Second World War* (London 1997); F. Fischer, *Germany's Aims in the First World War* (London 1967); N. Rich, *Hitler's War Aims: The Establishment of the New Order* (London 1974); M. Kitchen, *Nazi Germany at War* (London 1995).

The Holocaust is an ever expanding area of study. Among recent works particularly recommended are: J.C. Friedman (ed.), *The Routledge History of The Holocaust* (Abingdon 2011); R. Hilberg, *The Destruction of the European Jews* (Chicago 1961); D. Cesarini (ed.), *The Final Solution: Origins and Implementation* (London 1994); G. Hirschfield (ed.), *The Policies of Genocide* (London 1986); A. Barkai, *From Boycott to Annihilation* (London 1989); C.R. Browning, *The Origins of the Final Solution* (London 2004); D.J. Goldhagen, *Hitler's Willing Executioners: Ordinary Germans and the Holocaust* (London 1997); G. Eley (ed.), *The 'Goldhagen Effect'* (Ann Arbor, MI 2000); O. Bartov, *Germany's War and the Holocaust* (Ithaca, NY 2003); O. Bartov (ed.) *The Holocaust: Origins, Implementation, Aftermath* (London 2003); M. Postone and E. Santner (eds) *Catastrophe and Meaning: The Holocaust and the Twentieth Century* (Chicago 2003); M. Housden, *Hans Frank: Lebensraum and the Holocaust* (London 2005); D. Lipstadt, *Denying the Holocaust: The Growing Assault on Truth and Memory* (London 1993); R. Breitman, *Official Secrets: What the Nazis Planned, What the British and Americans Knew* (New York 1968); D. Bloxham, *Genocide on Trial: War Crimes Trials and the Formation of Holocaust History and Memory* (Oxford 2001); L. Rothkirchen, *The Jews of Bohemia and Moravia: Facing the Holocaust* (Lincoln, NE 2005); J.T. Gross, *Neighbours: The Destruction of the Jewish Community in Jedwabne, Poland* (Princeton, NJ 2001); T. Cole, *Holocaust City: The Making of a Jewish Ghetto* (London 2003); R. Ioanid, *The Holocaust in Romania* (Chicago 2000); G. Corni, *Hitler's Ghettoes: Voices from a Beleaguered Society 1939–1944* (trans. N.R. Iannelli) (London 2003); I. Trunk, *Judenrat: The Jewish Councils in Eastern Europe under Nazi Occupation* (London 1972); L. Dobroszycki and J.S. Gurock (eds), *The Holocaust in the Soviet Union* (New York 1993); and I. Ehrenburg and V. Grossman, *The Complete Black Book of Russian Jewry* (New Brunswick, NJ 2000).

DICTATORSHIP IN SPAIN

In the fourth edition of this book, Spain has been entirely rewritten and given its own chapter. This means that an expanded bibliography includes the earlier entries and some newer publications.

General histories include: R. Carr, *Spain 1808–1975* (Oxford 1966); and R. Carr, *Modern Spain 1875–1980* (Oxford 1980). The Rivera dictatorship is covered in: S. Ben-Ami, *Fascism from Above: The Dictatorship of Primo de Rivera in Spain 1923–1930* (Oxford 1983); and J.H. Rial, *Revolution from Above: The Primo de Rivera Dictatorship in Spain, 1923–1930* (London and Toronto 1986). The Second Republic and the different aspects of the Spanish Civil War are dealt with in: H. Thomas, *The Spanish Civil War* (London 1961); G. Jackson, *The Spanish Republic and the Civil War 1931–39* (Princeton, NJ 1965); G. Jackson (ed.), *The*

Spanish Civil War (Chicago 1972); F.J.R Salvadó, *The Spanish Civil War: Origins, Course and Outcomes* (Basingstoke 2005); P. Preston (ed.), *Revolution and War in Spain 1931–1939* (London 1984); G. Eisenwein and A. Shubert, *Spain at War: The Spanish Civil War in Context 1931–1939* (London 1995); J. Casanova, *The Spanish Republic and the Civil War* (trans. Cambridge 2010); A. Beevor, *The Battle for Spain: The Spanish Civil War 1936–1939* (London 2006); W.J. Mommsen and L. Kettenacker (eds), *The Fascist Challenge and the Policy of Appeasement* (London 1983); S.G. Payne, *The Spanish Civil War, the Soviet Union and Communism* (New Haven and London 2004); R.H. Whealey, *Hitler and Spain: The Nazi Role in the Spanish Civil War 1936–1939* (Lexington, KY 1989); and S.G. Payne, *Falange: A History of Spanish Fascism* (Stanford, CA 1961).

Franco and his regime are covered in: B. Crozier, *Franco: A Biographical History* (London 1967); J.D.W. Trythall, *Franco: A Biography* (London 1970); P. Preston, *Franco: A Biography* (London 1993); S. Ellwood, *Franco* (Harlow 1994); M. Gallo, *Spain under Franco* (trans. J. Stewart) (London 1973); P. Preston, *The Politics of Revenge* (London 1990); N. Townson (ed.), *Spain Transformed: The Late Franco Dictatorship, 1959–75* (Basingstoke 2007); and J. Grugel and T. Rees, *Franco's Spain* (London 1997).

Three books provide new perspectives on the whole Franco period: A.C. Sanchez, *Fear and Progress: Ordinary Lives in Franco's Spain 1939–1975* (Chichester 2010); J. Treglown, *Franco's Crypt: Spanish Culture and Memory Since 1936* (London 2013); and C. Jerez-Farrán and S. Amago (eds), *Unearthing Franco's Legacy: Mass Graves and the Recovery of Historical Memory in Spain* (Notre Dame, IN 2010).

DICTATORSHIP ELSEWHERE IN EUROPE

I found the most readable books on Salazar's Portugal to be: J.M. Anderson, *The History of Portugal* (Westport, CT 2000); R.A.H. Robinson, *Contemporary Portugal: A History* (London 1979); T. Gallagher, *Portugal: A Twentieth-Century Interpretation* (Manchester 1983); H. Kay, *Salazar and Modern Portugal* (London 1970); N. Bruce, *Portugal: The Last Empire* (London 1975); D. Birmingham, *A Concise History of Portugal* (Cambridge 1993); L.S. Graham and H.M. Makler (eds), *Contemporary Portugal: The Revolution and its Antecedents* (Austin, TX 1979); G.A. Stone, *Spain, Portugal and the Great Powers, 1931–1941* (Basingstoke 2005); T.C. Bruneau, *Politics and Nationhood: Post-Revolutionary Portugal* (New York 1974); M. Soares, *Portugal's Struggle for Liberty* (trans. London 1975); D.L. Raby, *Fascism and Resistance in Portugal: Communists, Liberals and Military Dissidents in the Opposition to Salazar, 1941–1974* (Manchester 1988); and A.C. Pinto, *The Blue Shirts: Portuguese Fascists and the New State* (New York 2000).

Dictatorships in central and eastern Europe are effectively covered in: R.J Crampton, *Eastern Europe in the Twentieth Century – and After* (London 1997); J.C. Swanson, *The Remnants of the Habsburg Monarchy: The Shaping of Modern Austria and Hungary* (New York 2001); R. Steininger, G. Bischof and M. Gehler (eds), *Austria in the Twentieth Century* (New Brunswick 2002); E. Barker, *Austria 1918–1972* (London 1973); M. Kitchen, *The Coming of Austrian Fascism* (London and Montreal 1980); C.E. Richardson, *The Heimwehr and Austrian Politics 1918–1936* (Athens 1978); E.B. Bukey, *Hitler's Austria: Popular Sentiment in the Nazi Era, 1938–1945* (Chapel Hill and London 2000); G.-K. Kindermann, *Hitler's Defeat in Austria 1933–1934: Europe's First Containment of Nazi Expansionism*, trans. S. Brough and D. Taylor (London 1984); P. Ignotus, *Hungary* (London 1972); E. Pamlényi, *A History of Hungary* (London 1975); J.K. Hoensch, *A History of Modern Hungary*, second edition (London 1996); M. Molnár, *A Concise History of Hungary* (trans. A Magyar) (Cambridge 2001); L. Kontler, *A History of Hungary* (London 2002); D. Sinor, *History of Hungary* (London 1959); P.F. Sugar (ed.), *A History of Hungary* (London 1990); J.K. Hoensch, *A History of Modern Hungary*, second edition (London 1996); A.C. Janos, *The Politics of Backwardness in Hungary 1825–1945* (Princeton, NJ 1982); J.C. Kun, *Hungarian Foreign Policy: The Experience of a New Democracy* (Westport, CT 1993); P. Kenez, *Hungary from the Nazis to the Soviets: The*

Establishment of the Communist Regime in Hungary, 1944–1948 (Cambridge 2006); A.J. Prażmowska, *A History of Poland* (Basingstoke 2004); J. Lukowski and H. Zawadzki, *A Concise History of Poland* (Cambridge 2006); N. Davies, *God's Playground, A History of Poland. Volume II: 1795 to the Present* (Oxford 1981); H. Roos, *A History of Modern Poland: From the Foundation of the State in the First World War to the Present Day* (trans. J.R. Foster) (London 1961); K. Syrop, *Poland: Between the Hammer and the Anvil* (London 1968); P.D. Stachura, *Poland Between the Wars, 1918–1939* (London 1998); A. Polonsky, *Politics in Independent Poland, 1921–1939: The Crisis of Constitutional Government* (Oxford 1972); E.J. Patterson, *Pilsudski: Marshal of Poland* (Bristol 1935); W.F. Reddaway, *Marshal Pilsudski* (London 1939); A. Garlicki, *Józef Piłsudski,1867–1935* (trans. and ed. J. Coutouvidis) (Aldershot 1995); V.S. Vardis and R.J. Misiunas (eds), *The Baltic States in Peace and War 1917–1945* (University Park, PA 1978); G. Smith (ed.), *The Baltic States* (New York 1994); J. Hiden and P. Salmon, *The Baltic Nations and Europe: Estonia, Latvia & Lithuania in the Twentieth Century* (London 1991); G. von Rauch, *The Baltic States: The Years of Independence. Estonia, Latvia, Lithuania 1917–1940* (trans. London 1974); and R. Misiunas and R. Taagepera, *The Baltic States: Years of Dependence 1940–1990* (London 1993).

The Balkans and south-eastern Europe are dealt with in: L.S. Stavrianos, *The Balkans since 1453* (New York 1958); B. Jelavich, *History of the Balkans*, Vol. 2, *The Twentieth Century* (Cambridge 1983); M. Biondich, *The Balkans, Revolution, War and Political Violence since 1878* (Oxford 2011); T. Gallagher, *Outcast Europe: The Balkans, 1789–1989 from the Ottomans to Milošević* (London 2001); D.B. Hupchick, *The Balkans from Constantinople to Communism* (New York and Basingstoke 2001); R. Ristelhueber, *A History of the Balkan Peoples* (trans. S.D. Spector) (New York 1971); S. Pollo and A. Puto, *The History of Albania* (trans. C. Wiseman and G. Cole) (London 1981); K. Frasheri, *The History of Albania* (Tirana 1964); B.J. Fischer, *King Zog and the Struggle for Stability in Albania* (New York 1984); G. Bokov (compiler), *Modern Bulgaria: History, Policy, Economy, Culture* (Sofia 1981); V. Dedijer (ed.), *History of Yugoslavia* (New York 1974); S. Clissold (ed.), *Short History of Yugoslavia* (Cambridge 1966); L. Benson, *Yugoslavia: A Concise History* (Basingstoke 2001); F. Singleton, *Twentieth-Century Yugoslavia* (London 1976); J.R. Lampe, *Yugoslavia as History: Twice There was a Country* (Cambridge 2000); J. Ridgeway (ed.), *Burn this House: The Making and Unmaking of Yugoslavia* (Durham and London 2000); A.N. Dragnich, *The First Yugoslavia: The Search for a Viable Political System* (Stanford, CA 1983); D. Djokić (ed.), *Yugoslavism: Histories of a Failed Idea 1918–1992* (London 2003); J.B. Allcock, *Explaining Yugoslavia* (London 2000); C. Bennett, *Yugoslavia's Bloody Collapse: Causes, Course and Consequences* (London 1995); J.K. Cox, *The History of Serbia* (Westport and London 2002); S. Pavlowitch, *Hitler's New Disorder: The Second World War in Yugoslavia* (London 2008); D.N. Ristić, *Yugoslavia's Revolution of 1941* (London 1966); K. Hitchins, *Rumania 1866–1947* (Oxford 1994); S. Fischer-Galati, *Twentieth-Century Rumania* (New York 1970); various authors, *Horthyist-Fascist Terror in Northwestern Romania* (Bucharest 1986); R. Ioanid, *The Sword of the Archangel: Fascist Ideology in Romania*, trans. P. Heinegg (New York 1990); J.V. Kofas, *Authoritarianism in Greece: The Metaxas Regime* (New York 1983); M. Petrakis, *The Metaxas Myth: Dictatorship and Propaganda in Greece* (London and New York 2006); P.J. Vatikiotis, *Popular Autocracy in Greece 1936–41: A Political Biography of General Ioannis Metaxas* (London and Portland 1998); D.H. Close, *The Origins of the Greek Civil War* (London 1995); R. Clogg, *Greece 1940–1949: Occupation, Resistance, Civil War* (Basingstoke 2002).

Twentieth-century Turkey, first included in the third edition of this book, is well covered by: N. Berkes, *The Development of Secularism in Turkey* (London 1988 edition); R.H. Davison, *Essays in Ottoman and Turkish History, 1774–1923: The Impact of the West* (Austin, TX 1990); B. Lewis, *The Emergence of Modern Turkey* (New York 2002 edition); D. Quataert, *Social Disintegration and Popular Resistance in the Ottoman Empire, 1881–1908* (New York 1983); and E.J. Zürcher, *Turkey: A Modern History* (London 1993).

DICTATORSHIPS vs DEMOCRACIES

This is a new chapter, added to the fourth edition of this book. Its purpose is to reflect the attitudes of the democracies to their wartime invaders and to explain the methods used by the dictatorships that occupied or tried to subdue the democracies. The bibliography is therefore more restricted than in other sections.

For the section 'Democracies destroyed', the following were particularly useful: V.S. Mamatey and R. Luža (eds), *A History of the Czechoslovak Republic 1918–1948* (Princeton, NJ 1973); J. Korbel, *Twentieth-Century Czechoslovakia: The Meanings of Its History* (New York 1977); V. Mastny, *The Czechs under Nazi Rule: The Failure of National Resistance, 1939–1942* (New York and London 1971); H.S. Nissen (ed.), *Scandinavia during the Second World War* (Minneapolis 1983); P.M. Hayes, *Quisling: The Career and Political Ideas of Vidkun Quisling* (Newton Abbot 1971); O.K. Hoidal, *Quisling: A Study in Treason* (Oslo 1989); H.F. Dahl, *Quisling: A Study in Treachery* (Cambridge 1999); V. Mallinson, *Belgium* (London 1969); J. Newcomer, *The Grand Duchy of Luxembourg: The Evolution of Nationhood 963 A.D. to 1983* (New York and London 1984); I. Ousby, *Occupation: The Ordeal of France 1940–1944* (London 1999); T.R. Christofferson and M.S. Christofferson, *France during World War II: From Defeat to Liberation* (New York 2006); J.F. McMillan, *Twentieth-Century France: Politics and Society 1898–1991* (London 1992); and H.R. Kedward, *Resistance in Vichy France* (Oxford 1978).

The section 'Democracies marginalized' owes a great deal to the following: J. Steinberg, *Why Switzerland?* (Cambridge 1996); J. Wraight, *The Swiss and the British* (Michael Russell 1987); J.-R. De Salis, *Switzerland and Europe: Essays and Reflections* (London 1971); N. Kent, *A Concise History of Sweden* (Cambridge 2008); *Sweden, the Swastika and Stalin: The Swedish Experience in the Second World War* (Edinburgh 2011); J. Lydon, *The Making of Ireland* (London and New York 1998); G. Morgan and G. Hughes (eds), *Southern Ireland and the Liberation of France* (Bern 2008); C.J. Carter, *The Shamrock and the Swastika* (Palo Alto, CA 1977); J.P. Duggan, *Neutral Ireland and the Third Reich* (Dublin 1985); and C. Wills, *That Neutral Island: A Cultural History of Ireland During the Second World War* (London 2007).

For the section 'Democracies defiant' the following are directly relevant: R. Pope, *War and Society in Britain 1899–1948* (London 1991); R. Chickering, S. Förster and B. Greiner (eds), *A World at Total War* (Cambridge 2005); F. Singleton, *A Short History of Finland* (Cambridge 1989); and A.F. Upton, *Finland 1939–1940* (London 1974).

Index

Page numbers in *italic* refer to figures. Page numbers in **bold** refer to tables.